RESTLESS IDEAS

RESTLESS IDEAS

CONTEMPORARY SOCIAL THEORY
IN AN ANXIOUS AGE

TONY SIMMONS

FERNWOOD PUBLISHING
HALIFAX & WINNIPEG

Editing: Brenda Conroy
Cover design: John van der Woude
Printed and bound in Canada

Published by Fernwood Publishing
32 Oceanvista Lane, Black Point, Nova Scotia, B0J 1B0
and 748 Broadway Avenue, Winnipeg, Manitoba, R3G 0X3
www.fernwoodpublishing.ca

Fernwood Publishing Company Limited gratefully acknowledges the financial
support of the Government of Canada, the Canada Council for the Arts, the
Manitoba Department of Culture, Heritage and Tourism under the Manitoba
Publishers Marketing Assistance Program and the Province of Manitoba, through
the Book Publishing Tax Credit, for our publishing program. We are pleased to
work in partnership with the Province of Nova Scotia to develop and promote our
creative industries for the benefit of all Nova Scotians.

Library and Archives Canada Cataloguing in Publication

Title: Restless ideas : contemporary social theory in an anxious age / Tony
Simmons.
Names: Simmons, Anthony M. (Anthony Michael), 1945- author.
Description: Includes bibliographical references and index.
Identifiers: Canadiana 20190137517 | ISBN 9781773630953 (softcover)
Subjects: LCSH: Social sciences—Philosophy. | LCSH: Social history—21st
century. | LCSH: Sociology.
Classification: LCC H61 .S56 2019 | DDC 300.1—dc23

CONTENTS

*I dedicate this work to all my global sisters
and brothers — near and far — in their
struggles for recognition and social justice.*

"What may appear as Truth to one person will often
appear as untruth to another person. But that need
not worry the seeker. Where there is honest effort, it
will be realized that what appear to be different truths
are like the countless and apparently different leaves of
the same tree." —Mohandas Gandhi (1951: 109), "On
the Meaning of Truth" (January 1, 1927) from *Non-
Violent Resistance (Satyagraha)*, Shocken Books.

ACKNOWLEDGEMENTS

I would like to thank the entire Fernwood team who made the publication of this book possible: Wayne Antony for his early endorsement of this project; and especially my managing editor, Tanya Andrusieczko, whose erudite advice, scrupulous reviews and constant encouragement greatly enriched this text; and also Beverley Rach, Brenda Conroy, Debbie Mathers and John van der Woude, who magically transformed my manuscript into a real book. Thanks, as well, to the working people of Alberta for subsidizing the sabbatical leave that allowed me to complete this project, and to my wife, Sybil, for her constant encouragement and support.

THE CHANGING FACE OF CONTEMPORARY THEORY

THE WANING OF THE WESTERN WORLDVIEW

Today, perhaps more than at any time since the Second World War, we live in an age of uncertainty and anxiety, an age characterized by rapid social and technological change and by the erosion of many customary boundaries and borders — whether these are geographical, political, cultural, occupational, racial, sexual, public or private. For many of us, the world has become an increasingly uncertain and precarious place where the assumptions and expectations of earlier generations — whether of stable employment and secure residence, or the validity of customary beliefs and social norms, or even our hopes and prospects for the future — have become unsettled and thrown into doubt. And although these feelings of crisis and confusion are far from unprecedented and have periodically arisen at other times of profound historical change, the shocks and aftershocks of these uncertain times reverberate through all aspects of our lives. As Karl Marx (1969 [1848]) said many years ago when he described the social impact of the rise of industrial capitalism: "All fixed, fast-frozen relations, with their train of ancient and venerable prejudices and opinions, are swept away, all new-formed ones become antiquated before they can ossify." These shockwaves are felt throughout society: on factory shop floors, in corporate boardrooms and government offices — and even behind the cloistered walls of universities and colleges, at the desks of scholars and social theorists.

Social theory, like everything else in our anxious age, has been heavily impacted by the social, cultural, geopolitical, technological and environmental changes that are transforming our social worlds and redefining our ideas and our identities. Many of the assumptions and conceptual frameworks of past social theories are being critiqued by a new generation of social thinkers whose ideas and experiences have, until recently, been overlooked or excluded by most Western theorists. Many theorists from this new generation are presently engaged in re-examining, nuancing and reworking earlier theories in order to reflect the complex, changing and different lived experiences from those that informed earlier theories. In many ways, this is an exciting yet challenging time to study social theory; there is much to consider and much to learn.

The most penetrating criticisms by the new generation of global social theorists target the "Eurocentric," or "Western," worldview, which, until fairly recently, was the dominant paradigm for constructing, teaching and learning social theory in North America, Europe and around the world. Most social theory — whether classical or contemporary — has remained embedded in this Eurocentric worldview. This worldview has come under increasing scrutiny, especially from social theorists and other scholars whose ideas have been shaped by their experiences of material, psychological and epistemic oppression and violence which

The Eurocentric Worldview: Reason, Liberty and Progress

The Eurocentric worldview emerged during the European Enlightenment (Age of Reason), which spanned the mid-seventeenth to the mid-eighteenth centuries. It was based on a number of assumptions and key concepts, the most distinctive of which are the following:

Rationalism: the belief that true knowledge of the world can only be gained through reason, rather than through religious faith.

Humanism: the belief that our understanding of the world and our moral and ethical values should be based on actual experience rather than on religious doctrine or mystical revelation.

Secularism: the belief that public life — government, education, the judiciary etc. — should be separated from all religious influence or authority and that religion should be relegated to the private sphere.

Modernity: the belief that modern societies — in contrast to traditional or "primitive" societies — have evolved institutions for greater technological innovation, greater economic growth and greater individual liberty.

Progress: the belief in so-called "human perfectibility": that through the application of reason to human affairs, the history of humanity is destined to show continuous linear advances in self-improvement and in the solution of natural and social problems. Humanity, rather than God, shapes its own fate.

are unexpressed and unrepresented in this once dominant paradigm of social theory.

The Eurocentric worldview has allowed "the West" to mythologize its own history, knowledge and practices as a paragon of human civilization and as a rationalization and legitimization of its colonization of non-European cultures and communities around the world. However, the recent history of the West — the brutal conquest and colonization throughout the Global South; the Nazi holocaust; the genocide of Indigenous Peoples; the construction of nuclear bombs and other weapons of mass destruction; the unchecked extinction of many species; and the looming climate crisis — has served to discredit the naïve self-promotion of the European worldview. At the same time, this Enlightenment paradigm has lasted for several centuries and has provided motivation and direction for most intellectual projects at home and abroad. But times are changing, and today this Eurocentric worldview is being challenged by critical thinkers who bear no allegiance to a colonial narrative of knowledge and who have every interest in overthrowing this narrative. Nowhere are these intellectual struggles more apparent than in the quarrelsome world of social theory.

EUROCENTRISM AND ITS DISCONTENTS

Today, the Eurocentric worldview, which is embedded in all classical and many contemporary social theories, including most of those included in this book, is being challenged from several angles: by feminist critics, who expose the male-oriented, or androcentric, biases and assumptions that continue to frame the perspectives of many social theorists (*Kanter 1993 [1977]; Smith 1987;* Sydie 1994; Marshall and Witz 2004); by queer theorists, who question the heteronormative biases underlying much contemporary social theory (Green 2007; Seidman 1996; Namaste 1994); and by scholars from the Global South and Indigenous and racialized peoples in the Global North (Alatas and Sinha 2017; Al-Hardan 2018; Bhambra 2014; Chakrabarty 2000; Churchill 2002; Go 2016). These critics identify the numerous unexamined presuppositions of Eurocentric theory that limit its relevance and applicability for understanding the diversity of human experience around the world. Some of the more common criticisms of Eurocentrism are described below.

Figure 0-1: Common Criticisms of Eurocentrism

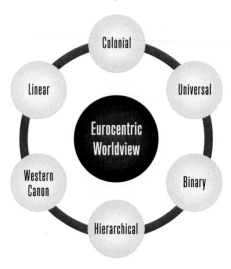

The Western Canon

A major criticism of the Eurocentric narrative and of the established works traditionally included in the "canon," or foundational literature, of classical and contemporary social theory is that this canon has been dominated by white Western (mostly male) theorists and has excluded non-European theorists from the Global South — both scholars from former colonies and Indigenous and other racialized scholars from within the metropolitan colonial states. Some of the more illustrious non-European pioneers of social theory include Ibn Khaldun (Tunisia); W.B. DuBois, Richard R. Wright, Booker T. Washington, Ralph Ellison (United States); Jose Rizal (Philippines); Said Nursi (Turkey); and Benoy Kumar Sarkar (India), among many others (Al-Hardan 2018). And, of course, there are prominent Indigenous social thinkers in North America, Australia, New Zealand and elsewhere, including Marie Battiste and Lee Maracle (Canada); Ward Churchill, Robert Allen Warrior and Vine Deloria (United States); Stephen Muecke and Marcia Langton (Australia); and Linda Tuhiwai Smith (New Zealand). Today, the traditional canon of social and sociological theory is being reconfigured, and the narrow roster of white Western males, or "old dead white guys" (see, for example, Bancroft and Fevre 2010; Inglis and Steinfeld 2000), has become the object of intense criticism from postcolonial theorists, feminists, queer theorists, critical race and Indigenous theorists and scholars from the Global South. These social theorists from around the world seek to decolonize social theory, to fully recognize previously excluded women and racialized theorists and to widen the horizons of social thought and social research (Alatas and Sinha 2017). We shall meet some of these contemporary theorists as we progress through later chapters of this book.

Universal

Another criticism made of Eurocentric theories of society is their "false universalism." Whether these are macrosocial theories, such as structural functionalism, structural conflict theory and systems theory, or micro-social theories, such as ethnomethodology and rational choice theory, the underlying assumption is that they are universally applicable to all societies — past, present and future. However, an increasing number of critical theorists from the Global South show that these supposedly universal theories are often unable to adequately conceptualize or interpret local, non-European cultures and communities. Eurocentric theories have often proven to be insensitive ("tone deaf") to the cultural, traditional and local conditions of human existence beyond the beltway of Europe and North America. This "pseudo universalism" has provided an ideological legitimation for European policies of imperialism and colonialism around the world. The epistemology of universalism is closely linked to the global history of colonialism. This false universalism has also been termed "metrocentrism" by recent critical theorists (Go 2013). Indeed, some critics of metrocentrism have even disparaged such anti-imperialist perspectives as postcolonial theory and Marxism for their own metrocentic premises: namely, that these critiques of metrocentrism carry their own brand of false universalism. In order to avoid the trap of metrocentric and universal theories (whether these are colonial, anticolonial or postcolonial perspectives), some theorists (Go 2014; 2016) insist on privileging the viewpoint of the colonized "underdog" — that is, adopting a "subaltern standpoint."

Linear

The adoption of a Eurocentric worldview has produced many distortions and misunderstandings of non-European societies, cultures and communities. For example, Eurocentric theories of society have invariably imposed their own linear concepts of "time" and "history" (as well as "territory" and "space") on other cultures that have not shared these concepts. For Europeans — and their North American cousins — history is seen as an evolving linear chronology in which the past is safely behind us, the present is currently with us and the future remains unopened before us. History from this perspective is invariably considered a progressive development, though which humanity emancipates itself from superstition and ignorance and moves forward to ever greater enlightenment and individual liberty. For some cultures, history may be understood as circular, or cyclical, rather than linear. Some cultures may have conceptions of space and time that cannot be collapsed into a Eurocentric narrative. For others, the boundaries of the past, present and future may be experienced as more fluid and porous than the hard distinctions of the Eurocentric worldview, including movement between "dreaming time" and "real" time (McLean 2009).

Binary

Eurocentric conceptual frameworks have frequently imposed their own binary categories on cultures for which such categories are meaningless and even invasive. This may be seen in rigid binaries like male/female and homosexual/heterosexual, which ignore the full range of genders and sexualities. As LBGTQ theorist Scott Lauria Morgensen suggests, the Indigenous and sexual identities of two-spirited individuals cannot be easily inserted into a homo/hetero binary gender dichotomy, but their recognition and expression provide new opportunities for personal liberation and decolonization: "Thus Two-Spirit presents an Indigenous epistemology rooted in Native traditions, articulating Native modernities — that challenges colonial knowledges, alters power relations with non-Natives, and incites new registers through which Native people can join and hold non-Natives accountable to work for Indigenous decolonization" (2011: 86).

The problem with Eurocentric binary conceptual systems is that they suppress ambiguous or fluid spaces between the opposed categories, so that any overlap between categories of man/woman, child/adult or friend/stranger become impossible to identify. Unfortunately the history of social theory is closely aligned with — and has often reinforced — the history of colonialism, as may be seen in such fundamental binary categories as — colonizer/colonized, white/Black, settler/Indigenous, civilized/savage, primitive/modern, good/evil, superstition/reason, human/beast, among many others. Many recent critics regognize these close ties between social theory and colonialism and call for the "decolonization" of the narratives and conceptual frameworks of contemporary Eurocentric theories (Connell 2007; Smith 2012; Comaroff and Comaroff 2011; Ascione 2016).

Hierarchical

Hierarchy has always been an essential and ineradicable aspect of imperial and colonial social relations. European conquest and colonization have inevitably stratified and divided the colonized from the colonizers. In most cases this imperial legacy has also imposed a racial stratification on subjugated, or subaltern, populations: white colonizer over racialized colonized; settler over Indigenous Peoples. Imperial and colonial perspectives have also imposed other hierarchal classifications — including those based on class, gender, sexuality, ethnicity, language and religion. Hierarchy is deeply embedded in the Eurocentric worldview.

Colonial

Many critics of both classical and contemporary European and North American social theory point to the role of the Eurocentric paradigm in the project of colonialism. While gender and queer theorists expose the androcentric and heteronormative biases of Eurocentric theory, its deepest roots — according to postcolonial, Indigenous, and critical race theorists — are to be found in its "imperial or colonial episteme," or colonial worldview (Go 2016). Some commentators note that there is a well-defined infrastructure maintained by the gatekeepers of most disciplines to regulate the portals of publication and public recognition (Crane 1972). However, postcolonial, Indigenous and critical race theorists are contesting much social theory for its implicit prejudices and biases and for the gaps and silences around the colonial origins of this discourse. Among the many targets of postcolonial criticism are the "origin narratives" of Eurocentric theory. A popular origin narrative is the "Protestant ethic" myth, which — from the time of Max Weber to contemporary modernization theory — has attributed the Industrial Revolution, of the late eighteenth century, to a uniquely Western combination of economic enterprise and moral discipline, originally centred in Britain and later to spread throughout Europe and North America and eventually the rest of the world. For postcolonial critics, this narrow and insular historical perspective, focused exclusively on the apparent self-sufficient rise of industrial capitalism in the West, ignores the role of colonialism in funding and financing the Industrial Revolution — with capital accumulated through trade and commerce in enslaved peoples, sugar, tea, tobacco and cotton — among many other colonial cash commodities. Postcolonial critics argue that the modernization of the West was only achieved through the exploitation of colonial land, labour and natural resources, such as gold, silver and copper. Scholars from the Global South (such as Eric Williams 1944; Walter Rodney 1972; C.L.R. James 1938) who emphasize these interconnections until recently remained outside the established canon of Eurocentric social theory.

Besides the failure to acknowledge the economic and material role of colonialism and slavery in the rise of Western industrial capitalism, postcolonial critics also challenge the ethnocentric biases and racial stereotypes typically used to portray non-European cultures in most classical and many contemporary social theories. Palestinian-American philosopher Edward Said (1978) developed a postcolonial critique of Eurocentric narratives of Eastern or Asian societies in his most famous book, *Orientalism*, and his critical framework has encouraged later theorists to contest and challenge the (sometimes explicit but often implicit) ethnocentric and racist preconceptions embedded in many contemporary social theories. Indigenous and critical race theorists also critique Eurocentric theoretical narratives for viewing non-European cultures and communities only through "Western eyes," because these perspectives have frequently misunderstood and distorted local alternative realities. The "East," or the "Orient," has typically been portrayed as "mysterious" or "inscrutable" in Western texts, and European studies of Asian societies traditionally made references to what was perceived as Oriental backwardness, degeneracy and inequality (Said 1978). Similarly, Indigenous cultures have long been described by colonial anthropologists and sociologists as "primitive," "savage," "barbaric" and "uncivilized." At the very least, many premodern non-European societies, cultures and communities have been defined as "foreign," "alien" and "different" — or more basically, as the "Other." Said and other critical scholars (Hailey 1944; Gough 1960; Asad 1973; Pathy 1981; Steinmetz 2013) emphasize that these Eurocentric traditions of theory and research are inextricably tied to the culture, ideology and discourse of colonialism — the colonial episteme. The sad fact is that, over the centuries, these and other racialized stereotypes and caricatures have distorted the reality and diminished the humanity of the West and have legitimized the occupation and dispossession of colonized populations. Ideas have real consequences, and the Orientalist fictions of colonial discourse have always served to rationalize and reinforce the harsh and often brutal policies and practices of colonialism and imperialism.

THE CRUMBLING CANON OF SOCIAL THEORY: THE CLASSICS

The task of identifying the canon of social theory has become increasingly politicized. The more conservative custodians of social theory continue to insist upon the centrality of the classics — especially the holy trinity of Marx, Durkheim and Weber. For these commentators, the long-established classics still represent the highest standards of scholarship within social theory. This attitude is articulated by Mouzelis (1997: 1): "I consider the writings of Marx, Durkheim, and Weber indispensable, in the sense that we shall not be able to put them on forgotten library shelves as easily as chemists or physics do with their own classical texts. This is because they inform current research, scholarship and debate." Theorists who strongly defend the traditional definition of the canon often oppose any attempts to broaden it. Attempts to incorporate women, Black, Indigenous and other social theorists of the Global South into the classical tradition are resisted on a number of grounds; for example, appeals for the inclusion of neglected theorists may be dismissed as evidence of a "creeping relativism," often seen to be driven by external political pressures ("political correctness") or by a general lowering of standards within the discipline.

For conservatives, the traditional classics represent the highest standards of research and scholarship. Demands for the inclusion of such figures as Charlotte Perkins Gillman or African American sociologist W.E.B Du Bois, for example, are seen, not as opportunities to deepen and widen the focus of social theory but as special pleading by political groups and movements. One defender of the status quo (Mouzelis 1997: 3), disparages these efforts: "I do not at all see why W.E.B. Du Bois or Charlotte Perkins Gilman should be admitted to the club.... Until I am presented with more convincing arguments, I am bound to assume that [t]his proposal is based less on intrinsic/cognitive and more on extrinsic values. (For those unfamiliar with their names, Du Bois is black and Gilman is a feminist)."

However, it is clear that these reactionary attempts to discourage a more inclusive and global understanding of social theory — and social theorists — are doomed to failure. Gerald Davis and Mayer Zald observe: "The radicalization of the curriculum and the pressure from suppressed groups for recognition of 'their' classics forced an examination of how the canon was constructed, why some forms of literature or art were included, and others excluded, why few women and African-Americans authors or artists were included in the then acceptable curricula" (2009: 638). Today, most theory textbooks and journals include the contributions of non-European theorists; the Eurocentric paradigm has already lost its paramountcy, and its theoretical canon is rapidly crumbling (see, for example, Connell 2007; Go 2016; Rodriguez, Boatcă, and Costa 2016; Benzecry, Krause, and Reed 2017).

In so many ways, the conservative defenders of the traditional canon are swimming against the tide of recent history. There is a rising swell among theorists across the social sciences and humanities in favour of a more inclusive definition of the classics. This new wave signals the mounting challenges from contemporary theoretical perspectives, such as postmodernism and poststructuralism, as well as from feminist and queer theorists; standpoint and intersectionality theorists; and from the interdisciplinary areas such as gender studies, cultural and multicultural studies, global studies and Indigenous, critical race and postcolonial studies. Many of these critics conclude that traditional social thought remains severely compromised by androcentric perspectives and by Eurocentric assumptions of Western superiority, what some call the "imperial gaze." One writer declared: "Sociology was formed within the culture of imperialism and embodied a cultural response to the colonized world. This fact is crucial in understanding the content and method of sociology as well as the discipline's cultural significance" (Connell 1997: 1519). The broadening scope of theoretical perspectives, which now includes the contributions of theorists from the Global South and from marginalized Indigenous and minority cultures within the Global North, greatly enhances the relevance of social theory both at home and abroad. The present generation of theory is more cosmopolitan, interdisciplinary and global than ever before. Instead of the narrow Eurocentric worldview that prevailed for much of its history, social theory now provides us with a far more accurate picture of the world and a more reflexive methodology that registers the diversity and variety of social life on our planet.

There has never been a better time than the present to broaden our understanding of our shared global heritage of social theory, to include some of the formerly excluded classics of past social thinkers and to open the doors to current social theorists from the Global South. Several scholars are already reclaiming some of these neglected masterpieces from Western societies and beyond (see Abdo-Zubi 1996; Alatas and Sinha

2001; Alatas 2006; Churchill 1996). Indeed, this process is underway in many other disciplines as well (Naidoo 1996; Ramose 2002; Thiong'o 1981/1986). In many ways, social theory may be viewed as a debate between different theorists. For example, Karl Marx's work may be seen as a critical response to at least three different traditions of theory: French utopian socialism, British political economy and German historical idealism. While Marx ridiculed these early utopian socialists for what he considered their wholly unrealistic goal of returning modern capitalist society to a pre-industrial state of harmony and for their attempts to rise above class conflict, he appropriated their ideas of "class conflict" and "class struggle." Similarly, although he dismissed much of the classical tradition of political economy, Marx appropriated the "labour theory of value" into his own more critical "theory of surplus value." Also, Marx replaced Hegel's theory of "historical idealism" with his own theory of "historical materialism" (sometimes called "dialectical materialism"). In a memorable phrase, Marx proclaimed that he had "turned Hegel on his head" and had "extracted the rational kernel from the mystical shell" of Hegel's dialectical theory of history (Marx 1961: 20). All theories are originally formulated as responses — sometimes explicit, often implicit — to past as well as prevailing theories. Most classical theorists "settled their accounts" with their predecessors and with their contemporaries. In this sense, theories are all about argument, debate and deliberation; they never fall out of a clear blue sky.

Much as theorizing may be thought of as a debate or an argument — with a partner or against an opponent — the same holds true for definitions of the canon. Although the chronology of social theory may appear — at least to the outside observer — as a simple matter of historical record, the inclusion of theorists in this record has remained a "contested terrain." Indeed, it would be accurate to say that the canon is "constructed" rather than simply "discovered" or "reclaimed." This is because the criteria used to construct the canon are unavoidably ideological and are liable to change from one generation to the next. The canon of social theory, therefore, is not only a living legacy, subject to periodic change and transformation; it is also a reflection of the struggles and conflicts of different social groups for recognition and respect. The early histories of social thought published at the turn of the twentieth century faithfully reflected, for the most part, the worldview of the predominantly white, androcentric, ethnocentric, patriarchal, heterosexual, middle-class professoriate of that time. The construction of the canon during this period expressed the predilections and prejudices of the educated elite in Europe and North America. For many years, even the works of Karl Marx were either trivialized or excluded from many standard histories of social and economic thought (Williams 1964). Indeed, Marx was contemptuously dismissed by one famous economist as a "minor post-Ricardian" (Samuelson 1962; and Brewer 1995). To be fair, Paul Samuelson added the following qualification: "Marx's bold economic or materialistic theory of history, his political theories of the class struggle, his transmutations of Hegelian philosophy, have an importance for the historian of 'ideas' that far transcends his facade of economics" (14).

Today, postcolonial, Indigenous and critical race theorists, as well as feminist, gender and queer theorists, have all begun to deconstruct and reconstruct the traditional canon of social theory. Past social thinkers who were previously overlooked because they were women or came from non-Western cultures are now being taken seriously and incorporated into an expanding global conception of our shared intellectual heritage. Once again, the historical canon has become an object of contestation, negotiation and revision. Earlier criteria for inclusion in the canon are being expanded; the criteria for constructing the classics are more open and cosmopolitan than ever before. The intellectual excitement of these times is well captured by Davis and Zald: "The classics and the canon evolve. ... We have no idea whether there are hidden jewels out there, just waiting for some scholar to make claims about their importance for current or future thinking" (2009: 644).

This is the spirit of the present text. In addition to the usual list of social thinkers included in the contemporary tradition, this book also includes feminists, postcolonial, Indigenous and critical race theorists. But even the best-intentioned efforts at reconstructing the historical canon of social theory still suffer from what has sometimes been called the "Anglocentric gaze": an over-reliance on Euro-American sources to the virtual exclusion of other cultural contributions. As one eminent critic (Collins 1997: 1564) suggests, "What we need is to broaden out to the formation of canons in other disciplines and in other parts of the world.... Perhaps someday there will be a genuinely cosmopolitan account." When viewed through the eyes of another culture or another gender, such classical theorists as Marx, Durkheim and Weber exemplify the many cultural and gender prejudices of their age. While this is not a

THE CHANGING FACE OF CONTEMPORARY THEORY 13

justification for consigning their works to the ash heap of history, it is a
reason to recognize their limitations. As in all things, we can only take one
step at a time — even when dismantling the past legacy of Eurocentrism,
Orientalism and androcentrism.

THE EXPANDING HORIZONS OF CONTEMPORARY SOCIAL THEORY

The recent rise of critical and global perspectives has led to a major re-
evaluation of Western social theory. Eurocentric theories that claimed to
be universal in their scope increasingly appear parochial and provincial
in their theoretical focus and methods of inquiry. Postcolonial critics in
particular insist that many of the conceptual frameworks and methodologies of Eurocentric theories have little or no relevance for the experiences
and perspectives of many groups and individuals residing in the Global
South. Eurocentric theories were narrowly constructed within the local
contexts of Europe and North America even though they tacitly assumed
a universal and global validity. Today, these assumptions are being challenged by postcolonial theorists and others who not only reject the false
universalism — or metrocentrism — of Eurocentric concepts and methods, but also the underlying colonial worldview — or colonial episteme
— which has until now remained largely unquestioned. The Western
copyright on social theory is no longer privileged within the discipline.
Postcolonial theorists, in particular, contest and challenge the hegemony
of Eurocentric theory in a number of different ways.

Globalization of the Canon

For most social theorists today, especially those from the Global South,
the Eurocentric canon of classical and modern social theory is viewed as
wholly unrepresentative of the past and present diversity of social theory.
At the same time, contemporary critiques of the Eurocentric canon are
also critiques of European colonialism, which elevated European thinkers
to the privileged status they have occupied over the past few centuries.
The power and influence of the European canon has always reflected
the power and influence of European colonialism. This globalization of
the Eurocentric theory canon has passed through a number of different
stages, or "waves," and each successive wave has expanded the inclusion and incorporation of theorists from around the world. According
to some recent commentators (Go 2016; and Al-Hardan 2018, for
example), the first wave, anticolonial theorists, included W.B. DuBois

and other original founders of the Atlanta School of Sociology (United States) and Pan-African "Negritude" thinkers such as Aimé Césaire (Martinique), Léopold Senghor (Senegal) and Franz Fanon (Algeria). The second wave, postcolonial theorists, included Edward Said (a Palestinian American), Homi K. Bhabha (India) and Gayatri Spivak (India), and the third wave, de-colonial theorists, includes Syed Fari Alatas (Malaysia), Dipesh Chakrabarty (India), Raewyn Connell (Australia), Gurminder Bhambra (United Kingdom), Bonaventura de Sousa Santos (Portugal) and Encarnación Gutiérrez Rodríguez (Spain), among many others. Together, these theorists have transformed the face of contemporary social theory, expanding and globalizing the scope and scale of its intellectual inheritance.

At the same time, many contemporary critics argue that the transformation and globalization of social theory needs to go far beyond the simple addition of global theory texts to the crumbling Eurocentric canon. As Ina Kerner (2018: 554) suggests,

> decentering the canon by addition of non-Western theories appears as an important, but not a sufficient step to tackle and possibly to even fix the problems Eurocentrism entails. This is because ... enlarging the canon this way cannot guarantee to result in more than adding-the-non-Western-and-stir — for it does not necessarily engage in ... further tasks that, against the backdrop of my broad conception of Eurocentrism, seem crucial, as well.

The decolonization of social theory also requires a critique of the underlying "colonial episteme" — a worldview that has inscribed binary, linear, hierarchical, parochial and provincial assumptions and concepts into its discourse. And, of course, decolonization has to include a counter-narrative of colonial history in which the perspectives of the colonized are fully recognized and represented. Only then can we more fully comprehend the ways in which colonial discourse has contributed to and reinforced the oppressive practices and policies of colonialism and imperialism.

Counter-Colonial History

Postcolonial critics insist that social theory needs to address and correct the sanitized history of Western colonialism. Classical social theory, in particular, has long overlooked the extent to which the colonization and exploitation of overseas territories and Indigenous communities enriched European imperial states, funded their industrial and technological revolutions and contributed to their political and cultural hegemony. This neglect has led to what Manuela Boatcă (2013) describes as "the systematic omission of exogenous factors such as colonial rule and imperial exploitation from social scientific explanations — [which]has alternately been referred to as typical of the 'gestures of exclusion' (Connell 2007: 46) of metropolitan theory and as responsible for the 'silences,' 'absences' (Sousa Santos 2004: 14ff.) or 'blind spots' (Hesse 2007) of mainstream sociological analysis." The absence of the history of colonization and exploitation from the "origin narratives" portrayed in Eurocentric theory is particularly evident in the works of theorists such as Auguste Comte, Herbert Spencer, Adam Smith, Emile Durkheim and Max Weber — especially Weber, who attributed the rise of industrial capitalism to the rationality, moral discipline and economic enterprise of the Protestant ethic, without any acknowledgement of the role of conquest, colonization and exploitation in funding these historical innovations. For this reason, postcolonial critics of Eurocentric theory seek to provide a counter-colonial history from the perspective of the colonized, subjugated and exploited by showing how "the development of capitalism and modernity is not a tale of endogenous development in Europe, but of structural interconnections between different parts of the world that long predated Europe's ascendance and, moreover, provided the conditions for that ascendance" (Seth 2014: 312).This project involves a critique, not only of the Western canon, but also of the colonial, or imperial, episteme: the Eurocentric worldview, which has portrayed Indigenous populations in racial stereotypes of "primitivism," "irrationality," "innocence," "savagery" and "barbarism." The Eurocentric history of colonialism underlying most classical and much modern social theory has served to reduce the "subaltern" (or the oppressed) identity to silence and invisibility, while celebrating the rationality, modernity and universality of the Western worldview (Sousa Santos 2014).

Subaltern Standpoint Perspective

Postcolonial critics also challenge and contest the colonial episteme, the "imperial gaze," which has, until now, structured the conceptual framework and methodological focus of most Eurocentric theory. This decentring, deconstruction and decolonization of the colonial episteme requires that the experiences, perspectives and agency of the "subaltern" — marginalized, oppressed, colonized or Indigenous communities and individuals — be fully represented in the discourse of social theory. However, as Gayatri Chakravorty Spivak (1988) suggests, the very act of attempting to "give a voice to those who have been silenced" is, in itself, a colonial and patronizing project that is, in its own way, a form of "epistemic violence" against the subjugated and the silenced. Trying to give a voice to the oppressed is tantamount to withholding the right of the subaltern to speak in their own voice, a common error committed by intellectuals, who tend to romanticize subaltern identities and statuses. The recognition of an alternative subaltern standpoint also requires that Eurocentric theory be recognized for what it actually is: a product of a limited local cultural context, rather than a universal worldview with global validity. In practice, therefore, decentring the colonial episteme implies a "recontextualization" of Eurocentric social theory — an acknowledgement that its validity is limited to the local, parochial and provincial contexts of its original formulation and elaboration. This recontextualization is sometimes referred to as the "provincialization" of social theory (Chakrabarty 2000), a recognition that all theory is local and that no theory is universal — in either its validity or in its scope of application. "This does not necessarily mean that they are 'merely' European and therefore parochial, but it does require that scholars remain alert to the possibility that the analytical categories which the social sciences presume to be universal — land, labor and capital, state, individual, civil society, and so on — may not in fact transcend the European history from which they originate" (Seth 2014: 316).

This recontextualization of theory also recognizes that the "knowledges" generated by any theory are always partial, provisional and perspectival and never universal or incontrovertible. The postcolonial critique of the colonial episteme, therefore, is a demand for recontextualization and reflexivity when assessing the meaning and truth of Eurocentric theory or any other tradition of social theory. For postcolonial theorists, there are no "master narratives" that can offer universal causal explanations of social or cultural phenomena. All theoretical narratives reflect the local birthmarks of their origins and should be engaged with accordingly.

Figure 0-2: Elements of Contemporary Social Theory

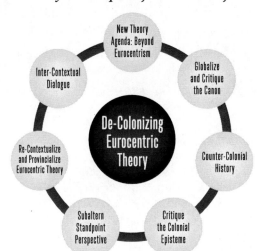

BEYOND EUROCENTRISM

The primary goal of the present volume is to provide a readable and accessible introduction to some of the more influential social theories of our time. Although most of these theories may be critically appraised as Eurocentric in their content and methods of analysis, they are all integral to the contemporary canon of social theory and for this reason are worthy of our interest and attention. However, they should be studied not as scriptures of a sacred theoretical canon but as malleable conceptual frameworks that may be altered, modified and adapted for use in very different societal, cultural and interpersonal contexts. Although such key concepts as "system," "structure," "network," "function"; metropole/colony; and core/periphery, for example, originated in the West, they may also — with some cultural translation — have value for analyzing aspects of social relations and social interaction elsewhere.

In addition to the landmark Eurocentric theories that have built the academic infrastructure of contemporary social theory throughout the twentieth and early twenty-first centuries, we also include some of the critical perspectives that question and challenge their scope, scale and relevance within a global context. Today, many of these critical global perspectives articulate the experiences and perceptions of subaltern, marginalized populations in former colonial regions of the Global South and of Indigenous and other minoritized populations in the Global North. These postcolonial, poststructuralist, Indigenous and critical race perspectives are striking examples of the expanding horizons of contemporary social theory. And if social theory often appears to be a quarrelsome and critical mode of discourse, this is because it remains a reflective mirror of the turbulent social world that conceived and delivered it.

References

Abdo-Zubi, Nahla (ed.). 1996. *Sociological Thought: Beyond Eurocentric Theory.* Canadian Scholars' Press.

Al-Hardan, Anaheed. 2018. "The Sociological Canon Reconfigured: Empire, Colonial Critique, and Contemporary Sociology." *International Sociology*, 33, 5 (September 11): 545–557. <https://doi.org/10.1177/0268580918791967>.

Alatas, Syed Farid. 2006. *Alternative Discourses in Asian Social Science.* Sage Publications.

Alatas, Syed Farid, and Vineeta Sinha. 2001. "Teaching Classical Sociological Theory in Singapore: The Context of Eurocentrism." *Teaching Sociology*, 29, 3: 316–331.

___. 2017. *Sociological Theory Beyond the Canon.* Palgrave MacMillan.

Asad, Talal (ed.). 1973. *Anthropology and the Colonial Encounter.* London: Ithaca Press.

Ascione, Gennaro. 2016. *Science and the Decolonization of Social Theory: Unthinking Modernity.* Palgrave Macmillan.

Bancroft, Angus, and Ralph Fevre. 2010. *Dead White Men and Other Important People: Sociology's Big Ideas.* London: Palgrave Macmillan.

Benzecry, Claudio E., Monika Krause and Isaac Ariail Reed. 2017. *Social Theory Now.* University of Chicago.

Bhambra, Gurminder K. 2014. *Connected Sociologies.* Bloomsbury Publishing.

Boatcă, Manuela. 2013. "'From the Standpoint of Germanism': A Postcolonial Critique of Weber's Theory of Race and Ethnicity." *Political Power and Social Theory*, 24: 55–80 (Emerald Group Publishing Limited).

Brewer, Anthony. 1995. "A Minor Post Ricardian: Marx as an Economist." *History of Political Economy*, 27, 1: 111–145.

Chakrabarty, Dipesh. 2000. *Provincializing Europe: Postcolonial Thought and Historical Difference.* Princeton: Princeton University Press.

Churchill, Ward. 1996. *From a Native Son: Selected Essays on Indigenism 1985–1995.* Boulder, CO: South End Press.

___. 2002. *White Studies: The Intellectual Imperialism of Higher Education.* Citizens International.

Collins, Randall. 1997. "A Sociological Guilt Trip: Comment on Connell." *American Journal of Sociology*, 102, 6: 1558–1564.

Comaroff, Jean, and John Comaroff. 2011. *Theory from the South: Or, How Euro-America Is Evolving toward Africa.* Routledge.

Connell, R.W. 1997. "Why Is Classical Theory Classical?" *American Journal of Sociology*, 102, 6: 1511–1557.

___ . 2007. *Southern Theory: The Global Dynamics of Knowledge in Social Science*. Cambridge: Polity Press.

Crane, Diana. 1972. *Invisible Colleges: Diffusion of Knowledge in. Scientific Communities*. University of Chicago Press.

Davis, Gerald F., and Mayer N. Zald. 2009. "Afterword: Sociological Classics and the Canon in the Study of Organizations." In Paul Adler (ed.), *The Oxford Handbook of Sociology and Organization Studies: Classical Foundations*.

Go, Julian. 2013. "For a Postcolonial Sociology." *Theory and Society*, 42, 1: 25–55.

___. 2014. "Beyond Metrocentrism: From Empire to Globalism in Early US Sociology." *Journal of Classical Sociology*, 14, 2: 178–202. <http://citeseerx.ist.psu.edu/viewdoc/download?doi=10.1.1.915.3681&rep=rep1&type=pdf>.

___. 2016. *Postcolonial Thought and Social Theory*. Oxford University Press.

Gough, Kathleen. 1960. *Anthropology and Imperialism*. Ann Arbor, MI: Radical Education Project. <http://faculty.arts.ubc.ca/menzies/documents/MR-019-11-1968-04.pdf>.

Green, Adam Isaiah. 2007. "Queer Theory and Sociology: Locating the Subject and the Self in Sexuality Studies." *Sociological Theory*, 25, 1: 26–45.

Hailey, Lord. 1944. "The Role of Anthropology in Colonial Development." *Man*, 44: 10–16. doi:10.2307/2791896.

Hesse, B. 2007. "Racialized Modernity: An Analytics of White Mythologies." *Ethnic and Racial Studies*, 30, 4: 643–663.

Inglis, Laura Lyn, and Peter K. Steinfeld. 2000. *Old Dead White Men's Philosophy*. Toronto: Humanity Books

James, C.L.R. 1938. *The Black Jacobins: Toussaint L'Ouverture and the San Domingo Revolution*. London: Secker & Warburg.

Kanter, Rosabeth Moss. 1993 [1977]. *Men and Women of the Corporation*, 2nd ed. New York: Basic Books.

Kerner Ina. 2018. "Beyond Eurocentrism: Trajectories towards a Renewed Political and Social Theory." *Philosophy and Social Criticism*, 44, 5: 550–570.

Marshall, B., and A. Witz. 2004. *Engendering the Social: Feminist Encounters with Sociological Theory*. Maidenhead, England, UK: Open University Press.

Marx, Karl. 1961. *Capital*, Vol. I, trans. S. Moore and E. Aveling. Moscow: Foreign Languages Publishing House.

___. 1969 [1848]. *The Communist Manifesto*: Chapter I. "Bourgeois and Proletarians." In *Marx/Engels Selected Works, Vol. One*. Moscow: Progress Publishers.

McLean, Ian. 2009. *White Aborigines: Identity Politics in Australian Art*. Cambridge: Cambridge University Press.

Morgensen, Scott Lauria. 2011. *Spaces Between Us: Queer Settler Colonialism and Indigenous Decolonization*. University of Minnesota Press.

Mouzelis, Nicos. 1997. "In Defence of the Sociological Canon: A Reply to David Parker." *Sociological Review* (May): 244–253.

Naidoo, A.V. 1996. "Challenging the Hegemony of Eurocentric Psychology." *The Journal of Community and Health Sciences*, 2, 2: 9–16.

Namaste, Ki. 1994. "The Politics of Inside/Out: Queer Theory, Poststructuralism, and a Sociological Approach to Sexuality." *Sociological Theory*, 12, 2: 220–231.

Pathy, Jaganath. 1981. "Imperialism, Anthropology and the Third World." *Economic and Political Weekly*, 16, 14 (Apr. 4): 623–627.

Ramose, M.B. 2002. *African Philosophy Through Ubuntu*. Harare, Zimbabwe: Mond Books.

Rodney, Walter. 1972. *How Europe Underdeveloped Africa*. London: Bogle-L'Ouverture Publ; Dar es Salaam: Tanzania Publ.

Rodriguez, Encarnacion Gutierrez, Manuela Boatcǎ, and Sérgio Costa. 2016. *Decolonizing European Sociology: Transdisciplinary Approaches*. Routledge.

Said, Edward. 1978. *Orientalism*. Pantheon Books.

Samuelson, Paul A. 1962. "Economists and the History of Ideas." *The American Economic Review*, 52, 1 (Mar.): 1–18.

Seidman, Steven. 1996, *Queer Theory Sociolog*. John Wiley and Sons.

Seth, Sanjay. 2014. "The Politics of Knowledge: Or, How to Stop Being Eurocentric." *History Compass*, 12/4: 311–320.

Smith, D.E. 1987. "Women's Perspective as a Radical Critique of Sociology." In H.E. Longino and E.F. Keller (eds.), *Feminism and Science*. Oxford, UK: Oxford University Press.

Smith, Linda Tuhiwai. 2012. *Decolonizing Methodologies: Research and Indigenous Peoples*. Zed Books.

Sousa Santos, Boaventura de. 2004. "A Critique of the Lazy Reason: Against the Waste of Experience." In I. Wallerstein (ed.), *The Modern World-System in the Longue Dure´e*. Boulder, CO: Paradigm Publishers.

____. 2014. *Epistemologies of the South. Justice Against Epistemicide*. Boulder, Co; London: Paradigm.

Spivak, Gayatri Chakravorty. 1988. "Can the Subaltern Speak?" In Cary Nelson and Lawrence Grossberg (eds.), *Marxism and the Interpretation of Culture*. Chicago: University of Illinois Press.

Steinmetz, George. 2013. "A Child of the Empire: British Sociology and Colonialism, 1940s–1960s." *J Hist Behav Sci.*, 49, 4 (Fall): 353–378. <https://pdfs.semanticscholar.org/5d04/3514fe42d56a33167a0c1098b6ed7a1cd21d.pdf>.

Sydie, R. 1994. "Sex and the Sociological Fathers." *Canadian Review of Sociology & Anthropology*, 31: 117–138.

Thiong'o, Ngugi wa. 1981/1986. *Decolonising the Mind — The Politics of Language in African Literature*. London: James Currey; Nairobi: Heinemann Kenya; New Hampshire: Heinemann

Williams, Eric. 1944. *Capitalism and Slavery*. University of North Carolina.

Williams, William Appleton. 1964. *The Great Evasion: An Essay on the Contemporary Relevance of Karl Marx and on the Wisdom of Admitting the Heretic into the Dialogue About America's Future*. Quadrangle Books.

CHAPTER 1

WHY DO WE THEORIZE?

LIVING ON THE BRINK

There can be little doubt that we are living in troubled times — indeed, we appear to be "living on the brink." The daily headlines in our news feeds bring us pictures of conflict and death: frontline stories from endless wars, the crisis refugees are facing, suicide bombings and mass shootings around the world, the devastation of ancient cities such as Palmyra in Syria, the rising evidence of climate change and extreme weather events and so on.

We are learning what it means to live in a global society. Whatever happens in one part of the world can easily spill over into our own backyard. Aerial bombardment of ISIS positions in Syria and Iraq can lead to reprisal attacks in Paris, Brussels and San Bernardino, in Manchester and London, as well as in Ankara and Lahore. And Canadians have grown more conscious of how we fit into the big picture of global trade and commerce. Many of us have come to realize that the coffee we drink and the running shoes we wear are often produced for us in the semi-slavery conditions of the EPZs (export processing zones) in the Philippines, Taiwan, Hong Kong, Brazil and other "investment platforms" of the Global South (Klein 2000). We have seen the protests against corporate globalization by movements for global justice — in Seattle, Genoa, Stockholm, Quebec City and other places — and the rise of the World Social Forums, first in Porto Alegre, Brazil in 2001 and later in other major cities. More than ever before, our lives are affected by things that happen in other parts of the world. There is no longer any "elsewhere"; our doorstep now extends across continents and oceans.

This is most obviously the case with environmental disasters. When the destruction of the Amazon rainforests by ranchers and oil companies leads to a deterioration of the ozone layer — not to mention the physical and cultural genocide of Indigenous communities — none of us can escape the global effects of these changes. Or when our production of hydrocarbons and other greenhouse gases leads to climatic change, none of us can escape these consequences. The writing has been on the wall for some time now: our planet is shrinking in cultural terms, and whatever happens in one part of the world is going to affect all of us.

What does it mean to live in a global society? What does it mean to live on the brink of war, of climate catastrophe, of acute and chronic social and economic global inequality, of global pandemic diseases and of other as yet unknown threats to our very existence? How has our sense of time and space been altered by the worldwide spread of telecommunications — the internet, satellite television, smart phones and tablets — and other aspects of the new technoculture? Where do our primary obligations as citizens and as human beings lie? Who really pulls the strings that control our lives? These kinds of questions have always been asked by the more curious among us, but they have a renewed urgency, if only because the present appears so unstable and insecure, the future so uncertain and the stakes so very high.

While every generation experiences its own challenges and its own disasters, the advent of the twenty-first century has already produced its own troubled agenda of horrors, threats and uncertainties. Starting on September 11, 2001 (9/11), the hijacked airliner attacks on the World Trade Centre and the Pentagon in the US signalled the "war on terrorism" and led directly to the ongoing wars in Afghanistan, Iraq, Libya and Syria and to the destabilization of other regions throughout the Middle East, North Africa and Central Asia — among other places. Other pressing social problems of this new century include the climate crisis; the catastrophic scale of global poverty, inequality, malnutrition and disease; the displacement of civilian populations from war zones, resulting in increasing numbers of refugees and migrants; and the rise of anti-immigrant, xenophobic and far-right nationalist political parties and social movements in Europe and North America. All of these problems pose threats to human security. And to these clear dangers we could also add the ever-present threat of nuclear weapons in the economic, political and military rivalry between such major powers as the US, China and Russia — with North Korea and Iran in the background. We live in an anxious geopolitical age which has passed through the bipolar stage of the Cold War (between the US and the former USSR) and has also passed through the brief unipolar stage of the 1990s into the far more dangerous multipolar world (between the US, Russia, China, India, North Korea, Iran, Pakistan, Israel and other potential nuclear states) of the early twenty-first century. In addition to these problems, we need to confront the rapid depletion of conventional energy sources and the urgent need for a non-carbon economy.

SOCIAL THEORY IN AN ANXIOUS AGE

Social theory has an important role to play in helping us to make sense of this anxious age in which we live. Theories allow us to see our own social worlds, and those of others, from a number of different and sometimes unfamiliar perspectives. Different theoretical perspectives can provide us with different "theoretical languages" — new ways of speaking about our lives and experiences. Theories also allow us to construct simplified models of our social relations. Using these models, we can reduce the complexity of social life to a set of key variables that we may wish to focus on, analyze and explain. Many different theoretical perspectives have been used to analyze the complex phenomena of social life.

By focusing on particular aspects of our social lives, we can try to understand what is happening to us — on a local and on a global level. Theories can help us to find explanations for the things that trouble us and challenge us in our everyday lives. Theories can also help to simplify the worlds in which we live. They can help to reduce the complexity of modern life and enable us to find answers to the questions we pose. And, perhaps, most importantly, theories can provide us with new languages to describe and analyze our observations and experiences of contemporary social life.

Whatever model, or interpretation, of social reality we use, any theoretical perspective offers a simplified version of our social lives and allows us to think more analytically, critically and empathically about our social worlds. Globalization is a case in point. How we talk about globalization greatly depends on how we think about it. Indeed, whether we believe that we are living in a "global society," a "postmodern world" or an age of "neoimperialism" depends to a large extent upon which theory we are using. Making sense of our worlds involves the use of theories. If we see global society as a conflict of interest between the rich multinational capitalist corporations and the exploited workers, we are likely to be drawn to a Marxist theoretical perspective. On the other hand, if we are more preoccupied with how telecommunications have compressed our global understanding of space and time, we may be attracted to theories of postmodernity. In any event, theories always help to reduce and simplify the complexity of social life.

AN AGE OF INDETERMINACY

The turbulent and dangerous world that confronts social theorists in the twenty-first century is also a world of unprecedented opportunity for the progressive development of human potential. As always in the course of human affairs, every new generation brings with it the potential for greater construction or destruction. It is in this sense that we live in an age of uncertainty — in fact more than uncertainty; we live in age of "indeterminacy." By indeterminacy, we mean not simply that our knowledge of social life is uncertain, or insecure, but that the very content of social life (social interactions, social structures and social processes, even personal identities) has become unstable, fluid and subject to constant disruption and change. In other words, it is not only our *knowledge* of social life that is unstable and uncertain but *social reality* itself now outpaces the explanations, hypotheses and descriptions offered by social theorists. Social theory can barely keep up with the accelerated pace of changing times. We live in a time of constant flux — in technology and also in our beliefs and practices, in our social activities and even in our personal identities. Our ways of "knowing" (our epistemologies) and also our ways of "being" (our ontologies) have grown increasingly uncertain, unreliable and impermanent. This is what we mean by indeterminacy. It refers to the growing complexity, changeability, fluidity and unpredictability of our social lives; nothing ever stays the same for very long; everything is in a state of constant and rapid flux. Indeterminacy comes in many different forms.

Many social theorists have addressed the indeterminacy of the present age in their theories and key concepts. One of the foremost contemporary theorists, Zygmunt Bauman (1999), introduces the concept of "liquidity" to describe modern society. By liquid, Bauman means that contemporary societies are no longer held together by the solid ties that previously formed the basis of social order. What was once perceived as long-term, stable and permanent has become increasingly short-term, transient and precarious. For example, many of the past generation of industrial workers and professionals could realistically expect life-long employment in their jobs and careers; today increasing numbers of workers in the labour force must expect to move continuously from one short-term job to the next, from one contract to the next and from one form of contingent employment to another. In place of the earlier term "proletariat," which classical social theorists used to describe the stable working class, some recent theorists use the term "precariat" to emphasize the precarious nature of employment for the working class today (see Standing 2011). Indeed, "gig economy" has become a popular term to describe our insecure employment sector: an unregulated market system in which temporary positions are common and organizations contract with freelancers, independent contractors, project-based workers and temporary or part-time hires for short-term engagements. The days of secure employment are over for many workers, who now face a future of job insecurity and uncertainty in the so-called "job churn" (see CBC Radio 2016). This indeterminacy in the lives of many marginalized Canadian, American and British workers could be experienced on several fronts, including the loss of manufacturing jobs through transnational trade deals that appear only to benefit the rich and powerful; the changing ethnic composition of the electorate through mass immigration and (what seemed to many older and rural voters in the US) the erosion of traditional cultural and religious values — through threats to their Second Amendment gun ownership rights and the imposition of a new "politically correct" permissiveness towards abortion and same-sex marriage. The greatest political upset in US history was caused by the threats of indeterminacy to the American underclass. And similar concerns had been expressed in Britain by those voters who succeeded in winning the right to leave the European Union during the June 2016 Brexit referendum.

Another example of indeterminacy identified by contemporary social theorists is revealed in work of Michael Hardt and Antonio Negri (2000), who focus on what they call the "de-territorialization" and "de-materialization" of social relations. De-territorialization refers to the present historical trend away from fixed territorial locations and boundaries towards an increasingly borderless and globalized social world. This process of de-territorialization may be seen in the ability of multinational and transnational corporations (MNCs and TNCs) to relocate their manufacturing plants and call centres to low-wage labour markets, to transfer their assets to off-shore tax shelters and shell companies and to conduct their global operations beyond the regulations and control of national governments and international government organizations (IGOs). In a very different example, de-territorialization may be seen in the ability of terrorist groups such as Al-Qaeda and ISIS — among others — to conduct their military operations in an increasingly borderless world, without regard to national boundaries or the traditional rules of international warfare. In Europe, the provisions of the Schengen Agreement abolished passport and other types of controls at the borders of twenty-six countries in the European Union (EU) and thereby transformed much of Europe into a borderless territory. While there is a growing trend towards de-territorialization, there have also been some recent reversals. The Brexit referendum vote in the UK called for a withdrawal of Britain from the EU and for the re-imposition of "hard" border controls. The rise of far-right nationalist political parties and social movements in many European countries and the unexpected election of Donald Trump in 2016 as president of the US are also indications of a growing populist resistance to the policies of de-territorialization.

At the same time, de-materialization refers to the growing trend towards the conversion of what were previously material, solid and real products and services into virtual, digital and abstract forms. The corporate branch plants that once manufactured actual products have increasingly been transformed into call centres or data centres that produce and distribute information. Similarly, where once the transfer of wealth within the international financial system involved the transfer of real assets — such as money, cheques or even gold bullion — today these transactions are accomplished through data flows which are often difficult (for governments) to track and trace. The de-materialization of products and services is yet another symptom of the indeterminacy of contemporary social life. As Karl Marx (1848) once famously proclaimed, "All that is solid melts into air, all that is holy is profaned, and man is at last compelled to face with sober senses, his real conditions of life, and his relations with his kind" (see also Berman 1982).

Many postmodernist writers also emphasize the accelerated pace of social and technological change and show how these changes are transforming our interactions with each other, as well as our perceptions of social reality. According to the French postmodernist theorist Jean Baudrillard, we now spend most of our lives — via the internet, social media and television — observing "simulacra" of real events rather than experiencing the actual events. Baudrillard (1995) illustrates his theory most provocatively in his controversial monograph *The Gulf War Did Not Take Place*, in which he argues that for most us, the first Gulf War (in 1990–91) was indirectly observed only on our TV screens as though it were just another video game — geographically and emotionally remote from our real lives. In the age of digital communication, war has become just another "spectacle" (see Debord 1970), another form of entertainment, and news stories have become "infotainment." In this sense, the indeterminacy of our social world is inherent in the media we use to watch, listen to and "experience" our world. We may believe that we keep abreast of global and local events, but in fact, we remain spectators within secondary virtual worlds of representation and illusion. This indeterminacy has been exacerbated — at least in the US — since Donald Trump began deflecting criticisms of his administration by charging the established news media with distributing "fake news." The lines separating fact from fiction, truth from falsehood, have become increasingly blurred and indistinct.

LOOKING BACK AT TWENTIETH-CENTURY SOCIOLOGICAL THEORY

Although there are some obvious overlaps and continuities between the "modernist" sociological theories of the twentieth century and the contemporary social theories of the twenty-first century, there are also major differences. Looking back at the modernist theories of the past century, we can identify a number of basic characteristics that distinguish them from the social theories that preoccupy us today.

Modernist sociological theories were primarily "sociological" in content; they were mostly constructed to enhance and enrich the discipline of sociology and to increase the explanatory potential of this discipline. By contrast, many of the contemporary theories reviewed in this book are far more "interdisciplinary" in content and draw their inspiration from a variety of areas of study, including literary, cultural, gender and global studies, philosophy, psychology and political science — among others. This wider interdisciplinary focus and broader range of theoretical perspectives is what distinguishes contemporary "social" theories from the previous generation of "sociological" theories (Seidman 1991).

Another important distinction between modernist sociological theories and contemporary (i.e., late modernist and postmodernist) social theories is the tendency for modernist theorists to construct their theories in the form of "grand theories" and "metanarratives" (or grand narratives). By grand theories, we mean theories of total societies that are typically constructed in general and abstract terms — often with little or no concern for empirically testable hypotheses and propositions. The term "grand theory" was first introduced by C. Wright Mills in his book *The Sociological Imagination* (1959) as a criticism of structural functionalist theory. The best example of grand theory is to be found in the highly abstract theoretical frameworks of Talcott Parsons, who conceptualized society as a set of functionally interrelated systems and subsystems, each with its own set of "functional imperatives" which need to be satisfied in order to ensure the stability and sustainability of the system. The construction of grand theories was ubiquitous among modernist theorists and included not only structural functionalism, but also systems theory, conflict theory and critical theory, as well as various versions of exchange theory, rational choice theory and network theory. Even the later contributions of sociobiology and evolutionary psychology only served to further reinforce the prominence of grand theory in sociology.

Many modernist theories were also constructed as "metanarratives" (also called "grand narratives" or "master narratives"), by which we mean a theory that claims to have a universal validity and applicability because it is supposedly constructed from the perspective of a "universal subject." Such universal subjects have included the "working class," in classical Marxism and historical materialism; the "voluntaristic social actor," in Parsons' social action theory and structural functionalist theory; "humanity," in many social and philosophical theories of the Enlightenment; "mankind," in many evolutionist theories; and even the universal subject identity of "women," as adopted by first and second wave feminist theorists. Metanarratives are often closely associated with macro-sociological theories (of total societies). However, they may also refer to micro-sociological theories (of social action and social behaviour). Some micro-sociological metanarratives focus on the universal "self" (in Mead and Blumer's symbolic interactionism and Goffman's dramaturgy) and "rational man" (*homo economicus*) of exchange theory, rational choice theory and analytical Marxism.

In the simplest terms, a metanarrative is a "big story" that is told about "society," "history," "humankind," "civilization" or some other broad or generic category, from a viewpoint (or perspective) that claims to speak on behalf of everyone within that category (i.e., has universal validity).

The problem with metanarratives — from the perspectives of their critics (postmodernists, poststructuralists, feminists and others) — is that no metanarrative can ever truly speak for everyone; in fact, all metanarratives exclude from their accounts the perspectives and experiences of many groups in society that are marginalized and whose voices have rarely, if ever, been listened to in the sphere of public discourse. *All metanarratives conceal as much as they reveal.* Every metanarrative is full of silences and absences, all of which undermine its claims to universality and objectivity. Many twenty-first-century social theorists criticize both macro-sociological and micro-sociological modernist metanarratives of the twentieth century — for their silences and absences.

Social theory has an important role to play in encouraging exploration of diverse viewpoints, discourses and identities that have long been excluded or marginalized within our social worlds. In this respect, the study of contemporary social theory can contribute to the cultivation of an informed and enlightened citizenry. The chance to explore and experiment with diverse theoretical perspectives offers a challenge to dogmatism and intolerance and provides an opportunity to learn from diverse viewpoints. The new directions of social theory are broader and more inclusive than previous generations of sociological theory; social theory in the twenty-first century is characterized by its pluralism, diversity, reflexivity, interdisciplinarity and globalism. Unlike past sociological theory, which was always closely identified with national traditions — American, British, German and French sociologies etc. — contemporary social theory has become global in its scope and less Eurocentric. More than ever before, social theory is becoming an increasingly borderless intellectual project.

Many critics today perceive theories such as Marxism, critical theory, conflict theory and structural functionalism as gendered, androcentric, Eurocentric metanarratives that only represent the narrow viewpoints of their founders and chief proponents — notwithstanding the claims of these theories to objectivity and universality. Even micro-sociological metanarratives, such as Mead's or Goffman's theory of the social self, are often critiqued as a gendered view of the "self," constructed from a white, middle-class, heterosexual, male perspective. A recent reviewer comments on the prevailing view of the self in contemporary philosophy and social theory: "Prevailing conceptions of the self ignore the multiple, sometimes fractious sources of social identity constituted at the intersections of one's gender, sexual orientation, race, class, age, ethnicity, and so forth" (*Stanford Encyclopedia of Philosophy* 2015 [1999]). Although such criticisms are not designed to totally discredit or invalidate these metanarratives, they are intended to challenge them and to offer a skeptical appraisal of these major theoretical traditions. They also suggest the possibility of alternative theoretical strategies for analyzing the growing complexity, liquidity and indeterminacy of contemporary social reality.

LOOKING AROUND AT TWENTY-FIRST-CENTURY SOCIAL THEORY

In place of the grand theories and metanarratives of the twentieth century, many late modernist, postmodernist and postmillennial theorists of the twenty-first century propose rather different strategies for theorizing society, social relations and social identities. The strategy for many twenty-first-century theorists has been to construct "local narratives" — or what the French social theorist Michel Foucault called "counter-histories" — often from the perspective of particular minority groups and "subaltern" subjects. This has most obviously been the case for the new generation of feminist and gender theories, which tend to privilege the viewpoints of women and other sexual minorities. It is also the case for theories emerging from other marginalized communities; examples include Afrocentric theory, Indigenous theory and queer theory. Contemporary social theory is more "polyvocal" (speaking in different voices) in nature than the previous generation of sociological theory. At the same time, this new critical sensitivity towards the limitations of modernist metanarratives has encouraged the growth of other theoretical perspectives — such as standpoint theory, intersectionality theory, as well as poststructuralism and deconstructionism — that offer many more methodological and theoretical strategies for overcoming the traditional biases embedded in modernist metanarratives.

The theories of today are more deliberately "relativistic"; they are more likely to recognize and emphasize that the validity of any theory is always limited by the particular context in which it is constructed and applied. Many theorists today have largely embraced the values of historical, cultural, societal and other forms of relativism. In this sense, many twenty-first-century social theories have rejected the major assumption of positivism: namely, that a valid scientific proposition holds true irrespective of when, or where, or by whom it is stated. In this respect, these social theorists may be classified as post-positivists.

Many social theories today are interdisciplinary and pluralist in their content and scope, drawing their sources of inspiration from several different disciplines and areas of study. Indeed, the rise of interdisciplinary areas of study — cultural studies, communication studies, global studies, literary studies, gender studies, women's studies, queer studies etc. — is sometimes seen as a threat to the long-term viability and survival of sociology as an independent discipline. Irving Louis Horowitz claims that "sociology has largely become a repository of discontent, a gathering of individuals who have special agendas, from gay and lesbian rights to liberation theology" (1993: 12). He is embittered by what he sees as the destruction of the objectivity and authority of sociology.

The changing faces of contemporary social theories, including their greater relativism, reflexivity, localism, pluralism, polyvocality and interdisciplinarity, have greatly diversified the field of theory in sociology and throughout the social sciences and humanities. Whereas the earlier generation of modernist sociological theory was dominated by several major traditions — structural functionalism, conflict theory, critical theory, symbolic interactionism, dramaturgy, exchange theory and rational choice theory and ethnomethodology (EM) — the field has broadened considerably and has grown ever more intertwined and integrated. The "great debates" of the past generation — order versus conflict models of society, macro versus micro levels of social theory, objective (empirical or positivist) sociological theories versus subjective (interactionist or phenomenological) sociological theories — no longer hold centre stage as they once did in the discipline. Today, the field of social and sociological theory has become too broad and diverse, and often too intertwined, for these debates to retain their earlier significance.

KEEPING THEORY SIMPLE

For many students and general readers, the prospect of studying sociological or social theory is daunting and intimidating. Theory — because it is often formulated in abstract and unfamiliar jargon — may seem remote and largely irrelevant to the bustling everyday world of practical affairs and personal concerns. Many students enroll in theory courses at college or university not because they choose to but because they have to in order to complete their program. Part of the purpose of this introductory chapter, therefore, is to show how theory can help us to look more deeply into our social world and understand more clearly some of the social forces that impinge upon our own individual lives.

One interesting way of seeing theories — especially sociological or social theories — is as glasses, i.e., spectacles, that can equip us with x-ray vision: that is, a theoretical vision to see beneath, or behind, surface appearances to a deeper, less directly observable social reality. Theories provide the lenses through which we see the world in ways that are often unrecognized and unacknowledged by us. But more importantly, theories can also enable us to look more deeply into social structures and social relations and discern the *underlying causal mechanisms* of our actions that often remain unobservable to the naked eye. This "theoretical gaze" was used by political economist Adam Smith, who saw beneath the surface exchanges between buyers and sellers and discovered what he called the "invisible hand" of market forces (supply and demand), which, when left alone to balance themselves, were responsible for setting the level of wages, prices, rents and other basic economic transactions. Similarly, Karl Marx gazed beneath the cycle of the regular work day and discovered that the extraction of "surplus value" — through the "exploitation" of the unpaid labour power of the industrial worker — was the "hidden secret" (or causal mechanism) underlying the production of profit and the rapid accumulation of wealth under capitalism. Other theorists have also discovered what they believed to be underlying causal mechanisms that helped to explain aspects of human behaviour. Charles Darwin discovered the "law of natural selection," which he believed explained the evolution of all animal species and the relationship of humans to the higher primates. And Sigmund Freud, in his study of such psychological maladies as hysteria and neurosis, discovered the power of the "libido" (sex drive) in mental life and the ability of the unconscious mind to "repress" painful memories and erect psychological "defence mechanisms."

Throughout this book, we shall encounter a variety of social theorists, each with their own particular set of ideas of how best to understand the changing social world that we inhabit. To simplify the tasks of describing, analyzing, comparing and contrasting, critiquing and applying these theories, there are several basic dimensions that should be included in any discussion of a social theory. These dimensions are briefly outlined below:

All sociological theories may be understood as mini-languages (or discourses): Any social theory — whether it is Marxism, structural functionalism, symbolic interactionism, ethnomethodology, feminism, postmodernism etc. — may be thought of as a mini-language (or mini-discourse). Learning a theory, therefore, is akin to learning a new language. Each theory has its own vocabulary of key concepts and its own set of basic assumptions that form the foundation of the theoretical discourse. To understand a theory, therefore, it is necessary to be able to identify its key concepts, show how they relate to each other and be able to apply them to an empirical or historical example. Some microsocial theories focus on the face-to-face, or interpersonal, aspects of social interaction, and some focus on the internal, intra-personal or psychological dynamics of personality and identity. Macrosocial theories focus on the large-scale societal or global structures, systems, institutions or networks and social processes that impact our lives and sometimes determine our destinies.

One of the implications of treating sociological theories as languages or discourses is that the way we *speak* about society greatly influences the way we *observe* society. In an important sense, what we see and what we look for in society are very much dependent upon the concepts and categories that form the "conceptual frame" of our sociological discourse. If we speak the language of Marxism, we are likely to see many examples of class struggle, alienation, exploitation and false consciousness in the world. But when speaking the language of psychoanalysis, we are far more likely to observe examples of "Freudian slips" in our conversations with others or symptoms of unresolved Oedipal (or Electra) complexes or traces of projection, transference or repression. On the other hand, if we speak the language of structural functionalism, we are more likely to see examples of social systems, societal functions, statuses and roles, as well as norms and values in the world. Without some kind of language, it is difficult, if not impossible, to impose any conceptual order on the social world. This is what the philosopher Ludwig Wittgenstein (1922) meant in the concluding statement to his *Tractatus Logico-Philosophicus*: "Whereof we cannot speak, thereof, we must be silent" (7). How we speak about the world "frames" how we see the world; language and observation are intimately connected. This is particularly true for theoretical languages.

Another implication of treating sociological theories as modes of discourse is that what may count as a "fact" may differ from one theoretical language (or discourse) to the next. In this respect, we may say that the facts of sociological analysis are always constituted within a particular theoretical language. The way we distinguish facts from theories is another story. For the sake of brevity, we shall simply say that, for us, a *fact may be defined as a highly confirmed observation statement*, one that is testable either through direct or indirect means of observation. However, different theoretical perspectives and discourses may have different criteria of "observability."

In the psychological theory language of radical behaviourism, what count as facts are those aspects of the behaviour of an organism — whether that organism is a rat, a pigeon or a human — that are externally observable and measurable. Indeed, not only can all of the key concepts of behaviourism be observed by an independent researcher, but they can also be assigned numerical values (which is to say, they can be measured). You have only to think of typical behaviourist concepts such as "stimulus," "response," "reinforcement" and "extinction" to see that this is the case. This is very different from sociological traditions such as symbolic interactionism or structural functionalism, in which the key concepts are much more abstract and non-empirical in content. Concepts such as "social system," "value orientation" and "social self" cannot be directly observed in the same measurable way as behaviourist concepts.

All sociological theories may be understood as critical responses to other theories: Most social theories arise as a critique of (or counter-argument to) prevailing or previous theories within the discipline. They invariably emerge as a "critical response" to established or earlier theories that continue to exert a powerful intellectual influence on a discipline or area of study. Marx used the expression "settling of accounts" to describe his critique of the bourgeois tradition of political economy represented in the writings of Adam Smith, David Ricardo, Thomas Malthus and others. And while Marx may have built upon the foundations of their labour theory of value, he saw his own work as a critique and transcendence of classical political economy. He also saw his work as a critique of other intellectual traditions, such as German historical idealism (represented in the work of Hegel) and French utopian socialism (represented in the works of Saint-Simon, Proudhon, Fourier and others). Even structural functionalism, now commonly perceived as a conservative sociological theory, arose — with anthropologists such as Malinowski and Radcliffe-Brown — as a radical critique of earlier, often racist and ethnocentric, anthropological theories of evolutionism, social-Darwinism and diffusionism. Similarly, the environmentalist critique contained in radical behaviourism of Pavlov, Skinner, Watson and others may be seen as a powerful psychological critique of the hereditarian theories popular at the turn of the nineteenth century, as well as the psychoanalytic theories of the early twentieth century. To fully comprehend any social theory, it is necessary to retrace the intellectual steps that led to its construction and adoption. This often means revisiting the original theoretical argument that precipitated the critical response. When considering sociological theories as critical responses to prior or dominant theories within the field of discourse, we need to ask: Which traditions of theory are being challenged by the current theory?

All sociological theories may be understood as political practices or as guides to social action: Besides framing the way we speak about and observe social phenomena, social theories may also influence the ways in which we act within our social world. Our actions, or — as French social theorist Michel Foucault called them — our "discursive practices," are often informed by our theoretical (or ideological) views, beliefs and values. We may embrace a theoretical view openly and explicitly and fully acknowledge our commitment to a particular perspective. But sometimes, we may not always fully recognize or reflect upon the influence that a particular theory (or ideology) exercises over our beliefs or upon our conduct. In other words, theories may exert either a "manifest" (or conscious) and fully acknowledged influence over our interpretations and actions, or they may exert a "latent" (or unconscious) and unacknowledged influence over our opinions and practices.

Social theories usually entail their own corresponding social actions and political practices. Some theories may be explicitly "programmatic" in content: Marx's theory of history and society contains a clarion call to the working class for the revolutionary seizure of state power, while Herbert Spencer's libertarianism reads more like a manifesto of non-interference (or *laissez-faire*) with the rights of private property. Other social theories may carry subtler or more ambiguous recommendations for social action or public policy. Some social theories — such as Marxism, feminism and queer theory — have clear implications for social and political activism in support of greater social equality and social justice. These activist theories have often formed the intellectual basis for powerful social and political movements — for civil rights, workers' rights, gender and sexual equality, social reform or even for political revolution. Other social theories have less obvious implications for popular political action but may well direct government policy and guide state or corporate behaviour. Neoliberal theories of free trade and open markets have informed such practices as privatization, deregulation, out-sourcing and off-shoring jobs, low taxes and cutbacks in social services wherever this "discursive regime" has prevailed.

More academic or professional sociological theories — such as structural functionalism and symbolic interactionism — have less obvious connections to social action or political practice. But even these theories carry implications that may well influence public policy, although more indirectly. Whereas a macrosocial theory like structural functionalism emphasizes the power of social systems and social structures over the relatively passive and "oversocialized" individual (see Wrong 1961), a microsocial theory like social exchange theory or symbolic interactionism, by contrast, emphasizes the dynamism and creativity of the individual (or "social actor") who is seen as a significant "agent" in their social interactions and life experiences (see Homans 1964). This juxtaposition of "structure" to "agency" produces different images of the individual in society, images that have different practical and political consequences. At the same time, many contemporary social theorists attempt to transcend this earlier modernist dichotomy between structure and agency and often succeed in constructing more integrated and interdisciplinary perspectives on social life.

While all sociological theories may contain some implicit or explicit guides to action, explicating these guides is not always an easy task. There will frequently be disagreement among scholars over the message and practical implication of a social theory. When considering sociological theories as guides to action, we need to ask: Who are the major players represented in the theoretical discourse: capitalists/workers; men/women; individual/society? Whose interests are being served by these theoretical ideas, and *cui bono* — who benefits, or who profits?

There are many different ways to talk about and analyze social theories. This first chapter shows how theories may be thought of not simply as abstract systems of ideas, but as real social forces with strong practical implications. Far from being disembodied figments of the sociological imagination, theories are often the expression of social and material interests, which have real consequences for society. Talking about theories as *languages* (or *discourses*), *critiques* and as *guides to action* (or political *practice*) reminds us that theories have consequences for both thought and action.

Figure 1-1: Dimensions of Social Theory

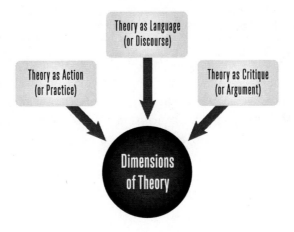

WHAT ARE GOOD SOCIAL THEORIES?

Having outlined some of the basic dimensions of a social theory, it remains for us to identify some of the attributes, or *desiderata* (desirable qualities), of a "good" theory — a theory that meets the prevailing expectations and standards of the scholarly discipline for which it was designed. While most of the theories covered in this book fail to meet all of these expectations, the following criteria provide a simple and useful framework for evaluating, comparing and contrasting different social theories. Indeed, we could even say that together, these criteria represent an *ideal type* of a good theory (also see Craib 1984).

Theories should be causal: Some of the most influential theories in the social sciences have been causal theories. These theories have discovered *underlying causal mechanisms* that explain the occurrence of particular events, processes or other types of social phenomena. Many of these causal mechanisms remained undetected by previous social scientists because they were not accessible to direct observation. Examples of causal mechanisms that operate beneath the surface of everyday social reality include the unconscious mind (discovered by Freud), the evolutionary process of natural selection (discovered by Darwin) and the production of surplus value (discovered by Marx). One of the constant criticisms made of much sociological theory is that it is largely descriptive and interpretative, rather than causal. Structural functionalism and symbolic interactionism, for example, have provided us with many ways of classifying, categorizing, analyzing, describing and interpreting social life. But they have added little to our knowledge and understanding of the *causes* of social action and social behaviour.

Theories should be systematic and logical: Theories should be constructed in a logical and systematic manner. Their key concepts should be unambiguous and clearly defined. Their major propositions should avoid any logical contradictions, and the conclusions of theoretical statements and hypotheses should follow logically from the premises of these statements.

Theories should be testable: Theories should be empirically testable. Propositions and hypotheses should be formulated in such a way that they can either be confirmed (verified) or falsified on the basis of available empirical evidence (or data). Many modernist sociological theories have been formulated at such a high level of abstraction and generalization that they are impossible to test empirically. Some critics of these untestable, abstract theories (such as C. Wright Mills) have dismissed them as examples of grand theory in sociology. Other critics (such as Robert Merton) attempted to introduce what he called "theories of the middle range," that is, more empirically testable versions of established theories.

Theories should be innovative: Theories should break new ground and generate new insights and new knowledge. The most valuable theories are those that detect previously unrecognized and unidentified social phenomena. Some humanistic social theories have opened up new perspectives for the interpretation and understanding of social life without offering empirically rigorous or formalized causal models of explanation and prediction. Many sociological theories fall into this category — interactionist, dramaturgical, functionalist and historical theories are all examples of *humanistic* rather than *naturalistic* (or positivistic) social theories.

Theories should promote empathy: A final indicator of a good social theory that is largely absent from standard reviews, but is significant for our discussion, is its ability to promote and increase empathy for marginalized groups and individuals in society — among both members of the discipline and the wider general public. Contemporary social theory allows us to view the world from diverse standpoints, including feminist and LGBTQ, Afrocentric and Indigenous, and the standpoints of many other marginalized groups and individuals. While standpoint and intersectionality theories provide frameworks for the expression and representation of minority perspectives, experiences, identities and discourses, poststructuralism allows us to detect and deconstruct the androcentric and ethnocentric biases, as well as the "absences and silences" in our supposedly universal or objective narratives. Social theory has an important role to play in encouraging exploration of diverse viewpoints, discourses and identities that have long been excluded or marginalized within our social world. In this respect, the study of contemporary social theory helps in the cultivation of an informed and enlightened global citizenry. The chance to explore and experiment with diverse theoretical perspectives challenges dogmatism and intolerance and offers an opportunity to learn from difference and diversity.

Throughout this book, social theories are never taught as doctrines to be uncritically embraced or as ideologies to be mindlessly defended. We see social theories as tools in a toolbox; while some theories may be useful for accomplishing certain tasks, other theories are valuable for different ones.

WHY STUDY SOCIAL THEORY?

The concept of "theory" is not necessarily held in high esteem in the bustling, businesslike world of the office, boardroom, sales counter or shop floor. "That's all very well in theory" is a common complaint against abstract and speculative ideas that have little obvious connection to the "real world." Theory, for many people, is synonymous with imaginative thinking that is, for the most part, untested and unproven and is not of practical use. Indeed, in the hard-headed worlds of government, industry, commerce, finance and the media, where hard work, practical experience and a good track record are prized above all else, theory may be seen to do more harm than good; it may be more trouble than it's worth. For most people, facts are more important than theory. Facts are, at least, proven and known phenomena. According to popular belief, facts never lie. Or do they?

One of the most important lessons to be learned from this book is that facts and theories are much more closely entwined than is normally recognized. Rather than standing on their own feet as objective building blocks of reality, facts — especially "social facts" — are better understood as products (or artifacts) of theories. Stripped down to their bare essentials, facts are nothing more than observation statements — albeit highly confirmed observation statements. We report something as a fact when we believe it to be true; it is an observation that is stable and unlikely to change. We do not expect that the date of the French Revolution (1789) will ever change or that the sun will ever rise anywhere but in the east.

FACTS AND THEORIES

Although our "common sense" assumes that the facts always speak for themselves, things are never quite that simple. Science historians (see especially Thomas Kuhn, Paul Feyerabend, Stephen Toulmin and Norwood Russell Hanson) have shown in their work that the "facts" of any accepted scientific paradigm may later be contradicted and superseded by the "facts" of a new paradigm. Indeed, the history of science suggests that facts are actually produced by scientific theories rather than simply discovered through objective methods of scientific research. Theories contribute to the search for new facts by providing new languages of observation. In this respect, new theories enable us not only to talk about our world in new ways, but also to *see* our world in unaccustomed ways. And, as a result of talking about and seeing our world in new ways, we are able to act in, and interact with, our world in innovative ways. Theories are the golden threads which link our ways of talking and seeing to our ways of acting in our world.

As we shall discover throughout this book, the social theories and the social observation terms that we use to talk about and observe society and its institutions all have a strong impact on how we act and interact in society. If, for example, we perceive society as a mechanical or organic system made up of many different yet interrelated parts, we probably elevate the system above the individual in our efforts to reach an understanding of how society works. Indeed, we may end up agreeing with the classical sociologist Emile Durkheim that society has a "reality" *sui-generis*, that is — over and above or external to that of the individuals who compose it.

If, on the other hand, like several contemporary social theorists, we perceive society as made up of relations of communication, our actions are likely to correspond with these beliefs. In this case, we may be concerned to free communication from the constraints imposed upon it by inequalities of power and wealth; we may be motivated — like Jürgen Habermas — to work towards "undistorted communication" in our professional, political, occupational and home environments. In other words, whether we think about and see society as a mechanical or organic system, as a public theatre of dramatic performances, as an evolutionary struggle for the survival of the fittest, as a social exchange of rewards and punishments, as a network of channels of communication or as an imaginary site constructed and deconstructed through different discourses, what we *see* will condition what we *do*. The language, or discourse, that we use to think about and observe our social surroundings strongly influences how we act in these surroundings. What we believe about society affects how we talk about and how we see society, and how we talk about and see society greatly influences how we act. This is the hidden power of theory — especially social theory.

SOCIAL OBSERVATION

Many examples could be used to show the power that theories have over our beliefs, perceptions and actions. Far from being inconsequential and superfluous, theories play an important role in our lives and in our relationships with others. As we proceed through this book, we shall distinguish some of the different ways in which theories may influence our lives and our perceptions of others. To simplify things, we propose the following distinction: some theories may be *consciously* accepted and defended — we classify these theories as "espoused" or "explicit." Other theories may be *unconsciously* accepted without us realizing that they are theories — we classify these as "tacit," "implicit" or "taken-for-granted" theories.

Among explicit theories, we may further distinguish between those that are conditionally accepted subject to testing and possible disproof (or falsification) and those that are unconditionally and uncritically accepted and defended — even in the face of overwhelming contradictory evidence. Theories that are unconditionally accepted may become institutionalized as "ideologies" — that is, they may become installed as official doctrines of states, organizations or political or religious groups and movements.

In all these cases, whether official or unofficial, explicit or tacit, any set of ideas that seeks to advance an explanation of human behaviour or social action can be regarded as a social theory and may be analyzed accordingly.

DECODING SOCIAL THEORIES

In the face of the diversity of theories, readers are encouraged to analyze the theoretical perspectives covered in the following chapters by examining a number of different elements. These elements may be used as a basis for explicating, comparing, contrasting and critiquing different theories and for assessing their respective strengths and limitations. We use the acronym SCAM as a reminder of the main elements of social theories: scale, concepts, assumptions, methodology.

Table 1-1: SCAM — Main Elements of Social Theories

Element	Question
Scale	What level of analysis is the focus of the theoretical perspective: macrosocial, mesosocial or microsocial?
Concepts	What are the key terms and concepts in the vocabulary of the theoretical language?
Assumptions	What are the basic assumptions of the theoretical perspective?
Methodology	Does the theoretical perspective use objective methods of analysis or subjective methods? Is the perspective oriented towards the explanation and prediction of social behaviour or the description, interpretation and understanding of social action? How are theoretical statements tested, confirmed, verified or falsified?

Scale: The first element for analyzing social theories is the scale. Does the theory focus on a microscopic social reality (nominalism) of face-to-face-interactions or a macroscopic social reality (realism or holism) of large-scale social structures, processes and events? In other words, does the perspective focus on the individual or on the collective? Or does the theory integrate or bridge both levels of social reality?

Concepts: The second element for analyzing social theories is the conceptual frame. What are the key concepts included in the vocabulary of the theory language? What are some of the basic observation terms? What are some of the underlying conceptual devices that help to systematize and structure the theory? What is the underlying social metaphor used in the narrative — society as a system, a game, a war, a market, a theatre, a discourse or an evolutionary environment — or something else? (see Rigney 2001).

Assumptions: The third element for analyzing social theories is the assumptions. Does the theory emphasize the need for consensus and social order or focus on the reality of conflict and change. Does the theory assume an independent social reality or a social reality constructed through discourse?

Methodology: The fourth element for analyzing social theories is methodology (i.e., the methods used to produce knowledge). Is the theory based upon a naturalistic (empiricist or positivist) theory of knowledge (i.e., an epistemology) or a humanistic (interpretative or hermeneutic) epistemology? Does the theory use objective (i.e., empirical or positivist) methods of analysis or subjective (i.e., interpretative or hermeneutic) methods? Is the theory primarily oriented towards the explanation and prediction of (externally observable and measurable) social behaviour or the description, interpretation and understanding of (subjectively meaningful) social action? How are theoretical statements (i.e., propositions, accounts, narratives) tested, confirmed, verified or falsified? Is the theory based upon an explanatory narrative (identifying underlying causal mechanisms), a descriptive narrative (historical, empirical or statistical) or an interpretative narrative (from an interactionist, dramaturgical or postmodernist perspective) or some combination of the above? What kinds of evidence may be used for assessing the truth claims of the theory? What kind of "facts" does the theory produce? What kind of hypotheses can be generated by the theory?

HOW TO TALK ABOUT SOCIOLOGICAL THEORY

There are many ways to define a social theory. Within the discipline of sociology there is little agreement over what constitutes a theory; theorists often differ in their definition of what a theory is depending upon their own theoretical preferences and perspectives. Some theorists define a social theory in formal terms that emphasize their preferred method of theory construction. One such definition is provided by Michael Faia

(1986: 134): "A theory is a set of interrelated propositions that allow for the systematization of knowledge, explanation and prediction of social life, and generation of new research hypotheses." Similarly, for Robert Merton (1949: 448), "the term 'sociological theory' refers to logically interconnected sets of propositions from which empirical uniformities can be derived."

Other sociologists define social theory more loosely in order to include ideas that have proven influential but cannot always be formally defined according to strict and narrow methodological criteria. Such a definition is provided by George Ritzer and Jeffrey Stepnisky (2018: 4):who suggest that social theories have "a wide range of application, deal with centrally important social issues, and have stood the test of time. These criteria constitute the definition of sociological theory used in this book." As Ritzer and Stepnisky put it, theories may often include those "big ideas" in sociology that have stood the test of time and that deal with major social issues, far-reaching in scope. Examples of these big ideas from the classical theorists include Marx's theory of class struggle, Weber's theory of Protestantism and capitalism and Pareto's theory of the circulation of elites. Today, some of the big ideas would probably include Bauman's theory of liquid modernity, Beck's theory of the risk society, Castells' theory of the network society, and Giddens' theory of the runaway society.

The conception of sociological and social theory used throughout this book has much more in common with the broad, inclusive definition proposed by Ritzer and Stepnisky than with the more formal definitions proposed by other writers. We are interested in the stories of society told by social theorists, irrespective of whether the validity of these stories can be tested according to the prevailing methods of empirical social research. Some of the most enduring and influential ideas of sociological and social theory have been those for which few satisfactory empirical indicators have been found. Weber's concept of "rationalization" surely falls into this category, as does Marx's concepts of "alienation" and "exploitation," as well as Mead's concept of the "reflexive self." The fact that these ideas have proven difficult to operationalize has not prevented them from being used in a rich and fertile tradition of descriptive social theory. For this reason, we retain as broad a definition of sociological theory as possible.

SOCIAL THEORY AND SOCIAL LITERACY

In the following chapters of this book, you will be introduced to some of the foremost social and sociological theorists of the twentieth and twenty-first centuries with up-to-date examples of how these theories and their related concepts may be used to enhance our understanding of contemporary events: both the small-scale (micro) events that we experience directly in our everyday lives and the large-scale (macro) events that we encounter indirectly as major news stories in the mass media. You will be equipped with a set of analytical and conceptual skills to use the theoretical perspectives, the observation terms and the methods of practical reasoning of these various social theories for a greater understanding of your own life experiences and of the social worlds that you inhabit. You will learn to read behind the headlines and to peer beneath surface appearances in order to grasp the deeper meaning of the personal, public and political events that influence our lives and shape our destinies. You will develop a proficiency in observing and analyzing the patterns of social interaction that combine to produce the social structures and the social processes that form the texture of our private and public lives.

Another way to describe the project of this book is to suggest that by acquiring a knowledge and ability to apply contemporary social theory to real-life situations, you will enhance your "social literacy": the ability to decipher the meaning of social events, social interactions, social identities and other social phenomena through understanding the underlying causal mechanisms and the ongoing practical logics that produce and reproduce these phenomena. Social literacy implies an ability to understand and interpret the deeper interactional infrastructures of social discourses and social practices much as literary theorists examine the semantic and syntactical structures of novels and poetry or as psychotherapists explore the deeper levels of consciousness. Social theories offer a variety of languages with which to analyze the many different aspects of our social reality. Rather than being a weakness, this "theoretical pluralism" provides a unique opportunity to engage with multiple interpretations, explanations, viewpoints, perspectives and worldviews and the many different social constructions of "reality."

References

Baudrillard, Jean. 1995. *The Gulf War Did Not Take Place*. Bloomington: Indiana University Press.

Bauman, Zygmunt. 1999. *Liquid Modernity*. Polity Press.

Berman, Marshall. 1982. All *That Is Solid Melts into Air: The Experience of Modernity*. Verso.

CBC Radio. 2016. "Are Short-Term Jobs the New Normal?" *The Current*, October 25. <http://www.cbc.ca/radio/thecurrent/the-current-for-october-25-2016-1.3818896/are-short-term-jobs-the-new-normal-1.3818898>.

Craib, Ian. 1984. *Modern Social Theory — from Parsons to Habermas*. London: Harvester-Wheatsheaf.

Debord, Guy. 1970. *The Society of the Spectacle*. Black & Red (in English).

Faia, Michael A. 1986. *Dynamic functionalism: Strategy and tactics*. London: Cambridge University Press.

Hardt, Michael, and Negri, Antonio. 2000. *Empire*. Harvard University Press.

Homans, George C. 1964. "Bringing Men Back In." *American Sociological Review*, 29, 6 (Dec.): 809–818.

Horowitz, Irving Louis. 1993. *The Decomposition of Sociology*. New York: Oxford University Press.

Klein, Naomi. 2000. *No Logo*. London: Flamingo.

Marx, Karl. 1848. *The Manifesto of the Communist Party*. Section 1, paragraph 18, lines 12–14.

Merton, Robert K. 1949. "On Sociological Theories of the Middle Range." In *Social Theory and Social Structure*: Chapter 35. New York: Simon & Schuster, The Free Press.

Mills, C. Wright. 1959. *The Sociological Imagination*. New York: Oxford University Press.

Rigney, Daniel. 2001. *The Metaphorical Society: An Invitation to Social Theory*. Rowman & Littlefield Publishers.

Ritzer, George, and Jeffrey Stepnisky. 2018. *Modern Sociological Theory*, 8th edition. Sage.

Seidman, Steven. 1991. "The End of Sociological Theory: The Postmodern Hope." *Sociological Theory*, 9, 2 (Autumn): 131–146.

Standing, Guy. 2011. *The Precariat: The New Dangerous Class*. Bloomsbury.

Stanford Encyclopedia of Philosophy. 2015 [1999]. "Feminist Perspectives on the Self." First published Mon Jun 28, 1999; substantive revision Mon Jul 6, 2015. <https://plato.stanford.edu/entries/feminism-self/>.

Wittgenstein, Ludwig. 1922. *Tractatus Logico-Philosophicus*. (C.K. Ogden, Trans.) (Original work published in 1921. London: Kegan Paul.

Wrong, Dennis. 1961. "The Oversocialized Conception of Man in Modern Sociology." *American Sociological Review*, 26, 2: 183–193.

CHAPTER 2

THEORIZING OUR HUMAN SYSTEMS

Structural Functionalism and Systems Theory

SYSTEMS ARE EVERYWHERE

On October 23, 1958, an underground earthquake (or "bump") shattered the mineshafts of the Number 2 colliery of the Springhill mine in in Cumberland County, Nova Scotia. At this time, the mine was one of the deepest in the world, reaching more than 1200 metres below ground level. By the time all rescue attempts were completed, seventy-five men had died. The last twelve survivors were brought to the surface at 2:25 a.m. on Thursday, October 30, 1958. They had spent five and a half days in the dark, trapped in a diminishing air-pocket, awaiting either rescue or death.

For most of us, the experience of remaining trapped so far underground, in total darkness, vulnerable to toxic fumes, rising water levels, and hunger, thirst and cold, would lead to an overwhelming sense of despair. And this was certainly true to a certain extent for these trapped miners. However, in many ways, their situation was more complex and interesting; from a sociological perspective, their collective (team) behaviour followed a pattern that could have been predicted and readily explained by the modern theory of structural functionalism.

According to reports collected from survivors — especially from the last twelve men to be rescued — the social interactions among the survivors followed a pattern familiar to sociologists. During the initial phase of their entrapment, several energetic workers tried hard to find an escape route through the blocked tunnels and collapsed mineshafts. This group was strongly task-oriented and more focused on the physical and technical challenges of their predicament than on the emotional distress of their workmates. When their best efforts to escape proved futile and they resigned themselves to the prospect of abandonment and death, other trapped workers began to play an empathic and emotionally supportive role within the group. These individuals were less task-oriented and far more motivated by feelings of sympathy, empathy and support towards fellow group members. This distinction between these two types of leadership was described by American journalist, author and filmmaker Sebastian Junger in reference to the Springhill mining disaster (2016).

What is of interest to us as students of social theory is that the famous structural functionalist theorist Talcott Parsons (along with his collaborator, Robert Bales) had earlier discovered that social groups struggling to solve a specific problem invariably produce two types of leader: the task-oriented leader (whom Parsons categorized as "instrumental"), who single-mindedly seeks a practical solution to the problem at hand; and the socio-emotional leader (Parsons's "expressive" leader), who tries to build consensus and cohesion within the group by recognizing and acknowledging the efforts and feelings of all group members. Parsons and Bales first reported the emergence of these two distinctive leadership styles when observing how jurors arrived at their verdicts in the often stressful and

The Springhill Mining Disaster

Canadian psychologists who interviewed the miners after their rescue determined that these early leaders tended to lack empathy and emotional control, that they were not concerned with the opinions of others, that they associated with only one or two other men in the group, and that their physical abilities far exceeded their verbal abilities. But all of these traits allowed them to take forceful, life-saving action where many other men might not. Once the escape attempts failed, different kinds of leaders emerged. In what researchers termed the "survival period," the ability to wait in complete darkness without giving up hope or succumbing to panic became crucial. Researchers determined that the leaders during this period were entirely focused on group morale and used skills that were diametrically opposed to those of the men who had led the escape attempts. They were highly sensitive to people's moods, they intellectualized things in order to meet group needs, they reassured the men who were starting to give up hope, and they worked hard to be accepted by the entire group.

Without exception, men who were leaders during one period were almost completely inactive during the other; no one, it seemed, was suited to both roles. These two kinds of leaders more or less correspond to the male and female roles that emerge spontaneously in open society during catastrophes such as earthquakes or the Blitz. (Junger 2016) combative settings in which jury deliberations typically take place (Bales 1951; also Parsons and Bales 1955).

Instrumental leaders are, by definition, task-oriented and primarily driven by their desire to find solutions to particular problems facing the group. They are largely indifferent to, or even impatient with, the need for group solidarity and cohesion. For this reason, they can be unpopular with other group members. On the other hand, expressive leaders try to extend a sense of inclusivity whereby the efforts and feelings of all group members are accorded recognition, respect and consideration.

This division between instrumental and expressive functions within small groups played a major role in Parsons' analysis of other social systems — including the nuclear family. However, as feminist critics point out, he employed a gendered stereotypical association of the instrumental role with the male (husband/father) status and the expressive role with the female (wife/mother) status. Some academic defenders of Parsons suggest that instrumental and expressive roles can be performed by either partner in a relationship — especially as the range of pair-bonded relationships has expanded greatly to include same-sex marriages; foster parents; stepparents; adoptive parents etc. (see, for example, Johnson 1993: 115–130).

Figure 2-1: Parson's Model of the Nuclear Family

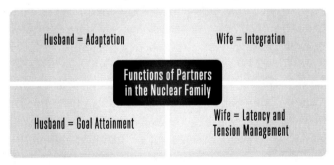

Source: see Finley and Schwartz 2006.

The story of the Springhill mining disaster shows how social life can be more thoroughly understood through the application of social theory. In this case, the harrowing experience of the trapped miners — as catastrophic as it was — may be studied in terms of the theory of small groups advanced by Parsons and his colleagues. The group dynamics of the miners resembled that of the jurors: both groups may be analyzed as small-scale social systems. According to Parsons — and his structural functionalist theory — all social systems have both instrumental and expressive needs that have to be satisfied if the system is to remain sustainable. For Parsons, all forms of human interaction may be analyzed as social systems and all social systems have basic functional needs (or "functional imperatives").

The story of the Springhill miners is simply one example of how social theory enables us to gaze beneath the level of surface appearances in order to discover the deeper structures of social relations and the underlying causes of the group dynamics that usually promote stability, although they may sometimes promote disruption and conflict within the system. This "theoretical gaze" allows us to observe the deeper structures and processes of social life.

We begin this chapter with a brief review of the theory of structural functionalism, which remained the dominant theoretical perspective in North American and Anglophone sociology for the first half of the twentieth century. Although its significance has been superseded by many other social theories, it is important — for historical and intellectual reasons — to examine the role this perspective played in shaping the development of modern sociological theory. As we shall see, the most important contribution of the structural functionalist theorists was to introduce the concept of "system" into the study of social relations. This general definition of "system" may be applied not only to mechanical systems (such as a car engine) but equally to biological systems (such as our own body), as well as to social systems — whether small-scale, like the family, or large-scale, such as the society or nation.

Although most of this chapter focuses on large-scale (or macro-sociological) systems of social relations (such as whole societies, institutions or organizations), the concept of system can also be applied to much smaller units of social analysis. A nuclear family can be described as a system composed of such elements as parents, children and the dog. In other words, the concept of system is flexible and adaptable. It can slide up and down the ladder of abstraction, from the most abstract system of a total society, to a more concrete system such as a household, a team of paramedics, a group of trapped coal miners — or to some other small group of individuals. There are also sub-atomic systems made up of elementary particles and cosmic systems made up of solar systems, galaxies and — for all we know — parallel universes. And then there are social systems made up of individual social actors who constitute the organized forms of collective life. For our purposes, we can define system as *a set of interdependent parts in which any change in one part will necessarily lead to changes in the other parts.*

We have become increasingly aware that our individual lives are directly connected to the lives of others — even those in faraway places, out of sight and out of mind. We live, as the Canadian media theorist Marshall McLuhan was fond of saying, in a global village: "Today, after more than a century of electric technology, we have extended our central nervous system itself in a global embrace, abolishing both space and time as far as our planet is concerned" (1964: 3). Global society has become a huge world system in which each of us is a small but thoroughly interdependent part.

As consumers of goods and services, we are all part of a system that links local, regional, national and international markets. If we were to follow the trail of our morning cup of coffee, we would find that it leads back to impoverished seasonal coffee pickers. Most of us who buy brand name products would be appalled to see how these items are produced in the sweatshops of the export-processing zones (EPZs) in Indonesia, China, Mexico, Vietnam, the Philippines and elsewhere (Klein 1999). In these regimented sweatshops of the Global South, the most famous brand name products are assembled for the consumer markets of the West. Nike running shoes, Tommy Hilfiger t-shirts, Gap pajamas, IBM computers, Old Navy jeans — all these products and more are produced in conditions that would probably have moved Charles Dickens to tears. If this were not bad enough, many luxury items originate from brutal conditions, e.g., the trade in blood diamonds, which has brought violence and bloodshed to Sierra Leone and the Congo (see the movie *Blood Diamond* 2006; also Brilliant Earth n.d.). We are part of an international system of production and consumption in which the consumer lifestyles of the rich nations are serviced by the super-exploitation of labour in the poorest regions of the planet.

Most of us take for granted the range of products available in our supermarkets and department stores. These products simply appear on the shelves. When purchasing them we rarely think about the human labour that went into their production or the conditions under which they were produced. Our failure to recognize any human dimension to commodities means that most of us remain ignorant of the underlying social relations that connect us to the products and services that we buy and consume. Every commodity involves a chain of labour that extends from the oil well, the mine, the plantation, the farm or factory and the sweatshop, through its refining and processing, through its transportation by road, rail, sea or air, to the supermarket and department store. Much of the industry associated with the production of commodities is organized through private companies — increasingly by large transnational corporations which produce for the global market. The huge profits accumulated by these corporations in the Global South and other regions is often extracted from workers (often children) who labour under conditions of semi-slavery, bonded labour or debt servitude (see Gausi 2018).

Over the past few decades some of the glaring inequalities of the global capitalist system have begun to receive more critical coverage. Everyday items such as coffee, lettuce and grapes are often produced by workers at home and abroad who are exploited for their labour and denied basic human rights, such as the right to form a union or to receive a minimum wage. The international economic system has never been a level playing field. The system that supplies consumers in the West with relatively cheap food and clothes is the same system that forces workers in the Global South to produce these goods under conditions of extreme economic exploitation and social misery. We are all parts of this system, even if we have never reflected on the roles we play within it.

LIVING IN SYSTEMS

Today, we are more aware than ever of our interconnectedness with others — of our own human species and of other species. Besides living in a globalized economic system, we also inhabit a global ecological system, and we are only beginning to understand how our local activities affect the rest of the world. In the last few decades, we have learned that our emissions of hydrocarbons in the industrial world have led to the process of global warming and climate change. Fossil fuel industries are responsible for climate change, which threatens the entire Earth. As we have recently seen, global warming has led to a sharp increase in severe forest fires and "wild" fires in North America, Australia and elsewhere, and its effects on rising ocean temperatures have led to an increase in the severity of violent storms and hurricanes in the US — Hurricanes Katrina (2005), Sandy (2012), Harvey, Maria and Irma (2017), in addition to those in other parts of the world, such as Hurricane Dorian, which killed hundreds of people in The Bahamas in 2019. We are all parts of the ecosystem, and any change in one part of this system has consequences for the total system.

The idea that we all live together in systems of social relations is hardly a novel one. Political philosophers have long described human societies as organisms, as living entities made up of numerous vital parts. One of the best examples of this image of society can be found in the writings of the English philosopher Thomas Hobbes, who titled his famous treatise on the state *Leviathan* — which means a huge creature or monster. Other philosophers equated the workings of society to those of a machine. By using the analogy, or metaphor, of a machine, many writers have implied that society can be reorganized or redesigned in the same way that a machine can be taken apart, stripped down and reassembled in a workshop. Images of society as a machine or as an organism can be traced back in European thought to the ancient Greeks and probably further back to other political thinkers from the Middle East, East Asia and other non-European civilizations.

A BRIEF HISTORY OF THE SOCIAL SYSTEM

The birth of the modern concept of "social system" can be traced back to the Enlightenment (1685–1815) and its aftermath in Europe. The discovery of the laws of gravity by Isaac Newton and the development of mathematics by René Descartes and others led the most advanced thinkers of the age to believe that the natural world could be fully explained in rational and scientific terms. Nature was seen as a mechanical system, much like a clock or any other human-made machine (see Dijksterhuis 1961). It did not take long for other thinkers to apply these ideas to the study of society. In France, social theorists such as Henri de Saint-Simon and his student Auguste Comte popularized the new discipline of "social physics" — later to be renamed "sociology" — as the new science of society. They believed that sociology would discover "laws of society" in the same way that physics had discovered laws of nature. The origins of modern sociological thought are closely related to the organicism of such writers as Henri de Saint-Simon, Auguste Comte, Louis de Bonald and Joseph de Maistre in France and Edmund Burke in England. The idea of society as a social organism also played an important part in the writings of such classical theorists as Emile Durkheim and Herbert Spencer (Levine 1995).

The French Revolution — with its attendant violence and cruelty — caused many conservative social thinkers to question the optimistic beliefs of the Age of Reason. For those intellectuals who spoke for the dispossessed French nobility, the Revolution embodied the worst features of the Enlightenment. These conservatives saw the Revolution as a catastrophe that had resulted in anarchy and violence. As part of their backlash against the Revolution, the conservatives rejected many of the ideas that had been used by the *philosophes* to justify the overthrow of the old order, the *ancien regime*. In particular, they rejected the universal and abstract declarations of the revolutionaries (liberty, equality, fraternity), as well as their blind belief in "human perfectibility" — the idea that the application of reason to human affairs was a guarantee of the inevitability of progress. Most of all, they rejected the mechanistic view of society. For them, society was not a machine that could be stripped down, redesigned and reassembled at will. Society was at best a social organism that had taken centuries to grow and mature. And like any organism, every part played a vital role in the survival of the total structure. It was no more possible to uproot social organs — institutions such as the monarchy and the church — than it was to uproot biological organs, such the heart and the brain, and expect the organism to survive. The idea of a social organism, in which all parts played a vital role, was the precursor of the later idea of a social system. Even today, this tension between human society conceived of as an organism (by conservatives) and society conceived of as a machine (by liberals and progressives) can be seen in how conservative commentators continue to oppose liberal and progressive reforms as "social engineering."

By the middle of the twentieth century, the idea of society as a social organism had evolved into the idea of society as a social system — a concept far more abstract and flexible than the earlier mechanistic and organic analogies. The notion of society as a social system has been used by a number of different social theorists, including the early British social anthropologists, American structural functionalists, the later neofunctionalists, German critical theorists, world-system theorists and many others.

It is clear that we all inhabit a number of different systems. Each of these systems places some constraints on the things that we can do and sets some limits on the range of possible actions we can perform. If a system is to remain viable and sustainable, the different parts of the system need to remain well integrated, well-regulated and fully functional.

THE LANGUAGE OF SOCIAL SYSTEMS THEORY

Most of us probably associate the term "social system" more with the theories of social scientists than with our own real-life experiences. What do social systems have to do with us? The truth is that many aspects of our lives can be understood clearly by invoking the concept of social system. This is especially the case when dealing with our relations and interactions with others. By focusing on how all of us are parts of a larger picture of social relations, we can often become more aware of the consequences that our actions may have for others. Seeing our lives as parts of larger social systems — as well as of ecosystems — gives us a broader perspective on how our social worlds are linked to those of others within our own communities and far beyond.

This is obviously true in terms of the big picture of how we fit into the systems of national or global social (as well as political, economic, eco- logical and cultural) relations. We have already seen that, as consumers of products from the sweatshop economies of nations in the Global South, our actions may perpetuate these conditions rather than improve them. We can begin to see how we fit into a global system of social relations and the international division of labour. This is also true when we analyze other large-scale systems of international relations. As citizens of Canada, we are part of the larger system of provincial and federal relations. We are also part of the North American system of free trade relations within what was once NAFTA, but which has become CUSMA (Canada-United- States-Mexico Agreement). Similarly, we are a part of other international systems, including NORAD, NATO and the United Nations.

Besides the large-scale systems of national, international and global relations, many other sets of social relations can be thought of as sys- tems. Most organizations can be represented as social systems, whether these are big oil companies, fast food franchises or small community or neighbourhood organizations, such as the local church, the Girl Guides and the United Way. For these systems to work efficiently and to sustain themselves over time, each part of the system needs to be fully integrated and fully functional.

The concept of social system is a master concept, or central concept, in several theoretical languages. Besides being central to the vocabulary of structural functionalism, it is also central to neofunctionalist theories (of Jeff Alexander and others), social systems theory (of Niklas Luhman and others), critical communication theory (of Jürgen Habermas), world-system theory (of Immanuel Wallerstein and others), as well as more recent general systems theories. Although some theorists have criticized some variations of social systems theory for conservatism, others have tried to integrate the concept of social system into Marxist and other critical analyses of capitalist and world capitalist societies. In this respect, social systems theory has proven to be one of the more adaptable and versatile theories of society.

A number of other concepts are used in conjunction with the concept of social system. Together, these concepts form a basic vocabulary in the language of social systems theory, although their meanings may be redefined from one theoretical tradition to another.

Social System: As we have already suggested, a system may be thought of as a set of mutually interrelated parts in which a change in one part results in a change to other parts in the system. If we think of the US federal government as a major social system, then a change in any of these parts will likely change other parts of the system. There is mounting evidence to suggest that the 2018–19 partial governmental shutdown ordered by President Trump had a number of dysfunctional effects — especially for those workers designated as "essential employees." Besides depriving all furloughed workers of their regular paycheques and sending many to foodbanks, loan companies and other short-term sources of funding and supplemental income, the shutdown still required many workers to perform their regular duties but without any pay. Air traffic controllers, airport security staff, members of the military, federal law enforcement agencies and homeland security officers were all required to report for work under increasingly stressful conditions. The shutdown disrupted many of the normal functions of the federal government social system and produced many social dysfunctions — such as increased house-hold debt, longer lineups at food banks, greater workplace stress and absenteeism. For the general public, the dysfunctional consequences of this presidential executive order were seen in longer airport lineups, increased travel risks and the closure of many public facilities, such as national parks and museums and the Bureau of Indian Affairs, to name only a few. The shutdown provided a classic example of how a major change in one part of the governmental system led to numerous changes in its constituent parts. And what is true for a federal government is also for other systems such as organizations, communities and whole societies.

Structure: Two other concepts which have figured prominently in the vocabulary of structural functionalist theorists are structure and function. Both of these concepts were originally linked to the biological metaphor of society as a social organism, which was popularized in nineteenth-century classical social theory by such writers as Emile Durkheim (in France) and Herbert Spencer (in England). According to this metaphor, society was seen as a social organism in a state of continuous evolution. The term "social structure" refers to the social organization of roles and statuses in a social system which are based upon recurrent and predictable patterns of social behaviour. As social structures grew increasingly complex over time, the component parts of these social structures became increasingly differentiated and specialized.

Equilibrium: According to Parsons and many other structural functional-ist theorists, social systems remain, for the most part, in a self-adjusting state of internal balance, or homeostasis. When external disturbances or internal changes happen, systems tend to correct themselves.

Function: The most obvious legacy of the biological metaphor in socio-logical theory can be seen in the concept of "function." The idea that societies, or social structures, are said to have functions is closely related to the idea that biological organisms are said to have needs. In much the same way that the different parts of an organism are indispensable to its overall vitality and survival, so too may the different parts of a society or organization be essential for its overall vitality and survival. Once sociologists adopted this theoretical perspective, the discipline became increasingly preoccupied with showing how the different parts of society (organizations, institutions, sets of beliefs or practices) are all functional for its long-term survival. This, in a nutshell, is the essence of classical structural functionalism: every system is made up of a set of interrelated parts and each part has an important role in the overall survival of the system. Anything that is functional helps the system maintain its internal cohesion and also helps it to adapt to its external environment. In a fam-ily setting, parents are functional not only as agents for the socialization of children but also as providers: they help the family unit adjust to its external environment and they help their children integrate into the family unit by internalizing common norms and values. Any social system — large or small — needs to ensure that its parts are fully functional in order for the system operate efficiently and effectively.

However, not all parts of a social system necessarily make a positive contribution to the maintenance of the system. Not all parts are necessarily functional. When we think about the different parts of a social system we normally include not only the individuals — or groups — who make up the system, but also the beliefs, practices, norms and values of these social actors. In any social system there are likely to be some parts that are "dysfunctional" — that is, they reduce the internal cohesion or the external adjustment of the overall system. Instead of contributing to the long-term sustainability and survival of the system, dysfunctional parts may contribute to its breakdown and disintegration.

The assessment as to what is functional or dysfunctional within a social system is not always clear-cut. It very much depends upon the viewpoint that is adopted. For example, although the institution of slavery in the United States and Canada was clearly dysfunctional for those who were sold into slavery, it was functional for those who made a profitable business from buying and selling and owning enslaved people. Similarly, in a classic contribution, the American theorist Lewis Coser, in his book *The Functions of Social Conflict* (1956), showed how various forms of social conflict could, in fact, be functional for the long-term sustainability of a society or social system.

FROM ANTHROPOLOGY TO SOCIOLOGY

Although the theoretical language of classical functionalism was developed in the writings of Spencer and Durkheim, much of the empirical research was undertaken by social anthropologists. Earlier studies in anthropology and ethology — especially during the late Victorian era — were strongly influenced by intellectual currents such as evolutionism, which had been introduced into the natural and social sciences through the ideas of Charles Darwin. However, many theorists of this time, such as Thomas Huxley, William Henry Flower, Francis Galton and Edward Tylor, extended these ideas beyond Darwin into theories of social-Darwinism, which celebrated the "survival of the fittest" in the struggle for existence — invariably with strong racist overtones (Lorimer 1988).

Victorian theorists invented a number of measures, including cerebral indexes and other specious craniometric measures from pseudo-scientific perspectives like phrenology and eugenics to construct racial taxonomies and racial hierarchies which were intended to demonstrate the innate "superiority" of the "Caucasian race" and the corresponding inferiority of the "primitive and savage races." These attempts to demonstrate the superiority of the "white race" coincided with the golden years of European imperialism. Today, we would hope that those vintage Victorian connections between anthropology and racism are long gone, but this is not the conclusion of a recent survey. In an article titled "Anthropology as White Public Space?" the authors ask: "How far has anthropology come in becoming racially inclusive?" Their answer is not very far at all: "Our argument is that anthropology departments have not done well when it comes to decolonizing their own practices around race. This is neither true of all departments nor true all of the time — but is still true all too often" (Brodkin, Morgen and Hutchinson 2011: 545).

At the same time, some anthropologists during the early twentieth century criticized and countered the racism and ethnocentrism of anthropological evolutionism and social-Darwinism. Two British anthropologists in particular, Bronislaw Malinowski and A.R. Radcliffe-Brown, pioneered important studies of non-literate societies using the language of classical functionalism. For these anthropologists, the rise of structural functionalism began as a critical encounter with the traditions of social evolutionism, historicism and cultural diffusionism (see Szacki 1979). Malinowski and Radcliffe -Brown — as well as Franz Boas and Ruth Benedict in the US — rejected the ethnocentrism and imperialism of the social evolutionists (Gough 1960). Instead of analyzing so-called "primitive" societies as examples of less biologically and culturally evolved populations, many functionalists adopted a perspective of "cultural relativism." Every society — whether literate or non-literate — was assumed to be well adapted to its environment. And every society could be analyzed as an efficient social system in which the basic structures and essential functions all contributed to meeting the long-term survival needs of the population as a whole. Anthropologists studying non-literate traditional societies held together by strong religious and magical beliefs (e.g., Malinowski's studies of the Trobriand Islanders of the South Pacific) had no trouble in showing how these societies were made up of mutually interdependent and functionally coordinated parts. These early anthropological functionalists focused on the complexities of societies that had been subjected to racist characterizations as exotic, simple and even non-human. And for this advance in our understanding, functionalism deserves considerable historical credit. However, while Malinowski and Radcliffe-Brown both rejected the racist theories and practices of evolutionism and social-Darwinism of their time, their embrace of cultural relativism continued to privilege literate over non-literature cultures, and in this respect, they remained locked into a Eurocentric perspective. As we shall see in a later chapter on Indigenous knowledge, contemporary anthropologists recognize the cultural significance of oral histories, ancestral stories and narratives as well as other "non-literate" ways of recording and transmitting knowledge and communal experiences.

Eventually, structural functionalist analysis showed itself to be less useful when more stratified horticultural, agricultural and especially industrial societies became the focus of study. Whereas smaller, well integrated hunting and gathering societies were normally based upon a fundamental social consensus — manifested in their unitary beliefs and social practices — stratified societies were invariably based upon sharp conflicts of interests — between slave owners and enslaved people; aristocrats and commoners; capitalists and workers. In other words, the primary assumption of structural functionalism, that society is based upon a fundamental consensus, became increasingly problematic in those more stratified societies in which social conflict was more apparent than social consensus.

Talcott Parsons (1951) and Robert Merton (1949) pioneered the use of structural functionalist ideas to describe and analyze industrial societies. Throughout the immediate postwar decades of the 1940s, 1950s and into the early 1960s, the ideas of Parsons dominated Western sociology and soon acquired the status of orthodoxy. While Parsons' earlier work displayed an interest in integrating the study of how the individual social actor is motivated to act within the collective structures of society, his later work appeared to lose sight of the individual and focused almost entirely on the structures and functions of social systems. In fact, Parsons' theoretical work may be divided into three distinct phases, beginning with his "voluntaristic" theory of social action — in which he focused on how the individual social actor selected particular means for the achievement of specific goals. This phase combined aspects of utilitarianism (the study of rational action) with aspects of idealism (the study of subjectively meaningful social action). In the second phase of Parsons' theoretical career he switched his emphasis to more "deterministic" aspects of the social systems that invariably regulate and constrain social action — through the institutionalization and internalization of norms, sanctions and societal goals. The third phase emphasized the process of societal evolution, whereby all institutions and organizations constantly increase their levels of structural complexity and functional differentiation.

Figure 2-2: The Three Phases of Parsons' Work

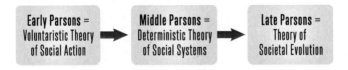

Parsons' switch in focus from the individual to (the collective) large-scale societal systems, earned Parsons a growing number of critics, some of whom took issue with his apparent neglect of the individual social actor, while others rejected what they perceived as Parsons' brainwashed, programmed or "oversocialized" conception of the individual social actor in society (Wrong 1961). Still other critics attacked what they saw as the conservative political premises of Parsons' ideas because if all parts of a social system are seen as functional, this amounts to a blanket endorsement of all institutions in our society, even those which reproduce injustices such as social inequality, economic exploitation, environmental degradation, gender oppression, racial prejudice and discrimination, and other social evils often associated with entrenched cultural beliefs and traditional social practices. In other words, for a growing number of critics, functionalism was seen as little more than a defence of the status quo (see, for example, Lockwood 1956; Dahrendorf 1959; Rex 1961; Horton 1966; Atkinson 1971).

It is no accident that structural functionalism was put in the hot seat in the mid-1960s — a time of considerable social conflict and social change. The rise of the civil rights movement, the anti-Vietnam War movement, the feminist movement and the radical students' movement, as well as "Third-World" liberation support movements, all contributed to an unprecedented breakdown of the national consensus in the United States. In this climate, the prevailing assumptions of structural functionalism seemed increasingly out of touch with the new realities of American society. The critics in the street were quickly joined by critics in the class-room as well as in the pages of journals and textbooks.

By the end of the 1970s, structural functionalism, the orthodoxy in North American sociology for almost half a century, appeared largely spent as a significant theoretical influence. In its place, an increasing diversity of new theoretical perspectives populated the sociological stage. These included various sociologies of everyday life (symbolic interaction-ism, dramaturgy, frame analysis, exchange theory, social phenomenology and ethnomethodology), various types of conflict and neo-Marxist theory, feminism, sociobiology and, more recently, postmodernist, poststruc-turalist and postcolonial, as well as structuration, queer, diaspora and multicultural, globalization and late modernity theories. In a new age of theoretical pluralism and intellectual diversity, structural functionalism appeared to have outlived its usefulness.

Even though the popularity and credibility of structural functionalism has declined, the fundamental question posed by these theorists remains important. The basic question underlying the work of theorists such as Talcott Parsons and others was: How is social order possible? Or, to put it another way: What are the necessary and sufficient conditions that enable societies (or other social systems) to continue to function in an orderly way over time? In a time of escalating global tension and the rise of conflict, violence, global terrorism and war in the world, this question remains relevant. For this reason alone, structural functionalism deserves some attention and discussion in this book.

THE STRUCTURAL FUNCTIONALISM OF TALCOTT PARSONS

Parsons began his theoretical career with a strong interest in the "volun-taristic" sources of social action. In his 1937 book *The Structure of Social Action,* he was interested in learning how an individual with a free will chose to pursue certain goals over others. Later in his career, in *The Social System* (1951), Parsons turned from the voluntaristic sources of social action to a more "deterministic" interest in how the individual's ideas and actions were regulated by the larger society. In this later work he focused on the systems and structures that determined all forms of social action and interaction. Parsons became increasingly preoccupied with how the actions of individuals were "institutionalized" within society and how the motivations of social actors derived from the "internalization" of cultural norms and values. The process of socialization implies the internalization of beliefs and values that are shared by most members of society. When individuals violate commonly held societal norms, they may be subject to the formal mechanisms of social control (through law enforcement and criminal justice systems) in order to ensure the maintenance of social order. Or they may face informal methods of social control (through social disapproval or sometimes even ostracism). Institutionalization refers to the integration of roles and sanctions within a generalized value system or normative framework which all members share.

This shift from voluntarism to determinism is not peculiar to Talcott Parsons. Many other social theorists who began their work by empha- sizing the free will of individuals in society ended up emphasizing the deterministic role of structures and systems. Karl Marx's early works on alienation, class consciousness and class struggle focused on the volun- taristic aspects of human activity, but in his later works, he concentrated on the inner workings of capitalist society as a system of commodity production. More recently, social theorist Erving Goffman, whose early work in dramaturgy emphasized the subjective aspects of the self in social interaction, later focused in his frame analysis on how objective social structures combined to "frame" the subjective self-concepts and identities of individual actors in particular social situations.

For many of his critics, Parsons's work does not deserve to be called theory at all. If theories are defined as explanations that link particular cases to the application of more general principles or laws, Parsons' achievement seems to have been the classification and categorization of social relations. He tried to construct a general conceptual scheme that could be used for the classification of all aspects of social action.

The Social System

Although Parsons's ideas have been widely criticized as deterministic, as ideologically biased (towards a consensual view of society) and as con- servative (for its apparent defence of the status quo), they were important to the historical development of sociological theory. Indeed, Parsons laid the foundation for what later came to be called social systems theory, a perspective that has influenced many other social theories. Rather than dismissing Parsons outright, therefore, it makes sense to ask: How can Parsons' work contribute to an understanding of our contemporary social worlds? What were some of the key concepts Parsons introduced in his theory of society? For Parsons, the concept of "system" was central to his analysis of modern societies. All systems (whether large or small) had to meet four basic needs, or functional imperatives, in order to survive. These imperatives have become known as the AGIL schema: adaptation, goal attainment, integration and latency/tension management.

Figure 2-3: The AGIL Schema

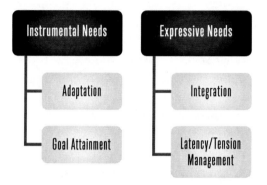

AGIL: The Functional Imperatives of Social Systems

Adaptation is accomplished by securing necessary resources from the environment and distributing these resources throughout the system through the processes of production, distribution and exchange.

Goal attainment is accomplished by prioritizing system goals and using resources to attain these goals.

Integration is accomplished by coordinating sustainable relationships among the different parts of the system in order to maintain the overall organization and functional integrity of the whole system.

Latency (or pattern maintenance) is accomplished by ensuring that members of the social system internalize the necessary motives, norms, values, beliefs and role-playing skills and practices to contribute to the long-term viability of the system. *Tension management* is accomplished by resolving the internal tensions, stresses and strains experienced by social actors within the system through conflict resolution strategies and social control mechanisms.

Parsons also analyzed social action in terms of four main "action systems" that extend from the micro- to the macro-level of analysis. These action systems include the behavioural organism, the personality system, the social system and the cultural system. The most important of these systems, for Parsons, was the social system, which can be broken down into a number of constituent subsystems. All of these systems and subsystems are made up of different parts, and each part performs an important function in maintaining the structure of the total system. What is important to understand in reading Parsons' work is that the concept of "system" is an abstract and highly flexible concept to organize social reality. This is why Parsons' work appears to operate at such a high level of abstraction and generalization.

Figure 2-4: Functions of Action Systems

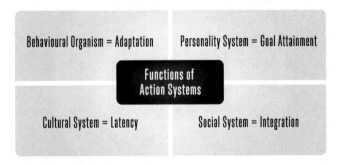

Figure 2-5: Functions of Social Systems

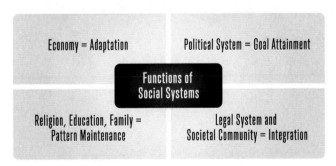

Throughout much of his work, Parsons represented social relations as a set of systems within systems — rather like Russian nesting dolls, one stacked into another in progressively smaller sizes. The social system was only one of four major action systems. Similarly, "society" was also composed of four subsystems, each of which performs an essential function, or functional imperative, directly related to the survival of the society. Parsons was primarily interested in those social forces that contributed to the sustainability of the social system. The underlying question that runs through much of his work is: What prevents society from dissolving into a war of all against all? Or, to put the matter another way: What conditions are necessary for societies to survive and persist over time?

Because he was primarily focused on the conditions that preserve and reproduce social relations, Parsons emphasized certain basic assumptions and key concepts. He assumed, for example, that all societies are based upon a consensus of basic values. He also suggested that societies typically maintain a state of equilibrium (or homeostasis) and that, although this equilibrium could be temporarily disrupted by intense social conflict or abrupt social change, most societies eventually return to a state of equilibrium.

Figure 2-6: Conditions that Preserve and Reproduce Social Relations

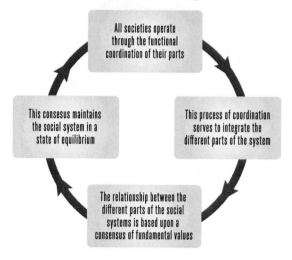

Parsons was one of the major social theorists of modern sociology. He was a system builder who sought to understand how societies operate by examining their systems and subsystems, their structures and functions. More than anything else, he emphasized the importance of the common beliefs and values that serve to integrate individuals (or social actors) and

Functionalism and Failed States

Recent political commentators have introduced the concept of "failed state" to describe a society in which social order and legitimate authority have collapsed, leaving entire populations at the mercy of warring political, religious and military factions. Besides the death, injury and displacement of large numbers of people, as well as the destruction of private and public property, the failure of a state invariably brings in its wake famine, starvation, disease, poverty and other catastrophic social problems.

Examples of failed states are Sierra Leone, Liberia, Democratic Republic of the Congo (DRC), Somalia, Southern Sudan, Rwanda (formerly), and Afghanistan and Iraq (after the US invasion and occupation of these countries), as well as Syria and Libya. Some cases can be found in the West; for example, the breakup of Yugoslavia into the warring territories of Serbia, Croatia, Bosnia and Kosovo. What, if anything, can the theoretical perspective of Talcott Parsons teach us about these tragic events?

First, Parsons would probably emphasize the negative consequences of a collapse in the consensus of values that formerly held these states together. When the citizens of Yugoslavia no longer defined themselves as Yugoslavs, but as Serbs, Croats, Bosnians and Kosovars, or when the colonization of Rwanda imposed a division between Hutus and Tutsis, the collapse of a consensus of national values occurred.

Second, Parsons would examine how the collapse of value consensus led to the breakdown of other subsystems in society. In most failed states, the economy (which performs the function of adaptation) is often severely weakened, sometimes resulting in famine and starvation, as in Sudan, DRC and many other countries. Similarly, the societal community (which performs the function of integration: law enforcement and social control) may also be weakened, leading to problems of security and safety for the civilian population (as in Sudan, Afghanistan, Iraq, Somalia and other combat zones). The fiduciary system (which performs the function of latency: education, socialization and the transmission of cultural values) may also be disrupted or destroyed (as in Afghanistan and many failed African states). Finally, the polity (which performs the function of goal attainment and the management of resources) is often destroyed and replaced by a puppet government or by a number of competing rebel and warlord governments.

Third, Parsons would understand that when the formal structures of a nation state begin to fail, members of that society are likely to revert to informal, or premodern, structures in order to meet their basic needs — adaptation (food, shelter, livelihood etc.), goal attainment (political administration), integration (safety and security) and latency (education, socialization and cultural/religious values). In many failed states, the breakdown of the formal government structures has resulted in the rise of more traditional structures of administration. In Iraq, for example, the collapse of central political authority led to the rise of ethnic and religious administrations among the Sunni, Shia and Kurdish populations. These are the conditions that produced ISIS. In Palestine and Lebanon, the breakdown of central authority led to the rise of religious militias, such as Hezbollah and Hamas, which took over many civic responsibilities, including employment, health, education and welfare, law enforcement and defence. In Afghanistan, Pakistan and Somalia, the weakening of the central government corresponded to the rise of tribal governments that ran their regions as semi-autonomous states. None of this would have surprised Parsons, who would likely have predicted that the decline of "universalism" and "achieved" social status would result in the rise of "particularism" and "ascribed" social status.

Many of the problems of failed states can be analyzed by using a systems theoretical perspective. In addition to this analysis of the societal systems of failed states, however, Parsons would probably suggest that parallel studies could be conducted on the cultural, personality and environmental (biological-organic) systems of these territories.

to motivate them to perform their roles in modern societies. Without such consensus, Parsons concluded, modern societies would come into crisis and cease to function as unified social systems. As with any social theory, the ultimate value of Parsons' theoretical perspective depends upon its intelligibility and its general applicability and relevance. What can Parsons' theory of society teach us about the contemporary social world? How can the language of structural functionalism help us to understand some of the pressing social issues of our time? One application of Parsons' theory of social systems — particularly when considering the conditions which may result in their disruption, disintegration and collapse — may be seen in current concerns with "failed states," whether Iraq, Syria, Yemen, Libya, the Democratic Republic of Congo or elsewhere.

Parsons and His Critics

There were many criticisms levelled at structural functionalist theorists during the 1960s and 1970s. Some of these criticisms were substantive — i.e., they were directed against the substance, or content, of structural functionalist theories of society. Functionalism was dismissed as ahistorical, as too macrosocial, as unable to conceptualize the processes of social change or social conflict, as rationalizing the existing status quo and as politically conservative. Other criticisms were directed against the logic and methodology of structural functionalism, which were often dismissed as too vague, abstract or ambiguous, as teleological or as tautological (Turner 2012). The following summary represents some of the more trenchant criticisms that have been made of this theoretical perspective:

- Parsons' theories and concepts focus on large-scale (macrosocial) structures and processes to the exclusion of small-scale (microsocial) face-to-face social relations and everyday social encounters. The criticism comes from theorists of social phenomenology, symbolic interactionism, dramaturgy, exchange theory, ethnomethodology and others.

- Especially in his later work, Parsons' conceived the social actor as "oversocialized" (i.e., programmed or indoctrinated) and he focused on the constraints that social systems and social structures impose upon individuals (see, for example, Wrong 1961). In much of Parsons' work, individual social actors are portrayed as passive subjects whose actions are influenced and determined by larger social forces over which they have little or no control. In other words, Parsons largely emphasized structure over agency in his theoretical perspective. Harold Garfinkel describes the structural functionalist characterization of the individual social actor as "cultural dope," "judgmental dope" and "psychological dope." Such a "dope" is not a real person but is instead a theoretical construct, an oversimplified ideal type that acts "in compliance with pre-established and legitimate alternatives of action that the common culture provides" (Garfinkel 1967: 68).

- Parsons paid little attention to the importance of social conflict or social change. These inescapable aspects of social life remained marginal to Parsons' main interest, namely, how social order is possible. This neglect of conflict and change leads many critics to conclude that Parsons' theory of society greatly overemphasizes the stable, orderly, balanced and consensual aspects of social relations and thereby underemphasizes the changeable, conflictual and contradictory aspects of social life (Dahrendorf 1959; Rex 1961; Lockwood 1956).

- Parsons' version of structural functionalism is ahistorical because its concepts are abstract, and its categories and typologies are intended to be universal in their application. Postmodernists are especially critical of Parsons' "metanarratives" of history and society — in other words, his belief that a general, standardized description and explanation of social reality is valid for everyone — irrespective of their ethnicity, sexuality, gender, social class etc.

- For critics on the left, Parsons' version of structural functionalism is biased in favour of existing social institutions, which makes it conservative. This criticism has also been made of Kingsley Davis and Wilbert Moore's structural functionalist (1945) "principles of social stratification," which argued that social inequality is both an inevitable and a necessary feature of all modern societies (Mills 1959; Gouldner 1970).

- Parsons relied on gendered categories and concepts, especially in his stereotypical gendered division of the nuclear family into male/ instrumental roles and female/expressive roles. Feminist scholars critique this approach (see Alway 1995; Sydie 1994; and Johnson 1993) .

- Parsons assumes that social action is motivated primarily by "ideational" factors (norms, values and beliefs); he has an apparent disregard or neglect of material factors (see Lockwood 1956; Dahrendorf 1959; Gouldner 1970).

- Parsons's work does not even constitute "theory" in any meaningful sense of this term. Many critics have dismissed Parsons' theories and concepts as "ungrounded," unverifiable, non-empirical and far too abstract and speculative. If theory involves the formulation of testable propositions and the construction of hypotheses that can be empirically verified or falsified, then much of Parsons' work clearly fails to meet these criteria. Michela Bowman et al. (n.d.) conclude:

> One problem with the theory, perhaps its most fatal flaw, is that it is unverifiable. Even supporters of the general theory of social action have been unable to test it in a satisfactory way. It does not readily offer itself for empirical analysis as good theories do. Which raises the question of if it can even really be deemed a theory by definition.

Parsons spent much of his time constructing abstract categories and classifications (boxes within boxes) rather than formulating testable theories. For many critics, Parsons was not so much a theorist as he was a taxonomist — someone who simply classified things according to categories or classes.

What is often overlooked by critics is that past functionalist writers, especially anthropologists, often played a progressive role in the history of social theory. Functionalism criticized dominant racism in anthropology through a critical encounter with the ideas of the social evolutionists and social Darwinians, who believed that all societies could be classified along a general scale of evolutionary development with so-called "primitive" societies falling close to the bottom of the scale and — surprise, surprise — white, Anglo-Saxon Protestant societies, such as Great Britain and the United States, at the top. These ideas had considerable currency at the start of the twentieth century (see, for example, Hofstadter 1992 [1944]), and they influenced immigration policies and the treatment of foreigners and minority populations, colonial policies and policies targeted at the poor. Social-Darwinism played an important ideological role in rationalizing the policies of imperialism abroad and the politics of class oppression at home. The apotheosis of these racist and imperialist ideas came with the rise of the Third Reich in Nazi Germany, in which eugenics and racist "social science" played an important role in rationalizing a state ideology of racial supremacy (Weiss-Wendt and Yeomans 2013).

Although structural functionalism is now largely dismissed as a conservative theory of society, there are some striking examples of how social theorists influenced by functionalist ideas played a progressive role in their respective societies. The Swedish social scientist Gunnar Myrdal, in his epic book *An American Dilemma*, showed how the eradication of racial segregation in America could usher in social consensus and commitment to universal values in that society. Although not a mainstream structural functionalist, Myrdal was influenced by functionalist ideas. Maxwell Caughron (2014: 109) suggests: "A second common feature between the Structural Functionalist model and Myrdal's understanding was the necessity to expand and reinforce values that transcended traditional, communitarian, religious, and ethnic lines and reinforced national cohesion." Similarly, American sociologist Seymour Martin Lipset (1950; Lipset, Trow and Coleman 1956), who was initially attracted to structural functionalism, published several progressive studies in his early career. His book *Agrarian Socialism* described how the newly elected socialist (Co-operative Commonwealth Federation, or CCF) provincial government in Saskatchewan was constantly frustrated in its attempts to introduce reforms by the conservative legacy of the civil service. And in another book, *Union Democracy*, Lipset showed how the "iron rule of oligarchy" — or the entrenchment of a "labour aristocracy," could be prevented by enforcing fixed terms for all union officials and their swift return to the shop floor after their term of office had expired. In his later years, however, Lipset became more conservative in his thinking — and even turned towards neoconservative ideas. Having said this, however, is not to defend structural functionalists from their contemporary critics nor to minimize the force of these criticisms

APOLOGISTS FOR SOCIAL INEQUALITY: DAVIS AND MOORE

One of the best known and in some quarters — most notorious — theoretical statements to come out of the functionalist tradition was the theory of social stratification. In a famous paper originally written in 1945, Kingsley Davis and Wilbert Moore set out to explain why all contemporary industrial societies are characterized by some degree of social inequality and social stratification. They argue that social stratification is not only a universal, but an inevitable and necessary feature of all societies. For them, social stratification — based on a hierarchy of social and economic inequality — ensures that the best people are always attracted and motivated to aspire to the most "important" positions in society. In all modern societies, there is a hierarchy of occupational positions which needs to be filled if the main institutions of society are to function efficiently. The core of this argument rests on the assumption that, in order to recruit and retain individuals to the most difficult and challenging positions in the occupational hierarchy, it is necessary to provide strong incentives — both income and prestige. Without a differential reward system, these theorists concluded, the most challenging positions in society would be difficult to fill with properly motivated individuals. This viewpoint argues for the necessity of social and occupational inequality in modern society, and it dismisses the hopes of more egalitarian social reformers as unrealistic and utopian "social engineering." The principles of stratification enunciated by Davis and Moore have been widely criticized by other social theorists. There is no doubt that this is a very conservative argument: don't plan on eradicating inequality, because inequality guarantees that the best people will always reach for the top positions in any society — that is, inequality is functional for the entire social system.

Criticisms of the Functionalist Perspective on Social Inequality

Various criticisms have been levelled at the functionalist model over the years. Perhaps the most famous was offered by Melvin Tumin (1953), whose concerns can be reduced to a series of critical questions:

1. Certain positions in any society are functionally more important than others.
   Question: How do you know what positions are functionally more important?
2. Only a limited number of individuals in any society have the talents that can be trained into the skills appropriate to these positions.
   Question: Couldn't stratification systems create obstacles to discovering talent?
3. The conversion of talents into skills involves a training period during which sacrifices of one kind or another are made by those undergoing the training.
   Question: Is training for a functionally important position (e.g., attending college) really a sacrifice?
4. In order to induce the talented persons to undergo these sacrifices and acquire the training, their future positions must result in privileged access to scarce and desired rewards.
   Question: Couldn't people be attracted to functionally important positions and motivated to do them by feelings of workmanship, duty or service? Don't these positions offer more satisfaction anyway?

Of the several criticisms of the functionalist theory of stratification, many are from conflict theorists, who strongly disagree with the premises and conclusions of structural functionalism. The conflict perspective embraces a broad range of theoretical approaches — including the conflict theories of Georg Simmel, Lewis Coser, Ralf Dahrendorf, John Rex and Randall Collins and also the traditions of Marxism, critical theory and other neo-Marxian and dialectical conceptions of social relations. The conflict perspective should be understood as a broad, generic orientation that includes a number of distinct theoretical approaches. Most conflict theorists begin their analysis of social relations with the assumption that every social system exhibits a differential allocation of power and authority. Unlike the functionalist perspective, which assumes the existence of a common value system and an underlying community of interests, the conflict perspective rests on the assumption that in any social system (whether a large-scale society or a small-scale organization) some people come to dominate and coerce others by virtue of their wealth and power. In other words, the fundamental characteristic of all social systems is this division between those who dominate within the structure of social relations and those who are dominated.

The cumulative effect of these criticisms over the past thirty years or so has been to dislodge the functionalist perspective from its formerly privileged status in sociological theory. These criticisms and others have succeeded in clearing the ground for the emergence of new theoretical perspectives that have challenged the basic assumptions of the functionalist tradition and which now compete with it for legitimacy and acceptance within the discourse of sociology. Of these new perspectives, the conflict perspective offers the most direct and explicit alternative to functionalism.

The conflict perspective provides an inverted image of the functionalist perspective. Where the functionalist model stresses stability, the conflict model stresses change. Where the functionalist model stresses integration, the conflict model stresses division and dissensus. Where the functionalist model stresses the positive functions of all parts of the social system, the conflict model stresses their negative functions (or dysfunctions). Where the functionalist model stresses a consensus of values, the conflict model stresses domination and coercion. In summary, the modern conflict model of social relations and social inequality represents an attempt to revise and update Marx's conception of class conflict in ways that render it more acceptable for analyzing the social conflicts of contemporary capitalist societies. In this respect, modern conflict theory offers a more universal theory of social conflict, a theory that is applicable to all modern societies, whether capitalist, socialist or post-capitalist.

A further influence on contemporary studies of social inequality since the 1980s is feminist theory and criticism. The focus of much feminist criticism is the traditional exclusion of women as objects of sociological theory and analysis. This concern about the gendered nature of sociological theory has contributed to the diminished significance of the consensus/conflict debate in sociology. Feminist writers are more preoccupied with particular theoretical questions, such as the institutional significance of patriarchy and its relationship to social inequality, the importance of the household as a social and economic unit in society and the role of women in the largely unacknowledged sphere of domestic production, among many other issues.

Before we dismiss the structural functionalist theory of social inequality out of hand as hopelessly biased, its argument has proven to be influential; similar sentiments have been heard in the mouths of politicians, conservative commentators and social scientists (Herrnstein and Murray 1994). While it may seem that particular social theories have bitten the dust and disappeared from public view, this has rarely proven to be the case. Theories that were formerly discredited have often returned in new forms. Functionalism is a case in point. Who would have thought that the apparent demise of structural functionalism in the 1970s would have been followed in the 1980s by the rise of neofunctionalism?

THE REVISED STRUCTURAL FUNCTIONALISM OF ROBERT MERTON

Many structural functionalists eventually became dissatisfied with Parsons' brand of grand theory. Robert K. Merton was one such theorist who attempted to bring structural functionalism down to earth and to make it more compatible with the tradition of empirical social research. He believed that earlier structural functionalists were too mechanistic and dogmatic in their analyses of social and cultural systems. Merton, who began his sociological career as a student of Parsons, grew increasingly impatient with the highly abstract and unverifiable nature of the theory, which delighted in classifying and categorizing social relations but only rarely applied these ideas in empirical research. Merton was also troubled by structural functionalism's conservative political bias. He certainly disagreed with Davis and Moore's conclusion that social inequality was a necessary and desirable feature of all modern societies, and in his own work, Merton tried to show how structural functionalist analysis could by applied in critical and even radical ways.

Merton set out to transform the "mechanistic and dogmatic" framework of anthropological functionalism into a more flexible and empirical framework for sociological analysis. This he tried to accomplish in several ways: first, he challenged the traditional anthropological "postulates" of structural functionalism (Merton 1967). Second, he introduced new concepts — such as functions/dysfunctions; manifest/latent functions, net balance of functions — that would enable sociologists to study the negative and the unintended consequences of social institutions. Third, he advanced the strategy of constructing "theories of the middle range" — theories that could be used to guide empirical social research.

Although Merton disagreed with several aspects of Parsons' version of structural functionalism — especially his assumption that all or most social institutions had survived because they performed positive functions for all members of society and that all societies were based upon a fundamental consensus of basic values — he still accepted the basic framework of functionalist analysis. He believed that the study of society began with the study of large-scale (or macrosocial) systems of social relations and that all social systems (institutions, organizations and other collectivities) could be analyzed in terms of their consequences (positive and negative, intended and unintended) for other members of society. Thus, although Merton had criticisms and revisions of structural functionalism, he never abandoned the perspective in favour of another theoretical framework. He remained an internal critic and did his best to change structural functionalism from within. His main concern was to convert structural functionalist analysis into a more practical framework that could be used to guide empirical studies of societies, institutions and organizations.

Challenging the Postulates of Structural Functionalism

Merton began his revision of structural functionalism with a critique of some of its basic assumptions, or "postulates." These postulates presupposed that all observed beliefs and practices in a society enabled that society to successfully adapt to its external environment and to survive as a viable social system. In other words, all observed beliefs and practices, especially when organized into institutions such as kinship structures, magical or mythological belief systems, age grading ceremonies, economic activities such as hunting and food gathering and so on, were assumed to be functional for the social system as a whole. Most structural functionalist theorists believed that traditional beliefs and practices had first arisen as responses to basic societal needs, or functional imperatives. The persistence of these needs, it was felt, was the explanation for the persistence of the beliefs and practices.

In some ways, the assumption that all cultural beliefs and practices have positive functions for the entire social system is reminiscent of the naïve optimism of Dr. Pangloss (the absurd optimist satirized in the novel *Candide*, by the eighteenth-century French writer Voltaire), who repeatedly declared: "We live in the best of all possible worlds." The assumption made by the early structural functionalist theorists was that the structures of any society persist because they continue to perform positive functions. Although Merton conceded that these early claims of structural functionalism may have made sense to anthropologists who studied close-knit and tightly integrated societies, he argued that these postulates were no longer valid for sociologists who studied modern industrial societies. Whereas many traditional hunting, gathering and foraging societies remained more egalitarian than most horticultural, agricultural or industrial societies — with common worldviews and strong bonds of social solidarity — modern societies were typically stratified by divisions of class, race, gender and region (Moore 1966). Thus, the early structural functionalist assumptions of the functionality of all beliefs and practices did not apply to modern societies and stood in need of drastic revision.

New Concepts for New Times

In addition to questioning the validity of the classical postulates of structural functionalism, Merton introduced a number of new concepts. Among the more important of these new concepts was the distinction that Merton made between positive functions and negative functions, or dysfunctions. Whereas traditional structural functionalist theorists assumed that all beliefs and practices have positive functions for the entire society, Merton suggested that some practices may have negative consequences for some members of society. By introducing the possibility that some institutions could have negative, or dysfunctional, consequences for some members of society, Merton sought to correct the theory's conservative bias. In many ways, Merton's study of anomie and social structure can be seen as a critique of the infamous endorsement of stratification earlier enunciated by Davis and Moore. The concept of "anomie," first introduced into sociology by Durkheim, refers to a condition of rootlessness, anxiety and moral confusion experienced by individuals at times of social instability resulting from a breakdown of traditional standards and values, or from rapid social or technological change.

Figure 2-7: Key Concepts in Merton's Version of Structural Functionalism

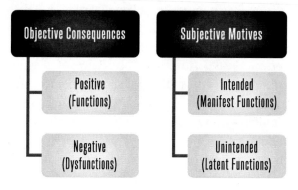

Besides the distinction between functions and dysfunctions, Merton also introduced the distinction between "manifest" and "latent" functions (and dysfunctions). Manifest functions are those consequences of beliefs or practices which are both intended and acknowledged as "official" functions. For example, two of the manifest functions of a university are to disseminate knowledge (by teaching students) and to produce knowledge (through faculty research). However, Merton recognized that any practice or belief can also have unexpected, unintended and unacknowledged consequences. Some of these "unofficial" consequences may be positive for some members of society (latent functions), while other unintended consequences may be negative (latent dysfunctions). Thus, a latent function of the university may be to create a "marriage market" for young, eligible adults. However, a latent dysfunction of the university may be to prolong the period of financial precarity of many university students. The framework for evaluating the functions and dysfunctions may be wide enough to encompass whole societies, or narrow enough to focus on families or other small social groups. Merton also recognized that any assessment of whether a set of beliefs and practices is functional or dysfunctional for a particular social group can only be based on a calculation of the "net balance" of functions, that is, whether the observed positive consequences outweigh the negative consequences, or vice versa.

The following summary identifies and defines some of the key concepts that Merton introduced into his version of structural functionalist analysis:

- *Functions* are observed consequences of social action that contribute to the adaptation or adjustment of the system.
- *Dysfunctions* are observed consequences of social action that lessen the adaptation or adjustment of the system.
- *Manifest functions* are observed consequences of social action that contribute to the adaptation or adjustment of the system and are both intended and recognized by the social actor.
- *Latent functions* are observed consequences of social action that contribute to the adaptation or adjustment of the system and are neither intended nor recognized by the social actor.
- *Manifest dysfunctions* are observed consequences of social action that lessen the adaptation or adjustment of the system and are both intended and recognized by the social actor
- *Latent dysfunctions* are observed consequences of social action that lessen the adaptation or adjustment of the system and are neither intended nor recognized by the social actor.

Theories of the Middle Range

Merton's attempts to refine structural functionalist theory and adapt it to the needs of empirical social research led him to advance a conception of theory that he called "theories of the middle range." According to Merton, theories of the middle range are designed to avoid the polar extremes of much social thought. On the one hand, they sought to avoid the highly abstract theories of Parsons and others while, on the other hand, they tried to rise above the mere counting and collection of "facts" in the manner pursued by statisticians and number crunchers. Merton's theories of the middle range sought to find a middle ground between the "grand theory" of the abstract theorists and the "abstracted empiricism" of the bean counters. Whereas grand theory had produced "theories without facts," abstracted empiricism had produced "facts without theories." Theories of the middle range were designed to produce testable hypotheses, theoretical statements (propositions) whose validity could be verified or falsified through the methods of empirical social research. Merton attempted to provide examples of middle range theories in his own work, the most enduring of which is his classic 1938 study of social structure and anomie.

Merton's attempts to revise the structural functionalist perspective in ways that would combine theory and empirical social research led him to formulate a "paradigm of functional analysis." This paradigm was a

Blowback and Latent Dysfunctions

A dramatic example of Merton's concept of latent dysfunctions may be seen in some cases of US foreign policy and military intervention. From 1969 to 1973, during the height of the Vietnam War, President Nixon secretly authorized the clandestine bombing of Cambodia. The intended purpose of the bombing was to disrupt the supply lines of the "Vietcong" and North Vietnamese Army and to deny "the enemy" sanctuary within Cambodia. However, an unintended negative consequence (or latent dysfunction) of these aerial attacks was the destabilization and overthrow of the neutral government of Prince Norodom Sihanouk and the rise to power of the fanatical Maoist party, the Khmer Rouge, under the leadership of Pol Pot. The Khmer Rouge seized power in 1975 and installed a regime which was eventually responsible for the genocide of around 1.5 million of its own citizens (see Shawcross 1979).

More recently, from 1979 to 1989, the US government — via the CIA — provided covert military and moral support to the Afghan resistance as it battled the Red Army during the invasion and occupation of Afghanistan by the Soviet Union. However, the support given by the CIA to the Afghan warlords led to the unintended consequence (or latent dysfunction) of strengthening the jihadist mujahedeen, including the Taliban and al-Qaeda. After the Red Army was driven from Afghanistan, some of those same religious militias turned against the US and later executed the attacks of 9/11. This is another example of how unintended consequences may sometimes follow the implementation of official policies (or manifest functions).

A further example of the latent dysfunctions of US foreign policy is illustrated in the work of Chalmers Johnson. His book *Blowback* describes how the invasion and occupation of Iraq in 2003 by US and "coalition" forces increased rather than diminished the role of the terrorist organization al-Qaeda. While the Bush administration justified the Iraq War — and the regime change — as a way of containing terrorism, the US military intervention only served to strengthen the influence of jihadist organizations, which led to the rise of ISIS in Iraq and Syria. The unintended consequence of these aspects of US foreign policy is now often referred to as "blowback" (see Johnson 2004).

conceptual framework that offered a set of explicit procedures for researching organizations or other social systems from a structural functionalist
perspective. Although in his later years Merton became increasingly
preoccupied with studies in the history and sociology of science, he is still
remembered as the theorist who finally brought structural functionalism
down to earth.

BEYOND FUNCTIONALISM: NEOFUNCTIONALISM

A new generation of functionalists emerged during the 1980s. Calling
themselves, "neofunctionalists," these theorists have tried to reinstate functionalism as a viable theoretical framework. The neofunctionalists derived
their inspiration from earlier generations of structural functionalism but
have attempted to avoid previous pitfalls and fallacies. Neofunctionalist
writers have introduced the concept of "differentiation" — a process
of continuous evolutionary social change. Neofunctionalists also have
given more prominence to the role of material factors in the organization
and development of societies than did their functionalist predecessors.
Parsons, in particular, was preoccupied with ideational factors — norms,
values, beliefs and need dispositions — to the neglect of material factors
— such as environment and geography.

Neofunctionalists have shown a new willingness to theorize the issues
of power, inequality and conflict in societies without invoking conservative assumptions about the necessary stability and equilibrium of social
systems. Many have also embraced cross-fertilization with other perspectives — both macro- and micro-social — in an effort to encourage some
integration and fusion of sociological theories. The present generation of
neofunctionalists advances its ideas less rigidly and dogmatically than did
its predecessors. For this reason, modern functionalism is viewed by its
adherents more as an "intellectual tendency" than as an integrated body
of theory and research. While functionalism may continue to be identified
in terms of a common core of tenets, these tenets are defined in far looser
and more flexible ways than in the past, permitting them to coexist with
a wide diversity of theoretical perspectives. Thus, concepts drawn from
social action theory and systems theory have migrated from functionalism and taken root in critical theory, world-system theory and even in
some versions of social phenomenology and symbolic interactionism.

Perhaps the most important step forward made by neofunctionalists,

such as Jeff Alexander and Paul Colomy, has been their attempt to reintroduce the individual social actor back into the functionalist framework.
This reintegration of agency and structure has been influenced by similar
efforts in other theoretical schools, most notably in Anthony Giddens'
theory of structuration and in Jürgen Habermas' version of critical communication theory. For these more recent writers, neofunctionalism,
stripped of its conservative ideological baggage and freed from its fundamentalist biological metaphors, is seen as a noble attempt to resolve
the classical oppositions of micro/macro, subjective/objective and order/
conflict. However, the excitement over neofunctionalism appears to have
been short-lived, as the initial enthusiasm for this revised version of functionalism has largely dissipated in the opening decades of the twenty-first
century. Today, the legacy of structural functionalism may best be seen
in the rise of systems theory, exemplified in the work of the late German
sociologist Niklas Luhmann. A brief outline of his ideas is included in
the final section of this chapter.

Differentiation Theory

Another important refinement of neofunctionalism may be seen in its
updated theory of social change. During the first wave of criticism in the
1950s, structural functionalism was attacked mercilessly for its alleged
inability to account for conflict or change in social systems. On top of
this, functionalism was criticized for what many saw as its abstract and
non-empirical character. To meet such objections, neofunctionalists have
attempted to develop a theory of social change consistent with the other
tenets of the functionalist tradition that can be readily applied to real-life
empirical and historical case studies.

Differentiation theory, as it is now known in sociology (Alexander and
Colomy 1990), offers a general theory of social change that is intended to
appeal to a wide range of social scientists, including those who remain
outside the theoretical boundaries of modern functionalism. Instead
of viewing the development of societies as a series of linear (evolutionary) stages, neofunctionalists recognize a general historical process of
differentiation — or what they call a "master trend" — that is active in
most, if not all, human societies. Simply stated, the trend towards greater
differentiation refers to the increasing specialization in the division of
labour, apparent everywhere in the social world and one of the most
potent forces in transforming pre-industrial societies into industrial (and

post-industrial) societies. In our own society, the process of differentiation has resulted in the gradual (sometimes spectacular) decline of multi-purpose structures and their replacement by more highly specialized single-purpose units. The days when an eye doctor would examine your eyes and also make up your glasses have gone. Eye care has become the responsibility of a more specialized division of labour, including opticians, optometrists and ophthalmologists. Similarly, churches used to run the parochial schools and charitable social agencies, but these functions of education and social work have been delegated to more specialized secular institutions such as school boards and government departments. For neofunctionalists, the concept of differentiation can be used to explain many of the changes taking place in contemporary societies.

Unlike earlier functionalists, who were inclined to view differentiation as an irreversible, inevitable evolutionary tendency of modern life, today's functionalists are less dogmatic. While differentiation is seen as the master trend, it does not preclude the possibility of counter-processes that may appear to swim against the general evolutionary tide. Among current theorists, there is also a greater recognition that the process of differentiation may lead to social conflict, resulting in "structural strains" for the social system. This explicit acknowledgement of the importance of power, conflict and inequality stands in marked contrast to the bland consensualism of earlier structural functionalists. Neofunctionalists have shown themselves more willing than their predecessors to apply their analysis to concrete empirical and historical case studies in order to overcome the theoretical abstraction that characterized functionalist writings of an earlier period.

Although the future of neofunctionalism is still far from clear, the resurgence of this tradition should warn us against the presumption that any social theory is ever finally "dead and buried." Social theories have always reflected the changing times and events of their founders and supporters. No theoretical tradition in sociology ever remains frozen in time. Theoretical traditions are constantly changing. Sometimes these changes may be so subtle as to go unrecognized, or they may be dramatic and spectacular. Wherever theories are used, formulated and reformulated by new generations of theorists, they will continue to grow and change like all living things. Sometimes the changes introduced into a theoretical tradition by a new generation of theorists attempt to resolve ambiguities and inconsistencies, and respond to external critiques of the tradition, but do not modify the core of the theory (its assumptions and key concepts). Other changes may be more profound and may involve new ways of articulating the core of the theory that break with all previous interpretations.

Theorists such as Jeff Alexander attempted to distinguish themselves from structural functionalists like Parsons in a number of ways. They explicitly recognized that although social order and consensus may be the basis of social integration for many societies, many other societies are characterized by division and conflict. They also abandoned Parsons' static conception of social systems by emphasizing the continuous process of change and differentiation inherent in the evolution of and occasional revolution in) actual societies. But although they opened up their theoretical framework for an analysis of conflict, power and inequality, much of their work remains as abstract and as theoretical as that of structural functionalism. This finally led Jeff Alexander, a founder of neofunctionalism, to abandon the theory and move on in search of alternative theoretical frameworks. However, there has been something of a revival of interest in neo-functionalism — especially among political scientists who have used many of its core theoretical concepts to study the problems and challenges of political and social integration within the European Union (Rosamond 2000; Eilstrup-Sangiovanni 2006; Schmitter and Lefkofridi 2016; European Studies: Hub, n.d.).

THE SYSTEMS THEORY OF NIKLAS LUHMANN

In many ways, structural functionalism has disappeared, at least for now, from the current agenda of social theory. It is largely extinct in its original (classical) form, relegated to the museum of social thought. The writings of Parsons, Merton and Davis and Moore retain only historical interest for most contemporary sociologists. At the same time, the path blazed by these early structural functionalists has been followed by more recent theorists who have revised and updated these theoretical ideas and converted them into new social theories. One of the most prominent of the intellectual descendants of structural functionalism was the German systems theorist Niklas Luhmann, who died in 1998.

Luhmann only became known in North America in the late 1980s and 1990s when many of his works were translated into English. Before then, Luhmann was known mostly in Germany, where his work was hotly debated among German sociologists and where it exerted considerable influence on the growth of contemporary social theory. Some of the most well-known debates over his work and ideas occurred between Luhmann and the famous German critical theorist Jürgen Habermas. These exchanges were collected and published as part of the history of contemporary German social theory (Bausch 1997).

Like Parsons, Luhmann's work is abstract and dense, though his ideas challenge us to see the world in a radically new way and to talk about social reality with a radically new vocabulary of concepts. Luhmann's theoretical perspective diverges from the earlier tradition of structural functionalism. The most important point of departure is in his definition of the concept of "system." For Parsons, a social system was composed of a set of individual social actors who had internalized the norms and values of the larger culture and society. The individual was connected to society through the internalization of norms and values, while the society was connected to the individual through the institutionalization of these basic elements. In Luhmann's perspective, however, the individual social actor largely disappears from view.

Systems and Environments

For Luhmann, social systems are not conceived as systems of interrelated human actions, or "action systems" (à la Parsons), but as systems of communication. The purpose, or function, of all systems of communication, according to Luhmann, is the "reduction of complexity." All systems may be understood as simplified representations of their respective environments. Systems evolved as mechanisms for simplifying the otherwise infinite complexity of the external environment. Thus, economic systems reduce the complexity of the world to communications about the production, distribution and exchange of goods and services (through the medium of money). Similarly, the system of science reduces the complexity of "the world" to communications about the search for "facts" (through the medium of truth). In some ways, Luhmann's concept of system can be likened to a computer software program that opens a particular "window" in the context of a larger environment. Everyone understands that these windows offer only simplified representations of a far more complex external environment. However, it is only through such simplified systems that selected aspects of an environment can ever be (partially) known and understood. Systems, therefore, are only understandable as ways of reducing the complexity of their surrounding environments.

For Luhmann, social reality is only knowable through the different systems of communication that are used to represent and to simplify this reality. For Parsons, social systems were models of social relations, whereas for Luhmann, systems are ways of talking about social relations. In this respect, Luhmann's systems are like "discourses," "texts," or even "windows" that allow us a partial and highly simplified view of the forms of communication that are commonly used to represent — and extrapolate from — selected aspects of an infinitely complex external environment.

Autopoietic Systems

According to Luhmann, all types of communication about social relationships are analyzable in terms of systems. Thus, while communication about economic relations may be represented (and simplified) through a specific system, so also may communication about other, far more intimate social relations — even something as personal as "love." When analyzing different systems of communication, Luhmann distinguishes between the "medium" and the "code." Thus, the modern economy — conceived as a system of communication — uses the medium of money. At the same time, the code of any system is always expressed as a binary code (+ versus -). In the case of the economy, the binary code is the presence (or payment) of money versus the absence (or non-payment) of money. The religious system, on the other hand, uses the medium of faith, and its binary code is expressed in belief or non-belief.

Luhmann conceives of his analytical systems as "autopoietic" systems. An autopoietic system, according to Luhmann (who borrowed this term from the cognitive biologists Maturana and Varela 1980), is a self-referential and self-reproductive closed system. In other words, autopoietic systems are self-generating systems which provide simplified representations of an external environment without allowing any of the elements of the environment to penetrate or enter the system. Luhmann's systems are always — and only ever — systems of communication. They should never be misunderstood as direct representations of social beliefs and practices, whether these systems relate to the law, the economy, religion, romance or to anything else in the complex social environment.

In this sense, Luhmann's systems are always systems that reflexively refer to their own communication about how other social actors in the larger environment have communicated about law, economy, religion etc. In other words, Luhmann's conception of system analysis is based upon what we might call a "second order" observation of society. His systems enable us to observe the observers and to describe the descriptions (and representations) that have been made of particular aspects of the global environment. This reflexive, or self-referential, conception of system is very different from that of Parsons, for whom systems were analogical models that directly corresponded to action systems as institutionalized patterns of social interaction.

System Differentiation

In a way that is somewhat reminiscent of structural functionalism, Luhmann subscribes to an evolutionary theory of society. He suggests that through the process of system differentiation, social systems divide themselves into subsystems that are part of the environment of other subsystems of the same system. In his classification of social systems, Luhmann distinguishes between three different types: "interactions," which are based upon face-to-face communications; "organizations," which are based upon positions held and roles performed in official settings; and "society," which is the largest and most comprehensive of all these systems. For the most part, Luhmann suggests that in human societies, organic (or biological) processes of evolution have now been superseded by symbolic (or communicative) processes of evolution. Biological evolution has been superseded by sociocultural evolution.

The process of system differentiation, much like the process of cellular division and subdivision, is part of the ongoing evolution of all societal systems. This differentiation of societal systems, which results in the multiplication of social systems, leads to three possible types of change in the relationship of a system to its environment: 1. changes in relation to the societal system; 2. changes in relation to other social systems; and 3. changes in relation to the system itself.

For Luhmann, the actions and choices of the individual — even in matters as personal as intimate relations — are best understood and analyzed in terms of evolving systems of communication. The individual is viewed as a site of intersecting and evolving systems, each with its own media of communication and its own codes. Rather than seeing the individual as a decision-making agent in the process of social change, Luhmann sees the individual as a product of intersecting and evolving systems of communication.

Love as an Autopoietic System

A brief illustration of how Luhmann's systems theory can be applied to the sociology of intimate relations may be seen in his analysis of the changing meaning of the idea of "love." The topic of love is usually addressed as an individual and personal experience, at least in popular culture and romantic literature. But in Luhmann's work, the individual is mostly invisible. Whereas for Parsons the individual was initially conceived of as a voluntaristic, or free-willed, social actor motivated by values, norms and goals (although later as a passive recipient of internalized and institutionalized norms and values), Luhmann views the individual merely as the site of intersecting systems: biological, biochemical, neurological, psychological and so on. In other words, Luhmann does not grant the individual any independent agency. Instead, the individual is seen as determined by intersecting systems of communication. How, then, does Luhmann address the topic of love?

For Luhmann, the communication systems of intimate interpersonal relations have undergone important evolutionary changes over the past millennium. During the Middle Ages (in Europe), when women were the property of men, the medium of "love" was sharply differentiated from the media of sex (pleasure) and marriage. In other words, neither love nor sex had any necessary relationship to the institution of marriage. Because of the relative unattainability of women, love was coded by heterosexual men as a passion. A "passion," by definition (from the Latin: "passio"), is related to suffering and is normally experienced as a passive rather than an active sentiment. Individuals are said to be "caught in the grip" of a passion, or "overwhelmed" with passion. Love was usually expressed in medieval literature and poetry as an ideal rather than an actual state. This was the tradition of "courtly love."

With the Enlightenment, in the eighteenth century, and the greater independence of women, new media of intimate relations emerged — such as friendship (non-sensual relations) with the opposite sex. But more significantly, the sharp differentiation between love, sex and marriage was eroded as these media were recoded and recombined. With the weakening of patriarchy, the medium of sex was gradually incorporated into the medium of love. Once love was recoded and redefined to include reproduction, then marriage was also recoded and incorporated into a modernized representation of love. The recombination of love and sex, with the eventual goal of marriage, signals the evolution of the earlier code (of courtly love) into a modernized code (of romantic love).

During the twentieth and twenty-first centuries, the media and codes of intimate relations have changed again, and new forms of differentiation and recombination have emerged. With the rise of feminism and the impact of the sexual revolution, the linkages between reproductive, recreational and romantic sex have weakened, and earlier codes linking romantic love to marriage are frequently dismissed as patriarchal and archaic. Casual sex has emerged as a separate code from that of marriage. And with the advent of gay rights and same-sex marriage, even the traditional binary gender code of marriage is being redefined.

Summarizing Luhmann

As we have seen, Luhmann's systems theory is not an easy theory to comprehend. It is formulated in very abstract terms and, for this reason, presents at least as many challenges to the reader as does Parsons' version of structural functionalism. The following summary identifies and defines some of the key concepts that Luhmann introduced into his version of autopoietic systems theory:

- Autopoietic social systems are composed of mutually interrelated parts (or elements), which together differentiate the system from its environment.
- The systems cannot operate beyond their boundaries.
- The systems are closed, self-referential and self-reproducing.
- The function of the systems is to reduce the infinite complexity of the environment to the finite complexity of the systems.
- Autopoietic social systems are systems of communication, rather than, as they were for Parsons, systems of action. However, systems of communication normally (mis)represent themselves as systems of action.
- Autopoietic social systems are distinguished from other systems (such as organic or physical systems) by the fact that they operate as "meaningful" systems. They are reflexive and self-referential; they reflect upon their own patterns of communication. In this respect, the autopoietic theory of social systems represents a second-order observation of society whereby observations are made of observations.
- Autopoietic social systems operate through the specific languages (or media) of communication, which are expressed in particular (binary) codes.
- Autopoietic social systems divide into subsystems through a

process of system differentiation. This division and subdivision convert the original system into the environment of the subsystem.

Luhmann saw himself as a grand theorist in the tradition of Parsons and other classical social theorists. Luhmann has remained a somewhat controversial figure in contemporary social theory and has been criticized by some well-known adversaries, such as Jürgen Habermas, as a neoconservative. Luhmann's popularity has also been limited by the impenetrability of his writing. Indeed, Luhmann himself described his theory as "labyrinth-like" and "non-linear" and admitted to formulating his ideas in deliberately enigmatic language in order to prevent them from being understood too quickly or too superficially. One student shared:

> Luhmann wishes to liberate his theorizing from the "stranglehold of understandability." By virtue of its distance to ordinary language concept definitions, Luhmann's theoretical language is supposed to create a certain controllability of understanding.... Luhmann requires his readers to "go the extra mile" of coming to grips with the obscurity of his writing style. This renders the interpretation of Luhmann's writings particularly difficult. (Kirsch 1998)

Predictably, this apparently deliberate obfuscation led some critics to accuse Luhmann of elitism. Notwithstanding these negative judgements, Luhmann offers us a new and intriguing way to analyze social relations, and the hard work involved in understanding his ideas is repaid by the fresh insights they provide.

Many sociologists have found Luhmann's version of systems theory a particularly useful way to conceptualize and analyze environmental and ecological problems. The "greening" of social theory has brought a new-found interest in his work. This is because Luhmann insisted on understanding social systems as systems that are always located in environing systems. More than any previous systems theorist, Luhmann emphasized the significance of environmental crises (such as climate change) for the analysis of social systems. For these reasons, Luhmann is regarded by many European sociologists as a pioneer in the study of the social impact of environmental change.

Luhmann was one of the earlier contemporary social theorists to include the external environment, as an ecosystem, in his theoretical project. For Luhmann, the theoretical and practical problems posed by the natural environment were methodologically similar to that of any system confronting its outside environment: the problems of complexity and uncertainty. To address these problems, especially the maintenance of what Luhmann calls "environmental equilibrium," he argues that we need to analyze the environment as a system of communication and information, if we are ever to reduce the complexity and uncertainty of the raw natural environment that lies beyond the borders of our autopoietic system. For Luhmann, this is the fundamental theoretical and methodological problem: "A system can never have sufficient variety to match in a point-for-point fashion the possible states an environment might exhibit. The environment is much more complex. It therefore requires a selective process and we must question what type of organized selection is possible given these circumstances" (1993: 530).

According to Luhmann, until we begin to address the epistemological problems of complexity and uncertainty in environmental and ecological systems of communication and information, we will not "possess the cognitive means for predicting and directing action" (530). For this reason, he is a strong proponent of what he calls "risk research" — an academic field that has more recently become associated with the work of another German sociologist, Ulrich Beck, whose ideas are discussed in a later chapter of this book. Luhmann's conclusions are perhaps best expressed by one of his recent students:

> Before rushing towards answers, we need to carefully reflect upon the questions we pose, and upon the way in which we frame our problems.... our society currently alarms itself with regard to its environmental conditions. The situation seems to necessitate urgency and speed.... Apparently, we do not have much time left. But this is also a self-protective device. We have, then, not enough time for reflection. In this light, it makes sense to be guided by the Utopia of rationality: to see whether and how particular social systems can be used to provide solutions to problems that are more rational and include more parts of the environment. (Vanderstraeten 2005: 480)

I once asked Luhmann how he first became interested in social theory, especially in the theory of social systems. He explained that his fascination with social structures began at the end of the Second World War. The liberation of Germany by the allied forces brought about the downfall, not only of the Nazi state, but of all the local representatives of that state. Luhmann described how petty neighbourhood dictators — such as police chiefs, city mayors, postmasters, and other local officials — who had drawn their power from the Nazi party were suddenly transformed into buffoons and comic figures. When the walls of the Third Reich finally came tumbling down and the once-solid structures of society evaporated into thin air, even as a young man, Luhmann was made painfully aware of the fragility of social structures. It was this experience, he claimed, that gave him a lifelong interest in social systems and the constitution of society.

Luhmann's systems theory differs from that of Parsons in a number of ways. Parsons constructed his social system in a direct correspondence to patterns of social action in the real world: his four action systems — cultural system, social system, personality system and behavioural organism — are first-order systems and are meant to correspond to actual patterns of behaviour in the real world. They are analogical systems. On the other hand, Luhmann's autopoietic systems are reflexive, second-order systems: they are intended to decode the communications used by social actors in their interactions with each other and with their complex environments into meaningful information. Whereas for Parsons, the environment of any specific system is always contained, subsumed or nested in other more general systems; Luhmann saw the environment of any specific system in more phenomenological terms as simply that which is different from, outside of or beyond the system itself. For Luhmann, the system represents (relative) simplicity; while the environment represents (infinite) complexity.

Also, whereas Parsons identifies general functions (or functional imperatives) that every system needs to fulfill in order to remain sustainable — such as the AGIL schema — for Luhmann, any specific system encounters its own particular functional needs in order to survive. The functional problems encountered in global systems of economic or environmental relations, science or international law are very different from those confronting local systems of sport, urban planning or education, or from interpersonal systems of intimate relations.

In the final analysis, Luhmann's theory may be seen as a further development of Parsons and of structural functionalism — beyond social systems theory into a theory of communication systems. Luhmann reformulated

Parsons' theory of media exchange into a theory of communication media (including such media as money, power, truth and love). He also reformulated Parsons' theory of differentiation. Like Parsons, Luhmann does not directly address such critical social problems as social inequality and social conflict; these topics are only ever considered at high levels of abstraction and generality within the coded systems of information that comprise his theory of communication systems.

Today, the novelty of Luhmann's theory of autopoietic systems has already been superseded by newer and more interdisciplinary theories — involving complexity theory, chaos theory and other theoretical frameworks imported into the social sciences from the mathematical and natural sciences. One theorist who has expanded our conceptual horizons in systems theory is Sylvia Walby (2007). In her work, she has combined some aspects of complexity theory with those of intersectionality theory — already a major feminist perspective. In the hands of theorists such as Walby, the concept of "system" now promises to have a new lease of life — without the static, fixed, frozen and dogmatic assumptions that led to the demise of both structural functionalism and neofunctionalism.

References

Alexander, Jeffrey C., and Paul Colomy (eds.). 1990. *Differentiation Theory and Social Change: Comparative and Historical Perspectives.* Columbia University Press.

Alway, Joan. 1995. "The Trouble with Gender: Tales of the Still-Missing Feminist Revolution in Sociological Theory." *Sociological Theory*, 13: 209–228.

Atkinson, D. 1971. *Orthodox Consensus and Radical Alternative: A Study in Sociological Theory.* London: Heinemann Educational.

Bales, Robert Freed. 1951. *Interaction Process Analysis: A Method for the Study of Small Groups.* Cambridge, MA, Addison-Wesley.

Bausch, Kenneth C. 1997. "The Habermas/Luhmann Debate and Subsequent Habermasian Perspectives on Systems Theory." *Systems Research and Behavioral Science*, 14, 5 (September/October): 315–330.

Blood Diamond. 2006. [Film.] Director: Edward Zwick; Writer: Charles Leavitt.

Bowman, Michela, Amy LeClair, Michelle Lynn, and Robert Weide. n.d. "Talcott Parsons: *Toward a General Theory of Action*." <https://www.nyu.edu/classes/jackson/calhoun.jackson.theory/papers/A--Parsons.pdf>.

Brilliant Earth. n.d. "Blood Diamond Exposé." <https://www.brilliantearth.com/blood-diamond/>.

Brodkin, Karen, Sandra Morgen and Janis Hutchinson. 2011. "Anthropology as White Public Space?" *American Anthropologist*, 113: 545–556.

Caughron, Maxwell C. 2014. "Whither Myrdal? An Inquiry into the Theoretical and Educational Contributions of the Asian Drama." <http://r-cube.ritsumei.ac.jp/repo/repository/rcube/6416/K77_dis.pdf>.

Coser, Lewis. 1956. *The Functions of Social Conflict*. Simon and Schuster.

Dahrendorf, Ralf. 1959. *Class and Class Conflict in Industrial Society*. Stanford: Stanford University Press.

Davis, Kingsley, and Wilbert E. Moore. 1945. "Some Principles of Stratification." *American Sociological Review*, 10: 242–249.

Diamond, Stanley. 1974. *In Search of the Primitive: A Critique of Civilization*. New Brunswick, NJ: Transaction Books.

Dijksterhuis E.J. 1961. *The Mechanization of the World Picture*. Translated by C. Dikshoorn. New York: Oxford University Press.

Eilstrup-Sangiovanni, M. (ed). 2006. *Debates on European Integration*. Palgrave Macmillan.

European Studies: Hub. n.d. "Neo-Functionalism – University of Portsmouth: <http://hum.port.ac.uk/europeanstudieshub/learning/module-4-theorising-the-european-union/federalism-functionalism-and-transactionalism/2-functionalism-neo-functionalism/>.

Garfinkel, Harold. 1967. *Studies in Ethnomethodology*. Englewood Cliffs, NJ: Prentice-Hall.

Gausi, Tamara. 2018. "The Many Faces of Labour Exploitation." *Equal Times*, 3 August. <https://www.equaltimes.org/the-many-faces-of-labour#.XEnocWnNu2w>.

Gough, Kathleen. 1960. *Anthropology and Imperialism*. Ann Arbor, MI: Radical Education Project.

Gouldner, Alvin. 1970. *The Coming Crisis in Western Sociology*. Basic Books.

Herrnstein, Richard J., and Charles Murray. 1994. *The Bell Curve: Intelligence and Class Structure in American Life*. Free Press.

Hofstadter, Richard. 1992 [1944]. *Social Darwinism in American Thought, 1860–1915*. Philadelphia: University of Pennsylvania Press.

Horton, John. 1966. "Order and Conflict Theories of Social Problems as Competing Ideologies." *American Journal of Sociology*, LXXI, 6: 701–713.

Johnson, Chalmers. 2004. *Blowback: The Cost and Consequences of American Empire*, 2nd edition. Holt Paperbacks.

Johnson, Miriam M. 1993. "Functionalism and Feminism: Is Estrangement Necessary?" In Paul England (ed.), *Theory on Gender/Feminism on Theory*. New York: Aldine de Gruyter.

Junger, Sebastian. 2016. *Tribe: On Homecoming and Belonging*. HarperCollins Publishers.

Kirsch, Jochen H.Ch. 1998. "The Military of Guatemala and Niklas Luhmann's Theory of Autopoietic Social Systems." Thesis submitted to the Faculty of the Virginia Polytechnic Institute and State University, May 8, 1998. <https://pdfs.semanticscholar.org/3316/52adabe45df6b91f18a6ae050b8577ca68bf.pdf>.

Klein, Naomi. 1999. *No Logo: Taking Aim at the Brand Bullies*. Random House of Canada, Picador.

Kuper, Adam. 1988. *The Invention of Primitive Society: Transformations of an Illusion*. Routledge.

Levine Donald N. 1995. "The Organism Metaphor in Sociology." *Social Research*, 62, 2, The Power of Metaphor (Summer): 239–265.

Lipset, Seymour Martin. 1950. *Agrarian Socialism: The Cooperative Commonwealth*

Federation in Saskatchewan: A Study in Political Sociology. University of California Press.

Lipset, Seymour Martin, with Martin Trow and James S. Coleman. 1956. *Union Democracy: The Internal Politics of the International Typographical Union.* Free Press.

Lockwood, David. 1956. "Some Remarks on 'The Social System.'" *British Journal of Sociology,* 7, 2 (Jun): 134–146.

Lorimer, Douglas. 1988. "Theoretical Racism in Late-Victorian Anthropology, 1870–1900." *Victorian Studies,* 31, 3: 405–430.

Luhmann, Niklas. 1993. "Ecological Communication: Coping with the Unknown." *Systems Practice,* 6, 5.

Maturana, H.R., and F.G. Varela. 1980. *Autopoiesis and Cognition: The Realization of the Living.* Reidel, Dordrecht.

McLuhan, M. 1964. *Understanding Media: The Extensions of Man.* London and New York. <http://beforebefore.net/80f/s11/media/mcluhan.pdf>.

Merton, Robert K. 1938. "Social Structure and Anomie." *American Sociological Review,* 3, 5 (Oct.): 672–682.

___. 1949. *Social Theory and Social Structure.* New York: Free Press.

___. 1967. *On Theoretical Sociology.* Free Press.

Mills, C. Wright. 1959. *The Sociological Imagination.* Oxford University Press.

Moore, Barrington. 1966. *Social Origins of Dictatorship and Democracy: Lord and Peasant in the Making of the Modern World.* Boston: Beacon Press.

Parsons, Talcott. 1937. *The Structure of Social Action.* Glencoe, IL: Free Press.

___. 1951. *The Social System.* Glencoe, IL: Free Press.

Parsons, Talcott, and R.F. Bales. 1955. *Family, Socialization and Interaction Process.* Glencoe, IL: Free Press.

Rex, John. 1961. *Key Problems of Sociological Theory.* Routledge & K. Paul.

Rosamond, B. 2000. *Theories of European Union Integration.* Basingstoke: Macmillan.

Shawcross, William. 1979. *Sideshow: Kissinger, Nixon, and the Destruction of Cambodia.* Simon & Schuster.

Schmitter, Philippe, and Zoe Lefkofridi. 2016. "Neo-Functionalism as a Theory of Disintegration." *Chinese Political Science Review* 1, 1.

Sydie, Rosalind. 1994. *Natural Women, Cultured Men: A Feminist Perspective on Sociological Theory.* UBC Press.

Szacki, Jerzy. 1979. *History of Sociological Thought.* Westport, CT: Greenwood Press.

Tumin, Melvin M. 1953. "Some Principles of Stratification: A Critical Analysis." *American Sociological Review,* 18, 4: 387–393.

Turner, Jonathan H. 2012. *Contemporary Sociological Theory.* Sage Publications.

Vanderstraeten, Raf. 2005. "System and Environment: Notes on the Autopoiesis of Modern Society." *Systems Research and Behavioral Science,* 22: 471–481.

Walby, Sylvia. 2007. "Social Inequalities, Complexity Theory, Systems Theory, and Multiple Intersecting." *Philosophy of the Social* Sciences, 37: 449–470.

Weiss-Wendt, and Anton and Rory Yeomans (eds.). 2013. *Racial Science in Hitler's New Europe, 1938–1945.* Lincoln and London: University of Nebraska Press.

White, Michael. 2013. "Ed Miliband and Diane Abbott: Better to Keep Your Enemies Close?" *The Guardian,* 9 October.

Wrong, Dennis H. 1961. "The Oversocialized Conception of Man in Modern Sociology." *American Sociological Review,* 26, 2 (Apr): 183–193.

CHAPTER 3

THEORIZING OUR CONFLICT ZONES

Conflict Theories of Society

THE HUMAN HABIT OF SOCIAL CONFLICT

Social conflict is perhaps the single most important topic of social theory and social research. Indeed, it is in many senses the root and raison d'être of the social sciences. A failure to understand the causes and motives of human conflicts and our inability to find ways of managing and resolving these conflicts will continue to pose the greatest threat to our collective existence on this planet. Although social theory and social research cover a broad range of human problems and dilemmas, the problem of conflict remains among the most intractable and pressing of all these concerns.

While there are many ways of studying human conflict, we are primarily concerned with how social theorists have studied the causes and motives of conflict. In other words, we are focused on the study of *social* conflict. Some theorists — such as sociobiologists and evolutionary psychologists — have been fixated on the biological and genetic traits that supposedly predispose human populations to aggression, violence, territoriality, dominance and competition. According to these perspectives, these inherited propensities for aggression and conflict have remained an important part of our evolutionary heritage over the several millennia of our collective existence. On the other hand, most social theorists have focused on the environmental causes and contributory factors to human conflict, whether these are social, economic, cultural, political or ecological. The ongoing debate between hereditarian and environmental explanations for human conflict, while no longer a primary focus of theory or research, remains an underlying division between different approaches to the study of human conflict.

Modern and contemporary social theorists have pursued many different aspects in the study of human conflict. Some theorists — Randall

Collins (1974, 1975), for example — focused on violent rather than non-violent social conflict. Other theorists — such as Ralf Dahrendorf (1958, 1959) — studied the social conditions that contribute to both non-violent and violent conflict groups in society. Some theorists have focused on the microsocial (or interpersonal) conditions and situations that lead to conflictual encounters, while other theorists have studied the larger scale mesosocial or macrosocial influences that contribute to conflict situations in organizations, communities and societies or between nation states. Thus, conflict theorists differ in the scale and scope of their theoretical, historical or empirical studies of human conflict.

One of the more significant limitations of twentieth-century conflict theory was not only its Eurocentrism (in common with much social theory) but also its androcentrism and gender-blindness. Social theorists and sociologists traditionally paid very little attention to the major social problem of violence against women. This has been the case from the origins of the discipline, as Hearn (2014: 17) remarks: "Many canonical writers and texts in sociology, sociological theory and social theory, both 'classics' and more contemporary landmark texts, have not made such domestic violence a central concern. The founding fathers of sociology, as men of their own historical time … were generally not well attuned to foregrounding interpersonal violence against women."

Typically, early sociological theories of conflict and violence and those of more modern theorists, such as C. Wright Mills, Lewis Coser, John Rex, Ralf Dahrendorf, Randall Collins and Michael Mann, were formulated in abstract terms that that failed to distinguish violence against women. In other words, gendered violence has remained largely invisible in social theory and also in the methodology of crime data collection. Until fairly recently, police statistics on recorded incidents of violent crime also failed to specify the gender status of offenders and victims or the relationship between the two — even in cases of intimate-partner violence (Walby, Towers and Francis 2014: 196). This gender blindness has, unfortunately, extended into twenty-first century social theory. Slavoj Žižek (2009: 10, 174) argues that a "fascination" with "subjective violence" (individual and interpersonal violence) only serves to distract the theorist from the more serious analysis of "systemic violence" (structural, more impersonal and objective violence generated by the institutions of the state, the media, law enforcement agencies, criminal justice administration systems etc.). But by overemphasizing the structures of systemic violence, Žižek in his own way, renders invisible gendered violence against women. And another celebrity theorist of the twenty-first century, Pierre Bourdieu (2000), perpetuates the marginalization of violence against women by suggesting that many victims of violence are complicit in their own victimization because they have invariably internalized the values of inequality that (symbolically and structurally) legitimate the ideologies and practices of power.

This overemphasis on systemic violence at the expense of subjective interpersonal violence, combined with the low visibility (or invisibility) of violence against women in social theory — has led to the propagation of some deeply embedded "myths" about sexual violence — both in public discourse and in social theory. It is still a common, though mistaken, belief for example, that violence against women is typically perpetrated by strangers or acquaintances when most violence is actually inflicted by intimate partners in domestic household situations (Midgley 2003). For many years, until intimate-partner violence was first widely recognized as a social problem in the 1970s, the topic had already "had a long history of being treated as a private matter that did not warrant research or attention outside the family" (Lawson 2012: 573). Similarly, though most reports of sexual violence in war zones or other combat zones have often focused on rape as a weaponized crime by military forces, more common locations of sexual violence, such as refugee camps, workplaces and families, remain overlooked and underreported (Midgely 2003; McKie 2006). For this reason, it is worth remembering, in any survey of contemporary conflict theory, that much everyday violence perpetrated against women in our society and around the world has gone unnoticed and unrecorded in the annals of social theory. With the growth of transnational women's movements such as #MeToo and #TimesUp, we may hope that the era of gender blindness is finally coming to an end. There are some promising signs: a number of scholars have already contributed to a growing theoretical and empirical literature focused on violence against women — including Sylvia Walby (Walby, Towers and Francis 2014), Jeff Hearn (2014), Linda McKie (2006) and Jennifer Lawson (2012), among others. The victims of gender violence are no longer invisible or inaudible.

As we shall briefly see later in this chapter, the study of human conflict has a long and venerable pedigree among historians, philosophers, dramatists, military strategists and many other thinkers and theorists down throughout the ages. The ancient Greek historian Thucydides (*History of the Peloponnesian War*), the ancient Chinese military strategist Sun

Tzu (*The Art of War*) and the early modern military strategist Claus von Clausewitz (*On War*) each helped to lay the foundations for later studies of armed conflict. The roots of conflict theory extend back in time to the ancient philosophers on several continents — many of whom have yet to be recognized and acknowledged in the global canon of conflict theory. For some commentators (Dahrendorf 1959), the ancient Greek philosopher Thrasymachus is seen as a pioneer of conflict theory; for others it is Heraclitus; other commentators suggest the Islamic philosopher Ibn Khaldun (Alatas 2014). The search for the progenitors of conflict theory continues among the ancient political philosophers of China, India, Africa and other pre-European traditions of social thought. But in the social sciences, the groundwork for much theoretical, historical and empirical research on human conflict was prepared by such writers as Nicolai Machiavelli, Karl Marx, Vilfredo Pareto, Georg Simmel and Max Weber, among many others.

It is hardly surprising that many scholars who contributed to theories of social conflict as well as to empirical and historical studies of social conflict have come from regions with a strong legacy of conflict and institutional violence. Many scholars from former colonies of European states or from internal colonies within these states have written about the historical and empirical experience of colonial violence, slavery and racism. Algerian theorist Frantz Fanon wrote extensively about French colonialism; Trinidadian scholars C.L.R. James and Eric Williams wrote about slavery in the American South and French colonial violence in Haiti. Walter Rodney, who was assassinated in his home country of Guyana, wrote about European colonialism. African American scholars, such as W.E.B. Du Bois, Ida B. Wells, Franklin Frazer and Oliver Cromwell Cox, wrote about slavery and racism, while Indigenous writers, such as Vine Deloria, Lee Maracle and Richard Wagamese, deepened our understanding of the internal colonialism and cultural genocide experienced by Indigenous Peoples. Contemporary postcolonial writers from around the world provide a global context for theories as well as empirical and historical studies of social conflict. The study of social conflict has proven to be an enduring topic in social theory and social research, one that has preoccupied some of the greatest thinkers in the annals of social thought.

OPTIMISM, PESSIMISM OR REALISM?

Theorists have, through the ages, differed in their explanations of the causes of human conflict and also in their prognoses for social conflict in future human societies. Today, there is a marked division between theorists who conclude that the recent history of modern societies — over the past few centuries — has witnessed a significant decline in violent and cruel expressions of human conflict, and theorists who remain deeply skeptical of what they perceive to be these optimistic and utopian claims.

One contemporary writer who advances an optimistic view is Stephen Pinker. His popular book *The Better Angels of Our Nature: Why Violence Has Declined* (2011) argues that violence, including tribal warfare, homicide, cruel punishments, torture, child abuse, animal cruelty, domestic violence, lynching, pogroms and international and civil wars, have all declined over the past few centuries. To support his claim, Pinker argues that prehistoric and premodern armed encounters were far more lethal than is generally recognized. The proportion of fatalities in premodern societies — when measured as a percentage of the total population (of the band, tribe, clan or nation) — was far greater than the losses of life in modern wars and armed conflicts. Pinker also suggests that the end of public executions, public torture and public physical punishment — as well as advances in human rights, which have ended the persecution of racial, ethnic and sexual minorities in many countries — is further evidence of the historical decline of officially sanctioned violence and cruelty and an indication of a "humanitarian revolution" and an evolutionary trend towards the progressive "civilization" of human conflict. Although Pinker is one of the more optimistic commentators on the decline of violent and cruel conflicts, he is not alone in his sanguine interpretation of human history. Joshua L. Goldstein presents a similar view in his book *Winning the War on War: The Decline of Armed Conflict Worldwide* (2011), as do Azar Gat in *War in Human Civilization* (2008), political scientist John E. Mueller in *Retreat from Doomsday: The Obsolescence of Major War* (1989) and philosopher Peter Singer in *The Most Good You Can Do: How Effective Altruism Is Changing Ideas About Living Ethically* (2015).

However, this optimistic view of human conflict is not shared by everyone. In his 1977 book *Discipline and Punish*, Michel Foucault traces the decline of public torture and execution and the corresponding birth of the prison and privatized punishment. Foucault argues that these "humane" reforms of the penal system in France were motivated by the need for the state to exercise greater control over criminals and all other members of society. In place of overt corporal punishment (such as public flogging, branding, amputation and other forms of mutilation, as well as public torture and execution) that sought to control the body and to symbolize the direct power of the sovereign, the rise of the prison and the privatization of punishment sought to control the soul (or the mind) of the criminal, (Rose 1990). The privatization of punishment avoided possible public outrage over the spectacle of official violence and cruelty and reduced the opportunity for popular revolt in opposition to, or discontent with, the legal or political system. Although Foucault documented the reform of earlier barbaric punishments, he concluded that the new "disciplinary practices" (such as solitary confinement, total surveillance and regimentation, coercive psychiatric treatment etc.) perpetrated new forms of violence against social outcasts in private rather than in public settings, using psychological rather than physical methods of coercion and punishment. Foucault did not subscribe to any optimistic or utopian belief in the decline of violence or cruelty in modern society; he simply documented their changing forms.

Another writer who rejects the claim that violent social conflict has declined is the sociologist Randall Collins (1974, 1975). While Collins concedes that face-to-face, or interpersonal, violent conflict may have declined in contemporary Western societies, he concludes that other, more lethal, forms of violence have replaced it. Collins suggests — in his theory of human conflict — that earlier "ferocious" forms of face-to-face violent combat (such as prehistoric raiding parties or trench warfare) have been superseded by more "callous" or remote forms, such as aerial bombardment, missile attacks and drone strikes. At the same time, contemporary examples of "ferocious" face-to-face violence may still be seen in combat zones such as the Iraq-Iran War, 1980–88; the Rwandan genocide, 1994; the Cambodian (Kampuchean) genocide, 1975–79; the rise of ISIS in Iraq and Syria and of Boko Haram in northern Nigeria; and other paramilitary and rebel militia groups, such as the Lord's Resistance Army in the Central African Republic, the Democratic Republic of the Congo and Uganda. According to Collins, human conflict remains endemic around the globe, and far from declining, it has become more lethal and more efficient.

In summary, the subject of conflict remains a central topic in social theory and throughout the social sciences and humanities. However, for social theorists, the challenge has always been to reduce the complexity of the existing historical and empirical research literature on human conflict to some general themes and explanations. All theories of social relations or social behaviour necessarily draw upon a vast repository of documented fact and accumulated knowledge. But the construction of social theory inevitably relies upon the oversimplification of these research resources in order to search for the general causes, conditions and consequences of various types of human conflict. It is only by identifying generalizable causal explanations of human conflict that it becomes possible to develop informed and practical strategies for managing, ameliorating or even resolving these conflicts.

ORIGINS OF CONFLICT THEORY

We shall now examine the development of conflict theory in modern sociology and locate the sources of some of these ideas. Although conflict theory emerged as a distinct theoretical discourse in sociology (within the past sixty years or so), its roots may be found in ideas that go back to the ancient Greek philosophers and historians, such as Heraclitus and Thucydides, and to medieval Arab philosophers, such as Ibn Khaldun. It is important to acknowledge these early influences in order to show that every theoretical perspective in sociology has its roots in the ideas of earlier social thinkers. Another important reason for acknowledging the influence of classical Greek, Roman, Chinese and Arab thinkers on the tradition of conflict theory, is to counter the Eurocentric bias of traditional historical accounts of social theory. To judge from many standard text-book accounts of the development of social theory, it has only been dead, white guys who made any significant contribution to our understanding of society. This kind of ethnocentrism and androcentrism blinds us to the influence of distinguished scholars from non-European civilizations whose ideas anticipated many of the concepts that have become fashion-able in contemporary sociological theory.

More modern origins of conflict theory can be traced back to Enlightenment theorists, who proposed new ideas that were in contradic-tion with the established beliefs of the old order, or *ancien regime*. From the French Enlightenment, which included thinkers such as Jean Jacques Rousseau, Voltaire, Denis Diderot, Marquis de Condorcet and Henri de Saint-Simon, came the radical criticisms of the monarchy, nobility and clergy that paved the way for the French Revolution. From the more moderate British (or more accurately, Scottish) Enlightenment scholars, which included Adam Smith, John Stuart Mill, David Hume and Thomas Malthus, came the liberal criticisms of the economy, polity and society.

Some of the early ideas about competition were influenced by Adam Smith's *laissez-faire* theories of free trade and the marketplace. These ideas later found their way into conservative social Darwinian versions of conflict theory (including Herbert Spencer, Ludwig Gumplowicz, Gustav Ratzenhofer and more recently, Leo Strauss and Carl Schmitt) in which relations between different social classes or racial groups were portrayed as a struggle for the "survival of the fittest." These and similar notions found their fullest expressions in the fascist and Nazi ideologies of the early twentieth century. Ominously, in the opening decades of the twenty-first century, some of these ideas appear to have been resurrected by far-right white nationalist and neo-Nazi parties in Europe, the United States and Canada (see *New York Times* 2016).

More radical versions of conflict theory were associated with French and German thinkers of the eighteenth and nineteenth centuries (including Saint-Simon, Lorenz von Stein, Georg Hegel, Georg Simmel and Georges Sorel, among others), but above all with the ideas of Karl Marx and his followers. Marx is the great genius behind modern conflict theory, and although many writers rejected his universalist view of class conflict, the influence of his ideas was felt by everyone.

It is important to remember that like all social theories, the ideas of conflict theorists did not fall out of the sky but were influenced by some of the major historical events of their times. Chief among these events were the democratic revolutions of the seventeenth and eighteenth centuries (English Revolution of 1689; American Revolution of 1776; French Revolution of 1789). In addition to these political revolutions were the eighteenth-century agricultural and industrial revolutions in Britain, which, even more than the political revolutions, contributed to the transformation of traditional into modern societies. All of these major events were part of the historical background to the birth of many of the ideas of modern conflict theory.

The emergence of modern conflict theory in the 1960s was not only an intellectual challenge to the pre-eminence of structural functionalism in most of the English-speaking world but also a political challenge to the climate of complacency and consensus that was part of the postwar ethos in many of these societies. It is no accident that conflict theorists began their sociological critiques of functionalism around the same time that more practical critiques of the Vietnam War, universities, patriarchy and sexual and racial discrimination were taking place in the classrooms, courtrooms, boardrooms and streets of North America and Europe. There is an important sense in which conflict theorists were inspired by the struggles of the civil rights, antiwar, women's liberation and student movements of the 1960s, much as their philosophical predecessors had been inspired by the turbulent events of the eighteenth and nineteenth centuries. Theory is always informed by events that unfold within our social worlds, and it offers us images of these events that are reflected back to us in sometimes strange and unfamiliar ways.

The first wave of modern conflict theory during the 1960s was preoccupied with critiquing and contesting functionalism as the prevailing sociological orthodoxy. Much of the key literature of conflict theory during this period was polemical in nature. Theorists such as Ralf Dahrendorf (1959), C. Wright Mills (1956), John Horton (1966), Alvin Gouldner (1970) and John Rex (1961, 1981) argued that North American sociology had become frozen in a static and conservative view of the social world, which they identified with structural functionalism, especially the version associated with the work of Talcott Parsons. Some of the most representative writings of this period take the form of elaborate theoretical, political and even methodological refutations of structural functionalism. It was during this period that the "consensus/conflict debate" became the major controversy of modern sociology (Demareth and Petersen 1967; Bernard 1983).

In the early twenty-first century, conflict theorists are no longer preoccupied with mounting a challenge to functionalism, as its reign as a sociological orthodoxy has long since ended. Conflict theory has broadened considerably, ranging from microsociological studies of conflict between small groups, to the large-scale historical studies of conflict and social change. Later in this chapter, we shall review examples of the work of some of the foremost conflict theorists of the modern and contemporary periods.

MODERN SOCIOLOGICAL CONFLICT THEORY

Since the emergence of conflict theory in the 1960s, it has become a popular theoretical perspective in Europe and North America. Along with other perspectives, such as the microsocial traditions (symbolic interactionism, social phenomenology, ethnomethodology, exchange theory, rational choice theory etc.), as well as feminism, critical theory and neo-Marxism, and more recently, structuralism, postmodernism and poststructuralism — conflict theory helped to dislodge structural functionalism from its dominant position in Anglophone sociology. However, conflict theory includes a broad range of theorists with diverse intellectual backgrounds and, in many ways, has proven to be a less unified tradition than structural functionalism.

Whereas for functionalists, social order in all social systems is explained in terms of such concepts as "functional interdependence and coordination," "integration," "equilibrium" and "consensus," conflict theorists view society and other social systems as arenas in which competing social groups struggle for dominance, power and control. From the perspective of conflict theory, any resolution of conflict can only be achieved when one group is able to successfully dominate other groups, even if only temporarily.

In the most general terms, the following three basic assumptions underlie most versions of conflict theory:

1. Any social group has definite material interests or strategic resources that are common to all members of the group, although these interests may not always be fully recognized and articulated. The corollary to this assumption is that different social groups may be in competition with, or in opposition to, each other in their efforts to protect, secure or restrict access to particular material interests or strategic resources. In some cases, the opposition between social groups may produce deep divisions within society, such as those between capitalists and workers (according to Marx). In other cases, these divisions may be focused on specific struggles for strategic resources, such as those between anti-abortion and pro-choice groups over access to abortion, or LBGTQ groups and their opponents over the legalization of same-sex marriage.
2. Power, or authority, is the basis of all social relationships. Power is distributed unequally in society and forms the root of social

conflict as different groups struggle against each other for power. However, as many social theorists emphasize, there is an important distinction between the concepts of "power" and "authority." "Power" may be defined as the ability of some social actors to enforce their will through the coercion or manipulation of other social actors. "Authority" may be defined as the ability of some social actors to enforce their will over others by virtue of the position, status or office they hold within society. In other words, as Max Weber suggested, authority is "legitimated power," exercised as the legitimate right of a particular office-holder in society. Whereas individuals or groups need to impose their power on others through force or manipulation, office-holders can expect their authority to be accepted as legitimate by most members of society. Whereas power is exercised through coercion, authority is exercised through public consent or compliance. When a police officer steps out into the middle of the road in order to halt or redirect traffic, she is obeyed not because she is physically powerful or intimidating, but because she possesses legitimate authority to act in this way.

3. Values and ideas are often used by different groups to advance their own ends, to defend their privileges and to justify their causes. These values and ideas differ from one group to another and from one historical period to the next. Some groups try to justify their struggle for power by using religious ideas (Christian Crusades, Islamic jihads etc.), while other groups resort to ideas about race, ethnicity, language, gender, age or social class to advance their interests. The list of ideological justifications for advancing group interests is a long one. Most groups that have found themselves in struggles for power have tried to win support for their actions (whether military, political, cultural or economic) in terms of some appeal to popular sentiments. Many groups engaged in social conflict have attempted to win the hearts and minds of the people by invoking ideas and values that appear to have popular support. At different times these values have included "democracy," "freedom," "civilization," "the believers" or "the faithful," "the master race," "the nation," "the working class" and so on. Marx used the concept of "ideology" to describe how the ruling class of each historical period imposes its ideas and values on all other classes in society. Pareto used the concept of "derivations" to describe how powerful

elites spread their own ideas and values in order to dominate and manipulate the masses under their control and jurisdiction. Each conflict theorist has found their own way to analyze the role of ideas in the struggle for power between opposing social groups.

Modern conflict theories may be divided into two distinct traditions. These traditions differ in at least two important ways: first, in terms of their views of social science, and second, in their beliefs as to whether conflict can ever be eradicated from social relationships. These two traditions of conflict theory are:

1. *Analytical tradition*: Social theorists included in this category generally regard conflict as an inevitable and permanent aspect of social life. These theorists subscribe to the view that the social sciences should be value-free scholarly disciplines committed to "objectivity" and "ethical neutrality." According to this view, social scientists should not let their political beliefs interfere with the goal of scientific objectivity. For these analytical conflict theorists, a sharp distinction is made between facts on the one hand and values on the other. Some of the major theorists in this analytical tradition include Max Weber, Georg Simmel, Lewis Coser, Ralf Dahrendorf, John Rex, Randall Collins and Michael Mann.

2. *Critical tradition*: Theorists in this category recognize a political and moral responsibility to undertake a "critique" of modern society. These theorists reject the distinction between fact and value proposed by the analytical theorists as spurious and otiose. The critical conflict theorists insist that it is never possible to separate the practice of social theory and research from the political values of the investigator. They argue that the choice of research topic, the use of particular research methods and the purposes to which the research results are put are all related to the basic political and moral values of the researcher.

Critical conflict theorists also believe that it is possible to envision a society in which many of the modern sources of social conflict (such as class exploitation, racial discrimination, gender oppression and religious persecution) have been eliminated. The work of many of these theorists is informed by a strong socialist, feminist, Marxist or even utopian intellectual influence. In place of ethical neutrality, therefore, critical conflict theorists emphasize a strong normative commitment to their particular vision of theory and research.

Some of the most important of the critical conflict theorists have been associated with various schools of neo-Marxism. Several of these schools have made significant contributions to the development of social thought. The school of Hegelian Marxism, for example, was established through the works of Georg Lukacs, Antonio Gramsci and Karl Korsch, among others. A generation later, the Frankfurt School of Critical Theory became internationally known through the ideas of such theorists as Theodor Adorno and Max Horkheimer and later through the ideas of Herbert Marcuse and Jürgen Habermas. In yet another variation of neo-Marxist theory, Immanuel Wallerstein popularized his version of world-system theory. And more recently, theorists such as Frederick Jameson as well as Lucio Magri, Michael Hardt, Ernesto Laclau and Chantal Mouffe have tried to reconcile Marxist analysis with the contemporary perspective of postmodernism. Although the fall of the USSR and the Soviet bloc in 1989 has been viewed by some critics as evidence of the failure of the communist project, Marxism as an organic intellectual tradition remains a vital force in the world of social theory.

THE STRUCTURAL CONFLICT THEORY OF RALF DAHRENDORF

The first modern conflict theorist we shall discuss in this chapter is the German sociologist Ralf Dahrendorf (1929–2009). He can be categorized as an analytical conflict theorist, and his work achieved its greatest impact during the closing years of the 1960s and throughout the 1970s. During this time, Dahrendorf became known as a severe critic of the structural functionalist perspective of Parsons, and most of his work attempted to provide an alternative to the consensus model of society. Dahrendorf also pursued careers in politics and education administration. He served as an elected representative to the German Bundestag (parliament) and was also a member of the Commission of European Communities (later called the European Commission). From 1974 until 1984, he served as director of the London School of Economics. More than many other modern social theorists, Dahrendorf was not afraid to get his hands dirty in the real world of politics.

Although Dahrendorf's work has long been overtaken by more recent conflict-oriented theories of society, we include him because his ideas represent a clearly formulated alternative to structural functionalism.

Indeed, he was one of the key theorists of the mid-twentieth century to challenge the hegemony of structural functionalism and to advance a serious alternative theory of society. Unlike Parsons, who remained convinced that social order was almost always based on a consensus of basic values — a "social contract" of some kind — Dahrendorf proposed that social order is invariably based on the domination of some groups in society by others. For Dahrendorf, therefore, order in many types of social relations — whether in organizations, small groups (such as the family) or most especially in society itself — is often maintained through coercion rather than through voluntary consensus. Many organizations and institutions in society are run by those who have the power or the authority to command others. In place of the "integration model" of society advanced by the structural functionalist theorists, Dahrendorf offers us a "coercion model" of society, which, he believed, provides a more realistic picture of how social organizations work. What then, are some of the key concepts and basic assumptions that Dahrendorf used to construct his coercion, or conflict, theory of society?

Power and Authority

Following in the footsteps of Max Weber, Dahrendorf introduced the important distinction between "power" and "authority." Power is normally defined as the ability of some social actors (either individuals or groups) to enforce their will through the coercion of other social actors. Some institutions, even in our own society, are governed by the age-old rule that "might is right" and use their material or symbolic resources to dominate others and control and manage social relations. Some institutions that are evidently governed by brute force include the modern street gang or the criminal syndicate. In those largely coercive organizations, power is projected through physical force and increasingly through economic wealth accumulated through narcotics, gambling, auto theft, human trafficking, prostitution etc. Authority may best be defined as the ability of some social actors to enforce their will over others by virtue of the office or official position they hold in society. The authority of a social actor is always linked to and limited to a particular office or position; it is not supposed to exceed these limits. A police officer may have the authority to divert traffic but not to demand that you clean up your room or wash your dishes. This distinction between power and authority is central to Dahrendorf's theory of social conflict.

Imperatively Coordinated Associations

In place of the concept of "social system," which played such a central role in Parsons' theory of society, Dahrendorf uses the concept (also taken from Max Weber) of the "imperatively coordinated association." Unlike the social system, which, according to Parsons, is based upon consensus, equilibrium and the functional coordination and integration of the constituent parts of the system, the imperatively coordinated association (ICA) is based upon coercion, inequality, conflict and social change. An ICA, according to Dahrendorf, whether analyzed in the form of an organization, a social group or a total society, is based upon a fundamental conflict of interest between groups that dominate social relations and groups that are dominated. In any social situation, there is always an actual or potential conflict of interest between superordinate versus subordinate social groups.

For Dahrendorf, all units of social organization can be analyzed as ICAS. Every social organization, from a small group to an entire society, is characterized by the unequal distribution of authority among members of the organization. In any organization, some individuals or groups possess authority, while others do not. In this sense, authority, unlike income or education, is an absolute rather than a relative concept. One cannot have more or less of it; one either has it in any particular situation or one does not. At the same time, Dahrendorf recognizes that authority is a pluralistic concept in that an individual may possess authority in one context but not in another. While someone may only be a janitor in her workplace, she may be the pastor or deacon at her local church.

One of the best, or purest, examples of an ICA is the prison. In a custodial institution, the structure of authority relations is clearly defined: the warden and guards exercise a monopoly over authority, while the inmates have none. Other examples of "total institutions," to use the terminology of Erving Goffman (1961), or "carceral institutions" from Michel Foucault, include the military (division between officers and lower ranks), residential schools (staff versus students) and some religious institutions (monasteries, convents etc.). In each of these examples, some have authority, while others do not. However, Dahrendorf's point is that many other institutions in society exhibit some of the characteristics of the ICA: the boardroom, the classroom, the shop floor, the office, for instance.

Theory of Intergroup Conflict

Dahrendorf believes that any set of social relations always involves a basic division between those individuals or groups who occupy a superordinate status (have authority) and those individuals or groups who occupy a subordinate status (without authority). Dahrendorf also recognizes that individuals who occupy a subordinate status do not necessarily have any shared consciousness of their common situation. In other words, while many individuals or groups in low status positions may have common interests, these interests may remain unrecognized and unacknowledged. As long as their common interests remain unrecognized, these interests can never become the basis for mobilizing collective action directed towards social change. It is only when individuals begin to recognize their common interests that collective action of any kind becomes possible.

Dahrendorf uses the term "latent interests" to describe a situation in which individuals who share certain objective interests fail to subjectively recognize these common interests and thereby fail to collectively act upon them. For example, the tenants of a large apartment complex may find themselves paying huge rent increases to the property management company while at the same time receiving reductions in service. If tenants regard themselves as isolated individuals, then the common interests of all tenants remain unacknowledged and no collective action to protest rent increases will result.

Dahrendorf uses the term "quasi-group" to define a collection of individuals who together occupy a common set of subordinate statuses but who have no shared consciousness of their common situation (i.e., their "structural identity"). They may have common objective interests but do not have a shared subjective recognition or understanding of their common situation. There are, of course, many different quasi-groups in our society whose members may have no common recognition of their shared interests. Consumers may have a strong collective interest in regulating price increases and preventing reduced retail services. However, as long as members of this quasi-group remain isolated and privatized in the face of soaring price increases, they are only potential rather than actual groups in society.

On the other hand, according to Dahrendorf, an "interest group" is one whose members have a conscious recognition and understanding of their common status and of their relationship to other groups in society. An interest group is a group in which the formerly latent interests of its members have become transformed into "manifest interests," which are fully recognized and acknowledged and which may form the basis for collective action. An interest group, therefore, is organized around a common set of manifest interests. It possesses what Dahrendorf calls a "conscious identity," which may bring the group into antagonistic relations with other groups. An interest group may eventually be transformed into a "conflict group," whose members may see their interests in conflict with, or in opposition to, the manifest interests of another group or groups in society. In summary, quasi-groups may evolve into interest groups or even into conflict groups, when the latent interests of group members become manifest and thereby begin to function as a basis for collective action.

A recent striking example of how Dahrendorf's theory may be applied to a current conflict situation can be seen in the development of the Idle No More movement that arose in Canada in 2012, led by several Indigenous women who protested the introduction of Bill C-45 by the Conservative government of Stephen Harper. Among other things, this bill proposed to remove the protections for forests and waterways and raised concerns among Indigenous communities and environmentalists. These concerns were expressed in numerous acts of protest that included round dances in public places and blockades of rail lines. Eventually, with the formation of Idle No More as a mass grassroots movement, protests spread to include opposition to other projects seen as harmful to Indigenous Peoples and in violation of existing treaty rights, such as pipeline protests (against the Enbridge Northern Gateway Pipelines project), hunger strikes and demonstrations about other concerns of Indigenous communities, such as housing, suicide and contaminated drinking water. Idle No More has quickly become one of the largest Indigenous mass movements in Canadian history — sparking hundreds of teach-ins, rallies and protests across Turtle Island and beyond.

Using Dahrendorf's conceptual framework and vocabulary, we could say that Indigenous Peoples living in rural and urban areas across Canada constituted a quasi-group, a potential group that shared a number of common threats and experiences — even though these commonalities were not always collectively recognized or openly acknowledged. However, the arrogance of the Harper government triggered outrage among Indigenous Peoples, which led to a public acknowledgement of commonly perceived injustices, including broken treaties, government indifference to Indigenous grievances and the erosion of Indigenous sovereignty. Idle

No More has also brought together several solidarity groups and allies in opposition to governmental policy that impacts collective rights, social safety nets and environmental protections. In this sense, we can see how the quasi group of Indigenous Peoples, which was always potentially united around a set of — unacknowledged and unmobilized — latent interests, was dramatically transformed into a fully awakened and mobilized interest group, and eventually into a conflict group, united around what had become stridently articulated manifest interests.

Plenty of other examples can be used to illustrate how Dahrendorf's conceptual framework and vocabulary may be used to analyze the formation, growth and maturation of protest groups — and their fuller development into social movements. The rise of feminist activist groups such as #MeToo and #TimesUp, which originated as a national protest against the culture of powerful celebrity male sexual predators in the US, has become a global social movement, bearing witness to the sexual victimization of women around the world. What started as the emergence of an "interest group" from a "quasi-group" of a much larger population of victimized women has now become an organized and formalized "conflict group" — dedicated to the exposure and accountability of sexual harassment and sexual abuse. Indeed, #MeToo has its own website, Twitter account and other publicity channels, and its impact has been felt in many major institutions — including media industries, politics and government, organized religion and even in the military. It offers a textbook example of the growth and transformation of a quasi-group into an interest group and eventually into a conflict group.

Another example of an interest group is the high school protest group March for Our Lives, which emerged in the wake of the horrific high school shooting in Parkland, Florida, on February 14, 2018, in which seventeen students and staff members were killed and another seventeen were seriously injured. This protest group later become the basis of support for the more organized Never Again MSD (Marjory Stoneman Douglas High School) campaign, a student-led campaign for greater gun control in the US. This is yet another example of an interest group that emerged from the larger population (quasi-group) of vulnerable high-school students into a more organized and formalized social movement, a conflict group — with its own publicity media, political lobbyists and national audience. Dahrendorf's framework can be used to analyze the growth and transformation of many other collective struggles, from potential quasi-groups, into interest groups, into more formalized social protest movements (conflict groups). These groups have emerged in different social contexts — from Indigenous communities (Idle No More), among anti-capitalist activists (Occupy) and — most recently — among populist consumer protestors (Gilet Jaunes/Yellow Vests) in Europe and a new generation of environmentalist activists (Extinction Rebellion).

Figure 3-1: Dahrendorf's Model of Inter-Group Conflict

Dahrendorf outlines some of the conditions which favour the transformation of quasi-groups into interest and conflict groups. According to Dahrendorf, there are at least three sets of conditions — technical, political and social — which facilitate the formation of interest/conflict groups and which may lead to the growth of inter-group conflict.

Technical conditions: relate to the formalization of the structure of the groups. Technical conditions may include the publication of a charter (or constitution), membership lists, a program or platform, the election (or appointment) of group leaders or representatives, the distribution of literature (or propaganda) and — more recently — the construction of websites and blogs. An example of the formation of large and powerful interest group is the rise of the Christian right in the US through the influence of televangelism. Similarly, environmental groups (Greenpeace, Extinction Rebellion), hate groups, global justice groups and even jihadist groups (ISIS) have benefited from the resources of the internet. Most recently, women protesting sexual harassment and sexual assault have organized around the online Twitter hashtag #MeToo and have suddenly become a potent political force in the US and beyond.

Political conditions: relate primarily to whether political activity can be open and public, or whether it has to be clandestine and underground. The formation of interest groups is much easier in liberal democratic societies, where freedom of speech and assembly are tolerated or even encouraged, than in repressive societies, where these freedoms are denied or repressed.

Social conditions: relate to the ecology of social interaction. Social conditions which centralize interactions among individuals, such as a factory or construction site, are more conducive to group formation than social conditions in which individuals are spatially or geographically dispersed (such as peasants or farm workers in rural areas). Factories, cities and universities (or other centralized locations) provide greater opportunities for communication and recruitment to groups than the more isolated conditions of rural life. With the advent of more mobile forms of communication (through the internet, cell phones, social media etc.), the gap between the dense communication of urban areas and the more sparse communication of rural areas has undoubtedly narrowed.

Historical Flashback

It is worth noting that Dahrendorf borrowed and modified his concepts of quasi-, interest and conflict groups from a distinction introduced by Karl Marx. In his book *The Civil War in France,* Marx distinguished between a "class-in-itself" (such as the peasantry in France) and a "class-for-itself" (such as the working class, or proletariat). Whereas the former can be defined objectively in terms of its relationship to the means of production and to other classes, most members of a class-in-itself remain highly individualized and fail to achieve any collective class consciousness. For Marx, a class only becomes fully developed when its members arrive at a subjective recognition and understanding of their real class interests and of their actual position in society. A class-for-itself, therefore, is a class that has evolved beyond a mere aggregate of individuals into a fully developed "class conscious" social group.

In practical terms, the key distinction between a class-in-itself and a class-for-itself is that whereas the former remains a *passive* actor in the structure of social relations, the latter may easily become an *active* force for collective action and sometimes revolutionary social change. The big difference between Marx's theory of class formation and Dahrendorf's theory of group formation lies in the different scope of each analysis. For Marx, a "class" is always defined in terms of its relationship to the means of production: ownership or non-ownership of productive property. For Dahrendorf, on the other hand, a "group" is defined in terms of its

The Athabasca Pulp & Paper Mill: A Local Example of Group Conflict

A useful application of Dahrendorf's theory of social conflict can be made to an event that occurred not far from Athabasca University. In 1993, the provincial government announced its approval of a large pulp and paper mill (the Alberta-Pacific or Alpac mill) in northern Alberta. This announcement was greeted enthusiastically by some sectors of the local community, but with dismay by others. Those who opposed the mill did so on a number of grounds. Environmentalists were concerned that the effluent discharged from the mill would result in much higher levels of toxicity in the river system. Farmers were concerned that toxic leakage from the mill could infiltrate the water table and contaminate arable farmland. Several Indigenous communities were concerned that higher levels of toxicity could poison the fish stocks that constituted part of their traditional livelihood.

The opposition constituencies quickly coalesced into a formalized interest group. This group soon acquired a name — Friends of the Athabasca — as well as a constitution and a mailing list of members. They held rallies and meetings to demand that the provincial government hold an environmental impact assessment hearing in the town of Athabasca. In the space of a few weeks, a quasi-group made up of individuals from various backgrounds rapidly evolved into an interest group with a clear, conscious common identity. In response to the formation of an interest group in opposition to the mill, a counter group made up of supporters of the mill soon emerged — Friends of the Mill. Among those who supported the mill were realtors (who anticipated rising residential property values), store owners and managers (who anticipated increased sales of goods and services) and local politicians (who hoped to take some credit for the location of the pulp mill and thereby enhance their own chances of re-election).

In the months that followed the announcement of the mill, relations between these two groups grew increasingly antagonistic. At public meetings to discuss the project, members of one group were sometimes insulted or verbally abused by members of the rival group. Indeed, the controversy over the mill sharply divided the community. In the end, the forces promoting the mill proved more powerful than those opposing it, and the mill began its operations in August 1993.

The controversy provides an informative case study which can be analyzed by using some of the key concepts from Dahrendorf's theory of social conflict. Some years later, a study was published of the different arguments which were used to support and to oppose the mill (at the environmental hearings). Readers can access this publication for a more detailed discussion of this controversy (see Richardson, Sherman and Gismondi 1993).

relationship to authority: the ability to command versus the obligation to obey. In other words, Dahrendorf attempts to widen Marx's theory of inter-group conflict from a historically specific theory of class conflict into a universal theory of social conflict.:

One question that was asked of Dahrendorf is whether he viewed the conflict model of social relations as the preferred alternative to that of the consensus model of structural functionalism or as a complementary but equally necessary model. Interestingly, Dahrendorf provided different answers to this question at different times. In his famous article "Out of Utopia" (1958: 127), Dahrendorf conceded that both consensus and conflict perspectives have a role to play in analyzing what he calls the "two faces" of social reality: "I do not intend to fall victim to the mistake of many structural functional theorists and advance for the conflict model a claim to comprehensive and exclusive applicability.… It may well be that in a philosophical sense, society has two faces of equal reality: one of stability, harmony and consensus and one of change, conflict and restraint."

In a passage from another book, *Class and Class Conflict in Industrial Society* (1959: 159), Dahrendorf again suggested that there may be certain problems in the study of society for which the consensus perspective is best suited and other problems for which the conflict perspective is more appropriate: "There are sociological problems of which the integration theory of society provides adequate assumptions; there are other problems which can be explained only in terms of the coercion theory of society; there are, finally, problems for which both theories appear adequate. For sociological analysis, society is Janus-headed, and its two faces are equivalent aspects of the same reality."

However, in a later essay, "In praise of Thrasymachus" (1968: 149–150), Dahrendorf appears to have changed his mind and argued instead for the superiority of the conflict over the consensus perspective as a sociological theory of social relations:

> I no longer take the tolerant view that the two approaches discussed are essentially equivalent ways of understanding a given problem or understanding two different sets of problems. It can be argued, I think — and I have tried to argue — that the constraint approach is superior to the equilibrium approach … the constraint approach being more general, more plausible, and generally more informative about the problems of social and political life, should for these reasons

replace the approach now so surprisingly in vogue in social science.

In later publications, Dahrendorf remained silent on the question of the relative priority of these two perspectives. Readers are encouraged to make up their own minds regarding the relationship of the consensus to the conflict perspective.

RANDALL COLLINS'S SOCIAL THEORY OF CRUELTY

We now turn to the work of one of the foremost conflict theorists in modern sociology, Randall Collins. According to Collins, modern conflict theory developed as an alternative to the Marxian approach to the study of social conflict. Marxists believe that all forms of social conflict have their roots in class conflict. Conflict theorists assume that social conflict may come from many different sources, of which class is but one. Indeed, some traditions of conflict theory have developed in clear opposition to Marxism. This is especially true of what we may call the "Italian tradition of elite theory," which extends back to Machiavelli and includes such theorists as Vilfredo Pareto (1935), Gaetano Mosca (1965) and Robert Michels (1959) (although Michels was a German contributor to this tradition). More generally, however, modern conflict theory regards Marxism (or class analysis) as a limited case of a more general approach to the study of social conflict. Collins concludes that conflict theorists see themselves as competent to study the same social phenomena as Marxists, but in a more systematic, empirical way and without any of the philosophical baggage that many Marxists carry.

One of the central points Collins makes is that modern conflict theory has moved beyond the debating stage and has now become a fully developed theoretical perspective with its own research tradition. Unlike in the 1960s, which saw conflict theory emerge as a critical echo of structural functionalism, it has become one of the more integrated perspectives in social theory, combining macrosociological and microsociological studies in ways that blend theory with empirical research. Collins believes conflict theory is about much more than social conflict and that it has developed into a fully independent theory of society in which the realities of power and property, domination and struggle have been elevated to major research priorities.

Collins provides us with concrete examples of how modern conflict theorists go about developing theories of particular social phenomena that are rich in historical or empirical detail. In an earlier formulation of his theory of violence and cruelty, Collins invites us to consider how standard historical and sociological accounts of past societies have tended to overlook many of the daily realities of ordinary people. This is because many accounts have focused on the "big picture" and have emphasized the dominant personalities and the major events of the societies in question. What has often been left out is any consideration of the perspectives and experiences of ordinary people, who are the foot soldiers of history and the building blocks of society.

One of the most easily forgotten facts of everyday life for countless individuals in past and present societies is the reality of *cruelty*. Although it may be unpleasant to contemplate, the record of cruelty endured by previous generations of ordinary people is one of the great silences in standard historical and sociological accounts of past societies. The history and sociology of cruelty is one of the great untold stories of our time. To rectify this situation and to shine some light on this neglected dark side of the social world, Collins proposes to show how conflict theory may help us to understand the pattern of cruelty in human history. This is the kind of macrosociological topic that is ideally suited to conflict analysis. After reflecting on the few sociological references to cruelty and violence in the works of Alexis de Tocqueville (1966 [1856]) and Georges Sorel (1950), Collins decided that Durkheim's theory of society offers a useful framework for classifying and analyzing the phenomena of violence and cruelty in past and present human societies.

In his study of religion, Durkheim shows that the way in which individuals are treated is a function of how they are classified within a society. Individuals who are seen to fall outside of the boundary of a group are, in an important sense, beyond the limits of human sympathy and morality that define group membership. To be outside the group means to be outside the structures of social solidarity and collective consciousness that provide group members with their sense of collective identity. Those who exist beyond the moral boundaries of the group (who may be variously defined as pagans, heathens, infidels, unbelievers, apostates, heretics etc.) have no appeal to group codes of mercy or justice.

Durkheim's theory of society contained an evolutionist logic; for example, he explains how repressive legal codes (characteristic of traditional societies based upon mechanical solidarity) are superseded by restitutive legal codes (characteristic of more modern societies based upon organic solidarity). In much the same way, Collins attempts to construct a theory of human cruelty that, although not evolutionist in any linear sense, shows how manifestations of cruelty may be related to the socio-historical development of societies.

Three Types of Violence and Cruelty

Collins suggests that when we examine the sad history of human cruelty from a macrosociological perspective, several types of cruelty may be distinguished. These types correspond to different stages in the socio-historical development of societies and extend from the use of "ferocious violence" in early stratified advanced horticultural societies, to the use of "callous violence" in large-scale bureaucratic societies, to the growth of "ascetic violence" in highly ideologized puritanical societies (both religious and political).

It is important to note that while Collins explains the growth of different types of violence in terms of the changing socio-cultural structure of historical societies, he is quick to reject the notion that the pattern of history shows any consistent evolutionary trend away from cruelty and violence towards greater kindness and happiness. Indeed, he is at pains to note that the emergence of the great world religions — most of which universalized ideals of brotherhood — were often used by secular and religious authorities to sanctify violence in the pursuit of secular or religious ends. Similarly, the advent of modernity led not to the elimination of

Randall Collins' Views on Cruelty in Society

There is no evolutionary trend towards kindness and happiness. Ferociousness once increased, then declined; callousness and asceticism now oppose each other as defenders and challengers of the status quo. ... The demons can be exorcised, but only by seeing them for what they are. Those who claim that the demons can be exorcised only by action in the world, not by theorizing about them, seem to be possessed by demons of their own, especially the demon of asceticism; one senses here the communal hostility of the ascetic to the individual luxury of intellectual contemplation. And here is the danger. Those who deny everything for the self, deny it as well for others; our altruism, taken too exclusively, is an infinite regress, passing a bucket from hand to hand that never reaches the fire. When we act, we call out the demons to meet us. Be careful: they are ourselves. (Collins 1974: 415–440) violence, but to its rationalization, mechanization and depersonalization. Whether we choose to call him a "pessimist" or a "realist," for Collins, there is no light at the end of the violent historical tunnel.

The theory of violence and cruelty outlined by Collins provides us with an example of the kind of theorizing undertaken by the new generation of conflict theorists. The focus of modern conflict theory is no longer on debates with structural functionalists over whether order or conflict models provide the best analyses of contemporary societies. More recent conflict theorists are interested in developing rich historical and empirical case studies that analyze certain features of modern societies — often associated with power, property, domination and struggle — which are invariably overlooked in other theoretical perspectives.

JACK GOLDSTONE'S THEORY OF REVOLUTION

Another political sociologist, Jack Goldstone (2002), focuses on developments in theories of revolutions. Over the past few decades, the study of revolutions has become a well-defined topic for a growing number of sociologists, especially those with an interest in conflict theory. In his survey of contemporary theories of revolution, Goldstone distinguishes several generations of theory, each of which emphasizes a distinct set of causal factors. From his account of these theories, it is clear that contemporary conflict theory has evolved far beyond those earlier debates of the 1960s and 1970s with structural functionalists.

Conflict theorists today are far more interested in real (i.e., historical or empirical) situations of conflict than in abstract models. Many have tried to explain real revolutionary situations in such places as Russia, China, Cuba, Iran, Philippines and Nicaragua, as well as in other countries (see, for example, Foran 1992). Also, today's conflict theorists are much more concerned than were their predecessors with methodological and conceptual issues. One major concern is whether to ascribe revolutionary upheavals to objective changes in societal structures (the state, class and elite structures, the economy etc.) or to subjective actions of groups and individuals (influenced by ideology, cultural values, leadership etc.). This debate over the relative priority of *structure* versus *agency* has largely replaced mid-twentieth century debates over the relative priority of conflict and consensus in society.

According to Goldstone, theories of revolution have made considerable progress and some notable successes in recent years although, as he concedes, there have been some conspicuous failures. Among the obvious failures was the inability of theorists to anticipate or predict the collapse of the USSR and other communist states of the Soviet bloc after 1989. Along with the rest of the world, conflict theorists were completely surprised by these momentous events and also by the regime changes in Tunisia, Egypt, Libya and other countries during the Arab Spring of 2010–11.

However, several theorists correctly diagnosed and predicted the inherent instability of many dictatorial "strongman" regimes. This instability was especially pronounced for regimes in which the personal demagogic qualities of the leader were not fully institutionalized into the military or state apparatus. Such regimes have sometimes been characterized as "neo-patrimonial," "sultanistic" or "personalist," and examples of these dictatorships have been found throughout the developing world, in Africa, Southeast and Central Asia and in Latin America. The overthrow of dictatorships in the Philippines (Ferdinand Marcos), Zaire (Sese Seko Mobutu), Indonesia (General Suharto) and Egypt (Hosni Mubarak) demonstrated the accuracy of some of these predictions.

The Classical Legacy of Marx and Weber

Traditional theories of revolution were very much influenced by the Marxian interpretation of class conflict. According to this view, revolutions result from the rise to prominence of powerful social classes that were able to successfully challenge and overthrow traditional ruling classes. The basis of this class conflict lies in the struggle of different social classes to dominate the means of production (that is, the institutions in society that create wealth). The standard Marxian interpretation of the French Revolution, for example, sees it as the victory of the ascendant commercial and industrial bourgeoisie over the old landed nobility. It was a struggle between two ownership classes in which the old land-owning aristocracy was overthrown by the new class of commercial and industrial capitalists.

The standard Marxian theory of ideology forms a similar piece with the theory of revolution. For Marx, the ruling ideas of any period were the ideas of the ruling class. In the case of the French Revolution, as in other European revolutions of the eighteenth and nineteenth centuries, the ideology of the new bourgeoisie was well represented in the ideas of the Enlightenment — ideas that amounted to a frontal assault on the doctrines of the *ancien regime,* such as royal absolutism, mercantilism and the "Great Chain of Being."

Although later writers rejected some aspects of the Marxian theories of revolution and ideology, the idea that revolutions were led by rising classes, elites or modernizing social groups continued to play an important role in post-Marxian and even in some anti-Marxian theories. It is only within the past thirty or so years that there has been profound rethinking of traditional theories of revolution. Part of the reason for this is the impact that recent revolutions and other political crises have had on traditional interpretations of these events. Whereas earlier interpretations were largely based on the European experience, more recent interpretations have been influenced by revolutionary events that have taken place in many other parts of the world.

This result of this shift of focus in theories of revolution has been the increased attention paid to the role of the peasantry in revolutionary uprisings. Although peasants may not have played a major role in the European revolutions of the eighteenth and nineteenth centuries, they have certainly done so in many of the twentieth-century revolutions in Asia, Africa and Latin America (see Wolf 1969). Another result of the shift of focus has been a greater preoccupation with the role of the state. Current theorists examine factors that bring about the breakdown of the state during a revolutionary situation. Indeed, whether or not a breakdown of the state occurs during a political crisis has become one of the yardsticks in deciding if a successful revolution has actually taken place.

Goldstone suggests that Marx's general analysis of revolutions has, in the eyes of many contemporary critics, proven inadequate in some essential respects. Because of Marx's assumption that revolutions were much more likely to occur in the advanced industrial states of the West than in the underdeveloped countries of the Global South, he overestimated the importance of the industrial working class (or proletariat) as the agent of revolutionary change, and underestimated the role of other classes — most notably, the peasantry — as potential revolutionary classes. Marx also assumed that revolutions were always driven by conflicts between social classes (the proletariat versus the bourgeoisie). He failed to take into account that revolutions could be precipitated by competition between different "fragments" of the ruling class, or between different political, corporate or military elites, or by combinations and alliances between different classes. Nonetheless, Goldstone admits that Marx's influence on the study of revolutions has been seminal.

One of the legacies of Marx's theory of revolutions, as Goldstone acknowledges, was the theory and practice of revolution adopted by the Russian revolutionary leader Vladimir Lenin. Lenin organized a "vanguard" party (the Bolsheviks), which was led by a group of full-time professional revolutionaries (or "cadres") and which subjected all party members to strict internal party discipline (or "democratic centralism"). The successful organization of the Bolshevik Party enabled Lenin to achieve the revolutionary seizure of state power and the overthrow of the old regime in a country where capitalism was relatively underdeveloped. This model of revolution was later copied in China, Cuba, North Korea and Vietnam, countries in which both capitalism and an industrial working class were virtually non-existent. These were all revolutions which would have confounded Marx's expectations and predictions.

Max Weber also contributed a number of ideas that proved useful in the study of revolutions. He emphasized the long-term historical trend of rationalization and bureaucratization in society and predicted that revolutions would invariably expand the scope and scale of state control over the individual. Weber also explained that for any regime or administration to obtain popular acceptance, it was necessary for the regime to be seen as a "legitimate" authority, either through the continuity of tradition, the rational administration of law or the inspirational "charisma" of its leadership. Weber emphasized the importance of "values" in revolutions, whether these values were based upon secular, religious or other ideologies. In order for a regime to consolidate a revolution, it was necessary for its values to effectively replace those of the old regime it had overthrown. Together, these various insights have greatly influenced contemporary approaches to the study and theory of revolutions.

Paradigm Shifts in Theories of Revolution

Goldstone suggests that the development of theoretical knowledge (the explanation and prediction) of revolutions has followed a pattern similar to the growth of knowledge in other fields of science and social science. Successful theories are those which satisfactorily explain and predict the occurrence of particular events. When an established theory is confronted by new empirical evidence that cannot be satisfactorily explained by the theory, then it is time to replace the discredited theory. However, it is only a matter of time before the new theory is confronted by anomalous facts which cannot be satisfactorily explained. Thus, all theories are sooner or later superseded by new theories in an endless series of "scientific revolutions" (see Kuhn 1962).

In reviewing modern theories of revolution, Goldstone maintains that there have been three distinct paradigm shifts, or scientific revolutions, during the twentieth century, and that a fourth generation of revolution theory has appeared in the early twenty-first century. There are, he suggests, clear-cut criteria which can be used to distinguish earlier theoretical perspectives from those which have more recently evolved:

> Third-generation theories of revolution pointed to the structural vulnerabilities of regimes as the basic causes of revolutions. In the last decade, critics of structural theories have argued for the need to incorporate leadership, ideology and processes of identification with revolutionary movements as key elements in the production of revolution. Analyses of revolutions in developing countries and in communist regimes have further argued for incorporating these factors and for the inadequacy of structural theories to account for these events. Rather than try to develop a list of the "causes" of revolutions, it may be more fruitful for the fourth generation of revolutionary theory to treat revolutions as emergent phenomena, and to start by focusing on factors that cement regime stability. (Goldstone 2001: 139)

As Goldstone also makes clear, revolutions are extremely complex historical events made up of many different elements, including causes and consequences, leaders and supporters, ideologies, counter-revolutions, the state, the economy and so on. No single theory of revolution has yet come close to offering a complete explanation which incorporates all of these different elements. Most theories have only focused on a few of these elements and have tried to explain how these elements are interrelated. Earlier theories of revolution remained largely Eurocentric in their orientation and focused almost exclusively on the so-called "great revolutions "in England (1640 and 1689), the United States (1776), France (1789), Russia (1917) and China (1949). Later theories expanded their scope to include the anti-colonial and national independence revolutions of the post-Second World War era and the guerilla campaigns and armed struggles of the mid-twentieth century. Notwithstanding the significant differences between these various revolutionary situations, Goldstone proposes that all revolutions share at least some key defining criteria: (1) an actual or attempted overthrow of established political authority; (2) popular mobilization; and (3) the replacement of established institutions and values with new revolutionary institutions and values. Any revolution worthy of the name can be defined according to these key criteria.

Goldstone traces the history of revolution theory from its earliest beginnings in the work of the classical social theorists. He singles out the works of Tocqueville, Marx and Weber as especially important for the theoretical analysis of revolutions. At the risk of oversimplification, it may be helpful to classify these three theorists along an ideological continuum: conservative (Tocqueville), radical (Marx) and liberal (Weber). Each of these theorists viewed revolutions from a different perspective, and each had something of value to contribute to our understanding of revolutions as significant historical and social events.

Tocqueville, as a more conservative theorist, emphasized a number of points still relevant to the study of revolutions in our own time. He suggested that (1) reforms by an established regime — such as limited extension of the franchise, the introduction of more progressive taxation, including a tax on the nobility, constitutional rather than absolute monarchy or greater powers for popular assembly — may actually accelerate, rather than slow down, the development of a revolutionary crisis in society. This idea was later reformulated as the "revolution of rising expectations" (McElroy 2016); (2) new revolutionary regimes may introduce more centralized and more far-reaching systems of total (totalitarian) state control than those which they replaced, and (3) new revolutionary regimes may show less tolerance towards political, religious, racial, ethnic, national and sexual minorities than the regimes they replaced. In other words, revolutionary governments may often sacrifice individual freedoms in the name of "class solidarity" (communism), "racial purity" (fascism), "national (or internal) security" (militaristic), "divine law" (theocratic or religious fundamentalist) or some other version of a collectivistic ideology.

Looking back over the past several decades, Goldstone distinguishes three major theoretical perspectives, or paradigms, that have, at different times, dominated this field. These perspectives may be labelled as the "natural history" approach, the "modernization" approach and the "structural model" approach.

The "natural history" perspective studied revolutions in the same way that early biologists studied plant and animal life. These theorists compared and contrasted different types of revolution and outlined a cycle of stages through which all revolutions passed. These stages included criticism and reform, revolutionary crisis, revolutionary moderates, revolutionary radicals, state terror, military rulers, and pragmatism and progress. However, as Goldstone notes, while the natural history approach advanced the study of revolutions in some directions, it failed to address other outstanding questions. These limitations eventually led to the rise of a second major theoretical perspective.

Modernization theorists emphasized the role that changing values, beliefs and practices played in the revolutionary transition of societies. Some theorists, influenced by the ideas of the structural functionalists, saw revolutions as part of the historical process of rationalization and modernization through which traditional societies are transformed into modern societies. For these theorists, modernization was the underlying process that explained such diverse revolutions as the anti-colonial, communist, fascist, populist, nationalist and even religious, or theocratic, revolutions of the twentieth century. Each of these revolutionary upheavals could be explained in terms of the promotion of, or resistance to, modernization. Some theorists who rejected structural functionalism proposed radical alternatives to modernization theory. Thus, "mobilization theory" was adopted by critics who felt that general theories of modernization paid little or no attention to how revolutionary movements and revolutionary parties were organized and led. Neo-Marxists also proposed alternative theories to modernization theory.

After several decades of debate and disagreement, the structural model of Theda Skocpol (1979) emerged as the dominant perspective of the late twentieth century. Among other theoretical innovations, the structural model analyzed each revolution within the context of the world system. Skocpol suggested that revolutions often result from external political or military interference (through wars, invasions and/or occupations), as well as from economic competition or other international pressures. Skocpol also noted that conflicts between state rulers and traditional elites could sometimes precipitate revolutionary crises, in addition to the presence of social movements and political parties which could mobilize popular support and direct collective action. Taken together, these three factors were seen as necessary and sufficient conditions for the occurrence of major social revolutions. Although Skocpol's theory became the dominant perspective, it was tested and challenged by a number of events, most notably the revolutions in Iran and Nicaragua (1979), the Philippines (1986) and by the fall of communism (1989). Each of these events highlighted factors which had been largely neglected in Skocpol's theory of revolution. These factors included the importance of urban protest and the transformative power of secular or religious ideology.

Further attempts to refine the structural theory of revolution were made by Goldstone, among others. In his research, Goldstone paid particular attention to population growth as a major cause of revolutionary change. He suggested that population change contributed to fiscal crises of the state, conflicts within and between elites, and popular unrest. In a step beyond Skocpol, Goldstone emphasizes the crucial role of ideology in revolutionary situations. Ideology often determines the choices made by a revolutionary regime and may thereby determine the eventual outcome of a revolution. In addition to their theoretical sophistication, Skocpol and Goldstone pioneered innovative methods of research by supplementing historical narratives with statistical analysis. However, Goldstone concludes that even revised versions of the structural model are not immune from criticism. Rational choice theorists, using highly formalized mathematical models, critique structural models for their inability to analyze individual behaviours. Other critics maintain that structural models do not adequately explain the revolutions of the late twentieth century. One way or another, structural models remain under siege from a number of adversaries.

FUTURE THEORIES OF REVOLUTION

In the wake of these criticisms, a new theory of revolutions — the fourth generation — seems destined to make its appearance soon. This new perspective promises, among other things, to link the theory of revolutions to broader theories of social movements and collective action using a version of network analysis. The new perspective also promises to investigate the complex role of ideology in revolutions more fully and creatively than previous theories. The acid test for any current theory of revolutions is its ability to explain the causes of the revolutions of the late twentieth and early twenty-first centuries. Many of these revolutions overthrew modern dictatorships based upon "personalist" or "neo-patrimonial" regimes.

Recent theorists increasingly focus on the impact that international pressures had on these domestic revolutions. In particular, the influence of the US government in initially providing and later withdrawing support for many of these dictatorial regimes dramatically illustrates the role of international intervention in revolutionary crises. This was evidently the case when the US withdrew its former support for such leaders as Saddam Hussein (Iraq); Muammar Gaddafi (Libya) and Manuel Noriega (Panama). At the same time, international or global ideologies — whether secular or religious — may also play a major role in mobilizing support for revolutionary collective action.

As we can see from these few examples, the new conflict theorists are distinguished not only by their sweeping macrosocial focus but also by the richness of their historical studies. Goldstone no longer believes that revolutions are primarily made by insurrection from below, as much recent evidence suggests that they are often brought about by a collapse from above. In examining the factors that contribute to the collapse of state power, Goldstone shifts attention away from the role of revolutionary social classes, in contrast to traditional interpretations. This new emphasis on the role of state breakdown in revolutions is shared by other conflict theorists working in this area, most notably by Skocpol (1979).

Besides the debates over structure versus agency, contemporary theorists of revolution also differ on a number of other issues, including the relative importance of urban versus rural forms of protest and rebellion, the role of external (international) versus internal (domestic) factors in the crisis and breakdown of the state, the autonomy or relative dependency of the state, and Eurocentric studies versus studies of revolutions in the Global South.

As we have already suggested, recent attempts to integrate and synthesize these different approaches to the study of revolutions have led to the rise of a fourth generation of theorists. These theorists try to avoid the methodological and conceptual pitfalls of previous generations. They show how large-scale institutional structures — such as the state and the economy — are formed and reproduced through the long-term accumulated beliefs and practices of groups and individuals. To a greater extent than ever before, the various aspects which make up any study of revolution — the state, culture, ideology, leadership and mobilization of individuals into groups — are closely integrated in current theories of revolution. Many fourth-generation theorists have undertaken detailed studies of particular revolutionary situations — in Kenya, Iran, Nicaragua and elsewhere.

In many ways, we may find that contemporary conflict theories are more closely related to actual events in the "real world" of war, conflict and violence than were the earlier, more abstract, theories of social conflict. Contemporary theories provide us with enhanced conceptual tools with which to analyze recent revolutions. Distinctions such as "neo-patrimonial" (or "sultanistic") versus "institutional" types of revolutionary regimes can be used to distinguish between those revolutions closely identified with powerful leaders (such as Fidel Castro, Ayatollah Khomeini, Hugo Chavez) versus those more closely identified with institutional structures of a political party, as in China, or an ethnic constituency, as in South Africa (with the African National Congress).

CONFLICT THEORY AND TERRORISM

Finally, we shall briefly review a topic that has recently attracted the interest and attention of conflict theorists: terrorism. Although historians have chronicled the occurrence of terrorist activities at least since the time of the French Revolution, social theorists only began to focus on this topic after the highly publicized attacks on the World Trade Center in September 2001 (9/11). For the most part, the subject of terrorism has remained the province of conflict theorists.

The tendency for much recent social theory has been to focus on localized theoretical narratives and to avoid the broader, more universalized theoretical statements (grand theories and metanarratives). Unlike many of the sociological theorists of the twentieth century — such as Talcott Parsons, Ralf Dahrendorf, Herbert Marcuse and even Jürgen Habermas — all of whom attempted to formulate highly generalized and systematic theories of society, most theorists today develop more specific theories of local social issues. In this chapter, we have seen how many contemporary theorists have studied particular localized events, including revolutions, wars (inter-state and civil), inter-ethnic or inter-communal violence, terrorism and genocide, among various other forms of human conflict. Contemporary conflict theorists pay far greater attention than did their twentieth-century counterparts to the detailed historical and social conditions of particular cases of reported or recorded human conflict.

The topic of terrorism, in common with other controversial objects of social inquiry, has been studied from a number of vantage points. How individual or institutional researchers define "terrorism" or "terrorist" is always closely related to their political perspectives and political agendas. It remains, of course, a truism that one person's "terrorist" is another person's "freedom fighter." Policy-oriented researchers with a strong interest in public security and social control are likely to advance research programs that attempt to profile the typical characteristics of a terrorist and analyze the networks of terrorist groups and organizations. Researchers with a strong interest in social justice and social movements are more likely to analyze the social causes of terrorism and the socio-historical conditions — such as colonialism, invasion and occupation — which have led to the growth of violent forms of political protest and armed struggle. For a more systematic review of left, right and centrist discourses on terrorism, see Klein (2007).

Contemporary conflict theorist Austin Turk (2004) provides a brief survey of recent sociological research on the topic of terrorism and identifies a number of the major themes in the research literature that have begun to define the sociological study of terrorism. As Turk illustrates, "terrorism" is a socially constructed category. Who is defined as a terrorist and what is classified as a terrorist incident are closely allied to the political preferences and ideological biases of the observer/researcher. Whereas violent attacks by Muslim/Arab armed organizations are normally labelled in the US as terrorist incidents, violent attacks by domestic groups in the US — such as the 1995 Oklahoma City bombings, high school rampages and animal liberation, pro-life and Ku Klux Klan bombings — have rarely been classified in these terms. Today, many commentators on Muslim armed violence distinguish between global jihadist groups — such as ISIS, Al-Qaeda, Al-Shabaab, Boko Haram etc. — versus nationalist or resistance groups — such as the PLO (Palestinian), Hamas (Palestinian), PKK (Kurdish) and Hezbollah (Lebanese). Jhadist groups are driven by strongly religious motives, while nationalist and resistance groups are primarily secular and anti-colonial in their motivations for combat (see, for example, Bondokji 2014). Terrorism, in other words, is what "they" do to "us," not what "we" do to "them" or even what we may sometimes do to ourselves. In much of the current popular literature on what has been called the "global war on terror," especially in government reports and media coverage, "terrorism" is used primarily as a label with which to stigmatize the "enemy" rather than as a precise, defined concept with universal applicability.

Beyond the problems of conceptualizing and defining terrorism, Turk distinguishes a number of broad approaches to the study of terrorism as political violence. While some perspectives, such as functionalism, see terrorism as nothing more than a deadly type of deviant behaviour, more critical and radical perspectives see terrorism as an understandable or predictable response to overwhelming oppression and exploitation. Terrorism, in this sense, is often seen as a "weapon of the powerless." From a more analytical perspective, terrorism may be strategically understood as an option, or choice, made in the context of the shifting power game of geopolitics or, in some cases, domestic politics. What becomes clear from the research findings reported by Turk is that terrorism cannot be satisfactorily explained either by individual pathology (crazy bombers) or by relative or absolute deprivation (driven by poverty and acute need).

In recent times, many terrorists have come from relatively privileged, educated and affluent backgrounds. Osama bin Laden was a textbook example. Their acts of political violence appear to be driven more by their burning sense of indignation and outrage than by any material deprivation. These individuals (both male and female) have, for all intents and purposes, sacrificed their social statuses and their lives in order to retaliate for what they perceive as personal humiliation (as with the "Black Widow" Chechen female suicide bombers) or for the larger suffering inflicted upon their communities. It is for this reason that jihadist terrorists in many parts of the world are considered "martyrs" (or shahids/shaheeds) and their acts of political violence — especially suicide bombings — defined as "martyrdom operations." While this view of terrorism may appear perverse to Westerners, it remains the popular view in many other conflicted parts of the Islamic world.

More recently, as Turk suggests, the motivation and organization of terrorism have undergone some important changes. Unlike terrorism of the nineteenth and early twentieth centuries, which was often motivated by strong secular political or nationalist beliefs, many of today's terrorist acts are motivated by religious fundamentalism — whether Muslim, Jewish, Christian, Hindu, Sikh or Buddhist. Whereas earlier terrorist acts were undertaken by small, tightly knit organizational cells, many terrorist acts in the US and Western Europe are now committed by singular individuals ("lone wolves") without any group affiliation. In other words, terrorist acts committed in societies with strong individualistic cultures (such as the United States and Europe) are likely to be motivated and organized very differently from those terrorist acts committed in more traditional collectivistic cultures (such as those in the Middle East, North Africa and South, East and Central Asia), where networks and webs of group affiliation (such as ISIS, Al-Qaeda, the Taliban, Hamas, Hezbollah, Al-Shabaab, Boko Haram, the PKK, or other religious or ethno-national-religious groups) are likely to be more common.

Much of the limited research on contemporary terrorism focuses on how individuals are socialized, radicalized and converted into terrorists. Most of this research now discounts earlier explanations that were based on assumptions of individual psychopathology or acute material deprivation. The single most plausible explanation for the radicalization of individuals to terrorism appears to be their exposure to ideologies — often through internet websites or social media — that justify the use of violence for political ends. Whether this ideological influence comes from the extreme left (such as the Weather Underground in the US, the Baader-Meinhof Gang in Germany or the Red Brigades in Italy), the extreme right (white nationalist, neo-Nazi, anti-immigrant or other anti-government militia groups), armed nationalist and resistance groups (such the Provisional IRA, the PLO, Hezbollah, Hamas, the PKK, the Tamil Tigers, the Basque ETA, the Quebec FLQ or Sikh separatists) or religious fundamentalists (ISIS, Al-Qaeda, Al-Shabaab, Boko Haram, Christian pro-life groups), the common thread that connects all contemporary terrorists is their exposure to ideologies that justify violence in pursuit of political objectives.

For social scientists, the study of terrorism raises significant problems. Many of the government defence and security agencies concerned with the collection and analysis of data on terrorism block access to official sources of information on this sensitive topic. Outsiders often find their access to information on terrorism restricted or even denied. Similarly, funding for research into terrorism is typically directed towards studies which are most likely to lead to the containment, control and prevention of terrorism, rather than to studies which seek to understand and interpret the phenomenon. Policy-driven studies which produce operational findings are much more highly valued in government and military circles than theoretical studies, which often have broader academic and less practical implications.

Nevertheless, there have been a number of theoretical studies of terrorism undertaken over the past few years. Indeed, one indication of the rising theoretical interest in this topic may be seen from the publication of a special issue on terrorism in the academic journal *Sociological Theory* (March 2004). One example of a conflict-oriented approach to research on terrorism is a study which employed a world-system perspective to analyze periodic cycles in the rise and fall of terrorist violence (Bergesen and Lizardo 2004). Another theoretical paper on terrorism, written by a former neofunctionalist theorist, analyzes terrorism from a neo-dramaturgical perspective (Alexander 2004). Terrorism, it would seem, has become a hot topic of investigation for a growing number of social theorists.

LOOKING AHEAD

Contemporary conflict theory has evolved beyond the typical debates of the mid-twentieth century. These earlier debates focused on such central sociological topics as consensus versus conflict interpretations of social relations; microsocial versus macrosocial studies of social conflict; analytical versus critical theories of social conflict; and optimistic versus pessimistic projections of future social conflict. Today, in the second decade of the twenty-first century, conflict theory has matured in a number of ways. Contemporary conflict theories are increasingly interdisciplinary in their content. They have become social rather than sociological theories. They are more cross-cultural, comparative and global in their scale and scope of analysis than earlier sociological theories, which tended to focus on national (primarily US, UK and European) situations and settings. Contemporary conflict theories are decidedly more analytical than critical in their basic assumptions and methods of analysis. They tend to eschew dogmatic or doctrinal classical interpretations of social conflict (such as historical materialism or elite theories) in favour of empirical, value-neutral and heuristic inquiries. Critical conflict theories are commonly associated with the successive generations of critical theory.

One of the ways in which modern conflict theory has benefited from cross-fertilization with other theoretical traditions in sociology may be seen in the work of Michael Mann, an influential contemporary social theorist. In his book *The Sources of Social Power* (1986), Mann proposes a method of studying large-scale societal conflict and social change which employs an analytical classification of four dimensions of power: geopolitical, political, economic and cultural. By focusing on each of these distinctive dimensions of power, Mann is able to research case studies of conflict and change that are rich in empirical and historical detail. His work provides an excellent example of how contemporary conflict theory has developed into an independent research tradition and has restored the reputation of macrosocial studies of social change. Moreover, Mann is only one of several contemporary writers who have made important contributions to the contemporary tradition of conflict theory. It is an area that promises to add much to our understanding of the macrosocial tradition of theory and research of conflict and social change.

Finally, contemporary conflict theorists — for the most part — have grown disenchanted with optimistic or utopian prognoses of future conflict-free societies. Most conflict theorists today, except those optimists mentioned earlier in this chapter — share a rather bleak "realism" regarding future prospects for global peace and conflict resolution. This grim realism is best expressed by Mann (2018: 58):

> The history of violence I have presented suggests that periods and regions of war alternate with periods and regions of peace. This will probably continue for a good while yet. It is clear that we cannot explain war or peace by relying on universals like human nature or the essential nature of societies, as historical pessimists did. But nor can we support the evolutionary theories of the past and present. Peace has to be metaphorically fought for. This is an admittedly uncertain ending, but wars have been the product of human choices which might have gone differently, and which might go differently in the future. I wish I could share the cheerful optimism of the 250 year-old liberal tradition, culminating in recent writers like Mueller, Pinker, Goldstein, and Gat. Yet what they say about history and the future represents more hope than experience.

References

Alatas, Syed Farid. 2014. *Applying Ibn Khaldūn: The Recovery of a Lost Tradition in Sociology*. Routledge.

Alexander, J. 2004. "From the Depths of Despair: Performance, Counterperformance, and September 11." *Sociological Theory*, 22, 1: 88–105.

Bergesen, A.J., and O. Lizardo. 2004. "International Terrorism and the World-System." *Sociological Theory*, 22, 1: 38–52.

Bernard, T. 1983. *The Consensus-Conflict Debate: Form and Content in Social Theories*. Columbia University Press.

Bondokji, Neven. 2014. "The Nationalist Versus the Religious: Implications for Peace with Hamas." Brookings, March 18. <https://www.brookings.edu/opinions/the-nationalist-versus-the-religious-implications-for-peace-with-hamas/>.

Bourdieu, Pierre. 2000. *Pascalian Meditations*. Cambridge: Polity Press.

Clausewitz, Claus von, Carl. 2012 [1832]. *On War*. CreateSpace Independent Publishing Platform (January 21).

Collins, Randall. 1974. "Three Faces of Cruelty: Towards a Comparative Sociology of Violence." *Theory and Society*, 1, 4 (Winter): 415–440.

___. 1975. *Conflict Sociology: Toward an Explanatory Science*. New York: Academic Press.

Dahrendorf, Ralf. 1958. "Out of Utopia: Toward a Reorientation of Sociological Analysis." *American Journal of Sociology*, 64, 2 (Sept.).

___. 1959. *Class and Class Conflict in Industrial Society*. Stanford, CA: Stanford University Press.

___. 1968. *Essays in the Theory of Society*. Stanford University Press.

De Tocqueville, A. 1966 [1856]. *The Ancient Regime and the French Revolution*, trans. Stuart Gilbert. London: Collins.

Demerath, N.J., and R.A. Peterson. 1967. *System, Change, and Conflict: A Reader on Contemporary Sociological Theory and the Debate over Functionalism*. Free Press.

Foran, John. 1992. "A Theory of Third World Social Revolutions: Iran, Nicaragua, and El Salvador Compared." *Critical Sociology*, 19, 2.

Foucault, Michel. 1977. *Discipline and Punish*. Pantheon Books.

Gat, Azar. 2008. *War in Human Civilization*. Oxford University Press.

Goffman, Erving. 1961. *Asylums: Essays on the Social Situation of Mental Patients and Other Inmates*. N.Y: Anchor Books.

Goldstone, Jack. 2001. "Toward a Fourth Generation of Revolutionary Theory." *Annual Review of Political Science*, 4: 139–187.

___. 2002. "Theory Development in the Study of Revolutions." In J. Berger and M. Zeldich (eds.), *New Directions in Contemporary Social Theory*. Rowman and Littlefield Publishers.

Goldstein, Joshua L. 2011. *Winning the War on War: The Decline of Armed Conflict Worldwide*. Plume; Reprint edition.

Gouldner, A. 1970. *The Coming Crisis of Western Sociology*. New York, London: Basic Books.

Hearn, Jeff. 2014. "Why Domestic Violence Is a Central Issue for Sociology and Social Theory: Tensions, Paradoxes, and Implications." *Gender, Equal Opportunities Research*, 15, 1: 16–28. ISSN 1213-0028.

Horton, J. 1966. "Order and Conflict Theories of Social Problems as Competing Ideologies." *American Journal of Sociology*, 71, 6: 701–713.

Klein, J. 2007. "Where Should We Stand to Get the Best Perspective on Collective Violence?" *Critical Sociology*, 33, 5/6: 957–980.

Kuhn Thomas. 1962. *The Structure of Scientific Revolutions*. University of Chicago Press.

Lawson, Jennifer. 2012. "Sociological Theories of Intimate Partner Violence." *Journal of Human Behavior in the Social Environment*, 22: 572–590.

Mann, Michael. 1986. *The Sources of Social Power*, Vol. 1. New York: Cambridge University Press.

___. 2018. "Have Wars and Violence Declined?" *Theory and Society*, 47, 1: 37–60.

Marx, K. 2009 [1872]. *The Civil War in France*. Dodo Press.

McElroy, Wendy. 2016. "The Revolution of Rising Expectations." The Future of Freedom Foundation, May 1. <https://www.fff.org/explore-freedom/article/revolution-rising-expectations/>.

McKie, Linda. 2006. "Sociological Work on Violence: Gender, Theory and Research." *Sociological Research Online*, 11, 2: 1–9. <https://doi.org/10.5153/sro.1252>.

Michels, R. 1959. *Political Parties*. New York: Dover.

Midgley, M. 2003. *The Myths We Live By*. London: Routledge.

Mills, C.W. 1956. *The Sociological Imagination*. New York: Oxford University Press.

Mosca, G. 1965. "The Ruling Class." In H.D. Kahn (ed. and rev.), *Elementi di Scienza Politica*. New York: McGraw-Hill.

Mueller, John E. 1989. *Retreat from Doomsday: The Obsolescence of Major War*. Basic Books.

New York Times. 2016. *Europe's Rising Far Right: A Guide to the Most Prominent Parties*. December 4. <https://www.nytimes.com/interactive/2016/world/europe/europe-far-right-political-parties-listy.html>.

Pareto, V. 1935. *The Mind and Society*. [Trattori di Sociologia Generale] (4 Vols.), ed. Arthur Livingstone. New York: Harcourt Brace Jovanovich.

Pinker, Stephen. 2011. *The Better Angels of Our Nature: Why Violence Has Declined*. Viking Books.

Rex, John. 1961. *Key Problems of Sociological Theory*. London: Routledge and Kegan Paul.

___. 1981. *Social Conflict: A Theoretical and Conceptual Analysis*. London: Longmans.

Richardson, M., J. Sherman and M. Gismondi. 1993. *Winning Back the Words: Confronting Experts in an Environmental Public Hearing*. Toronto: Garamond.

Rose, N. 1990. *Governing the Soul: The Shaping of the Private Self*. Taylor & Frances/Routledge.

Singer, Peter. 2015. *The Most Good You Can Do: How Effective Altruism Is Changing Ideas About Living Ethically*. Yale University Press.

Skocpol, T. 1979. *States and Social Revolution: A Comparative Analysis of France, Russia and China*. Cambridge, UK: Cambridge University Press.

Sorel, George. 1950. *Reflections on Violence*, with an introduction by Edward A. Shils, translated by T. E. Hulme and J. Roth. The Free Press.

Sun Tzu. 2002 [5th century BC]. *The Art of War*, trans. John Minford. New York: Viking Books.

Thucydides. 1989 [431 BC]. *History of the Peloponnesian War*. University of Chicago Press.

Turk, A. 2004. "Sociology of Terrorism." *Annual Review of Sociology*, 30: 271–286.

Walby, S., J. Towers, and B. Francis. 2014. "Mainstreaming Domestic and Gender-Based Violence into Sociology and the Criminology of Violence." *The Sociological Review*, 62 (Suppl 2): 187–214.

Wolf, Eric. 1969. *Peasant Wars of the Twentieth Century*. Harper & Row.

Žižek, Slavoj. 2009. *Violence: Six Sideways Reflections*. London: Profile Books.

CHAPTER 4

THEORIZING OUR CLASS DIVISIONS

Neo-Marxist and Post-Marxist Theories of Society

THE MODERN LEGACY OF KARL MARX

This chapter highlights some modern updates of what has arguably been the most powerful and influential social theory of the past century: Marxism. More than those of any other social theorist, the ideas of Karl Marx have inspired the hopes and actions of countless people in their struggles for social justice and social change. During the course of the twentieth century, Marxism, specifically Marxism–Leninism, became not only an ideology of revolution against the capitalist system but also the official state ideology of the former USSR. And, as a state ideology, Marxism–Leninism rapidly changed from being a theory of social change and human emancipation to one of domination and social control. For these reasons, Marxism has a mixed and controversial legacy. But in order to understand the power and influence of Marxist ideas and the legacy of Marxist theory, we need to return to Marx's own social thought: his critique of capitalism.

Marx's Critique of Capitalism

The essence of Marx's critique of capitalism is that he believed the development of capitalist society would produce a fundamental contradiction, or irreconcilable conflict, between what he called the private nature of the "relations of production," that is, how the productive forces were increasingly owned as private property by the capitalist class, versus the increasingly social nature of the "forces of production," that is, how the whole society had become increasingly dependent upon the means of production, distribution and exchange. In other words, Marx believed that as capitalist society developed, the fact that the technology used to power society remained under private ownership, and thus not under democratic control, would become a major social problem for most members of society.

This is because decisions that are made about how to use technology affect all of us in some way or another — in terms of our jobs, our communities, our environment, our children, our standards of living, our health and welfare etc. — even though we may have no say in these decisions. As we grow more dependent upon the technology of modern society, our inability to exercise democratic control over it becomes the major social problem, or contradiction, of our time. In effect, those who manage technology manage our lives. According to Marx, this is the central "contradiction" of capitalist society, which can only be resolved by taking the forces of production (technology) out of the hands of private corporations and placing them under popular democratic control. Only in this way can decisions about the use of technology come under public scrutiny and enter the arena of public debate. Only then can decisions that have massive public consequences also have full public accountability.

At the root of Marx's critique of capitalism was his belief that there is an irreconcilable antagonism between the capitalist and the worker. Marx believed, in common with many political economists of his time (such as David Ricardo and Joseph Schumpeter), that the value of any commodity was based upon the amount of "socially necessary," or "average," labour time used to produce it. Thus, raw petroleum that remains in the oil sands of Alberta has no value until it is extracted, refined and transported to consumer markets. Only then does it become a commodity, and its value is calculated by the amount of labour time used in its production. And while the "price" of petroleum may rise and fall with fluctuations in supply and demand, the "exchange value" of the commodity is fixed by the labour time embodied in its production. Among the economists of the nineteenth century, this perspective was called the "labour theory of value." However, Marx went beyond the labour theory of value when he introduced his own "theory of surplus value." In simple terms, Marx argued that the worker under capitalism is only paid for a part of their labour time during the workday; Marx called this part "necessary labour time." Beyond this, the worker (usually without their knowledge or awareness) is engaged in "surplus labour time," and the value produced by surplus labour is "surplus value." Surplus value is the value produced by the worker for which they are not paid and which is extracted by the capitalist in the form of "profit." Although the worker may believe that they receive a fair day's wage for a fair day's work, Marx was convinced that he had discovered the "hidden mechanism" for the creation of profit and the accumulation of wealth. The secret is that the worker is not paid for the surplus value produced during the working day. The injustice, according to Marx, is that the same process which enriches the capitalist simultaneously impoverishes the worker. This is the process that Marx called "exploitation."

For Marx, the only long-term solution to the private ownership of strategic resources that are needed by everyone in society is the overthrow of the capitalist system and its replacement by a more democratic and egalitarian political, social and economic system. But this would necessarily involve a "class struggle" between the "bourgeoisie" (the capitalist class, who retains wealth, power and privilege) and the "proletariat" (working class, who are impoverished and powerless). In order to mobilize mass support for the transformation of a capitalist into a socialist, and eventually communist, society, Marx believed that members of the working class would need to develop a "class consciousness," an understanding of their common class interests and a revolutionary vision of a more humane society, based on social justice and economic as well as political democracy. This was his revolutionary mission — as a theorist and as a political activist.

Varieties of Marxism

After Marx's death, his ideas developed in many directions. The earliest generation of Marxists seized upon his work as a practical guide to the task of transforming capitalist into socialist societies. Many of these followers of Marx were themselves active revolutionaries seeking to transform their own societies by any means necessary. For this reason, the versions of Marxism developed by revolutionary intellectuals like Vladimir Lenin, Leon Trotsky, Joseph Stalin, Rosa Luxemburg and others tended to emphasize what they believed to be the "scientific" aspects of Marx's work. Today, their interpretations may strike us as deterministic and mechanistic, but this is because they saw Marxism as a science revealing the internal laws of capitalist society, much as Newton's work revealed the laws of gravity.

Over the course of the twentieth century, many versions of Marxism emerged, each of which provided a distinctive reading and interpretation of Marx's ideas. Some of these versions, such as the social democratic

Marxism of Karl Kautsky and the revisionist Marxism of Eduard Bernstein, broke with the revolutionary tradition by asserting that Marx had shown that the iron laws of capitalist development would lead inevitably to the collapse and transformation of the capitalist system. With such an evolutionist view of history, the role of revolutionary politics was seen as redundant and counterproductive.

The evolutionist version of Marxism was challenged during the 1920s and 1930s by a group of intellectuals who became known as the Hegelian Marxists. Led by theorists Georg Lukacs (1971), Antonio Gramsci (1968, 1971) and Karl Korsch (1972), these Marxists rejected what they saw as the positivism and dogmatism of Marx's "historical materialism" (the view that objective historical and economic conditions would determine the downfall of capitalism) in favour of a more humanistic interpretation of his ideas. Among other things, they emphasized the role of revolutionary politics, class struggle and political consciousness in bringing down the capitalist system. Hegelians believed that political action, or "praxis" — which requires the subjective collective consciousness of the working class — is the vital spark needed to ignite the revolution. It was this emphasis on the importance of subjectivity, consciousness and action that led the humanistic (sometimes called "voluntaristic") Marxists to rediscover the Hegelian roots of Marxism and to distance themselves from the more deterministic and economistic interpretations of the historical materialists and other "vulgar" Marxists.

The humanistic tradition of Marxism was also continued in the works of the Frankfurt School of critical theory. The school consisted of a group of German Marxists who began their studies of contemporary society in the 1920s. In the following decades, critical theory emerged as the leading tradition of humanistic Marxism, and it brought together an interdisciplinary group of scholars who pioneered new areas of Marxian research and analysis. Much of their work involved the analysis and critique of capitalist society in ways that had not been done before. Unlike the orthodox Marxists, who focused on the economics of capitalism almost to the exclusion of everything else, the critical theorists focused their studies on the culture and ideology of capitalism, aspects of society that had previously been treated as residual. Their analysis resulted in a number of influential studies of mass society, including, for example, Wilhelm Reich's (1970 [1933]) study of the "mass psychology of fascism," Theodor Adorno's (1982) studies of the "authoritarian personality,"

Herbert Marcuse's (1964) study of "one-dimensional man" and Erich Fromm's (1941) studies of "alienation."

Since the 1970s, there has been a dramatic increase in the number of Marxian sociologists who have proliferated different versions, or schools, of Marxism and expanded sociological theory. Some of these modern schools of Marxism, such as critical theory, structuralism, post-structuralism and postmodernism, originated in Europe, where their influence quickly spread to English-speaking sociological communities. Others, such as world-system theory, analytical Marxism and economic Marxism, have their roots in North America, where they have begun to develop a local tradition of Marxian and neo-Marxian scholarship. Some traditions, such as socialist feminism, have been influenced by scholars from Europe, North America and other parts of the world. The schools of Marxism and neo-Marxism are among the most cosmopolitan of all current sociological traditions. Many of the leading Marxist scholars come from Latin America, Africa and Asia, as well as from North America and Europe. More than any other tradition of social theory, Marxism remains global in the application and appeal of its ideas.

Marxism Today

Marxism today has reached a crossroads. The last half of the twentieth century saw the rebirth and proliferation of Marxism in Europe, North America and in other parts of the world. However, after the fall of the Soviet Union in the early 1990s and the subsequent breakup of the communist "peoples' democracies" of Eastern Europe, the fate and future direction of Marxism has often seemed uncertain. The fall of communism left an ideological vacuum now filled by other religious and political movements. But although some earlier critics argued that Marxism is a spent force, both as a model of a new society and as a critique of the present, many contemporary social theorists are not so sure. Social theories are remarkably resilient over time, and whenever a once-popular theory seems to have sunk from sight, it often reappears, albeit in a modified form, to win over a new generation.

Today, for many social commentators, Marx's critique of capitalist society has never seemed so relevant or so prescient in its ability to speak to the problems and pathologies of our own age of neoliberalism and global capitalism. Academic Marxism underwent a renaissance in North America and other Anglophone countries during the last half of

The Rich and the Rest

The globe's richest 1% own half the world's wealth, according to a new report highlighting the growing gap between the super-rich and everyone else.... The increase in wealth among the already very rich led to the creation of 2.3 million new dollar millionaires over the past year, taking the total to 36 million... These millionaires — who account for 0.7% of the world's adult population — control 46% of total global wealth that now stands at $280 trillion.... At the other end of the spectrum, the world's 3.5 billion poorest adults each have assets of less than $10,000 (£7,600). Collectively these people, who account for 70% of the world's working age population, account for just 2.7% of global wealth. (Neate 2017)

the twentieth century. The current popularity of Marxism among social scientists stands in stark contrast to the situation at the height of the Cold War, during the late 1940s and throughout the 1950s. This was a period of intense anti-communism in the United States, when much public political life fell under the shadow of Senator Joe McCarthy whose Government Committee on Operations of the Senate — also known as the House Un-American Activities Committee — targeted and criminalized left-wing activists and academics. In this Cold War climate, all interest in Marxism was denounced as tantamount to treason. It was only when a new generation of political activists emerged in the 1960s — from the antiwar, civil rights, feminist and student power movements — that an interest in Marxism reawakened in the classrooms, on college campuses and on the streets.

So why have many of Marx's ideas come back into fashion, and which aspects of his work resonate most strongly with our contemporary conditions and experiences? For now, we shall only summarize some aspects of Marx's extensive work that appear most relevant to our present predicament.

Marx predicted that socio-economic inequality would greatly increase with the development of advanced capitalism. And most indicators today show an unprecedented and deepening inequality between the super-rich and the rest of the population — both within nation-states and around the world. Marx also predicted the growing centralization and concentration of capital and the rise of monopolies and oligopolies in both national and global markets. Today, there are many prominent examples of multinational and transnational corporations that dominate manufacturing industries, retail and distributive trades, the arms and weapons trade,

The Capitalist State: Karl Marx to Donald Trump

Marx (and Engels 1992/1848) famously described the state in a capitalist society in the following terms: "The executive of the modern state is nothing but a committee for managing the common affairs of the whole bourgeoisie." Today, with Donald Trump as the billionaire president of the US, surrounded with a plutocratic cabinet of other billionaire secretaries and advisors, Marx's description of the capitalist state appears particularly apposite (see Burleigh 2017). Marx also remained convinced that capitalist states — in their drive for expansion and globalization — were always prone to escalate their international competition into armed conflict, or even war. And, as we have seen over the past several decades, US oil companies have often benefitted from the concessions awarded through their government's interventions and invasions — as in Afghanistan, Iraq and Libya. For Marx, capitalism was predisposed to international competition, conflict and war in order to secure and expand its markets and energy resources (see Ahmed 2014).

natural resource extraction and refining industries, and information, communications and financial markets. Marx also suggested that the domination and distortion of the market by giant enterprises, with the resultant decline in competition, would inevitably lead to constant economic crises: repetitive business cycles extending from "boom" to "bust." And our historical experience — from the Great Depression (1929) to the most recent recession (2008) confirms this prediction.

Other aspects of Marx's critique of capitalism are particularly relevant today: his description of "commodity fetishism" provides a useful framework for a deeper understanding of the hyper-consumerism of our own times, and his concept of "false consciousness" offers us an explanation for why so many marginalized members of the white working class voted for Donald Trump and why so many white workers support far-right nationalist parties and anti-immigrant movements in Europe and elsewhere. We live in troubled times, and Marx always addressed himself to tumultuous and turbulent times.

Over the past few years, the dramatic resurgence of interest in Marx and his ideas has resulted in a tsunami of books published about Marx, many of them designed to rehabilitate his reputation and reprise his key concepts and major theories. Among the recent flood of commentaries on Marx, the following titles have received much attention and interest: *Reclaiming Marx's "Capital,"* by Andrew Kliman (2006); *Why Marx was*

Right, by Terry Eagleton (2011); *The Revolutionary Ideas of Karl Marx,* by Alex Callinicos (2012); *Capital in the Twenty-First Century,* by Thomas Piketty (2013); *Karl Marx,* by Jonathan Sperber (2013); *Marx, Capital and the Madness of Economic Reason,* by David Harvey (2017); and *Karl Marx,* by Gareth Stedman Jones (2017). In addition to this revival of interest among Euro- and andro-Marxists (i.e., white male theorists), it is important to note that many non-European and feminist theorists have also contributed to the revitalization of Marxist theory, including African theorists Kwame Nkrumah and Frantz Fanon; Afro-Caribbean Marxists C.L.R. James, Eric Williams and Walter Rodney; African-American Marxists W.E.B. Du Bois and Oliver Cromwell Cox; as well as a whole new generation of socialist and Marxist feminist theorists, such as Tithi Bhattacharya, Keeanga Yamhatt Taylor, Angela Davis and Cinzia Arruzza. Far more than any other past intellectual celebrity, Marx has inspired many later social theorists to update and revise his work: to expand and extend his vocabulary of theoretical concepts and to adapt his critical analysis to the changing conditions of contemporary capitalism. Marxism is, without doubt, the most controversial of any social theory. Marx's ideas can evoke passionate commitment and passionate opposition to an extent unheard of in connection with the ideas of other social theorists. How

Figure 4-1: Marxism after Marx

many people declare themselves to be avid "Comteans," "Durkheimians" or "Weberians" with the same passion that many still declare themselves to be Marxists? Marxism was one of the most influential ideologies of the twentieth century. And although there may be some social theorists who regard themselves as Durkhemians or Weberians, only Marx has inspired whole groups, or schools, of later theorists who have remained committed to the continuation and renewal of his ideas. We shall now turn to review some of these intellectual descendants of Marx: these different branches, or schools, of Marxism, neo-Marxism and post-Marxism.

Orthodox Marxism

After the Russian Revolution, in 1917, Marxism was transformed from a critical method of social analysis into the official doctrine, or state ideology, of the USSR. Because of its importance as a tool of revolutionary change, the early Marxism of this first generation of theorists was viewed more as a "science" than as a critical method of social analysis. In the USSR this tendency to proclaim Marxism as a science was most evident, after the Bolshevik Revolution, when Marxism became known as the science of "historical (or dialectical) materialism," or "Marxism–Leninism." Marxist–Leninists in particular saw Marxism as a method for discovering what they believed to be the fixed and natural laws of historical and social change, much as physical and biological scientists had discovered the fixed and natural laws of nature (e.g., Isaac Newton's laws of universal gravitation, Charles Darwin's law of evolution by natural selection and the laws of thermodynamics). Most scientific laws are assumed to have a universal validity: they are true irrespective of the context — the place and time — in which they are stated. They are conceived as positivist laws: they are not only based on sensory experience (empiricism), but they also express a universal truth. The early Marxist theorists subscribed to a positivist interpretation of the theories of historical materialism, such as the concentration and centralization of capital, the falling rate of profit etc., and believed that these theories expressed universal laws, even though Marx himself recognized that these were "laws of tendency" (i.e., probability) rather than iron laws of historical necessity. On the other hand, the more humanistic traditions of Marxism — such as Hegelian Marxism and critical theory — downplayed the significance of "objective historical conditions" and placed a much greater emphasis on the role of collective action (praxis) in bringing about social and political change. This distinction between Marxists who believed in the historical inevitability of socialism and ultimately communism and those who emphasized the need for class consciousness and organized political action is sometimes referred to as the division between "deterministic" interpretations of Marxism versus "voluntaristic" interpretations.

In the decades leading up to the First World War and the Russian Revolution, other revolutionary leaders and intellectuals emerged to claim the true legacy of Marx's ideas. One of the greatest was the Russian revolutionary leader Vladimir Ilyich Ulyanov (better known as Lenin). In many ways, Lenin remains a somewhat paradoxical figure in the history of Marxism. At times in his writings he seemed like a hard-nosed deterministic Marxist. At other times, in works such as *The State and Revolution* and *What Is to Be Done?*, he strongly opposed the fatalism and political quietism of some of the more revisionist political intellectuals — including social democrats such as Karl Kautsky and Karl Mehring in Germany, Edouard Bernstein in France and Otto Bauer and Rudolph Hilferding in Austria. These theorists interpreted historical materialism as a non-revolutionary theory of social evolution. They believed that the inevitable and final collapse of capitalism was already predetermined by iron laws of historical necessity. These versions broke with the revolutionary tradition by asserting that the iron laws of capitalist development would lead *inevitably* to the collapse and transformation of the capitalist system. Thus, the role of revolutionary politics was seen as redundant and counterproductive. Lenin, who had become the leading theoretician of the Bolshevik Party, did not believe that "objective historical conditions" alone would bring about the transformation of capitalist societies. It was necessary, in Lenin's view, to create highly disciplined revolutionary vanguard parties led by a cadre of professional revolutionaries.

THE MANY FACES OF CONTEMPORARY MARXISM

Since the mid-twentieth century, the dramatic increase in the number of Marxian social theorists and sociologists and the resultant proliferation of versions, or schools, of Marxism and neo-Marxism have added greatly to the diversity in sociological and social theory. Some of these modern derivative schools of Marxism — such as critical theory, structuralist Marxism, poststructuralism, postmodernism, post-Marxism and post-colonial theory — originated in Europe, although their influence quickly spread to Anglophone sociologists. Others, such as world-system theory, analytical and rational choice Marxism and economic sociology, have their roots in North America, where they have developed independent traditions of Marxian and neo-Marxian scholarship. Some traditions, such as socialist feminism, appear to have been influenced by scholars from around the world.

Figure 4-2: Twentieth Century Marxism

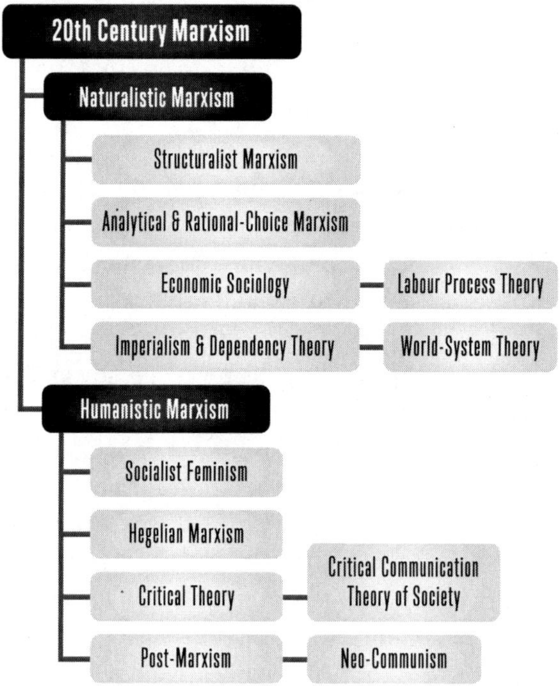

Hegelian Marxism

One of the earliest branches of Marxism to dissent from the official Soviet state ideology of Marxism–Leninism was Hegelian Marxism. The theorists associated with this school of Western Marxism included Georg (György) Lukács (from Hungary), Antonio Gramsci (from Italy) and Karl Korsch (from Germany). These Marxists believed that Marxism needed to rediscover its tradition of social activism and mass political struggle. Each of these writers, in his own way, returned to the Hegelian roots of Marxism in order to rediscover a view of humans that was creative, active and not over-determined by "objective historical conditions." These humanized versions of Marxism played an important role in the later sociological "rediscovery" of Marxism in the mid-twentieth century. They were to prove particularly attractive to the student radicals of the antiwar and student power movements of the 1960s and 1970s, and they partly informed the new left social critique that emerged from these decades.

Figure 4-3: Hegelian Marxism

In contrast to the doctrinaire approach of many orthodox Marxists, who emphasized the "historical inevitability" of the overthrow of capitalism and the ultimate victory of socialism and communism, the Hegelian Marxists emphasized the necessity for the active role of class struggle, ideology and revolutionary theory and practice. These theorists restored the critical and reflexive elements to Marx's theory of history and society. Hegelian Marxists believed that political action, or praxis — which required the subjective collective consciousness of the working class — was the vital spark needed to ignite the revolution. It was this emphasis on the importance of subjectivity, consciousness and action that led these humanistic Marxists to distance themselves from the deterministic and economistic interpretations of the historical materialists and other vulgar Marxists, who downplayed the role of conscious political action and overemphasized the role of objective material and historical conditions in the transformation of societies. From the work of the Hegelian Marxists, a number of new terms and concepts were introduced into the vocabulary of modern Marxism, including "totality" and "reification" (Lukacs), "hegemony" and "civil society" (Gramsci) and "practical socialism" and "historical specificity" (Korsch). Over time, the influence of the Hegelian school of Marxism spread to other theorists and contributed to the development of other schools of modern Marxism, or neo-Marxism — especially the Frankfurt School of critical theory.

CRITICAL THEORY

The other major tradition of humanistic Marxism that influenced modern social theory was that associated with the Frankfurt School of critical theory. This tradition of critical theory was originally composed of a group of German Marxists who began their studies of contemporary society in 1923 at the Institute of Social Research in Frankfurt am Main. In the following decades, critical theory emerged as a leading tradition of humanistic Marxism, a tradition that brought together an interdisciplinary group of scholars who pioneered new areas of Marxian theory, research and analysis. Much of the work undertaken by the critical theorists involved the cultural analysis and critique of capitalist society in ways that had never been done before. Unlike the orthodox Marxists, who had focused primarily on the economics of capitalism, almost to the exclusion of everything else, the critical theorists studied the psychology, culture and ideology of capitalism, aspects of society that had previously been overlooked or treated as residual. A fuller discussion of critical theory and its most recent representatives is left for the next chapter of this book.

STRUCTURALIST MARXISM

Besides the critical theory associated with the Frankfurt School, many other traditions of neo-Marxism emerged and evolved throughout the twentieth century, and some of these traditions continue to influence social theory in the early decades of twenty-first century. The history of Western Marxism — in common with the general history of social thought — has been characterized by the rise and fall of successive theoretical perspectives. Or, to state the matter more accurately, a particular perspective (or interpretation of Marxism) has often generated a counter-perspective (or backlash). The history of Marxist theory may be seen as the progressive emergence, opposition, conflict and transformation of different interpretations of Marx's ideas. The growth of these Marxist intellectual traditions, much like the growth of social theories more generally, has often followed a "dialectical" pattern, whereby the appearance of one theory or interpretation has often provoked the rise of an alternative or opposing version; it is a conflict that later results in the fusion or combination of these previously opposed traditions. This pattern is dialectical in the sense of Hegel's theory of history, which analyzed the development of ideas as a pattern of thesis, antithesis and eventual synthesis, after which this pattern is regenerated with the emergence of a new thesis. For example, existential Marxism (Jean-Paul Sartre), which emphasized the importance of individual choice and revolutionary commitment, was later challenged by the school of structuralist Marxism (Louis Althusser), which emphasized the importance of the objective institutional structures that program or socialize individuals into the ideologies of capitalist society through the process of "interpellation" (or internalization). Today, Marxist theorists Slavoj Žižek and Alain Badiou have tried to blend these opposing traditions into a new theoretical synthesis.

Figure 4-4: Structural Marxism

Voluntaristic versions of Marxism — those that emphasize the free will (or agency) of the social actor (such as the Hegelian school and the Frankfurt School of critical theory) — eventually generated a counter-movement of more deterministic versions of Marxism. One of the more prominent examples of this anti-humanist and more deterministic trend was seen in the rise of structuralist Marxism in the 1970s, associated with Louis Althusser, Nicos Poulantzas and Maurice Godelier, among others. Whereas the voluntaristic versions of Marxism emphasized the importance of the "active agents" of revolutionary change (class consciousness, ideology, class struggle etc.), structuralists emphasized the decisive role played by "objective material conditions," including such large-scale structures as the economy, the state and the various institutions or "apparatuses" of the state. In other words, structuralists focused almost exclusively on the structures of total societies rather than on the actions or agency of individual or collective social actors. At the same time, structuralist Marxists — especially Althusser — tried to recover the scientific prestige of Marxism, a viewpoint which had long been dismissed as "positivistic" and "scientistic" by earlier critical and Hegelian theorists. Althusser sharply distinguished between what he called the early "ideological" writings of Marx from the later "scientific" writings.

By the mid-1980s, structuralism in all its forms (in sociology, anthropology and literary and cultural studies) had been critiqued, challenged and largely supplanted by the rising tides of poststructuralism and postmodernism. Under the influence of poststructuralist writers, such as Michel Foucault and Jacques Derrida, and postmodernist writers, such as Jean-Francois Lyotard and Jean Baudrillard, all previous traditions of Marxism (as well as most other social theories) were critiqued and condemned as "grand narratives." According to postmodernists, all grand narratives — including Marxism — represented the illegitimate attempts of privileged social identities — typically white, Western, heterosexual, metropolitan men — to universalize and totalize their worldviews, discourses and related social practices to entire societies and populations.

Marxian Economic Sociology

In the mid-twentieth century, another important tradition of neo-Marxism — sometimes called Marxian economic sociology — had an impact on modern social theory. This general classification can include several different generations of theorists. The focus of much Marxian economic social theory and research has been on advanced or late capitalist societies, e.g., Canada, United States, United Kingdom, Japan and member states of the European Union. Some of this work has analyzed the social division of labour and class relations in capitalist societies, while other theory and research has focused more specifically on the technical division of labour within particular capitalist enterprises.

Two important American Marxists who pioneered the study of advanced capitalism in the United States are Paul Baran and Paul Sweezy. Their research extends across the decades of the 1950s, 1960s and 1970s. Their most influential publication was *Monopoly Capital*, which first appeared in 1966. In this and other works, Baran and Sweezy analyze how the earlier stage of competitive capitalism in the US — from the midnineteenth to the opening decades of the twentieth century — was later transformed into the stage of monopoly capitalism. The rise of the giant corporation and the growth of multinational and transnational enterprises have changed the face of contemporary capitalism. Large corporations are no longer run by individual entrepreneurs in the way that Henry Ford once ran the Ford Motor Company, or in the way that other American tycoons — such as the Carnegies, the Mellons and the DuPonts — once ran their industrial empires. The large national and multinational corporations of today rely on a class of salaried professionals to manage the day-to-day business of the company. The owners have little to do with the direct operations of these companies and only make their presence known at the annual shareholders' and boards of directors' meetings. Besides this new phenomenon of the separation of ownership from control, Baran and Sweezy studied other characteristics of monopoly capitalism. One of the more important of these modern features is the growing problem of "surplus." How is the monopoly capitalist ruling class able to manage the vast surplus accumulated by the new technology and rising productivity of labour? According to Baran and Sweezy, much of this surplus is invested in the military, and much of it is disbursed as waste. The imperatives of monopoly capitalism, therefore, have created an economy that is driven by a dependency on military and other non-productive forms of investment as strategies for managing crises of overproduction. We have witnessed the birth of what Herbert Marcuse, in his book *One-Dimensional Man* (1964), called "the warfare/welfare state," or what former president Dwight Eisenhower called the "military-industrial complex." The phrase describes the link between government agencies and defence manufacturing companies: both sides gain in this partnership; the military gets the equipment needed for war, while defence companies get multi-million- or multi-billion-dollar contracts.

Marxist Labour Theory

An important tradition of theory and research that is related to the Marxian school of economic sociology is sometimes referred to as labour process theory. This perspective includes a number of Marxist writers who have analyzed the workplace in advanced capitalist society as well as the technical division of labour that is used to manage, exploit and control the contemporary labour force. One of the pioneering works in this tradition, written in 1974 by Harry Braverman, is entitled *Labor and Monopoly Capital: The Degradation of Work in the Twentieth Century*. This book had a major impact on the study of work throughout the 1970s and 1980s and inspired the growth of labour process theory in the United States and elsewhere. In many respects, this perspective represented a continuation of the earlier tradition of Marxian political economy popularized by Baran and Sweezy (1966). Other writers who became associated with this tradition include Richard Edwards, who wrote *Contested Terrain* (1979), and Michael Burawoy, who wrote *Manufacturing Consent: Changes in the Labor Process under Monopoly Capitalism* (1979) and *The Politics of Production: Factory Regimes Under Capitalism and Socialism* (1985), among other works. Throughout the 1970s, 1980s and beyond, Marxian social scientists increasingly turned their attention to the workplace and to the changing nature of work in the 1990s. There was much talk of "dual labour market theory," "split labour market theory," "labour market segmentation theory" and other perspectives that emphasized the disparities within the contemporary labour force and the gradual cheapening and casualization of work towards the end of the twentieth century.

This was also a time when many feminist theorists began to analyze the unpaid work of women in the household, or the "domestic sphere of production," as a striking example of the exploitation of women under the system of patriarchal capitalism. Many of these feminist writers were critical of orthodox Marxist accounts of exploitation, as even Marx primarily discussed the exploitation of "waged" labour, but within this analytical framework, the unpaid domestic labour within the household was never defined as "exploitation." By the mid-twentieth century, the domestic exploitation of women became a burning political issue for an increasing number of feminist writers. Some of the landmark texts of this period include *The Double Ghetto: Canadian Women and Their Segregated Work* by Pat and Hugh Armstrong (2001); *Hidden in the Household: Women's Domestic Labour under Capitalism* by Bonnie Fox (1980); *The Second Shift: Working Parents and the Revolution at Home* by Arlie Hochschild (1989); *More than a Labour of Love: Three Generations of Women's Work in the Home* by Meg Luxton (1980); and *Woman's Work: The Housewife, Past and Present* by Ann Oakley (1976). Not since the appearance of Karl Marx's *Capital* has the working world of the working class figured so prominently in academic and scholarly accounts.

Dependency Theory

A development that has helped to reshape Marxian political economic theory and research over the past several decades is the ubiquitous trend of *globalization*. During the 1960s, Marxist and other radical social theorists from Latin America popularized dependency theory in their studies of development and underdevelopment. The purpose of these studies was to show the extent to which the "development" of the industrialized economies of the Global North was only made possible through the "underdevelopment" (via the extraction and processing of the raw materials, and the exploitation of the cheap labour) of the Global

South. Development and underdevelopment were seen as complementary aspects of a single process, or as opposite sides of the same coin. In many ways, these dependency studies were an extension of earlier research on imperialism authored by first-generation Marxist writers such as Vladimir Lenin, Nikolai Bukharin and Rosa Luxemburg.

The dependency perspective was originally formulated as an explicit critique and refutation of the "modernization theories" of a number of leading American social scientists. As a growing number of commentators (Latham 2000; Engerman et al. 2003; Gilman 2003; Ekbladh 2009) have observed, modernization theory — as an economic doctrine and as a political ideology — played a vital role in the postwar mission of the US to spread its cultural influence and extend its hegemony over many regions of the Global South (at that time called the Third World). Indeed, one of the most prominent modernization theorists, Walt Rostow, served as special assistant for National Security Affairs to US President Lyndon B. Johnson from 1966 to 1969. His most famous book, *The Stages of Economic Growth* (1960), was explicitly subtitled *A Non-Communist Manifesto*. The rise of modernization theory, therefore, has to be understood in the climate of the Cold War, which overshadowed international relations after the Second World War. The theories and policies of the modernization perspective were tools in the American crusade against communism and were used by the US to plan and engineer the societies and economies of developing countries in many parts of the world — including Latin America, South Korea, Vietnam and Iran.

Many modernization social scientists (particularly those who had been influenced by structural functionalism) believed that in order to achieve economic growth, countries of the Global South —so-called "underdeveloped" countries — should imitate Western countries by importing their democratic institutions and market economies in order to achieve the necessary preconditions for a "take-off" into sustained economic growth and social development. In order to reach the first stage of take-off, it was necessary for "modernizing elites" within Global South countries to play a leading role in sponsoring capital accumulation and fostering the entrepreneurial spirit. This point of view was put most forcefully and influentially by various American scholars in addition to Rostow, such as A.F.K. Organski, in *The Stages of Political Development* (1965) and David Apter, in *The Politics of Modernization* (1965). Other social scientists, such as sociologists Talcott Parsons and Seymour Martin Lipset, along with political scientists like David Easton and Gabriel Almond, also contributed to the broad tradition of modernization theory.

Marxists roundly criticized modernization theorists' proposition that Global South societies needed to imitate the historical conditions experienced by the Western democracies in order to achieve economic growth and political stability. They argued that this perspective totally overlooks the historical impact of colonialism and imperialism on developing countries. The fiercest critics of modernization theory, who proclaimed that the economic and political "underdevelopment" of many countries and regions around the world was inexorably linked to their domination and exploitation by the "developed" states of the Western hemisphere, became known as dependency theorists. Contrary to modernization theorists, dependency theorists showed how much of the economic and political power exercised by the "industrialized North" over the "underdeveloped South" was a direct legacy of European colonialism and imperialism, a legacy that had always enriched the North and impoverished the South. In other words, the same process that enriched the neocolonial countries of the North also impoverished the underdeveloped countries of the South, and these theorists argued that the "development of underdevelopment" is an active and ongoing process. Dependency theory, therefore, began as a critique of the neocolonial structures of power and wealth that continued to intensify the unequal relations between the rich and the poor nations of the world. For dependency theorists, the very factors that contributed to industrial take-off in the West — such as the slave trade and enslaved labour, the plunder of raw materials and natural resources and later cheap labour — were the same factors that directly contributed to the "underdevelopment" of the countries of the Global South. According to dependency theorists, in order to achieve growth and stability, low income countries had to resist and sever their ties from the global system of capitalist exploitation, not embrace and endorse it.

The dependency perspective was first introduced to Anglophone readers by Paul Baran in 1957 with the publication of *The Political Economy of Growth*. However, it was German American theorist Andre Gunder Frank who popularized this perspective among Anglophone readers with his book *Capitalism and Underdevelopment in Latin America: Historical Studies of Chile and Brazil* (1967). Interestingly, Frank's critical perspective on modernization theory was not much appreciated by border officials in Canada and the US. In fact, he was repeatedly denied entry to Canada in the 1970s as "a threat to national security." In 1965 the US, refused him permission "to return to unrelinquished domicile in the USA" as "contrary to the best interests of this country" because of his "further identification with the Communist Chinese position of world revolution and the destruction of the capitalist system." These refusals were undoubtedly linked to his strong criticism of US foreign policy in Latin America and around the world, and to his association with anti-imperialist movements — especially in Chile and Cuba. His critical stand against American imperialism during the Cold War secured his reputation as a "national security threat" within the US administration and among some of its closest allies, such as Canada.

Other writers of the dependency school, such as Fernando Henrique Cardoso, Celso Furtado, Samir Amin, Giovanni Arrighi, Arghiri Emmanuel and Walter Rodney, later contributed their own critical studies of development and underdevelopment and of "unequal exchange." More recently, Marxist research on globalization has benefited from the work of Immanuel Wallerstein, who pioneered a series of historical studies into the development of the international capitalist system. Wallerstein's theoretical perspective has become known as world-system theory.

World-System Theory

The work of Immanuel Wallerstein in the United States grew out of the work of Latin American and African dependency theorists, or *dependentistas*, who studied the dependency relations that continued to subordinate the Global South to the power and control of the modern industrial capitalist states. The dependency theorists tried to show how the gap between the metropolitan industrial capitalist states and the undeveloped hinterland countries was growing rather than declining. They also showed how relations of inequality and dependency among states were being reproduced within underdeveloped countries, between the urban metropolitan and rural hinterland areas.

Immanuel Wallerstein developed these ideas into a more comprehensive theory of the modern world system. He analyzed the historical conditions that led to the rise of the Western capitalist states and showed how these states contributed to a vast system of global inequality and dependence that has continued to define relations between rich and poor nations. He also refined some of the key concepts of dependency theory, for example, the terms "metropolis" and "hinterland" were replaced with "core," "periphery" and "semi-periphery" states. And while Wallerstein's work has attracted the criticism of some Marxists for paying insufficient attention to class relations, he has advanced the study of capitalism as a global system of exploitation and accumulation.

Figure 4-5: Wallerstein's World System

Unlike the modernization (or developmentalist) perspective, which sees the Western industrialized world as the model — based on a "linear stage theory" — for the future modernization of the Global South, the world-system perspective rejects the notion that Eurocentric paths of development can be imposed on cultures and societies of the Global South. The fundamental problem for these countries, according to this perspective, is not the absence of development models, but rather the structures of domination and exploitation that continue to lock these countries into dependency relationships with the industrialized capitalist states.

One of the important points made by Wallerstein in his critique of the prevailing linear stage theory underlying the modernization perspective is that this view of development is held not only by liberal ("bourgeois") modernization theorists, but by some vulgar Marxists as well. For this reason, challenges to the modernization perspective also involve challenges to the traditional Marxian view of economic development (historical materialism), which assumed that all nations had to pass through several stages on the road to socialism. Many of these challenges pose as large a problem for orthodox Marxian views of development as they do for modernization theorists. Why did the first "proletarian" revolution succeed, not in an advanced capitalist country — as Marx expected — but in a largely rural nation like Russia (1917) and later in largely agrarian societies such as North Korea (1948), China (1949), North Vietnam (1954), Cuba (1959), Laos (1975) and Venezuela (1999)? Similarly, why did socialist revolutions fail to materialize in the heartlands of capitalism, in Great Britain and the United States, contrary to Marx's expectations? These and other apparent "anomalies" — such as the recent unexpected resurgence of hard nationalism across the globe — have provided developmentalists of all stripes, Marxist and non-Marxist alike, with serious theoretical headaches.

For Wallerstein, many of these theoretical questions can be satisfactorily answered within the world-system perspective. By focusing on the world system as a whole, rather than on individual nation-states, shifts in the distribution of power and wealth between the cores (i.e., the industrial states), peripheries (the underdeveloped states) and semi-peripheries (the transitioning states) of the world system can best be understood historically. What appears to be "regression" in some states is only part of a much larger picture that will include corresponding "progress" in other states. As the balance of power shifts globally, along with changes in the international division of labour, what were once "core" states may become "semi-peripheral" or "peripheral" states at a later time. And of course, what were once semi-peripheral nations — such as China or India — are now well along the way to becoming core states and economic powerhouses. In other words, the changing kaleidoscope embracing the economic fortunes of individual countries can only be understood in all its complexity against the larger background of world history, rather than as a mechanistic linear and evolutionary stage process, as envisaged in both modernization and classical Marxist theory. Wallerstein also outlines some of the social forces that have been responsible for consolidating the modern world capitalist system over the past four centuries: military conquest, the enslavement of Indigenous workers, the exploitation of raw materials and the imposition of colonial terms of trade that enriched the colonial powers and impoverished the colonies. He argues that each of these forces carries within it the seeds of opposition and conflict that can lead to changes in a different direction.

Wallerstein's later writings took on a more apocalyptic tone in which, among other things, he announced the "disintegration of the modern world-system of capitalism as a civilization" (Wallerstein 1999: 33). Indeed, in his latest works, Wallerstein appears to have abandoned his earlier historical materialist analysis in favour of a more ideological and more eclectic approach to the study of globalization. In his recent predictions, the decline of the capitalist world-system is attributed less to materialist contradictions (such as intensified class conflict or destabilizing business cycles) and more to cultural contradictions. These contradictions, or "crises," have arisen through the failure of earlier containment strategies of the West (such as universal suffrage, the welfare state and national self-determination, as well as modernization and development programs) to successfully divert the revolutionary aspirations of the oppressed and impoverished peoples of the world into long-term reformist "solutions."

According to Wallerstein, the decline of the world capitalist system has deepened as a result of a number of developments. The collapse of the USSR and the disappearance of the former communist states of Eastern Europe have weakened the power and political influence once exercised by the United States over its partners and allies. At the same time, heavy overseas borrowing by the US Federal Reserve Bank has made the US more dependent on its foreign creditors, specifically China, South Korea and Japan. For Wallerstein, all of these factors signal the incipient decline of the US as the remaining global superpower.

In a 2004 work, which is a collection of Wallerstein's "web commentaries on the state of the world" from 2001 until 2004, Wallerstein speculated further on the decline of the US as a world superpower. As one critic has suggested (Hirsch 2006), this work represents something of an uneasy conflation of at least two different voices of Wallerstein: that of the social scientist and that of the political pundit. For some critics, Wallerstein became more of an ideologue than a scholar and now "appears attached to a more ultra-Leftist political tradition … than some of those other world-systems and dependency thinkers, such as (early) Frank or Samir Amin" (el-Ojeil 2014: 16). One such critic, Stephen Sanderson (2005: 204), advises Wallerstein to return to his central academic interests and to eschew such "foolish things" as ideological and prophetic predictions of the imminent decline of the world capitalist system. These and other critics argue that Wallerstein's predictions of the imminent downfall of the U.S. as a global power were given without rigorous analysis or carefully presented factual evidence. Although the 2008 financial crisis certainly destabilized the US economy and drove it into recession, predictions of the death of US capitalism have proven to be premature.

Analytical Marxism

Analytical Marxism springs from the efforts of some academics — including Gerald Cohen (1978), John Roemer (1986), Jon Elster (1985), Adam Przeworski (1985) and Erik Olin Wright (1994) — to redefine Marxism according to the methods of analytic philosophy and empirical social science — especially those of economics. This perspective is one of the more interesting branches of modern Marxism to appear in recent years. In many ways, analytical Marxism is of the classroom rather than of the streets. It represents an attempt by some academic Marxists to formulate their key ideas and concepts using the standard methodological principles of the social sciences. These analytical Marxists, and their close cousins, rational choice Marxists, have attempted to remove from Marxian analysis what they regard as all elements of dogma, ideology and metaphysics, such as Hegel's theory of the dialectic contained in his philosophy of historical idealism. In place of abstract philosophy, analytic and rational choice Marxists remain committed to the methods of empirical observation and logical reasoning as the best ways to advance the emancipatory goals of Marxist analysis. The goal of these theorists has been to reformulate Marx's ideas according to the modern *positivist* principles of economics, game theory and rational choice theory. They have attracted the criticism of more traditional Marxists, for whom analytical Marxism is nothing more than a bourgeois dilution of Marx's ideas and an abandonment of his historical and dialectical analysis of society. At the same time, analytical Marxism has proven attractive to intellectuals whose goal has been to reformulate Marx's ideas as rigorous propositions and hypotheses capable of empirical verification (or falsification) through the accepted methods of social science research.

Analytical Marxists reject what they see as the many unscientific, or even anti-scientific, uses of Marxism, ranging from the untestable and ideological linear stage theory of historical materialism to the abstract philosophical ideals of critical theory — such as Jurgen Habermas' "ideal speech community" based upon a "rational consensus," which some critics (Larsen and Wright 1993) have dismissed as "a new, sociolinguistic frame [of] Marx's utopian classless society ... devoid of hierarchy and social tension, which Marx held to be the terminus *ad quem* of history." However, the same critics also suggest: "One might add that Habermas' analysis is at odds with the most powerful contemporary emancipatory force, the multicultural movement, which has sought to empower minorities and broaden participation in social and economic institutions by arguing that the perspectives of minorities are unique, that no universalizing consensus can capture those perspectives." Notwithstanding the claims of Marx himself to have discovered a materialist, or scientific, conception of history and society, many Marxists have misused the label of science to sanctify Marxism as a set of unquestionable and unassailable truths. Far from using the proven methods of social science research, much orthodox Marxism degenerated into dogma especially when institutionalized as an official ideology in the former USSR and in the days of Mao's regime in China. At least this is the contention of analytical Marxists.

What is of interest to us is the recognition that for analytical Marxists, Marxism is best understood as a "family of theories united by a common terrain of debate and questions" (Wright 1994: 178), rather than as a unified theory with well-developed boundaries. In other words, Marxism has been divided and subdivided by many of the same ontological and epistemological debates that have preoccupied most other social theorists over the past several decades. The state of *methodological and theoretical pluralism*, which has been endemic throughout the social sciences, has also been true of the theoretical tradition of Marxism.

Analytical Marxists believe that in order for Marxism to tell us anything new about the social world it has to be transformed from an ideology into a rigorous social science. This involves analytical Marxists making a series of specific commitments to uphold the proven methods of social science — and analytic philosophy — when defining Marxian concepts, constructing theoretical arguments and formulating rational explanations. Only in this way can Marxism achieve the rigour and respectability normally reserved for scientific disciplines. And more importantly, only in this way can Marxism become a truly self-critical and reflective social theory that is capable of discovering new things about the social world instead of restating its own doctrinal "truths."

The desire of analytical Marxists to use the methods of social science to formulate Marxist ideas represents a clear departure from many orthodox Marxists who rejected the social sciences as "bourgeois" and undialectical. This commitment to methodological rigour has become the hallmark of analytical Marxian research and may be seen in many examples of this type of work. Among the examples of methodological rigour is the attempt by some analytical Marxists to find a precise operationalization for the concepts of "working class" and "middle class," concepts that have often been used imprecisely in traditional Marxian analyses of class structure.

In another, some analytical Marxists have borrowed or imported methods from the social sciences, in particular the rational choice model used by Adam Przeworski (1985), to clarify the conditions under which social democratic parties can participate in general elections, either by maximizing their share of the popular vote by broadening their appeal beyond a traditional working-class constituency (like Tony Blair and his program for New Labour in the UK and Bill Clinton's bi-partisan political coalitions in the US) or by consolidating their traditional working class base and minimizing their share of the popular vote but remaining true to a traditional socialist agenda (like Bernie Sanders in his US presidential campaigns and Jeremy Corbyn in his successful bid for leadership of the British Labour Party in 2015). What is novel about these examples is the way in which analytical Marxists are prepared to use the methods of modern economics to construct simplified models of social reality. Although such models are necessarily oversimplifications of reality, they are regarded as useful "thought experiments" that enable the researcher to refine the internal logic of a causal model under controlled conditions before it is generalized to a wider field of application. Although Przeworski identifies as an analytical Marxist, he remains skeptical of the possibility for any profound transformation of capitalist into socialist social relations — at least through the "bourgeois" electoral system. In order to secure a popular mandate in most elections, progressive political parties are obliged to pursue social democratic rather than socialist goals and reformist rather than revolutionary agendas. And because of what he sees as "the structural dependence of labour on capital," he sees no real possibility of redistributing the extreme inequalities of wealth or income or of achieving any radical democratization of class relations in contemporary capitalist societies (see Mohun and Veneziani 2019). These tensions between reformist and revolutionary politics are particularly evident today — in the divisions between the "radical" and "moderate" wings of the Democratic Party in the US, the Labour Party in the UK — and in other progressive parties in Europe and elsewhere.

Analytical Marxism has been roundly criticized by other, more humanist or cultural, Marxists for dabbling in the methodology of bourgeois social science, especially modern economics, the most capitalistic of all the social sciences. Among the more stinging criticisms to be raised against analytical Marxism is the charge of "methodological individualism," which involves the belief that the structural properties of societal systems, such as economies, societies, polities etc., are fully reducible to the sum of their individual parts. Simply stated, this means that instead of examining the large-scale structural units of society, such as the state, class structure, or mode of production, methodological individualists are more interested in looking at how the actions of individuals are motivated by rational choices made within a set of social constraints.

It is, to say the least, rather unusual to see the charge of methodological individualism levelled against Marxists, because most versions of Marxism have remained committed to analyzing concrete historical societies as *ensembles* of social relationships. However, according to analytical and rational choice Marxists, this charge is unjust because it wrongly assumes that analytical Marxists are willing to reduce large scale social forces to the actions of individuals, when all they are really doing is making use of conventional methods of social science to cast new light on the core concepts of Marxism. The attempts by analytical Marxists to theorize the micro-foundations of a macro-structural theory such as Marxism is part of a general trend of modern and contemporary social theory that includes the work of such illustrious figures as Jürgen Habermas (1975; 1979; 1984; 1987), Anthony Giddens (1981; 1984; 1991), Pierre Bourdieu (1977; 1990) and Axel Honneth (1995; 2007). All of these theorists have, in their own ways, tried to integrate micro-theories of the individual social actor with macro-theories of social structure.

POST-MARXISM

The closing decades of the twentieth century and the opening decade of the twenty-first century saw the rise to prominence of a theoretical tradition that has become known as post-Marxism. Although there is as yet no final consensus on exactly how to define post-Marxism, or even how to distinguish it from neo-Marxism and other recent radical left-wing perspectives, the title appears to have stuck, and some of the major social theorists of our age are now labelled with this new brand. Generally, the category of post-Marxism embraces the theorists who have moved beyond Marxism even though they may continue to invoke Marx's political and intellectual project as a source of inspiration. Post-Marxism no longer uses any of the key concepts of Marxism. Post-Marxist writers like Michael Hardt and Antonio Negri, for example, have replaced many of the central concepts of classical Marxism. Instead of the "proletariat" or working class, they now identify the global "multitude" as the primary social category of the oppressed, exploited and immiserated. Instead of the capitalist ruling class, they now identify a global "hegemony," and instead of the capitalist or imperialist state, they now speak of "Empire" as "a diffuse, anonymous network of all-englobing power" (Balakrishnan 2000: 143). The means of production have now become "de-territorialized," and the actual products of labour have become "dematerialized," the production of "information" often replaces the production of actual material commodities. In this respect, post-Marxism differs from what is usually recognized as neo-Marxism (the critical theory of the Frankfurt School, associated with such writers as Herbert Marcuse, Theodor Adorno and of course, Jürgen Habermas). While it is true that critical theory departed from classical Marxism in a number of important ways, it retained much of the vocabulary of, as well as a political and ideological attachment to, Marxism — albeit a version of Marxism reinterpreted through Hegel, Weber and Freud, along with more modern intellectual influences.

Postmodernism has also influenced the ideas of some contemporary Marxists, despite the hostility that postmodernists have shown towards Marxism and other grand narratives of social theory. At the heart of the postmodernist rejection of Marxism (and of other general theories of society) is the rejection of the so-called grand narrative, or metanarrative, upon which Marxism and other general theories are based. In other words, postmodernists do not believe that any general theory of society that claims to speak on behalf of a collective historical subject, whether this is Marxism speaking on behalf of the "working class," structural functionalism speaking on behalf of "the social actor" or even feminism speaking on behalf of "women," can ever speak to the experiences and perceptions of everyone. However, several attempts have been made to incorporate postmodernist insights into revised interpretations of Marxism and post-Marxism, and several examples are particularly notable.

Post-Marxist Theorists

Although our general discussion of post-Marxism has treated it as though it were a single perspective, the truth is rather more complicated. A number of different theorists today are variously described as post-Marxist, neo-Marxist or even neo-communist. The conceptual boundaries used to define post-Marxism are vague and highly fluid, indicating that there is no final consensus as to which theorists should be included in this classification. At the same time, it is possible to identify several prominent theorists who have been classified as post-Marxist and whose work is often cited as an example of the post-Marxist theoretical perspective.

Figure 4-6: Post-Marxist Theorists

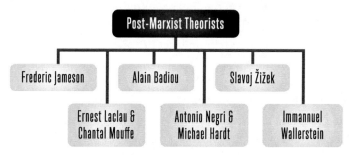

Fredric Jameson: He was one of the earliest theorists to introduce a post-Marxist perspective into contemporary social theory. Indeed, Jameson (along with David Harvey 1989) was one of the first Marxist theorists to fully acknowledge the transformative impact of the late twentieth-century revolutions in information and communication technology, as well as the growing globalization of economic relations (in finance, trade, commerce, manufacturing and services) on the contemporary world system. His recognition of the transformative effects of the "space-time compression" on information retrieval and real-time communication, as well as his acknowledgement of the ideological and political effects of hyper-consumerism on class relations in capitalist societies, led him into a close relationship with postmodernist and poststructuralist theorists at a time when most Marxists reviled and rejected these emergent theoretical perspectives. When his most famous book, *Postmodernism, or, the Cultural Logic of Late Capitalism,* was published in 1991, Jameson was among the very few Marxist writers to form a pact with postmodernism and poststructuralism.

However, Jameson does not abandon all aspects of a historical materialist analysis of contemporary capitalism. In his most famous contribution to the study of contemporary, or postmodern, capitalist society, Jameson argues that postmodernism may be understood as the particular worldview, or "cultural dominant," that corresponds to a specific stage in the linear development of contemporary capitalism. It reflects the new era of space and time compression, of *simulacra*, of floating signifiers, as well as the hyper-consumerism and global spread of Westernization. Postmodernism corresponds to the most recent stage in the development of capitalism: the stage of multinational or transnational capitalism.

Jameson suggests that postmodernism corresponds to the multinational stage of capitalist development, much as modernism corresponded to the monopoly capitalist stage and realism to the market or competitive stage. Jameson — following another Marxist economic theorist, Ernest Mandel (1975) — distinguishes three stages in the growth of capitalism. The first stage, competitive, or market, capitalism is characterized by the production and manufacture of products for a national market, especially during the nineteenth and early twentieth centuries in the West. The second stage, monopoly capitalism, signals the rise of large-scale capitalist corporations and the growth of monopolies through the acquisition and take-over of smaller capitalist companies. The once competitive market becomes dominated and administered in the interests of fewer and larger corporations. The third stage is characterized by the rise of multinational and transnational corporations whose power, wealth and scale of operations have become global. At the same time, Jameson suggests that each economic stage corresponds to a distinct cultural stage — or what he calls a "cultural dominant." For Jameson, the cultural content of these stages may be seen in cultural products, such as literature, films, architecture etc. Thus, the stage of competitive or market capitalism corresponds to the cultural dominant of realism; the stage of monopoly capitalism corresponds to the cultural dominant of modernism; and the third stage, multinational capitalism, corresponds to the cultural dominant of postmodernism. The realism of market capitalism may be seen in the books of Charles Dickens and Emile Zola, who describe the raw realities of life under early capitalism. The modernism of monopoly capitalism may be seen in the more introspective and reflective works of James Joyce, T.S Eliot, Virginia Woolf and Samuel Beckett, with their techniques of stream of consciousness and literary allusions. But for Jameson, the third stage, postmodernism, represents a distinct break from these earlier traditions. In the literary works of Thomas Pynchon, Don DeLillo and Kurt Vonnegut and in movies like *Blade Runner* and *Pulp Fiction*, there is no longer a grand narrative or sense that history guides a central plot or orders a cast of characters. Jameson distinguishes postmodern cultural products by a number of features, including superficiality, shallowness of emotion, a lack of any sense of history or linear time and new technologies (which can compress space and time). Jameson's periodization of capitalism and its successive cultural dominants is his attempt to acknowledge the new period of postmodernism and to incorporate its distinctiveness into his own grand narrative. While some theorists have applauded this effort, others have been more critical. According to Steven Best and Douglas Kellner, "His work is an example of the potential hazards of an eclectic, multiperspectival theory which attempts to incorporate a myriad of positions, some of them in tension or contradiction with each other, as when he produced the uneasy alliance between classical Marxism and extreme Postmodernism" (1991: 192; see also Ritzer 2008: 499).

Postmodernism represents a cultural development beyond the previous stage of late (or high) modernism associated with monopoly capitalism, and far beyond the even earlier era of realism associated with the stage of market capitalism. For Jameson, therefore, postmodernism, with all its political vulnerabilities, may best be understood as a cultural expression of the global stage of capitalism. Jameson has also focused on the more individualistic consequences of the present postmodernist age — for personal identity, psychic processes, and for the instability and liquidity of contemporary social relations. In this respect, Jameson's theoretical interests and concerns overlap with those of some late modernist theorists, such as Jacques Lacan, Zygmunt Bauman, Slavoj Žižek, Manuel Castells and Ulrich Beck, all of whom we shall visit later in this book.

In retrospect, the great achievement of Jameson has been to apply a Marxist historical materialist methodology and analysis to the unprecedented cultural conditions of the present postmodern age. Jameson has tried to explain these unique conditions: the growth of global networks of information and communication; the fragmentation and plasticity of personal identities; the instability and liquidity of social relations; the global reach of transnational capitalism with its outsourcing and off-shoring of manufacturing and call-center jobs; its international flows of capital and speculative finance; and the rise of hyper-consumerism and global commodification — all within an historical materialist theory of capitalist development. What past Marxists did for political economy, Jameson has tried to do for cultural studies.

Ernesto Laclau and Chantal Mouffe: Another much celebrated example of a post-Marxist perspective is reflected in the book *Hegemony and Socialist Strategy*, by Laclau and Mouffe (1985). These authors provide general guidelines for a new progressive politics that, although inspired by Marx's original project, moves far beyond Marx in a number of ways. The authors propose a new agenda for radical social change that embraces the "multiformity" of a wide range of "democratic struggles." Their stated goal is to advance towards a "deeper" and more "deliberative" democracy that is both radical and pluralist in nature.

Their work is intended both as a critique of dominant, or hegemonic, discourse and as a guide to a new progressive and emancipatory politics. Orthodox Marxism is dismissed for its classism, statism and economism. According to the authors, these tendencies installed Marxism as a dominant metanarrative and conditioned it to rationalize and endorse totalitarian political regimes. In place of a Marxism that privileges a classical conception of an industrial proletariat and reduces its blueprint for revolution to the satisfaction of economic needs, the authors propose a post-Marxist pluralist, more inclusive and radical democratic revolution in which human emancipation is defined in terms of both equality and liberty.

For traditional Marxism (at least in Marxist-Leninist interpretations), the revolutionary overthrow of capitalism was always dependent upon the mobilization of a class-conscious proletariat led by a revolutionary communist or socialist political party. This conception of revolution is often called "vanguardism" because of its reliance on a revolutionary vanguard, or professional cadre, — to lead the masses. Laclau and Mouffe jettison this "elitist" conception of revolutionary change, which is based upon a single, dominant metanarrative, in favour of a far more inclusive and pluralist theory and practice of revolutionary politics. Instead of a unified working class led by a revolutionary vanguard, post-Marxists embrace an alternative strategy aimed at bringing together disparate and diverse political subjects, drawn from the ranks of the new social movements.

These political subjects, which have come to represent the socially marginalized, stigmatized and victimized, compose the new forms of popular resistance to power and domination in our society. In place of the vanguard politics of the recent past, post-Marxism endorses the identity politics of the postmodern present. In order to mobilize popular resistance to the national and transnational powers of states, corporations and international agencies, the authors propose a socialist strategy based upon the recognition of and respect for diversity within political populations. They insist that any popular resistance must be based upon the formation of "counter-hegemonic alliances." These are political partnerships between NGOS, political parties, new social movements, spontaneous protest groups, social media campaigns, flash mobilizations, and other networks which recognize and respect the independence and autonomy of all collaborating groups. The emphasis on the mutual independence of alliance and coalition members distinguishes the decentralized politics of post-Marxism (and postmodernism) from the more centralized politics of the recent past and present. It is the difference between the politics of the World Social Forums (held in Porto Alegre, Mumbai and other cities); the spontaneous eruptions of the Occupy, Black Lives Matter, Idle No More and #MeToo movements, on the one hand, and the earlier centralized politics of established political parties; civil rights organizations; trade union bureaucracies and even the old Communist International (COMINTERN) in the days of Stalinist politics.

Michael Hardt and Antonio Negri: Another work that is often cited as an example of post-Marxism is the book *Empire*, by Hardt and Negri, and its sequel, *Multitude*. In these works, the authors present a post-Marxist theory of globalization that is intended to show us the face of the future. Their "Empire" of global capital supposedly represents a postmodern world in which the present quasi-imperial reach of the sole remaining superpower, the United States, has been replaced by the global sovereignty of an empire without any territorial borders and without any circumscribed material base. The Empire of global capital to which Negri and Hardt refer is de-centered, de-materialized and de-territorialized, without fixed boundaries and beyond the limits of any particular nation state. It is a realm of pure sovereignty — a conjunction of overlapping economic, political and biopolitical sources of wealth and power. And in this realm of absolute sovereignty, production is globally socialized, while labour — through the use of digitalized information and communication technologies — is increasingly de-materialized.

Confronted with the de-territorialization of sovereignty, with rapidly expanding circuits of capital and with the eclipse of the nation-state, traditional resistance to Empire is no longer possible. Instead of invoking the spectre of a working-class revolution (in a traditional Marxian sense), the authors posit a new postmodern source of resistance and revolt.

According to them, the postmodern resistance to Empire will come from the "multitude" — the global masses imprisoned by poverty, economic exploitation, gender oppression, racialization and biopolitical domination. It is the multitude that will confront Empire, rise up against it and ultimately overthrow it. "The autonomy of the multitude and its capacities for economic, political and social self-organisation take away any role for sovereignty. Not only is sovereignty no longer the exclusive terrain of the political, the multitude banishes sovereignty from politics. When the multitude is finally able to rule itself, democracy becomes possible" (Hardt and Negri 2004: 340). In this postmodern allegory of future global domination and resistance, the authors have painted a political landscape which is as dark and inscrutable as it is nebulous.

However, not everyone has applauded this post-Marxist view of politics and social change. Several prominent theorists — including Todd Gitlin (1995), Terry Eagleton (1996) and Ellen Meiksins Wood and John Bellamy Foster (1997) — have each critiqued these poststructuralist revisions of Marxism and have strongly advocated a return to a class-based politics and social analysis.

THE "POST" IN POST-MARXISM

Any attempt to combine postmodernism or poststructuralism with theories such as Marxism, feminism and critical theory has usually turned out to be something of an uneasy alliance. Although poststructuralism, or deconstructionism, has sometimes proven useful for exposing the unacknowledged and unexamined androcentric, ethnocentric, Eurocentric, racist, classist, elitist, homophobic, ageist, ableist and other "hidden signifiers" embedded in traditional discourses, any alliance with poststructuralism comes at a price. Both poststructuralism and postmodernism — as we shall see more fully in a later chapter — ultimately lead to the critical analysis of all discourses (including Marxism), to the disbelief in the categories of all collective subjects (including the "working class") and to the questioning of all metanarratives (again, including Marxism). However, as many progressive theorists insist, without a collective subject, or solid constituency, like the working class, there can be no basis for collective action. And where there is no basis for collective action, there can be little possibility for significant social change. This is the dilemma that confronts any theorist who seeks to combine the methods of postmodernism with more traditional theories of social change (see, for example, Epstein 1995). Some theorists have sought to escape from this dilemma by distinguishing a tactical, or strategic postmodernism from a more radical, or substantive, postmodernism (see, for example, Charles Lemert's advocacy of "strategic postmodernism" in his 2005 book *Postmodernism Is Not What You Think*). This distinction implies that it is possible to use the methods of poststructuralism — such as the critical analysis, or "deconstruction," of texts in order to discover their "silences," "absences" or other sources of gender, racial, class etc. bias without a commitment to the underlying theory and logic of postmodernism. Some theorists believe that it is possible to enjoy the benefits of postmodernism while rejecting its costs, or negative consequences (see, for example, the "strategic essentialism" once advocated by Gayatri Chakravorty Spivak, although since 2008, Spivak appears to have renounced the use of this term). Many other theorists, however, have remained skeptical and continue to search for ways to move beyond postmodernism.

The most important attribute linking Marxism to neo-Marxism, however, is what we may call the shared political optimism of both traditions. This optimism, inherited from the Enlightenment, is best expressed in the shared commitment to Enlightenment values such as reason, liberty, equality and progress. Although many critical theorists abandoned some of the basic assumptions of classical Marxism, they retained a belief in the viability of a revolutionary project, even if the working class was no longer seen as the main agent of revolutionary change. For Herbert Marcuse (1968: 248), the old industrial proletariat, which Marx saw as the revolutionary agency that would eventually rise up and transform capitalism into socialism and ultimately communism, had been replaced by a "new working class" led by alienated radical students of the new intelligentsia and other non-integrated sectors of the population, including racialized minorities and other "outsiders."

Post-Marxism, as its name suggests, is a tradition that has fallen under the spell of postmodernism and poststructuralism. Post-Marxists have an aversion to metanarratives such as classical Marxism's linear stage theory of the history of productive regimes, from primitive communism, or tribal society, through to ancient society, feudal, capitalist, socialist and eventually communist modes of production and social formations; they also reject critical theorists' endorsement of the emancipatory project of the Enlightenment and share a common concern with the role of discourse in politics and ideology. In other words, post-Marxism has replaced radical political thought in the humanities and social sciences with a concern about discourse and language in political theory and social action. Unlike traditional Marxists and many critical theorists, who have remained committed to some version of universal human emancipation, most post-Marxists have abandoned grand or metanarratives in favour of more localized narratives arising from particular cultural contexts.

In contrast to traditional Marxists, who sought to uncover the underlying laws of society, post-Marxists seek to decode the signs and representations of different social discourses. Instead of viewing the economy as an objective aspect of social reality, post-Marxists examine economic discourse as a particular linguistic code — or system of significations — composed of its own vocabulary of concepts and reproduced through its own discursive practices. For post-Marxists, as for all poststructuralists, *the world only exists through discourse.* For this reason, post-Marxists resist all attempts to transform or essentialize concepts such as the "working class" or "mode of production" into *real* material entities. Post-Marxists are opposed to treating the products of discourse as though they were real things existing externally in the outside world beyond discourse. They remain opposed to the essentialism and foundationalism that, in their eyes, characterizes much modernist political discourse.

POLITICS AND POST-MARXISM

In addition to its discursive break with Marxism, post-Marxism has also been influenced by some of the social events that helped to shape late twentieth and early twenty-first century politics. The fall of communism in the USSR and Eastern Europe in the 1990s shattered the discourses of the Cold War and began to redefine the scope of conventional politics. The rise of social movements in the 1960s coalescing around civil rights (National Association for the Advancement of Colored People), student politics (Students for a Democratic Society), anti-war, anti-nuclear (Campaign for Nuclear Disarmament) and trade unions have also redefined radical politics in the West. Today, social movements are concerned with LGBTQ rights, racial justice (Black Lives Matter), Indigenous sovereignty (Idle No More), economic justice (Occupy, Fight for $15) and environmental and animal rights, as well as social movements on the right, including neo-Nazi, white supremacist, sovereign citizen militias and other far-right patriot groups such as the Tea Party in the US.

As we have seen in Canada, the US, Europe and elsewhere, the rising tide of new social movements has also witnessed the emergence of a more radical politics — from both the hard left and the hard right. In this sense, "radical" means returning to the "roots" of a political ideology, i.e., to a form of political fundamentalism. Thus, under the left-wing leadership of Jeremy Corbyn in the UK, there was renewed demand from party members to implement the socialist Clause Four of the Labour Party constitution which involves the full nationalization of the "means of production, distribution and exchange" and the redistribution of wealth and income. This clause was opposed by more conservative leaders of the Labour Party such as Tony Blair. Similarly, calls for a return to more traditional socialist principles and ideals can be seen in the US, with politicians such as Bernie Sanders and Alexandria Ocasio-Cortez. On the other hand, radical right-wing fundamentalism can move towards fascist calls for a white ethno-state and for a return to racial segregation, anti-miscegenation (racial inter-breeding) and anti-non-white immigration. Radical right-wing fundamentalism may also be expressed in neoliberal demands for full marketization, de-regulation and unconstrained free trade. The end of the Cold War and the articulation of human-rights politics through the last quarter of the twentieth century into the twenty-first century marked an important turning point in the politics of both progressive and reactionary social movements.

On a practical level, the vanguard politics — characterized by a professional centralized leadership elite, or cadre — of the mainstream parties of the left and right increasingly gave way to a more decentral-ized politics with an emphasis on local issues. In place of the old mass movements spearheaded by conventional political organizations — such as those representing the working class, women, civil rights etc. — the new "identity politics" is oriented to the local and to the specific. In particular, some post-Marxist politics emphasizes "autonomism" and "anti-authoritarianism." Autonomism implies freedom and independ-ence from centralized political structures, while anti-authoritarianism is often directed against the control exercised by traditional parties of the left over their members and supporters. For a while, the Zapatista move-ment of Indigenous Peoples in the Mexican province of Chiapas became an icon for these new progressive grassroots protests celebrated by some post-Marxists. The new politics of the left requires a political vision that on the one hand recognizes and respects the diversity of interests and identity groups, and on the other hand the ability to build coalitions and alliances between these diverse groups in support of particular political actions and strategies. Today, the anti-authoritarian politics of the street may also be seen in the rise of the yellow vests, or *gilet jaunes*, movement, which arose France in 2018 as a protest against rising food and fuel prices, later demanded more general economic reforms and is an example of an autonomist and anti-authoritarian movement composed of members from both the far left and the far right. This example shows how contemporary populist movements may either remain autonomist in their politics or be attracted to demagogic leaders, such as Donald Trump (US), Nigel Farage (UK) and Marine LePen (France). Populist politics may evolve in different ways. As we have already seen, the disintegration of a mass working-class political constituency for the left finds its theoretical counterpart in the abandonment of the traditional metanarratives of Marxism. Today, many post-Marxist theorists have turned towards versions of feminist, psycho-analytic and linguistic theory in their search for alternative discourses and radical re-readings of Marxism. In some ways, these developments undoubtedly signal a crisis for orthodox Marxist theory; in other ways, however, they point towards a radical regeneration of Marxist ideas — unencumbered by the Cold War legacy of the past century.

PROSPECTS FOR POST-MARXISM

Numerous criticisms have been directed at the emergent tradition of post-Marxism, many of them from more traditional Marxists. Some critics dismiss Laclau and Mouffe and their post-Marxist perspective as inherently *idealist* and as too influenced by the "linguistic turn" in poststructuralism and deconstructionism. These critics allege that post-Marxism is driven more by theoretical concerns (i.e., its "theorism") than by serious analysis of the actual material conditions of contemporary capitalist accumulation and exploitation. For these critics, post-Marxism fails to analyze the economic, technological, social and political conditions that have together transformed capitalism in the twenty-first century. Henry Veltmeyer (2000) concludes that post-Marxism "is an abandon-ment, not a renewal, of Marxist thought and that as such it is part of a long tradition of idealist anti-Marxist criticism that should be rejected for its theoretical flaws and misplaced criticism." Other critics also reject the *relativism* of post-Marxism and insist on retaining the revolutionary overthrow of capitalism as the unchanging and absolute project of Marxist theory and practice.

Although the vision of a "radical democracy" as a project for deepening and extending the liberal democratic order of many Western societies remains controversial in the eyes of many of its critics, it would appear that this vision still has a future. Without a doubt, the collapse of communism has contributed to the present crisis not only of orthodox Marxism, but also of socialism, both as a theory and as a political practice. The spectre of the failed state of the USSR and of its satellite "peoples' democracies" continues to cast a long shadow, as may be seen in attempts to discredit current socialist projects by its adversaries on the political right — whether by US Republicans or conservatives in the UK and Europe, or by the radical rhetoric from the far Right. At the same time, the hegemonic status of the capitalist ideology of neoliberalism, as a doctrine and as a set of global policies, requires an effective critique as well as a practical alternative. The vision of a radical democracy advocated by post-Marxists is not without its weaknesses and shortcomings, but in the absence of any significant alternative — and confronted by the extreme inequalities of wealth and income produced by neoliberal policies — this vision remains a vital project for progressive social thinkers and activists.

From this brief review of the various schools of contemporary Marxism (including neo-Marxism and post-Marxism), it is evident that the broad tradition of Western Marxism has remained a productive and prolific source of critical, radical and progressive social theory. While the fall of communism in the former USSR and Eastern Europe posed some fundamental questions of theory and practice, it has certainly not signalled the demise of Marxism as an organic tradition of social thought. In the past, Marxism was critiqued by critical theorists for its scientism and determinism, by Hegelian theorists for its vulgar materialism, by structuralists for its idealism and voluntarism, by new left theorists for its vanguardism and elitism, and by analytical theorists for its ideological dogmatism. None of these criticisms proved fatal, and Marxism in one form or another has always bounced back as a vigorous theoretical tradition. In many ways, the global financial crisis of 2008–09, along with the wars in Afghanistan and Iraq, the politics of regime change, the so-called "global war on terror" and the plutocracy inaugurated by Donald Trump have all succeeded in reinvigorating Marxism as a critical perspective on world affairs. We may conclude — with a nod to Mark Twain — that the news of Marxism's death has been greatly exaggerated. However, the postmodern debate over the fate of Marxism is far from over, and there is little prospect of any closure of this debate in the immediate future. As always, readers will have to navigate their own ways through these debates and form their own conclusions.

References

Adorno, T.W., et al. 1982. *The Authoritarian Personality*. [Abridgment of original 1950 work.] New York: Norton.

Ahmed, Nafeez. 2014. "Iraq Invasion Was About Oil." *The Guardian*, 20 March. <https://www.theguardian.com/environment/earth-insight/2014/mar/20/iraq-war-oil-resources-energy-peak-scarcity-economy>.

Apter, David. 1965. *The Politics of Modernization*. University of Chicago Press.

Armstrong, P., and H. Armstrong. 2001. *The Double Ghetto: Canadian Women and Their Segregated Work*. Toronto, ON: Oxford University Press.

Balakrishnan, Gopal. 2000. "Hardt and Negri's Empire." *New Left Review*, 5 (September–October).

Baran, Paul A. 1957. *The Political Economy of Growth*. New York: Monthly Review Press.

Baran, Paul A., and Paul Sweezey. 1966. *Monopoly Capital*. Monthly Review Press.

Best, Steven, and Douglas Kellner. 1991. *Postmodern Theory: Critical Interrogations*. New York: Guilford Press.

Bourdieu, P. 1977. *Outline of a Theory of Practice*. London: Cambridge University Press.

___. 1990. *In Other Words: Essays Towards a Reflexive Sociology*. Cambridge: Polity.

Braverman, Harry. 1974. *Labor and Monopoly Capital: The Degradation of Work in the Twentieth Century*. Monthly Review Press.

Burawoy, Michael. 1979. *Manufacturing Consent: Changes in the Labor Process under Monopoly Capitalism*. The University of Chicago Press.

___. 1985. *The Politics of Production: Factory Regimes Under Capitalism and Socialism*. Verso Books.

Burleigh, Nina. 2017. "Meet the Billionaires Who Run Trump's Government." *Newsweek*, 4/5. <http://www.newsweek.com/2017/04/14/donald-trump-cabinet-billionaires-washington-579084.html>.

Callinicos, Alex. 2012. *The Revolutionary Ideas of Karl Marx*. Haymarket Books.

Cohen, Gerald. 1978. *Karl Marx's Theory of History: A Defence*. Oxford: Oxford University Press.

Eagleton, Terry. 1996. *The Illusions of Postmodernism*. Oxford: Blackwell.

___. 2011. *Why Marx Was Right*. Yale University Press.

Edwards, Richard. 1979. *Contested Terrain: The Transformation of the Workplace in the Twentieth Century*. New York: Basic Books.

Ekbladh, David. 2009. *The Great American Mission: Modernization and the Construction of an American World Order*. Princeton, NJ: Princeton University Press.

el-Ojeili, C. 2014. "Reflections on Wallerstein: The Modern World-System, Four Decades on." *Critical Sociology*, 41, 4–5: 679–700. <https://doi.org/10.1177/0896920513497377>.

Elster, J. 1985. *Making Sense of Marx*. Cambridge: Cambridge University Press.

Engerman, David, Nils Gilman, Mark Haefele and Michael Latham (eds.). 2003. *Staging Growth: Modernization, Development and the Global Cold War*. Amherst, MA: University of Massachusetts Press.

Epstein, Barbara. 1995. "Why Post-Structuralism Is a Dead End for Progressive Thought." *Socialist Review*, 25, 2: 83–119.

Fox, Bonnie (ed.). 1980. *Hidden in the Household: Women's Domestic Labour under Capitalism*. Toronto: Women's Press.

Frank, Andre Gunder. 1967. *Capitalism and Underdevelopment in Latin America: Historical Studies of Chile and Brazil*. New York: Monthly Review Press.

Fromm, E. 1941. *Escape from Freedom*. New York: Farrar and Rinehart.

Giddens, A. 1981. *The Contemporary Critique of Historical Materialism*. Berkeley: University of California Press.

___. 1984. *The Constitution of Society: Outline of the Theory of Structuration*. Berkeley: University of California Press.

___. 1991. *Modernity and Self-Identity: Self and Society in the Late Modern Age*. Stanford, CA: Stanford University Press.

Gilman, Nils. 2003. *Mandarins of the Future: Modernization Theory in Cold War America*. Baltimore, MD: Johns Hopkins University Press.

Gitlin, Todd. 1995. *The Twilight of Common Dreams: Why America Is Wracked by Culture Wars*. New York: Henry Holt and Company.

Gramsci, A. 1968. *The Modern Prince and Other Writings*. New York: International Publishers.

___. 1971. *Selections from the Prison Notebooks* New York: International Publishers.

Habermas, J. 1975. *Legitimation Crisis*. Boston: Beacon Press.

___. 1979. *Communication and the Evolution of Society* Boston: Beacon Press.

___. 1984. *The Theory of Communicative Action*, Vol. 1: *Reason and the Rationalization of Society*. Boston: Beacon Press.

___. 1987. *The Theory of Communicative Action*, Vol. 2: *Lifeworld and System: A Critique of Functionalist Reason*. Boston: Beacon Press.

Hardt, Michael, and Antonio Negri. 2000. *Empire*. Harvard University Press.

___. 2004. *Multitude: War and Democracy in the Age of Empire*. New York: Penguin Press.

Harvey, David. 1989. *The Condition of Postmodernity: An Enquiry into the Origins of Cultural Change*. Oxford: Basil Blackwell.

___. 2017. *Marx, Capital and the Madness of Economic Reason*. Profile Books.

Hirsch, M.L. 2006. "*Alternatives: The United States Confronts the World* by Immanuel Wallerstein." [Book review]. *International Social Science Review*, 81, 1/2: 95–96.

Hochschild, Arlie. 1989. *The Second Shift: Working Parents and the Revolution at Home*. New York: Viking Press.

Honneth, Axel. 1995. *The Struggle for Recognition: The Moral Grammar of Social Conflicts*. Polity Press.

___. 2007. *Disrespect: The Normative Foundations of Critical Theory*. Polity Press.

Jameson, F. 1984. "Postmodernism, or the Cultural Logic of Late Capitalism." *New Left Review*, 146: 53–92.

___. 1991. *Postmodernism, or the Cultural Logic of Late Capitalism*. Durham, NC: Duke University Press.

Jones, Gareth Stedman. 2017. *Karl Marx: Greatness and Illusion*. Penguin.

Kliman, Andrew. 2006. *Reclaiming Marx's "Capital": A Refutation of the Myth of Inconsistency*. Lexington Books.

Korsch, K. 1972. *Marxism and Philosophy*. London: New Left Books.

Laclau, Ernesto, and Chantal Mouffe. 1985. *Hegemony and Socialist Strategy*. Verso.

Larsen, Val, and Newell D. Wright. 1993. "A Critique of Critical Theory: Response to Murray and Ozanne's *The Critical Imagination*." In Leigh McAlister and Michael L. Rothschild (eds.), *Advances in Consumer Research*, 20. Provo, UT: Association for Consumer Research: 439–443. <http://acrwebsite.org/volumes/9863/volumes/v20/NA-20>.

Latham, Michael E. 2000. *Modernization as Ideology: American Social Science and "Nation Building" in the Kennedy Era*. Chapel Hill and London: University of North Carolina Press.

Lenin, V.I. 1916/1965. *Imperialism: The Highest Stage of Capitalism*. Peking: Foreign Languages Press.

Lukacs, G. 1971. *History and Class Consciousness*. London: Merlin Press.

Luxton, M. 1980. *More than a Labour of Love: Three Generations of Women's Work in the Home*. Toronto, ON: Women's Educational Press.

Mandel, Ernest. 1975. *Late Capitalism*. New Left Books.

Marcuse, Herbert. 1964. *One-dimensional Man: Studies in the Ideology of Advanced Industrial Society*. Boston: Beacon Press.

___. 1968. *Negations*. Boston: Beacon.

Marx, Karl, and Friedrich Engels, 1992/1848. *The Communist Manifesto*. David McLennan, ed. World's Classic: Oxford University Press.

Mohun, Simon, and Roberto Veneziani. 2019. "Social Democracy and Class Compromise." <https://www.researchgate.net/publication/252191118_SOCIAL_DEMOCRACY_AND_CLASS_COMPROMISE>.

Neate, Rupert. 2017. "Richest 1% Own Half the World's Wealth, Study Finds." *The Guardian*, 14 Nov. <Https://Www.Theguardian.Com/Inequality/2017/Nov/14/Worlds-Richest-Wealth-Credit-Suisse>.

Oakley, Ann. 1976. *Woman's Work: The Housewife, Past and Present*. New York: Random/Vintage.

Organski, A.F.K. 1965. *The Stages of Political Development*. New York: Alfred A Knopf.

Piketty, Thomas. 2013. *Capital in the Twenty-First Century*. Harvard University Press.

Poulantzas, Nicos. 1978. *Political Power and Social Classes*. London: Verso.

Przeworski, Adam. 1985. *Capitalism and Social Democracy*. Newbury Park, CA: Sage.

Reich, Wilhelm. 1970 [1933]. *The Mass Psychology of Fascism,* ed. M. Higgins and C. Raphael; trans. V. Carfagno. New York: Noonday Press.

Ritzer, George. 2008. *Modern Sociological Theory*. McGraw-Hill.

Roemer, J. (ed.). 1986. *Analytical Marxism* Cambridge: Cambridge University Press.

Rostow, W.W. 1960. *The Stages of Economic Growth: A Non-Communist Manifesto.* Cambridge, UK: Cambridge University Press.

Sanderson, Stephen. 2005. "World-Systems Analysis After Thirty Years: Should It Rest in Peace?" *International Journal of Comparative Sociology,* 46, 3: 179–213.

Sperber, Jonathan. 2013. *Karl Marx: A Nineteenth-Century Life.* Norton.

Spivak, Gayatri Chakravorty. 1988. "Can the Subaltern Speak?" In Cary Nelson, Lawrence Grossberg, Henri Lefebvre, Chantal Mouffe, Catharine A. MacKinnon, Etienne Balibar, and Gajo Petrovic (eds.), *Marxism and the Interpretation of Culture.* University of Illinois Press.

Veltmeyer, Henry. 2000. "Post-Marxist Project: An Assessment and Critique of Ernesto Laclau." *Sociological Inquiry,* 70, 4 (October): 499–519.

Wallerstein, Immanuel. 1999. *The End of the World as We Know It: Social Science for the 21st Century.* University of Minnesota Press.

___. 2004. *Alternatives: The United States Confronts the World.* Boulder, CO: Paradigm Publishers.

Wood, E.M., and J.B. Foster (eds.). 1997. *In Defence of History: Marxism and the Postmodern Agenda.* New York: Monthly Review Press.

Wright, Erik Olin. 1994. "What is Analytical Marxism?" In *Interrogating Inequality: Essays on Class Analysis, Socialism and Marxism.* Verso.

CHAPTER 5

THEORIZING OUR DOMINATED LIVES

Three Generations of Critical Theorists

THE CRITICAL VISION OF THE FRANKFURT SCHOOL

Critical theory is not a favourite perspective with everyone. Michael Walsh, a former editor of *Breitbart News*, the preferred far-right news source for President Donald Trump and his entourage — dismissed the critical theorists as nihilistic "cultural Marxists" who disrespected and disowned American core values and who pursued a political and ideological agenda that was destined to bring only "destruction, division, hatred, and calumny" to the American republic. Fortunately, not all of us see the world through the narrow lens of the American far-right Republican worldview. The present chapter offers a more balanced assessment of the history, ideas and major representatives of the Frankfurt School of critical theory.

Criticism of Critical Theory from the Far Right

Few … ideas have proven more pernicious than those of the so-called Frankfurt School and its reactionary philosophy of "critical theory." At once overly intellectualized and emotionally juvenile, Critical Theory — like Pandora's Box — released a horde of demons into the American psyche.

When everyone could be questioned, nothing could be real, and the muscular, confident empiricism that had just won the war gave way, in less than a generation, to a fashionable Central European nihilism that was celebrated on college campuses across the United States. Seizing the high ground of academe and the arts, the new nihilists set about dissolving the bedrock of the country, from patriotism to marriage to the family to military service. They have sown (as Cardinal Bergoglio — now Pope Francis — has written of Satan, who will play a large role in our story) "destruction, division, hatred, and calumny" — and all disguised as a search for truth that will lead to human happiness here on earth. (Excerpt from Walsh 2015)

The Frankfurt School of critical theory was first established in 1923 at the Institute for Social Research in Frankfurt, Germany. This institute began as a left-wing think tank that published the works of socialist and Marxist scholars who were deeply critical of unfolding historical events in Europe, especially the rise of the Third Reich, the Nazi state of Adolph Hitler. For these critical theorists, many of whom were Jewish, the technological power and military might of the Third Reich and the institutionalization of anti-Semitism combined to make the new Nazi state a colossal threat to the life, liberty and dignity of humanity. However, it was not only the rise of Nazism that preoccupied the early critical theorists. The rise of Stalinism in the USSR was also seen as a catastrophic event for the future of Marxism. These critical theorists were among the first to acknowledge that the birth of these totalitarian regimes was made possible by unprecedented forms of political and technological domination. Later critical theorists have also sounded the alarm at the increasing concentration and centralization of power and wealth in late capitalist societies, especially those — such as the United States — in which the locus of power is based on what has become known (since the term was introduced by US President Eisenhower on January 17, 1961) as the "military-industrial complex." Over time, critical theorists moved beyond critiquing fascist and communist totalitarian regimes to more general critiques of many aspects of modern Western capitalist society, especially the growth of large state or corporate bureaucracies. The rise of these monster bureaucratic institutions has been seen by many critical theorists as a threat to the freedom and dignity of the individual. Although the Frankfurt School is sometimes discussed in an oversimplified way, as though it represented a singular homogenous tradition of social theory, the works produced by the leading theorists of this school may be divided into three different generations.

THE FIRST GENERATION

The first generation of the Frankfurt school remained very close to its Marxist roots. Many of the works produced at this time were studies in the political economy of nation states and of societies. An example of this is the critical study of Nazi Germany by Franz Neumann (1944) entitled *Behemoth: The Structure and Practice of National Socialism, 1933–1944*. However, many of the later works of this first generation signalled a

Figure 5-1: The Three Generations of the Frankfurt School

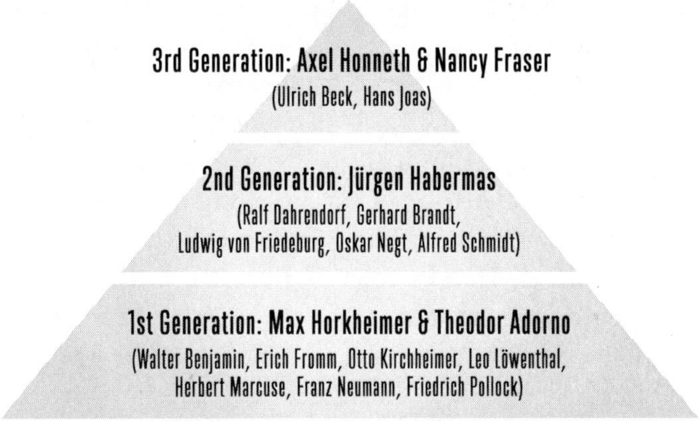

3rd Generation: Axel Honneth & Nancy Fraser
(Ulrich Beck, Hans Joas)

2nd Generation: Jürgen Habermas
(Ralf Dahrendorf, Gerhard Brandt,
Ludwig von Friedeburg, Oskar Negt, Alfred Schmidt)

1st Generation: Max Horkheimer & Theodor Adorno
(Walter Benjamin, Erich Fromm, Otto Kirchheimer, Leo Löwenthal,
Herbert Marcuse, Franz Neumann, Friedrich Pollock)

radical departure from orthodox Marxism. Under the directorship of
Max Horkheimer, theorists such as Theodor Adorno, Erich Fromm,
Walter Benjamin, Herbert Marcuse and Wilhelm Reich began to study
the popular culture, ideology and social and psychological relations that
prevailed in modern societies. While the impulse for much of this research
began as an investigation of the conditions that led to the rise of Nazism
and Stalinism, its scope soon expanded to include more general studies of
domination, manipulation and exploitation in modern society, including
contemporary capitalist societies, such as the United States.

Although the Frankfurt School was, in part, made up of a number of
prominent Marxist scholars, they became profoundly disillusioned with
the orthodox Marxism-Leninism that had become the official ideology
of the USSR. Part of this criticism was political: the Frankfurt theorists
saw that under the harsh, bureaucratized police state of the Stalinist USSR,
Marxism had become an instrument of social control and repression,
rather than of liberation and humanization. But part of the criticism
was also philosophical: the critical theorists rejected the determinism,
economism and scientism, or positivism, that lay at the heart of Marxism-
Leninism or, as it was sometimes called, "scientific socialism." Because
of their opposition to these deterministic interpretations of Marx's ideas,
the critical theorists focused much of their attention not so much on the
economy, or mode of production, but on the popular culture, psychology, ideology and lifestyles to be found in late capitalist societies. During
the 1930s, many of the leading theorists of the first generation combined
the ideas of Marx with those of other social theorists, including not only

Hegel, but also Max Weber and Sigmund Freud. Much of this early work remained philosophical in content. Theorists such as Max Horkheimer and Theodor Adorno published philosophical critiques of the forms of rationality that had come to dominate modern societies.

After the rise of the Third Reich, many of the critical theorists were forced into exile in order to to escape inevitable persecution from the Nazi state. Some relocated to other European countries, while others went to Great Britain. Some also emigrated to the United States, where they continued to publish critical studies of modern society. This American period produced some important works of critical theory. Perhaps the most distinctive aspect of the works associated with the first generation of critical theorists was their common interest in reinterpreting Marx's theories through the ideas of other social theorists — such as Hegel, Freud and Weber. Although most of the early critical theorists remained convinced Marxists (or neo-Marxists), they also recognized that traditional, or orthodox or classical, Marxism had always focused primarily on the economic, or material, "base" of society — that is, the forces and relations of production. However, the rise of fascism in Germany and the conversion of Marxism into the dogmatic and doctrinaire official ideology in the USSR (known as historical or dialectical materialism or Marxism-Leninism), convinced many critical theorists that Marx's critique of capitalism needed to be extended into a critique of the culture, psychology and politics of all "administered societies," including the capitalist state and its institutions.

The extension of critical theory beyond its initial focus on the twin totalitarianisms of Nazism and Stalinism to include late capitalist societies signalled the emergence of what was to become a major theme of the Frankfurt School: the critical study of "domination" in all modern societies. This theme of domination was particularly apparent in the work of Herbert Marcuse, who described the late capitalist society in the West — with its market manipulation of "false" consumer needs; its conversion of the "citizen" into the "customer"; its privatization of the individual; its ahistorical focus on the immediate present and its cultural "amnesia" towards the historical past — as aspects of a "one-dimensional society" that most of us currently inhabit.

This tradition resulted in a number of memorable works on mass society, including, for example, Wilhelm Reich's (1970 [1933]) research into the "mass psychology of fascism" and sexual politics; Theodor Adorno's (1964 [1950]) study of the "authoritarian personality," which showed how certain personality types were predisposed to supporting fascist and right-wing political ideologies; Walter Benjamin's (1969 [1935]) studies of the mass media; and Erich Fromm's (1965 [1941]) studies of "alienation," to mention only a few. Some of these works attempted to combine a Marxist perspective with new and more radical interpretations of Freud's ideas. Reich and Fromm used radical psychoanalytic theories to analyze how the subjective life of the individual is repressed, oppressed and manipulated under capitalism. But the greatest achievement of these American years was probably the publication of Marcuse's *One-Dimensional Man*, a treatise on the new forms of power and domination used in contemporary industrial societies. Marcuse's work offers an analysis of capitalism from a neo-Marxian perspective, but one strongly influenced by the writings of Weber and Freud. In many ways, this first generation of critical theorists produced some of the most exciting and innovative studies to come out of the Frankfurt School.

The first-generation critical theorists also focused their attention on one of the most obvious features of contemporary (late) capitalist societies: the prevalence of the consumer culture, which has increasingly morphed into a state of "hyper-consumerism." Hyper-consumerism is reflected in the passion that many of us exhibit when buying new products and in the need we feel to update these products when new versions appear in the marketplace. Many of us develop a fierce attachment, or loyalty, to particular brands or logos. Indeed, it is worth recalling that this over-attachment and idolization of consumer goods is partly what Karl Marx had in mind when he coined the term "commodity fetishism" to describe how individuals were seduced into a kind of secular worship of the goods produced and sold in the capitalist marketplace. And although the early critical theorists (Horkheimer, Adorno, Fromm and Marcuse) originally focused on the social and psychological conditions that accompanied the rise of totalitarian states in both Germany and the USSR, they later broadened their focus to include the rise of what they referred to as the "administered," or "authoritarian," late capitalist societies in the West.

The critical study of how Western societies are able to dominate our lives through applying the techniques of "soft" totalitarianism — including the culture of hyper-consumerism — became a hallmark of the first and second generations of the Frankfurt School. Horkheimer, Adorno and Marcuse documented the rise of "instrumental reason" and the corresponding decline of "practical reason"` in Western societies. Whereas instrumental reason is focused on the attainment of rationally planned and calculated ends without regard to ethical, moral or subjective values, practical reason is motivated by a conscious belief in the value, for its own sake, of some ethical, moral, political, religious or other action, irrespective of its prospects for success. This focus on the struggle between instrumental and practical reason signals the re-appropriation of Weber's earlier distinction between formal, or goal-oriented, rationality (*Zweckrationalität*), versus substantive, or value-oriented, rationality (*Wertrationalität*). Weber's differentiation between these two basic types of rationality had great significance for the critical theorists. For Weber, although formal rationality, or instrumental reason, has realized the promise of greater technical efficiency and progress in the material conditions of social life — through science, technology and rational organization — there was also a darker side to this type of rationality. Weber predicted that the domination of formal rationality and the decline of substantive, or value, rationality would eventually result in what he called the "irrationality of rationality" (see Gronow 1988).

Weber foresaw the possibility that, without the influence of moral, ethical or any other value rationality, formal rationality (based only on technical efficiency) could also be used to accomplish irrational ends that could degrade, depersonalize, dehumanize and even destroy humanity. Today, as we contemplate some of the "irrational" and pathological consequences of a technical progress without moral or ethical values — such as the rise of totalitarian and bureaucratic dictatorships; the Holocaust; the construction of atomic and nuclear weapons; and the growing threats of environmental degradation, climate change and global warming — Weber's early warning of irrationality has never seemed so prescient. The early critical theorists seized upon Weber's critique of technical rationality and, in combination with Hegel's critical analysis of history, along with Marx's critical analysis of capitalist society and Freud's critical analysis of the conscious mind, they developed an interdisciplinary paradigm for the critical study of modern society. A prime example of how the first generation of critical theorists addressed some of the problems of late capitalist society may be seen in the work of Herbert Marcuse.

HERBERT MARCUSE

Herbert Marcuse was one of the most influential critical theorists of the first generation of the Frankfurt School. Along with other Marxist scholars, such as Adorno and Horkheimer, Marcuse was forced to take refuge in the United States during the 1930s when Hitler and the Nazi Party came to power. Of all the critical theorists, Marcuse was probably most committed to a Marxian framework of analysis, even though his own interpretation of Marxism was far from orthodox. Marcuse's work also shows the influence of Weber's theories of society. This is hardly surprising, given the fact that Marcuse was a student of the Hungarian Marxist Georg Lukacs, who had studied under Weber. Marcuse's work draws its characteristic pessimism from the Weberian disenchantment with the rationalization of the modern world. Weber remained highly ambivalent about the role of large bureaucratic organizations in modern societies, and towards the end of his life he became deeply pessimistic that the increasing rationalization of the world would eventually trap humanity in an "iron cage" of modernity. As Weber famously proclaimed, the instrumental rationality of the modern world had succeeded in producing "specialists without spirit, sensualists without heart; this nullity imagines that it has attained a level of civilization never before achieved" (1958: 182). Marcuse incorporated the pessimistic features of Weber's ideas into his own work. He had seen his country swept up in a nationalistic fervour that resulted in the victory of National Socialism and the installation of Adolph Hitler as chancellor of the Third Reich. It was not long before Marcuse and his colleagues of the Frankfurt School had to flee the growing hostility the Nazi state exhibited towards anything remotely influenced by Marxism or sponsored by "cosmopolitan" (read Jewish) intellectuals.

Marcuse's critical study of late capitalism — based in large part on his observations of the United States — is a part philosophical and part sociological analysis of the popular culture, psychology and lifestyle of a contemporary capitalist society. In *One-Dimensional Man*, Marcuse tries to answer the central question of contemporary Marxism: why have modern capitalist societies failed to generate the structural crises that Marx predicted would lead to their collapse and transformation? How have modern capitalist societies remained so resilient? Marcuse sets out to explain why the working classes in these societies are no longer agents of revolutionary change, as they were in the nineteenth and early twentieth centuries. For Marcuse, much of the apparent resilience of late capitalist societies may be traced to the new forms of domination and social control that emerged throughout the twentieth century. These forms of domination are different from earlier forms because they operate not simply in the realm of production but, increasingly, in the realm of consumption. Today, the imperatives of the capitalist system have become fully internalized by the working class through a process referred to by Marcuse as "introjection." The ideology and false consciousness that were once imposed externally on the working class by the ruling class have now become fully internalized and self-maintaining. This historic transformation in the forms of domination corresponds to the growth of the culture of consumerism in late capitalist societies and, through globalization, around the world.

The Allure of Consumerism

The culture of consumerism is central to Marcuse's study of late capitalism. He proposes that the culture of contemporary capitalism is best understood as a one-dimensional society in which most people have lost the ability to think critically about their surroundings or even about their own lives. By "critical thinking," Marcuse means the ability to question the rationality of the real and to ask whether the existing status quo is the best of all possible worlds. In this sense, critical thought refers to a consciousness that can transcend the boundaries of the present and speculate about alternative futures, i.e., whether there are different and perhaps better ways to organize society. The problem with one-dimensional societies — such as our own — is that they seem to lock us into an "eternal present," where we lose the perspectives of both the past and the future. This is what Marcuse means when he talks about "mimetic" behaviour as behaviour that imitates, or is fully conditioned by, the exigencies of the present.

Increasingly, we live in social worlds characterized by social "amnesia," a rapid forgetting of what happened yesterday. This is particularly noticeable in the short attention span of the mass media, whether on television, in the tabloid press or on the internet. The stories of today are forgotten by tomorrow, while the stories of tomorrow are destined to be forgotten by the day after. We live in a world where only the present is real, and only the real is rational. Under these conditions, there appears to be no radical alternative to the status quo, and all discussions of other possible ways of organizing our society are seen as unrealistic, irrational, utopian or even dangerously subversive. Contemporary capitalist society, according to Marcuse, is characterized by a pattern of one-dimensional thought and behaviour that results in mental imprisonment in the present and indefinite complacency and compliance with the established political and economic order. The only way to break free of this one-dimensional consciousness is through the rediscovery of dialectical, or critical, thought, which shows that all things exist in a state of flux and that the present already contains within it the seeds of the future. Dialectical thinking allows us to see that the possible and the potential already exist within the actual, that all things are transformed by history and that nothing ever remains the same. Without critical thought, radical social or political change is literally inconceivable, and thus, impossible.

An important concept introduced by Marcuse is that of "false needs." According to Marcuse, one of the ways in which late capitalist societies differ from earlier capitalist societies may be seen in the forms of social control that are used to dominate and manipulate the working classes. Today, there is less need for externally imposed social controls — such as the army, police and ideologies of religion and politics — because the working classes have fully internalized the values and goals of late capitalism. Nowhere is this acceptance of capitalist values more apparent than in the culture of consumerism. Most of us are caught up in the endless rat race to buy newer and better products — upgrading our electronics, trading-in our cars for the newest models, buying speedboats, ATVs or other "toys," selling and buying houses, donning the latest trends in clothing and so on.

For Marcuse, this endless drive to acquire newer and better commodities is an example of how late capitalist societies generate an infinite number of false needs and thereby facilitate the internalization of the alienation that all of us experience in these societies. Marcuse refers to the need to acquire these commodities as an expression of false needs because the demand for these products is artificially driven by the advertising and marketing departments of the industries that produce and distribute them. The drive to satisfy our false needs has largely replaced our attempts to fulfill our more authentic, or true, needs for personal growth, self-actualization, freedom, autonomy, meaning, purpose and other more liberating and humanizing needs. In fact, private, individualized acquisitive needs often displace public, collective needs for clean environments, safe neighbourhoods and adequate health care, social services and education. Although Marcuse is noticeably reticent about providing examples of "true needs," it is clear that, for him, the satisfaction of false needs integrates us more tightly into, and makes us more dependent upon, the alienated forms of production and consumption of late capitalism; whereas the satisfaction of true needs would serve to advance our individual and collective freedom, autonomy and humanity. In the end, false needs can never be truly satisfied.

Marcuse's critique of consumerism/false needs is linked to his critiques of instrumental reason and positivism/scientism. In common with other members of the Frankfurt School, Marcuse believed that one of the central contradictions of late capitalism was the gradual eclipse of "practical reason" (or what Max Weber called "substantive rationality") by instrumental reason (or "formal rationality"). By practical reason, Marcuse meant the rationality associated with the Enlightenment values of freedom, self-knowledge, autonomy and humanity. By "instrumental reason," he meant the rationality associated with science, technology, efficiency, productivity and profitability. Under the conditions of late capitalism, Marcuse saw that the struggles for individual and collective freedom, autonomy, meaning and purpose have been overshadowed by the drive for increasing efficiency, productivity and profitability. The domination of technology is no longer externally imposed on a resistant and recalcitrant working class, as was the case in the nineteenth century. Today, the demands of technology have become fully internalized, or "introjected," into the popular consciousness (as false needs); the masses are now fully complicit in their own social subjugation and exploitation.

Technological Rationality and Social Irrationality

For Marcuse, the Enlightenment age, when the goal of practical reason had been the emancipation of the individual, has long since been transformed into an age in which the goal of instrumental reason is the domination and control of the individual by technology. No aspect of the social world has escaped the power of technological rationality, or instrumental reason, and in our present age, every effort is made to fit the individual into society according to the demands of modern corporate technology. Under such conditions, individual potential for self-actualization is sacrificed to the need for increasing efficiency, productivity, profitability and technological rationality. The machine is no longer made for people; people are now made for the machine.

Such is the gloomy picture Marcuse paints of the modern world. Reason has been turned upside down. Instead of leading to the self-development of individuals, reason now leads to their domination by technological forces of production over which they are no longer able to exercise any effective control. There is a strong undertone of Marx's theory of aliena- tion in Marcuse's critical account of modern technology, which, when combined with Weber's ambivalence towards modernity, produces a strikingly pessimistic view of the world.

The drive for ever greater efficiency, which underlies the growth of technological rationality, has become a pervasive and inescapable feature of the modern world. Although the Holocaust may have provided the most horrific modern example of the power of heartless instrumental reason (see Bauman 1989), this rationality has now pervaded all mod- ern industrial societies. Thus, Marcuse's account cannot simply be seen as a critique of fascism, or even of capitalism, for he was later to write a further critique of Soviet society in which he targeted the bureaucratic system of state socialism (Marcuse 1958). The target of Marcuse's criti- cism, therefore, is any example of modern industrial society in which technological rationality has overshadowed the needs of the individual for self-development and any society in which technological rationality also creates false needs. It is in this sense that Marcuse refers to all such societies (whether fascist, communist, social-democratic or liberal capi- talist) as "totalitarian" — either "hard" totalitarian or "soft" totalitarian.

Current examples of the omnipresent power of technology would have to include the impact on our lives of telecommunications and digital forms of connectivity, including mobile phones and tablets and sites such as Facebook, Twitter, Snapchat, WhatsApp, Instagram etc. What we have seen over the past twenty years or so is the decline of the mass media and the rise of social media. Whereas the mass media (such as national newspapers, movies, major TV news channels, documentary programs etc.) involved the centralized transmission of news and information to a decentralized audience of numerous individual viewers or readers, social media now involve both the decentralized transmission and the decentralized reception of news, information and other forms of digital communication. Although this decentralized technology allows for greater freedom of communication, it also provides far greater scope for both cor- porate and state surveillance and manipulation of all members of society.

This surveillance can be conducted in many ways: tracking individual visits to websites, emails, cell phone activity and movement or travel through smart-phone GPS records. In addition to these personal communication devices, the movements of individuals are also tracked in many urban areas through CCTV (or CCC, closed circuit cameras) mounted in many city locations. Some indication of the vast potential scope of this so-called "dragnet" state surveillance of the individual was exposed by Edward Snowden, a former Central Intelligence Agency (CIA) employee and contractor for the United States government, who copied and leaked classified information from the National Security Agency (NSA) in 2013. His disclosures of the NSA files to the *Guardian* newspaper revealed numerous global surveillance programs, many run by the United States' NSA and the Five Eyes intelligence alliance, also including Australia's ASD, New Zealand's GCSB, the UK's GCHQ and Canada's CSEC, with the cooperation of telecommunication companies and European governments. Snowden showed that

> the NSA was harvesting millions of email and instant messaging contact lists, searching email content, tracking and mapping the location of cell phones, undermining attempts at encryption, and that the agency was using cookies to piggyback on the same tools used by Internet advertisers "to pinpoint targets for government hacking and to bolster surveillance." The NSA was shown to be secretly accessing Yahoo and Google data centres to collect information from hundreds of millions of account holders worldwide by tapping undersea cables using the MUSCULAR surveillance program. (Wikipedia n.d.)

One useful source of information on Snowden's revelations is provided by Glenn Greenwald, an American journalist and author known for his role in a series of reports on American and British global surveillance programs, in his 2014 book *No Place to Hide*.

The rise of social media provides countless members of society with new and convenient forms of interpersonal connectivity that overcome the barriers of time and space as never before. At the same time, this new technology also provides both governments and private corporations with unprecedented means for spying on individuals in ways that not even Marcuse had dreamt of. In this respect, the new technology has brought all of us closer to the sinister world envisioned by George Orwell in his dystopic novel *Nineteen Eighty-Four*. This point was forcibly made by the British journalist Rachel Holmes (2016) in a review of the increasing power of the online technology of social media to monitor our personal preferences and to use this information for crass commercial interests:

> The technology we thought we were using to make life more efficient started using us some time ago. It is now attempting to reshape our social behaviour into patterns reminiscent of the total surveillance culture of the medieval village, East Germany under the Stasi, or the white supremacist state of South Africa in which I grew up.... In an increasingly online everyday life, our use of social media has become a medium for normalising the acceptability of intrusion and behavioural correction. We are bombarded by "helpful recommendations" on education, health, relationships, taxes and leisure matched to our tracked user profiles that nudge us towards products and services to make us better citizen consumers. The app told you that you only took 100 steps today. The ad for the running shoes will arrive tomorrow.

Towards the end of *One-Dimensional Man*, Marcuse speculates on how the conditions of technological rationality might actually pave the way for an eventual democratization and humanization of society. Because technology brings with it the potential to abolish scarcity and liberate human beings from material want, Marcuse allows himself to project the possibility of a future in which the domination of technology has given way to the collective self-development of all groups in society. There is a real sense, however, in which Marcuse's account reflects a tension between the pessimism of his critical theory and the optimism of his Marxism. In his later writings, Marcuse resolved this tension in favour of the pessimism of his critical theory. Whereas for Marx, technology was a sword with a double edge — a means of oppression and exploitation in the hands of the bourgeoisie, but also a means of emancipation in the hands of the workers — for Marcuse, technology is primarily only a means of domination.

There are very few ways to escape from the one-dimensional trap of instrumental reason. According to Marcuse, even the working class — the historical agent of revolutionary change — has lost its revolutionary potential and is now fully integrated into the structures of late capitalism. What, if any, is the point of resistance to one-dimensional society? On this question, Marcuse is far from clear. At the individual level, he suggests that personal acts of rejection and resistance are still possible for those who have not fully internalized the norms of late capitalism. More collective forms of resistance will only come, according to Marcuse, from the margins of society. During the 1960s, when *One-Dimensional Man* was written, the most spectacular acts of protest came from student, civil rights, anti-war and racialized groups. These groups had little or no investment in the status quo (no mortgages, no pensions, no jobs), i.e., they were the least integrated into the consumerism of late capitalist society. And during the 1960s, the popularity of Macuse's writings made him almost a "patron saint" of the student protest and other activist movements. But this celebrity status among radical students also earned him notoriety among university administrators. In 1965, Marcuse was fired from Brandeis University for his radical views before he joined the philosophy department at the University California, San Diego, where he supervised civil-rights activist and Black feminist Angela Davis as a graduate student. Marcuse's radical views drew the ire of other groups, including the American Legion, as well as death threats from the Ku Klux Klan (see Castro 2013).

Today, other protest groups have arisen from the margins of contemporary society, including anti-racist movements like Black Lives Matter, Indigenous sovereignty movements like Idle No More and social and economic justice movements like Occupy, as well as radicalized intellectuals and political activists. There are also grassroots feminist groups such as #MeToo and Time's Up, the LGBTQ movement, animal rights groups, new environmental groups such as Extinction Rebellion (XR), anti-gun violence groups like March For Our Lives and many others, as well as urban revolts and rural rustbelt rebellions from the poor, unemployed and disenfranchised. It is from these marginal groups that we are most likely to see the impetus for what Marcuse called the "Great Refusal," during which the cracks in our contemporary social world will begin to appear.

THE SECOND GENERATION

At the end of the Second World War, the leading theorists of the Frankfurt School returned to Germany, where they re-established the Institute for Social Research. But some of the earlier theorists found it difficult to adjust to the new conditions of postwar Germany. Adorno, in particular, was uncomfortable with the anti-Vietnam War mobilizations and student protests of the 1960s, and he was dismissed by many student radicals as far too conservative. At the same time, however, the student activism of the 1960s and 1970s gave rise to a whole new generation of critical theorists. This second generation is most often associated with the work of its leading representative, Jürgen Habermas.

JÜRGEN HABERMAS

More than any other theorist, Jürgen Habermas represents the development of the Frankfurt tradition during the last quarter of the twentieth century. However, Habermas's work signals a growing departure of Frankfurt critical social theory from its Marxian roots. Whereas the earlier generation of theorists largely repudiated what they labelled the "bourgeois" sociological tradition, Habermas has tried to integrate his ideas with some of the main schools of modern sociological theory, and his work may be seen as an elaborate synthesis of a number of distinctive theoretical traditions, especially those of structural functionalism and systems theory. This makes Habermas a challenging theorist to read, for his work demands a certain level of theoretical erudition (i.e., the ability to spot different intellectual influences).

Habermas's analysis of late capitalist society represents a blend of critical theory, structural functionalism and modern systems theory, with a dash of phenomenology thrown in. Habermas is sometimes described as a systems theorist, albeit one with a critical neo-Marxian perspective. Much of his most recent work was influenced by the two leading social systems theorists of our time: Talcott Parsons (from the United States) and Niklas Luhmann (from Germany). Habermas has tried to use his own perspective to analyze the different systems that hold late capitalist societies together and to identify the sources of tension within and between these systems. He is also interested in showing how the systemic structures of the state, and of large corporations, increasingly "colonize" the private spaces of our own "lifeworlds." Throughout his work, Habermas has continued to see himself as a late representative of the modernist tradition — as a critical modernist — at a time when this tradition has been under attack from postmodernist, irrational and conservative forces in society. In the face of these attacks, Habermas has tried to uphold and keep alive the "emancipatory project" of modernity: the Enlightenment belief in the capacity of reason to free us from ideological, political, technological and economic forms of domination.

In his early work, Habermas traced the decline of what he called the "public sphere" (local spaces of free and open criticism, discussion and mobilization of popular opinion) and its gradual eclipse by the growing power of the state and large corporations. His later work includes a critique of positivism in the social sciences (a theme that had earlier been explored by Horkheimer and Adorno), as well as a classification of different types of knowledge (empirical/analytic; historical/hermeneutic; critical/emancipatory) and their underlying human interests. Habermas became famous for his "communication theory of society," a perspective that borrows heavily from other intellectual traditions, such as linguistics, systems theory, hermeneutics and phenomenology. Since the advent of Habermas's communication theory of society (or "universal pragmatics"), the legacy of the Frankfurt school has split into a number of perspectives, many of which continue to claim some affiliation with the tradition of critical social theory. Although the original distinctive tradition of the Frankfurt School has been overtaken by more contemporary theorists, some of the defining themes of critical theory have endured. Among these are (1) the critique of positivism; (2) the conflict between instrumental reason (strategic or purposive-rational action) and practical reason (communicative action); and (3) the domination of civil society by the state and large corporations — or what Habermas calls the colonization of the "lifeworld" by the "system."

Habermas also provides us with a striking example of what we may call "a public intellectual" — someone who has intervened on numerous occasions in the significant theoretical debates of our time. Among his many interventions, Habermas has debated the issues of positivism with students of the philosopher Karl Popper; hermeneutics with Hans Gadamer; systems theory with Niklas Luhmann; student politics with the German SDS (Socialist German Student Union); Holocaust denial with German revisionist historians; and postmodernism with Jean-Francois Lyotard. Besides these academic debates, Habermas has commented on other pressing public issues, such as German reunification, the collapse of communism and the legacy of Nazism.

For Habermas and others in this second generation, the overwhelming existential, philosophical and moral problem of the postwar world was the terrible legacy of the Holocaust and the sense of national guilt felt among

Germans for the Nazi wartime crimes against humanity. This legacy dominated literary, artistic and cultural life in postwar Germany, and in much of Europe, and cast a long shadow over the social sciences — including the ideas of the critical theorists. The theory and practice (the ideology and politics) of the second generation of critical theory were inexorably shaped by a sense of collective guilt for the Holocaust and by the need to atone for it and prevent any future repetition of these terrible events. These concerns motivated many social theorists and social scientists in the immediate postwar era, and none more than Habermas. The shadow of the Holocaust can be seen in much of Habermas's early work, and it determined many of his intellectual priorities and choices. Habermas's version of critical theory and his later communication theory of society are characterized by a number of features that express his postwar sensibilities: (1) his "internationalism," i.e., the assimilation of Anglo-American traditions of social theory and the avoidance of any parochial German nationalist theory; (2) his "constitutionalism," i.e., the emphasis on legal and constitutional rights and the focus on deliberative democracy and universal principles of justice; and (3) his "universalism" and his hostility to postmodernism and poststructuralism, i.e., the rejection of moral or epistemological relativism and pluralism and the commitment to moral and ethical universalism.

More recently, Habermas has contributed to other public debates , including those related to the "cosmopolitan project" of the European Union; the 2008 debt crisis within the Eurozone; the plight of refugees and migrants to Europe; and the growth of populist and far-right political parties and social movements — especially after the UK referendum on Brexit in 2016 and the 2016 election of Donald Trump as president of the US. In this respect, there has been an admirable consistency between what Habermas has preached in theory and what he has practised in his own life work (see, for example, Habermas 2016a, 2016b).

As with most major theorists, Habermas's ideas have evolved over the course of his intellectual career. But there is an underlying thread linking the writings of many critical theorists, including those of Marcuse and Habermas. The work of these writers can often best be understood as a response to the question: Why is it that the advanced industrial capitalist states have not become springboards for socialist revolutions in the way that Marx fully expected? Much of the work of critical theorists has tried to account for the apparent resilience of late capitalism and its success in securing the loyalty and consent of the working classes. In one way or another, this question is an underlying theme, or problematic, in the work of both Marcuse and Habermas. But whereas Marcuse incorporated Freudian psychological concepts, such as "repressive desublimation" and "introjection," to explain how the capitalist ruling class had successfully manipulated the working class to "internalize" the ideology of capitalism in a "one-dimensional society," Habermas introduced linguistic and phenomenological concepts, such as "systematically distorted communication" and "colonization of the lifeworld," to account for the erosion of the "public sphere" and the domination of corporate power in late capitalist society.

Like all major theorists, Habermas has passed through a number of stages in his work: his early interest in a theory of knowledge, his middle interest in reconstructing the foundations of historical materialism and his later interest in developing a theory of communicative action. One persistent theme for Habermas that has haunted much of his sociological theory is how the demands of instrumental reason (or what Habermas calls strategic, or rational-purposive, action) and practical reason (or communicative action) can be reconciled in advanced industrial societies. Although the terminology for addressing this theme has changed at different points in his work, an understanding of the centrality of this issue for Habermas gives us a key with which to unlock his academic writing.

Throughout his work, Habermas's main objective has been to defend the emancipatory project of Enlightenment rationalism and to show how the power of reason can be used to liberate and progressively humanize social relations in the contemporary world. In this respect, Habermas departs from the first generation of critical theorists — especially Horkheimer, Adorno and Marcuse — who emphasized the power of instrumental reason to dominate ordinary members of society and subject them to "totally administered" or "one-dimensional" forms of technical control, market manipulation, economic determinism and political domination. In contrast, Habermas reminds us that reason has always been two-sided: it can be used for the liberation and emancipation of humanity or for its domination and control.

Erosion of the Public Sphere

The prevalence of popular protest and social activism in the 1960s and thereafter persuaded Habermas that even though the political power of the state and enormous wealth of the big corporations exercised considerable control over ordinary members of society, this domination was far from total. There were still sectors of society where state or corporate control had not fully penetrated and where resistance to this control was still possible. In his earlier work, Habermas traced the origins of civil society, especially areas of free and open discussion, deliberation and debate, to the growth of the "public sphere," the coffee shops and literary salons, as well as to the newspapers and broadsheets of early modern (eighteenth century) Europe (Habermas 1989 [1962]).

Habermas's early work on the importance of the public sphere established a theme that was continued through much of his later work. Habermas argues that in late capitalist society social forces have eroded the public sphere, that public space in which the free exchange of ideas takes place. With the expansion of corporate, state and bureaucratic control over our lives, Habermas believes that our opportunities to exert democratic and rational control over our social institutions have been progressively diminished. Rational discussion and criticism have gradually been displaced by the demands and exigencies of economic efficiency, technological necessity and political and administrative expedience. There are many examples of this trend towards the growing instrumental rationality in modern societies. Discussions of free trade and neoliberal corporate globalization are driven by the arguments of economic inevitability and business rationality — in the face of much popular opposition. Even on a local level, full public discussion over health care, education and environmental issues is often shortcircuited by government appeals to "economic realism" or corporate appeals to "sound business strategy."

Among other things, Habermas suggests that social actors who confront each other from radically different positions of power will find it difficult, if not impossible, to reach intersubjective understanding or consensus. Habermas suggests that the public sphere for democratic discussion is in danger of being overtaken by the demands, or imperatives, of the state and big business. The space for communicative interaction has fallen increasingly under the shadow of political-administrative domination and control and under the ruling media of power and money. There are significant long-term problems associated with the erosion of the public sphere, and one of the most serious of these, according to Habermas, how the "system" (the state and large corporations) can secure the loyalty and consent of social actors when these actors no longer believe that the system works in their best interests. When the experiences of social actors in their lifeworlds come into serious contradiction with the needs of system-integration, this may well result in what Habermas calls a "legitimation crisis" for the state.

Habermas's early focus on the growth of the public sphere later evolved into a study of how the free and intersubjective lifeworld of the individual in society was gradually dominated and constricted by the overarching power of the system — these anti-democratic forces of state and corporate bureaucracies. His later discussions of the problem of "distorted communication" owe much to his earlier concerns about the erosion of the public sphere. For Habermas, "systematically distorted communication" refers to the constraints imposed on the exchange of ideas and on the production of knowledge by unequal power relations. Whether we are talking about the relations between Palestinians and Israelis in the Occupied Territories, the relations between Indigenous Peoples and politicians here in Canada, or the attempts by gun control advocates in the US to pressure the government to enact gun control legislation and resist the influence of the National Rifle Association and its political lobbyists, we are a long way from enjoying what Habermas calls an "ideal speech situation." An ideal speech situation is, for Habermas, a model of political and social relations in which free and undistorted communication on the basis of a deliberative democratic consensus is possible and realizable.

Critical Communication Theory of Society

Habermas's career has spanned over six decades, from the 1960s until the present. Much of his work has focused on the reconstruction of historical materialism into a critical theory of communicative action. Whereas Marx placed the category of "labour" at the centre of his emancipatory theory of social change, Habermas places "communicative action" at the centre of his own theory. For Habermas, social emancipation implies a condition of "non-distorted communication" in which the free and open communication between individuals and social groups is no longer mediated by inequalities of power or wealth. This is a far more general understanding of social emancipation than that proposed by orthodox Marxists. For orthodox Marxists, emancipation has always meant the socialization of the technological and organizational forces of production, the overthrow of capitalist relations of production and an end to alienated forms of labour. For Habermas, however, as with earlier members of the Frankfurt School, the alienation and exploitation of labour under capitalism are seen as particular cases of a more general problem: the dominance of strategic action, or instrumental reason, over all other forms of rational action in society. This is the key to understanding Habermas's theory of society and to his framework for connecting the social actor to the social structures of society.

Concern with the domination of instrumental reason (variously expressed as scientism or positivism, and more generally as economic or technological determinism) has continued to preoccupy Habermas in his later works. In his book *Legitimation Crisis*, Habermas distinguishes two sectors of our contemporary social worlds: "system" and "lifeworld." As we have already mentioned, system refers to those large-scale, top-down processes that govern our lives from above. Decisions made by governments and by private corporations may have far-reaching consequences for us and for those around us, but as ordinary citizens, most of these decisions are arrived at without any real discussion or participation on our part. The decisions are often justified in the name of greater efficiency, technological necessity and economic or political realism. These decisions are driven by what Habermas calls "strategic action," or "instrumental rationality." In contrast, the lifeworld is that sector of our lives — including family, friends, community and other informal social and cultural relations — in which the processes of communication and interaction play an important role. Within the lifeworld, social actors try to reach agreement or consensus through intersubjective understanding. While the system is characterized by social relations of domination and technical efficiency, the lifeworld is characterized by social relations of communicative (inter)action and consensus. For Habermas, one of the most serious problems of contemporary capitalist society is that of the "colonization" of the lifeworld by the system.

Colonization of the Lifeworld by the System

According to Habermas, the world of the social actor is formed within the lifeworld. The lifeworld, for all of us, is the world of subjectively meaningful social action, in which our self-understandings are formed and our informal interaction and communication with others takes place. This is the world of communicative action, or practical reason. The system, by contrast, refers to the more objective structures of our society that dominate and formally regulate our actions in many different ways. We are regulated through bureaucracies, the criminal code, our employment contracts, our financial ties and obligations and the manifold requirements of administrative authorities. The system, therefore, is the world of strategic action, or instrumental reason. For Habermas, the problem of connecting "agency" to "structure" is seen most sharply in the "colonization of the lifeworld." This expression refers to the tendency of the impersonal objectified forces of the system to invade the world of the individual social actor. The strategic (instrumental) rationality of the system is characterized by the goals of efficiency, calculability, predictability and control (Ritzer 1996). The communicative (practical) rationality of the lifeworld, on the other hand, is characterized by such goals as freedom, self-understanding, personal growth, sociality and humanity. Living in modern societies, most of us have experienced how growing state and corporate power can penetrate and intervene in our lives and regulate our everyday activities. Those who hold the power and the purse-strings exert undue influence on the decisions of stakeholders while bypassing consensus-oriented communication, or rational dialogue, which is characteristic of the lifeworld. The lifeworld is thus devalued and becomes less important in the daily lives of people. In the context of Habermas's ideas, the struggle for free and open communication and for social interaction undistorted by inequalities of power and wealth may be seen as a reformulation of the classical Marxian notion of class struggle. It has become the historic struggle of the twenty-first century.

The colonization of the lifeworld by the administrative, corporate and technical systems of society has also resulted in the restriction or even blockage of possibilities for communicative action. The relatively free and open channels of communication once associated with the lifeworld, within the public sphere, are increasingly dominated by the authoritarian media of power and money. The colonization of the lifeworld has led to social relations characterized by "systematically distorted communication." An example of the colonization of the lifeworld may be seen in the attempts by the Republican Party in the US to dismantle Obamacare (Affordable Health Act) in order to divert funds to their tax reform bill for the wealthy — even though the majority of ordinary Americans are opposed to these health-care cuts. In Canada, the decision to construct the

Keystone XL and Kinder Morgan Trans-Mountain oil pipelines — over the protests of Indigenous Peoples and environmentalists — could also serve as an example of the colonization of the lifeworld (of local communities) by the system (of government and oil companies). What Habermas suggests is that the opportunities for reaching consensus between individual and collective social actors through rational deliberation and discussion are diminishing. The "validity claims" of arguments advanced in discussions and debates are more likely to be assessed — and accepted or rejected — in terms of the authority or profitability of these claims, rather than by rigorous evaluation of the supporting evidence.

The problem of systematically distorted communication may be understood as a metaphor for the growth of authoritarian and anti-democratic institutions in contemporary societies, and Habermas believes that the public should struggle to restore free and open channels of communication in all sectors of our society and thereby advance towards what he calls an "ideal speech situation." An ideal speech situation is one in which all speakers, or interlocutors, have an equal right to be heard and where all arguments, or validity claims, are judged on their intrinsic (empirical and factual) merits, not on the wealth or power of those who advance them. In other words, it is through extending the areas of free and open discourse in our society that we can deepen and broaden our democratic rights and freedoms.

In many ways, the best example for Habermas's ideal speech situation and, by extension, his model for a deliberative, democratic and rational society, may be found in the scientific community. In their debates (i.e., in presenting their competing validity claims) over what can and cannot be accepted as proven scientific fact, scientists are expected to appeal only to observable (empirical or logical) evidence. They are not entitled to appeal to traditional, popular or institutionalized religious or political beliefs in support of their validity claims. Nor are they entitled to appeal to expedient economic interests in their objective evaluation of evidence. Scientific disagreements are normally resolved through a dispassionate assessment of the data, and scientific consensus is built upon these procedures. Another example of an ideal speech situation suggested by some theorists is the World Social Forums, originally held at Porto Alegre, Brazil. These popular forums (which are held as counter-forums to official government-sponsored World Economic Forums of the G-8 and G-20) encourage the free and open communication between speakers and audiences.

Some critics have taken Habermas to task for promoting what they consider to be an oversimplified and highly idealized view of science. Several historians and philosophers of science (for example, Paul Feyerabend [1975]) have been quick to observe that the actual practices of scientists often fail to live up to the high-minded principles of science. According to these critics, scientists have at various times throughout the history of science resorted to deception, fraud, dogma and even outright coercion to justify their knowledge claims. In this respect, it would seem that science remains as vulnerable to corruption as any other human institution.

It does not require much imagination to apply Habermas's critical communication theory to some of the events currently unfolding in the world. Many critics cite the trend towards neoliberal corporate globalization as an example of the increasing colonization of our lifeworlds by the demands for greater system integration. Most of the transnational free trade agreements have been signed by governments without regard for the concerns of average citizens over the possible loss of their jobs through out-sourcing and off-shoring to low wage economies in the Global South. The demands of economic efficiency and political necessity have far outweighed concerns for democratic or popular consultation. And, although the anti-globalization and global justice movements — as seen in Seattle, Quebec City, New York, Genoa, and other places — once seemed to have the potential to create legitimation crises in many societies around the world, this potential appears to have faded in recent years. Today, it may well be younger environmental groups — such as Extinction Rebellion (XR) — that are more likely to trigger a political crisis. The popular grassroots resistance to both major political parties in the 2016 US election, expressed in the campaigns of both Bernie Sanders and Donald Trump, and the Brexit referendum to withdraw the UK from the European Union, are further indications of ordinary citizens feeling alienated from the political and economic elites who currently control the centres of power and wealth — or what Habermas calls the system.

Late Capitalist Societies
In addition to his critical communication theory of society, Habermas also analyzes the structures of late capitalist societies in more conventional sociological terms. His analysis owes as much to the perspectives of structural functionalism and systems theory as it does to Marxism. Habermas

outlines what he believes to be the basic systems of a late capitalist society and identifies the inherent crises that periodically destabilize these societies. He begins his account of the structure of late capitalist society by distinguishing three different systems for the purposes of analysis.

The first system of all contemporary capitalist societies is the "economic system," which is made up of three different sectors: the public and monopolistic (corporate) sectors, both of them primarily capital intensive (such as the oil, electronics, aerospace, armaments industries) and the competitive sector, which is primarily labour intensive (such as the retail and distributive and service industries). The public and monopolistic industries tended in the recent past to offer employment in what is sometimes referred to as a "primary labour market," characterized by relatively high wages, job security, career paths, collective agreements, full benefits packages, pensions and so on. The competitive sector, on the other hand, tends to offer employment in a "secondary labour market," characterized by relatively low-wage and frequently dead-end employment, in which positions are typically temporary or casual, precarious, unprotected by collective agreements and without full benefits.

The second system, the "administrative" system, refers to those structures and functions of the state apparatus that are responsible for regulating and planning the business environment of late capitalist societies. This is seen to be the joint responsibility of public and private sectors of the economy. This has been the case in the United States since the end of the Great Depression, when the Democratic administration of Theodore Roosevelt launched the New Deal, and in Great Britain since the end of the Second World War, when the Labour government of Clement Attlee introduced the National Health Service and other provisions of the welfare state. Today, the governments of most late capitalist societies play an active role in managing many aspects of the economy. Such measures include the regulation and direction of investment, the provision of loans or subsidies to businesses, the tendering of government contracts to private sector companies, establishing price guarantees through marketing boards, the legislation and enforcement of environmental regulations, the review of unfair trade practices, foreign ownership and anti-monopoly commissions and so forth. In addition to these direct interventions, most governments work to stabilize the economy indirectly through investments in the material and social infrastructure of the nation (roads, housing, education, research and development etc.). By sharing the responsibilities for planning economic growth with the private sector, governments of late capitalist societies try to prevent the dangerous instabilities of earlier business cycles, which alternated between periods of growth and periods of recession (boom and bust). The purpose of the state, therefore, is to stabilize the economic system and to minimize the downward swings of regular business cycles. Today, with neoliberal economic policies that began with Ronald Reagan in the US and Margaret Thatcher in the UK, many Western governments have abandoned the earlier policies of welfare capitalism in favour of deregulation, privatization of public enterprises, cuts to social services and corporate tax cuts. These policies have eroded the welfare state and the safety nets and protections for low income and vulnerable members of society.

The third system, the "legitimation system," is the main focus of Habermas's analysis. In his classification, the legitimation system refers to the political and ideological superstructures of the Western states — the system of liberal democracy and its associated set of values and beliefs — through which the governments of late capitalist societies secure the consent and compliance of the governed. According to Habermas, it is through the legitimation system that the ruling classes of these societies develop the strategies and mechanisms for gaining the mass loyalty of the population and for defusing the tensions and conflicts that could otherwise lead to wholesale dissatisfaction and revolt against the capitalist system.

The legitimation of the ruling class is typically achieved through emphasizing the individual civil rights of citizens (such as voting rights, freedom of speech, property rights, collective bargaining and trade union rights etc.) while de-emphasizing the need for active participation in the political and economic institutions of the nation. Members of society are increasingly encouraged to define themselves in terms of their individual identities (as members of families, churches, ethnic, racial, sexual or gender groups) rather than their collective social, political or economic identities (as citizens, workers or consumers). Habermas refers to this emphasis on (passive) individual identities and the corresponding de-emphasis of (active) class or collective group relations as "civic privatism" — an important part of the mechanism of class compromise. Civic privatism emphasizes intimate relationships, as well as a strong focus on personal life, and the consumption of goods and services at the expense of civic involvement. This withdrawal from civic culture leads to a surrender of public life to institutions, interest groups, corporations and powerful individuals like Rupert Murdoch, Donald Trump and the Koch brothers in the US, and Jim Pattison (business magnate), David Thompson (media mogul), the Irving family (oil, pulp and paper) and Galen Weston (food processing, sales and distribution) in Canada, and others who control information and the media and who have the power to influence and manipulate public opinion. In this respect, civic privatism erodes the capacity of publics to participate in any deliberative democratic process. In Habermas's words, "Issues of political discourse become assimilated into and absorbed by the modes and contents of entertainment. Besides personalization, the dramatization of events, the simplification of complex matters, and the vivid polarization of conflicts promote civic privatism and a mood of antipolitics" (2006: 27).

In late capitalist societies, the management of industrial conflict (in the monopolistic and public sector industries) through such compromises as collective bargaining and price administration has destroyed working-class solidarity in a number of ways. Besides the growing segmentation of the labour force into high- and low-wage sectors, the monopolistic control of the economy has led to a permanent crisis in government finances, in which private sector companies have fought to advance the process of capital accumulation at the expense of public sector institutions. The social costs of maintaining profitable rates of accumulation (especially in the face of global competition) have been passed down to the working class. Because these costs are experienced as differential problems for particular constituencies (the sick, the elderly, the unemployed, the homeless, the racialized, commuters, consumers, students, parents), the effect of these costs is to divide the population into special interest groups and to further destroy the basis for more general working-class unity and solidarity. In this way, late (or organized) capitalism compels us to define ourselves as individuals (rather than as members of the working class) and to seek individual solutions to our political and economic (structural) problems.

Crises of Late Capitalism

Having distinguished the economic, administrative and legitimation systems, Habermas also identifies what he considers to be the main global and domestic crises facing late capitalist societies. According to Habermas, four major crises threaten the organization and stability of the present world capitalist system.

Figure 5-2: Crises of Late Capitalist Society

1. The crisis in the *ecological balance* is brought on by the problem (or what earlier Marxists would have called the "contradiction") of reconciling the two different needs, or imperatives, of the world capitalist system:

    · the continual need for economic growth and the accumulation of capital, which has always been achieved through the exploitation of natural resources; and

    · the need for environmental protection and conservation, especially as this relates to the depletion of non-renewable energy resources, and to the long-term degradation of the environment.

    For Habermas, the growing need to set environmentally friendly limits to economic growth (in order to deal with such major ecological problems as pollution, deforestation, the climate crisis) means that in the future, economic decisions will have to be made more by rational social planning than by the marketplace. This need for more centralized social planning, in Habermas's view, will be very difficult to satisfy within any capitalist system in which production for profit remains paramount.

2. The crisis in the *anthropological balance* refers generally to the increasing problem that many late capitalist societies are already experiencing in successfully socializing their members into the values and norms that have traditionally motivated and morally regulated

social participation. We can already see evidence of this crisis in our own society. When government cutbacks result in underfunded schools and unemployment in the public and private sectors, many students become increasingly cynical about the need for high school or college education. Matriculation certificates or university degrees are no longer guarantees of future employment in a world in which good jobs have become increasingly scarce. In the same way, Habermas believes, other traditional norms and values that have served to legitimate participation in capitalist society, such as the work ethic, will lose their power to motivate and regulate the actions of members of society.

3. The crisis of the *international balance* refers to the way in which the stockpiling of nuclear weapons has led to the real danger of global destruction through a thermonuclear war. As Habermas sees it, the pressure to produce nuclear and other high technology weaponry comes from the long-term need of late capitalist societies to advance the process of capital accumulation (in the monopolistic/public sectors of the economic system) through the state's demand for non-productive goods. The armament industries are driven as much by the need for capital accumulation as they are by the need for national security. For this reason, late capitalist societies will find it difficult to dismantle these industries without radically reorganizing their privatized ownership, even when external threats to national security have been removed (as with the fall of the communist states and the end of the Cold War). However, as we have recently seen, the removal of one threat, such as the former USSR, may be replaced by another threat, a resurgent nationalist Russia.

4. The *legitimation crisis* refers to how the state secures the loyalty and commitment of the population to work within the structures of late capitalism. According to Habermas, it is the need for increasing efficiency in the process of capital accumulation that comes into conflict with the need for legitimation. The need for increasing efficiency is met by the intervention of the state, through the administrative system, which attempts to coordinate, regulate and stimulate the business environment of late capitalism. However, although the activity of the state may eliminate the worst features of traditional business cycles, this is only accomplished at a price. This price, paid by the working classes, takes the form of perma-

nent inflation, financial crisis (as in balance of payments, national deficit, national debt, public and private bankruptcy etc.) and the long-term impoverishment of the public sector (through cutbacks in education, health care, public transportation, social services etc.). Thus, there is an almost paradoxical sense in which the expansion of the role of the state in late capitalist societies brings with it an ever-increasing need for legitimation.

In its efforts to rationalize the planning and steering of societal structures and institutions for the efficient accumulation of capital, the state may challenge established values and practices that have become embedded in the traditional culture of capitalism. At such points, the efficiency needs of late capitalism come into conflict with the cultural values of traditional capitalism. Conflict brings with it the danger that the traditional mechanisms for socializing the population into the culture of capitalism may break down, causing a crisis of legitimation. In crisis, traditional ideologies that have functioned to integrate members of society into the structures of late capitalism may be abandoned in favour of alternative and more radical prescriptions for social action.

In many ways, these possibilities are already beginning to unfold in Western societies. The administrative needs of the capitalist state, which have led to unemployment and underemployment and cutbacks in health care, education and social services, have already generated legitimation "emergencies" that always threaten to become "crises." We have seen the popular protest vote in the US which led to the election Trump. Similarly, in many European states, far-right nationalist and fascist parties have capitalized on the discontent and despair of disgruntled voters who fear for their jobs and strongly oppose immigration into their countries. The Brexit vote in the UK is yet a further indication of a developing legitimation crisis: in which whole regions of the population appear to have lost confidence in the urban political elites who run the country. Some writers have described these protests and social divisions as evidence of a "revolution of falling expectations" (see, for example, Goldhammer 2016). And for Habermas, the legitimation crisis has become the central crisis of late capitalism.

Habermas's Politics

Habermas has projected many of his theoretical commitments into his practical politics — i.e., his political *praxis*. He sees the still-incomplete project of the European Union as a continuation of the Enlightenment "emancipatory logic" of communicative action and rationality and as an example of a "deliberative democracy " — although not without its serious faults. For better or worse, the European Union, with its open borders, single market and single currency, remains for Habermas the best defence against a resurgence of xenophobic nationalism and fascism in Europe.

In place of nationalism, which has long been the driving force in international affairs, Habermas calls for what he refers to as "constitutional patriotism." Unlike nationalism, which places the interests of a particular nation, or ethnic group, above all other interests, Habermas suggests that the time has come to place the rule and procedures of law (the constitution) over and above all other political or economic interests and motivations. According to Habermas, only when the rule and procedures of law (both nationally and internationally) become the final arbiters of human conduct can societies elevate the principles of communicative action above those of instrumental, or strategic, rational action. Towards this end, constitutional patriotism represents the highest development of communicative action within the nation state, while "cosmopolitan constitutionalism" represents the highest embodiment of communicative action between nation states within the international community.

The closest actual example of Habermas's idea of cosmopolitan constitutionalism is the European Union. However, in view of the opposition of some European states — notably France and the Netherlands — to endorsing a common European constitution, even this is not a perfect example. But in principle, the evolution of a common constitutional and legislative treaty for all member states of the EU would represent a triumph of communicative action within a framework of undistorted communication. For all intents and purposes, a common EU constitution would come as close as possible to a transnational ideal speech situation.

Canada is an example of how Habermas's model of constitutional patriotism works in practice. Canada is composed of many different regional, ethnic, racial, sexual and gender, religious, cultural, political and ideological groups with different ideas of what constitutes right and wrong, or justice versus injustice. However, instead of choosing between, or negotiating between these different views, the actual governance and law enforcement of the country is based upon a generalized set of procedures (the Charter of Rights and Freedoms and the Criminal Code) designed to provide each citizen with equal treatment, fairness, justice and due process under the law. However, even this is not a perfect example as the disproportionate incarceration of Indigenous individuals shows that the law enforcement, legal and penal systems in Canada are still seriously flawed by racism and discrimination. Besides protecting the rights and freedoms of all Canadians, the Charter and the Criminal Code also offer a set of procedural remedies for violations of these rights and for offences against society. The Charter, in particular, is designed to address perceived injustices and to resolve significant social disputes. In other words, it is designed to provide a framework for resolving conflicts through a process of undistorted communication (in which each party to the dispute has an equal right to speak) instead of allowing these conflicts to be "resolved" through force or violence, coercion or manipulation, or administrative diktat (i.e., by systematically distorted communication). Some conflicts may still occasionally erupt into violence (pro-life/pro-choice conflicts; seal hunts/animal rights; pipeline proponents versus pipeline protestors), but most disputes are settled through procedural means. This is what Habermas means by the term "constitutional patriotism."

Criticizing the Critical Theorist

By the time Habermas had more fully developed his communication theory of society, younger colleagues had begun to express dissatisfaction with some aspects of his theoretical perspective. In particular, his discourse theory of truth and morality was critiqued by third-generation critical theorists for its abstraction and idealism. Habermas's attempt to broadly conceive of major social problems — such as inequality, prejudice, discrimination, conflict and even terrorism — as examples of systematically distorted communication or as colonization of the lifeworld was increasingly seen as inadequate. In the eyes of many third-generation critical theorists, he has attempted to reduce real social problems — with their very real material causes and consequences — to abstract problems of communication. This new generation of critical theorists is not persuaded by Habermas's "linguistic turn" in critical theory. Conflict theorist Pierre L. van den Berghe dismissed Habermas's communication theory as the idealism of someone who proposes a mere "thought revolution," instead of practical and material actions for social change. None of these critics believe that fundamental social change can be accomplished by communication alone, without corresponding political action. Feminist critics have also admonished Habermas for what they perceive as his gendered description of the lifeworld, a description that fails to acknowledge the entrenched subordination of women within the typical patriarchal household and more generally, throughout the institutions of civil society (see, for example, Nancy Fraser 1989).

The other big problem that younger theorists have perceived in Habermas's work is his apparent failure to logically justify his own theoretical perspective — in other words, his failure to provide rational grounds for the normative foundations for his own viewpoint. While Habermas remains committed to a universal set of principles — which form the basis of his communicative ideals of cosmopolitanism and deliberative democracy — and while he also remains strongly opposed to the relativism and pluralism of postmodernism, he has so far been unable to provide a logical and compelling argument for prioritizing his own theoretical perspective. For many theorists of the new generation, this failure to provide a theoretical self-justification exposes yet another major weakness of his theory.

But Habermas's work remains significant. Like many other Germans of his generation, Habermas has had to come to terms with his nation's recent past. The terrible legacy of Nazi Germany has helped to shape Habermas's cosmopolitan and constitutional vision and his progressive humanistic values. He is a strong advocate for the European project, a defender of the human rights of refugees and a firm believer in the power of rational consensus and deliberative democracy to address the geopolitical and diplomatic challenges of our present age. Above all, he is a theorist who not only talks the talk, but who also walks the walk.

THE THIRD GENERATION

The rise of the third generation of the Frankfurt School is primarily associated with the work of Axel Honneth — as well as his main critic, Nancy Fraser. Honneth's theoretical perspective differs from that of Habermas in a number of ways: (1) Honneth's main focus is on the politics and morality of recognition and respect rather than on communication structures and discursive practices within society; (2) he focuses on the concrete subjective experiences of marginalized, or denigrated, groups and individuals, unlike Habermas, who is fixated on abstract structural entities, such as the system and the lifeworld; (3) he incorporates the various viewpoints and concerns of different identity groups in society into a universalistic program for social justice and ethical action; and, (4) unlike Habermas, who remains hostile to pluralism and relativism, and therefore to postmodernism and poststructuralism, Honneth recognizes and respects difference and diversity, albeit within a generalized emancipatory project for social and political action.

The third generation of the Frankfurt School is well illustrated in the works of Axel Honneth, who is the primary representative of twenty-first century critical theory. Along with other theorists of his generation, Honneth represents a departure from the relatively abstract theorizing of Habermas towards a more concrete concern with the actual subjective lived experiences of individuals and social groups in the twenty-first-century social world. Although more fragmented, the critical theory tradition lives on in North America in the works of several third generation theorists, including Axel Honneth, Nancy Fraser, Hans Joas and others. Many of these theorists have focused on how the new technologies of telecommunication have transformed social relations and social interactions around the world. Others have examined how the rise of the new social movements has changed the nature of political and social action in the postmodern world.

AXEL HONNETH

Axel Honneth is the leading figure and most prominent theorist of the third generation of critical theorists. Born in 1949, he came of age during the time of the fall of the Berlin Wall, the collapse of the USSR and the end of the Cold War. The opening years of the twenty-first century also saw the terrorist attacks on the World Trade Center (9/11) and the subsequent US military interventions in Afghanistan, Iraq and Libya. These years also marked the beginning of the indefinite war on global terrorism, as well as the destabilization of the Middle East and North Africa — with ongoing wars in Afghanistan, Iraq, Libya, Syria, Sudan, Yemen, Somalia and in other "failed states" and conflict zones around the world.

Honneth, like Habermas, witnessed the progressive development of the European project: the Schengen Agreement in 1985 and the Amsterdam Treaty in 1995 on borderless European states; the adoption of a single currency within the Eurozone; and the growth of a single European market for trade and commerce. These changing political conditions made a strong impression on the third generation of critical theorists like Honneth and changed the analysis of social interaction and communication, as well as of social conflict and social change. Although Honneth has much in common with Habermas's theoretical perspective, he also diverges from Habermas in a number of significant and innovative directions.

New social movements: One of the strongest influences on Honneth's social and moral thought has been the growth and spread of the new social movements and the role that the new networks of information and communication have played in the activism and advocacy of these movements. The proliferation of these new social movements, and the corresponding rise of identity politics during the transition from the twentieth to the twenty-first century, has played a major role in shaping Honneth's theoretical perspective and in advancing the critical theory paradigm beyond the framework established by Habermas. Over the past several decades, we have seen the rise of the LGBTQ movement; the growth of environmental and ecology movements; the spread of movements for global justice and international labour rights; and anti-nuclear and animal rights movements, among many others. And more recently, we have witnessed the rebirth of radical movements for civil, racial, ethnic and other rights — such as Black Lives Matter, Idle No More, Occupy and #MeToo.

Concrete rather than abstract: Honneth is interested in the concrete lived experience of individuals and social groups. Whereas Habermas has focused on the more abstract parameters of social interaction and communication — such as the problems of systematically distorted communication and the colonization of the lifeworld — Honneth has focused much more on the feelings and the actual experiences of individuals and social groups.

Identities rather than institutions: Honneth's greater interest in the concrete lived experiences of individuals and social groups in contemporary societies has resulted in his greater focus on identity and subjectivity, rather than on institutional structures. Whereas Habermas emphasizes the institutional dominance of the system over the lifeworld and the eclipse of communicative rationality by strategic, or instrumental, rationality,

Honneth shows far greater interest in how identities are formed (or deformed) and recognized and respected (or denigrated and disrespected) in contemporary societies, as well as how identities and subjectivities can be emancipated (or oppressed).

Diversity rather than unity: The influence of the new social movements on the current generation of critical theorists can also be seen in Honneth's emphasis on the diversity and plurality that characterizes contemporary societies and his concern for the greater inclusion, tolerance and accommodation of cultural, ethnic, racial and sexual minorities as well as other expressions of social diversity and difference. This emphasis differs somewhat from Habermas, who has remained more focused in his discourse theories of universal pragmatics and communicative action, on the communicative and constitutional procedures for reaching consensus and unity within a deliberative democracy.

Theory of recognition versus a theory of communicative action: These differences between Habermas and Honneth have led to two distinct theoretical perspectives: Habermas's theory of communicative action versus Honneth's "theory of recognition." Unlike the more abstract and institutional theory of Habermas, Honneth focuses on the social, political and psychological conditions that contribute to the growth of recognition and respect (for oneself and others), and also to the growth of denigration and disrespect (for oneself and others).

Honneth's Theory of Recognition
Perhaps the simplest way to summarize Honneth's theory, or philosophy, of recognition is to say that, unlike many traditional conflict theorists — including Marxists and the first-generation critical theorists — Honneth proposes that many, if not most, social conflicts and social struggles today are motivated more by *moral* than by *material* disputes. What Honneth means by this is that many current conflicts arise from the failure of a particular community or group to recognize and respect the aspirations, values, dignity or even perspective of another community or group with which it remains locked in an antagonistic relationship. In other words, it is not so much the material inequalities of wealth or power that generate social conflict, as it is the moral failure to recognize and respect what are perceived as the "rights" of the Other to justice and equity. Some of

the most brutal and violent conflicts of our times have arisen over the non-recognition by one side of what the other side regards as its rights and entitlements. In this sense, according to Honneth, many contemporary conflicts may be understood as conflicts over unacknowledged or disrespected "moral claims" rather than over purely material interests. Honneth's theory of recognition is closely related to his corresponding theory of "identity formation." Honneth's theoretical perspective has been strongly influenced by both Hegel's writings on the philosophy of rights, including his discussion of the master/servant relationship, and by the theory of the self, developed by George Herbert Mead and the symbolic interactionists. Honneth outlines the following three stages of identity formation: (1) The stage of acquiring self-confidence is achieved in early childhood through positive and supportive interactions with primary group relations (family and friends). (2) The stage of acquiring self-respect is achieved in later years when entering into legal and moral relations with others in organizations, associations and other collectivities. Each of these social connections helps to define the autonomous individual as a person with human, legal, civil and employment rights that need to be acknowledged within the larger society. (3)The stage of acquiring self-esteem is also achieved in later years in work organizations and other communities of practice where the contributions of the individual are recognized and honoured by others. But within these communities, the individual also learns to participate in structures of social solidarity in which the rightful accomplishments of others also need to be recognized and respected. This sense of solidarity demonstrates the reciprocal nature of the rights and norms that govern recognition and respect in social interactions with others.

Figure 5-3: Honneth's Theory of Identity Formation

For Honneth, the three stages of identity formation (self-confidence, self-respect and self-esteem) correlate with the three main forms of social recognition: love, individual rights and social solidarity. And each of these stages also corresponds to a different "sphere of interaction": personality, social organization and culture. Although this theoretical perspective is intended to trace the relationship between the positive self-development of the individual or group and the forms of social recognition and respect that support and reinforce this process of self-development, there is also a darker side to Honneth's theory of recognition.

Table 5-1: Honneth's Three Forms of Recognition in Identity Formation

Stages of Identity Formation	Forms of Recognition	Spheres of Interaction	Forms of Disrespect	Aspect of the Self under Assault
Self-confidence	Love	Personality — through primary relations of family and friends	Neglect, abuse, emotional neglect	Physical integrity & psychological damage
Self-respect	Rights	Social organization — through legal and moral relations with others	Violation of legal, civil, employment and human rights	Social integrity: autonomous individual treated as an object
Self-esteem	Solidarity	Culture — through community of practice, respect & solidarity	Bullying, ignoring, excluding, constant negative feedback	Honour, dignity

Source: Adapted from Fleming 2011

Honneth suggests that the failure of individuals and groups to receive appropriate recognition and respect, or their negative experience of receiving non-recognition, degradation and disrespect, will — over an extended period of time — likely have serious negative consequences for individual and collective self-development. These consequences may lead to various oppositional behaviours ranging all the way from individual criminal offences and lawful social protests and civil disobedience, to retributive acts of violence and even to terrorism. In other words, Honneth believes that the denial of recognition and respect to individuals or to groups may easily become an underlying cause for any number of social struggles and conflicts. In other words, the triggers for many social conflicts today have their roots in moral rather than material causes. A sense of outrage over a perceived injustice, humiliation or other mark of disrespect can become a powerful and enduring motivation for individual or collective revenge and retribution. According to Honneth, many contemporary conflicts can be analyzed as a consequence of these apparent failures of recognition and perceived signs and symbols of disrespect.

A powerful example of how contemporary social conflicts may be fueled more by problems of disrespect and by what Honneth calls "mis-recognition" than by problems of poverty and economic hardship, may be seen in some of the major factors that drive young Muslim "foreign fighters" to travel to war zones in Iraq, Syria, Libya and other countries to join ISIS, al-Qaeda and other jihadist groups. As Aamna Mohdin (2016) observes, many of these fighters who were born and/or have resided in Western countries and are well educated and relatively affluent, have been motivated more by the discrimination, disrespect, non-recognition and non-inclusion they feel within their host societies than by economic deprivation. This is also the explanation offered in a major World Bank study into the causes of radicalization: "While terrorism is not associated with poverty and low levels of education, the lack of inclusion seems to be a risk factor of radicalization into violent extremism" (Devarajan et al. 2016). But one of the more compelling confirmations of Honneth's thesis of disrespect and "misrecognition" comes from Peter Neumann, a professor of security studies at Kings College, London, and director of the International Centre for the Study of Radicalization in his submission to the UN Security Report (2015) on the radicalization of young foreign fighters:

> However different the foreign fighters my colleagues and I have found and spoken to may be; however different their profiles and characteristics, what many, if not most of them, have in common is that they do not feel that they have a stake in their societies. They have often felt that, because of who they are, how they look and where their parents or grandparents came from, they still were not part of us, they were not European, they did not belong, and they would never succeed in Europe however hard they tried. And if you do not feel you belong; if you do not feel that you are part of

your society, it becomes easier to leave and it becomes easier to hate, and it becomes easier to go against the very society whose passport you hold and whose language you speak.... What I am trying to say is that exclusion — that sense of not feeling you belong or part of your own society — opens your mind. It opens your mind to an ideology that says, "The West is at war with you; Europe is at war with you; your country is at war with you; you cannot live among these people; you cannot be European and Muslim at the same time."

Honneth's Politics of Recognition

Before turning to other aspects of his work, we shall briefly summarize some of the more obvious social and political implications of Honneth's third generation perspective on critical theory. By emphasizing the importance of recognition and respect in social relations, and by illustrating the significance of non-recognition and disrespect (what Honneth also calls "misrecognition" or "diremption") as potential causes of social conflict, Honneth has introduced a new dimension into the study of social relations. Unlike the first-generation critical theorists, such as Adorno and Marcuse, who often focused on the *individual* in modern (one-dimensional) society, or the second generation theorists, like Habermas, who focused on the pragmatic and communicative *structures* of social relations, such as the lifeworld and the system, Honneth focuses on the relations between social *groups*. And because he emphasizes the role of recognition and respect in social relations, Honneth sometimes defines his perspective as one which focuses on the "moral grammar" of social relations and social conflict.

Honneth's theoretical and moral perspective reminds us of the importance of subjectivity and emotionality as factors to consider when studying the causes and consequences of social conflict and when analyzing the rise of populist movements, whether these are social protest movements, social reform movements, religious fundamentalist movements or even terrorist networks and armed struggles. These subjective factors have often been neglected and overlooked in previous explanations, such as those offered by orthodox Marxists and structural conflict theorists, who traditionally focused on external or material factors like socio-economic inequality or material deprivation. Honneth's emphasis on recognition and respect, in both interpersonal and intergroup relations, not only opens a new window on the study of social conflict and social change but also points towards potential strategies for conflict management, mediation, reconciliation or resolution through focusing on the theoretical and practical importance of mutual recognition, mutual respect and reciprocal empathy.

Issues of recognition and respect have played a major role in a number of contemporary social conflicts and have entered into the very different narratives that opposing social groups may tell about themselves and each other. Recognition and respect have certainly been important, albeit often overlooked, variables in the conflicts between Catholics (nationalists and republicans) and Protestants (loyalists and unionists) in Northern Ireland; Sunni, Shia and Kurds in Iraq and Syria; Turks and Kurds in Turkey; Israelis and Palestinians in Israel and the Occupied Territories; Tutsi and Hutu in Rwanda; Sinhalese and Tamils in Sri Lanka; Dinka and Nuer in South Sudan; and in countless other combat zones, civil wars and trouble spots around the world.

Closer to home, according to some observers, much of the support for the election of Trump came from the white working-class constituencies in regions of America who felt unrecognized and disrespected by the political elites of both major political parties (see Vance 2016; Hochschild 2016). Similarly, the surprising 2016 Brexit referendum vote reflected a silent and overlooked constituency from the rural and economically depressed regions, as well as the wealthier and more conservative "leafy shires" of "middle England," whose sense of alienation from the central government in London was manipulated by a campaign of misinformation and false promises from right-wing populist politicians such as Nigel Farage and his United Kingdom Independence Party, and other hard-right parties such as Britain First and the English Defence League. Whether we are talking about the de-industrialized regions of the US or the rural and suburban voters in the UK, these protest voters have raised their voices in anger and fear and have voted for leaders who they believe are also "outsiders" to the political elites and genuine spokespersons for the overlooked white working class. Although those with strong feelings of marginalization and alienation may sometimes be attracted to socialist and left-wing "outsider" politicians, like Bernie Sanders in the US and Jeremy Corbyn in the UK, the growth of far-right or fascist parties and anti-immigrant movements in European countries may be further evidence of the voices of the disaffected, who feel that they are unrecognized, disenfranchised, disrespected and betrayed within the political process.

Honneth's theory of recognition may also help us to understand some of the most violent conflicts of our time. Many observers have concluded that the rise of ISIS may be directly attributed to the disrespect shown to the Sunni majority tribes by the Shia minority after the US installation of a Shia government following the invasion of Iraq in 2003. The disrespect and persecution of the Sunni tribes by these successive Shia governments made the Sunni population fertile ground for the spread of a jihadist ideology and for the rise of al-Qaeda and later of ISIS (see, for example, Cockburn 2015).

Criticisms of Honneth

Honneth's "ethical turn" in critical social theory and his focus on the "moral grammar of social conflict" have not gone unopposed. There have been a number of critics of Honneth's theory of recognition, and one of the most prominent is Nancy Fraser, who is, herself, a member of the third generation of critical theory. In an earlier work, *Unruly Practices* (1989), Fraser critiqued Habermas's communication theory of society for its allegedly androcentric perspective and for its failure to acknowledge the particular standpoint and "positionality" of women and of other sexual, racial and social minorities. In a later work (co-authored with Honneth in 2003), *Redistribution or Recognition* (2003b), Fraser argues that in order to reclaim the "socialist project" that underlay critical theory, it is necessary to return to the *material* basis of many struggles for social justice, which are often centred around the problem of inequality and, more specifically, the maldistribution of wealth and power. For this reason, Fraser argues that critical theory needs to refocus on redistribution, alongside recognition. Although Fraser concedes the importance of recognition in struggles for social justice, she contends that the problem of maldistribution and the struggle for redistribution cannot be subsumed under the struggle for recognition. Honneth has mounted his own defence against these criticisms, and the dialogue continues.

Some critics (Cheng 2014; Petherbridge 2011) also express concern that in Honneth's focus on the non-recognition, disrespect and denigration often experienced by marginalized and minoritized social groups, he may inadvertently legitimize some anti-social and morally reprehensible and indefensible groups, such as neo-Nazi, white supremacist, homophobic, xenophobic, anti-Semitic and other racist and terrorist groups. This was certainly the concern of Fraser (2003b: 32), who cautions that it is imperative to "avoid the view that everyone has an equal right to social esteem. That view is patently untenable." Other critics (Mark 2014; Van den Brink and Owen 2007) argue that, in dispensing with any metanarrative or moral universalism, Honneth has no logical or moral basis from which to distinguish between "progressive" and "reactionary," "benign" and "malign," "virtuous" and "villainous" groups — all of which have, at one time or another, experienced "non-recognition," "disrespect," "disremption" and "denigration" — at least in their own eyes. If you are focused on listening to and recognizing the voice of the Other without fear or favour, then how do you distinguish the "good" from the "bad"?

Recognizing Honneth

At the very least, Honneth's theoretical perspective may help us achieve a deeper understanding of some of the most pressing and urgent problems of the present age, including the growth of terrorism, both local and global. Many oppositional groups may come to see themselves as victims of disrespect and may mobilize around demands for what they perceive as social justice. According to Honneth, the strongest motive driving many of these groups is not so much their immediate material self-interests but rather their need to gain recognition and respect and to be heard and included in the turbulent postmodern and neoliberal world. Their key demand is to be acknowledged and admitted into the universe of political discourse and to be fully included in the "intersubjective" channels of communication that are an essential part of contemporary social relations. However, although this theory of recognition may be used to explain and justify the aspirations and activism of many oppositional groups in society — on both the political left and the political right, there is a big problem when we come to analyze terrorism. Even though terrorists may see themselves as "victims of disrespect," most of us remain unwilling to condone their actions, especially when those actions involve the killing of innocent civilians through the use of car bombs, improvised explosive devices (IEDs), suicide bombers, mass shootings, weaponized vehicles or knifing rampages. Indeed, several critics have alleged that Honneth's theory of recognition offers an unintended and inadmissible defence of terrorism — through a logical loophole that betrays a basic weakness and naïveté in his theory.

Honneth denies that his theory of recognition can ever be used to justify terrorism because, unlike many non-violent, extra-parliamentary and civil disobedience oppositional groups, terrorists are not interested in entering into a relationship of mutual recognition or respect with their opponents and intended targets. Rather than seeking social justice through the law, or through changes to the law, terrorists are primarily committed to unilaterally imposing their own worldviews and practices on others without any intersubjective communication or mutual recognition. In this sense, Honneth insists that terrorists may best be understood as "moral absolutists," secure in their belief that only their perspective is fully valid.

For Honneth, the injuries and traumas of disrespect and non-recognition can only be cured through the achievement of social justice. And social justice requires an accommodation between victim and perpetrator; social justice requires the achievement of mutual recognition and respect between opposing parties. In other words, social justice can only be achieved, in Honneth's words, through "legitimacy and normativity" — through recognizing and upholding the legal and human rights of all parties within a reformed constitutional framework of agreement. Sometimes, subaltern paramilitary groups that have been labelled as "terrorist" — such as the Provisional Irish Republican Army (PIRA), the Palestine Liberation Organization (PLO) and the African National Congress (ANC in South Africa) — may reach an accommodation through truth and reconciliation commissions, restorative or transitional justice tribunals or other negotiated settlements with state actors (such as the British government, the Israeli government or the former South African Apartheid government). Many of these state actors have, themselves, been accused of "state terrorism" by their paramilitary opponents. Only under these settlements based on negotiated mutual recognition and respect can the required conditions for social justice outlined by Honneth be said to have been fulfilled.

CRITICAL THEORY AND THE CHARGE OF EUROCENTRISM

In recent years, the Frankfurt tradition of critical theory, along with most other perspectives associated with what we have called the crumbling canon of contemporary social theory, has attracted growing criticism for its alleged Eurocentrism and its apparent indifference to the problems of domination and exploitation in societies of the Global South. Most of the work associated with the first and second (and arguably the third) generations of critical theorists has remained squarely focused on European and North American societies. Indeed, many recent critiques of Eurocentric narratives, such as Michel-Rolph Trouillot's *Silencing the Past* (1995),

Jack Goody's *The Theft of History* (2006) and Sanjay Subrahmanyam's *Europe's India* (2017), argue that the underlying assumptions, as well as the key concepts of critical theory, remain firmly rooted in the European historical experience (see also Vázquez-Arroyo 2018).

These criticisms and concerns about the Eurocentric biases of critical theory have recently come to a head with the publication of a major critical review of critical theory by Amy Allen, *The End of Progress: Decolonizing the Normative Foundations of Critical Theory* (2016). For Allen, a primary symptom of the current weakness of critical theory is its neglect of other critical traditions — most notably feminism, as well as postcolonial and decolonial social theories. According to Allen, this failure to engage with these and other critical traditions has left critical theory increasingly unable to relate to the postcolonial and neocolonial world of today — in other words, critical theory is losing its relevance to the real world.

The main target of much recent criticism of critical theory is the European concept of "progress," which underlies the rationale and motivation of critical theory. Critical theorists of the Frankfurt tradition have typically subscribed to a view of progress that privileges the European historical experience and measures the political goals of progress, modernity and freedom against the baseline of European history (Dussel 1995; Vázquez-Arroyo 2018). Allen suggests that this Eurocentric worldview constitutes an "imperialist metanarrative," based on the idea "that European, Enlightenment modernity — or at least certain aspects or features thereof, which remain to be spelled out — represents a developmental advance over premodern, nonmodern, or traditional forms of life" (2016: 3–4). Other critics note that this teleological assumption of progress has had further negative implications for critical theory — epistemological, theoretical and political. The epistemological tunnel vision of critical theory, which sees only European development as "progressive," also assumes that European moral values and standards are superior to those from other regions, especially the Global South. Thus, Yves Winter (2018: 786) reminds us: "As postcolonial theorists have shown again and again, civilizational schemas that treat the Euro-Atlantic space as more developed than the rest of the world are inextricably entangled in colonial and racist logics."

The Eurocentric perspective of critical theory has also had unfortunate political consequences for earlier and the current generation of Frankfurt critical theorists. Arnold Farr (2017: 65–66) observes that the critical theorists who arrived in the US as refugees from Nazi Germany during the Second World War were largely oblivious to the institutionalized racism against African Americans that pervaded all aspects of American society — in strict Southern school segregation, Jim Crow laws and terrorism of the KKK, as well as in less violent forms such as housing and employment discrimination:

> It is amazing that when members of the Frankfurt School were exiled to the US, segregation and various forms of and manifestations of white supremacy, as well as sexism were very visible. However, they by and large remained silent on these issues. The lack of writing on racism and the black struggle for liberation by members of the Frankfurt School depicts a certain blindness that one can only attribute to their inability to see the world through non-European lenses.

Even today, a similar myopia seems to inhibit the most famous critical theorists from commenting on, or critiquing, some of the more intractable problems of domination and exploitation in the Global South. Thus, as Winter (2018: 788–789) records, nearly all Frankfurt theorists have refused to take a public position on the Israeli occupation of Palestinian land and the oppression of the Palestinian people. Even Habermas declined to directly address this issue in various media interviews. Although it may be argued that his reticence on this issue arises from the collective sense of historical guilt still felt by many German intellectuals towards the state of Israel, Winter (2018: 789–790) is less charitable in his criticism of what she sees as a moral, theoretical and political abdication of responsibility, as well as a blind spot in contemporary critical theory: "But when it comes to Palestine, Habermas collaborates in concealing the crimes of the Israeli state, not because of insufficient epistemic or metanormative humility about non-Western culture or religion, but as a result of failures of moral and political judgment."

These debates between the Frankfurt critical theorists and their postcolonial and feminist critics are ongoing and in many ways unresolved. On the one hand, recent critics have effectively exposed the Eurocentric roots of critical theory and the colonial assumptions implicit in Eurocentric concepts such as "progress," "modernity," "freedom" and, of course, the "civilizing mission." This epistemological and theoretical battle has largely been won, with victory already declared. However, the more problematic issues concern the moral and political questions arising from postcolonial demands for greater theoretical pluralism and epistemological inclusiveness. While the demand to extend equal recognition to the contrasting narratives of the colonized and the colonizer is now generally conceded, the demand for moral equivalence between the values and practices of non-Western and Western societies is more problematic. Thus, while cultural relativism may be extended to offer equal recognition and acceptance of different religious beliefs, societal worldviews and conceptions of the natural world, there is still resistance from many Eurocentric scholars to assign moral equivalence to more alien values and practices of some non-Western cultures — such as the execution of heretics, blasphemers, apostates, adulterers, people from the LGBTQ community etc. or sexual stratification and gender apartheid. For many Western theorists, there are limits to their acceptance of cultural relativism. In this sense, therefore, although chastened and critiqued, it may be premature to announce the death of the "emancipatory project" of Frankfurt critical theory.

THE LEGACY OF CRITICAL THEORY

Perhaps the major legacy of critical theorists over the past three generations has been their embrace of the emancipatory project of the Enlightenment. In other words, critical theorists have remained committed to their critique of domination and exploitation and to the project of advancing human freedom and autonomy in the complex and often heavily structured environments of modern society. This is the golden thread that runs throughout much critical theory in the twentieth and early twenty-first centuries. It can be traced back to the early critiques of totalitarianism and authoritarianism — of Nazism and Stalinism — in the early works of Franz Neumann, Theodor Adorno, Max Horkheimer, Erich Fromm and Herbert Marcuse and to the later critiques of mass society and mass culture in the works of Emil Lederer, Jürgen Habermas, Nancy Fraser and Axel Honneth, among others.

This passionate concern of critical theorists with human freedom is very much in the spirit of Georg Hegel, one of the major intellectual influences on the original Frankfurt School. As Friedrich Engels wrote (1969 [1894]: 136–137), Hegel cryptically defined "freedom" as "recognition of necessity." What he meant by this definition is that humans can only realize their potential for free and autonomous action by recognizing and fully understanding the natural and social constraints that may obstruct, impede or limit their capacity for conscious rational action. It is only after they have discovered and made fully transparent the natural and social forces that have blindly conditioned their existence and conduct, that people can free themselves from those previously unknown and unrecognized determinants of their behaviour. But as long as we remain oblivious to the unknown external and internal forces that impact our lives, we will continue to be controlled by them, and as Engels (1969: 137) stated: "*Freedom therefore consists in the control over ourselves and over external nature, a control founded on knowledge of natural necessity; it is therefore necessarily a product of historical development.*" For example, it was only after humans learned to control fire by generating heat through friction that fire became a tool for human development rather than simply an unaccountable and unpredictable force of nature. This is the lesson that the critical theorists learned from Hegel.

Most of the classical social theorists who influenced critical theory had already uncovered hidden and hitherto unrecognized natural and social forces that had long determined the course of human conduct — and the fate of human lives. Karl Marx discovered what he regarded as the "hidden secret" of capitalist accumulation: the extraction of surplus value through the exploitation of the working class. Sigmund Freud exposed the power of the unconscious mind to blindly shape our thoughts and motivate our actions. Charles Darwin revealed the laws of evolution and natural selection that have shaped many of our characteristics as a human species. These and other theorists have helped to uncover the underlying "generative mechanisms" of our thoughts and actions. And only by recognizing and negotiating these natural and social laws can we progressively free ourselves from their blind imperatives.

The first and second generations of critical theorists moved beyond the earlier critiques of totalitarian societies and began to focus on the more subtle forms of domination, manipulation and control exercised by the corporate elite in the mass societies of industrial and late capitalism. Marcuse analyzed the ahistorical consciousness and historical amnesia prevalent in modern mass culture, a condition which he famously referred to as "one-dimensional society," while Habermas laments the erosion of the "public sphere" in late capitalist societies and warns of the growing threats of "systematically distorted communication" and the "colonization of the lifeworld by the system." These and other critiques of popular culture paved the way for a new generation of home-grown critiques of

American culture and society that appeared during the 1950s. Among the most famous of these were David Riesman's analysis of the culture and ideology of individualism in *The Lonely Crowd* (1950); Vance Packard's exposé of the manipulative and subliminal techniques of commercial advertising in *The Hidden Persuaders* (1957); and the sociological critiques of corporate power and the degradation of labour provided by C. Wright Mills in *The Power Elite* (1956) and *White Collar* (1951). All these writers were influenced — either directly or indirectly — by the second generation of critical theorists who had established their base in the United States.

Today, the emancipatory project of critical theory has passed to a younger generation of theorists — including Axel Honneth, Nancy Fraser, Hans Joas and more recently, Thomas McCarthy and Rainer Forst, among others. And although they confront the new political and theoretical challenges of the contemporary age, it would seem from their writings and interventions that they remain committed to the original (Hegelian) premise of critical theory: that freedom is founded on a "recognition of necessity" — on the need to reveal the underlying determinants of our ideas and actions.

References

Adorno, T.W., F. Frenkel-Brunswik, D.J. Levinson, and R.N. Sanford. 1964 [1950]. *The Authoritarian Personality*. New York: John Wiley.

Allen, Amy. 2016. *The End of Progress: Decolonizing the Normative Foundations of Critical Theory*. New York: Columbia University Press.

Bauman, Zygmunt. 1989. *Modernity and the Holocaust*. Ithaca, NY: Cornell University Press.

Benjamin, Walter. 1969 [1935]. *The Work of Art in the Age of Its Technological Reproducibility, and Other Writings on Media*. New York: Schocken Books.

Castro, Javier Sethness. 2013. "Herbert Marcuse and Absolute Struggle in 2013." *Counterpunch*, December 16. <https://www.counterpunch.org/2013/12/16/herbert-marcuse-and-absolute-struggle-in-2013/>.

Cheng, Sinkwan. 2014. "Terrorism, the Subaltern, and the Politics of Recognition: Rethinking Hegel and Honneth." *Journal of Law and Conflict Resolution*, 6, 3 (June): 56–66. <https://pdfs.semanticscholar.org/08bc/e82d6f649229c776ba909af90b9fbeb5d2f4.pdf>.

Cockburn, Patrick. 2015. *The Rise of Islamic State: ISIS and the New Sunni Revolution*, revised ed. Verso.

Devarajan, Shanta, Lili Mottaghi, Quy-Toan Do, Anne Brockmeyer, Clément Joubert, Kartika Bhatia, and Mohamed Abdel Jelil. 2016. "Economic and Social Inclusion to Prevent Violent Extremism." *Middle East and North Africa Economic Monitor*(October), Washington, DC: World Bank. <http://documents.worldbank.org/curated/en/409591474983005625/pdf/108525-REVISED-PUBLIC.pdf>.

Dussel, E. 1995. *The Invention of the Americas,* trans Michael D. Barker. New York: Continuum.

Engels, Friedrich. 1969 [1894]. *Anti-Dühring.* Moscow: Progress Publishers.

Farr, Arnold. 2017. "Where Is Critical Theory? Eurocentrism and Marginalization In European and American Critical Theory." *Comunicações Piracicaba,* 24, 2 (maio-agosto): 57–70. DOI: <http://dx.doi.org/10.15600/2238-121X/comunicacoes. v24n2p57-70>.

Feyerabend, Paul K. 1975. *Against Method: Outline of an Anarchist Theory of Knowledge.* New Left Books.

Fleming, Ted. 2011. "Recognition in the Work of Axel Honneth: Implication for Transformative Learning Theory." In M. Alhadeff-Jones and A. Kokkos (eds.), *Transformative Learning in Time of Crisis: Individual and Collective Challenges.* New York & Athens: Teachers College, Columbia University & The Hellenic Open University. <http://www.tedfleming.net/doc/Honneth_on_Recognition_byTed_ Fleming.pdf>.

Fraser, Nancy. 1989. *Unruly Practices.* Minneapolis, MN: University of Minnesota Press.

Fraser, Nancy, and Axel Honneth. 2003a. *Redistribution or Recognition.* London; New York: Verso.

_____. 2003b. "Social Justice in the Age of Identity Politics." In Nancy Fraser and Axel Honneth *Redistribution or Recognition.* London; New York: Verso.

Fromm, E. 1965 [1941]. *Escape from Freedom.* New York: Avon.

Goldhammer, Arthur. 2016. "The Revolution of Falling Expectations." *Le Monde diplomatique,* English edition (October). <https://mondediplo. com/2016/10/03expectations>.

Goody, Jack. 2006. *The Theft of History.* Cambridge University Press.

Greenwald, Glenn. 2014. *No Place to Hide: Edward Snowden, the NSA, and the U.S. Surveillance State,* 1st ed. London: Hamish Hamilton.

Gronow, Jukka. 1988. "The Element of Irrationality: Max Weber's Diagnosis of Modern Culture." *Acta Sociologica,* 31, 4: 319–331.

Habermas, Jürgen. 1989 [1962]. *The Structural Transformation of the Public Sphere: An Inquiry into a Category of Bourgeois Society.* Cambridge: Polity.

_____. 2006. "Political Communication in Media Society — Does Democracy Still Enjoy an Epistemic Dimension? The Impact of Normative Theory on Empirical Research." Paper presented to the ICA Annual Convention, Dresden, Germany.

_____. 2016a. "The Players Resign: Core Europe to the Rescue: A Conversation with Jürgen Habermas about Brexit and the EU crisis." *Zeit Online,* 26, 12 (July). <http:// www.zeit.de/kultur/2016-07/juergen-habermas-brexit-eu-crises-english>.

_____. 2016b. "For a Democratic Polarisation: How to Pull the Ground from Under Right-Wing Populism." *Social Europe,* 17 November. <https://www.socialeurope. eu/democratic-polarisation-pull-ground-right-wing-populism>.

Hochschild, Arlie Russell. 2016. *Strangers in Their Own Land: Anger and Mourning on the American Right.* The New Press.

Holmes, Rachel. 2016. "We Let Technology into Our Lives. And Now It's Starting to Control Us." *The Guardian,* 28 November.

Honneth, A. 1987. "Critical Theory." In Anthony Giddens and Jonathan Turner (eds.), *Social Theory Today.* Stanford, CA: Stanford University Press.

Horkheimer, M. 1972 [1937]. *Critical Theory: Selected Essays*, trans. M.J. O'Connell. New York: Herder and Herder.

____. 1974. *Critique of Instrumental Reason.* New York: Seabury Press.

Horkheimer, M., and T.W. Adorno. 1972 [1944]. *Dialectic of Enlightenment*, trans. J. Cumming. New York: Herder and Herder.

Marcuse, Herbert. 1958. *Soviet Marxism: A Critical Analysis.* New York: Columbia University Press.

____. 1964. *One-dimensional Man: Studies in the Ideology of Advanced Industrial Society.* Boston: Beacon Press.

Mark, D. Clifton. 2014. "Recognition and Honor: A Critique of Axel Honneth's and Charles Taylor's Histories of Recognition." *Constellations*, 21, 1.

Mills, C. Wright. 1951. *White Collar: The American Middle Classes.* Oxford University Press.

____. 1956. *The Power Elite.* Oxford University Press.

Mohdin, Aamna. 2016. "ISIL's Foreign Fighters Are Surprisingly Well-Educated, According to the World Bank." Quartz, October 6. <https://qz.com/802276/the-foreign-fighters-of-isisislamic-state-are-surprisingly-well-educated-according-to-the-world-bank/>.

Neumann, Franz. 1944. *Behemoth: The Structure and Practice of National Socialism, 1933–1944.* Frank Cass Publishers.

Packard, Vance. 1957. *The Hidden Persuaders.* Longmans Green and CO.

Petherbridge, Danielle (ed.). 2011. *Axel Honneth: Critical Essays: With a Reply by Axel Honneth.* Social and Critical Theory, Vol 12. Brill.

Reich, Wilhelm. 1970 [1933]. *The Mass Psychology of Fascism*, eds. M. Higgins and C. Raphael; trans. V. Carfagno. New York: Noonday Press.

Riesman, David, with Nathan Glazer and Reuel Denney. 1950. *The Lonely Crowd: A Study of the Changing American Character.* Yale University Press.

Ritzer, G. 1996. *The McDonaldization of Society*, revised ed. Thousand Oaks, CA: Pine Forge.

Subrahmanyam, Sanjay. 2017. *Europe's India: Words, People, Empires, 1500–1800.* Harvard University Press.

Trouillot, Michel-Rolph. 1995. *Silencing the Past: Power and the Production of History.* Beacon Press.

United Nations. 2015. S/PV.7432. Security Council Seventieth year, 7432nd meeting, Thursday, 23 April, 10 a.m. New York. <https://www.securitycouncilreport.org/atf/cf/%7B65BFCF9B-6D27-4E9C-8CD3-CF6E4FF96FF9%7D/spv_7432.pdf>.

Van den Brink, Bert, and David Owen (eds.). 2007. *Recognition and Power: Axel Honneth and the Tradition of Critical Social Theory.* Cambridge University Press.

Vance, J.D. 2016. *The Hillbilly Elegy.* Harper Collins.

Vázquez-Arroyo, Antonio Y. 2018. "Critical Theory, Colonialism, and the Historicity of Thought." *Constellations*, 25: 54–70.

Walsh, Michael. 2015. *The Devil's Pleasure Palace: The Cult of Critical Theory and the Subversion of the West.* Encounter Books.

Weber, Max. 1958. *The Protestant Ethic and the Spirit of Capitalism*, trans. Talcott Parsons. New York: Charles Scribner's Sons.

Winter, Yves. 2018. "Formally Decolonized but Still Neocolonial?" *Political Theory* 46, 5.

CHAPTER 6

THEORIZING OUR SOCIAL SELVES

Microsocial Theories of Symbolic Interactionism and Dramaturgy

THE RISE OF MICROSOCIAL THEORIES

This chapter, which introduces some important microsocial theories of society, focuses on the social world as experienced by individual social actors. Whereas earlier chapters dealt with the big pictures of the social world as described in the grand theories and metanarratives of structural functionalists, conflict theorists, critical theorists, neo-Marxists and others, this chapter and Chapter 7 focus on the local settings in which individuals interact in the course of their everyday activities. The first theoretical perspective we discuss is that of "symbolic interactionism." This perspective — along with the related "dramaturgical" perspective — has proven to be one of the more popular theories in modern sociology because its concepts and theoretical framework are so readily applicable to the study of everyday life. Although symbolic interactionism is generally acknowledged to be an American theoretical invention associated with the University of Chicago, its roots can be traced to the work of German social theorist Georg Simmel.

Simmel's sociological ideas were first introduced into North America by Albion Small, who had been Simmel's student in Germany and who became the first chair of the Department of Sociology at the University of Chicago, at the end of the nineteenth century. The University of Chicago was fertile ground for Simmel's ideas, which, in combination with other philosophical influences, led to the development of symbolic interactionism — the first home-grown American sociological tradition. Symbolic interactionism merged a number of intellectual influences in addition to the ideas of Simmel and other German idealist thinkers, which were spread by Small, Robert Park and others. The University of Chicago was also a major centre of American pragmatist philosophy, associated with philosophers John Dewey, Charles Pierce, Charles Horton Cooley and, most importantly, George Herbert Mead. More than anything else, Mead's philosophy of social behaviourism, which was a critical response to the earlier psychological theory of classical conditioning behaviourism, associated with Ivan Pavlov and John B. Watson, laid the groundwork for the sociological tradition of symbolic interactionism.

Unlike macrosocial theories, such as structural functionalism, structural conflict theory, systems theory and various Marxist theories, which emphasize the large-scale social forces that influence or determine human behaviour, symbolic interactionism focuses on the thoughts, beliefs and self-images that lead social actors to make their decisions and select their course of action. In other words, symbolic interactionism is interested in human "agency": how social actors see themselves and others; how they construct symbolic meanings in their social worlds; and how they acquire their sense of self and personal identity. Whereas many other theories are interested in the externally observable and measurable aspects of human *behaviour*, symbolic interactionism is centred on the subjectively meaningful sources of human *action*.

Mead emphasized that the study of human behaviour was qualitatively distinct from the study of animal behaviour inasmuch as human interaction and communication were primarily based upon the use of "significant symbols," especially language, while animal interaction and communication were wholly based upon the use of "instinctual signs." From this distinction, Mead elaborated his notion of the "social self" as the reflexive ability that human beings have to experience themselves as both the subject and the object of their own consciousness, in a way that no other creature is able to do — as far as we know.

This notion of the "self" has remained a central concept for theorists of the Chicago School, and under the later influence of Herbert Blumer, the major interpreter of Mead's work, the concept of self became the distinguishing hallmark for subsequent generations of symbolic interactionist theory and research. Other theorists who expanded upon the concept of self included Charles Horton Cooley with his concept of the "looking-glass self" and W.I. Thomas with his theorem of the "definition of the situation," in which he pronounced that, "if men [sic] define a situation as real, it becomes real in its consequences." In many ways, Thomas's theorem became the foundation of other theoretical perspectives that emphasized the power that public perception of an individual (even when these are incorrect perceptions) can have on an individual's self-concept and social acceptance.

The power and relevance of Thomas's theorem can be seen in the smear campaign conducted by Donald Trump against other candidates during the 2016 presidential election in the US. Trump stigmatized many of his competitors with pejorative labels that were designed to discredit and degrade them. Nicknames such as "Crooked Hillary," "Low energy" Jeb Bush, "Lying" Ted Cruz, among many others, were used in an attempt to redefine the public perception of these candidates, and once these perceptions took hold, they became "real" in their consequences. One political commentator observed:

> Once a negative label is placed on someone, people's brains start to recognize and cherry pick the information that fits that label. When new information came out about Clinton's email scandal or speculation about pay for play in the Clinton Foundation, people became more and more assured that Clinton was "crooked." ... Whether there was truth to Clinton's scandals made no difference, Trump's stigma stuck. When it comes to symbolic interactionism, it's people's perceptions that matter.... The mainstream media and the public now accept the idea that Trump ignored facts, science, and even common decency ... and still got elected.... facts don't matter. (Johnson 2017)

In the run-up to the 2020 campaign, Trump is using the same tactics against his opponents in the Democratic Party — with "Sleepy" (or "Creepy") Joe Biden; "Pocahontas," for Elizabeth Warren; and "Crazy" Bernie (Sanders).

One perspective derived from symbolic interactionism is that of labelling theory, which is often used in criminological studies. For example, we could think of a traveller who is mistaken for someone else with a similar name on a no-fly list and prevented from boarding a plane; or Maher Arar, who was wrongly subjected to extraordinary rendition to Syria and detained for almost a year, during which time he was tortured, because he was misidentified as a member of Al Qaeda (Mazigh 2008). Once you are defined in a certain way, even if the definition is incorrect, the definition, or the label, carries real and sometimes frightful consequences.

Besides the Chicago School of symbolic interactionism, the Iowa

School of symbolic interactionism arose at the University of Iowa. It was founded by Manfred Kuhn, a leading symbolic interactionist of his time who taught at Iowa from 1946 until his death in 1963. Carl Couch was another important figure in the Iowa School and served as its ambassador until his death in 1994. The Iowa School emphasized defining symbolic interactionist concepts, such as the "self," the "other," "primary, secondary and reference groups" etc., in ways that would permit these concepts to be used in empirically testable theoretical hypotheses. In other words, the Iowa School researchers favoured empirically testable concepts over the more subjective and abstract concepts pioneered by theorists such as Blumer, and later by Erving Goffman. Whereas the Chicago tradition relied more on subjective, impressionistic and even anecdotal evidence, the Iowa School researchers were more hard-nosed in their demand for objective, measurable evidence. The Chicago School relied primarily on participant observation research. In this sense, the Chicago school was anthropological in orientation inasmuch as it focused on understanding and interpreting the meaning system of an individual or group of people, rather than uncovering generalizable patterns in human behaviour.

OTHER MICROSOCIAL THEORIES

Symbolic interactionism was only one of a number of microsocial theories that took root and flourished in North America. In the decades following the 1960s, a variety of microsocial theories emerged in the United States to challenge the dominance of structural functionalism and to reassert the primacy of small-scale studies of social actors in local settings. Microsocial theories that have appeared over the past fifty or so years are exchange theory, rational choice theory, network theory and the ever-popular dramaturgical theory, of Canadian sociologist Erving Goffman. One of the more intriguing of these traditions was that of ethnomethodology, a form of social analysis pioneered by Harold Garfinkel and closely associated with California universities

Ethnomethodologists are interested in studying the methods used by ordinary people to make sense of, and produce order in, their everyday lives. Unlike symbolic interactionists, however, who looked inside the social actor for evidence of self, meaning, purpose and other internal subjective indicators, ethnomethodologists looked only at the externally observable, recordable and measurable evidence of the common sense methods — or what ethnomethodologists call "methods of practical reasoning" — that ordinary people use to accomplish their everyday activities. As we shall see in a separate chapter on ethnomethodology, these are the taken-for-granted methods that we all use to accomplish many routine activities, such as navigating our way through a crowded shopping mall; learning when to laugh, when to stay silent and when to show disapproval in the company of others; knowing when and how to approach strangers and countless other unspoken methods we use and rules we follow to act in predictable and expected ways towards others. Ethnomethodologists, therefore, are committed to using only what they regard as objective methods for observing, recording and analyzing social interaction. And it is no accident that the emergence and growth of ethnomethodology corresponded to the popularization of the new recording technologies in the 1960s and thereafter: the tape recorder, the video-camera or camcorder and now smart phones.

Ethnomethodologists have progressed from being the *enfants terribles* of sociology departments to respected as serious scholars in their own right, with their own academic journals and research traditions. And although the rise of ethnomethodology first appeared to be a distinctly American — even Californian — phenomenon, the roots of this sociological tradition are to be found in the phenomenological ideas of European philosophers such as Edmund Husserl and Alfred Schutz. Today, ethnomethodology has become a vigorous and respected sociological tradition that, besides its own considerable achievements, has influenced other traditions, such as Marxism, feminism and symbolic interactionism. We shall return to this theory in the next chapter.

Another microsocial theory that emerged in the late 1960s to challenge the ascendancy of structural functionalism was exchange theory. In some ways, exchange theory can best be understood as a sociological version of the psychological theory of behaviourism. Exchange theory applies the principles of "operant conditioning behaviourism" (associated with B.F. Skinner) to *social,* rather than to individual behaviour. Unlike the *psychological* theory of behaviourism, which focuses on the externally observable behaviour of individual subjects (whether rats, pigeons or humans), *sociological* exchange theory is focused on the *social interaction* between individuals, rather than on the isolated individual subject. While both perspectives study how subjects are conditioned by rewards and punishments, the psychologist is centred on the individual, while the sociologist is centred on the interaction (between individuals).

Pioneered by Harvard social psychologist George Homans, exchange theory was later extended by German-born organizational theorist Peter Blau, to the analysis of collective behaviour — that is, to the study of organizations, institutions and other social structures.

Some of the key concepts of exchange theory are built upon the notions of positive and negative reinforcement (rewards and punishments, benefits and costs) derived from the basic principles of operant conditioning behaviourism. However, exchange theory is perhaps better understood as a theory that employs a model of "rational social action" in much the same way that modern economic theory employs a model of rational economic action. In other words, much as economic theory — or utilitarianism — postulates that the economic individual, or *homo economicus*, is primarily motivated by rational self-interest to maximize rewards and minimize costs in the marketplace, exchange theory extends this assumption of rational self-interest to all other areas of social interaction.

Exchange theorists are strongly committed to the idea that all sociological explanations should in principle be reducible to propositions about interacting individuals and to the conditions that influence individual behaviour in a social context. Homans has been highly critical of holistic, or macrosocial theories, regarding these theories as "reifications" of social reality (that is, as explanations which mistakenly attribute the properties of real things to abstract concepts such as "social system"). However, unlike symbolic interactionists, who study the internal cognitive processes of the social actor, exchange theorists are only interested in the externally observable and measurable behaviour of the individual in interaction with others. Internal cognitive processes that cannot be "scientifically" observed and measured, according to exchange theorists, are wholly speculative and without empirical foundation. However, although their emphasis on outwardly observable behaviour may appear to resemble the orientation of the ethnomethodologists, there are also important differences between these two traditions.

Whereas the positivist inclinations of exchange theorists (as well as rational choice and network theorists) lead them to formulate propositions about human behaviour that are assumed to be universally valid, the phenomenological influences on ethnomethodologists lead them to emphasize the relativity and "indexicality" (i.e., the contextually dependent nature) of all sociological descriptions and generalizations. Thus, while ethnomethodologists are strongly empiricist in their research, they are, at the same time, anti-positivist. On the other hand, exchange theorists (as well as their close cousins, the rational choice theorists, game theorists and network theorists) are strongly positivist in their research orientations. In other words, positivists believe that their propositions are universally valid: that is, the meaning and truth of these propositions remain constant, irrespective of where, when or by whom they are stated — just as the law of gravitation is presumed to be true, irrespective of where or when it is stated. What these differences demonstrate, therefore, is that microsocial theories, no less than their macrosocial counterparts, are deeply divided along epistemological and ideological lines.

Yet another microsocial theory is the dramaturgical perspective, which is associated with the work of Erving Goffman. Goffman's early work on the "presentation of self" in everyday life may be seen as a further development of the ideas of symbolic interactionism, especially his notion of the self as a social actor. His ability to portray the most routine encounters in social life as "performances" staged for particular audiences by the social actor in the different settings where interaction takes place, has given Goffman's work a popularity unusual for most theoretical writing in sociology. In his later work, however, which begins to focus on the more stable structural elements of social interaction, Goffman returns to themes pursued by Durkheim in his studies of how the "collective representations" of society arise from and structure definite patterns of social interaction. Goffman's work evolved from his earlier interactionist theory of dramaturgy to a later, more structuralist theory of frame analysis. Whereas dramaturgy was primarily focused on individuals as social actors who performed for their audiences, frame analysis introduced the idea of the frame as a culturally or institutionally determined definition of reality that strongly influences, or even determines, how people to make sense of objects and events. For example, an evangelical frame is likely to project a strongly pro-life idea of abortion, emphasizing biblical injunctions to uphold the sacredness of "God-given" life — even if many evangelicals still support capital punishment. But for many feminists, the issue of abortion is likely to be framed in terms of a pro-choice perspective, emphasizing the inherent right of a woman to exercise control over her body.

These are some of the different microsocial perspectives which evolved during the closing decades of the twentieth century and which have greatly enriched the discourse of contemporary social theory. In some ways it may appear as though contemporary social theory has become a modern version of the Tower of Babel: a confusion of different voices, all speaking past each other with nothing in common. (For another text which discusses different sociological perspectives as a Tower of Babel, see Phillips 2001). The reality, however, is less daunting and more optimistic. The proliferation of perspectives has in many ways strengthened rather than weakened the enterprise of social theory. Old traditions that appeared in danger of growing moribund, such as structural functionalism, have become revitalized (as neo-functionalism) due in part to their exposure to new traditions of social thought. More than at any time in its recent history, social theory is alive with fresh ideas which are cross-pollinating between different traditions and contributing to new and intriguing ways of deciphering our social worlds.

GEORGE HERBERT MEAD: ORIGINAL PIONEER OF SYMBOLIC INTERACTIONISM

The two most prominent theorists of symbolic interactionism were George Herbert Mead and Herbert Blumer. Each of these theorists contributed important ideas that helped to shape the symbolic interactionist perspective. However, it is again worth noting that one of the most important intellectual traditions to influence symbolic interactionism was the philosophy of "pragmatism" as it was preached and practised at the University of Chicago. The essence of pragmatism lay in the belief that "truth" is not something that exists out there beyond us, awaiting discovery. For pragmatists, there is no absolute or objective truth that somehow corresponds to an independent or external "reality." Instead, "truth" is seen as the specific solution to any particular intellectual or practical puzzle. In other words, what is found to be true for one situation is not necessarily true for a different situation. "Truth" is always defined within a particular context, and a knowledge claim is only certified as true when it has a positive practical outcome (i.e., when it "works"). Thus, even though the law of gravitation appears to be an absolute truth, some argue that it is actually a relative truth inasmuch as it is assumed that this truth is stated by someone located on Earth — and the laws of gravitation are not the same in an extra-terrestrial environment. In this sense, therefore, it may be asserted that there is no absolute truth. Any conception of "truth" is always dependent upon time, space, place, beliefs and context. The late astrophysicist Stephen Hawking, for example, also championed a pragmatic perspective on truth and facts in scientific discourse: "If there are two models that both agree with observation ... then one cannot say that one is more real than another. One can use whichever model is more convenient in the situation under consideration" (see Jones 2017).

This conception of truth is sometimes known as the "coherence," "contextual" or pragmatic theory of (meaning and) truth. It stands in contrast to the "referential" or "correspondence" theory of (meaning and) truth, which assumes that the truth of any knowledge claim lies in its direct correspondence to an independent or external "reality." The pragmatic theory of truth assumes that the truth of any knowledge claim is only what competent or suitably qualified people agree is the truth. And it is this pragmatic theory of truth that forms the epistemological basis of symbolic interactionism.

Besides the concept of "truth," another concept central to the concerns of symbolic interactionists is "meaning." The search for meaning marks, on one important level, the great divide between the lives of humans and — from what we can observe — the lives of other animals. Humans, as far as we can tell, are the only animals able to question the meaning of their own lives, as well as the meaning of everything else. We can also assume that no action or object carries any inherent meaning (in itself); the meanings assigned to all actions and objects are defined, in practical terms, within the pragmatic contexts of their occurrence and use. "Meaning," therefore, is defined by *use* rather than by correspondence to some external and unchanging "reality."

For example, the meaning a totemic animal — such as an eagle or bear — has in a traditional hunting and gathering society may be very different from the meaning that an image of the same animal has in a colonial settler, industrial society. The diverse meanings attributed to objects within different cultures or worldviews can often be seen in the different uses made of these objects. Thus, whereas grasshoppers may simply be regarded as an agricultural nuisance in many Western societies, in other regions — such as the Central Valleys area of Oaxaca in Mexico, where they are called *chapulines* — they are prized as a food delicacy and an important source of protein (Cohen et al. 2009). For pragmatists, this example shows how everything is thoroughly dependent for its meaning upon the context of its occurrence and use. Symbolic interactionists are also very sensitive to the diversity and relativity of meanings in human societies.

For symbolic interactionists, the meaning attributed to any act or object is always defined within a social or cultural context, i.e., within a social interaction or a social relationship. In other words, the meaning that we attach to things grows out of the relations we have to other people — to other social actors. When we encounter a person who is crying, for example, the meaning we attach to this act, whether the person is sad or happy, will depend upon the cues and responses we receive during our interaction with this individual. Meanings emerge through the process of social interaction. And in human societies, meanings are constructed through the use of "symbols."

Mead first developed many of his symbolic interactionist concepts as a critical response to the tradition of classical conditioning behaviourism, which originated with Pavlov and further evolved under the influence of Watson, a former student of Mead. This tradition reached its height with the later operant conditioning behaviourism of Skinner in the 1950s, as the influence of behaviourism declined in recent decades. What needs to be understood is that Mead saw his ideas as an extension of the principles of behaviourism from the animal world to the social world (that is, the human world). Mead referred to his own ideas as "social behaviourism" to emphasize both their differences and their continuities with the evolving tradition of psychological behaviourism.

THE VOCABULARY OF INTERACTIONISM

The term "symbolic interactionism" was never used by Mead and was only introduced by Herbert Blumer several decades later. As Mead's ideas developed more fully, it became evident that his brand of social behaviourism was essentially incompatible with the principles and concepts of psychological behaviourism, which had first been developed for the study of animal (non-human) forms of behaviour. In this respect, Mead's ideas were always in tacit opposition to those of the behaviourists because he always insisted that the concepts used to study non-human behaviour were inadequate for the study of human behaviour. It was on this assumption that Mead's theoretical perspective was founded, and it has been this assumption that has guided the subsequent growth of symbolic interactionism.

Symbols, Signs and Gestures

The distinction between a "sign" and a "symbol" is an important one. A sign provides us with physical evidence of a relationship between one natural object, or one behavioural act, and another. In many higher primates, raised hackles accompanied by growling noises is a sign of anger that is likely to lead to aggression. Smoke pouring from a house is normally a sign that a fire is burning within the house. The smoke is a natural sign that is instantly understood not only by all humans, irrespective of their nationality or culture, but by most other animals as well. The meaning of signs is based upon our immediate reactions to the natural world. For this reason, humans and most animals *react* to signs instinctively through our conditioned and unconditioned reflexes.

Unlike a sign, which indicates a relationship between "natural objects," or natural acts, such as smoke and fire or anger and aggression, a symbol represents a relationship between "social objects," or social acts. The meaning of a symbol is based upon our response to the social world. For this reason, we *respond* to symbols through our shared social and cultural understandings. These understandings may vary from one culture to another, and symbols from one culture are not always understood in another culture. For many people around the world, one of the most potent symbols is a flag. The significance of a flag has very little to do with its material characteristics — such as the quality of its cloth or its colours — but from what it symbolizes. Thus some flags can be divisive: in the US, for example, the Confederacy flag (the Stars and Bars) may be seen in some white communities as a symbol of Southern heritage and tradition, whereas for many African Americans and many Northerners, it is a symbol of slavery, racism and bigotry. While symbols may be readily understood by everyone within a particular society, they can both unify and polarize communities.

Symbols in human communication are "invented" during the course of interacting with others. The most powerful sets of symbols used in human communication are those which make up languages. Language is our primary medium of symbolic communication. Language also provides us with good examples of the essential characteristics of any symbol. In general terms, symbols possess three important characteristics: (1) they are arbitrary; (2) they are abstract; and (3) they are reflexive. What do we mean by these characteristics? Linguistic symbols, i.e., words, are obviously *arbitrary*. There is no natural, or necessary, reason why the yellow food we eat with bread or crackers should be called "cheese," "fromage," "Käse," "formaggio," "queso" or " сыр." The name and meaning of this symbol simply express an arbitrary, or conventional, agreement reached within a particular linguistic community. Symbols are *abstract* because we can talk about and think about the object referred to by the symbol in its absence. We can refer to the referent (cheese) in recollection or in anticipation of its use, but it does not have to be present in order for us to talk about it. Symbols allow us to conjure up the idea of objects or acts any time, any place. Symbols provide us with the abstract powers of displacement and projection in time and space. Finally, symbols are *reflexive* in that when we communicate a symbol to other members of our community, they can conjure up the image of the object in their own minds. These are powers that only humans possess.

As we all know, humans not only communicate with each other through the use of verbal symbols but also through the use of what Mead called "significant gestures." These are often non-verbal acts which carry a strong symbolic meaning. In recent years, the "high five" action has been a commonly shared gesture signifying congratulations or celebration over a frequently minor practical accomplishment. At the opposite end of the moral spectrum, significant gestures may also be used to communicate insults or threats. In Canada, raising a middle finger, or "flipping the bird," signifies a strong insult to those at whom it is directed. Significant gestures, of course, vary from one culture to another. Thus, while the raised finger insult is readily used and understood in North America, comparable insults may be expressed differently in other parts of the world.

The Social Self

The heart of all symbolic interactionist discourse is the concept of the "self." It is in their possession of a socialized self that humans are most clearly distinguished from the higher primates. Most importantly, the self is the product of social interaction with others. The self emerges through the process of "role-taking," that is, through our learned ability to put ourselves in the place of another and to see ourselves from the perspective of another. The ability to take the roles and perspectives of others evolves through a number of stages. Childhood socialization is sometimes broken into three distinct stages: the preparatory stage, the play stage and the game stage. In the preparatory stage (0–2 years), children imitate or mimic the actions of their parents: they may attempt to "read" a newspaper, even if holding it upside down. In the play stage (2–6 years), children learn to create an inner world of make-believe in which they pretend to perform different activities without really taking others into account: the young girl with her doctor set; the small boy with his building blocks. But it is only in the final, game stage (7 years or more), that children learn to respond to the needs and expectations of others — often by participating in group activities — such as hockey, board games, dancing — for which there are rules that need to be recognized and followed (see Medley-Rath 2016).

As young children learn to recognize and respond to the expectations of others, they acquire the capacity to see themselves from the vantage point of others. They first learn to respond to the expectations of those closest to them (parents, siblings etc.), or what are referred to as their "significant others." Later, they learn to respond to the more general expectations of other members of society, their so-called "generalized others." The social and emotional development of a child is only complete when they have learned to "internalize" the expectations of generalized others, because these generalized expectations represent the norms of society.

According to Mead, the fully developed self is "reflexive," i.e., capable of conducting an "internal conversation" within itself. Every reflexive self is composed of two aspects: the spontaneous, impulsive and creative aspect, which is known as the "I," and the socially responsible and moral self, which is known as the "me." Whereas the "I" is driven by the primal energy of self-interest, the "me" is socially conditioned by the expectations of others. In most healthy individuals, the self is engaged in a perpetual dialogue — or internal conversation — between itself as subject (the I) and itself as an object (the me). In incompletely socialized individuals, however, the self may be largely driven by perceived self-interest without regard for the expectations of others. Such individuals, who may be largely devoid of empathy, are sometimes defined as "psychopaths" or "sociopaths."

For symbolic interactionists, the self is wholly a product of social interaction. Without such interaction, individuals are incapable of developing a reflexive self in any meaningful sense. There have been a few documented cases of individuals who have grown up beyond the boundaries of society without any human contact. Many of these cases involve abandoned babies who were later adopted and raised by other animals, most notably by wolves or apes. When later "discovered" by humans, these feral children were only able to communicate through animal — often canine or simian — sounds, such as barks, growls, grunts etc. Their behaviours were largely motivated by instinctual drives. In many cases, these feral children were unable to learn even the most rudimentary social skills; their early potential for self-formation often remained unrealized — sometimes because they had experienced severe human abuse and isolation even before their abandonment into the wilderness.

According to Mead, the ability of humans to act in a subjectively meaningful way may be broken down into several distinct phases: impulse, perception, manipulation and consummation. Together, these different phases suggest that human action is a far more complex behaviour than the purely instinctual behaviour of most other animals. Human action is subjectively meaningful and involves the elements of choice, reflection and conscious decision-making. Also, as Mead further suggested, the capacity for meaningful social action is closely linked to the emergence of a "mind." The mind, like the self, is also a product of social interaction.

MICROSOCIAL THEORIES AND THE MICROSCOPIC FOCUS

The primary theoretical and methodological focus of symbolic interactionism is on the interactions that take place between "real" social actors, rather than on the transactions between large-scale structures of social relations, such as "societies," "institutions" and "social systems." In this sense, symbolic interactionism is a microsocial theoretical perspective that is committed to the idea that *the structure of the social whole is always reducible to the sum of its individual parts*. This idea is known as the "postulate of methodological individualism," or "nominalism." The opposite assumption is known as the "postulate of methodological holism," or "realism"; it proposes that *the structure of the social whole is greater than the sum of its individual parts*.

Symbolic interactionists are critical of traditional sociological and social theories, which frequently ascribe to abstract concepts — such as society, institution, social system, organization etc. — the properties of real things. This process of treating abstract concepts as though they are real things is known as "reification." Symbolic interactionists reject the use of reified concepts when used in macrosocial theories such as Marxism, structural functionalism, conflict theory, critical theory and so on. Besides their strong microsocial focus on social actors (i.e., agency) rather than on large-scale social systems (i.e., structure), symbolic interactionists have pioneered the techniques of qualitative social research. In particular, Herbert Blumer systematized some of the guiding principles of social research from a symbolic interactionist perspective.

Although symbolic interactionism is compatible with both qualitative and quantitative research methodologies, symbolic interactionists place heavy emphasis on understanding the cognitive processes involved in the social construction of meaning and on the subjective processes underlying the social construction of identity. Unlike more macrosocial perspectives, symbolic interactionists maintain a sharp focus on how social actors choose to act and how the meaning of their actions is always "negotiated" between actors in any particular situation or context.

In many ways, symbolic interactionism is a quintessentially American theoretical perspective. Its emphases on the free will of the social actor, the fragility and impermanence of our social structures and the mutability of our social identities reflects a society in which individualism, innovation and change have always been prized more highly than stable tradition and established authority. From its earliest beginnings at the University of Chicago, symbolic interactionism has represented the promise of a more open society and new opportunities for the individual — a society that, at least in theory, rejected the authority of fixed and frozen structures of social relations in favour of constant innovation and social change. And although these promises and opportunities remain unrealized for many Americans today, symbolic interactionism still displays the ideological birthmarks of its origins (Plummer 2000).

Some of the most significant changes in our understanding of the modern world can be enhanced from a symbolic interactionist perspective. This is especially true for some of the major political and ideological shifts that have taken place in our societies over the past several decades. One observer comments at length on how political changes have often altered our shared perceptions and understanding of our social worlds:

> Socially shared meanings are extremely powerful in shaping our perception of the world. They can change our behaviors, influence our thinking and motivate our actions. The fact that these meanings can be shifted has been the essential insight behind the advertising industry, but also behind social movements. The civil rights movement sought to shift the meanings that society at large associated with African Americans, and the LGBT movements have sought to do the

same thing for their constituents. Both have been successful in powerful ways. But if the study of symbolic interaction teaches us anything, it is that meanings can be reshaped, meaning that the victories of social movements, like the legalization of same-sex marriage, abortion rights and voting rights, are not necessarily permanent. Many other movements are fighting hard under the belief that they can undo these changes, using the same methods, to shift public meanings and change society to fit their own vision of what reality should be. (Kincaid 2017)Q

HERBERT BLUMER: FIRST AMBASSADOR FOR SYMBOLIC INTERACTIONISM

More than any other social theorist, Herbert Blumer attempted to sys-tematize and codify the tradition of symbolic interactionism around a set of key concepts and basic assumptions. Throughout much of his career, Blumer acted as an interpreter and ambassador of the ideas of George Herbert Mead. Mead himself published very little during his lifetime, and it was left to his students to collect, collate and organize his lecture notes into a coherent presentation of his ideas. This is how Mead's most famous book, *Mind, Self and Society,* was finally published. After Mead's death in 1931, Blumer refined some of his key concepts and popularized the theory of symbolic interactionism.

Blumer highlights a number of key concepts introduced by Mead that helped define the evolving tradition of this theoretical perspective. One of these is the concept of "interpretation." For Blumer, interpreta-tion distinguishes the symbolic interactionist perspective from that of behaviourism. If the behaviourist paradigm is definable in terms of the "stimulus-response" paradigm (S-R), then the symbolic interactionist paradigm is distinguished by its emphasis on "interpretation" as a factor which mediates, or intervenes, between the stimulus and the response (S-I-R). Blumer's point is that whereas animals invariably respond automatically to environmental stimuli on the basis of their instincts, humans respond to such stimuli on the basis of the meanings that such stimuli hold for them. This is what Blumer means when he suggests that human actions are social "constructions" rather than instinctual "releases." Human responses are constructed through the process of "self-indication," whereby humans are able to discriminate the objects of their environment and assign particular meanings to these objects. In order to do this, humans use mental constructs, or symbols, to label objects and to communicate the symbolic meaning of these objects to other humans. This capacity to invest the objects of their environment with symbolic meaning most distinguishes human *action* from animal *behaviour*.

The process of self-indication and the development of the self that is implied by this process constitute the real starting points for Blumer's study of society. For Blumer, the structures of society are fully reducible to the actions of individuals who take each other into account (take the role of the other) in the course of their everyday activities. It is this capacity to take the role of the other that provides a basis for collective action and ensures that much of this action is routinized in stable and predictable ways. What may appear to be large-scale collective societal forces that combine to produce social order are, in fact, reducible to the consequences of countless inter-individual decisions to take the role of the other during everyday activities. Social order arises from the reciprocal actions of individuals and not from the monolithic influence of large-scale structural units of society.

Blumer remained strongly committed to a version of sociological individualism and was critical of macrosocial theoretical perspectives based upon sociological holism. He was particularly critical of social theories and explanations that rely upon some form of what he refers to as "sociological determinism." By this he means social theories that seek to explain the actions of individuals by reference to larger social forces that influence, regulate or in other ways determine these actions. Such sociological theories are said to be "deterministic" because they overlook entirely the fact that all social action originates with individuals, who possess reflexive selves and whose freedom of action is always based upon the subjective meanings that any such action has for them. In other words, Blumer always emphasized the importance of *agency* over *structure* in his theoretical contributions.

Because the starting point for Blumer's conception of sociology is the study of the interpretative actions of individuals, he is especially critical of social theories that seek to explain the actions of individuals in terms of larger external social causes. Thus, Blumer rejects the notion that individual actions can be meaningfully understood as expressions of "social norms," performances of "social roles," the consequence of "functions," the result of an "institutionalization of value orientations" or the reflection of patterns of "collective representations." None of these formulations — typically used by structural functionalists — acknowledge the active and creative aspects of individual actions that are part of the process of self-indication and interpretation.

The major target of Blumer's criticism, therefore, is the language of structural functionalism, which describes social relations in terms of structural units such as "social system," "social structure," "culture," "institution," "status position" and so on. According to Blumer, all of these terms help to conceal the fact that society is made up of individuals, all of whom possess selves which interpret stimuli from the social world in countless different ways. The great problem with the language of structural functionalism, or any other macrosocial perspective, is that it portrays the actions of individuals, or of groups, as though these actions are produced by larger structural units of society. Social actors are said to "internalize" the patterns of norms which have been institutionalized through the larger cultural system. Similarly, in the language of Marxism, individuals may be bearers of "false consciousness" or "class consciousness," depending upon their political orientation. Other types of group action may be defined as "functions" or "dysfunctions" depending on the consequences of these actions for the larger societal structure of which they are a part. In these and similar examples, individual or group actions are portrayed as a reflection of larger social forces that exercise a determinate influence on the outcomes of the conduct of groups or individuals. This is what Blumer objects to most strongly, and this is the reason that Blumer dismisses structural functionalism as a prime example of sociological determinism, or "sociologism."

At the same time, Blumer concedes that the symbolic interactionist perspective is not entirely incompatible with more macrosocial and structurally oriented forms of social theory and social analysis. He suggests that larger structural concepts of society, such as "organization," "culture," "social system" etc., may best be understood as frameworks, or limits, within which symbolic interaction between individuals actually takes place. In other words, to the extent that symbols and other cultural codes may originate from the larger structures of society that have predated, and will also outlast, the individual, these cultural influences may be thought of as "external" to the individual. Indeed, Blumer even introduces the term "joint action" to describe the combined and collective actions of individuals which may result in the construction of social relations that are greater than the actions of any single individual. However, Blumer emphasizes that these social relations are always dynamic "processes," forever changing and never stable or frozen "structures" independent of individuals. Blumer's point is that these larger structural elements of society only come alive in the hands of real interacting individuals. In this sense, he regards the terminology of structural functionalism as unavoidably abstract because it does not directly refer to the interactions of real individuals with selves, purposes, interpretations and intentions. By contrast, the language of symbolic interactionism, which refers directly to the intentions and actions of real individuals, remains, for Blumer, the concrete language of the real social world.

Blumer's contributions show us how symbolic interactionists emphasize the active, creative and interpretive aspects of social interaction. During its heyday in the 1960s and 1970s, symbolic interactionism offered one of the more effective challenges to structural functionalism from a microsocial theoretical perspective. Today, many of its key concepts and basic assumptions have become assimilated into other sociological theories, including some macrosocial theories of society. We have moved far beyond the age of theoretical confrontation between macrosocial and microsocial theories and entered a period of cross-fertilization and greater theoretical pluralism and theoretical diversity. However, before we conclude this chapter, we shall briefly trace some of the more recent developments of symbolic interactionism and show the growing influence of this perspective on other traditions of sociological and social theory.

The World as Theatre

With the richness of his kaleidoscopic thought, there are few better interpreters of modern metropolitan life than Erving Goffman: every day in our cities people play their ever-changing roles, then gripe about them in dark bars at the end of the working day. We all try to "pass," or desperately scramble to protect our secrets; each of us suffers sudden disappointments that require consolation, and to every man or woman there eventually comes a moment of decision and the chance to act with courage or generosity. To Erving Goffman we human beings are all on the same merry-go-round, but each of us displays a different attitude to the ride. In the meantime, around and around we go! (Dirda n.d.)

THE DRAMATURGICAL THEORY OF ERVING GOFFMAN

Erving Goffman's work has influenced several generations of sociology scholars and students, and his insights have helped to reshape the face of contemporary social theory. Goffman prepared one of his more influential articles, "The Interaction Order," as his presidential address to the American Sociological Association (ASA), but his untimely death in 1982 led to the address being delivered posthumously in 1983. It is something of a testament to the changing times in which we live that an institution as traditionally conservative as the ASA could finally bestow the imprimatur of respectability and acceptance upon one of modern sociology's most illustrious outsiders.

Goffman first became known through early works that focused on how our social selves and identities are shaped and reshaped during the course of our interactions with others in a variety of social settings. Those early works, most notably *Presentation of Self in Everyday Life* (1959), *Asylums* (1961a), *Encounters* (1961b), *Behavior in Public Places* (1963b) and *Stigma* (1963a) secured Goffman's reputation as a leading representative of interactionism in modern social theory and as a fascinating observer of the rituals and encounters of everyday life. We can trace Goffman's career from its beginnings as an extension of symbolic interactionism to its later development as a version of micro-structuralism. Goffman's early work was characterized by his introduction of the theory of dramaturgy, while his later work inaugurated the theory of frame analysis. This evolution from dramaturgy to frame analysis reflects a shift in Goffman's concerns from the early "voluntaristic" study of how social actors present their selves and perform their roles, to the later more "deterministic" study of how the micro-structures of ritualized encounters combine to frame, and thereby define and shape, the identities and performances of social actors. In other words, Goffman's career advanced from the early study of voluntarism (freely acting individuals) to the later study of determinism (constraining frames and structures). In this respect, Goffman followed in the footsteps of other major theorists — including Karl Marx and Talcott Parsons — whose early voluntaristic perspectives evolved into more deterministic frameworks in their later works.

The dramaturgical perspective is a good example of the social theory of everyday life. Goffman was primarily interested in how individuals, or "social actors," present their selves in public places and how they perform for the various "audiences" in their lives. As the word "dramaturgy" suggests, Goffman's theoretical perspective is based upon a metaphor of the theatre. Each of us, according to Goffman, is an actor who performs one way when on a public stage (a "front") and another way when in a private place (a "back region").

Much of Goffman's early work analyzes the different ways in which individuals perform their public roles, try to sustain their public identities and protect these identities against risks, threats or challenges to their credibility. Like any other social theorist worth their salt, Goffman develops a theoretical language with a rich vocabulary of concepts. He introduces these concepts in the hope that they will provide us with new and refreshing ways to speak about and observe the interpersonal social relations of our everyday life.

Goffman and Symbolic Interactionism

Part of the interest of Goffman's work is his independence from the established tradition of symbolic interactionism by repudiating what have often been seen as some of its most cherished assumptions. In doing this, Goffman not only confirms his own status as a highly original and inventive social thinker, but he also helps us to critically reappraise the theoretical possibilities of the interactionist tradition. In some of his early work, Goffman sets out to explode a couple of widely held assumptions, or "dogmas," about the analysis of society from an interactionist perspective. The first of these dogmas is the assumption that interactionist accounts of social life necessarily presuppose a "normative consensus" around which social order is structured. Indeed, Goffman goes to considerable lengths to show not only that an interactionist perspective may remain independent of these functionalist assumptions, but that it is equally compatible with the assumptions of a more conflict-oriented perspective. These are fascinating observations, and in his analysis of the possible range of motives and consequences leading individuals to participate in the "interaction order," Goffman moves beyond traditional interactionist sources into the realms of Marx, Durkheim and Weber.

A second dogma long associated with interactionism that Goffman disagrees with is the assumption that an interactionist analysis privileges the small-scale microsocial aspects of social reality over the large-scale macrosocial aspects. In other words, he challenges the idea that the large-scale structures of social reality can only ever be properly understood as aggregations and extrapolations of the face-to-face encounters which take place in myriad local settings. When confronting these expressions of "ontological nominalism" traditionally associated with symbolic interactionism, Goffman explains why he finds these claims to be unconvincing and, to use his own word, "uncongenial."

The Interaction Order

One of the key concepts Goffman uses in his study of interpersonal, or face-to-face, social relations is that of the "interaction order." For Goffman, the interaction order is the primary locus of social action and interaction, much as the economic order may be seen as the primary locus of economic behaviour. Analytically, the interaction order may best be understood as the site of social practices that are governed, or regulated, by a set of "enabling conventions" in much the same way that the use of language is governed by the rules of syntax or that the use of automobiles is governed by the Highway Code.

However, as Goffman is at pains to point out, although the interaction order is the site of the routinized face-to-face encounters of everyday life for countless individuals, we should be careful not to draw unwarranted conclusions from this fact. We should not assume, for example, that everyone who participates in the interaction order does so because the rewards of participation necessarily outweigh the costs. In other words, the interaction order should not be seen as a kind of "social contract" by means of which individuals voluntarily surrender some personal freedoms in order to secure the greater good for the community of which they are a part. According to Goffman, what may be viewed as a desirable interaction order by some members of the community could just as easily be viewed as undesirable by other members. What was viewed as desirable by the religious orders who ran the residential schools in Canada was viewed very differently by the Indigenous children (and their families) who suffered in these schools. Thus, the interaction orders may be sites of contestation and conflict, or they may be areas of cooperation and consensus. But part of Goffman's originality lay in his suggestion that the interaction order could be viewed through the lenses of conflict theory as well as of consensus theory (i.e., functionalism). For this reason, the "contractarian" assumptions (treating all forms of social interaction as though they were based on agreement, as in a "contract") that have traditionally been associated with interactionist views of the social world are dismissed by

Goffman as dogmas which have no place in his analytical framework. Goffman concludes, therefore, that the interaction order, as the site of face-to-face encounters, may sometimes be structured more around relations of inequality and conflict than around relations of cooperation and consensus. Unlike most previous interactionists, who typically assumed that individuals engage in face-to-face interactions on the basis of a voluntary consensus and freedom of choice, Goffman reminds us that not all forms of interaction are necessarily of this kind: "Individuals go along with current interaction arrangements for a wide variety of reasons, and one cannot read from their apparent tacit support of an arrangement that they would, for example, resent or resist its change. Very often behind community and consensus are mixed motive games" (1983: 5).

For some social actors, participation in the interaction order may result from the ability of more powerful groups and individuals either to coerce them through the actual or implied use of force or to obtain their compliance through intimidation, deceit or manipulation. Wherever the interaction order is structured around relations of inequality, any suggestion that all social actors participate on the basis of a voluntary consensus of values becomes highly questionable. It is in observations such as these that Goffman appears open to the influences of Marx, Weber and Durkheim, whose concepts of "ideology," "false consciousness," "legitimation" and "collective representations" also focused on how social order was maintained in stratified societies.

Besides questioning the contractarian and consensualist assumptions, or dogmas, traditionally associated with the interactionist perspective, Goffman also challenges the inherent "nominalism" of interactionism. In other words, unlike most interactionist theorists, who begin their analyses of social life with the assumption that the microsocial processes and events of face-to-face interaction are somehow *more real* than the macrosocial structures of social relations, Goffman goes out of his way to disavow this kind of nominalism and reductionism. In his view, all forms of sociological description, whether of encounters in a local setting, or of large-scale societal structures and processes, may equally be seen as social constructions, or in his own words, "somebody's crudely edited summaries" (1983: 9). According to Goffman, if face-to-face interactions in a local setting are more open to systematic analysis than studies of large-scale social structures, this is only because the forms of daily interaction have been "worn smooth by constant repetition on the part of participants"

(9) and because the subjective aspects of interaction are more open to the empathic understanding of the observer. These factors should not be misunderstood as ascribing any ontological priority to microsocial over macrosocial constructions of reality.

What makes Goffman atypical of most interactionist theorists is not only the fact that he resists the temptation of seeing microsocial processes as somehow more real than macrosocial structures, but that he allows that there may be "a loose coupling" between interactional practices and social structures. In ways that are more reminiscent of Durkheim than of Mead, Goffman discusses how certain forms of face-to-face interaction may have considerable significance for the larger structures of the state and of civil society. As an example, he cites the larger political significance of such face-to-face interactive events as the Carnival celebrations of the Caribbean community in the UK or, in a very different vein, of the Nuremberg rallies in Nazi Germany. In these and other collective happenings, Goffman suggests, it is often possible to trace the connections between local settings and the larger structures of the polity, economy or society in which these settings are situated. Goffman's discussion of these ceremonies and the ways in which social interaction among individuals is connected to broader societal structures reveals the clear influence of Durkheim's ideas and points in the direction of an analysis that is more structuralist than interactionist.

The Dramaturgical Self

Goffman is far more interested in the form of an interaction, i.e., the rules followed and the techniques employed, than in its content. And, as he repeats throughout much of his work, the underlying concern for most social actors is to protect their selves from embarrassment and to repair any damage to their selves caused by inconsistencies, exposure or other incongruities. One of the most controversial and heavily criticized parts of Goffman's work is his concept of the "self." Many critics have berated Goffman for having what they perceive as a "situational" definition of the self. Because the dramaturgical metaphor of the theatre is so central to Goffman's early work, many commentators have concluded that, for Goffman, the self is perpetually reinvented by the social actor for every new audience. This conclusion has led many critics to accuse Goffman of cynicism in his assessment of the self in social interaction: "His apparent cynicism is such that his work often appears to be a prime example of the con-games he sees in the public behaviours he studies, thereby stubbornly defying our attempts to place it and assess its significance" (Dawe 1973: 246).

Goffman is often castigated for suggesting that all social actors — which means all of us — are little more than con-artists who are willing to resort to deception, fraud or manipulation in order to stage a convincing performance. These critics have also reproached Goffman for abandoning any conception of a core self in favour of an infinitely plastic self, wholly conditioned by the need to opportunistically influence or manipulate any particular audience. Such a conception of the self marks a clear departure from the mainstream tradition of symbolic interactionism, which, from the time of Mead, has always distinguished between a core self (the I) and a socially conditioned self (the me).

However, much of this criticism of Goffman may have been misplaced. Far from denying the existence of a core self, or identity, Goffman has — in some of his work — distinguished between three different types of identity: a social, personal and ego identity. For Goffman, the personal identity refers to the unique and specific characteristics of an individual that enable them to have a relatively stable self-image based on their particular social, cultural, personal and biographical experiences. As Chriss (2015: 17) observes, this concept leads to the idea "that nobody can walk in another person's shoes, meaning that no two persons share the exact same socialization experiences." A social identity, on the other hand, is the societal, or supra-individual, identity given to an individual — which is normally accepted by them as an authentic representation — that arises from broader social or cultural categories or criteria. A person's gender, ethnicity, nationality and even age are usually aspects of their social identity. The ego identity differs from both of the other identities as it is often defined in the context of a particular situation or context. Thus, when facing extreme situations — such as the prospect of death in combat or on a mountainside, or when experiencing some other traumatic event — individuals may discover an unrealized potential in themselves, a deeply intimate identity with which they were previously unacquainted. As Williams (2000: 7) explains, the central characteristic of ego identity is "the capacity of individuals to choose among a set of available attributes, and a concern with the coherence and consistency discernible within the variety of chacterisations accepted by individuals to be true of themselves independent of time and location."

The Vocabulary of Dramaturgy

The basic terms and concepts of Goffman's dramaturgical perspective are by now pretty well known. All of us, as social actors, present our selves in public performances in a variety of different "fronts." Each front may be analyzed in terms of its "setting," "appearance" and "manner." Most of our public performances are staged in cooperation with a performance "team" of other social actors. Together, we cooperate in staging orderly and credible performances. When we retreat from our public fronts, we enter the "backstage" areas of our private lives, where we can relax and escape from the expectations of a public audience. Backstages, however, can be transformed into fronts at any time and in any place.

Goffman reminds us that social actors can show different degrees of attachment to the roles they play in public. Sometimes, actors will display considerable "role distance" in their performance of a role towards which they feel some ambivalence. This is particularly the case for actors who feel that their roles are beneath them or fail to fully express their personalities. Goffman's famous example of role distance is that of teenage boys riding on a merry-go-round. Although these boys apparently enjoy their ride, they also show — by their horseplay and goofing around — that they do not take the activity too seriously. In contrast, the seriousness and gravity of a lawyer observing courtroom etiquette is probably a good example of "role embracement" — the opposite of role distance.

In addition to these basic dramaturgical terms, Goffman introduces other concepts into his analysis of the presentation of self. Among other things, Goffman was interested in how the performance of a social actor could be disrupted by the exposure of unwelcome information. Such information could reveal a discrepancy between the projected identity, or "virtual self," of the actor and their real identity, or "actual self." Performances may sometimes be disrupted when personal information that the actor seeks to conceal is inadvertently revealed. Goffman refers to any type of negative information that is known about an actor as a "stigma." Some stigmas ("discreditable" stigmas, such as a despised sexual orientation, unpopular political or religious beliefs or even a criminal record) are able to be concealed from public view. Other stigmas ("discredited" stigmas, such as speech impediments, disfigurations and defects and physical or mental disabilities) are immediately apparent. Much of the "work" of any public performance involves concealing discrepant information from other actors and "repairing" any damage arising from unwanted revelations.

When a disruption occurs during a performance or presentation of the self, most social actors take immediate remedial action to repair the damage to their social identities. Goffman refers to this repair work as a "corrective process," which involves a number of different "moves," including "challenge," "offering," "acceptance" and "appreciation." In this way, the actor seeks to re-normalize the social interaction and to salvage the credibility and believability of their projected self. Most of the time, however, social actors prevent serious disruptions by using what Goffman calls "techniques of impression management." These are strategies designed to protect the self from risks, challenges and threats which may arise during social interaction.

In his dramaturgical studies of everyday life, Goffman distinguished between "focused encounters" and "unfocused encounters." Focused encounters are those face-to-face meetings that take place between actors engaged in a sustained interaction of some sort. This interaction may be between friends or relatives, between work or college associates, or between other social actors who interact for a limited period of time. "Unfocused encounters," on the other hand, include the casual and often fleeting interactions that most of us experience throughout a normal day — in the street, shopping mall, parking lot, at the bus stop or railway station, or in any number of other public places. Although these unfocused encounters are usually of minor significance to us in the overall scheme of things, Goffman suggests that even these interactions are guided by a set of unspoken rules and unconsciously agreed-upon conventions. However, as in other aspects of life, the expectations underlying unfocused encounters are most clearly revealed when they are violated or broken. When someone cuts in front of us at the supermarket line-up for the checkout, or stares at us for too long in the elevator, or fails to hold the door open when entering a building before us, we experience how the unspoken rules that normally guide unfocused interactions may be broken.

From Dramaturgy to Frame Analysis

Goffman is anxious to show how even the most transitory and fleeting of social encounters may, upon close scrutiny, reveal a degree of structure and organization that the social actors are largely oblivious of. For Goffman, what happens at the level of face-to-face interaction invariably has implications for larger structures of human relations. It is this interest in examining what are sometimes called the "deep structures" of social interaction that coloured Goffman's work in the later stages of his intellectual career and pointed it in the direction of structuralist analysis. Indeed, in his last works, *Forms of Talk* (1981) and *Frame Analysis* (1974), Goffman's debt to Durkheim becomes ever more apparent, and his theoretical interests move closer to, although still remaining distinct from, those of ethnomethodology. Goffman moved beyond dramaturgy and began to experiment with a new perspective he called "frame analysis." This perspective led Goffman to emphasize the interpretative schema, or "frames," used by social actors to organize their actions and to reduce the complexity of social reality. According to Goffman, each of us "processes" our interactions and our casual encounters by viewing these events through a frame, i.e., a personalized definition of the situation. Every frame represents a simplification of an encounter; the frame allows us to include some things and to exclude others. It is a way of reducing the complexity of everyday life. Frames may also be "keyed" in a number of different ways. Each of these keys helps to further define the situation we encounter, whether as make-believe or as a contest, a comedy, a celebration, an interview, a ceremony and so on.

Goffman suggests that all our social interactions are mentally organized into frames. These frames enable us to simplify the meaning of any social encounter and to respond to the cues we decipher from other social actors. Frames are more than simply "definitions of the situation." They are ways of reducing the complexity of social life. Over time, with the benefit of past experience, frames and their keys may become virtual templates for social interaction, enabling us to slip into accustomed roles with well-rehearsed performances.

The Legacy of Goffman

While it may be premature to write an epitaph for Goffman's work, it is certainly not too early to render a judgment on his ideas or to anticipate their likely fate in the years ahead. Goffman has earned his place in the hall of fame of sociology and social theory. Although his work was initially dismissed by some critics as trivial, banal, superficial and "unscientific," and was later condemned as cynical and pessimistic, times have changed. Today, Goffman is widely regarded as an original thinker and founder of several important theoretical perspectives, including dramaturgy and frame analysis. In these respects, Goffman deserves our respect as one of the great contemporary social theorists and as a pioneer in the sociology of everyday life. The questions and challenges that may be raised against Goffman's ideas are no longer those of the past generation of critics. We no longer need to be persuaded of the value of studying everyday life, nor are we scandalized by the possibility that Goffman was both cynical and pessimistic in his assessment of the motives underlying self-presentation. Today, our concerns are likely to have a more contemporary relevance. In an age that has become fixated on the issue of identity — how it is constructed, sustained and even transformed — both Goffman and the symbolic interactionists have some important questions to answer.

One of these questions pertains to the representation of the self. In the traditions of both dramaturgy and symbolic interactionism, the self was always conceived in neutral terms: neither male nor female, neither Black nor white, neither straight nor gay, neither young nor old. But in the real world, our selves are always socially constructed around the basic demographic dimensions of age, gender, sexual orientation, race, nationality, religion, language etc. And today, binary classifications — such as those relating to gender, sexual orientation and race — are often discarded in favour of more complex classifications that represent the greater diversity of social identities. The challenge for interactionist theories is to recognize and respect this diversity in their evolving theoretical perspectives. To do otherwise is to fly in the face of facts and to create an oversimplified social world of neutral identities. It is hardly surprising that the point of departure for many contemporary standpoint theories, such as postmodernism, feminism, Indigenous and Afrocentric theory, and queer theory, among others, is a rejection of the past neutralization of the self and a corresponding demand for the recognition of sexual, racial, ethnic and chronological identities. What standpoint theories — as well as postmodernist and poststructuralist theories — show us is that the neutralization of identity to a single generic profile is not only a problem of knowledge (an epistemological problem), but also a problem of power (a political problem). Grand narratives and metanarratives constructed from the viewpoint of an unacknowledged "zero signifier" — who has traditionally been a white, heterosexual Western male — have always served to express the viewpoint of the privileged and powerful and to suppress the viewpoint of the exploited and oppressed.

Another limitation of dramaturgy is its traditional preoccupation with face-to-face interactions and encounters. But in an age of emergent cyber-identities that interact through social networking sites, many of the assumptions and even the concepts of dramaturgical analysis require revision and further refinement. Concepts such as the "front" and "backstage" regions take on a different meaning when interaction is mediated through a computer or social media site. Indeed, there is a growing literature on the presentation of self in cyberspace. And while some of Goffman's conclusions may have been rendered obsolete by technological change, many of his concepts and ideas have been recycled into a new sociology of telecommunication and virtual interaction. No one has yet suggested that Goffman's work is wholly redundant. For this reason, readers are encouraged to reflect on whether or not they believe that Goffman has any continuing relevance to their own cyber-worlds.

THE ONLINE SOCIAL SELF

A growing number of theorists have tried to evaluate the relevance of Goffman's dramaturgical perspective for analyzing online social interactions on social networking sites, such as Facebook, Twitter, Instagram etc. (see, for example, Zarghooni 2007; Cunningham 2013; Tashmin 2016). The main purpose of this discussion is to determine whether or not Goffman's perspective and key concepts — such as "impression management," "front ," "backstage," "teams" and "stigma" — are still of relevance when analyzing online social interactions and interpersonal encounters. Goffman's research was focused exclusively on face-to-face encounters between social actors and their audiences, and all of his original concepts were designed to analyze real life interactions in actual social situations. The question remains, however, whether Goffman's work applies in an age of interactions in virtual social settings.

After comparing some of the differences and some of the similarities and overlaps between face-to-face (actual) and online (virtual) forms of social interaction and communication, Sasan Zarghooni (2007) concludes that, although there are some unique features to online interactions, many of Goffman's dramaturgical concepts can still be useful for analyzing these interactions. This is because the main point of most social networking sites is *self-presentation*. And while Goffman's work addresses the tactics of self-presentation and the techniques of impression management in face-to-face settings, his perspective may also be used to analyze the popular new forms of self-presentation on the internet. As Zarghooni makes clear, several different tactics of self-presentation are available to most social actors, including self-description, attitude statements, non-verbal behaviour and social associations. And while these tactics may be used in face-to-face settings, they can also be employed by actors who are self-presenting, or performing, on a social networking site or a social media site. Indeed, the writer introduces some recent tactics of self-presentation that were never mentioned by Goffman. Some terms, or neologisms, for these new tactics include BIRGing (basking in reflected glory), CORFing (cutting off reflected failure) and "burnishing" and "boosting." BIRGing refers to how some individuals when networking on social media publicize their association with famous or successful social units, by name-dropping their prestigious connection. By CORFing, on the other hand, individuals seek to conceal their association with losing sports teams, unpopular entertainers or discredited public figures. These and other techniques are used as strategies to reveal or conceal those attributes that can be projected as part of an online performance and personality. In many ways, the increased attention often given to the detailed tactics of self-presentation in a virtual environment only serves to illustrate how narcissistic our popular culture has become. Whether on social networking sites or on reality television, everyone now wants to be an instant celebrity.

Zarghooni also discusses the problem of self-presentational "predicaments." These are embarrassing situations or negative factors which threaten to undermine or contradict the public presentation of the self by a social actor to their audience. Thus, the performance of an actor may be undermined or contradicted by "normative public deficiencies." Examples of celebrities whose public selves have been threatened in this way include the growing list of males accused of sexual improprieties, ranging from sexual harassment to sexual assault, including media heavyweights like Harvey Weinstein, Kevin Spacey, Bill Cosby, Charlie Rose, Roger Ailes, Matt Lauer and Mark Halperin, as well as numerous politicians, such as US Rep. John Conyers, US Senator Bob Packard, US Senator Al Franken, US Senate candidate Roy Moore, British Defence Secretary Michael Fallon. The list is long and growing. In light of the well-publicized accounts of sexual misconduct, these powerful men have undermined their own public images and damaged the appeal of their commercial "brands."

Another threat to an actor's social self may come from a damaging association with discredited groups or individuals. In his first presidential campaign, Barak Obama was forced to disassociate himself from some previous acquaintances, particularly Rev. Jeremiah Wright, who was caught on YouTube "cursing" America, and Bill Ayers, who was once associated with the violent radical political group Weather Underground. Each of these former acquaintances attracted adverse publicity. And so, to maximize his chances of electoral success, Obama cut these individuals loose. Anytime a social actor confronts a self-presentational predicament, there is often a need for "damage control," or what Goffman referred to as "repair work." Thus golf celebrity Tiger Woods faced down his global audience in a public confession of his misdeeds, while Barak Obama publicly disowned acquaintances whose notoriety threatened to discredit him. On the other hand, Donald Trump, who has been accused of sexual improprieties by multiple women and has been caught on camera making insulting and degrading comments about women (in the *Access Hollywood* tape) — and has also appeared to defend neo-Nazis and Ku Klux Klansmen — seems to have chosen a different strategy for damage control and repair work. Pugnacious politicians like Trump may simply choose to provoke a further personal controversy as a means of distraction, in order to divert public attention from a more serious threat to their image and "brand."

When comparing the process of self-presentation on a social networking site to self-presentation in a face-to-face setting, there are some intriguing differences and some similarities. While the concept of the "front" can be used to describe a personal profile that appears on a website by a social actor, it is not the same as the front used in a face-to-face setting. In a virtual setting, although the profile represents the actor's self-presentation, the real flesh and bones actor sits at home in front of a computer, detached, invisible and away from the front. The separation of the real actor from their virtual front is sometimes referred to as "detached self-presentation." Also, the management of stigma is, in many ways, easier in online self-presentations than in a face-to-face setting.

However, there are some constraints which may discourage actors from grossly misrepresenting themselves online or from engaging in blatant deception or fraud. For one thing, the profile that an actor posts online is often monitored by friends and acquaintances. Many of these individuals have intimate personal knowledge of the actor and would easily spot any blatant untruths. Social actors are also aware that, sooner or later, they may have face-to-face meetings with their online correspondents, especially those on dating and friendship websites. The knowledge that a "virtual" identity may someday have to justify its "actual" existence in a face-to-face setting provides a strong incentive for social actors to remain relatively truthful in their online self-presentations. For inhibited or shy social actors, the anxiety that is experienced in face-to-face interactions is greatly reduced in online interactions. And even when an online personal profile elicits a critical or negative response, the actor may compensate by using such self-presentation tactics as "burnishing" or "boosting" their profile.

One of the more obvious differences between online and face-to-face presentations of the self lies in the factor of spontaneity. Whereas face-to-face interactions are more likely to appear relatively spontaneous, online interactions are far more controlled and, some would say, "contrived." In order to compensate for the more structured environment, a number of novel features have been introduced into online communications that are designed to re-inject spontaneity as well as some emotional involvement. The use of icons known as "smileys" and other animated "emoticons" to humanize online communications has become widespread. These icons represent a broad spectrum of emotional expressions ranging from humour and friendship, through to disappointment and displeasure.

More recently, the range of emotional expressions and non-verbal forms of self-presentation has been extended through the use of other applications designed to increase the intimacy of interpersonal contacts. Earlier and now discontinued Facebook applications such as "poke," "superpoke," "vampire-bites" and "throwing a sheep" were once introduced as simulated forms of physical contact between individuals online. These outdated online gestures have been replaced on users' profiles with new forms of quick interaction collectively referred to as "greetings" (Ghoshal 2017). Zarghooni (2007) coined the term "computer-mediated tactility" to refer to these simulated acts of physical contact. These recent applications are normally used to enhance the online performance of an actor for their audience.

In general, it appears as though many of Goffman's dramaturgical concepts are able to provide a framework for analyzing online as well as face-to-face interactions. However, the online setting has some unique characteristics, and a new vocabulary of concepts may be needed to describe and analyze these novelties.

THE FUTURE OF SYMBOLIC INTERACTIONISM

A number of major changes to the symbolic interactionist perspective have taken place over the past several decades. The accumulated effect of these changes has been to lift interactionism out of its earlier isolation within the discipline of sociology and to place it at the busy crossroads of contemporary theory, where its ideas and concepts have become commonplace to many other theoretical perspectives. The time when symbolic interactionism reprised the lonely role of "loyal opposition" to the regime of structural functionalism is now past. Today, its ideas are used by theorists of different persuasions, and its once distinctive set of concepts is shared by a growing number of social theories. These changes signalled the end of interactionism as we once knew it — as an exclusive and distinctive body of social thought — and brought about the dispersal of its ideas among a widening number of intellectual currents and traditions. What is less clear, however, is what these changes have meant for the fate of modern interactionism. Does the widespread acceptance and assimilation of interactionist concepts by other theoretical traditions signal the end of symbolic interactionism as an independent theory in its own right, or does this new acceptance indicate that this perspective has now achieved its greatest influence within the discipline? Is it dead, or has it triumphed and been reborn?

Although the intellectual origins of interactionism are associated with the University of Chicago, especially with the work of George Herbert Mead, it was only under the later influence of Herbert Blumer, one of Mead's students, as well as the more empirical orientation of the Iowa School (under Manfred Kuhn), that modern interactionism became fully codified as a coherent theoretical perspective. However, the codification of modern interactionism led to a subtle reinterpretation of Mead's work by Blumer and his colleagues, a reinterpretation that exaggerated those elements in Mead's social thought that were most compatible with the premises of modern interactionism and overlooked those elements that were less compatible. Thus, Mead's preoccupation with the meaning of significant symbols and his theory of socialization and the social self were highlighted by modern interactionists, while his continuing attachments to evolutionism and behaviourism were downplayed. It may be noted in passing that this kind of retrospective reinterpretation, or "rational reconstruction," of major theoretical figures is far from uncommon. It can also be seen in the way that different schools of thought have reinterpreted the works of theorists as diverse as Marx, Darwin and Freud, for example.

Another issue is the diversity of approaches currently subsumed under the rubric of "interactionism." While this may come as a surprise to those superficially acquainted with the literature of interactionism, its tradition has been influenced by many intellectual currents and may be analyzed according to the diversity of these influences. One of the principal fault lines running through the interactionist tradition is between those theorists who focus on the "self" and those who focus on the "situation." This is a difference in conceptual orientation that can be traced back to the works of Mead and Cooley on the one hand, and to the works of Robert Park and W.I. Thomas on the other. Today, this difference of emphasis may be discerned by comparing the works of Blumer and his students with those of Goffman and his students. There remains a tension in interactionist circles centring upon the priority given to either the "self" or the "situation" (or to put it another way, "agency" or "structure") in accounts of social interaction in local settings. This is also a major split in many other traditions of sociological and social theory. This tension may be seen most clearly in Goffman's evolution from dramaturgy to frame analysis. He abandoned his earlier, more voluntaristic perspective of how actors freely choose to perform in front of their audiences in favour of a more structured, even deterministic, perspective of how each actor performs within a "knowledge-producing system" (Hill 2014) that structures their interactions within a framework of contextual rules, conventions and background assumptions. Goffman redirects his theoretical focus from the "agency" of the individual — the primary concern of classical symbolic interactionism — to the cognitive and normative micro "structures" that constrain an actor's freedom of choice and select for some responses rather than others. At the same time, it should be noted that Goffman's dramaturgy contained implicit structuralist aspects regarding the context of a performance (front, backstage, outside etc.), while, at the same time, his frame analysis retained aspects of his earlier sense of the actor's agency.

Even a brief review of these different branches of interactionism is enough to show that the scope of this intellectual tradition has broadened considerably over the past decade or so and, like other theoretical perspectives covered in this book, has opened up to a variety of hitherto unacknowledged intellectual influences. Interactionists, like other social theorists, have become far less exclusive in how they define the concepts, methods and topics of their field, and far more open to the influence of other theoretical perspectives. This is, after all, the age of diversity and cross-fertilization in social theorizing much as it has become the age of globalization in our everyday lives.

Many recent interactionist writers have moved beyond the traditional limits of interactionism and have succeeded in overcoming its segregation from other theoretical perspectives, especially in areas of collective action, globalization, culture and art, and in social identity and social problems theory, in which the traditional distinction between interactionism as a microsocial theory and other more classical macrosocial theories has increasingly been rendered redundant. In each of these substantive areas of theory and research, interactionist writers have shown how the vocabulary of symbolic interactionism may be used to describe and analyze macroscopic structures and processes in the larger society. In other words, interactionist studies are no longer confined to the face-to-face encounters that take place in local settings, but are now often broad enough to link local settings to the larger structures of social action and social relations.

Several research projects have begun to combine interactionist with more critical macro-theoretical perspectives:

> A few authors have brought the perspectives of symbolic interactionism and critical perspective together in theoretical discussions and in research studies. The term "critical interactionism" was suggested by Sandstrom and Fine (2003) to describe this convergence of the two perspectives. They discussed ... "developing a framework for critical interactionist's analysis of power, politics, and policy formation and ... making linkages between local actions and extralocal inequalities." Reynolds (1998: 35) also blended critical theory with an interactionist perspective stating, "A skillful welding of the radical sociology of Karl Marx with the liberal social psychology of George Herbert Mead is where to start; it holds the key to a viable future for our discipline [sociology]. (Burbank and Martins 2010: 25)

Over the years, there has been a resurgence of academic interest in developing a more critical version of interactionist theory. There have, for example, been several attempts at reconciling and synthesizing some aspects of the works of Marx and Mead (Batiuk and Sacks 1981; Goff 2016). These attempts have often sought to combine Marx's early focus on class consciousness and revolutionary action with Mead's insights into the socially conditioned nature of the self and identity. More recently, the works of third-generation critical theorists, such as Axel Honneth, have shown how Mead's ideas can provide an intersubjective understanding of Hegel's concept of "recognition." As recognition is seen by Honneth as the normative ground for social conflict, social struggle is both motivated by the need for recognition and necessary for achieving "more encompassing recognition relations" (Petherbridge 2013: 106). From Mead, therefore, Honneth emphasizes the conception of "practical intersubjectivity," which expands intersubjective communication and collective modes of cooperative action. And by emphasizing social role-taking in the formation of the self, Mead provides a social-psychological basis to struggles for recognition, in which self-confidence, self-respect and self-esteem are fundamental modes of self-determination. By displacing Freud with Mead in contemporary critical theory, Honneth and others, including Charles Taylor, have sought to modernize the classical Marxist theory of class struggle into a theory of recognition (and misrecognition) and respect (and disrespect and humiliation) (Petherbridge 2013).

Similarly, the boundaries between interactionism and other allied theoretical perspectives, such as phenomenology and ethnomethodology, have become less rigid and more permeable. At the same time, the search for connections between these perspectives has served neither to erase, nor even to blur, their respective boundaries, for each of these theoretical traditions continues to acknowledge a distinctive intellectual heritage and way of conceptualizing the social world. There has been, however, an end to the isolation of symbolic interactionism from other major theories of society and a greater encouragement of interactionist studies of social actors that are more multidimensional in scope and more informed by structural context and historical process.

Some of the advances by the new generation of interactionist writers may be seen in the areas of sociolinguistics, organization theory, social identity theory and the sociology of emotions. All of these areas represent breakthroughs for the interactionist tradition, which, until fairly recently, remained preoccupied not only with the study of face-to-face interaction in local settings, but with cognitive (largely devoid of any affective or emotional dimensions) interactions. Within the past decade or so, this somewhat oversimplified framework for studying social interaction has been enriched and enhanced through exposure to a growing number of other sociological traditions.

Several recent writers have offered some suggestions for the revitalization of the symbolic interactionist perspective in contemporary sociology (see, for example, Benzies and Allen 2001; Charmaz and Belgrave 2013; Kotarba 2014). A common recommendation is that this tradition should be seen not simply as a theoretical perspective but also as a methodological and empirical research program. In other words, many recent writers make a strong plea for the reintegration of theory and method in symbolic interactionist research. Part of the task of revitalizing symbolic interactionist research requires a return to the roots of this perspective and a recollection of some of the simple yet powerful research requirements first articulated by Blumer. Above all, the distinctive character of symbolic interactionist research has always been its ability to represent an insider view of the social actor — a view that attempts to make transparent the biases and preconceptions of the researcher. In many ways, the task of re-centring sociological research around the perspective of the social actor has been made easier by recent advances in social theory. Contemporary traditions such as postmodernism, post-structuralism, feminism and other standpoint theories all emphasize the "positionality" of social actors and the socially constructed nature of their identities and social realities. In this respect, the time for revitalizing the future agenda of symbolic interactionism as a major sociological tradition of theory and method has never seemed so propitious.

A new generation of theorists is championing a more political and ethical role for symbolic interactionism as a contemporary social theory. Ken Plummer, for example, has insisted that in order for symbolic interactionism to adapt to the twenty-first century, it needs to extend its scope beyond North America and Europe to become a genuinely cosmopolitan social theory for the present age. Plummer (2012) describes his own version of cosmopolitan interactionism as critical humanism:

> There are many pathways ahead for symbolic interactionism — whatever names it may pass under. I believe its theory of human social life — symbolic, reflexive, grounded, processual and political — is too compelling an account of how we humans live in this universe to be ignored.... I have suggested just one way forward in the twenty first century — of

making symbolic interactionism a much more global and cosmopolitan theory in the international world.

Other contemporary interactionists (such as Norman Denzin) also stress the importance of recognizing the politically progressive implications of symbolic interactionist theory and research. They believe that an interactionist perspective should focus on such aspects as empathy, equality and social justice, as well as other basic human values.

Today, symbolic interactionism has acquired a strong political conscience, perhaps more than any other current theoretical perspective in sociology. And nowhere has the new politics of interactionism been stated more clearly and explicitly than by Denzin and Yvonne Lincoln (2005: 13):

> The social sciences are normative disciplines, always already embedded in issues of value, ideology, power, desire, sexism, racism, domination, repression and control. We want a social science that is committed up front to issues of social justice, equity, non-violence and peace, and universal human rights. We do not want a social science that says it can address these issues if it wants to. For us, that is no longer an option.

References

Batiuk, M., and H. Sacks. 1981. "George Herbert Mead and Karl Marx: Exploring Consciousness and Community." *Symbolic Interaction*, 4, 2: 207–223.

Benzies, K.M., and M.N. Allen. 2001. "Symbolic Interactionism as a Theoretical Perspective for Multiple Method Research." *Journal of Advanced Nursing*, 33, 4 (Feb): 541–547.

Burbank, Patricia M., and Diane C. Martins. 2010. "Symbolic Interactionism and Critical Perspective: Divergent or Synergistic?" *Nursing Philosophy*, 11, 1: 25–41.

Charmaz, K., and L.L. Belgrave. 2013. "Modern Symbolic Interaction Theory and Health." In *Medical Sociology on the Move: New Directions in Theory*. Springer Netherlands.

Chriss, James J. 2015. "Goffman, Parsons, and the Negational Self." *Academicus International Scientific Journal*, 11 (January): 11–31. Entrepreneurship Training Center Albania.

Cohen, Jeffrey H., Nydia Delhi Mata Sanchez and Francisco Montiel-Ishino. 2009. "Chapulines and Food Choices in Rural Oaxaca." *Gastronomica*, 9, 1 (Winter): 61–65.

Cunningham, Carolyn (ed.). 2013. *Social Networking and Impression Management: Self-Presentation in the Digital Age*. Lexington Books.

Dawe, Alan. 1973. "Review: The Underworld-View of Erving Goffman." *The British Journal of Sociology*, 24, 2 (Jun): 246–253.

Denzin, Norman, and Yvonne Lincoln. 2005. *Handbook of Qualitative Research*, 3rd edition. Sage Handbooks.

Dirda, Michael. n.d. "Waiting for Goffman." *Lapham's Quarterly*. <https://www.laphamsquarterly.org/city/waiting-goffman>.

Ghoshal, Abhimanyu. 2017. "Facebook's New 'Greetings' Buttons Are Like Pokes on Steroids." *The Next Web*, December 7. <https://thenextweb.com/facebook/2017/12/07/facebooks-testing-greetings-buttons-that-are-like-pokes-on-steroids/?utm_source=social&utm_medium=feed&utm_campaign=profeed>.

Goff, Tom. 2016. Marx *and* Mead, 1st edition. Routledge Library Editions: Social Theory.

Goffman, Erving. 1959. *Presentation of Self in Everyday Life*. Garden City, NY: Anchor.

___. 1961a. *Asylums*. New York: Doubleday.

___. 1961b. *Encounters: Two Studies in the Sociology of Interaction*. Indianapolis, IN: Bobbs-Merrill.

___. 1963a. *Stigma: Notes on the Management of Spoiled Identity*. Englewood Cliffs, NJ: Prentice-Hall.

___. 1963b. *Behavior in Public Places: Notes on the Social Organization of Gatherings*. Glencoe, IL: Free Press.

___. 1971. *Relations in Public: Microstudies of the Public Order*. New York: Basic Books.

___. 1974. *Frame Analysis: An Essay on the Organization of Experience*. New York: Harper Colophon.

___. 1981. *Forms of Talk*. Philadelphia: University of Pennsylvania Press.

___. 1983. "The Interaction Order: American Sociological Association, 1982 Presidential Address." *American Sociological Review*, 48 (Feb): 1–17.

Hill, Michael R. 2014. "'Bomb Talk' and Erving Goffman's Frame Analysis." Sociology Department, Faculty Publications. <http://digitalcommons.unl.edu/sociologyfacpub/313>.

Johnson, Elijah. 2017. "How Did Trump Win?" *Finance and Liberty*, May 26. <https://www.financeandliberty.com/original-analysis-trump-win/>.

Jones, Andrew Zimmerman. 2017. "What Is Model-Dependent Realism?" *ThoughtCo*, September 2 <https://www.thoughtco.com/what-is-model-dependent-realism-2699404>.

Kincaid, John. 2017. "Why Smoking Makes You Free." *Sociology in Focus*, March 20. <http://sociologyinfocus.com/2017/03/why-smoking-makes-you-free/>.

Kotarba, Joseph A. 2014. "Symbolic Interaction and Applied Social Research: A Focus on Translational Science Research." *Symbolic Interaction*, 37, 3 (Aug): 412–425. <https://www.ncbi.nlm.nih.gov/pmc/articles/PMC4159952/>.

Mazigh, Mona. 2008. *Hope and Despair: My Struggle to Free My Husband, Maher Arar*. McClelland & Stewart.

Mead, G.H. 1962 [1934]. *Mind, Self and Society: From the Standpoint of a Social Behaviorist*. University of Chicago Press.

Medley-Rath, Stephanie. 2016. "Rules? What Rules? Mead's 3 Stage Role-Taking Process." *Sociology in Focus*, January 11. <http://sociologyinfocus.com/>.

Petherbridge, Danielle. 2013. *The Critical Theory of Axel Honneth*. Lexington Books.

Phillips, Bernard. 2001. *Beyond Sociology's Tower of Babel: Reconstructing the Scientific Method. Responsibility*. New York: Aldine de Gruyter.

Plummer, Ken (ed.). 2000. "Symbolic Interactionism in the Twentieth Century." In B. Turner (ed.), *The Blackwell Companion to Social Theory.* Oxford: Blackwell.

___. 2012. "Towards a Cosmopolitan Symbolic Interactionism?" In Andrea Salvini, Joseph A. Kotarba, and Bryce Merrill (eds.), *The Present and Future of Symbolic Interactionism,* Vol 1. Pisa, Italy: FrancoAngeli. <https://kenplummer.com/2012/07/07/cosmopolitan-symbolic-interactionism/>.

Tashmin, Nushrat. 2016. "Art of Impression Management on Social Media." *World Scientific News*, 30: 89–102. <http://www.worldscientificnews.com/wp-content/uploads/2015/10/WSN-30-2016-89-102.pdf>.

Williams, Robin. 2000. *Making Identity Matter: Identity, Society and Social Interaction.* Durham, UK: Sociologypress.

Zarghooni, Sasan. 2007. "A Study of Self-Presentation in Light of Facebook." Institute of Psychology, University of Oslo (Autumn). <https://pdfs.semanticscholar.org/5b09/38b252864d120a318d885be668392c88af7f.pdf>.

CHAPTER 7

THEORIZING OUR METHODICAL LIVES

Ethnomethodology

THE METHODS IN OUR MADNESS

Think about the many unspoken and taken-for-granted rules that we follow and the methods that we use to make sense of and to produce order in our everyday lives. Most of the time we follow these rules and use these methods without thinking about them because they normally work to ensure harmonious relations in our interactions with others. For example, when we first get into an elevator, we usually follow the "rule of civil inattention" (Goffman 1972: 385); although we may make brief eye contact with other passengers in the elevator, we are careful to avoid staring at them or showing inappropriate interest, which could result in their personal discomfort. The rule of civil inattention involves the unobtrusive and peaceful scanning of others so as to allow for neutral interaction; we neither ignore the other passengers (which would be discourteous), nor do we impose our presence on others (which would be presumptuous). Civil inattention enables us to maintain a polite privacy within an anonymous group through a culturally accepted convention of "self-distancing" (Baldwin 2004: 276, 396).

People whose job requires frequent and unpredictable contact with the public may try to reduce the uncertainty of these random encounters by categorizing individuals according to criteria designed to make sense of, anticipate and predict their likely behaviour. For example, a highway patrol officer who has just clocked a motorist exceeding the posted speed limit will probably switch on their flashing lights and pull the driver over. Imagine as the officer approaches the vehicle that the driver appears reticent and ignores the officer's initial greeting. A failure to respond may alert the officer as they try to decide what type of person they are dealing with. Several possibilities may come to mind:

- This driver may be unwell and unable to speak for some medical reason.
- This driver may be ashamed at having been stopped and is intimidated by the police.
- This driver is defiant of authority and is resentful at having been pulled over but is basically harmless.
- This driver is an unknown quantity: he could be a criminal, a fugitive from justice or even a psychopath and should be treated with extreme caution, maybe even requiring backup.

The highway officer "screens" the driver in order to decide how to proceed. Peter Eglin and Stephen Hester showed that patrol officers will scan environments for visual confirmation that "all is well" within what some researchers call the "territory of normal appearances" (1992: 131). These researchers used the term "incongruity procedure" to describe how police scan for any evidence of outsiders or for other potential sources of disruption or conflict. In many cities, these incongruity procedures have often been used to profile — sometimes lethally — innocent citizens. In a society riven by severe social inequality and long-term racial prejudice and discrimination, the categories used by police officers can often lead to racial and class stereotyping and profiling. Thus, the carding process in Canada, stop-and-frisk laws in the US and the "sus" laws in the UK have long been selectively enforced against racialized people. The methods of practical reasoning can often reinforce racial profiling and ethnic prejudice.

Most of us use similar categorizations when interacting with strangers. However, these screening precautions are so embedded in the "routine practices" of everyday social interaction that we are largely unaware of these subtle and subliminal strategies we often use to quickly assess the motives and the character of people we meet. Even the most routine and intimate aspects of our everyday encounters and interactions can become the focus of rigorous observation and theoretical analysis. In the above examples, what has most interested social theorists are the "methods of practical reasoning" used by members of society to make sense of, and produce order in, their everyday activities. But who would be interested in such apparently trivial and insignificant details of daily life? The answer is: ethnomethodologists!

STUDYING THE COMMON SENSE METHODS OF EVERYDAY LIFE

Ethnomethodology is one of the more intriguing perspectives in contemporary social theory. When it first made its appearance in the late 1960s, many sociologists refused to take it seriously as a legitimate area of theory and research. It was greeted with ridicule, skepticism and hostility by many prominent and established sociologists (see Bauman 1973). To scholars used to researching social class and stratification, socialization and the social self, work and leisure, race and ethnic relations, and deviance and crime, the pretensions of ethnomethodology and its practitioners seemed absurd by comparison. Ernest Gellner (1975) famously dismissed ethnomethodology as a "Californian way of subjectivity." Why would anybody want to study how police patrolled local neighbourhoods, or how sex workers screen and categorize their potential customers, or how people walked or how they laughed, applauded or booed at public events? Why would sociologists want to study how jurors performed their duties, or how scientists and doctors talked about their work? For some critics, the methods used to collect data — tape and video recording — seemed uncreative, un-sociological, subjectivist and reductionist (Gordon 1976).

Several factors contributed to the hostile reception ethnomethodologists received when they made their appearance in sociology departments during the late 1960s and early 1970s. The resistance arose in part from the defensiveness of mainstream sociologists towards an unfamiliar approach that appeared to challenge the most basic assumptions of their discipline. At the same time, many leading ethnomethodologists deliberately distanced themselves from mainstream sociology and criticized its traditional tenets and knowledge claims. Part of the problem resulted from the almost inevitable misunderstandings that developed between the academic sociologists and what they sometimes regarded to be the emerging "cult" of ethnomethodology. Moreover, the style in which much ethnomethodological research was written — especially by the founder, Harold Garfinkel — was often obscure and difficult to understand. If Parsons' work was regarded by many sociologists as hard to read, Garfinkel's work was, by comparison, almost impenetrable.

This chapter provides a broad overview of the current state of ethnomethodology as an area of theory and research. Among other things, we shall briefly review some of the defining methodological and theoretical characteristics; some examples of ethnomethodological research;

the vocabulary of ethnomethodology; and some of the contributions of ethnomethodology. In addition to reviewing the current state of ethnomethodology, we shall focus on the growth of conversation analysis as a distinctive branch of ethnomethodological research.

Ethnomethodology may seem at first glance to be a perplexing way of looking at the social world, appearing to be a superficial, even trivial, branch of sociology. Today, however, ethnomethodologists have ceased to be the *bêtes noires* of sociology departments. (That honour was later accorded to postmodernists and poststructuralists.) Not only has ethnomethodology found general acceptance within the discipline of sociology, but insights arising from its studies have had widespread influence on other traditions of social theory and social research. This is very much a sign of the times for, as we have seen, the cross-fertilization and fusion of social theories has become increasingly commonplace and has overtaken the former isolation of rival sociological perspectives.

The starting point for all ethnomethodological research is a commitment to study the methods that people use to accomplish ordinary, routine activities. Ethnomethodology can thus be described as "the study of common-sense practices in everyday life." Although it may appear to resemble the dramaturgical perspective in some respects, it differs from Goffman's approach in important ways. In more precise terms, ethnomethodology can be defined as "the study of the methods of practical reasoning that members of society use in order to make sense of, and produce order in, their everyday worlds and to accomplish their everyday activities." Although this may seem to be a longwinded way of expressing a simple idea, this definition makes use of some of the key concepts of ethnomethodology. The following quick reference points may help to place ethnomethodology on the map of contemporary social theory and to illustrate some of the ways in which it may be distinguished from more mainstream sociological theories:

Everyday Practices

Like symbolic interactionism and dramaturgy, ethnomethodology is a partially microsocial perspective. It focuses on the "methods of practical reasoning" used by members of society to make sense of and produce order in their everyday social worlds. Unlike other social theories (such as symbolic interactionism, dramaturgy and even structural functionalism, which refer to "social actors"), ethnomethodology refers to "members," who are understood not simply as individuals but as any social agent that can produce an "account" that can be practically converted or translated into a social fact. In short, members of society make sense of, and produce order in, society through their routine methodical practices. In this sense, ethnomethodology is at the same time both macro and micro oriented in that members can produce social facts at an individual level through their interpersonal interactions or at an institutional level through their collective interactions.

Ethnomethodologists are interested in studying the routine practices and unspoken rules that guide and structure our everyday/everynight interactions with others — within our families, communities and institutions of the larger society. Whether we are obeying the unwritten rules of etiquette when waiting in line at the supermarket checkout, or when walking through the local shopping mall, or when sitting through a job interview. or when riding an elevator, or when hosting a family Christmas dinner, all our actions are normally guided and constrained by a set of conventions that are socially designed to make our public behaviour predictable and acceptable to others. And whenever we transgress or violate this unwritten and unspoken code of behaviour, there is always a price to pay! Ethnomethodology focuses on the minutiae of daily life: the routine practices that get us through each day and night and enable us to interact with others in an orderly and predictable manner. Thus, ethnomethodology is the study of the methods of practical reasoning that help all of us to maintain social order in our everyday lives. Ethnomethodology examines the "local settings" in which face-to-face interaction takes place rather than the abstract structural entities of social system, state and social class, which have preoccupied structural functionalists, system theorists, Marxists, conflict theorists and other macrosocial theorists.

Hard Data

Ethnomethodology focuses on the "externally observable" and "objectively reportable" aspects of social interaction, unlike other microsocial theories (such as symbolic interactionism and dramaturgy), which focus on the internal cognitive states of the social actor. This means that ethnomethodologists are only interested in studying those features of social interaction that can be *seen* or *heard* (i.e., they only study what people actually do and what people actually say), using what they call "objective" methods (audio and video recording) to collect data that may be corroborated and replicated by any qualified observer in the field. Ethnomethodologists see themselves as using objective methods of social research, in contrast to the evident subjectivism and intuitionism of symbolic interactionism and dramaturgy, which profess to look *inside* the individual to study the subjective meanings that social action has for the social actor.

Empiricism versus Positivism

Although ethnomethodology is committed to the rigorous empirical analysis of all objectively collected (i.e., recorded) data, this does not mean that ethnomethodology can be classified as a "positivist" perspective. While ethnomethodology is rigorously "empiricist" in its research orientation, it remains at the same time resolutely "anti-positivist" in its philosophical (epistemological) outlook. Unlike positivist theories (such as behaviourism, exchange theory, rational choice theory, network theory and game theory), ethnomethodology does not believe in the possibility of constructing universal propositions whose meaning and truth remain independent of the original contexts in which these propositions were formulated. For ethnomethodology, all propositions are "indexical," i.e., fully dependent upon their original contexts for their meaning and validity. While ethnomethodology, exchange theory and behaviourism all profess to focus on the externally observable aspects of the individual, ethnomethodology rejects the possibility and the desirability of constructing "general covering law" causal explanations, in the tradition of exchange theory and behaviourism. This is because, unlike behaviourism and exchange theory, ethnomethodology is not committed to a causal analysis of human behaviour. Indeed, its phenomenological roots make ethnomethodology deeply skeptical of *any* generalizing or *universalizing statements* — scientific or otherwise.

Topic versus Resource

Unlike more mainstream social theorists and sociologists, ethnomethodologists avoid using abstract concepts such as the "self," "norms," "values" and "functions" to analyze or explain social action. Instead, they restrict themselves to what they describe as a "formal analysis of members' accounts." Ethnomethodologists have always been vocal in their criticisms of traditional social theory and research — or what is referred to as the "normative paradigm" of social research (Wilson 1970). Their main criticisms are, first, that most social theorists impose their own sense of social reality on the social world they purport to study. They do this primarily by imposing their own abstract theoretical and methodological concepts on the data that they are observing. Thus, social actors are variously assumed to "internalize norms," to "be motivated by value orientations" to "suffer from false consciousness" and so on. These "descriptions" of social reality are, in fact, constructed from the theorist's own vocabulary of concepts. Even symbolic interactionists are guilty of imposing their own concepts — such as those of the "self," the "generalized other," the "I" and the "me" — on the raw experiences of those they study. By contrast, ethnomethodologists begin their studies with members' own accounts — the raw, unmediated data of the social world.

Figure 7-1: Ethnomethodology versus Sociological Theory

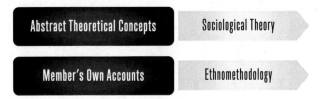

Mainstream social theory and social research are criticized by eth-nomethodologists for using indicators to measure sociological concepts that are based on the theorist's own sense of reality rather than those of the members themselves. Concepts such as "values," "norms," "motives," "alienation," "anomie" are not directly observable. They can only be indi-rectly observed (i.e., inferred) and measured through the use of concepts and indicators. Social researchers typically use questionnaires, interviews and other "pen and paper tests" as empirical indicators. However, the indicators used to measure these concepts are constructed from the researcher's own sense of reality rather than from those of the members themselves. Sometimes this has led to serious misrepresentations and distortions of social reality. In a famous critical study, Aaron Cicourel (1974) re-analyzed some sociological data on fertility and family planning in Argentina. He found that the low divorce rates — which had been used as an indicator of family stability — concealed quite a different reality. Because divorce was expensive and difficult to obtain in Argentina, the incidence of marital break-ups among the lower-income classes was not recorded in the official statistics. However, when members' own accounts were examined, it was clear that marital splits and common-law unions were much more common than conventional indicators had shown. Reliance on these indicators had resulted in a serious distortion of social reality.

Social researchers have been criticized for confusing what ethnomethodologists distinguish as "topic" and "resource." This is a problem related to the way in which researchers have processed everyday speech — the things that people say in conversations and in response to questionnaires and interview questions. Most sociologists normally accept what people say at face value and proceed to interpret this "evidence" or "data" in terms of their preferred theoretical concepts. What people say is often taken as direct evidence of what they actually do. Expressed attitudes and opinions are typically accepted as reliable indicators of "values," "norms," "class consciousness," "the convict code" or whatever other concept is privileged by the researcher. Ethnomethodologists, on the other hand, make no such theoretical or methodological leaps from data to speculative theory. Their studies begin and end with members' accounts. Their job is to describe and analyze the "formal properties" of these accounts and to uncover the underlying methods and rules of practical reasoning that have been used to produce them.

In a groundbreaking conversation analysis, Pamela Fishman (1977: 178) demonstrated the difference between using everyday speech as a resource and as a topic. Using a sample of university students, she showed that the attitudes expressed in the everyday speech of these students did not correspond to the methodical practices used to organize this speech. While all of the students professed strong egalitarian and feminist values, the actual organization of the speech was highly gendered. Men dominated the topics of conversation, set the conversational agendas, interrupted when women were speaking and switched topics whenever they felt like it. Women, on the other hand, performed the "menial labour" of the conversation. They made supportive statements and reassuring noises and generally followed the men's lead. They played a subordinate part in the conversational division of labour. We shall return to this case study in our further discussion of conversation analysis later in this chapter.

Sociologists using this example of everyday speech as a "resource" — that is, taking at face value what was said by all participants — would probably see evidence of strong egalitarian values being typical of educated middle-class students. An ethnomethodologist using this same speech as a "topic," however, saw evidence of strong interactional patterns of dominance/deference, revealed through observation and analysis of actual speaking practices. Herein lies an important methodological difference between traditional sociology and ethnomethodology.

WHAT ETHNOMETHODOLOGISTS STUDY

It is only by observing social actors (or what Garfinkel calls "members") in their natural settings and by studying the "accounts" given by members of their activities within these settings that ethnomethodologists are able to uncover the fine-grained details of the surrounding social structure. Members are always studied directly in their local settings, for these are the sites of social interaction where real things happen. In this sense, ethnomethodology has unavoidably become the sociology of the local, the immediate and the "here and now." It has no use for the abstract theoretical concepts such as "social system," "social class," "the state," "social solidarity" etc., upon which much of classical and modern social theory has been based.

For some critics, it has seemed that a social theory focused wholly on the local settings of social interaction, disavowing any interest in larger-scale theory construction or causal analysis, strikes at the very heart of the classical sociological enterprise. This focus on the local context of what people do and what people say was a major cause of the antipathy that many sociologists initially felt towards ethnomethodology. In a discipline that has traditionally been preoccupied with the big pictures of social class, social structure, culture, socialization and society, the ethnomethodological focus on the local has often seemed unworthy of the serious attention.

Today, the most important point of contact ethnomethodology has with other theoretical perspectives, including structural functionalism, symbolic interactionism, exchange theory and even conflict theory, is the study of "order." It could be argued that every theoretical perspective — not excluding the various versions of Marxism and neo-Marxism — has a profound interest in the problem of order, i.e., how social order is maintained in society. In other words, ethnomethodologists are interested in studying how ordinary people produce and reproduce orderliness in their daily interactions and routine encounters. All of us do so by following rules, by using various methods of practical reasoning and by "working" at producing order in our encounters with each other. This is why ethnomethodologists emphasize that all forms of social interaction should be thought of as "accomplishments" that require work in order to succeed. This is true irrespective of whether the interaction is something relatively simple like "doing walking," "doing laughing" and "doing applause," or more complex things like "doing being a woman," "doing being a juror," "doing being a student or a store assistant" and so on. In studies, the focus remains on the local setting and on what the person actually says or does. Ethnomethodologists record the "accounts" of the people they study from within the perspective of the "world as it happens" (Boden 1990).

With their greater acceptance within the discipline of sociology, ethnomethodologists have made important contributions to some of the burning issues of contemporary social theory, such as the agency/structure debate, the embeddedness of social action, the idea of "rationality" and the notions of "time" and "history." They have also contributed to the sociology of knowledge, science, medical sociology and the professions. In addition to these advances, particular branches of ethnomethodology, such as conversation analysis, are enjoying a new acceptance in such areas as media studies and cultural studies. With such an upsurge in its popularity, it is easy to conclude that ethnomethodology has arrived and is here to stay.

THE VOCABULARY OF ETHNOMETHODOLOGY

In the course of conducting their studies, ethnomethodologists have evolved a specialized language to describe and analyze the taken-for-granted methods that members of society use and the unspoken rules that they follow in accomplishing their practical, everyday activities. This terminology is used to describe and analyze the methods used by members in their verbal and behavioural accounts. For example, the concepts of "accomplishment," "work," "accounts/accounting," "indexicality" and "reflexivity" are central to the discourse of ethnomethodology. Similarly, concepts such as "the etcetera principle," "letting it pass," "glossing," "the documentary method of interpretation," "topic," "resource" and "breaching demonstration/experiment" are also part of the basic vocabulary of ethnomethodology.

One way to view current sociological and social theories is as a set of different languages, each with its own particular vocabulary of concepts. A language is not only a way of speaking about the world but also a way of observing the world and of orienting oneself to act within it. The languages we choose as social theorists provide us with a particular set of observation and theory terms. These terms — and the relations between them — play an important role in helping us to decide what counts as a "fact" in our "universe of discourse" and what practical implications arise from these "facts." All facts may be understood as well-confirmed, or incontrovertible, observations — observations that have been seen by so many people on so many occasions that their objective existence is beyond reasonable doubt. It is a fact that the sun rises every morning in the east and sets every evening in the west. It is also a fact that the British colonized what is now Canada by 1760. However, which of all the potentially infinite observations are certified as "facts" depends on which language we use and what activities we wish to accomplish. Every language has its own rules for certifying facts and its own criteria for linguistic competence.

Using the language of Marxism, for example, we will see factories, oil companies, banks and insurance companies as capitalist institutions in which workers are exploited for the surplus value they produce. If, on the other hand, we use the language of Emile Durkheim's functionalism, we will see the statistical fact of a high suicide rate for combat veterans or young victims of homophobic abuse as evidence of anomie caused by low levels of social solidarity and a weakened collective consciousness. It is only through language that the facts of the "world" — or, more properly, of "our social worlds" — come into existence for us. Without language, there would be no "facts" in any meaningful sense of this term. This is easily demonstrated in the case of highly specialized languages. It is only through the language of quantum physics that such facts as sub-atomic particles — electrons, protons, neutrons and quarks — have any meaning. These facts have been produced through the language and associated practices of quantum physics. They are "products" of the language of physics. And the same may be said of other specialized discourses, whether we are speaking of molecular biology, necromancy or demonology, or of meteorology or geomorphology. We shall now provide a more detailed introduction to some of the key concepts in the language of ethnomethodology.

Accomplishments

One of the main assumptions of ethnomethodology is that any kind of social order and any type of social activity may be regarded an interactional "accomplishment," something that results from the methods of practical reasoning used to produce these social outcomes. Even what some consider as taken-for-granted aspects of our social lives — such as our gender identities — have been produced by using practical methods of reasoning and action. This was clearly the case in Garfinkel's famous clinical study of Agnes, a trans woman who was interviewed as part of her application to have what was then called gender reassignment (now referred to as gender affirmation) surgery. In her interview, she recounts how her early life was transformed during adolescence when she began to openly identify as a woman. Garfinkel was interested in Agnes's story because it shows how her gender identity was *accomplished* through considerable thought and effort — what may be thought of as ethnomethodological "work." Garfinkel uses the story of Agnes to illustrate the different methods of practical reasoning that were used to accomplish her gender identity. The case study exemplifies some of the methods used by all of us to accomplish our identities — whether these are gender identities, occupational or professional identities, or personal and ethnic identities.

Work

Part of the mission of ethnomethodology is to discover exactly what kind of "work" is required in order to produce our social identities, our routine activities and our localized everyday lives. Once we understand that all aspects of social life are produced by using definite methods of practical reasoning and action and by following definite rules of interaction, we have grasped the essential viewpoint of ethnomethodology. Whether we observe how individuals, or members, *do* walking in public places (such as shopping malls or supermarkets), or how they *do* applause or booing at a public performance, or how they conduct a telephone or face-to-face conversation, or even how they present their gender, ethnomethodologists are primarily interested in the work that is necessary to successfully accomplish these activities. The ethnomethodological commitment to study the work, or what Garfinkel calls the "artful practices," that produce different kinds of social phenomena has proven to be deeply subversive toward many taken-for-granted assumptions — both in the everyday world of ordinary people and in the professional world of sociologists. In other words, ethnomethodologists have shown how many aspects of social reality normally assumed to be "natural" activities, such as walking in a public place, or "natural" identities, such as identifying with a particular gender, are the results of careful interactional work by all members of society.

Even the most mundane activities are produced by artful practices, and these practices are always guided by particular methods and rules of practical reasoning and action. What may appear to the casual observer as a natural or wholly spontaneous event or action is typically studied by the ethnomethodologist at a deeper and more formal level of analysis. What may be accepted by mainstream sociologists as incontrovertible and self-evident social "facts" may be seen by ethnomethodologists as "artefacts" of a particular theoretical perspective and a particular method of observation and research. For ethnomethodologists, therefore, "facts" are never simple reflections of a natural or independent objective "reality." They never "speak for themselves" or stand on "their own two feet." Facts are always produced according to particular methods of observation, categorization and measurement and interpreted from a particular theoretical perspective. Contrary to popular belief, "facts" are always *produced* rather than simply discovered; like everything else, the production of facts is an ongoing accomplishment of those who produce them. According to ethnomethodologists, the social world can never be taken for granted or at face value. Beneath the surface level of appearances lies a deeper structure of often unacknowledged practical methods and rules of social interaction that guide, frame and direct our day-to-day activities. The challenge posed by ethnomethodology is to uncover and analyze this deep structure of practical methods and rules of interaction — the ethnomethodological work of living our daily lives.

Accounts/Accounting
The starting point for ethnomethodological research is the study of members' accounts. "Accounts" is a broad concept referring to the descriptions, justifications, explanations, observations, interpretations, definitions and classifications used by members of society to make sense of and produce order in their everyday/everynight routine activities. Accounts may also be understood as ways of producing and processing "facts" — both in the everyday world and in the professional worlds of academia and science.

Even the ways in which sociologists produce and process accounts — whether these are through surveys, statistical analyses, clinical studies or ethnographic studies — may be studied in much the same way as those of ordinary members of society who produce their own "folk" accounts of their ongoing routine activities.

Accounts may be *verbal*, e.g., how a caller talks to a dispatcher on the 911 emergency lines. All of us provide accounts of our actions to those with whom we interact. In fact, accounts become part of the process of interaction. The most obvious accounts are those that are verbal — what people say about themselves and others. Verbal accounts are necessarily expressed as statements, or utterances: "The dog ate my homework." "For God's sake, stop nagging me." "You have the right to remain silent." In the absence of spoken words, accounts may be *behavioural*, i.e., what people do by themselves and with others, such as how an individual navigates through a crowded shopping mall while doing walking in a public place, or how a police officer pulls over and interrogates a speeding motorist, or how you take your place in the queue to wait for the bus in the morning. All accounts can all be empirically observed, and video or audio recorded. Accounts are "sense-making activities," ways in which individuals make sense of and produce order in their everyday lives.

By studying the verbal or behavioural accounts that members of society give to each other, ethnomethodologists are able to reveal the invisible methods and unspoken rules that make ordinary everyday social interaction possible. Unlike symbolic interactionists, phenomenologists and dramaturgical theorists, who study the inner thoughts and feeling of social actors by using subjective methods of social research, ethnomethodologists are strongly committed to using what they define as objective methods and measurement indicators. Ethnomethodology came of age at a time when the portable tape-recorder was first mass-produced. Since then, ethnomethodologists have also made extensive use of various forms of video cameras in their research. The availability of this technology has meant that members' accounts can now be studied using strictly objective methods of recording and analyzing data. Verbal accounts, in the form of conversations, are typically tape-recorded and transcripts produced for more detailed analysis and description. Similarly, behavioural accounts — of events like walking through a shopping mall or lining up to see a receptionist in a government department — can be video-recorded and replayed repeatedly for more detailed analysis and description.

The process of accounting also refers to the production of local facts. The ways in which members put together the experiences that make up their lives — through observing, selecting, describing, reporting, recording, explaining, interpreting, defining — results in the production of local facts. To study members' accounts, therefore, is to study how the "facts" of everyday life, or, in the case of academics, how the "facts" of science and social science, are produced as ongoing everyday accomplishments (see, for example, Latour and Woolgar 1986). Producing facts, however, also implies acting on those facts. Our actions are always based on our understanding of the facts. For this reason, the accounts we produce of our everyday activities are also "scripts" for these activities. This is why we define accounts not only as ways of making sense but as ways of producing order in our lives. The process of producing facts is the same process that produces actions. Our actions are reflections of our sense-making activities; our sense-making activities are equally reflections of our actions. This is what it means to say "all accounts are reflexive."

Of course, what are facts for one individual may not always be so for others. In my encounters with my boss, I may "produce" or "construct" an account of him as a disagreeable, irascible control freak — someone to be treated with caution and circumspection. I produce an account of him — I make him "accountable" — in a way that is, at one and the same time, both a "factual" description and a strategy for (inter-)action. His life partner, on the other hand, may produce a very different account of him. Which of these accounts is "true" is an unanswerable question. If each of these accounts is satisfactorily produced and reproduced over again, then both are "true" for the local settings in which they are produced. Ethnomethodology is not interested in the "ultimate truth" of knowledge claims, but only in how facts are locally produced in particular settings, using methods of practical reasoning, i.e., mundane reason.

Loose Concepts

Ethnomethodologists have discovered that all of us continually bend or break the rules of logic when giving our accounts. We often use "loose concepts" — concepts that are "fuzzy around the edges." What this means is that the accounts of what we do in our everyday lives are not always rigorously logical or consistent. For example, if your partner asks you whether it is raining and you reply, "Well, yes and no," you are using the terms "yes" and "no" loosely, and this is hardly a logical answer. In fact, this answer is, strictly speaking, meaningless. The reason that your answer is illogical is because it violates the "law of the excluded middle," i.e., something cannot be both included and excluded from a logical class at the same time. It has to be one or the other. However, although this may be a meaningless statement to a strict logician, it makes complete sense to you and your partner. Another way of interpreting your answer could be, "Well, it's raining on and off." The point is that you and your partner understand each other. Both of you are playing by the rules of your own language game. And sometimes you may bend, or even break, the formal rules of logic. So what? The point made by ethnomethodologists is that there are myriad examples of members' accounts that use a rough and ready logic that is easily understandable to others, even if it appears to be illogical in formal terms. Ethnomethodologists are interested in what works, in how we succeed in pulling off, or accomplishing, our everyday activities using our own homemade logics and our own methods of practical reasoning.

Rather than being sharply defined and mutually exclusive, loose concepts are imprecise and shade off into each other. There are plenty of examples of loose concepts. "Baldness" is another example. When is a man bald? When he has absolutely no hair on his head? When he has only one hair, or only two hairs? Who knows? And who cares? Everyday talk is full of loose concepts. Most people do not require the same degree of precision in their conversations that a logician or a physicist might expect from a logical proposition. Normal conversation would probably become impossible if we insisted that it strictly conform to the laws of logic. And so, if — as ethnomethodologists — we are going to make a model of the formal structure of members' accounts, it has to be based on how people actually give these accounts. What we have learned from ethnomethodological studies is that the methods of everyday practical reasoning follow their own rules and that these have little to do with the rules of logic. Each of these rules, in its own way, contributes to the flexibility and looseness that is required of all accounts if they are to be sustained in everyday conversations and interactions.

The Etcetera Principle

The etcetera principle (sometimes called "let it pass") is another rule governing the methods of practical reasoning. When we are engaged in conversation with someone, we usually allow unclear information to pass unanswered while we await further clarification. In other words, we do not normally insist on absolute or instant clarity of expression and meaning. We tolerate ambiguities and try to clear them up as we go along. An example might be when we ask our young daughter, "Why did you do that?" She may reply, "Because!" Her answer does not qualify as a logically meaningful response. However, we are likely to continue the conversation in the expectation that a further and fuller meaning will eventually be elaborated. All accounts are like this. We tolerate ambiguity as the price we pay for sustaining the conversation. This concept is related to the earlier discussion of conversational norms and conversational work. In most informal conversations, partners will not normally insist upon an immediate and full explanation of all statements and expressions. It is tacitly understood that truncated statements, abbreviated expressions and incomplete information will be tolerated in the expectation that further clarification will follow sooner or later. In other words, most of us do not push for instant unequivocal clarity of expression from our conversational partners. If we fail to fully understand a statement or to receive expected information, most of us will await clarification during the conversational exchange. This unwritten rule of etiquette was labelled by Garfinkel as the "etcetera principle" or "let it pass."

Reflexivity

All accounts are "reflexive." This concept refers to how individuals, or members of society, produce accounts of their thoughts and/or actions as part of their ongoing attempts to make sense of and create order in their daily lives. When we say that all accounts are reflexive, we mean that in giving an account — in an ethnomethodological sense — we are simultaneously making sense of and producing order in the local settings of our everyday lives. Another way of putting it is that accounts produce local facts. We act on our understandings of these facts. Accounts define and describe our reality while simultaneously producing that reality. This means that all accounts not only describe, explain or justify an action, but they also help to produce the action as well. Accounts are reflexive in the sense that a verbal account — such as "The dog ate my homework" or "For God's sake, stop nagging me" — also directly contributes to a corresponding behavioural account. In the first example, the student actually fails to submit a homework assignment; in the second, a person scowls and expresses anger while complaining about what they view as unjustified expressions of disapproval. In each case, the verbal account, expressed as a statement or utterance, contributes to and helps to produce the behavioural account, expressed as an action or gesture, of the individual.

Indexicality

Indexicality, which is closely related to reflexivity, refers to another important characteristic of all verbal and behavioural accounts. According to ethnomethodology, the meaning of any statement, utterance, gesture or action only becomes apparent when it is understood in the context, or in the local setting, in which it is produced. In other words, all accounts are "indexical." For ethnomethodologists, there is no such thing as an objective statement — i.e., a statement that has the same, universal meaning for anyone at any time. The meaning of any statement depends on the context in which it is produced. A single statement such as "it is raining" can have different meanings when produced in different contexts — after a prolonged drought, after a prolonged flood or on the day of my family picnic. My personal favourite is the admission, "I'm sorry I cheated." The meaning of this account changes depending upon the context in which it is produced; it could be said by a spouse in a marriage counsellor's office, a student to an examination invigilator or a business owner to a government tax official, among others Another example cited in ethnomethodological research is that of police officers responding to signs of disrespect from people living on the street in a skid row neighbourhood. When alone with these people, officers would sometimes tolerate profanities and backchat without retaliation. However, when bystanders were present, officers retaliate strongly against these taunts — in order to maintain their public credibility (see Bittner 1967). Although the accounts produced by the offenders were the same for both situations, the officers understood and treated the offenders in the first situation differently from those in the second. Each account was thoroughly indexical.

To claim that accounts are indexical is to say that, in order to comprehend or analyze any verbal or behavioural account, we must acquire the background knowledge of the context in which the account was produced. More controversially, ethnomethodology insists that *all* accounts and statements are indexical (as well as reflexive), and consequently there can be no such thing as a "universal" account — that is, an account which does not depend for its meaning on contextual knowledge of either where it was produced (in space) or when it was produced (in time). A universal account, for example, would be one that can be fully understood without reference to the context. Abstract scientific or logical statements such as "2+2 = 4" or "Ice floats on water" have been accepted as universally valid statements. But for ethnomethodologists, even these statements depend, in subtle and taken-for-granted ways, on certain contextual understandings that are normally "glossed," or assumed, in everyday speech. Indeed, there are some scholars (sociologists of knowledge, philosophers/historians of science, anthropologists) who suggest that even a so-called objective statement with a supposedly universal scope of application is dependent on a rationalized Western life-world for its meaning and validity. Even the stuff of scientific knowledge can be analyzed as accounts produced by local methods of practical reason. Readers should consider whether or not they regard as credible ethnomethodology's claim that all statements — including abstract logical, mathematical and scientific — are indexical, or whether, contrary to such claims, it is reasonable to conclude that universal statements are indeed possible.

Breaching Demonstrations/Experiments

Breaching demonstrations and experiments refers to deliberate attempts by ethnomethodologists and their students to violate the taken-for-granted norms and conventions in any particular social setting for the purposes of ethnomethodological research. The object of these exercises is to uncover and analyze the underlying presence and influence of these, often constraining, norms that govern most forms of social interaction. The most common examples of such breaches occur when an individual refuses to accept the conventions that structure most everyday conversations or other forms of expected and accepted behaviour. For example, some ethnomethodological researchers have chosen to breach the conversational norm of the etcetera principle. Instead of accepting the abbreviated and often incomplete expressions that are frequently used in informal conversations, a covert researcher intent upon exposing these conventions may insist upon a full clarification of each incomplete expression. This insistence often provokes confusion and even irritation or anger in the other conversation partner. For example:

Subject: "I had a flat tire."

Experimenter: "What do you mean, you had a flat tire?"

Subject: (appears momentarily stunned and then replies in a hostile manner): "What do you mean, 'What do you mean?' A flat tire is a flat tire. That is what I meant."

In one of his most famous breaching demonstrations/experiments, Garfinkel instructed a class of his students to return to their family homes and begin to act as though they were lodgers. Students were excessively polite to their parents and other family members; they asked permission to use the restroom and pretended to be ignorant of the comings and goings of the household. To the parents, this behaviour was incomprehensible, bizarre and disturbing, because the routine conventions and unspoken rules of how family members behave in their home were disrupted for no apparent reason. Another famous breaching experiment was conducted on the New York City subway in the 1970s, when experimenters boarded crowded trains and asked able-bodied but seated riders, with no explanation, to give up their seats. Reportedly, the experimenters themselves were deeply troubled by being involved in such a seemingly minor violation of a social norm. This experiment was supervised by Stanley Milgram.

Breaching demonstrations — especially those conducted on family members or on close personal friends — have sometimes resulted in resentment and hurt feelings from those who feel that they have been unfairly used as "guinea pigs" in a bizarre ethnomethodological experiment. For this reason, ethnomethodologists have often been warned against, and even disciplined for, conducting what more mainstream social scientists have sometimes condemned as "unethical research." Today, many of Garfinkel's and Milgram's early breaching experiments — which often involved deception — would be considered unethical because of their intrusive nature. Such experiments have contributed to increased ethical reviews of social science research human subjects, normally based on the principle of "informed consent."

Membership Categorization Analysis

Membership categorization analysis (MCA) is a qualitative methodology for studying how members of society interpret and understand the behaviour of others through the construction of categories. These categories are often intuitive and common-sense ways of organizing our experiences, our direct and indirect knowledge, and our expectations of another's behaviour. The production of local knowledge is accomplished by collecting information about the commonly believed or personally experienced attributes of a particular "other," and linking these activities to the more general stereotypical characteristics of the collective "other" (group) category. The link between particular individual activities, and more general group category characteristics is accomplished through "rules of application" which match *individual* representations to *group* typologies. For example, if I was suddenly assaulted in a city street and caught sight of a passing police officer, I would be strongly inclined to ask that officer for help because, as a white middle-class man, I belong to a member category that police tend to help. But the contents of the membership categorization are different for Black and Indigenous Peoples, whom police do not reliably help and for whom the group category characteristics matching "police" would likely be far more negative and threatening. Membership categorization analysis allows people to screen and categorize social interactions with members of the public. Each situation is defined by its own context; everything is indexical.

Membership categorization analysis originates from the work of Harvey Sacks. It examines the ways in which descriptions of, and orientations to, social categories and their associated activities are used in everyday contexts and shows how these categories are produced through methods of practical reasoning (see Silverman 1998). Besides illustrating how members construct their local knowledge, MCA is also useful in examining how stereotypes and prejudicial profiling takes place in the context of unequal and hostile social interactions (see, for example, Horwitz and Rabbie 1989). For an insightful account of how MCA was used to analyze the notorious case of Montreal gunman Marc Lépine, who shot twenty-eight people, killing fourteen women at the École Polytechnique in Montreal before killing himself, see Eglin and Hester (2003).

Ethnomethodological Indifference

Ethnomethodological indifference is the somewhat controversial principle of methodological and theoretical indifference, or agnosticism, towards the traditional humanistic values, beliefs, goals, concepts and vocabulary of mainstream sociology. In their observational studies of members' verbal and behavioural practices, ethnomethodologists try to avoid any conventional sociological jargon, or sociological beliefs, that may prejudice or in any way pre-structure, or frame, their own research observations or findings. Ethnomethodologists are focused on describing and recording the social reality — as experienced by members' themselves. Only after they have accurately and transparently reported and recorded members' accounts do they conduct analysis of these accounts in order to reveal the "deep structure" of members' practical methods for accomplishing their everyday identities and activities. But in order to produce an authentic report of members' practices, ethnomethodologists try to remain free from sociological and popular biases and prejudices. In this sense, as we have already emphasized, ethnomethodologists utilize members' verbal and behavioural accounts as a "topic" rather than as a "resource" for research and study. In some ways, the principle of "ethnomethodological indifference" reminds us of Max Weber's principle of "ethical neutrality," whereby he insists on a distinction between "facts" and "values," i.e., between empirical statements and value-judgments. Although this distinction is often difficult to make, according to Weber, it is important to recognize and apply it in order to maintain methodological rigour in the social sciences. For ethnomethodologists, the conscientious refusal to take a moral stand in research is what makes the social sciences "scientific." However, for more politicized and radical social scientists, this methodological principle of indifference may be misinterpreted as an indication of callousness or lack of empathy towards the research subjects. And for Polish sociologist Zygmunt Bauman, this principle of ethnomethodological indifference was not simply a sign of apolitical passivity but also a sign of intellectual arrogance, by which the theorist stood above the subject of their theorizing, claiming an objectivity and factual knowledge of the subject's actions that was unattainable by the subject themself. Paradoxically, ethnomethodology appeared to emulate the theoretical perspective that it most severely criticized — i.e., positivism:

> Neither phenomenology nor early existentialism tried to impose the necessity of programmatic indifference ... and they never tried to turn it into a virtue.... The one philosophy which dared to be boastfully explicit as to its deliberate indifference was positivism. The entities left in the pool of self-enforced neutrality and silence were values. In a sense ethnomethodology is, therefore, a more radical and consistent version of the positivist attitude: the pool of scientific silence has been enlarged to include truth. (Bauman 1973: 19–20)

Documentary Method

The primary methodology of ethnomethodology is known as the "documentary method" of social analysis. This means that ethnomethodology studies the actual evidence of what people *do* (their behavioural accounts) and *say* (their verbal accounts) in order to reveal an underlying pattern, or "deep structure," of social relations. In other words, ethnomethodology studies the things that people do or say as "texts" in their own right, texts that can be examined in order to reveal their underlying methods of production and rules of order. This can be done in a number of ways. When analyzing conversations — between callers and emergency dispatchers, for example — researchers normally produce a transcript from the audiotape of the conversation. This transcript becomes the hard empirical data that forms the basis of ethnomethodological analysis. A closer examination of the transcript data often reveals the formal structure of the account: how the conversation is started, how it is concluded, how turns are taken, how contextual information is taken for granted and so on. Similarly, ethnomethodologists would examine a videotape of an individual walking through a shopping mall for what it can tell them about "doing walking" as an "accountable" activity. In each case, they are examining the accounts of how members make sense of, and produce order in, their everyday activities. This is what distinguishes ethnomethodology from sociology.

Structure versus Agency

Ethnomethodology has changed forever the image of the social actor in all theoretical accounts. It is no longer acceptable to portray social actors as oversocialized and overdetermined puppets of larger social forces over which they exercise no control or autonomy. Even those macrosocial perspectives, such as structural functionalism, Marxism and conflict theory, that in the past have been most inclined towards deterministic interpretations of social action are now obliged to revise these interpretations in light of the insights of ethnomethodology.

The ethnomethodological perspective suggests a resolution to the old debate in sociology, namely: whether the proper study of society begins with the study of individual social actors (methodological individualism or nominalism) or with the study of large-scale structures and processes (methodological holism or realism). This debate over the relative priority of microsocial versus macrosocial analysis helped to define the growth of sociological theory and research throughout much of the twentieth century. From the ethnomethodology perspective, however, this outdated sociological debate has always been based upon a false dichotomy of (subjective) social actors versus the (objective) social world.

Since the work of Harold Garfinkel, social actors, or members of society, are typically seen as "knowledgeable agents" — knowing subjects who routinely use a variety of practical methods and follow various conventional rules in order to accomplish their identities and activities in everyday interactions. Indeed, Garfinkel famously critiqued structural functionalism for its representation of the social actor as a "judgemental dope" — someone who had fully internalized the norms and values of the social system and appeared to exercise little or no independent freedom of will or personal choice, i.e., no *agency*. Garfinkel (1967: 68) introduced the terms "cultural dope," "judgemental dope" and "psychological dope" as critical terms to denote how social — psychological or cultural — actors are portrayed in many sociological and psychological models of human action. He concluded that in many macrosocial theories — especially structural functionalism — the social actor is theorized without any recognition of a free will or capacity for independent action. Such a "dope" is not a real individual but is instead a theoretical construct, an ideal type that acts in conformity with the societal norms and values provided or imposed by the culture. In the words of another critic, Parsons offers us an "oversocialized" conception of the social actor (Wrong 1961). The social phenomenologist Alfred Schutz (1953) suggested a similar analogy between a "puppet" and the ideal-typical social actor in macrosocial theories

The whole point of ethnomethodology is to show how all forms of social order — whether interpersonal and small-scale or societal and large-scale — may be understood as the accomplishments of the ongoing and often routine activities of members of society in interaction with each other. In this respect, ethnomethodology is not really interested in whether or not large-scale social structures actually "exist." Ethnomethodology is primarily interested in the methods of practical reasoning that ordinary members of society use to make sense of and to produce order in their everyday interactions with each other. In combination with each other, these recurrent, or "recursive," interactions are what produce and reproduce on a daily basis the large-scale and more abstract social structures that appear to dominate our lives in so many ways. In this sense, we may say that ethnomethodology is interested in the deep structure of our social institutions: the interactional work that goes into the production and reproduction of social order.

DOING ETHNOMETHODOLOGY

Ethnomethodologists have pioneered a number of different methods and technologies for studying social interactions. This major research perspective has popularized the use of audio and video recorders in studies of social interaction. Video footage of how members "do" activities have become part of the established ethnomethodological research paradigm. Similarly, transcripts of conversational exchanges are also part of the legacy of ethnomethodological research.

In Garfinkel's case study of Agnes (the trans woman), he documented her process of transition, including learning dominant gender expectations. For example, when she was invited over to a friend's house, ostensibly to learn how to cook Indian food, she used this occasion to learn the most rudimentary arts of cooking in general. In this sense, according to Garfinkel, she was a "secret apprentice." But Garfinkel's main point is that all of us have to learn how to assume our gender identities and perform our gender roles in society; these skills are not encoded in our genetic make-up — they are only learned and taught through our contacts with others. In other words, gender identities are always "interactional accomplishments" — learned through acquiring the practical methods and skills through social interaction. The same is also true of our occupational identities; our ethnic and racial identities; and even our chronological identities — how to act as an old man or as a young woman. All our practical activities may be regarded as interactional accomplishments inasmuch as they all result from some kind of interactional "work."

Besides the case study, ethnomethodologists have also pioneered studies in "natural settings" and in "institutional settings" and, most importantly, in "conversation analysis." In their famous study of the "art of walking," Lincoln Ryave and James Schenkein (1974) were primarily interested in the "practical methods," or methods of practical reasoning, that members of a community use in making walking an interactional accomplishment. Unlike most social scientists, for whom walking has normally been taken for granted, ethnomethodologists see it as an interactive practice requiring explanation and analysis. In this respect, the study of "doing walking," like other studies of "doing laughing" or "doing applause," is typical of the way in which ethnomethodologists investigate the ordinary activities of everyday life and subject these activities to a formal description and analysis.

The researchers explain that the expression "doing walking" is meant to draw attention to the fact that walking is being studied as an "ongoing situated (interactional) accomplishment" of everyday life. Although the activity of walking may appear to be effortless and unthinking, the truth is that walking in a public space requires considerable competence and work on the part of the walker. By "work," these researchers mean that walkers have to use definite "methodical practices" and follow definite rules to successfully engage in the practice of public walking. What are these practices and rules? Of the various problems involved in "doing walking," the researchers focused on two in particular: the "navigational" problem and what might be called the "membership categorization" problem. The navigational problem refers to the need for all walkers in a crowded public space to avoid collisions with each other and with obstacles. Indeed, the fact that large numbers of walkers successfully avoid collisions is seen as evidence of the fact that walking is organized around definite methodical practices. The membership categorization problem refers to how walkers have to act depending upon whether they are walking alone or walking with somebody else. Indeed, there are different rules for walking together and for walking alone, and the competence of walkers depends upon their correctly categorizing their own and other walkers' relations to each other. While these distinctions may appear to be exercises in the obvious, for ethnomethodologists they are part of the fine detail of social interaction. What emerges from this type of ethnomethodological analysis is that the act of "doing walking" requires a considerable amount of "work," which is taken for granted by most individuals in their everyday lives. Upon closer observation, much of this work appears to be guided by definite methodical practices and other kinds of rule-following behaviour. It is only by examining these practices in detail that their significance as ongoing situated interactional accomplishments can be fully revealed.

Besides the intrinsic interest of the topic of walking, these kinds of ethnomethodological accounts have yielded other conceptual and methodological insights. In the research on "doing waking," the data on which the analysis is based is taken from videotaped footage of pedestrians in a "natural setting." This study also provides an example of what ethnomethodologists refer to as the "reflexivity of accounts," which means that walking is observed to be a reflexive activity. The act of walking involves the twin processes of "production" and "recognition." Simply stated, this means that walking, like most other interactional accomplishments, may be analyzed as both a cause and a consequence of interaction. While walkers must work to produce orderliness in their walking, they must also work to recognize the structures of order in their relations with other walkers. The act of walking produces the act of recognition that in turn becomes part of the act of walking. It is in this sense that reflexivity is seen to be a noteworthy feature of what people do, and of what they think or say about what they do. "Reflexivity" has become a key concept in the vocabulary of ethnomethodology. It is through concepts such as these that ethnomethodologists have pioneered their analyses of the actual lived experiences of everyday life.

"Institutional studies," on the other hand, have included studies of how patients are admitted to medical clinics and triaged to particular health-care professionals, or how clients in other public offices — social welfare, workers' compensation, unemployment etc. — are dispatched and distributed by receptionists to appropriate administrative officers. In all of these cases, the researchers are interested in analyzing the "formal properties" of the external, objectively recordable and reportable practical methods used by members to accomplish their routine activities.

One of the central issues of ethnomethodological theory and research is how to describe or explicate the formal structure of these accounts. In other words, how do we represent the ways in which people talk to each other, or interact with each other, in order to examine and analyze these accounts? How do we make a model of peoples' accounts that would enable us to examine these accounts for their common properties — for their similarities and for their differences? How do we make a model of the formal or underlying "structure" of these accounts? What ethnomethodologists have discovered from their studies is that the structure of members' accounts cannot be reduced to the principles of formal logic. In their conversations and interactions with each other, people often violate logical principles in any number of ways, as we have already seen in connection with the use of "loose concepts" and "indexical expressions."

CONVERSATION ANALYSIS

We turn now to a specialized branch of ethnomethodology known as conversation analysis (CA). Conversation analysis, along with membership categorization analysis, was first introduced by Harvey Sacks, who was a student of Harold Garfinkel. Most of Sacks' ethnomethodological research was centred on the analysis of conversational data — that is, on "talk." Much of this conversational data was derived from recorded and transcribed social (i.e., verbal) interactions. Sacks was less interested in the substantive content of these conversations than he was in their form, or deep structure. He believed that the deep structure of conversations provided some important indicators regarding the social relations between the interacting individuals. Much of Sacks' work in CA was developed in collaboration with Emanuel Schegloff and Gail Jefferson (see Schegloff 2007). .

The core of CA focuses on how most conversations are organized through a sequential pattern of "turn-taking." In other words, one individual is expected to speak at a time, while the speakers change and alternate throughout the course of the conversation. Although this basic description of a typical conversation may appear self-evident and even trivial, CA research has shown how all conversations are systematically organized and involve definite rules which guide or govern the interactions between different speakers. Thus, while conversations may superficially appear to flow naturally between two or more speakers, it becomes clear on closer examination that the speakers are following definite rules of order and are using identifiable methods of practical reasoning to accomplish their verbal interaction.

As a specialized branch of ethnomethodology, CA is able to demonstrate how social order is accomplished on a turn-by-turn basis. CA research has studied how each utterance in a conversation is always a response to a prior utterance and may be analyzed as a distinctive "turn" at talk. Any stream of conversation, therefore, may be understood as a set of turns, each turn being a response to a prior turn and a basis for the next turn. CA focuses on such features as turn design and composition, silences within or between turns, corrections and repair work, and the way that turns are organized sequentially. Each turn in a conversation reveals the other speaker's own perspective of what was meant and done in the prior turn. In this sense, CA offers both a description and an analysis of the speakers' own methods and rules for constructing a coherent conversational and interactional order.

The main interest of CA has never been the subjectively meaningful content of the conversation *per se*, but in the actual methods, practices, rules and inferences that are observed in social interaction. Close examination of the sequential organization of talk can reveal the practical sense-making methods and procedures of everyday social life that are routinely used to produce the interactional basis of social order. CA is very different from more traditional studies of communication, in which talk is analyzed as the transmission of information and meaningful messages. For CA — to borrow an expression from Canadian philosopher Marshall McLuhan — the medium, i.e., the methods of practical reasoning, is the message.

A famous and controversial study in CA, undertaken by Pamela Fishman (1977; 1978), analyzed the patterns and deep structure of talk between men and women, using transcripts of recorded conversations. The writer concluded that the data revealed a strongly gendered division of labour in the actual work involved in the production of these conversational exchanges. The data revealed that women do more conversational work than men and that the role of women in conversation was clearly subordinate to, and deferential towards, that of men. In other words, the data suggested that male-female conversations showed a recurrent pattern of inequality in the exercise of power and control in conversational exchanges. The men repeatedly demonstrated in the timing, sequencing and turn-taking of their utterances an ability to control, direct and redirect the topics of conversation. Women, by contrast, played a supportive and subservient role in conversation and consistently showed their deference to the male conversational agenda.

The sample size used in Fishman's research was actually quite small, with only three couples. The couples had been together for different periods, one for two years and the others for three and six months. However, they were all drawn from a similar occupational (professional) and age (25–35) demographic. All the subjects expressed support for the women's movement, especially the women, who were described as "avowed feminists." The conversational data revealed a number of interesting findings. The women apparently worked harder than the men in sustaining conversation, accomplishing this work by asking many more questions (150) than men (59). They demonstrated the same kind of subservience towards the men that children normally show towards adults by using deferential utterances such as: "D'ya know what?" In this respect, the data almost suggests the *infantilization* of women in their conversational exchanges with their male partners. The women also used many more attention-seeking expressions, such as "This is interesting" and "Y'know" (34) than the men (3), as well as other kinds of support work, such as "Yeah," "Umm," "Huh," etc. The data also showed that the men far more frequently initiated and redirected topics of conversation, and they frequently remained unresponsive to topics suggested by women. In other words, the men controlled the conversational agenda.

Fishman concludes that women are — if you will pardon her expression — the "shit workers" in their verbal interactions with men. They perform a subordinate and subservient role in the division of labour that underlies the production of a conversational, and by implication an interactional, order. Women who violate these conversational norms are usually perceived as deviant and may be pejoratively labelled as "domineering," "aggressive," "shrill" etc. From an ethnomethodological perspective, the subordinate work performed by women in the local production of conversational order is evidence of a recurrent methodical practice that in time, and in many places, helps to produce and sustain the larger and more abstract societal structures of patriarchy. The localized practices that produce interpersonal inequalities are, at the same time, both constituents and reflections of the larger structures of gender inequality in society. The whole point of ethnomethodology is to show how the work of producing personal identity and routine activity can best be observed at a local and microsocial level of analysis.

The dramatic and highly political conclusions that Fishman drew from her original study have been widely cited in diverse research literatures: e.g., communication studies, women's studies and cultural studies. More recently, there have been attempts to corroborate and replicate Fishman's findings in some follow-up studies. One such attempt was reported in a study by Linda McMullen, Anne Vernon and Tracy Murton, published in 1995. The researchers examined whether Fishman's reported findings could be (1) generalized to a different sample (namely, forty previously unacquainted males and females) and (2) replicated with a larger similar sample (namely, seventeen intimate, cohabiting male-female couples). These researchers also critiqued the methodological weaknesses of Fishman's original study for its very small sample size (only three cohabiting male-female couples), its impressionistic and non-statistical data analysis, its unreliable research design (no control group) and its extravagant claims for the generalizability of the research conclusions. In their own study, McMullen et al. concluded that Fishman's research findings could not be generalized to non-intimate couples and could not even be fully replicated with a larger sample of intimate co-habiting couples.

In fact, only two of Fishman's results were weakly replicated: (1) Men used a greater number of minimal responses than women at the end of their partners' talk, although they also used these minimal responses "in the stream" of their partners' talk. This ambiguous finding made it difficult to interpret this result as evidence of a male lack of interest. (2) Men sometimes failed to respond to women's attempts to introduce or change topics of conversation. However, the evidence for this unresponsiveness was far weaker than that reported by Fishman. Unlike the Fishman study, this later study found no evidence that the women performed more support work than their male partners. Instead, the later findings only showed that the women may have helped to sustain the conversations with their male partners simply by talking more.

Thus, the study by McMullen, Vernon and Murton (1995) suggests that the data provided by Fishman for her dramatic conclusions was based upon an unrepresentative sample and was collected and analyzed using non-rigorous and unreliable research methods. They conclude that the widespread appeal of her study has more to do with the fact that she may have "touched upon a mythic truth or deeply held cultural belief" than with the generalizability, replicability, reliability or validity of her conclusions. And according to McMullen et al., Fisher failed to convincingly prove the charge that localized conversations between men and women serve to expose the deep structure of institutionalized sexism and patriarchy that pervades the larger society. Where does all this leave the rest of us?

Notwithstanding the methodological weaknesses of Fishman's study, her use of CA helped to sensitize us to some of the practical methods used to produce conversational order and to some of the unspoken rules that help to sustain this order. Even if her study was based upon a very limited sample size and composition, it revealed that the men who portrayed themselves as committed feminists were unwilling or unable to forgo their gender power and privilege of controlling and directing the conversation, and that women who proclaimed themselves as "avowed feminists" played a subordinate and subservient role in the conversational division of labour with their intimate partners. This finding alone has made this a memorable study.

Other studies have corroborated Fishman's findings and reinforced her conclusions regarding the subtle ways in which sexist practices often relegate female conversational partners to a subordinate and dependent status in cross-sexual verbal interactions. Candace West and Donald Zimmerman (1975, 1983), reported a very similar outcome to that of Fishman's study: "We suggested that males assert an asymmetrical right to control topics and do so without evident repercussions. We are led to the conclusion that, at least in our transcripts, men deny equal status to women as conversational partners with respect to rights to the full utilization of their turn and support for the development of topics. Thus we speculate that just as male dominance is exhibited through male control of macro-institutions in society, it is also exhibited through control of at least a part of one micro-institution" (1975: 125).

In a later ethnomethodological review of how everyday patriarchal sexist practices can reinforce the gender oppression of women, Marsha Houston and Cheris Kramarae (1991) noted: "Some of the specific ways women have been silenced include: ridicule, enforcement of family hierarchies, male-controlled media, anti-woman educational policies, making women's bodies political battlegrounds, censorship, racism, homophobia, and terrorism. Some of the ways women have broken silence are through the analysis of silencing tactics, the re-evaluation of 'trivial' discourse, creative code-switching, linguistic creativity, and the organization of women's presses." From these and other examples, it is clear that ethnomethodological studies of the taken-for-granted everyday practices of social interaction can reveal some disturbing signs of gender inequality, or to put it another way, a "deep structure" of patriarchy and sexism. In their close observation and formal analysis of everyday behaviour, ethnomethodologists have shown how their studies can assist us in becoming more self-critical and reflexive in the ways we routinely interact with others in society.

ETHNOMETHODOLOGY IN A CRITICAL AGE

The story of ethnomethodology has proven to be a fascinating and instructive one. Once reviled by many professional sociologists as a bizarre and disruptive academic "cult," it is now a respected and fully accredited perspective in the social sciences. The influence of ethnomethodology has spread out into several theoretical directions. Garfinkel's original insistence on studying the methods of practical reasoning used by members of society to accomplish their identities and activities has now become a common feature of many other theorists — most obviously in the later works of Erving Goffman on frame analysis and forms of talk — but also in the structuralist writings of Anthony Giddens and Pierre Bourdieu and in the feminist writings of Dorothy Smith. These studies of the microfoundations of social order have helped to bridge the ontological and epistemological gap between macrosocial and microsocial theories of society, and in many ways, this old sociological dichotomy has now been rendered largely irrelevant to contemporary social theory.

The beauty of ethnomethodology is that it attends to what we do, rather than what we say. These practices may sometimes be at odds with the idealized ways in which we often think about ourselves and others and how we try to represent ourselves to others. This was certainly the case with several significant findings of conversation analysis — like those of Fishman (1977) and of West and Zimmerman (1983), which showed how patriarchal practices are often reproduced in verbal exchanges between men and women, even when the male conversational partners believe themselves to be egalitarian and non-sexist in their treatment of women. In addition to these studies of sexism and conversational practices, the techniques of membership categorization analysis have proven useful in showing how stereotyping and profiling is accomplished through the methods of misinformed practical reasoning.

At the same time, ethnomethodology has not escaped critical scrutiny. A new generation of global social theorists, feminists and critical gender theorists, committed to diversity, inclusion and insurgency, have critiqued some of the major assumptions, landmark studies and political implications of ethnomethodology. Ethnomethodology, which was once both celebrated and notorious for its debunking of many of the icons and shibboleths of the sociological canon has now, itself, been debunked for its own perceived methodological, theoretical and political inadequacies. These attacks have centred on several different issues:

Political conservatism: Garfinkel has been reproached by Baumann and others for his principle of "ethnomethodological indifference" as a prescription for ethical neutrality and methodological objectivity. For many contemporary critics, ethnomethodological indifference is seen as a patronizing view of the research relationship between the theorist and their subjects, in which the theorist assumes they know more about the subject than the subject knows about themselves. This principle of indifference also implies a false sense of objectivity and a refusal by the ethnomethodologists to reflexively account for their own standpoint, or viewpoint, within the structure of power relations. Through their own unreflexive practices, ethnomethodologists have continued to repro- duce the power relations that they refuse to acknowledge and account for. As Denis Gleeson and Michael Erben (1976: 474) suggest, "because ethnomethodology neglects to take into consideration the character of certain events, it borders close on being an ideology of conservatism.... Furthermore, certain misgivings are advanced concerning the failure of ethnomethodology to make explicit critical comments concerning those features of interaction which may exercise oppressive influence on the meanings of members."

Ethnomethodological indifference is seen by many recent critics as a betrayal of the reflexivity that ethnomethodologists have sworn to uphold in their own studies. This critique has focused on Garfinkel's famous study of Agnes. Critics have argued that by restricting his study to an obser- vation of Agnes's accomplishment of her transitioned gender identity, Garfinkel failed to analyze his own privileged masculine status, which defined the context of this study and the patriarchal power relations in which this context was situated. This lack of reflexivity is recognized by Rebecca Raby (2000: 27), who comments that Garfinkel "seems oblivi- ous to his own methods and to the wider power relations evident in his interviews," even though, "Garfinkel and particularly his masculinity are evident throughout the paper, a fact that suggests a need for him to reflect upon his own gender performance." And this concern is also expressed by Roslyn Bologh (1992: 200), who concludes: "Garfinkel's study fails to recognize its own complicity in that social construction. Garfinkel fails to notice how his passing as a man is implicated in Agnes's passing as a woman. Garfinkel's ethnomethodology lacks self-reflection, an unwilling- ness to apply its methods and strictures to itself."

Positivism: Ethnomethodologists have also been critiqued for their positiv- ism and lack of self-reflexivity and accountability in their own methods of inquiry. This may appear ironic in view of the strong critique of positivism expressed by most ethnomethodologists over the years. For positivists, the truth content of a proposition, or statement, always has a universal validity — irrespective of when, where or by whom it is uttered; but for ethnomethodologists, all statements or propositions are seen as "indexical," that is, as fully dependent for their meaning on the context in which they are uttered. However, for many critics, the failure of ethnomethodologists to practise reflexivity and accountability shows that they remain trapped in an objectivism that bears the all the hallmarks of positivism. Thus, for Bologh (1992: 201, 203), ethnomethodology

> ends up guilty of the same kind of "positivist science" that it decries — a dualistic separation between subject (researcher) and object (member's practices) as opposed to dialectical recognition that both subject and object are mutually constituted products of a form of life that they are engaged in (re) producing. … It engages in the reproduction and representation of an objective reality without acknowledging its own complicity in constituting that reality.

Determinism: Some critics of the Agnes study have also condemned Garfinkel for framing Agnes as a "deviant," with an "abnormal" or "pathological" sexual identity, thereby contributing to the process of "othering" Agnes rather than seeing her as an independent agent capable of making a free and rational choice concerning her identity and lifestyle (Raby 2000: 19). The framing of Agnes as a pathological identity illustrates what Jodi O'Brien (2016: 209) has called the "unexamined assumptions of heterosexuality" that are embedded in the Garfinkel study. While these assumptions may have been accepted in the "psychiatric-medical-heteronormative" script of the 1950s, this is clearly no longer the case. Today, with the rise of transgender studies, many of these earlier negative labels and stereotypes of trans people have been contested, as we can see from a more recent assessment of the Agnes study: "Agnes did not have a disorder of gender identity. Her gender identity was in excellent shape, thank you very much. Her immediate problem was that she had a boyfriend and a penis" (Connell 2009: 106–107). But Garfinkel remained completely and unreflexively trapped in the heteronormative and psychiatric scripts of his day that defined and diagnosed Agnes as a deviant sexual identity suffering from a gender dysphoria who was intending to "pass" as a woman. In recent years, the politics and the epistemology of gender studies — including trans studies — has changed dramatically. As O'Brien (2016: 312) observes: "The contemporary context is one of mutually constitutive bio-socio theories, a flourishing transgender studies, and richly complex trans activism." For many recent critics of ethnomethodology, it is high time to progress beyond unreflexive empirical observational studies and to jettison the positivist norm of methodological indifference in favour of a more passionate commitment to social justice, individual self-expression and gender sovereignty.

Beyond the particular case of the Agnes study, ethnomethodology has been criticized more generally for portraying members of society as passive automatons whose behaviour and daily actions are "scripted" by the rules and norms of society and by methods of practical reasoning that members use to conform to the expectations of others. This is a picture that strips the individual of any real agency or autonomy and represents an "oversocialized" conception of members of society that is reminiscent of the structural functionalist perspective, which ethnomethodologists have always critiqued. Several recent critics have noted this overdetermined view of the individual in ethnomethodological studies:

> Not dissimilar to the tradition of conventional sociology, the status of 'ethno-theory' rejoices in a hierarchic dominance over its subjects of research ("members"), who like puppets provide the 'magician' with evidence that they really are alienated beings. '"Members" are in fact treated as objects, as if in an experiment, and are seen as useful only as exhibitors of the routine, mundane and taken-for-granted order of things. (Gleeson and Erben 1976: 482)

O'Brien (2016: 325) also censures ethnomethodology for its oversocialized conception of the individual: "Much ethnomethodology is predicated on assumptions of mindlessness — the rote ways in which we practice everyday interaction routines, including frequently repairing breaches through well-established secondary elaborations." She sees another possible path for ethnomethodology: a more radical and progressive program of theory and practice committed to emancipatory and inclusive goals: "Far from being passive victims or blank receptacles, these people are likely to be the most aware of their social circumstances. The ways in which they grapple with the tensions and contradictions of hierarchical, oppressive, exclusionary social forms is the basis for a sociology of resistance and change; an ethnomethodology focused on potential disruption" (O'Brien 2016: 325). For the more critical ethnomethodologists of today, this may be the way forward.

References

Baldwin, Elaine. 2004. *Introducing Cultural Studies.* Pearson/Prentice Hall.

Bauman, Zygmunt. 1973. "On the Philosophical Status of Ethnomethodology." *The Sociological Review,* 21: 5–23.

Bittner, Egon. 1967. "The Police on Skid Row: A Study of Peace Keeping." *American Sociological Review,* 32: 699–715.

Boden, Deirdre. 1990. "The World as It Happens: Ethnomethodology and Conversation Analysis." In George Ritzer (ed.), *Frontiers of Social Theory: The New Synthesis.* New York: Columbia University Press.

Bologh, Roslyn. 1992. "The Promise and Failure of Ethnomethodology from a Feminist Perspective: Comment on Rogers." *Gender & Society,* 6, 2: 199–206. <https://doi.org/10.1177/089124392006002004>.

Cicourel, Aaron V. 1974. *Theory and Method in a Study of Argentine Fertility.* New York: Wiley Interscience.

Connell, Raewyn. 2009. "'Doing Gender' in Transsexual and Political Retrospect." *Gender and Society,* 23, 1: 104–111.

Eglin, Peter, and Stephen Hester. 1992. *A Sociology of Crime.* Routledge.

___. 2003. *The Montreal Massacre: A Story of Membership Categorization Analysis.* Waterloo, ON: Wilfred Laurier Press.

Fishman, P.M. 1977. "Interactional Shitwork." *Heresies,* 1, 2: 99–101.

___. 1978. "Interaction: The Work Women Do." *Social Problems,* 25, 4: 397–406.

Garfinkel, H. 1967. *Studies in Ethnomethodology.* Englewood Cliffs, NJ: Prentice Hall.

Gellner, E. 1975. "Ethnomethodology: The Re-enchantment Industry or the Californian Way of Subjectivity." *Philosophy of the Social Sciences,* 5, 3: 431–450.

Goffman, Erving. 1972. *Relations in Public.* Penguin.

Gleeson, Denis, and Michael Erben. 1976. "Meaning in Context: Notes towards a Critique of Ethnomethodology." *The British Journal of Sociology,* 27, 4: 474–483.

Gordon, Raymond. 1976. "Ethnomethodology: A Radical Critique." *Human Relations,* 29, 2 (February): 193202.

Horwitz M., and J.M. Rabbie. 1989. "Stereotypes of Groups, Group Members, and Individuals in Categories: A Differential Analysis." In D. Bar-Tal, C.F. Graumann, A.W. Kruglanski, and W. Stroebe (eds.), *Stereotyping and Prejudice.* Springer Series in Social Psychology. New York: Springer.

Houston, Marsha, and Cheris Kramarae. 1991. "Speaking from Silence: Methods of Silencing and of Resistance." *Discourse and Society,* 2, 4: 387–399.

Joas, H., and W. Knöbl. 2009. "Ethnomethodology." In *Social Theory: Twenty Introductory Lectures.* Cambridge University Press.

Kessler, S.J., and W. McKenna. 1978. *Gender: An Ethnomethodological Approach.* New York: Wiley.

Latour, Bruno, and Steve Woolgar. 1986. *Laboratory Life: The Construction of Scientific Facts.* Princeton, NJ: Princeton University Press.

McMullen, Linda, Anne Vernon, and Tracy Murton. 1995. "Division of Labor in Conversations: Are Fishman's Results Replicable and Generalizable?" *Journal of Psycholinguistic Research*, 24, 4: 255–268.

Mehan, H., and H. Wood. 1975. *The Reality of Ethnomethodology.* New York: John Wiley and Sons.

O'Brien, Jodi. 2016. "Seeing Agnes: Notes on a Transgender Biocultural Ethnomethodology." *Symbolic Interactionism*, 39, 2 (May): 306–329.

Raby, Rebecca. 2000. "Re-Configuring Agnes: The Telling of a Transsexual's Story." *Torquere: Journal of the Canadian Lesbian and Gay Studies Association*, 2: 18–35.

Ryave, Lincoln, and James Schenkein. 1974. "Notes on the Art of Walking." In Roy Turner (ed.), *Ethnomethodology.* Harmondsworth: Penguin.

Schegloff, Emanuel A. 2007. *Sequence Organization in Interaction: A Primer in Conversation Analysis, Volume 1.* Cambridge: Cambridge University Press.

Silverman, David. 1998. *Harvey Sacks, Social Science and Conversation Analysis.* Cambridge: Polity Press.

___. 2007. *A Very Short, Fairly Interesting and Reasonably Cheap Book about Qualitative Research.* Sage Publications.

West, Candace, and Donald Zimmerman. 1975. "Sex Roles, Interruptions and Silences in Conversation." In Barrie Thorn and Nancy Henley (eds.), *Language and Sex: Difference and Dominance.* Rowley, MA: Newbury House.

___. 1983. "Small Insults: A Study of Interruptions in Cross-sex Conversations between Unacquainted Persons." In Barrie Thorne, Cheris Kramarae, and Nancy Henley (eds.), *Language, Gender and Society.* Rowley, MA: Newbury House.

Wilson, Thomas P. 1970. "Normative and Interpretive Paradigms in Sociology." In Jack D. Douglas (ed.), *Understanding Everyday Life: Towards a Reconstruction of Sociological Knowledge.* Chicago: Aldine Publishing.

Wrong, Dennis H. 1961. "The Oversocialized Conception of Man in Modern Sociology." *American Sociological Review*, 26, 2 (Apr): 183–193.

CHAPTER 8

THEORIZING OUR DISCURSIVE LIVES

Postmodernism and Poststructuralism

THE POSTMODERN AGE

The postmodern age is often seen as an age of instability and insecurity, when longstanding traditions are uprooted, ancient truths are overturned, and formerly established "facts" are exposed as the privileged opinions of the powerful. In short, postmodernism is considered an expression of a contemporary crisis in the Western world. This crisis is expressed in the arts and humanities, the social sciences, the media and entertainment industries, politics and the ways in which we think about and live our lives. More than anything else, postmodernism and poststructuralism reflect a *crisis of uncertainty* and a recognition that the certainties of the past — even the recent past — may no longer be valid.

Many things have contributed to this uncertainty. North Americans and western Europeans are no longer masters of their own economic destinies. The days when American, British, French and German companies dominated the industrial, commercial and financial centres of the world economy are over. Today, the terms of trade are set by multinational corporations, as well as by such transnational agencies as the International Monetary Fund, the World Bank and the World Trade Organization, none of which owe formal allegiance to any particular country — even though the US continues to exert a disproportionate influence on their policies and practices. The days when the West occupied the undisputed centre of the world stage are gone. Instead, most of us are exposed, as never before, to the pressures of a highly competitive world marketplace in which our jobs, natural resources, social programs and even sense of national identity are likely to be unpredictably affected by the new age of global free trade and commerce. The dominant position that our industrial economies and liberal democracies once enjoyed in the world system has been displaced — or "decentred," to use a poststructuralist term — by the pressures of international competition. This decline of the West has been accompanied by a corresponding rise of new global industrial and political powers, most notably those of China, Russia, Japan, India and Brazil, with other nations, such as South Korea, Hong Kong and Taiwan, also affecting these dynamics. Indeed, we saw some of the fallout from the unpopularity of transnational free trade agreements in the 2016 election of Donald Trump as the US president and the 2016 Brexit referendum vote for Britain to leave the European Union.

Along with the economic decline and decentring of the West, globalization has added to our uncertainties in other ways. More than ever before, we have been forced to acknowledge our interconnectedness and interdependency with other parts of the world. The electronic media have brought about what postmodernists call a "space–time compression." We are able to watch what happens in different parts of the world without having to travel. In new and unprecedented ways, the affairs of other parts of the world may spill over into our own lives. Sometimes this broadens and enriches our experiences: we can read newspapers, listen to overseas radio programs or watch foreign video footage on the internet. Sometimes, however, this new global interconnectedness may be deeply troubling or even terrifying, as shown by the wars in Afghanistan, Iraq and Syria or terrorist attacks in Baghdad, Kabul, Ankara, Nice, Paris, San Bernardino, London, Manchester, Brussels and elsewhere. For better or worse, the world has shrunk into a global village, and all of us are affected by these changes in new and unpredictable ways (see McLuhan 2003 [1964]: 6).

There have been other important effects and side effects of the new networks of interconnectedness made possible through the internet, cable and satellite television, smartphones and other forms of electronic communication. As several postmodernist writers have suggested, even our sense of what is "real" has changed and become more confused. Our experience of the "real" world — the world directly observed through our own senses — has become increasingly displaced by the "virtual" world of electronic images. According to some postmodernists, we live in an age of "hyperreality," in which the boundaries separating the actual from the virtual have become blurred and indistinct. Whereas much of our traditional knowledge was based on direct experience of the world, today our knowledge is based more and more on electronic representations — "simulacra," or copies of the world.

How have these changes contributed to a crisis of uncertainty? The decline and decentring of the economic dominance of the West has opened the floodgates not only to products and services from other countries but also to ideas and beliefs from other cultures and communities. But although the erosion of old cultural borders and narrow nationalist worldviews provide unprecedented opportunities for sharing ideas and experiences around the world, for some groups these global changes represent a crisis of national identity. This blowback may be seen in the rise of nationalist and far-right political movements in Europe, North and South America, India, Turkey and other countries. While globalism has provided new opportunities for some, for others, it poses a threat. In this time of unprecedented pluralism, an increasing number of voices are joining our universe of discourse. The worldwide marketplace of commodities has also become a worldwide marketplace of ideas, expressed in a variety of voices that challenge dominant narratives and share experiences of being immigrants and refugees, people of colour, Indigenous Peoples, women, queer and non-binary people, workers and poor people, and so on. In its own way, the internet has become an icon for the proliferation and diversification of our universe of discourses in the postmodern age.

The rise of this new diversity has also meant a corresponding decline in the authority of established discourses. This, more than anything else, underlies the crisis of uncertainty in postmodernism. Conventional accounts of how our society is organized or of how it has developed have been challenged by many other voices. These are the voices of the "outsiders," who have traditionally been overlooked in conventional accounts (see Gilroy 1993; Giroux 2000). The days of universal historical accounts — of metanarratives, or general theories of society, are over.

Today, an ever-proliferating number of versions of the world are produced by an ever-increasing and fragmenting number of "standpoint positions" and "subject identities." The old versions of history and the old versions of social theory are now regarded by most postmodernist writers as grandiose stories told by privileged groups — invariably white, wealthy, heterosexual men — from their own powerful and parochial perspectives. Although these stories once claimed universality and generality, they never included the perspectives and experiences of those who were powerless to tell their own stories. Now voices from the margins are informing new social movements and disrupting the established politics of the traditional social order. And, in many ways, the theories of postmodernism and poststructuralism reflect these new social movements by "deconstructing" the established and traditional theoretical discourses of the recent past.

WHAT IS POSTMODERNISM?

"Postmodernism" is a rather slippery concept, difficult to define with great precision. The term has become ubiquitous, used in a number of academic disciplines and intellectual traditions that range from architecture to literary theory and criticism, to cultural studies, through to the social sciences and the humanities. In the simplest possible terms, "postmodernism" may best be understood as a rejection of modernism. By "modernism," we mean a belief in the essential capacity of humanity to perfect or constantly improve itself through the power of reason, that is, through rational thought. For contemporary social theorists, postmodernism represents, more than anything else, the end of the so-called "emancipatory project," a powerful idea rooted in the Enlightenment and handed down to us over many generations. The term refers to the long-held belief that the emancipation of humanity can be achieved through the application of reason to social problems and human affairs. "Emancipation" can mean freedom from political oppression, but it can also mean freedom from economic want, ignorance, disease and a multitude of problems. Most of the classical social theorists, especially Marx, Durkheim and Weber, were strongly influenced by the Enlightenment values of reason, liberty and progress. They believed that, through the application of reason to social problems, humanity could progressively liberate itself from the problems of and threats to human existence. These Enlightenment ideals have shaped the political thought of the Western world and have handed down to us a culture of optimism that is still apparent in the ideologies of liberalism, humanism, rationalism, socialism, communism, anarchism, feminism and many other "isms" of the modern age.

Postmodernism begins with a rejection of the proclaimed universality of the Enlightenment values of reason, liberty and progress and a deep-seated skepticism towards any universalizing or totalizing ideologies — the so-called grand narratives or metanarratives — that claim to speak on behalf of all of us. The history of the modern age, as far as postmodernists are concerned, has been the subjugation of the powerless by the powerful. And much of this subjugation has been rationalized through appeals to "universal" values or interests: "*Liberté, Fraternité, Egalité*" (French

Revolution); "Life, Liberty and the Pursuit of Happiness" (American Revolution); "Workers of the World, Unite!" (First International); and "Rule Britannia" (British Imperialism) — to cite only a few examples. In opposition to the specious universality of modernist ideologies and discourses, postmodernism celebrates the diversity, pluralism and difference that have entered our social worlds and social discourses through the new social movements of the late twentieth century and early decades of the twenty-first century. The apparent unity of our social world has fragmented the established discourses of the white Western wealthy world. The discourses that were once thought to be universal have been revealed, or "deconstructed," as privileged, or "hegemonic," discourses imposed by the powerful onto the rest of society.

CHARACTERISTICS OF POSTMODERNISM

The fragmentation, pluralism and relativism of postmodernist thought reflect the realities of the postmodern age. The apparent unity of the old established social and intellectual order has been overtaken by kaleidoscopic diversity. Many modernist thinkers have experienced these postmodernist upheavals as a series of *losses* of their formerly established certainties. The old stable frameworks of meaning and truth have been disrupted, and the foundations of much classical social theory have been radically undermined and subverted.

It is worth reflecting for a moment on what distinguishes postmodernism from other critical perspectives in social theory, such as ethnomethodology, symbolic interactionism, structuralism, and critical theory, among others. More than anything else, what distinguishes postmodernism is its preoccupation with *language* and *discourse*. For postmodernist theorists, the social world is only made available to us through particular forms of discourse and through the practices that produce and are produced by these discourses. For postmodernists, there is no world beyond that of discourse.

In order to understand why postmodernists attach such importance to the role of discourse in constituting the world, one only has to turn to the example of scientific discourse. For postmodernists, there is an obvious sense in which the natural world has become an artifact of scientific discourse. Without the vocabulary of concepts that make up the discourse of science, as well as the *practices* accompanying this discourse (i.e., the practical experiments and rigorous observations, as well as the methods and instruments of science), there would be no "atoms," "protons," "electrons" or "quarks" in the micro-universe of natural phenomena, any more than there would be "galaxies," "white dwarfs" or "black holes" in the macro-universe. What modern scientific discourse shows us is that "reality" is very much an artifact of discourse — and its discursive practices. For postmodernists, the "reality" of the social world is also seen to be an artifact of locally produced discourses, which suggests that there is no reality outside of, beyond or independent of discourse. It is for this reason that postmodernism is sometimes described as the "linguistic turn" in philosophy and social theory. The full significance of postmodernism for sociological and social theory is difficult to summarize in simple terms. However, it is clear that its influence has already been felt in the following ways:

- in the way that theorists today are more concerned than ever before with the problematics of *language and discourse.*
- in the way that traditional "grand theories" of society, with their concern for social totalities and metanarratives, have increasingly given way to *theories and micronarratives of local settings.*
- in the way that earlier attempts to find theoretical unity and synthesis have given way to a new tolerance, even celebration of, *diversity and difference* in sociological theory.

Some recent theorists describe the rise of postmodernism as a series of "deaths," inasmuch as postmodern theories now question and reject many things that were once accepted as certainties and established "truths" (see Flax 1990). These postmodern "deaths" include the following casualties:

The Death of Truth

This refers to the end of our belief in any universal standards of validity that can be used to adjudicate between the truth claims of different communities of discourse and practice. Communities may have different criteria for testing the truth content of their narratives and different criteria for the production of knowledge. Even the truth and validity claims of Western science are dependent on the rules of the "language game" of the scientific community. Postmodernists argue that even so-called "facts" are not objective parts of an independent "reality" but rather are simply "highly confirmed" observation reports that may always be contested and superseded by new "facts" in the wake of a "scientific revolution" (see Kuhn 1962; Feyerabend 1975 [1970]). The traditional assumption that science is based on the universal principles of reason is rejected by postmodernists and poststructuralists as ethnocentric, Eurocentric, androcentric, logocentric and politically oppressive. In the postmodern age, there are no longer any reasons to privilege one form of discourse over another. This leaves us without any transcendental or universal concept of "truth." Truth is only what "works" within any particular language game, or community of practice. The standards of truth of one community cannot be imposed on other communities. The death of truth, therefore, implies a rejection of the belief in any independent reality that exists outside or beyond discourse. Instead of searching for secure foundations for our knowledge claims, postmodernists invite us to celebrate the relativism, pluralism and reflexivity of all forms of knowledge. For radical postmodernists, the arbitrary nature of linguistic terms signals an end, not only to any absolute notions of "truth," but equally to any absolute notions of "reality," "identity, "society, "history" or any of the taken-for-granted "essences" of the human condition. As we shall later discover, this hostility to the "essentialism," or "fundamentalism," that has characterized most modernist social theories is a hallmark of postmodernism. The "inconvenient truth" of postmodernism is this: in an age without certain or secure ways of knowing the "truth" or of knowing "reality," we must learn to live with uncertainties and ambiguities. This is what being alive in the postmodern age all is about. Welcome to the age of uncertainty.

The Death of Reality

This refers to the end of our belief in an independent or objective "reality" that exists outside of ourselves and beyond the horizon of our personal ideas and experiences. For postmodernists, and for poststructuralists, reality is only accessible to us through language, discourse or text. It is only through our language that we are able to apprehend the "world" as a set of intelligible experiences. In other words, the "world" is only accessible through language. It is only through systems of signs and symbols that we are able to discriminate and organize our perceptions and experiences. None of us has access to any raw or uninterpreted sense data of a "real world" that lies outside of our linguistic and cognitive fields. The only "reality" we can ever know and experience is that which is accessed through the mental "texts" we use to process our sensory experiences.

The "world," therefore, is only available to us as text, or discourse. Some of these texts may be written — those which we read. Other texts may be verbal — those which we hear. Some texts may be visual — those which we see. And others may be sensual — those which we feel. But in the final analysis, all life is textual, or discursive. And as there are many different languages and many diverse private frameworks of personal experience, none of us can access an objective and independent reality which is the same for everyone. "Reality" as a universal concept is another casualty of the postmodernist perspective. One of the most intriguing qualities of postmodern culture is how our notions of what is "real" have become increasingly confused — and inseparable from — the representations of reality in such media as television, movies, video games and the internet and in make-believe worlds such as Disneyland and other theme parks. As we shall see later in this discussion, some postmodern theorists, such as Jean Baudrillard, argue that much of our "experience" of the social world is now primarily through copies, or simulacra (simulations), made available through media and other "virtual" forms of reality. In other words, most of us have less and less direct experience of the "real world," as we rely more and more on copies of the world made and distributed though the mass media and through the social media.

The Death of Society

This refers to the way in which we no longer share any common experience or understanding of "society." The society that each of us thought we inherited and inhabit has always been an abstraction constructed in the image of those with the power to impose their representations on the rest of us. For example, the society experienced by white men has always been different from that experienced by women of colour. Similarly, the society experienced by heterosexual women has always been different from that experienced by lesbians. Today, we have to face the possibility that the abstract concept of "society" has become a barrier to understanding the diverse social worlds experienced by the multiple subject identities living in proximity to each other. For many postmodernists, the very term "society," if it means anything at all, only refers to an abstraction, a fantasy, an "imaginary," or an illusion, which differs according to the imagination of each fantasist. Interestingly, this rejection of the term "society," has sometimes been used by neoliberal politicians, such as Margaret Thatcher, a former British prime minister, to justify reductions in government funding and cuts to social and public services — in the interests of private enterprise: "*There is no such thing as society*. There is living tapestry of men and women and people and the beauty of that tapestry and the quality of our lives will depend upon how much each of us is prepared to take responsibility for ourselves and each of us prepared to turn round and help by our own efforts those who are unfortunate'" (*The Spectator* 2013, emphasis added).

The Death of History

This refers to the way in which we no longer share any common sense of "history." The history that we thought we held in common has been shown to be written from a particular and limited viewpoint, or subject position, most frequently that of white Western, upper- or middle-class, heterosexual men. Many of the established texts of history have already been deconstructed by poststructuralists and postmodernists, who have revealed the androcentric, Eurocentric, ethnocentric and logocentric biases underlying these texts. The history that we thought we shared has invariably overlooked, excluded or even actively suppressed the stories and narratives of marginalized groups and communities in our social worlds. Today, we no longer have a shared common historical understanding of who we are, where we have come from or where we are going. The death of history, therefore, implies a rejection of the teleological narrative or established logic of "history," or what is termed "logocentrism" by some poststructuralists. It is, at the same time, a rejection of the idea of progress that is embedded in the modernist idea of history. Postmodernists reject the established grand narratives, or metanarratives, that have variously portrayed history as the "fall of humankind" (Christianity); "unfolding of Reason" (Hegel); "class struggle" (Marx); and "growth of patriarchy" (feminism), to name a few. All totalizing and universalizing ideas of history are rejected because, according to postmodernists and poststructuralists, these ideas have inevitably led to violence and oppression. For most post-modernist writers, the postmodern age, in which we now live, represents a sharp and discontinuous break with everything that preceded it.

The Death of Collective/Generic Identities

This implies a rejection of all collective or generic identities, such as "humanity," "humankind," "the working class" and even "men" and "women." There is no "conscious group subject" who "knows" or "acts" independently in the world. All "knowing subjects" are constituted in particular fields of discourse and are products of particular language games. Thus, the subject is "decentred" in postmodernist thought. According to many postmodernist theorists, all collective subject identities, such as "humanity," "the working class," "the nation" and even "women" or "people of colour," can be broken down, or "deconstructed," into multiple and plural subject identities. Thus, the category "women" conceals a number of suppressed identities, including, Black women, lesbians, working-class women, immigrant women and so on. Indeed, these multiple subject identities can be further deconstructed into other, more individualized identities. The death of the collective subject signifies the death of all those ideologies and social theories that have been based on some form of collective subject. Socialism and communism, for example, have appealed to the "working class or "proletariat." Fascism has appealed to the "people" (Volk) or to the state (Reich); feminism has appealed to the "sisterhood" of "women." Humanism has appealed to the abstract concept of "humanity," while liberalism and utilitarianism have appealed to the generic concept of the "rational actor," or "*homo economicus.*" Postmodernists believe that each of these grand narratives or metanarratives of history and society has been based on the suppression of the real diversity and difference that has always existed in every social setting. The tendency for major Western ideologies and social theories to subsume and suppress difference and diversity under supposedly "universal" collective subjects has played an important part in the "politics of oppression." Grand narratives have paved the way in theory for the later practice of political oppression (see Saul 1993).

Postmodernism is unlike anything we have seen before. While this may be experienced as a sense of loss of our traditional conceptions of society, history, collective identity, truth and so on, it may also be experienced as a sense of liberation from the dominant, or hegemonic, discourses and grand narratives of the past. Postmodernism may be understood as a celebration of the diversity and difference that have surfaced in our social worlds and of the proliferation of "voices" within our universe of discourse. In some ways, postmodernism signals the coming of age of those underdog, or "subaltern," discourses that have for so long remained in the shadow of dominant discourses.

THE ROOTS OF POSTMODERN THEORIES

The roots of postmodernism can be traced to France in the mid-1960s. This was a period of considerable social unrest throughout Europe and North America. The antiwar and student protest movements had spread from the United States to Europe. In France, these movements joined with spontaneous workers' protests and factory occupations that nearly succeeded in toppling the government of Charles de Gaulle in 1968. This was also the year of the so-called Prague Spring, before the tanks of the USSR and other Warsaw Pact countries rolled into Czechoslovakia to suppress the liberal reforms introduced by Alexander Dubček. In France, the 1960s was also a time of intellectual change and transformation. One of the most important changes was the decline in the influence of "existentialism," the philosophy of individual freedom associated with the work of Jean-Paul Sartre, Albert Camus, Simone de Beauvoir and others. This philosophy had dominated the postwar cultural scene in France and many other European countries. It was essentially a humanistic philosophy that emphasized the importance of individual autonomy and freedom of choice and the need for personal commitment in pursuit of the "authentic" life.

Partly in response to the many mass mobilizations during this period — the antiwar, civil rights and women's liberation movements, as well as the anticolonial and independence struggles of many nations in the Global South — social theory began to focus more on the large-scale structures of society. This switch in focus signalled a decline in the humanistic and "voluntaristic" influences of such philosophies as existentialism and the rise of more "deterministic" traditions of thought. In the United States, sociology remained dominated by the theory of structural functionalism until the close of the 1960s. In Europe — especially in France — this period saw the rise of the theory of structuralism. Unlike American structural functionalism, French structuralism focused not on social systems but on linguistic, semiotic and cultural systems. This increasing preoccupation with linguistics and semiotics, or semiology, became known as the "linguistic turn" in philosophy and social theory. Structuralism influenced many branches of the social sciences and humanities, including linguistics (Ferdinand de Saussure), anthropology (Claude Lévi-Strauss), Marxism (Louis Althusser, Nicos Poulantzas and Maurice Godelier), sociology (Roland Barthes) and history (Fernand Braudel). The main focus of structuralist studies was on the underlying structures that produced cultural phenomena. For anthropologist Claude Lévi-Strauss, it was the underlying structures of the human mind that produced systems of kinship, mythology and language. For the structuralist Marxists, it was the underlying structures of the modes of production that produced the other superstructures and systems of capitalism. For Roland Barthes, it was the underlying structures of signs and symbols that produced the representational systems of human culture. The common thread running through most structuralist studies was an interest in the "deep structures" of human interaction and communication — whether these were defined as linguistic, semiotic, economic or historical structures. This emphasis on deep structures made much structuralist theory appear anti-empiricist in character. Empiricism has always been associated with the study of surface (i.e., directly observable) phenomena, whereas structuralism has mostly concerned itself with the study of deep structures.

Figure 8-1: The Linguistic Turn

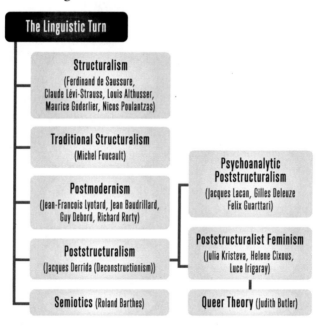

By the late 1970s, the structuralist movement in France and other parts of the world had run its course. A new intellectual movement arose that challenged the assumptions of structuralism and pointed the way towards a new tradition of literary, cultural and social theory.

This movement became known as poststructuralism. In some respects, poststructuralism may be understood as a continuation and radicalization of the linguistic turn in philosophy and in literary, cultural and social theory. Poststructuralists were also interested in the structures of language and meaning associated with all forms of human interaction and communication. But, unlike the structuralists, poststructuralists rejected the search for any definitive or fixed underlying deep structures. For poststructuralists, all structures of language and meaning remained arbitrary systems of representation that could always be "deconstructed" into multiple other interpretations. This philosophy of deconstructionism was pioneered by the French philosopher Jacques Derrida, who rejected any idea that a text could be said to have a definitive or authorized meaning. The different meanings of any text can be deconstructed in as many ways as there are active readers to deconstruct it. In the course of his work, Derrida popularized several key poststructuralist terms, including "deconstruction, "logocentrism, "play" and "*différance*." We shall return to deconstructionism shortly.

Over the past sixty years or so, a number of prominent postmodernist and poststructuralist thinkers have helped to reshape the course of social and sociological theory. The distinction between poststructuralists and postmodernists is not clear cut. For the most part, poststructuralists such as Derrida and others have remained preoccupied with the deconstruction of *texts*. Poststructuralism is best understood as a tradition of literary and cultural theory. Postmodernism, on the other hand, is a broader intellectual tradition — partly inspired by poststructuralism — that has influenced a wide range of disciplines, including architecture, history, sociology, anthropology, cultural studies and many others in the social sciences and humanities. Unlike poststructuralists, who have focused primarily on the written text, postmodernists have studied other forms of discourse, including those produced by institutions, professions, academic disciplines and the media.

MICHEL FOUCAULT: PIONEER OF POSTMODERNISM

Foremost among postmodernist theorists was the French social thinker, Michel Foucault. He may best be thought of as a transitional figure who bridges the divide between poststructuralism and postmodernism — his early work was greatly influenced by structuralism and poststructuralism, while his later work is a good example of postmodernism. Foucault's great contribution to the growth of postmodern social theory was to show how all forms of discourse are associated with specific discursive "practices." The most established and entrenched discourses of our social worlds have invariably been reinforced by, and intertwined with, the practices of power. Throughout his work, Foucault showed how the practices and institutions of power privileged some forms of discourse over others.

Michel Foucault was a forerunner of postmodernism who broke away from the mainstream traditions of social thought and sociological theory. His work and ideas connect mid-twentieth-century social thought, especially the French traditions of structuralism and semiotics, to the rise of the later traditions of poststructuralism and postmodernism. Foucault always rejected the labels that others tried to pin on his work and resisted all attempts to reduce his ideas to any rigid categorization or classification. As one reviewer of poststructuralism reminds us, "although Michel Foucault denies vehemently that he is a structuralist, he refrains from describing his work as 'post-structuralist,' preferring instead to call his approach a 'genealogy of the modern subject'" (Bell 2010: 55). He remained throughout his personal, political and professional life an iconoclast, an original thinker and an intellectual maverick. He was one of the greatest intellectuals of his generation, and his influence on social theory remains profound and lasting. However, much of Foucault's work is difficult to understand, especially when approaching it for the first time. Foucault's style is very different from that of many other more traditional social theorists. His subject matter traverses a number of disciplinary boundaries — philosophy, psychology/psychiatry, sociology, history, literature — and his methods of analysis are unusual, even unconventional, when compared to traditional studies in sociology or history.

Theorists are never exempt from the influences of their birth or background, and Foucault is no exception. Being French places him in a distinctive tradition of recent social theory, and one of the persistent themes of French social thought is what some observers have called the idea of *mentalités,* or "mentalities." This preoccupation with the collective cognitive/mental structures of particular societies, or cultures, reveals a legacy of idealism that has left its stamp on French social thought. It can be traced through Rousseau (*volonté générale*) to Comte (*consensus universalis*) to Durkheim (*conscience collective*) to Lévi-Bruhl (*mentalité*) to Lévi-Strauss (*pensée*) to Bachelard (épistémè), among many other theorists in the French tradition. Even as he rebels against it, Foucault falls into this tradition.

The other fact of Foucault's life that had a bearing on his social theory was his homosexuality. His sense of being a sexual minority sensitized him to the issues of identity, power, the body, sexuality, psychiatry, medicine and resistance. More than any theorist before him, Foucault managed to compress the large-scale societal structures of domination and repression into the private worlds of the body and personal identity. Foucault's work became a meeting point for the personal and the political; for the body and the state; for the private and the public. He set in motion a new kind of social theory that has spread in many different directions: feminism, queer theory, cultural studies, literary studies, film studies, sociology and a host of other humanities and social science disciplines. His intellectual influence dominated the last quarter of the twentieth century.

Archeology of Knowledge

As any reading of his work makes clear, Foucault's work can be periodized — that is, divided into at least two major periods. The first of these periods, the "archaeological period," includes such early works as *Madness and Civilization, The Birth of the Clinic, The Order of Things* and *The Archaeology of Knowledge*. The term "archaeology" is used to describe these early studies because Foucault set out to investigate, or excavate, the deep structure of knowledge contained within a number of different disciplines. In *Madness and Civilization*, for example, he shows how the study and treatment of "madness" underwent abrupt and radical changes at different times in the history of the Western world. These changes reflect dramatic paradigm shifts, or épistémès, in popular and clinical perceptions of "madness" and in the treatment of those who were labelled as "mad."

Foucault recounts how, during the Middle Ages, the mad were often free to roam at large and were often credited with having deeper insights into the meaning of life than those understandings vouchsafed to ordinary folk. This was often the case with the character of "the fool" in Shakespeare's plays and in such epic portrayals of madness as *King Lear* and *Don Quixote*. It was, according to Foucault, only during the late eighteenth century that people perceived as mad began to be locked up in asylums. This was the period of the "Great Confinement," when many other forms of coercion were used against the general population. Houses of correction first made their appearance during this time, joining workhouses, prisons, poorhouses, orphanages, press-gangs and other carceral institutions. For Foucault, these changes were evidence of a new way of thinking and speaking about madness. The age of the fool had given way — under the pressures of the new Age of Reason or the Enlightenment — to the age of the "madman." In other words, the mad had been redefined or reconstituted as objects of a new form of discourse: a discourse informed by the principles of reason.

Two points need to be emphasized in this account. The first is the importance of the concept of "discourse." For Foucault, the changes in the treatment of the mad — the end of their freedom and the beginning of their institutionalization — are consequences of the rise of a new form of discourse. It is through *discourse* that all aspects of social life are constituted as discursive objects — defined in relation to other objects within the discourse and treated in practical ways implied by the discourse. Discourses, as ways of thinking and speaking about things, always entail particular ways of behaving — discursive "practices." With the dawn of the Age of Reason, the figure of the fool, once tolerated at the margins of society, was reconceptualized as the "madman" — someone who violated and offended the spirit of the Age of Reason. Eventually, this trend led to the confinement not only of those classified as mad, but of all others who were constituted as "problems" in the new discourse of rationality. This penal form of discourse was later overtaken in the early nineteenth century by the medical discourse of "insanity" and, in the late nineteenth and early twentieth centuries, by the psychiatric discourse of "psychosis" and "schizophrenia." The mid-twentieth century saw a growing backlash to the "medical model" of mental illness, and critical perspectives emerged that encouraged the political mobilization of those groups that had traditionally been labelled and stigmatized by practitioners of the medical model, most notably psychiatrists. The 1960s saw the rise of the "anti-psychiatry" movement, represented in the writings of such critical psychiatrists as David Cooper (1967), R.D. Laing (1983), Thomas Szasz (1974 [1961], 1997) and Thomas Scheff (1975), sociologist Erving Goffman (1961) and scholars Gilles Deleuze and Félix Guattari (1972, 1980). Many of these writers opposed "deviant" or "pathological" labels and criticized the inhumane treatment and oppressive practices of the mental health system, including involuntary hospitalization, drugging and electroshock therapy. More recently, many of these critical concerns have received a renewed impetus in the rise of mad studies, an off-shoot of disability studies (LeFrançois, Menzies and Reaume 2013). Mad studies represents a growing political constituency of those who may identify as mentally ill, psychiatric survivors, patients or neurologically diverse individuals. Mad studies has developed from a variety of academic disciplines including women's studies, critical race studies, Indigenous studies and queer studies, among others. This brings us to the second point. As a result of his research into the history of madness, Foucault came to believe that the Age of Reason had a dark side that had been overlooked in earlier historical narratives. Besides being a time of new ideas and of free and critical inquiry, the Enlightenment was also a time of greater domination and regulation of social life — the age of the Great Confinement. This awareness led Foucault to distrust the power of reason and to emphasize its repressive force on society throughout history.

How does Foucault's archaeology of knowledge differ from more traditional studies of the history of ideas and science? There can be little doubt that Foucault intends his method to be both critical and subversive of traditional studies. Most traditional historians have seen the history of science as the progressive accumulation of "truth," that is, of factual statements about "reality" (also related to the so-called "Whig interpretation of history," Butterfield 1931). "Reality" has normally been seen as something external to the knowing subject, something that must be discovered through science. The progress of science, according to the traditional view, is measured by the incremental accumulation of true statements about reality. This progress results from the activities of knowing subjects who contribute to the growth of science through their collective efforts as a scientific community.

Like most postmodernists who followed, Foucault rejected the belief that history could be understood as an objective record of the past based upon an accumulation of incontrovertible facts. Foucault believed that any particular history was only one of an infinite number of possible histories. He concluded that all historical texts constitute records of the past written from the perspective of particular social groups. Most standard histories represent the perspectives of privileged groups, those which have had the power to tell their stories and to institutionalize these stories as the official narratives of entire societies or nations. Part of the novelty and genius of Foucault's historical method lies in the fact that he pioneered the method of "subversive" or "counter-history" — historical accounts written from the perspectives of those who were traditionally left out of or excluded from standard accounts of the past.

Foucault also rejected any belief that history constitutes an evolving record of human progress. He did not share the assumption of many of his contemporaries that history provides evidence of the progressive triumph of reason over superstition and prejudice; of truth over falsehood; of knowledge over ignorance; of humanism over barbarism. In other words, Foucault did not believe that the Enlightenment constituted a significant landmark in the march of humanity towards greater reason, progress and liberty. Instead, Foucault insisted that the Enlightenment introduced new forms of domination and oppression.

Foucault also rejected the positivist ideal of "truth" (the belief in the possibility of acquiring "objective knowledge" that is universally valid for all times and all places). For Foucault, the concept of "truth" can only be understood and elucidated in the context of its use. Much as the philosopher Ludwig Wittgenstein had earlier defined languages as "games," Foucault regarded "truth," or the certification of "truth," as a "language game." A game, by definition, involves a community of players who agree to observe a recognized set of rules and conventions. All games are collective activities or, as Durkheim suggested, "social facts." Nobody speaks a private, or individual, language (except those deemed insane), and nobody chooses their own personal truths. However, although truth is always a product of conventional community practices, different communities may vary widely in the languages they speak and on what they agree to accept as truths. There is no overarching or transcendental metalanguage — certainly not Western science — that can establish universal or absolute rules for certifying the truth of any observation or account. According to Foucault and those who have followed in his footsteps, truth is always a relative rather than an absolute concept. Its meaning can only be understood within a particular language and corresponding set of practices, which is to say within a particular truth or language game.

In Foucault's hands, therefore, the history of ideas takes on a different form. Instead of seeing the history of science as the gradual overcoming of falsehood by truth, Foucault sees history as a discontinuous series of épistémès, or "regimes" of thought, in which prevailing discourses are forever being displaced and replaced by new discourses. (This view in some respects resembles that of Thomas Kuhn in his theory of scientific "paradigms" — outlined in his seminal book *The Structure of Scientific*

Revolutions.) For Foucault, there is no independent reality that exists beyond discourse — awaiting "discovery" through the methods of science. What counts as "reality" is always specific to a particular field of discourse.

The "reality" of electrons and protons is produced by the discourse of the subatomic particle, or quantum, physics; whereas the world of the spirit-wrestler is produced by the discourse of spiritual practices. All objects of reality are constructed through discourse, and through its rules of formation and use. There is no transcendental or metadiscourse that can be used to evaluate the truth or falsity of different discourses. "Truth," like "reality," is internal to any particular discourse. In this respect, discourses are also independent of the knowing subjects who may speak their languages. Knowledge claims can only be made within the language of a particular discourse and this language exists independently of the knowing subject — in the same way that a system of monetary currency exists independently of an economic actor. This is what is meant by the expression "the decentring of the knowing subject."

Genealogy of Knowledge

Foucault's early preoccupation with the deep structures of discourse — the archaeology of knowledge — shifted in his middle years to a greater focus on the powerful forces that create and sustain different forms of discourse and different "regimes" of domination. This period of Foucault's work — known as his "genealogical period" — is best represented in such books as *Discipline and Punish* and *The History of Sexuality*. In these and other works, Foucault focused his attention on the changing forms of domination that hold our social and political institutions together. Foucault pioneered his own methods for studying historical and contemporary forms of domination — the genealogy of knowledge — which bear only faint resemblance to more mainstream sociological studies of social conflict. Foucault's studies of domination differ from standard sociological and historical accounts in several ways.

- *Local*: Foucault was never a systematic social theorist. Unlike most modern sociological theorists, he never tried to construct a general system of ideas that could then be applied to individual or singular cases. Foucault's studies were all local studies. He was interested in the particularities of any given historical example rather than in generalities. He was interested in what the details of the past could tell us about the present. But he was not interested in constructing grand theories or metanarratives with a wide range of application.

- *Micro-Power*: Foucault's idea of "power" is different from traditional sociological concepts of power. Foucault did not see power as something located at the top of an organization and imposed through a formal hierarchy or chain of command. Power grows out of the actions and interactions of individuals in myriad situations. Power is something that reaches through an organization like the arms of an octopus or the capillaries in the human body. Far from being an abstract sociological concept, power can be seen in how individuals treat each other in their public and private encounters. Foucault was primarily interested in what he called the "microphysics of power."

- *Bio-Power*: Foucault's genealogical studies focused on how power could be used to dominate and subjugate "the body" in a direct physical sense. This emphasis on the body has served to further distinguish Foucault's studies of power and resistance. Today, he is commonly regarded as a pioneer in the study of bio-power and his work on sexuality as an example of how powerful social forces may regulate or constrain the human body in many different ways. His studies of bio-power have influenced a number of recent intellectual traditions, including feminism, queer studies, penology, corrections and criminology, postcolonial theory, deep ecology and environmental studies — as well as the sociology of the emotions and the body. Foucault can be credited with putting the human body back into social theory.

- *Resistance*: In his studies of power and domination, Foucault has also drawn our attention to the ubiquity of resistance. Wherever there is power, there is always resistance to power. Foucault has shown how power and resistance are inseparable: the one feeds off the other.

If there is an underlying theme to Foucault's genealogical studies, it is that power is an enduring and pervasive presence in our lives. At every important turn, our lives are regulated and dominated by forces that seek to control us in a variety of ways and for a variety of purposes. The "purest" examples of the reality of domination may be seen in the prison and penitentiary. In these institutions, all aspects of inmates' lives are subject to formalized regulation and control. In his historical studies, Foucault has shown how the earlier forms of "traditional" domination — often applied in a harsh and even horrific way to the human body — were later replaced by "disciplinary" forms of domination applied to the "mind," the "soul" and the "will." His point in comparing the "hard" earlier forms of domination with the "soft" later forms is that our society remains, at heart, a carceral, or repressive, society. The prison is still the underlying model for all of our institutions. This is particularly true in its powers of observation and surveillance over inmates. Foucault describes the design of the Panopticon by Jeremy Bentham — a circular prison building that allowed the guards to maintain continuous surveillance of inmates without, themselves, being observed — and suggests that the Panopticon has become the paradigm of modern society.

The ways in which we are observed and monitored by others have multiplied. We have only to think of the internet, our credit card transactions, our police and hospital records, surveillance cameras in department stores and supermarkets, and street-surveillance cameras in inner-city and downtown locations. We have also witnessed the rapid growth of carceral institutions over the past century: prisons, mental institutions, poorhouses and workhouses, internment camps, residential schools and orphanages, and detention centres for refugees, undocumented migrants and "unlawful combatants." Prisons and mental institutions are overcrowded, and the number of offences for which we can be imprisoned under the Criminal Code is constantly increasing. In Canada and other industrialized countries, people of colour and Indigenous Peoples are over-represented in prisons. Young offenders, people with mental illnesses and addictions, and people living in poverty are also over-represented. In the US, the criminalization of marginalized groups has been steadily increasing through the racial, religious and discriminatory class profiling practices of the law enforcement agencies. And to make things even worse, the growth of privatized prisons in the US, where the use of slave labour has become normalized — along with extortionate and exploitative financial costs charged to inmates for a variety of "prison services" — has greatly increased the likelihood of recidivism for those inmates who default on repayment of these costs upon their release. According to statistics gathered by the American Civil Liberties Union, the United States, from 1970 to 2005, increased its prison population by about 700 percent (Hedges 2014). The private prison has proven very lucrative for big business.

Foucault's bleak prognostications are not original. To some extent,

they resemble the pessimism of Max Weber's later years and the apprehension that he felt about the growth of the "iron cage" of bureaucratic
organization. And Erving Goffman's descriptions of the growth of "total
institutions" resonate with some of Foucault's later concerns. Our lives
have become increasingly transparent. The protective barriers of privacy,
confidentiality and anonymity are being dismantled at an alarming rate.
The events of 9/11 and later terrorist attacks have only served to accelerate these trends. In these respects, the prison has become the paradigm
for the larger society. There are echoes in Foucault's work of a number
of other theorists. The ideas that all prevailing forms of discourse may
be seen as reflections of a "will to power" and that all institutions represent a particular "regime" of domination owe much to the influence of
Friedrich Nietzsche. Nietzsche's preoccupation with the motivation of
power in modern society and his cynicism and skepticism with respect
to the possibilities of progress and enlightenment in human history left
a profound stamp on Foucault's social thought. Recognition of these
influences has led critics such as Jürgen Habermas to condemn what
he sees as the "irrationalism" of poststructuralism and postmodernism
(see Isenberg 1991; Kelly 1994). At the same time, however, Foucault's
critique of the carceral society shares similarities with Weber's critique
of the rationalization and bureaucratization of modern society. Unlike
Weber, however, Foucault has no interest in providing us with a grand
narrative, or metanarrative, of a world-historical trend. Foucault provides
us only with localized historical snapshots that no single social theorist
can ever hope to complete.

The overall impact of Foucault's work has been profound. His ideas have
helped to reshape current thinking in the humanities and social sciences.
He remains one of the greatest intellectual figures of the late twentieth
century, and the legacy of his thought will be felt for many years to come.
He developed a method of social analysis that is particularly appropriate
for today's troubled times. It is a method that promises no happy endings
and makes no assumptions of common understandings. It questions the
motives of everyone. Instead of a bland optimism in the possibility of
future progress, it leaves us with an uneasy uncertainty about the past,
present and future.

JEAN-FRANCOIS LYOTARD: WARRIOR AGAINST TOTALITY

Another major postmodernist thinker was the French theorist Jean-François Lyotard. In his most famous book, *The Postmodern Condition*, Lyotard explains why he rejects all metanarratives, which applies to most classical and modern theories of society, including structural functionalism, systems theory, conflict theory, Marxism, critical theory and many others. In Lyotard's opinion these metanarratives fail to represent, and therefore exclude, the experiences and perspectives of many marginalized and powerless groups and identities in society. In other words, metanarratives are invariably composed from the perspective of prestigious and influential individuals, such as Talcott Parsons, Niklas Luhmann, Anthony Giddens and Jürgen Habermas, or of powerful groups and collectivities in society, such as white heterosexual middle-class men, academics, business leaders and capitalists, colonial officials and the organized labour movement. Lyotard expressed his skepticism towards all grand narratives because they have been used to construct specious "general" or "universal" theories of history and society. Lyotard denounced metaphysical abstractions such as "reason," "humanity" and "the working class" because, as general categories, or universal identities, they were often imposed, through manipulation or coercion, in order to homogenize a multitude of diverse and distinct identities.

For Lyotard, the major issue was the struggle against universal, or "totalizing," narratives of knowledge or society, and this is perhaps the hallmark of his work. According to Lyotard, one of the defining features of the postmodern age is what he describes as its "incredulity toward metanarratives." What does he mean by this phrase? Since the time of the Enlightenment, educated and influential men (very few women were privileged enough to join them) have tried to explain the human condition in compelling stories or "narratives." Such narratives not only functioned as descriptive stories of society and its history but also as prescriptive "moral messages," preaching values that were important to the storyteller or to the tradition of storytelling. Thus, the narratives associated with Enlightenment writers (such as Jean-Jacques Rousseau, Baron de Montesquieu, Adam Smith, John Stuart Mill, Immanuel Kant, Georg Hegel etc.) tend to emphasize, in one way or another, the values of reason, liberty and progress. In the EuroAmerican tradition, most modern ways of looking at the social world that have descended from the Enlightenment (such as socialism, liberalism, humanism, secularism, evolutionism, utilitarianism, feminism etc.) all generally remain committed to these values — even though the ways in which these values are interpreted have been contested between different Enlightenment traditions, for example, capitalism versus social-ism; androcentric versus feminist conceptions of the "social contract"; ideologized (racialized and gendered) versus empirical (and "value free") scientific rationality. However, the problem with these metanarratives, according to Lyotard, is that none of these powerful stories have ever spoken for everyone in society. Each of them represents the experiences, perspectives and observations of particular groups — traditionally those groups with enough power to have their stories told. This means, of course, that most of the metanarratives of history, philosophy and theory have always overlooked, or even suppressed, the lived experiences of those who are powerless to tell their own stories. Indeed, Lyotard goes as far as to argue that universal, totalizing theories have invariably proven to be blueprints for political repression and oppression in the hands and minds of those who have sought to impose their "universal" ideas and ideals on everyone else. For Lyotard all metanarratives carry within them the threat of political oppression: "'Traditional' theory is always in danger of being incorporated into the programming of the social whole as a simple tool for the optimisation of its performance; this is because its desire for a unitary and totalising truth lends itself to the unitary and totalising practice of the system's managers" (Lyotard 1984:131).

Although it is possible to detect the influence of Foucault in this rejec-tion of metanarratives, Lyotard put his own imprint on this critique and thereby became a poster child for postmodernism. Thus, the rational-ism of the Enlightenment paved the way for "The Terror" of the French Revolution under the Jacobins; Marxism paved the way for the terror of communism under Stalin, Mao Zedong and Pol Pot; evolutionism paved the way for the racist social Darwinist doctrines of European colonial-ism; and in our own time, neoliberalism has become the secular scripture which rationalizes the privatization, deregulation and full marketization of the global economy and which has led to the unprecedented growth of inequality at home and abroad:

> In countries with liberal or advanced liberal management, the struggles and their instruments have been transformed into regulators of the system; in communist countries, the totalis-ing model and its totalitarian effect have made a comeback

in the name of Marxism itself, and the struggles in question
have simply been deprived of the right to exist. Everywhere,
the Critique of political economy (the subtitle of Marx's
Capital) and its correlate, the critique of alienated society,
are used in one way or another as aids in programming the
system. (Lyotard 1984: 131)

But if the metanarratives of the modernist era represent the "bad news"
for Lyotard, then the fragmented, localized, provisional and partial narratives of the postmodern era represent the "good news." For Lyotard, all
"knowledge" in the postmodernist era has been revealed as provisional
and perspectival: knowledge, truth and facticity which provided grounds
for "certainty" and "objectivity" in the modernist era are now recognized
(as with Foucault) as products of a particular "language game," played
according to specific rules, always within a local context. The age of
universal reason, of empirical certainty and of objective truth is over. It
has been superseded by many different ways of knowing that are only
meaningful within particular contexts of discourse or particular communities of practice.

Lyotard proposes that in place of the discredited metanarratives of
history and society that often inspired the construction of brutal and
totalitarian regimes, we should turn our backs on metatheories and "wage
war on totality." What he means is that we should renounce any further
interest in metanarratives that falsely proclaim their universality and
turn instead towards the proliferating number of local narratives that
spring from the discourses, practices and interests of particular groups in
specific social settings. Lyotard directs our attention towards the growing
diversity, pluralism and difference of social theories, all of which, in an
important sense, mirror the growing diversity within our society. Today,
the old metanarratives of culture, society and history are revealed for
what they really were: stories told by the powerful and privileged about
themselves and others. The overthrow of these once dominant narratives has made it possible for a multiplicity of new narratives to appear
on the social scene. These new narratives tell the stories of those groups
whose discourses, interests and ideas were overlooked, despised and
often suppressed in traditional accounts of history, society and culture.
It is no accident that the postmodern age has become associated with a
new variety, relativity, plurality and diversity of social standpoints and
viewpoints. The voices of women, people of colour, Indigenous Peoples,

gays and lesbians, environmentalists, deep ecologists, terrorists and counter-terrorists, anti-abortion and pro-choice groups, and global justice and animal rights activists all clamour to be heard. Postmodernists such as Lyotard celebrate this diversity but, at the same time, recognize that for those who benefited from earlier and often unquestioned privileged perspectives, the present age of diversity marks an end to the comfortable certainties and securities of the past.

In the absence of metanarratives, there remain no universal standards of "truth," "justice," "reality" or anything else. Everything is relative, and what is considered true or just or real can only be decided within the context of a particular discourse. The modern age of dominant, or hegemonic, discourse is collapsing into a postmodern age of ever-proliferating "language games" in which notions of truth, justice and reality are locally produced, defined and defended. Perhaps one tentative example of the growing diversity of local discourses and discursive practices may be seen in the introduction of alternative systems of justice into the Canadian legal system alongside the established federal and provincial courts. In 1991, Ontario introduced the Ontario Arbitration Act for civil matters in order to relieve pressure from its heavily backlogged courts. Under the Act, both parties to a dispute must agree to arbitration and, if mutually acceptable, people can use a religious court for settlement of disputes. Jewish religious courts known as Beit Din and sentencing circles for Indigenous Peoples were established under the Act.

THE UNREAL WORLDS OF JEAN BAUDRILLARD

Of all the postmodernist social theorists, Jean Baudrillard is often considered to be the most radical and controversial. His vision of postmodern society as one in which real things have become increasingly displaced by replicas, simulated images or simulacra has had a major impact on contemporary views of culture and society. While most postmodernists reject the traditional assumptions of sociological and social theory, many contemporary social theorists have been influenced by postmodernist thought in one way or another. Feminists, for example, have made use of the deconstructive methods of poststructuralism to analyze the androcentric, phallocentric and masculinist biases underlying many forms and fields of discourse. Queer theorists have deconstructed the heteronormative and homophobic biases in many popular and scholarly discourses.

And postcolonial theorists have deconstructed the Eurocentric and ethno-centric biases of much traditional sociological and anthropological theory.

For Baudrillard, the modern age, in which peoples' experiences were based upon their interactions with the "real world" has been transformed into a new postmodern age in which most of our experiences are based upon our exposure to copies of real things rather than to the things themselves. In Baudrillard's view, our society is rapidly being transformed into a vast Disneyland in which our knowledge and experience of nature, of other cultures, indeed even of our own society, come from our exposure to replicas, or simulations, of these environments. Our experiences of the "Wild West" or of the wars in Afghanistan, Iraq and Syria, the Rocky Mountains or of countless other phenomena are now primarily gained through "representations of the real" that have now become the only "reality" that most of us will ever know. According to Baudrillard, therefore, our contemporary social world is made up of representations that refer to images produced within a "hyperreality" — a network of intersecting locally produced discourses, each with its own rules for producing "truth" and "reality." Within this chaotic postmodern world, there is no central point of reference, no absolute standards of truth or reality, no common sense of history and no shared understandings of who we are — as a collective social identity. All that was solid now melts into air.

It is this sense of the postmodern world constituted as a vast Disneyland, in which the reality of the modern age has been displaced by the hyperreality of the postmodern age, which makes Baudrillard's work distinctive. It is a world in which "signs" no longer refer to real objects but only to copies and to copies of copies. "In summer we ski indoors; in winter we spray snow on the slopes. Plastic surgeons sculpt flesh to match retouched photographs in glossy magazines. People drink sports drinks with non-existent flavors like 'wild ice zest berry.' We wage war on video screens. Birds mimic mobile-phone ring tones" (Van Mensvoort 2008). Among other things, Baudrillard shows how our sense of reality has been transformed by the explosion of images produced and reproduced through the television, movies, the computer, the satellite, phones and other electronic information and communication media. The proliferation of these digitalized images has profoundly changed our experience of the world. More than ever before, our experiences of the world are mediated and filtered through the electronic media.

Baudrillard suggests that the boundaries between reality and hyperreality, i.e., between our direct experiences of the world and our mediated experiences through digitalized images of the world, will grow increasingly blurred and confused. One of the conclusions that may be drawn from Baudrillard's picture of postmodern society is that we no longer have any secure grounds on which to base our knowledge claims. Our knowledge and experience of the world is often no longer based upon the real world at all but increasingly on copies and simulacra that are mass produced and constantly changing. This situation signifies, for Baudrillard, not only the end of "reality" as it was traditionally experienced but also of "truth" as it was traditionally known in the modern age.

The proliferation of signs and simulacra has been made possible by the unprecedented growth and expansion of the mass media and social media, which has led to the mass production, distribution and consumption of images. In our society, the mass production of signs and images is driven by profit — they are all manufactured as commodities to be bought and sold for their exchange values in the post-industrial marketplace. More than ever before, we live in a world where everything is potentially for sale. And in this world of commodities, information has become the hottest property of all.

> Knowledge in the form of an informational commodity indispensable to productive power is already, and will continue to be, a major — perhaps the major — stake in the worldwide competition for power. It is conceivable that the nation-states will one day fight for control of information, just as they battled in the past for control over territory, and afterwards for control over access to and exploitation of raw materials and cheap labor. (Lyotard 1984: 6)

It is a world in which our sense of reality has been transformed by the explosion of images produced and reproduced through the mass media and through the social media. These electronic media have profoundly changed our experience of the world, compressing time and space and creating a hyperreality made up of simulations of the real. And for Baudrillard, the boundaries between reality (direct experience) and hyperreality (digitalized images) are becoming increasingly indistinct in the postmodern age.

Today, we can also describe the postmodern world of digital reality as an "echo chamber" in which opinions, personal and political preferences and prejudices often replace any serious concern for "facts" or the "truth." In the worlds of Facebook, Twitter and other social media networks, rumours and accusations can — for protracted periods of time — replace facts. Conspiracy theories such as those surrounding Barack Obama's country of birth and fake news like Donald's Trump's claim that 3 to 5 million people voted illegally in the 2016 US presidential election or that the killers in the 2017 Quebec mosque shooting were militant Islamists often achieve a currency they do not deserve. There is a sense in which digital media, especially social media, encourage "tunnel vision" among members of these online communities, a myopic vision which reinforces an individual's own worldview and insulates this view from external scrutiny and criticism. Participants in online discussions may find their opinions and pre-existing beliefs constantly echoed back to them in ways that further reinforce and entrench their belief systems. Those who participate in digital echo chambers often do so because they feel confident that their opinions will be more readily accepted by others in the same online community. However, not only are these echo chambers natural breeding grounds for unverified rumours and unsupported conspiracy theories, they are also powerful means for the "tribalization" of social groups — especially for the tribalization of politics. Politics have rarely been so polarized. Political communities on the right and on the left maintain exclusive loyalty to their own sources of news and information — via the radio, TV, the internet and social media — and reject opposing news sources as purveyors of "fake news."

From Marxism to Postmodernism
One way to understand Baudrillard is to recognize him as a disenchanted — or even a renegade — former Marxist. Although Baudrillard began his intellectual career as a Marxist, he became disillusioned with the politics and ideology of Marxism after the events that took place in France in 1968. Like many other French intellectuals of that time, Baudrillard renounced the Communist Party and abandoned his Marxist beliefs after the failure of the student revolts and the apparent reluctance of the French Communist Party to embrace revolutionary politics. In this sense, his work may be read as a critique of Marxism. At the same time, Baudrillard used his knowledge of Marxism as a springboard for transcending and transforming his own political perspective: from a political economy of production into a "political economy of the sign." Such an analysis is needed, in his

view, to show how the hyperreality of our contemporary postmodern social worlds has been brought about through the mass production and commodification of signs and simulacra. The main criticism that Baudrillard levels at orthodox Marxism is that of economic reductionism and economic determinism, or "economism" — a perspective which has continued to emphasize the primacy of production over all other aspects of social and economic life. Baudrillard insists that because Marx was so committed to finding economic and materialist explanations of social life, he overlooked the significance of symbolic factors. For Baudrillard, one of the most important aspects of social life is the need for symbolic communication. Indeed, Baudrillard argues that the human need for representation and signification is as important as the need for labour and production. In other words, the need to find ways to communicate and interact in society is at least as important as the need to produce economic subsistence.

In some ways, Baudrillard's insistence on recognizing the importance of symbolic communication and exchange is reminiscent of Habermas's differentiation of several distinct forms of action, notably, purposive rational action (later called strategic action) versus communicative action. However, unlike Habermas, who always emphasized the complementarity of these different forms of social action, Baudrillard focuses almost exclusively on what he calls the "political economy of the sign." In his view, the labour theory of value and other associated Marxist concepts such as "surplus value" and "commodity fetishism" should be abandoned and replaced with new concepts that showcase the forms of symbolic exchange and signification that characterize contemporary postmodern capitalist societies. For Baudrillard, the problem of "production" in society has now been replaced by the problem of "meaning." In place of production, Baudrillard concludes that consumption now shapes and dominates the culture of postmodern society. In place of the exchange value of commodities — emphasized by Marxists — Baudrillard emphasizes the "sign value" of commodities, i.e., the symbolic value that these products represent in terms of prestige, status, style and reference group associations. In other words, people now shop more for brands than for products; the power and status of the sign or symbol has displaced the utility of the product.

Beyond his concern with consumption, Baudrillard came to recognize the strange new power of signs in the postmodern culture. Today, signs no longer necessarily designate, denote or correspond to actual objects.

Many signs simply exist independently of any concrete referents, as "float-ing signifiers." Baudrillard uses examples of fantasy settings — such as theme parks, amusement parks, video games, blockbuster movies and other spectacles — to illustrate his contention that many of the signs that populate our lives have little or no direct connection to any actual real-ity. They exist as copies and, in the case of Disneyland, often as copies of things that have never existed in the "real world."

For Baudrillard, we live in a world in which signs and images have been freed from the objects and events they may once have represented. In this new world of floating signifiers, consumers shop for the sign value or the brand rather than the use value of commodities. We no longer shop for functional footwear; instead, we compare the relative status and sign values of Nike versus Adidas. In our hunt for shirts, we are confronted by a com-parable system of signs and status symbols, ranging from Tommy Hilfiger and Gap to Old Navy, Roots and many others. Similarly, the purchase of a Harley Davidson motorcycle over a Yamaha or Kawasaki implies more than simply the choice of a different machine. It is also the choice of a distinct personal identity and cultural brand, a choice of lifestyle. In this brave new world of sign systems and images, the consumption of brands is far more important than the consumption of products. (For the global implications of these trends, see Naomi Klein's 2000 book, *No Logo*.)

This postmodern world, in which sign systems and images are removed from any direct correspondence to "reality," has ushered in an age of what Baudrillard calls "hyperreality," an artificial system of signs and images that portrays a number of different imaginary worlds. None of these "imaginaries" are real or have any independent existence beyond the images that constitute them. Thus, although reality television series all pretend to portray real situations, they are contrived and constructed performances manufactured for mass audiences. "The problem with much, if not all, of reality TV is that it isn't about real people or reality at all. These are highly scripted, performed shows, 'written' like a piece of fiction and as such they need the classic conflict-driven characters and soap opera melodrama" (Maguire 2017). In these surreal postmodern worlds, our experiences of "reality" have been transformed into experi-ences of imaginary and simulated "realities."

In Baudrillard's picture of postmodern society, there are no secure grounds on which to base our knowledge claims since knowledge and experience of the world are not based upon reality but only simulacra that are constantly changing. The long-term consequences of this conflation of the real with the spectacle can be seen in the growing passivity and privatization of the individual in postmodern society, as well as in the loss of any traditional notions of meaning, purpose and identity. In many ways, Baudrillard paints an even more depressing picture of our future than did Foucault.

Another way of understanding Baudrillard's ideas is to see his work as a history of the sign, as these signs have evolved throughout history. In fact, Baudrillard outlines four historical periods: premodern, the Renaissance, industrial and post-industrial (and postmodern). This periodization traces the changing uses of the sign in society from its direct representation of "reality" (in premodern societies), all the way to the end of representation in post-industrial society. According to Baudrilllard, today we live in an artificial world in which our experience and understanding of "reality" is totally mediated by signs, by simulations and by copies of reality for which no originals exist. Baudrillard's most famous example of a simulation which is unrelated to any existing reality is the entertainment or amusement park — such as Disney World at Orlando, Florida, and Universal Studios' Jurassic Park at Hollywood, California. Many of these theme parks show us a set of images, or signs, which do not correspond to anything in the "real" world. It is a world of fantasy, illusion and "spectacle." To an ever greater extent, the urban and suburban masses in our postmodern societies frequent and often inhabit unreal, or maybe "surreal," worlds, such as theme and amusement parks, amusement arcades, sports stadiums, shopping malls, reality television shows, video games, Facebook, YouTube and social media "echo chambers" and even major automobile highways, all of which are totally mediated by signs, simulations and copies of reality. Increasingly, our direct experience of the real world is morphing into our vicarious experience of an artificial world made up of signs and simulations. In our everyday lives, the "real" has been overtaken by the "spectacle" (see Debord 1994 [1967]).

For Baudrillard, then, the power of signs and virtual copies, or simulacra, of factual or fictitious objects and events has been propelled by the rapid development of information and communication technologies and the corresponding growth of the mass media and social media. Most of us inhabit an unreal world of simulacra and for much of the time, we have lost any direct connection or contact with "reality." It is this hyperreal world that Baudrillard describes as the "death of the subject." He means that any belief in the primacy of an autonomous or voluntaristic social actor or agent (so beloved of classical and modernist sociological theory) has been overtaken by a recognition of the primacy of the objects and events and their simulacra. In the postmodern world of today, it is these representations that define and shape the postmodern world; it is no longer done by the conscious social actor.

Postmodernism Politics

The advent of postmodernism has inevitably brought about changes in the self-conceptions and perceptions of individuals in society. As Baudrillard suggests, the firm, fixed sense of personal identity that most individuals experienced in the age of modernism has given way to a sense of the fragmentation, decentring and destabilization of identity in the postmodern age. Today, the identity of an individual is no longer clear-cut and autonomous. Most of us experience multiple identities — ethnic, sexual, class, age, occupational etc. — which may reinforce or contradict each other. Like other postmodernist signs, identity is changeable and unstable: it has become another commodity in a global marketplace of signs and images. Gender and sexual identities, which were traditionally seen as biologically determined, are no longer assumed to be fixed and unchangeable. Most postmodernists emphasize that all group and individual identities are fluid and capable of constant change and transformation — even those identities such as sex and race that once appeared to be frozen in time and space. However, postmodernists acknowledge that gender and racial fluidity are "social processes" rather than "individual choices." In other words, identity claims only become "real," or validated, when recognized and respected by society.

This postmodernist sense of fluid personal and collective identity raises serious political questions for many individuals and groups. The end of stable personal and collective identities has led to the decline of traditional social movements based upon collective identity politics. Some feminists (Epstein 1995; Alcoff 1988; Bordo 1990) have remained suspicious of, if not openly hostile to, postmodernist conversions of the feminist enterprise. For these writers, it is important to retain a unified collective constituency for feminist theory and praxis. Without a firm and stable generic constituency and metanarrative, some theorists fear that the feminist movement may have reached the limits of its ability to mobilize and organize its traditional constituency. Similarly, without a clear sense of the "working class," social democratic, socialist and communist parties, labour unions and related groups may appear to have experienced a crisis in their membership and organization. At the same time, postmodernism may have opened new opportunities and strategies for contemporary political action and social change. It has become apparent that a postmodernist feminist politics that recognizes and respects an inclusive and flexible approach to gender and sexuality and understands the need to build alliances and coalitions with other progressive groups represents the way forward to democratic social change. Postmodernism has taught us that strength lies not only in unity and commonality — but also in diversity and inclusiveness.

The full impact of Baudrillard's postmodernist theory of our hyperreal world only became apparent after the publication of his critical analysis of the first Gulf War, *The Gulf War Did Not Take Place* (1991). In this publication, Baudrillard argued that, as visual spectators observing this war through the media of TV, the internet and the movies, none of us had any actual experience or direct contact with the "reality" of this war. For most of us, this war never really happened; it was viewed as a video game — with drone strikes, smart bombs and other ordinance delivered from a distance via remote control — far away from the actual combat zones. We had all become mere spectators to an unreal, or hyperreal, war of the postmodern age. Baudrillard replicated this analysis in his account of the 9/11 terrorist attacks in his monograph *The Spirit of Terrorism and Requiem for the Twin Towers* (2002). These attacks, he argued, were only meaningful when understood as symbolic attacks on the financial heartland of Western capitalism: "Neither politically nor economically did the abolition of the Twin Towers put the global system in check. Something else is at issue here: the stunning impact of the attack, the insolence of its success and, as a result, the loss of credibility, the collapse of image" (82).

In order to understand Baudrillard's distinctive interpretation of global terrorism, we need to recall some of the key elements of his postmodernist perspective. Baudrillard believes that we inhabit a hyperreality constructed from simulacra, floating signifiers, signs, symbols and images. We rarely connect directly with the most dramatized and publicized locations of the "real world" — especially those locations that remain remote from us in space and time. But through TV, the internet and other media, we are *virtually* transported every day to far away locations — even to dangerous locations — such as war zones, areas of extreme poverty, disease epidemics and famine, hazardous refugee crossing points and so on. In other words, TV and the internet allow us to compress both space and time to virtually experience what would otherwise be impossible for us to actually experience. Even in this age of hypermobility, we often travel in a Western "bubble" and view foreign places and peoples through the lens of our Western "mediascape." As Lemert (1997) has suggested, reality has for all of us become "intertextual" and "discursive" in nature.

According to Baudrillard, the "space-time compression" made possible through our information and communication technologies, and the "hypermobility" made possible by through our transportation and travel technologies, are simply byproducts of the larger process of Western globalization, which has been underway for centuries, although accelerated in the present age of transnational capitalism. For Baudrillard, global terrorism — whether associated with al-Qaeda, isis, the Taliban, al-Shabaab, al-Nusrah Front, Abu Sayyaf Group, Boko Haram or other terror networks around the world — needs to be understood as a militant response to Western globalization. Those who fight against this globalization see themselves as soldiers or righteous warriors, engaged in a Fourth World War — against the predations of a Western global capitalist hegemony.

Although this sounds like a callous statement, for most of us without connections to war zones, war has become a spectator sport — not unlike a football or hockey game — viewed on TV, with periodic commercial breaks. The horrific violence of wars in Afghanistan, Iraq, Syria, Yemen and elsewhere, along with bombardments of Aleppo, Baghdad and Gaza and terror attacks in Paris, London, Ankara, San Bernardino, Nice and Manchester, are delivered to us via TV along with other highlights of the evening news. These events — horrific for those who experience them in real time, are transformed for most of us into media spectacles, as much for our entertainment as for our information. Baudrillard refers to the projection and mass distribution of these media images as "war processing," or "war pornography" (see Coulter 2015; Baudrillard 2005).

The hypermobility of our travels and the space-time compression of our information and communication technologies are simply aspects, or symptoms, of the growing worldwide reach of Western globalization. Western capitalism and secularism are spreading around the globe and are confronting and transforming Indigenous cultures as part of this process. For those committed to resisting and repelling this globalization, all Westerners have now become legitimate military targets in this Fourth

World War, wherever they are encountered. According to Baudrillard, this is why formerly safe tourist sites have now come under attack from members (i.e., soldiers/warriors) of terrorist groups, terror cells and terror networks. The world-wide spread of Western economics and culture has made all or any of us targets of anti-globalization resistance at home or abroad.

For Baudrillard, in order to comprehend the motives of terrorists, we need to view the world through their eyes rather than simply demonize them as evil, medieval, sick or barbaric. In order to achieve this perspective, we need to move beyond our own comfortable taken-for-granted assumptions, our own cultural norms and our own "universal truths." We need to realize that what we normally see as good, progressive and beneficial interventions by the West may be an anathema by those who do not share our beliefs and traditions. This ability to push beyond one's own conventional beliefs and values and enter the psychological and cultural space of the Other is, according to Baudrillard, what distinguishes "radical theory" from merely critical theory (Coulter 2015).

Baudrillard compares his own radical account and explanation of terrorism to that of other contemporary Western theorists, such as Slavoj Žižek, who, according to Baudrillard, remain trapped in their own liberal, humanist, socialist or other worldviews. Whereas Žižek has argued that jihadists and Islamists who murder, torture and rape Westerners, as well as their own peoples, are pseudo or inauthentic fundamentalists because they ignore the peaceful injunctions of their own religion, Baudrillard begs to differ. For him, Žižek's interpretation of contemporary terrorists as inauthentic or pseudo is simply wishful thinking. Žižek has attempted to assimilate these fundamentalists into a Western framework of humanist values, where they demonstrably fail the test of authenticity. But for Baudrillard, the actions of the jihadists cannot be adequately interpreted within a Western framework. They are, above all else, different and alien to our beliefs and values. And to understand them we need to try to enter their worldview and acknowledge how deeply and unalterably they hate the West and its pursuit of global hegemony. Whether we like it or not, says Baudrillard, the terrorists are not failed humanists; they stand apart from our culture and traditions: they will not be consumed by us.

JACQUES LACAN: POSTSTRUCTURALIST CRITIC OF THE POSTMODERN PSYCHE

We turn now to an overview of the theoretical perspective that has run parallel to postmodernism: the tradition of poststructuralism, in particular the psychoanalytic poststructuralism of Jacques Lacan, Gilles Deleuze and Félix Guattari and the textual poststructuralism of Jacques Derrida. We begin with a discussion of Lacan's work by briefly tracing his intellectual roots in French structuralism, a legacy which led to his emphasis on language and his focus on the power of the sign. Much like the French structuralists, Lacan and his colleagues deny that there is any natural or necessary link between a word and its object, or referent. There is no natural or necessary link between the word "dog," or "chien," or "hund," and the domestic pet that lives in your home. For Lacan, the link between the sign "dog" and its referent (the real animal) is *arbitrary*. The sign "dog" only acquires its meaning through its relation to other signs. For Lacan, "reality" cannot be experienced or understood outside of our written, verbal or mental "texts." Thus, the relationship between the signified (a dog) and the signifier (the word "dog") is always mediated by text or discourse; it is never a direct link from the symbol to the "real"; the "real" can only be accessed through language. That is, the object, dog, is similar in appearance but different from "cat" or "coyote," while the word "dog" is similar in sound but different from the word "hog" or "log." According to Lacan, our intelligible world is composed of a huge cultural dictionary of signs, and these signs acquire their meanings through their relations — which may include their divisions, exclusions, oppositions, equivalences etc. — with each other. It is through the cultural dictionary of signs that we construct and impose meanings on the world, rather than by recognizing any natural or necessary correspondence between a word and its denoted object.

Lacan's basic assumption, that the relation between a sign and its referent — the signifier and the signified — is arbitrary, leads to the central premise of his psychoanalytical theory of the psyche: namely, that the Ego, or self, is fundamentally self-divided, fractured or split. Lacan traces this fundamental split to what he calls the "mirror stage" of the child's psychosexual development, when the child first "misrecognizes" itself in a reflective mirror. This "misrecognition" is based on the child's narcissistic need to externally view itself as a complete and unified desirable image, while at the same time the child's internal subjective experience remains

divided and split (from its mother and from its neonatal world) and therefore remains essentially incomplete. In other words, the child's reflective
image projects a fantasy or an illusion which conceals the inner, or what
Lacan calls the "paranoid," feelings of loneliness, anxiety and separation.

This narrative — that we fantasize our relations with others and that
we project onto others our deep-seated, unconscious, need to find uni-
fication and completion in ourselves — has become a popular theme in
media representations of our emotional relations with and attachments
to others in our lives. This theme of incompletion has been represented
in the movies, on TV, in popular music and even in commercials and
advertisements. Some examples of movies with Lacanian themes are
Prom Night, *Orphan* and the aptly titled *Mirrors*. In each of these horror
movies, the moment of shock comes not from the reflection of the killer
in the mirror, but a friend, boyfriend or husband. Sometimes, as in *What
Lies Beneath*, the killer is the friend, boyfriend or husband.

For Lacan and his colleagues, our common perceptions of others and
of ourselves are bent and distorted — paranoid illusions and fantasies
— generated from the deep fissures and ruptures within our own Ego.
The underlying and disturbing message of Lacan's perspective is eerily
expressed by one particular film reviewer:

> If you want to test Lacan's theory about the alienating nature
> of the self-image out for yourself, here's a fun little game: try
> staring at yourself in a mirror for more than two minutes.
> As time passes, most people experience the strange sensa-
> tion that they are no longer looking at themselves — their
> image seems to change (some say to age, some say to blur)
> into something else. The experience is so unsettling for
> some that they can't bear it and have to break away. And so
> we can return to Lacan's wise words: "This illusion of unity,
> in which a human being is always looking forward to self-
> mastery, entails a constant danger of sliding back again into
> the chaos from which he started; it hangs over the abyss of a
> dizzy Assent in which one can perhaps see the very essence
> of Anxiety." (Hewitson 2013)

Although Lacan died in 1981, his influence on cultural studies and
film studies has been considerable. Lacanian film criticism has often
specialized in uncovering, or de-constructing, the ideological frames

and ideological codes that have been used to naturalize, i.e., make appear "realistic," the screen images and narratives in movie productions. While most major movies project structurally closed ideological frames — with fully naturalized characters and plots and a fake or fantasy "realism" — some movies project more structurally reflexive ideological frames — with characters and plots that seek to disrupt and explore the fake "realism" of normalized film narrative by exposing its arbitrariness and relativity. Examples of these more avant-garde reflexive, and poststructuralist, movies include *Pulp Fiction*, *Crash*, *Being John Malkovich* and *Natural Born Killers*, among many others.

The Return to Freud

Although Lacan was one of the most influential theorists of the mid to late twentieth century, whose ideas influenced many other social theorists, his writings are challenging and difficult to read and have often been critiqued for their alleged impenetrability. For this reason, we shall provide only a brief introduction to his main ideas: his themes and arguments, his key concepts and technical terms, and his basic assumptions. One of Lacan's great accomplishments was to reintroduce the work of Sigmund Freud back into the corpus of contemporary social theory. While some of the Frankfurt School critical theorists, such as Theodor Adorno, Erich Fromm and Herbert Marcuse, had earlier re-appropriated the ideas of Freud, Lacan's reclamation of Freud was somewhat different. Lacan remained strongly influenced by the structuralist theorists, particularly the anthropologist Claude Levi-Strauss, and Lacan's interpretations and applications of Freudian ideas were heavily indebted to the structuralist perspective.

The single most important difference that distinguishes Lacan's psychoanalytic theory and his vocabulary of key concepts and basic terms from those of Freud is Lacan's emphasis on the significance of *language* and the ways in which language constructs our sense of reality and our social world. For Lacan, "the Real" — which refers to the actual material world into which we are all physically born — is essentially unknowable to us and inexpressible by us, because it remains outside of, and beyond language, i.e., our linguistically constructed social universe. According to Lacan, we only have meaningful access to our linguistified world: a world in which we can observe and make sense of objects only through the medium of language; a world in which our relations with others and with ourselves is fully mediated through language; and a world in which the meaning of our lives and life experiences is, consciously and unconsciously, only available to us within a linguistic universe. This is not to say that the external material world, or the Real, never intrudes or imposes itself into our social "reality." But when the Real penetrates our reality, it is often as a surprise, a shock or a traumatic event. The unexpected lump in a breast, our car caught in a sudden skid on an icy highway or a bomb blast shattering our immediate setting are examples of how the Real may penetrate the non-linguistic raw substratum of our daily lives — and literally leave us speechless.

For Lacan, therefore, the world and our reality exist for us only as "discourse": we cannot escape the all-encompassing "oxygen" of language. It is the very existential air we breathe. We are like fish, fated to swim all our lives in a linguistic pond and only occasionally colliding with the raw pre-linguistic realm of the Real that lies outside language — beyond our capacity to fully comprehend or communicate. Because of the primacy he accords to discourse/language, Lacan is usually classified as a post-structuralist theorist.

Lacan's Vocabulary

Given the complexity and difficulty of Lacan's ideas, there are a number of possible entry points into his theoretical perspective. And so, as with other major theorists covered in this book, we shall try to summarize the main aspects of his psychoanalytic theory by explaining some of his key concepts and basic terms.

Signs: For Lacan, the world is only available to us through language, that is, discourse. The basic element of language can be reduced to the "sign." It is through signs that we construct, comprehend and communicate the "reality" of our social world. Lacan distinguishes two parts to the sign: the signifier and the signified. (This distinction was originally introduced by the structuralist linguist Ferdinand de Saussure, many years before Lacan). The "signified" refers to the representational function, or what Lacan calls the "concept image," of the sign — such as a painting of a horse, or the words "Ladies" or "Gentlemen" on a washroom door. The "signifier," or what Lacan calls "sound image," refers to the material or physical form of the sign — the spoken word "horse" or the spoken word "Ladies" or "Gentlemen." It is important to note that for Lacan, and for Saussure before him, the relationship of a sign to its referent is always arbitrary. There is no natural or logical reason to use the word "horse," or "cheval" (French), or "Pferd" (German), to refer to the four-legged animal. Our understanding of a horse is essentially a product of our language; we could have used any sign to designate this creature. Owen Hewitson (2010) explains the discursive and arbitrary link between the signifier and the signified in the following terms:

> The *signified* is not the thing *or* object in reality to which the *signifier* refers but instead the meaning.... This is why the *signifier* is primary according to *Lacan*. For example, when you look up a word in a dictionary you do not find the object itself but other *signifiers* that you use to ascertain its meaning. For Lacan, the signified refers to meaning, practically it "always refers to another signification," that is, to more signifiers and their potential signifieds as the latter slide underneath the former. If Lacan says that the signified is meaning ... then the signified is simply the discourse in which all signifiers are collectively bound up. This is why Lacan says that the "network" of the signified does not refer to a thing in reality but instead "always refers to another signification," another fleeting and transitory pairing of signifier with signified. The process of signification is therefore constantly in flux with what we might call meaning or sense created when the signified aligns with the signifier above it, until we move on to using another signifier.

These signs create a difference where it previously didn't exist: the washroom doors are the same but the signs demarcate the difference. In the same way, other nations use different signs to distinguish the genders: "hommes et femmes" (French); "Männer und Frauen" (German); "Fir agus Mná" (Irish); "мужчина и женщина» (Russian); "男女" (Mandarin). There is no necessary or natural link between the word (the signifier) and the object that it represents (the signified). In other words, all signs and symbols are arbitrary: no sign makes sense on its own, but only in relation to other signs.

For this reason, we understand "things" in the world not through a one-to-one correspondence between a word and its object, but only through understanding the function of a word (sign) within the context of a larger system, or discourse, of signs. The sign "horse" only acquires its specific meaning because it is distinct from and excludes other word-signs, such as "pig" or "sheep." Similarly, the word-sign "men" only acquires its specific meaning because it is distinct from and excludes other signs — most notably, "women." The only world we know, according to Lacan, is the world of signs.

Unlike Freud, who conceived of the psyche as several regions of the mind — the unconscious, the subconscious and the conscious — inhabited by elemental drives, instincts, repressed memories of past traumatic events and secret desires, Lacan has a rather different conception of the psyche. For him, the birth of consciousness and the path to full humanity only begins with the entry of the child into the world of signs and symbols — the world of meaning, of understanding and intelligibility. Whereas for Freud, the psyche was a region of psychic energy and psychic processes (of repression, projection, displacement, transference etc.), for Lacan, the psyche is a "zone of signification." To enter this zone is to begin the process of humanization. Lacan distinguishes three different "orders" of the human psyche: the Real, the Imaginary and the Symbolic.

The Real: For Lacan, the Real refers to the primordial and pre-linguistic state of nature that the child experiences before entering the zone of signification and language. In this neonatal stage, the child, without language, has yet to experience any differentiation or separation between its own body and that of its mother or between itself and the world. The child "owns" everything and exists in an undivided state of unity: a human cocoon. There is no gap between the child and the world, no split between the internal, subjective world of the child and the external, objective or material world of the mother, or the larger world beyond, no unfulfilled desire, no lack. It is a world in which primal needs are gratified and satisfied. But the Real can never be expressed or communicated as it lies beyond the zone of signification. Without language, it cannot be retrospectively restored, recalled or even remembered, because memories are composed from signs and symbols.

The Imaginary: Between six to eighteen months of age, the child experiences a profound — and for Lacan, a cataclysmic — transformation in its consciousness. This stage is known as the "mirror stage" and marks the beginning of the often-painful psychosexual process of development into maturity and adulthood. The mirror stage, for Lacan, occurs when the child first observes itself in a mirror, or some other reflective surface, as an external image, and the sight of its reflective "self" causes the child to "misrecognize," or misunderstand, its own image. For although this external image appears to show a stable, coherent and unified self, this external image is actually belied by the internally ruptured, fragmented and split sense of self that is subjectively experienced by the child. The mirror offers the child a narcissistic image which does not correspond to the sense of loss, alienation, anxiety and abandonment which comes with the child's realization that it is separate from its mother and displaced from the all-enveloping neonatal cocoon of its early infancy. Although the child is aware that the mirror reflects itself, what it does not realize is that the image is a fantasy, one that the child projects in order to compensate for its sense of loss or alienation from the Real. Seeing that image of itself creates a dissonance between the idealizing image in the mirror — one that is fully complete — and the chaotic reality of the child's body during this time of development. The child will therefore constantly strive to catch up to this idealized image of self — in both language and in life.

In this respect, entry into the Imaginary marks the sense of loss, of alienation and dislocation which generates a strong feeling of "desire." And this desire will, in many ways, continue to haunt the child into adulthood and for the remainder of its life. For these reasons, Lacan sees the Imaginary as an aspect of the psyche — and the origin of the Ego — composed of images and representations, but also of illusions, fantasies, deceptions and narcissistic "misrecognitions." It is a zone in which the Ego is tricked and deluded into believing that its fractured, fragmented, differentiated and separated self (and its "territorialized body," i.e., a body divided into different parts: genitals, anus, mouth etc.) is "really" the same as the unified, synthetic and autonomous fantasy image of the self that is reflected in the mirror.

The Symbolic: The Symbolic order represents for Lacan the field of language, or the "zone of signification." The child begins to function in this zone through the use of language and more precisely through following the rules of language. Language is always a social construct and, as the philosopher Ludwig Wittgenstein famously observed, there can be no such thing as a private language. Language is organized and structured through public rules, and it is by following these rules that the child learns to recognize, anticipate and fulfil the expectations of others. In this respect, language introduces the child into a social world of rules, laws, contracts, codes, norms and conventions that will regulate its behaviour and its subjective self for the rest of its life. Once the child enters into language, its thoughts, feelings and desires are forever entangled with the play of language. The Symbolic, through language, is in essence a contract between an individual and society. This contract encompasses many laws and restrictions that the child is required to follow in order to be accepted into society and to experience comfort and communication within a community.

Language is a metaphor and a template for social relations. It is in the Symbolic order that the child first confronts what Lacan (after Freud) calls the "name of the father." In a sense, this stage is equivalent to Freud's narrative of the Oedipal complex: the male child is forced to accept the primacy of the father, separation from the mother and the need to observe and conform to external rules and commands. For Freud, the father signals the (sexual) unavailability of the mother and the (symbolic) castration of the male child. For Lacan, the father is a surrogate for and symbol of the generalized power and authority of the larger society and culture — or what Lacan calls, the "big Other." Whereas the Imaginary remains within the order of nature, the Symbolic order represents the domain of culture.

It is also in the Symbolic order of the psyche that the child first experiences the powerful and enduring force of "desire." When still cocooned in the Real, the child experiences the primal need for unconditional love and care. But within the Imaginary, this need is transformed into a demand for narcissistic gratification, a demand that can never be satisfied because it is motivated by a fantasy image of the other, which is based upon a projection of the child's own idealized (fantasy) self, or Ego. But in the Symbolic order, under the constraints of language and linguistic and social rules, the child's demand is transformed into desire — i.e., a feeling of loss that is now articulated into speech.

Because "desire" is verbally expressed in speech and subject to the discipline of language and discourse, it differs from the more "primitive" pre-linguistic compulsions of "demand." Desire, in a sense, represents the "civilization" of demand within the zone of signification. For this reason, desire must follow the rules and conventions of social relations and is, therefore, influenced by culture and ideology. Desire is distanced from the raw compulsions of demand. And Lacan suggests that, in terms of psychosexual relations, desire can never be fully consummated; it will inevitably collide with the raw realism of demand, a force which springs from the pre-linguistic and unconstrained Imaginary. Desire, which arises from the Symbolic order, is destined to be disappointed, disabused and ultimately dissatisfied. Desire remains in pursuit of a gratification that is, at a deep level of the psyche, inexpressible and unattainable.

There can be little doubt that Lacan's ideas have radical, disturbing and unsettling implications for our understanding of social relations, especially for sexual relations and psychosexual development. According to Lacan, in our romantic attachments, we always view the object of our "desire" through narcissistic "spectacles." In searching for our ideal partner, we are searching for a perfect reflected image of ourselves which remains forever unattainable. Our idea of the other is always distorted by our desire for the completion of our divided and fragmented selves. In Lacan's reading of the deeper text of our psyche, the "other" is a screen onto which we project our inner fantasies, fantasies that arise from a need to re-unify what is divided and split within ourselves.

Table 8-1: Lacan's Developmental Theory of Psychosocial Development

Stage of Development	Response	Age
The Real: primal neonatal state; perfect unity of mother and child; no language	Need: for mother's breast, body & comfort	0–6 months
The Imaginary: the sense of self is misrecognized and misperceived in the mirror image	Demand: for recognition and love beyond physical stimuli and material objects	6–18 months
The Symbolic: entry into the world of language, rules and regulations, social norms and conventions, and the expectations of others (in the name of the father)	Desire: since the self has become alienated from its primary source and confronted with the power of the father and with the world of language, signs and symbols, i.e., society, the self now experiences an enduring sense of incompletion and lack	18 months onward for our lifetime

The Other: The Other refers to those within our social world, including our partners, with whom we interact. At the same time, according to Lacan, our understanding of others is always distorted by our projection onto them of our own Ego desires, fantasies and insecurities. We are only able to see in others what we project onto them; we seek in others the completion of our incomplete and fragmented selves. On the other hand, the Big Other refers to the symbolic order of rules, conventions and normative expectations that regulate our overt behaviours and our covert thoughts and feelings. The Big Other is originally associated with the all-embracing comfort and dependence upon the mother, but later becomes associated with the power and discipline of the father, and by extension of the larger society. However, the Other may also refer to that which cannot be assimilated or comprehended in terms of the learned rules of language and social interaction. In other words, the Other — as radical alterity — is beyond recognition or understanding. Many Lacanian theorists have developed explanations of racism, ethnocentrism, sexism, homophobia and other forms of social exclusion as examples of the perception and designation of unfamiliar or "foreign" subjects as the Other.

Lacan's Legacy: I Text, Therefore I am

The impact and influence of Lacan's theoretical perspective is ongoing. Indeed, Lacan's ideas continue to disrupt the premises of more traditional sociological theories, such as symbolic interactionism, dramaturgical theory, exchange theory and rational choice theory, which all presuppose the stability and autonomy of the individual self and the personal identity. Lacan puts this conventional sociological conception of the self into serious question. Perhaps the most important aspect to emphasize in Lacan's work is his conception of the psyche as a "zone of signification." According to Lacan, we are first and foremost creatures defined by language and verbal meaning. The conscious aspects of our social existence, even our introspective and reflexive self-consciousness, is only possible, i.e., intelligible, comprehensible and communicable, through language. For Lacan, the psyche exists as a textual domain that can be read, interpreted and deconstructed through the techniques of psychoanalysis. It is his emphasis on language, text and semiotics that links Lacan to the theoretical traditions of structuralism (Claude Levi-Strauss and Louis Althusser), but even more to the poststructuralists, such as Jacques Derrida and Judith Butler, and to other postmillennial theorists, including Slavoj Žižek, who have been deeply influenced by his work.

At the same time, Lacan's ideas have been pilloried for many reasons. Most frequently, he has been criticized for the alleged obscurity and impenetrability of his own theoretical language, and for his alleged misunderstanding and misuse of the Freudian and mathematical concepts employed in his writings. One of the more searing critiques of his work and that of other poststructuralists was published by Alan D. Sokal and Jean Bricmont in their 1998 book, *Fashionable Nonsense: Postmodern Intellectuals' Abuse of Science*. Another critique labelled Lacan as the "Shrink from Hell" (see Tallis 1997: 20). Besides these charges of obscurantism, Lacan has also been critiqued by some feminist writers, such as Luce Irigaray, for the androcentric, phallocentric and male-oriented perspective of his theories, a legacy from Freud. In addition to these scholarly critiques, other critics have focused on the more controversial details of his private life, especially his treatment of some of his students and colleagues.

On the political front, some critics have also faulted what they perceive as the overly skeptical, even conservative, implications of Lacan's deconstruction of the self (Anzieu 1978: 131; Webster 1994; Crews 1986: 176). In their view, Lacan's conception of the individual allows for no autonomy or agency and, therefore, no potential for self-actualization or self-determination. This skepticism around the possibility for self-emancipation separates Lacan's critical psychoanalytical theory from the critical theory of the Frankfurt theorists, who still embrace the emancipatory project of the Enlightenment. Similarly, other theorists have critiqued Lacan's "linguistification of the unconscious," whereby Lacan sees the acquisition of language as the most significant stage in the psychological and social development of the individual. These critics have invidiously compared Lacan's account of the unconscious mind to that of Freud, who recognized the significance of pre-linguistic drives, desires, instincts and raw biological urges. And finally, some critics have complained that Lacan fails to link his critical analysis of inner-psychic division and alienation to the prevailing material conditions of exploitation and inequality so prevalent in contemporary capitalist society. Lacan remains, even posthumously, something of an *enfant terrible*.

GILLES DELEUZE AND FÉLIX GUATTARI: ANTI-PSYCHIATRY ACTIVISTS

Another influential branch of social thought that emerged from the post-sociological theory of the late twentieth century was the radical anti-psychiatric perspective pioneered by Gilles Deleuze and Félix Guattari. Deleuze and Guattari both came of age during the radical student movement in France which reached its zenith in 1968 when students and workers united in their efforts to topple the government of Charles de Gaulle. Deleuze and Guattari were also associated with the anti-psychiatry movement, which — in the spirit of Foucault and Lacan — critiqued orthodox psychiatry for its dehumanizing and oppressive treatment of mental patients. (In Britain, a similar movement was associated with the work of R.D. Laing and David Cooper; while in the US, it was represented in the works of Ernest Becker, Erving Goffman, Thomas Szasz and Thomas Scheff, among others.) Deleuze died by suicide in 1995.

Deleuze established his reputation as a professor of philosophy during the 1960s, while Guattari was a psychoanalyst who had trained in the Lacanian tradition and had participated in the anarchistic "autonomy movement" — outside of the major political parties — in France. Perhaps more than most of the social theorists covered in these chapters, these theorists made a conscious effort to combine their radical politics with their critical and iconoclastic theoretical perspective. While the density and difficulty of their writings pose intimidating challenges for the average reader, their principal contributions may be summarized and simplified in a brief introduction to their key concepts.

Desire: The basis of Deleuze and Guattari's anti-psychiatric critique of psychoanalytic thought is to be found in their concept of "desire" — inherited, although partially revised, from Jacques Lacan. The concept of "desire" may be understood as a fundamental life-force, equivalent in some ways to Nietzsche's "will to power" or in other ways to Freud's sexualized notion of "libido." In their two primary works, *Anti-Oedipus* and *A Thousand Plateaus*, the authors argue that capitalism can be recognized as a schizophrenic system. By this they mean that in order to emancipate the individual from the repressive and alienating structures of capitalism, a new model for the liberation of "desire" needs to be recognized and followed. Deleuze and Guattari believed that the imperatives of capitalist society demanded that the basic desire of the individual had to be tamed and subordinated in order to meet the economic needs of society, and the particular needs for profit and production. But if this diagnosis of the distortion and subordination, or Oedipalization, of desire is partially influenced by the ideas of Marx and Freud, Deleuze and Guattari's remedy for the reclamation and return of desire is startling and controversial. Their conceptual ideal of the free and autonomous individual is the schizophrenic; not the pathological and medical schizophrenic, but the existential and political schizophrenic. But what do Deleuze and Guattari mean?

Schizoanalysis: For Deleuze and Guattari, schizophrenia in general and schizophrenic "desire," in particular, represent an escape from, or even a resistance to, the unconscious desire that is tamed, repressed and subordinated to the norms and conventions and the guilt of capitalist society — through the process of "Oedipalization." The ideal model of someone who can separate themselves from the alienating and debilitating constraints of capitalism is the schizophrenic. However, these authors are not idealizing the medical schizophrenic, who represents pathology, delusion and suffering, but the philosophical, or existential, "schizophrenic," who is capable of experiencing and expressing "productive desire" and is also capable of transgressing and resisting the limits and constraints of contemporary capitalist society (see Kingsmith 2016). The political objective of schizoanalysis is to confront and overcome the all-encompassing state of generalized "anxiety" produced under neoliberalism and to empower individuals to convert their passive anxiety into an active sense of outrage against the oppressive and divisive emotional and material structures of contemporary capitalism.

Unlike Lacan, who saw desire as rooted in a sense of loss, Deleuze and Guattari see raw and untamed "productive desire" as rooted in an anarchistic "force of production," which is rebellious, intense and potentially revolutionary. Schizoid or productive desire, unlike the repressed desire of conventional capitalist society, is "transgressive"; it can break all the rules and open up new paths for self-affirmation, unrestricted by the repression and commodification of desire under capitalism. Under the conditions of capitalist society, the productive desire of an individual can either submit to, conform to and embrace the power and authority of the state and its agents, including psychiatrists or, like the schizophrenic, can escape and reject these authorities in favour of transgressive and liberating expressions of productive desire. Then, and only then, according to Deleuze and Guattari, can the individual become a "nomadic subject": a free and autonomous subject living fully from moment to moment in a world of fluid and infinite possibilities. Needless to say, there has been no shortage of criticism and outright dismissal of Deleuze and Guattari's theoretical project and of their use of a schizophrenic analogy to critique psychiatry, capitalism and more generally the processes of socialization and internalization of social norms and conventions.

Rhizome: Another concept that is part of the theoretical vocabulary of Deleuze and Guattari, but which is now commonly invoked as a strategic principle of grassroots political activism, is that of the "rhizome." On the one hand, this concept is used by the authors as an alternative to the typical structure of knowledge and theory under the conditions of capitalist modernity. The rhizome — as understood in botany and agronomy — refers to the horizontal and subterranean network of root structures that connect and link crops and plants. This essentially "flat" mode of plant organization differs from the vertical and hierarchal structures of growth exemplified in tree and trunk-like structures of organization. Unlike the centralized root structure of a tree — which has an identifiable origin, history and linearity, a rhizomatic decentralized structure has no discernible beginning or end: everything is interconnected; everything is in a state of flux; and nothing is privileged. Similarly rhizomatic theory differs from more traditional theory inasmuch as it dispenses with hierarchical, binary and dualistic oppositions, in favour of multiplicity, plurality, symbiosis and unity. Rhizomatic political practices are typically decentralized, often spontaneous, grassroots and leaderless actions, as seen in the Occupy, Black Lives Matter, Idle No More, #MeToo and similar movements, which are frequently organized through social media as spontaneous mobilizations (see Nicholson 2005).

Deleuze and Guattari view capitalism as a schizophrenic system, always in danger of regressing into fascism. Capitalism is schizophrenic in the way it separates and alienates individuals and groups from their traditional social and moral "codes" rooted in family, community, church etc. and then reintegrates them into capitalist codes: the workplace, the market place, the company and corporation. This process of alienation and reintegration is described by Deleuze and Guattari as the "de-territorialization" and the "re-territorialization" of social groupings.

The practical politics of Deleuze and Guattari implies the growth and spread of informal social networks and leaderless configurations instead of more traditional structures of political parties and formalized movements. This rhizomatic strategy is intended to counter the de-territorialization of different spatial and territorial sectors of society, such as the separation and division of the family, church, community, outdoor recreational spaces etc., under the economic pressures of capitalism. Thus, rhizomatic politics is designed to re-territorialize these segmented and ruptured heterogeneous spaces into new forms of underlying unity and symbiosis. Under these conditions of struggle, the political actor becomes a "nomadic subject": a free autonomous and unrepressed individual with no fixed attachments who is able to negotiate a terrain of shifting possibilities for personal emancipation and self-actualization through a full expression of "productive desire" — a concept similar to Nietzsche's "will to power."

JACQUES DERRIDA: THE DECONSTRUCTION OF LANGUAGE AND LIFE

In Jacques Derrida, we encounter one of the pre-eminent theorists of language and discourse of the late twentieth century. In many respects, Derrida revolutionized our understanding of language and turned much of what had traditionally been assumed about the relationship between language and the social world onto its head. Today, Derrida is recognized as the founder of the contemporary perspective known as "poststructural-ism." Poststructuralism as an intellectual tradition originated as a critical response to the earlier tradition of structuralism. Although the influence of structuralism quickly spread across a number of disciplines, including structural anthropology (Claude Levi-Strauss); structural Marxism (Louis Althusser, Nicos Poulantzous); literary criticism (Roland Barthes); and history (Fernand Braudel) — Derrida was primarily influenced by the linguistic structuralism of Ferdinand Saussure.

Derrida's break with structuralism came as a result of a number of disa-greements over the relationship of language to "reality." Unlike Saussure and other structuralists who believed that written language, or text, was derived from speech, Derrida insisted on the primacy of text over speech. For him (as for Jacques Lacan), both "nature" and "society" — as expres-sions of "reality" — are only accessible to us through language. Like Lacan, Derrida suggests that it is only through our language-making capacity that we are able to apprehend "the world" as a set of comprehensible organized experiences. In other words, the "world" — in the only way we can experience it — is inscribed on our consciousness through language. It is only through systems of signs that we are able to discriminate and organize our perceptions and experiences of the outside world. In this sense, all life is textual, or discursive.

Although both structuralists and poststructuralists assert that "reality" is only knowable through language and that nothing can be experienced or understood outside of language, there are some very important ways in which these two theoretical perspectives differ from each other, including over the question of "meaning": how do we extract meaning from a text? In general, most structuralists believe that a close and methodical reading of a text — as a system of significations — can produce an accurate understanding of its "true" meaning. Althusser calls this a "symptomatic reading." A symptomatic reading is conceived by structuralists as a method for critically analyzing the "deep structures" of meaning that lie beneath the surface of traditional versions of textual analysis and literary criticism. A symptomatic reading stands in contrast to a more conventional "surface reading," which is preoccupied with an aesthetic appreciation of the text and an analysis of literary form and content. For Althusser, this method of critical analysis was inspired by the critical political economy of Karl Marx, who discovered that the deep structure of all societies lay in their mode of production; and also by Sigmund Freud, who discovered that the deep structure of human behaviour lay in the latent structures of the unconscious mind and in the sexual drives of the libido.

However, while structuralists believe that any text provides a stable and fixed system of linguistic signs (words and terms) that can be fully decoded and deciphered through a symptomatic reading, poststructuralists do not share this belief. Instead, they contend that all texts offer an infinite

Table 8-2: The Evolution of the Linguistic Turn

Structuralism	Transitional	Poststructuralism
Saussure, Althusser, Levi-Strauss,	Foucault, Barthes	Lacan, Deleuze, Derrida, Butler
Search for underlying authorized and definitive "deep structures" of texts; any text has a final and definitive meaning.	Historical study of paradigm shifts in "epistemes" and of different "discursive regimes"; archeological study of rules of formation and representation in systems of signification; genealogical study of discourse and power.	No fixed, stable or authorized structure to a text; all texts have an infinite number of possible meanings
Symptomatic reading	Discourse analysis	Deconstructive reading
Correspondence/ referential theory of meaning and truth	Pragmatic theory of meaning and truth	Coherence/contextual/ theory of meaning and truth

number of opportunities for "deconstruction"; there are no authentic, authorized or correct ways to interpret and understand a text. For them, no text can ever embody a fixed or definitive meaning; there is no such thing as an "authorized" meaning of any text. Instead, all texts contain multiple — even infinite — possible meanings. Any text opens up an endless number of possibilities. There are as many discoverable meanings in a text as there are readers to discover these meanings. Poststructuralism may be further distinguished from structuralism in its method of analysis: in the concepts it uses to analyze texts and in the assumptions which underlie these concepts. What are some of the main terms and concepts in the vocabulary of poststructuralism?

The Vocabulary of Poststructuralism

Text: For poststructuralists, text is the template of all discourse — whether spoken, written or simply thought. In this respect, it is possible to recognize some affinity with the ethnomethodologists, for whom all forms of human behaviour may be analyzed as "accounts" — either verbal accounts (which are audio-taped) or visual accounts (which are videotaped). Whereas for poststructuralists, the primary unit of analysis is the text, for some ethnomethodologists, especially conversation analysts, it is the transcript. The transcript reveals the template of all "accounts," much as the text reveals the template of all "discourse." Both structuralists and poststructuralists share a common preoccupation with language, discourse and the text. And both perspectives emphasize that any observation of experience of the "world" is only available to us through the texts of discourse. However, poststructuralists regard the text as a kaleidoscopic system of signs with multiple possibilities for different and contradictory meanings. In place of logocentric, i.e., definitive methods of analysis, poststructuralists advocate deconstructionism, a method employed to subvert the authorized meanings of the text and to reveal the hidden meanings, silences, absences and subtexts contained within the original. The radicalized poststructuralism introduced by Derrida into contemporary social theory has continued to reverberate throughout the social sciences, the arts and the humanities.

Arche-writing: For Derrida, arche-writing is an original form of language which is not derived from speech. It is a form of language which is unhindered by the difference between speech and writing. And for Derrida, text is always privileged over speech. Derrida believes that there is a powerful human need to mentally organize our sense impressions into a kind of cognitive template — a mental text — which he calls "arche-writing." It is these "mental texts," or cognitive compositions, which make human speech possible and which enable us to meaningfully apprehend and comprehend our environment. In this sense, the "world" only exists for us as text, or as Derrida also famously said: "There is no outside-text," although this quote is usually mistranslated as "There is nothing outside the text" by his opponents to make it appear that Derrida is claiming nothing exists beyond language (see, for example, Rich 2017).

Différance: For poststructuralists, the meanings of words and terms (linguistic signs) in a language, discourse or text are unstable, constantly shifting and impregnated with the "traces" of earlier, often remote, usages and interpretations. This sense of the unsettled and inherently unstable meaning of linguistic signs is captured in Derrida's concept of "différance." Différance implies the process of deferring: all meanings are constantly being redefined, reinterpreted and re-understood — with the passage of time and with a change of location. In other words, there are no "finalizable" meanings that can be attached to any linguistic signs. Derrida uses the term "différance" to describe the origin of presence and absence in discourse. In French, the verb "deferrer" means both "to defer" and "to differ."

Thus, différance may refer not only to the state or quality of being deferred, but to the state or quality of being different. The world of signs is constantly in motion, and texts are forever in a state of birth, maturation, death and rebirth. Nothing is permanent or fixed. The world of text plays by its own rules, and there are no fixed or final rules of meaning. Derrida coined the technical term "différance" to mean both a difference and an act of deferring, in order to characterize the way in which meaning is created through the play of differences between words. Because the meaning of a word is always a function of contrasts with the meanings of other words, and because the meanings of those words are in turn dependent on contrasts with the meanings of still other words, and so on, it follows that the meaning of a word is not something that is fully present to us; it is endlessly deferred in an infinitely long chain of meanings, each of which contains the "traces" of the meanings on which it depends. For this reason, there can never be a direct correspondence between a linguistic

sign (or word) and its referent (or object). The relationship between signifier and signified is arbitrary. Language is not a transparent medium
through which we can view "reality." The only "reality" we can ever know
is to be found in the discourse that surrounds us and that produces and
reproduces our sense of "reality."

All texts are organized around différance of one sort or another.
Différance refers to the distinctions, the discriminations, the polarities
and the binary oppositions that are inscribed by text upon "reality." All
so-called "natural" features of "reality," such as, space/time, truth/falsity,
reality/illusion, good/evil, male/female, light/dark etc., originate as cat-
egorical distinctions and binary oppositions, or "différance," in mental
texts. Text inscribes its categories and imposes its structure on the open
field of possibilities that we call "reality." This, according to Derrida, is
the violence we perpetrate on the "world" — the violence of abstraction.

Decentring: For poststructuralists, all texts are "decentred." This means
that texts are analyzed as autonomous systems of signification without
reference to any influences outside the text, such as an author, a com-
poser, a subjective "self" or any other external agency. "Decentring" also
implies that there is no central "meaning," no authorized interpretation of
a text; only a field of multiple, maybe even infinite, possibilities. Derrida
dismisses all attempts to discover the central or underlying meaning of a
text as "logocentrism": the search for, or imposition of, an authorized, or
definitive, "meaning" where none exists. Instead of designing a method
for uncovering a non-existent authorized "meaning," Derrida suggests a
more playful "deconstructivist" approach that juggles different meanings
and various interpretations of a text.

Logocentrism: Logocentrism is based on the view that speech, and not
writing, is central to language. According to logocentrist theory, writing
is merely a derivative form of language which draws its meaning from
speech. Logocentrism assumes that language originates as thought, which
produces speech, and that speech then produces writing. Logocentrism
is also based on the assumption that there is a realm of "truth" existing
prior to, and independent of, its representation by linguistic signs. This
assumption, according to Derrida, encourages us to treat linguistic signs
as distinct from their referents, rather than as inextricably bound up
with them. Thus, the logocentric perspective sees "truth" and "reality"

as existing outside of language — and as having an external and objective existence that is not reducible to the language which signifies their existence. This belief in an objective reality — independent of language, discourse or text — is critically dismissed by Derrida as the "metaphysics of presence."

Logocentric means literally "centred on the word," but for Derrida, logocentrism implies all forms of thought based on an authorizing foundation, an "essential" meaning, or a centre or Logos. In its ancient Greek philosophical and Judeo-Christian meaning, the Logos referred to how the universe was created by the words of God: "In the beginning was the Word." This conception assumes that there is an authoritative form of speech — Truth — through which language and reality intersect. Logocentrism, therefore, subscribes to a belief in an external objective reality which remains the ultimate test of the absolute truth of any statement. For this reason, Derrida rejects the logocentrism of structuralist theorists because their objectivism leads them to search for the "true" or "authentic" meaning of a text — the meaning that the author actually intended to communicate. But for Derrida, there is no "true" or authorized meaning; each text has an infinite number of possible meanings: all elements (words) in a text are unstable and unsettled in their meaning(s) as they are haunted by the ghostly "traces" of past or lost meanings, as well as by other absences and silences that can only be revealed through a deconstructivist analysis. According to Derrida, there can be no final authorized reading of any text.

Deconstruction: Most importantly, Derrida pioneered a method for reading texts which is known as "deconstruction." Deconstruction places the author and the reader of a text on a much more equal footing than was traditionally the case. To "deconstruct" a text means, first and foremost, to expose its hidden meanings. All texts contain a multiplicity of possible meanings. Some of these meanings may be hidden even from the author of the text. Thus, the author of a standard history of Canada, for example, may remain oblivious to the silences, absences or exclusions in his account of past events, which fails to include any references to the experiences and perspectives of women, children, Indigenous Peoples, members of the LGBTQ community, convicts, servants or slaves, the homeless or other excluded "standpoints" and subject identities. From the perspectives of these marginalized groups, the history of Canada may look very different from that contained in standard or official versions (Montgomery 2008; Khan 2016). The Truth and Reconciliation Commission stated: "Too many Canadians still do not know the history of Aboriginal peoples' contributions to Canada, or understand that by virtue of the historical and modern Treaties negotiated by our government, we are all Treaty people. History plays an important role in reconciliation; to build for the future, Canadians must look to, and learn from, the past" (2015: 8). The same concern has been raised regarding the silence or absence of women in Canadian history texts: "We conclude that women are underrepresented, misrepresented and marginalized in history textbooks. Women are portrayed as historically unimportant and incapable, contributing little to society outside of the domestic sphere" (Chiponda and Wassermann 2011). There is no longer any historical account of Canada, or of anywhere else, that has an absolute claim to universal validity. Far from constituting objective records of the past, most Canadian history books may be deconstructed as the narratives of white, middle-class, heterosexual men.

All texts may be deconstructed to reveal their hidden subtexts. Deconstruction produces a "critical reading" which exposes the asymmetries, the binaries, the hierarchies, the inequalities and power imbalances embedded in many texts. Most binary oppositions tend to privilege one identity over the other. Binary oppositions, as poststructuralist feminists have observed, often imply a hierarchy: a gendered ranking of more-valued against less-valued characteristics. A deconstructive reading is able to critically examine a text for its internal inconsistencies and contradictions, its unacknowledged preferences and its biases, as well as its silences and absences. Deconstructive readings have exposed many texts for their androcentrism, Eurocentrism, heterosexism, classism, racism, ageism and other sources of bias and privilege.

At the same time, the subversive methods of deconstruction have opened new theoretical doors for other critical perspectives to emerge. In its rejection of any metanarratives proclaiming the existence of an "objective" or transcendental "reality," deconstructionism has implicitly recognized the possibility of multiple "realities" constructed from the perspectives, experiences, discourses and local narratives of diverse social groups and different subject identities. If there is no fixed or immutable "reality," or no objective "history," then the time has surely come to recognize the existence of alternative "realities" along with counter-histories and counter-narratives of formerly excluded subject identities. In particular, the new acceptance of multiple realities and counter-histories has expanded our "universe of discourse" to include formerly marginalized, minoritized and other "subaltern" groups and individuals whose voices and narratives have until now remained absent or silent: suppressed, repressed or excluded.

PERPLEXITIES OF POSTMODERNISM

Among social theorists, the advent of postmodernism and poststructuralism has proven to be a double-edged sword. On the one hand, what might be called "strategic postmodernism" has had considerable appeal for those theorists intent upon rescuing and popularizing topics that have remained marginal to mainstream social theory (see Lemert 1997). The postmodernist critique of totalizing metanarratives has legitimized the proliferation of new areas of theory and research and has hastened acceptance of a greater diversity of perspectives within the discipline. This diversity may be seen in the appearance of altogether new areas, such as queer theory and postcolonial theory, as well as in the growing interdisciplinary areas of cultural studies, media studies, equity studies, diaspora studies, multicultural studies and Afrocentric and Indigenous studies. Formerly suppressed or subjugated discourses of marginalized and socially excluded groups are now in the arena of public discourse and contribute to the growing diversity of the social world.

On the other hand, many theorists remain hostile to what might be called "radical postmodernism" and reject many of the dominant assumptions of postmodernist thought. Sociologists in particular have found it difficult, if not impossible, to accept the postmodernist claim that such notions as "truth," "reality," "objectivity," "history" and "justice" cannot be defined in universal terms, but only within the contexts of particular discourses, or local "language games." It is one thing to celebrate the advent of a new diversity of social practices and discourses in public life. It is quite another to suggest that we no longer have any universal standards for assessing and testing the validity of competing knowledge claims derived from myriad theoretical and practical discourses. And, in practical terms, it is still highly controversial to suggest that any attempt to uphold universal standards of human rights, such as gender equality, racial or ethnic equality, or tolerance and understanding for racial, sexual or ethnic minorities, is simply a form of "cultural imperialism." Some of these ethical and political concerns have been expressed by major cultural critics — such as Jürgen Habermas (1981), Noam Chomsky (2017) and Christopher Hitchens (2007) — along with their criticisms of what they see as the obscurantism, irrationalism and impenetrability of much of the literature of postmodernism and poststructuralism. Many Marxist theorists have condemned postmodernism and poststructuralism for its idealism and retreat from historical materialism (Callinicos 1991; Eagleton 1996) and for its abandonment of "progressive" metanarratives of class unity and solidarity (Wood and Foster 1997; Gitlan 1995; Epstein 1995), while other Marxist thinkers have interpreted the relativism and subjectivism of postmodernism as an expression of the cultural logic of late capitalism and the policies of neoliberalism (Jameson 1991; Harvey 1989).

Radical postmodernists are likely to argue that there are no overarching objective standards of truth or falsity that can be externally imposed on local discourses. For this reason, postmodernism has been perceived by many social theorists as a slippery slope that leads inexorably to relativism, subjectivism and irrationalism in theory, and to passivism, solipsism and quietism in practice. While part of the appeal of postmodernism and poststructuralism lies in its ability to deconstruct the metanarratives and dominant discourses of mainstream social theory, its willingness to abandon all universal standards of objectivity is often still seen as an attack on the very epistemological grounds that make the construction of social theory possible, and on the empirical and practical grounds that make the pursuit of social justice possible and desirable.

To summarize, postmodernism has effectively advanced the critique of metanarratives and grand theories and has also shown how most attempts to construct universalizing or totalizing narratives are based upon privileged or unacknowledged assumptions. Poststructuralism has also emphasized the fluidity and contingency of many taken-for-granted categories of identity, including gender and sexual identity, racial and ethnic identity, and many other aspects of our personal and social identity. In this respect, postmodern theorists have offered support to the many new social movements, based upon identity politics, which have campaigned against fixed, frozen or essentialized identity labels and have advanced the struggle for the free expression as well as the recognition and respect of diversity and difference.

At the same time, postmodernism is not without its critics. Critics from both the political left and the political right remain concerned

370 RESTLESS IDEAS

that the indiscriminate celebration of diversity, difference and plurality, for its own sake, overlooks the darker side of the postmodernist condition. For while the new age of postmodern diversity has encouraged the recognition and expression of formerly suppressed and subjugated discourses and communities (such as feminism, queer theory, race theory and postcolonial theory), this celebration of diversity and difference has also opened the door for more malevolent identities and communities to express themselves. Thus, marginal communities such as neo-Nazis, white supremacists and white nationalists, racists and anti-Semites, and even terrorist groups have become part of the postmodernist mix of diversity and plurality. Clearly, many of these latter communities have no interest in progressive or emancipatory ideals or in pursuing generally recognized struggles for social justice.

Besides these concerns over the freer expression of hate speech and deeply divisive politics, other critics have pointed out what they regard as a logical contradiction in postmodernist theory. For while postmodernism claims to reject metanarratives and grand narratives in favour of local, fragmented and plural narratives, it is argued that this commitment to a diversity and plurality of perspectives actually constitutes, in itself, a "new postmodernist metanarrative" which seeks to replace earlier modernist metanarratives. Indeed, some critics have argued that postmodernism, far from eschewing all totalizing metanarratives, has produced one of its own. Postmodernism, for all its denials and disavowals, has become the new metanarrative of our times (see Jencks 1986). At the same time, many theorists are well aware of the dilemma posed by postmodernism and have tried, in a sense, to get the best of both worlds. While acknowledging the value of postmodernism as a source of deconstructive criticism of traditional social theory and as an inspiration for examining the impact of mass consumerization and commodification on popular consciousness, these critics have avoided its wholesale abandonment of all metanarratives and metatheory (see Best and Kellner 1991; Lemert 1997; Ritzer 1996; Seidman 1998).

References

Alcoff, L. 1988. "Cultural Feminism versus Post-Structuralism: The Identity Crisis in Feminist Theory." *Signs,* 13, 3: 405–436.

Anzieu, Didier. 1978. In Sherry Turkle, *Psychoanalytic Politics: Freud's French Revolution* London.

Baudrillard, Jean. 2002. "Hypotheses on Terrorism." *The Spirit of Terrorism,* trans.

Chris Turner. New York: Verso.

____. 2005. "Pornography of War." *Cultural Politics*, 1, 1: 23–26.

Bell, Duncan. 2010. *Ethics and World Politics*. Oxford University Press.

Best, S., and D. Kellner. 1991. *Postmodern Theory: Critical Interrogations (Critical Perspectives)*. London and New York: Guilford Press.

Bordo, Susan. 1990. "Feminism, Postmodernism, and Gender-Scepticism." In Linda J. Nicholson (ed.), *Feminism/Postmodernism*. New York: Routledge.

Butterfield, Herbert. 1931. *The Whig Interpretation of History*. London: Bell.

Callinicos, Alexander. 1991: *Against Postmodernism: A Marxist Critique*. Cambridge: Polity Press; Blackwell.

Chiponda, Annie, and Johan Wassermann. 2011. "Women in History Textbooks: What Message Does This Send to the Youth?" *Yesterday and Today*, 6: 13–25. <http://www.scielo.org.za/scielo.php?script=sci_arttext&pid=S2223-03862011000100006&lng=en&tlng=en>.

Chomsky, Noam. 2017. "Postmodernism Is an Instrument of Power." <https://www.youtube.com/watch?v=WwTfHv5dpPw>.

Cooper, David. 1967. *Psychiatry and Anti-Psychiatry*. Routledge.

Cooper, R. 1989. "Modernism, Postmodernism and Organizational Analysis 3: The Contribution of Jacques Derrida." *Organizational Studies*, 10, 4: 479–502.

Coulter, Gerry. 2015. "Baudrillard on Terrorism & War in Times of Hyper-Mobility." *International Journal of Safety & Security in Tourism/Hospitality*, January 1. <http://www.palermo.edu/Archivos_content/2015/economicas/journal-tourism/edicion13/03_Baudrillard_on_Terrorism_and_War.pdf>.

Crews, Frederick. 1986. *Skeptical Engagements*. Oxford: Oxford University Press.

Debord, Guy. 1994 [1967]. *The Society of the Spectacle*, trans. Donald Nicholson-Smith. New York: Zone Books.

Deleuze, Gilles, and Félix Guattari. 1972. *Anti-Oedipus*, trans. Robert Hurley Mark Seem and Helen R. Lane. London and New York: Continuum.

____. 1980. *A Thousand Plateaus*, trans. Brian Massumi. London and New York: Continuum.

Eagleton, Terry. 1996. *The Illusions of Postmodernism*. Blackwell.

Epstein, Barbara. 1995. "Why Post-Structuralism Is a Dead End for Progressive Thought." *Socialist Review*, 25, 2 (Spring).

Feyerabend, Paul K. 1975 [1970]. *Against Method: Outline of an Anarchist Theory of Knowledge*. Verso. First edition in M. Radner and S. Winokur (eds.), *Analyses of Theories and Methods of Physics and Psychology*. Minneapolis: University of Minnesota Press.

Flax, Jane. 1990. *Thinking Fragments: Psychoanalysis, Feminism, and Postmodernism in the Contemporary West*. University of California Press.

Foucault, M. 1969. *The Archeology of Knowledge and the Discourse on Language*. New York: Harper Colophon.

____. 1979. *Discipline and Punish: The Birth of the Prison*. New York: Vintage.

____. 1980. *The History of Sexuality*, Vol. 1. New York: Vintage.

Gilroy, Paul. 1993. *The Black Atlantic: Modernity and Double Consciousness*. Verso.

Giroux, Henry. 2000. "Racial Politics, Pedagogy, and the Crisis of Representation in Academic Multiculturalism." *Social Identities*, 6, 4 (December): 493–510.

Gitlan, Todd. 1995. *The Twilight of Common Dreams: Why America Is Wracked by Culture Wars*. Henry Holt & Co.

Goffman, Erving. 1961. *Asylums: Essays on the Social Situation of Mental Patients and Other Inmates*. New York: Doubleday.

Habermas, J. 1981. Modernity versus Postmodernity. *New German Critique,* 22: 3–14.

Harvey, David. 1989. *The Condition of Postmodernity: An Enquiry into the Origins of Cultural Change*. Blackwell Publishers.

Hedges, Chris. 2014. "The Prison State of America." *Truthdig,* Dec. 29. <https://www.truthdig.com/articles/the-prison-state-of-america/>.

Hewitson, Owen. 2010. "What Does Lacan Say About... The Signifier?" *LacanOnline.com* June 20. <https://www.lacanonline.com/2010/06/what-does-lacan-say-about-the-signifier/>.

___. 2013. "5 Lacanian Cinematic Clichés that Hollywood Loves – III." August 18. *LacanOnline.com*.

Isenberg, Bo. 1991. "Habermas on Foucault Critical Remarks." *Acta Sociologica,* 34, 4: 299–308.

Jameson, Frederic. 1991. *Postmodernism, or the Cultural Logic of Late Capitalism*. UK, Verso/U.S.A. Duke University Press.

Kelly, Michael (ed.). 1994. *Critique and Power: Recasting the Foucault/Habermas Debate*. Cambridge, MA: MIT Press.

Khan, Sheema. 2016. "When an Official Story Is a Monstrous Lie: The Textbook History of Canada's Indigenous People." *Globe and Mail,* August 12.

Kingsmith, A.T. 2016. "High Anxiety: Capitalism and Schizoanalysis." *Counterpunch,* December 23. <https://www.counterpunch.org/2016/12/23/high-anxiety-capitalism-and-schizoanalysis/>.

Kuhn, T.S. 1962. *The Structure of Scientific Revolutions*. Chicago: University of Chicago Press.

Laing, R.D. 1983. *The Politics of Experience*. Pantheon.

LeFrançois Brenda A., Robert Menzies, and Geoffrey Reaume. 2013. *Mad Matters: A Critical Reader in Canadian Mad Studies*. Canadian Scholars' Press.

Lyotard, J-F. 1984. *The Postmodern Condition*. Chapter 1. Minneapolis: University of Minnesota Press.

Maguire, Mercedes. 2017. "The Ugly Side of Reality TV: The Shows That Make You Cringe." *The Daily Telegraph,* June 9. <https://www.dailytelegraph.com.au/entertainment/television/the-ugly-side-of-reality-tv-the-shows-that-make-you-cringe/news-story/8d0517b65eadb7597b30160708750918>.

Marx, K. 1967 [1867]. *Capital: A Critique of Political Economy*, vol. 1. New York: International Publishers.

McLuhan, Marshall. 2003 [1964]. *Understanding Media*. Gingko Press.

Montgomery, Ken. 2008. "'A Better Place to Live': School History Textbooks, Nationalist Fantasies, and the Incarcerating Banality of White Supremacy." In J. Satterthwaite, M. Watts, and H. Piper (eds.), *Talking Truth, Confronting Power: Discourse, Power, and Resistance*, volume 6. Trentham Press.

Nicholson, Judith A. 2005. "Flash! Mobs in the Age of Mobile Connectivity." *The Fibreculture Journal,* 6: Mobility. <http://six.fibreculturejournal.org/fcj-030-flash-mobs-in-the-age-of-mobile-connectivity/>.

Rich, Bryce. 2017. "There Is Nothing Outside of the Text." 27 February. <http://www.brycerich.com/2011/02/there-is-nothing-outside-of-the-text.html>.

Ritzer, G. 1996. *Postmodern Social Theory*. New York: McGraw-Hill.

Saul, John Ralston. 1993. *Voltaire's Bastards: The Dictatorship of Reason in the West*. Vintage Books.

Scheff, Thomas J. 1975. *Labeling Madness*. Spectrum Books.

Seidman, S. 1998. *Contested Knowledge: Social Theory in the Postmodern Era*. Malden, MA: Blackwell.

Sokal, Alan D., and Jean Bricmont. 1998. *Fashionable Nonsense: Postmodern Intellectuals' Abuse of Science*. New York: Picador.

The Spectator. 2013. "Margaret Thatcher in Quotes." 8 April. <https://blogs.spectator.co.uk/2013/04/margaret-thatcher-in-quotes/>.

Szasz, Thomas. 1974 [1961]. *The Myth of Mental Illness: Foundations of a Theory of Personal Conduct*. Harper & Row.

___. 1997. *The Manufacture of Madness: A Comparative Study of the Inquisition and the Mental Health Movement*. Syracuse University Press.

Tallis, Raymond. 1997. "The Shrink from Hell." *The Times Higher Education Supplement*, 31 October.

Toynbee, A. 1947–1957. *A Study of History*, [Abridgement of Volumes 1–10 by D. Sommervell], New York: Oxford University Press.

Truth and Reconciliation. 2015. Commission of Canada Honouring the Truth, Reconciling for the Future: Summary of the Final Report of the Truth and Reconciliation Commission of Canada.

Van Mensvoort, Koert. 2009a. *A Society of Simulations*. April 13. <https://www.nextnature.net/2009/04/a-society-of-simulations/>.

___. 2009b. *What You See Is What You Feel: On the Simulation of Touch in Graphical User Interfaces*. Lambert Academic Publishing.

___. 2008. *Fake for Real*, December 9 <https://nextnature.net/2008/12/fake-for-real-%E2%80%93-essay>.

Webster, Richard. 1994. *The Cult of Lacan: Freud, Lacan and the Mirror Stage*. <http://www.richardwebster.net/thecultoflacan.html>.

Wood, Ellen Meiksins, and John Bellamy Foster. 1997. *In Defense of History: Marxism and the Postmodern Agenda*. Monthly Review Press.

CHAPTER 9

THEORIZING OUR GENDERED AND SEXUAL SELVES

Feminist and Queer Theories

FOR WOMEN, THE STRUGGLE CONTINUES

After centuries of indefatigable women's struggles on many different fronts, we could easily be tempted into believing that the worst is over. At least in the West, women have won the rights to vote, to hold property, to seek legal protection and redress against domestic abuse, to enter the professions and universities, and to extend their personal, including reproductive, freedoms, such as the rights of divorce, contraception, abortion, in vitro fertilization etc. These were all hard won gains that required tremendous sacrifice and suffering to attain. So, where are we now? Have we entered a new "post-sexual" age in which the burdens of gender inequality have finally been lifted from the shoulders of women? Unfortunately, like the delusion of a "post-racial" age, the answer has to be "no!" And, in some ways, the hands of the feminist clock have actually been ticking backwards.

Although the recent reversion to more demeaning and degrading forms of speech and action towards women may have been partially incentivized by the 2016 presidential election of Donald Trump, the scale of contemporary gender oppression is much broader and deeper than the Trump bully-pulpit. The past few years have seen many powerful men accused of committing sexual abuse, sexual harassment and sexual misconduct against vulnerable women, and some vulnerable men, in many different sectors of Western society (show business, news media, broadcasting, sport, politics). Although no one is seriously under the illusion that gender equality and gender justice have been fully implemented in Western societies, the proliferation of these cases has proven to be an ominous wake-up call. The struggle for women's rights is far from over.

We have seen a resurgence of feminist activism in the US and in other

Western societies; the misogynous speech and actions of President Trump mobilized millions of American women to take to the streets in public protests against his shamefully sexist and racist insults and demeaning comments. At the same time, the new connectivity of social media has galvanized many female activists to protest against the sexual misconduct committed by men in positions of power and privilege. A manifestation of this digital activism, the #MeToo movement, emerged in late 2017 as part of a popular protest against sexual misconduct revelations concerning Harvey Weinstein and others. Me Too was founded by African American social activist Tarana Burke to help sexual assault survivors realize they are not alone, and the hashtag was later used by actor Alyssa Milano, when she encouraged women to tweet in solidarity with other victims and survivors of sexual misconduct. In a relatively short time, this digital connection blossomed into a network of activists from countries around the world. #MeToo has become a global phenomenon, an example of how new technology has revolutionized the women's movement.

Many contemporary feminists recognize that their struggles for gender and sexual equality and inclusiveness are directly linked to parallel struggles against racism, trans- and homophobia, Islamophobia, poverty, ageism, ableism and legal status. Global feminism is increasingly focused on the systems and structures that generate oppression, including the structures of patriarchy, nationalism, capitalism and imperialism.

Knowledge about gender-based oppression and exploitation around the world has been reflected in the gradual globalization of the women's movement and in the corresponding growth and diversification of feminist social theory. The ethnocentrism and parochialism of earlier feminist theory is being increasingly transformed into more global and internationalist theoretical perspectives. Theorists from the Global South have critiqued the Eurocentric, colonial and imperial assumptions upon which many Western feminist theories were based (Mohanty 2003; McLaren 2017; Jacobs 2010). The earlier paradigms of first and second generation feminism, which were primarily focused on white, heterosexual, middle-class women in North America and Europe, are being superseded by perspectives that have broadened their focus to include women in postcolonial societies, women of colour, Indigenous women, lesbians, immigrant women and other "subaltern" women around the world. Feminist theory — along with other gender theories — is racing to keep up with the accelerated pace of contemporary social change.

This chapter critically reviews the classical, or "orthodox," feminist canon, which has classified the development of feminist theory and practice as a sequence of first, second and third waves, with some theorists believing that a contemporary fourth wave has made an appearance. This "wave" narrative of feminism is hotly contested by many contemporary theorists, who show how it has privileged white Western feminist theorists and excluded theorists from the Global South as well as theorists from racial, ethnic, sexual or other minority groups. We shall also briefly review the rise of the different branches, or schools, of feminism that emerged throughout the twentieth century, often in opposition to established feminist theories.

THE WAVE NARRATIVE OF FEMINISM

According to the orthodox account of the historical rise of feminism, it is possible to distinguish a number of different stages, or waves, in the social, political and intellectual development of the feminist movement. These waves correspond to different generations of feminist theorists. Although this wave narrative has been critiqued and rejected by many contemporary theorists, especially those from the Global South and other previously excluded groups, it is necessary to briefly outline this narrative in view of the authority it once commanded and the influence it once exerted over the feminist movement.

The "first wave" of feminism arose in the two centuries preceding the twentieth century and is associated with the writings of such thinkers as Mary Wollstonecraft, Catherine Macauley, Harriet Martineau, Harriet Taylor Mill and Charlotte Perkins Gilman, among others. Most of these women were white and came from relatively privileged upper-middle-class backgrounds, which gave them the freedom and opportunity to advance the political and social causes of women. This was the period of the so-called "blue-stockinged" women's movement. Although this first generation of feminist theorists and activists campaigned for social reforms in many areas of concern — such as temperance, divorce, domestic violence, passivism and anti-militarism, their greatest struggle in many Western nations focused on the suffrage: gaining the right to vote in national elections. For this reason, many early feminists were called "suffragettes." The right to vote was extended to women in most Western countries during the opening decades of the twentieth century.

We can refer to political and constitutional gains of this period as the "formal equality" of women, that is, their entitlement to political equality under the law and within the constitutions of their respective countries. However, the rights and benefits of formal equality remained limited in their range of application and were often nullified by barriers of social class, race, ethnicity and sexual orientation; in other words, the rights of formal equality did not extend into many other areas of women's lives.

Figure 9-1: Generational Waves of Feminism

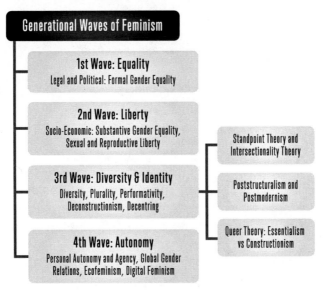

The "second wave" of feminism arose after the Second World War and came into its own during the 1960s with the writings of Simone de Beauvoir, Betty Friedan and later on Kate Millett, Germaine Greer, Gloria Steinem, Shulamith Firestone, Naomi Wolf, Susan Brownmiller, Barbara Ehrenreich and Sheila Rowbotham, among others. The activism in this period was then referred to as the "women's liberation movement": a movement inspired by the civil rights struggles and by the student protest and antiwar movements in the United States and elsewhere. Whereas the first wave was mostly led by women of privilege and wealth, the second wave was led by writers and activists who were supported by middle-class and working-class women. The goals and objectives of the second wave extended beyond the formal equality achieved by the first wave. Second wave feminists demanded greater workplace equality (equal pay for equal

Figure 9-2: Generational Representatives of Feminism

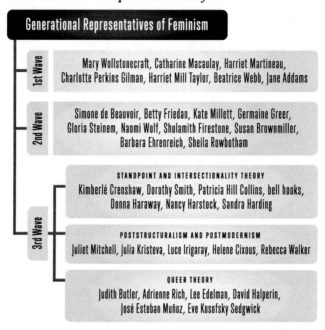

work), greater domestic equality (the sharing of domestic responsibilities), state support for childcare services and greater medical support for women (cervical and breast cancer screening clinics), among many other demands for social and economic equality. We can refer to the struggles of the second wave as struggles for "substantive equality." In addition to these equity goals, the second wave also demanded greater reproductive freedom (freedom of a woman's body), which included the right to obtain an abortion (pro-choice), the right to seek a divorce and the right to access contraception or in vitro fertilization and other assisted reproductive technologies. The fight for reproductive freedom was an important and distinguishing mark of second wave feminism.

The "third wave" of feminism came to prominence in the 1980s and 1990s. Third wave feminist writers express more varied and diverse viewpoints than those of their predecessors. The traditional ranks of white, middle-class, heterosexual women have now been joined by Black, Indigenous, immigrant, lesbian, transgender, working-class and other minoritized women. The viewpoints expressed by many of these women are often at odds with those of earlier generations of feminist writers. Indeed, many of the contributions of third wave feminists owe as much to the influence of poststructuralism and postmodernism as they do to mainstream feminism. Writers such as Juliet Mitchell, Julia Kristeva, Luce Irigaray, Helene Cixous, Judith Butler, bell hooks and Jane Flax, among others, have confronted the sexism, racism, classism, colonialism, homophobia and social inequality within feminism. Out of this mix have come some new areas of study, such as socialist feminism, ecofeminism, queer theory, standpoint and intersectionality theory, postcolonial theory, and diaspora and multicultural studies, all of which have influenced recent trends in social theory.

The Third Wave Legacy: Diversity, Plurality and Difference

Most third wave feminism represents a critical response to the certainties and strong moral convictions of second wave feminism. Susan Mann (2013: 63) even reports that "the refrain that second-wave feminists are their 'serious sisters' is echoed by other third-wave writers (Baumgardner and Richards 2000: 161)." This revolt against the perceived moralism and uniformity of second wave feminism is expressed most provocatively by the acknowledged founder of the third wave, Rebecca Walker, in her book *To Be Real*:

> A year before I started this book, my life was like a feminist ghetto. Every decision I made, person I spent time with, word I uttered had to measure up to an image I had in my mind of what was morally and politically right according to my vision of female empowerment. Everything had a gendered explanation, and what didn't fit into my concept of feminist was "bad, patriarchal, and problematic." (Walker 1995: xxix)

Third wave feminism arose, at least in part, from the growing doubts, confusion and skepticism that have appeared like cracks in the edifice of second wave feminism. As well, third wave feminists have been influenced by postmodernism and poststructuralism, which arose in the 1980s. Whereas, for example, second wave feminists took for granted the centrality and universality of the category of "women" as a collective identity and as a unified political constituency, postmodernism is highly skeptical of these and similar assumptions. Instead, the concept of "woman" has been deconstructed into a proliferating number of localized and more personalized identities: Black women, Indigenous women, working-class women, immigrant women, butch and femme women, girlie women and so on. At the same time, intersectional theorists have shown how the major structures of patriarchal domination, capitalist exploitation and racial and religious discrimination in modern societies combine to reinforce multiple axes of oppression, including race, religion, class, gender, ability, Indigeneity etc. Third wave feminists celebrate diversity among women and encourage the new visibility and audibility of previously marginalized groups of women. They also encourage a multiplicity of strategies and tactics for exercising individual choice and expressing personal freedom. More than anything else, the third wave represents a retreat from the "essentialism" and "foundationalism" implicit in universalized notions of "womanhood" and a rejection of all metanarratives or grand narratives built upon these ideas.

Of course, this new visibility of previously marginalized peoples, including racialized and Indigenous peoples and queer and trans people, doesn't always translate to equality. These "subaltern" voices have shown how the self-proclaimed universalism of second wave feminism was always based upon the historically and culturally limited ethnocentric and Eurocentric perspective of white, middle-class, heterosexual women in Europe and North America. The rise of postmodernism provided third wave feminists with a method for deconstructing and decentring the earlier metanarratives of second wave feminism and for advancing beyond the "modernist" world of middle-class feminism into a postmodernist world of cultural pluralism and political, moral and epistemological relativism. Besides postmodernism, other feminist perspectives have advanced our understanding of the multiple structures of oppression and exploitation of women in modern society and of how these structures interact and reinforce each other. Socialist feminism has focused on the commodification and stratification of women in the modern world, especially under the current policies of neoliberalism and global capitalism. These and similar studies have expanded our understanding of the status of women around the world and have also extended our definitions of justice and equality far beyond the parameters of liberal feminism.

Some commentators have even suggested the rise of a "fourth wave" of feminism that is strongly influenced by the new age of social media and instant connectivity. The postmodern age of digitalized information and communications technology has created new opportunities for self-expression and personal representation. Social networking sites such as Facebook, Instagram, Snapchat, Twitter and YouTube are platforms for media savvy feminists from a variety of backgrounds to develop a wide diversity of messages. Third wave feminism and maybe fourth wave feminism have been raised, at least in part, by the internet.

Although the strategies and tactics of the third wave may depart from those of earlier feminists, these differences do not signal a rejection of the traditional feminist goals of gender equality and social justice. If anything, the individualism and libertarianism of third wave feminism signal a strong commitment to the politics of personal choice. The longer term strategic implications of the politics of choice can be seen in a retreat from the traditional feminist politics of building a mass movement to a more postmodern politics of coalition-building. Third wave feminists are more likely to join with other groups in broadly based campaigns for social justice — including for racial, economic, global, antiwar, anti-racist, Indigenous, environmental and sexual justice, to name but a few — in their efforts to bring about political reforms and social change. This evident willingness of third wave feminists to work collaboratively with other social groups and social movements has been recognized by many other commentators; thus Mann (2013: 64) records:

> Because their generation also was "raised on a multicultural diet"… they argue that third wavers are more likely to branch out into other movements for social justice that reflect their commitment to intersectional differences, a claim echoed by other third-wave authors (Labaton and Martin 2004: xxxi; Mack-Canty in Reger 2005: 201; Dicker 2008: 126–127). *Feminism as a political movement thus becomes "less visible" but "more widely dispersed."* (Heywood and Drake 2004: 16, 20 — emphasis supplied)

Beyond the Third Wave: Beliefs and Practices of the Present Generation

Beyond the diversity and spread of the third wave, it remains an open question as to whether a new generation of fourth wave feminism has emerged onto the political and academic scene. The present generation embraces some new aspects of gender politics and gender culture while continuing to honour and acknowledge many of the legacies of the earlier feminist movements. Perhaps, more than anything else, the latest wave of feminism represents the aspirations, struggles and lifestyles of a younger generation of politically conscious and politically active women who were born into a global and technological environment. If we conclude that a fourth wave feminism has made its appearance in the twenty-first century, there can be little doubt that it has emerged as an outgrowth, or extension, of third wave feminism. Indeed, the boundaries separating the third from the fourth wave are blurred, with the differences being primarily of degree rather than of kind. The present generation has inherited many of the characteristics of the third wave. Among the most prominent of these legacies is the continuing influence of postmodernism and post-structuralism, with a corresponding emphasis on individualism, diversity, pluralism, relativism, inclusiveness and tolerance. These influences are manifested in the close relationships connecting the present generation to allied theoretical perspectives — such as standpoint and intersectionality theories and queer studies, among others. Given the obvious similarities that these later feminist waves share with each other, what are some of the distinguishing features of the present generation of feminism? Some of these differences include the following aspects, which, although not unique to the fourth wave, together combine to provide this latest feminist perspective with its distinctive and novel character.

Connectivity: The current generation of young feminists has been formed by the revolutions in digital information and communications technologies of the present age, including the internet and social media. They use these technologies to network within their own political and academic communities and to discuss, debate and publicize their current interests and projects. An example of this digital connection between contemporary feminist activists may be seen in the success in 2018 of the #MeToo campaign and the follow-up Time's Up campaign among celebrities to support victims/survivors of sexual assault and other forms of sexual misconduct committed by powerful men. Social media also helped to mobilize One Billion Rising, the 2017 Women's March and other protests across America and around the world that greeted the election of Donald Trump.

Internationalism: More than previous generations, fourth wave feminists show a greater interest in the global gender gap between men and women and the prevalence and persistence of severe forms of gender oppression and exploitation around the world. This focus on global gender relations in postcolonial societies is partly a consequence of the spread, speed and scope of global digital communications and partly a response to the pro-liferation of wars and combat zones in which women are invariably the victims of extreme forms of sexual and physical violence. This expanded focus has been led by many younger feminists who feel that traditional feminism remains Eurocentric and often irrelevant to the lives of women in the Global South. The focus of feminism in the twenty-first century has expanded beyond the local or the national to include a more global perspective than ever before.

Autonomy: Perhaps a more controversial aspect of present generation feminism has been the strong emphasis on individual agency and personal autonomy. Many younger liberal feminists redefine formerly stigmatized issues, such as prostitution and pornography, as matters of freedom of choice (either as freedom in the workforce or as freedom of expression), rather than as evil practices of a sexist patriarchal culture (Power 2009). Many younger members of the present generation also emphasize the celebration of femininity and womanhood. Many direct descendants of the second wave have condemned their younger contemporary counterparts for their (alleged) frivolity and for their apparent surrender or addiction to consumer culture and commercialization and commodification of femininity within the capitalist marketplace. These divisions, among others, illustrate some of the conflicts between different generations of feminist theorists and activists (see, for example, Sheinin et al. 2016).

Diversity: Fourth wave feminism also inherited from the third wave a strong focus and emphasis on diversity, pluralism and inclusivity. Thus, fourth wave theorists and activists recognize and respect the different dimensions of gender identity, including those of race, ethnicity, social class, sexual orientation, global location and age, as well as physical and mental ability. Many younger activists also express a preference for a more permissive and inclusive and less moralistic version of feminism that elevates collaboration above confrontation in advancing its beliefs and practices. Many prefer a more fluid and flexible definition of gender identity, one which openly recognizes and respects gay, lesbian, bisexual and transgender persons and which avoids the outdated essentialism of binary gendered identities. This inclusiveness in feminist theory and practice closely connects the fourth wave to allied branches of contemporary social theory, including standpoint theory, intersectionality theory, postcolonial theory and queer theory, among others. Although each of these perspectives emerged during the closing decades of the twentieth century, they have, along with fourth wave feminism, matured and diversified into the twenty-first century.

Environmentalism: Another focus of concern for contemporary feminism is the environment. Ecofeminism, as this movement was originally named, originated during the closing decades of the twentieth century. In many ways, the ecological branch of feminism further illustrates the growing globalization of the movement. Environmental feminists around the world have organized campaigns to prevent local deforestation, to protect wildlife and conserve bio-diversity, to protest pollution, environmental degradation and water contamination, to provide food security and end rural poverty and to publicize the threats from climate change and global warming.

Contesting the Canon: Dispelling the Waves

In previous chapters, we referred to the ongoing theoretical criticisms and revisions of the traditional historiography of social theory as the "crumbling canon" of social thought. The crumbling canon represents a rising dissatisfaction among many contemporary theorists with earlier, formerly paramount, historical and chronological narratives of social theory, especially in the discipline of sociology and allied fields. This dissatisfaction is also apparent in the changing historical and chronological narratives of feminist theory and feminist activism. The traditional feminist canon has long been exemplified in the narrative that describes the origins and historical development of feminist theory and activism as a sequence of generational waves, or stages. However, this wave chronology has come under increasingly critical scrutiny from many current feminist theorists, especially those from the Global South and from minoritized groups within the Global North (Laughlin et al. 2010; Berger 2006; Hewitt 2010; Jacob and Licona 2005; Akemi and Busk 2016). Kathleen Laughlin observes:

> The waves metaphor, like the earlier concept of separate spheres, has become a crutch that obscures as much as it organizes the past into a neat package. To make the feminist past understandable, if not relevant, to future generations, we must historicize both the creation of concepts and the lives and actions they categorize. One way to do this is to make

our "waves trouble" part of the discussion of the feminist past
and the Women's Studies present. (Laughlin et al. 2010: 81)

The wave narrative is now often seen as inherently Eurocentric, racially
exclusive and middle class in its focus. Beyond the biases of Eurocentrism,
racism, colonialism, classism, heterosexism and other inflexions of
Western capitalist societies, contemporary critics' political and epistemological concerns about the wave narrative are that it advances a unilinear,
unidirectional and unidimensional account of feminism. Today, feminists
from the Global South and from racially, ethnically, religiously, sexually
or other culturally marginalized groups are more inclined to see the heritage of feminism in multiple complex networks, or matrices, in which
diverse struggles invariably combined and intersected with each other.
Rather than viewing the history of feminism as a series of epic tidal waves
represented by a few celebrated thinkers and activists, many theorists
today see the theoretical and practical work of feminism as carried out
by ordinary women and men in various axes of oppression — sexism,
racism, ageism, homophobia and transphobia, poverty, slavery, among
others. This is the current view of feminism endorsed by many theorists
and eloquently expressed by Eileen Boris: "In short, feminisms developed
in various locations, sometimes tied to racial, class, religious, sexual, and
other identities, sometimes based on political — in the broadest sense
— philosophies, and usually derived from lived experiences as refracted
through the interpretative terms available during specific times and places"
(Laughlin et al. 2010: 93). Many leading feminist theorists of the early
twenty-first century have already abandoned the wave narrative in favour
of a much broader view of the feminist project, a view that recognizes the
diverse origins of feminist thought and activism and that seeks to include
those sources in a revitalized feminist canon.

THE MANY FACES OF FEMINISM TODAY

In the wake of the crumbling cannon of white, Western, heterosexual
feminism, contemporary feminism has fragmented into a number of
political perspectives. These perspectives cover the full spectrum of
feminism, including not only mainstream liberal-democratic approaches
to the problems faced by women in our society, but a variety of other
approaches ranging from Marxist and socialist, radical feminist perspectives, psychoanalytic and poststructualist feminist approaches, and even

cultural (see, for example, Gilligan 1982) and conservative versions of feminist studies (see, for example, Paglia 2017, 2018). While all of these perspectives are feminist in one sense or another, they represent some of the more intractable divisions and tensions within contemporary feminism, tensions that appear to have increased rather than diminished in recent years. What, then, are the essential differences between some of these political perspectives — in terms of their theories of gender relations and their practical implications for social and political action?

Liberal feminists over the past hundred years or more have remained committed to the classical goals of the women's movement: full integration into societal structures and institutions and full socio-economic and political equality. Strongly influenced by the civil rights movement in the United States, liberal feminists have pursued the goals of equality and integration through a variety of political and constitutional means. They have fought to end gender discrimination and gender inequality in many areas of public life: in the workplace, in politics and government, in education and so on. They have also fought to establish daycare centres, abortion clinics, women's shelters and other institutions for women. In their struggles for integration and equality, liberal feminists have relied heavily on constitutional, legislative and political solutions. Such solutions include section 28 of the Charter of Rights and Freedoms (Canada), the proposed Equal Rights Amendment (US), royal commission reports (Canada) and national political organizations, such as the antiwar Voice of Women (Canada), National Action Committee for the Status of Women (Canada) and the National Organization of Women (US). Both in their political analysis and political action — their theory and practice — liberal feminists remain in the mainstream of feminist politics. However, as many critics have charged, liberal feminism has often been seen to represent the interests and concerns of white, Western, middle-class heterosexual women and has overlooked the concerns of women of colour, working-class women, lesbians, women of different cultures and ethnicities and, most evidently, women from the Global South. In their theoretical perspectives and practical politics, liberal feminists have remained individualistic in their approach to the political and structural causes of gender inequality and sexism and have failed to address related problems of racism, homophobia and transphobia, as well as religious and cultural prejudice and discrimination, even when these problems intersect and reinforce the oppression of women at home and around the world. For many critics, liberal feminism has long been an expression of the wealthier women in Western society who have sought what they regard as their rightful seats at the table and their rightful places in the corridors of power and influence. As one critic tartly remarked, liberal feminism offers women a "piece of the pie as currently and poisonously baked" (Morgan 1996).

Marxist and socialist feminists have focused their analyses on the economic exploitation and political domination of women in capitalist society. Socialist feminists have drawn attention to the ways in which many women are minoritized, not only by their gender, but also by their race, ethnicity and class. Not all women experience the same degree of social oppression. Black, Indigenous, poor, lesbian and transgender and other minoritized women are oppressed and exploited not only by sexism but also by racism, colonialism, homophobia, xenophobia and economic hyper-exploitation. Socialist feminists target the institutions of patriarchal capitalism in their struggles for the liberation of women from all sources of domination and exploitation. Unlike liberal feminists, socialist feminists have little trust in the constitutional machinery of the capitalist state to bring about any real substantial change in gender relations. Problems of gender inequality and exploitation are caused, not only by ignorance and prejudice, but also by prioritizing profits and economic interests over social justice and gender equity. Consequently, problems will not be solved simply through education or constitutional reform, but through mass grassroots struggles for a wholesale transformation of our political and economic institutions: in short, a socialist revolution.

Radical feminists believe that the institutions of patriarchy have always existed in every human society since the dawn of humanity. The domination of women by men lies at the heart of all social organization and is rooted in the very nature of men, which has always been expressed through hierarchy, aggression, competitiveness, domination and violence. More than any other tradition of feminism, radical theorists have emphasized the role of physical aggression and brute force in gender relations. This emphasis on physical force has led to a focus on the patriarchal oppression of women's bodies — how they have been controlled, exploited and oppressed by men in modern societies through sex, rape, pornography, childbirth, female genital mutilation and female circumcision, medical-legal practices, gynecology and other forms of male domination. More than the other perspectives, radical feminism emphasizes the need for self-reliance in women's political struggles and discourages alliances with the enemy (i.e., with men). Some radical feminists have advocated lesbianism as the only form of intimate sexual equality possible in a patriarchal society (see, for example, Charlotte Bunch, Rita Mae Brown, Adrienne Rich, Audre Lorde, Marilyn Frye, Mary Daly and Monique Wittig), or, in the view of Adrienne Rich (2003 [1980]), as an escape from or resistance to the institutions and practices of "compulsory sexuality" in a coercively heterosexist and patriarchal society.

Many of these theorists have also eschewed what they perceive as male ideologies, including liberalism and socialism, in favour of wholly woman-centred, or gynocentric, wordviews. Some radical feminists have also essentialized the sexes, creating the sharp binary division between women and men and arguing that trans women should be excluded from the category of "women." In their exclusive focus on binary sexual relations, they have also overlooked other sources of women's oppression, such as racism, colonialism and capitalist exploitation. For this reason, radical feminism became the target of much criticism from intersectional feminism and Black feminism (Willis 1984).

One of the more interesting aspects of radical feminism has been its capacity for producing biting critiques of Marxism and other established theories of society. Typically, these critiques of Marxism have been about the apparent failure of Marxists to fully appreciate the primal cause of the oppression and exploitation of women (Bryson 2003: 163; Rowbotham 2000: 232). For radical feminists, the most important deficiency attributed to Marxism is the failure to recognize the importance of the woman's body and the necessity to free it from arbitrary restraint or external control. Thus, for Rich (1977: 285), "the repossession by women of our bodies will bring far more essential change to human society than the seizing of the means of production by workers." Other critics have focused on the failure of Marx to include the domestic work of women in the household as "productive labour" because it does not produce "surplus value" or directly contribute to the accumulation of capital. As Shulamith Firestone (1971), Mary O'Brien (1981) and others have pointed out, the domestic labour of women contributes much to the social reproduction, nurturing and care of workers and future workers: labour that is essential for the sustainability of the capitalist system. Other radical feminists, such as Andrea Dworkin, have located the source of women's oppression in the institution of the heterosexual patriarchal family and have suggested that the full emancipation of women can only ever be achieved through homosexual (i.e., lesbian) relationships. The development of what has come to be known as gay theory and queer theory may be seen as a further extension of these ideas into another branch of contemporary feminism and gender studies.

Postmodernist and poststructuralist feminists have emerged over the past several decades, greatly influenced by trends in postmodernism and poststructuralism. This tradition is inspired by the work of European, mostly French, intellectuals, such as Michel Foucault, Jean-Francois Lyotard, Jean Baudrillard, Jacques Derrida, Jacques Lacan and Julia Kristeva, among others. In common with other postmodernist theorists, feminists influenced by this tradition have focused on "discourse analysis" as their primary method of social, cultural and political criticism. For postmodernist feminists, power in society, including patriarchal power, is maintained and reproduced not only through specific practices, but also through particular discourses, or ways of viewing and speaking about the social world. Discourses not only frame the linguistic and ideological ways in which we apprehend the world, but they also rationalize our ways of acting within it. Discourses acquire their power and influence through discursive "practices": ways of acting which are informed by particular forms of discourse. For example, without a belief in witches and the demonization of women, there could have been no witch hunts, witch trials, tortures or executions.

Postmodernist and poststructuralist feminists have shown how most traditional accounts of history, culture and social theory have been written through the eyes of men. These androcentric discourses have always privileged the voices of the powerful over those of the powerless. Part of the attraction of poststructuralism for many feminists is that it provides a method for revealing the "silences," "absences" and "exclusions" of dominant discourses. This method, pioneered by Jacques Derrida, is known as deconstructionism. In most traditional cultural texts, there are many absences or silences, including the absent voices of women, racialized, Indigenous and ethnic minorities, as well as sexual and gender minorities, the poor, the disabled and many other overlooked or neglected social statuses and identities.

Following in the footsteps of Foucault, Lyotard, Baudrillard and others, postmodernist and poststructuralist feminists have targeted the dominant discourses of society because these texts have invariably marginalized or excluded the perspectives of socially powerless groups, including women. Besides excluding the voices of the powerless, dominant social texts — whether of history, theory, science, politics, religion, culture or art — have always proclaimed themselves to be general or universal accounts of the human condition. The dominant social texts — which have always expressed the voices of the socially powerful — have become the metanarratives of our society from which we construct our sense of history and our collective identity: whether this identity is expressed as empire, nation, class, race, sex or gender. Poststructuralist and postmodernist theorists have attacked these metanarratives as "totalizing," or universalizing, texts that have contributed to the suppression and subjugation of other forms of discourse, especially those of the socially powerless.

Serious tensions exist between the work of postmodernist feminists and that of their more socialist or radical colleagues. Because of the strong postmodernist and poststructuralist emphasis on discourse as a way of understanding the social world, socialist feminists have often accused postmodernist feminists of abandoning the material struggle for women's emancipation in favour of an abstract and esoteric intellectual critique. In place of the traditional demands of the women's movement for solidarity, postmodernist feminists are more likely to celebrate the virtues of diversity and difference. Thus, while some of the methods of poststructuralism have been endorsed by feminists, especially deconstructive critiques of standard male-oriented texts, other aspects of postmodernist feminism have drawn both criticism and opposition from more traditional feminist quarters (see, for example, Epstein 1995). In other words, as Jane Parpart (1993) suggests:

> Feminist scholars have reacted to postmodernism in a number of ways. Some reject it outright, while others call for a synthesis of feminist and postmodern approaches. Many scholars and activists concerned with Third World issues, especially poverty and development, have rejected both feminism and postmodernism, dismissing them as First World preoccupations, if not indulgences.

Psychoanalytic feminists have been influenced by contemporary psychoanalytic theories, especially those of European theorists such as Jacques Lacan, Gilles Deleuze and Félix Guattari. Whereas the influence of poststructuralism is often referred to as the "linguistic turn," we may perhaps refer to the equally strong influence of these European theorists as the "psychoanalytic turn" of contemporary feminist theory. This dramatic reappearance of the psychoanalytical perspective in the gender theory and feminist discourse of the last quarter of the twentieth century and into the twenty-first century is also referred to as the "return to Freud." And although a number of Anglophone feminists, most notably Juliet Mitchell, have also adopted a psychoanalytic perspective in their work, this psychoanalytic turn was primarily associated with contemporary French feminists, including Julia Kristeva, Luce Irigaray and Helene Cixous, among others.

Most of the third wave psychoanalytic feminists, especially the French feminists, were influenced much more by Jacques Lacan than by Sigmund Freud. However, some feminists, like Juliet Mitchell, insisted that this renewed interest in Freud corresponded to a new understanding of his work. For them, Freud was no longer seen as a phallocentric clinician intent on endorsing or legitimizing patriarchal institutions, especially the family, but rather as an analytical theorist who sought to explain and understand the psychodynamics that produced and reproduced these patriarchal intuitions.

For the French theorists, Freud was reinterpreted through the work of Jacques Lacan. Although Lacan's social theory makes full use of many of Freud's key concepts — Oedipal complex, castration complex, incest taboo, penis envy etc. — these concepts are reinterpreted through a poststructuralist lens. Lacan emphasized the critical role of language and signification in the early life of the individual. In this respect, Lacan is often credited with "de-biologizing" Freud's psychoanalytic concepts. Thus, when the French feminists began their "return to Freud," they did so through the filter of Lacan's poststructuralist psychoanalytic perspective.

In some ways, the rise of third wave feminism was a critical response to what many younger feminists have seen as the dogmatic and doctrinaire aspects of the second wave. In contrast to the activists and theorists of the second wave generation who, in the struggles against sexism, gender inequality and misogyny, often reduced sexual politics and gender issues to the binary opposition of male:female, third wave feminist have understood "identity" in more complex, flexible and fluid terms. The rise of the third wave coincided with the birth and increased visibility of the LGBTQ liberation movements and a growing recognition of the fluidity of personal identities. The third wave have strongly repudiated the notion that "biology is destiny" and, instead, reaffirmed the freedom of the individual to establish an independent identity, but at the same time, appealed to the larger community to recognize and respect that identity.

For this reason, the psychoanalytic framework of Lacan has largely displaced that of Freud, at least for most third wave feminists. Whereas for Freud, the early Oedipal experience of "castration fear" for boys and "penis envy" for girls was essentialized into biological terms, for Lacan, the Oedipal experience was understood primarily in linguistic, symbolic and semantic terms. Thus, the post-natal awareness of the father, or what Lacan calls the "name of the father," was interpreted as the entry of the child into the Symbolic order (of language, law and societal norms), rather than the fearful or envious recognition of the power of the biological penis.

This poststructuralist/psychoanalytic perspective of gender identity has met with considerable controversy and criticism among other feminist theorists (see, for example, Brodribb 1993; Nussbaum 1999). Some have simply denounced the entire psychoanalytic enterprise as "sexist." Others, however, have critiqued Mitchell and Lacan (Borch-Jacobsen 2001) for "essentializing" the present societal structures and hierarchies that generate contemporary gender identities and for treating these structures and identities as though they were fixed and immutable social hardware rather than fluid and changeable social software.

STANDPOINT THEORY

There are several perspectives that are often classified together under the headings of standpoint theory and intersectionality theory. Although standpoint perspectives represent an outgrowth from third wave feminism, they have provided frameworks for multiple "subject identities" to project their own specific viewpoints and to illustrate their own positions within the structure of social relations. In other words, standpoint theorists have shown us that the way in which people experience and understand their worlds is greatly influenced by their position within the social structures in which they interact with others, especially the structures of power and knowledge. Feminist standpoint theorists start from the assumption that the standpoint of women is different from that of men because of their differential position in structures of power and systems of social stratification. However, for feminist standpoint theorists, a standpoint is more than a perspective; it is a critical and reflexive understanding of a person's social position. In the words of Sandra Harding (1993: 141), "What grounds standpoint theories is not women's experience but the view from women's lives." And, as Harding (1991: 127) also emphasizes, a standpoint is achieved through a struggle to understand one's position within a structure of social relations, especially structures of power, wealth and social status:

> Only through such struggles can we begin to see beneath the appearances created by an unjust social order to the reality of how this social order is in fact constructed and maintained. This need for struggle emphasizes the fact that a feminist standpoint is not something that anyone can have simply by claiming it. It is an achievement. A standpoint differs in this respect from a perspective, which anyone can have simply by "opening one's eyes."

The standpoint of those who are subordinate in a structure of power relations may have an epistemic advantage over those who dominate them. The subordinate subject typically acquires a "double vision" — that of the outsider as well as that of the insider. Those at the bottom of a power structure need to learn the ways of the powerful, as well as their own ways, in order to survive. Conversely, the powerful have no need to learn from the powerless. This epistemic advantage is described by African American feminist critic bell hooks (1984: vii) in her narrative of growing up in small-town Kentucky: "Living as we did — on the edge — we developed a particular way of seeing reality. We looked both from the outside in and from the inside out ... we understood both." This is what makes the standpoint theoretical perspective so subversive and potentially radical: the oppressed learns about the oppressor; but the oppressor remains largely ignorant of the oppressed. As Harding (2004: 7–8) notes, oppressed groups "can learn to identify their distinctive opportunities to turn an oppressive feature of the group's conditions into a source of critical insight about how the dominant society thinks and is structured. Thus, standpoint theories map how a social and political disadvantage can be turned into an epistemological, scientific and political advantage."

As with other theories discussed in this book, the fortunes of standpoint theory have often been tied to real historical events and social changes. The rise of standpoint theory coincided with the advent of "identity politics" during the 1970s and 1980s and with the new social movements that began to campaign around contemporary political issues. These new social movements differed from some of the earlier movements, such as the labour movement, the antiwar movement and the civil rights movement, in the scope of their demands and in their constituencies. Whereas the earlier movements campaigned for universal material demands — such as collective bargaining rights, minimum wages, social security, an end to the Vietnam War, the right to vote, desegregation, integration and equality — the demands of the new social movements were focused more on identity, lifestyle and culture. These movements were also "new'" in the sense that they were not grounded in traditional party politics or in single-issue lobby groups directed solely towards influencing governmental decision-makers. Instead, many of these new groups began to express themselves in direct action politics, street demonstrations and marches and social media campaigns and by forming alliances and coalitions with similar groups. In these respects, the new social movements signalled a "cultural turn" in politics and a more "post-materialist" perspective than their predecessors.

An early inspiration for these later struggles was the rise of the second wave women's movement in the late 1950s and early 1960s, known at that time as the "women's liberation movement." Besides its universal appeal for gender equality in the workplace and in the wider society, the growing pluralism in the women's movement — with increasing recognition for Black women, Indigenous women, lesbians, ecofeminists, socialist feminists etc. — led to the rise of other activist movements. Some of the landmark events in the timeline of these new social movements include the 1969 Stonewall uprising, which marked the beginning of the movement for lesbian, gay, bisexual, transgender and queer rights; the founding of the Greenpeace organization (1971); the birth of the modern ecology/environmental movement; and the Campaign for Nuclear Disarmament in Britain during the early 1960s, which inspired the modern antiwar movements. As well, the global justice movement, originally called the "anti-globalization" movement, emerged from the World Social Forums (starting in Porto Alegre in 2001) and the protests against the World Trade Organization (in Seattle in 1999), International Monetary Fund and World Bank (in Washington in 2000 and 2002), the proposed Free

Trade Area of the Americas (in Quebec in 2001) and the G-8 (in Genoa in 2001). New social movements have proliferated at home and abroad, and today they include movements for the disabled, for consumers, for animal rights activists, for evangelicals, for pro-life and pro-choice, for the homeless and for the landless, as well as Occupy, Idle No More, Black Lives Matter, Extinction Rebellion and #MeToo.

The intellectual origins of standpoint theory can be traced back to the modern feminist movement and to some of the theorists who helped to shape the second and third wave feminist perspectives. The term "standpoint" was introduced by Sandra Harding and has become a central term in contemporary social and feminist theory. According to the original standpoint theorists (Dorothy Smith, Nancy Hartsock, Sandra Harding, Patricia Hill Collins and Donna Haraway), any standpoint reflects the social position occupied by an individual within a structure of social relations. A standpoint represents an individual's "epistemological perspective" — the ways in which they interpret and understand the world (Harding 2004). The main message of standpoint theory is that any standpoint is always conditioned by the social position occupied by the human subject. Any standpoint can only offer a partial view of social reality; different standpoints will always reflect the different social locations and social statuses occupied by individuals within a structure of social relations. For this reason, it is impossible to conceive of a "neutral" or "objective" view of society or social relationship because any view will always represent a particular standpoint. But most importantly, the subjugated subject understands much more about their oppressor than their oppressor understands about them — whether this relates to power relationships between women and men; colonized and colonizers; the racialized and the privileged; or any other hierarchical relationship.

Besides their inherent relativity, standpoints are also shaped by the structures of social inequality and domination that characterize all known societies. The early feminist standpoint theorists adopted the philosopher Georg Hegel's maxim — taken from his treatise on the master/slave dialectic — that it is always the members of subjugated and oppressed groups who have the clearest and most comprehensive view of society. Later standpoint theorists incorporated this insight into a methodological injunction to "study up," i.e., to begin any research project by defining the problem or topic from "below," to look at it from the standpoint of the "subaltern" or "underdog" group (Nader 1969). For most social researchers, a standpoint not only represented the objective position of an individual or group in society, but also the subjective individual or collective consciousness of that position.

This kind of standpoint consciousness was traditionally achieved through conflict and struggle. The standpoint of the oppressed was always "privileged" by many of the early (especially feminist) standpoint theorists and justified in terms of producing what they called a "strong objectivity," a term also introduced by Harding (1995). This political and methodological commitment to study social relations from the standpoint of the powerless inaugurated a tradition of "action-oriented" research. Many early standpoint theorists saw their engagement with research subjects as exercises in "consciousness raising" as well as opportunities for social research. For many theorists, social action and political practice, or praxis, were essential components of a standpoint philosophy, which emphasized both abstract theory and concrete research.

According to standpoint theorists, for example, there is no neutral way to observe and analyze the institution of slavery because the standpoint of the slave is very different from that of the master. Even the standpoint of the outside observer comes with its own biases and presuppositions. Similarly, within the patriarchal structure of marriage in our society, the standpoint of a woman is very different from that of a man. There is no neutral vantage point from which to view these institutions. We are all, in different ways, implicated in the complex web of ideologies, experiences and social practices that bind together and reproduce these sets of social relations.

It is clear from their embrace of "epistemological relativism" that standpoint theorists challenge some of the basic assumptions of conventional social science research. One of the goals of conventional empirical research has always been to acquire "objective" knowledge. The construction of empirical data-collection instruments (such as questionnaires, surveys, controlled experiments, interview schedules, content analysis, sampling techniques etc.) and the testing of research hypotheses have always been conducted in pursuit of "objective" knowledge. Objectivity and value neutrality are the *sine qua non* of conventional research methodology. In contrast to most accepted models, standpoint theorists have advanced their own conception of social theory and research. Every standpoint offers a limited and selective view of the social world, a view that is likely to be very different from and incommensurate with those of other social standpoints. It is incumbent upon theorists to strive for full transparency, to openly declare from the outset their preconceptions and presupposi-tions and, to the best of their ability, to acknowledge their cultural biases.

Dorothy Smith

Dorothy Smith, a Canadian feminist theorist, is one of the founders and foremost exponents of standpoint theory (1987). Smith succeeded in extending the boundaries of contemporary feminist theory by introduc-ing a new perspective that drew upon a number of different intellectual traditions. Although Smith's sources of intellectual inspiration were such traditions as Marxism, phenomenology and ethnomethodology, she effectively theorized the social world of the late twentieth and early twentieth-first centuries. Her analysis of Marxism, for example, is focused on the "knowledge economy" of the late twentieth century and on the corresponding growth of information and communication technologies, which in the West have increasingly displaced the industrial technolo-gies of the past two centuries. Smith felt that it was important to focus on the experiences and perspectives of those who were among the most marginalized and powerless in society. In practice, this meant that Smith has privileged the experiences of women and has ensured that their per-spectives are well represented in her theoretical perspective.

Feminist standpoint theory has, over the past several decades, opened up a new critical discourse for analyzing the experiences of women in patriarchal society. With the combination of her Marxian commit-ment to social equality and her ethnomethodological insight into how patriarchal ideologies are routinely sustained through recurrent and methodical social practices, Smith pioneered the development of a new vocabulary of feminist standpoint terms and concepts. Thus standpoint theory has helped to expose the "relations of ruling" (Smith 1990): those conceptual practices that so often exclude or marginalize women in the academic, corporate, entertainment, sports, medical and political worlds of men. These relations of ruling are frequently reproduced through the abstract and quasi-impersonal processes of knowledge and power that have traditionally privileged white, heterosexual, middle-class men and have, thereby, disadvantaged, or disenfranchised, women and other racialized, ethnic or sexual minorities. These relations of ruling may reveal themselves in many different ways: in publication requirements for professorial tenure; in the unwritten psychological profiles emphasizing aggressiveness, competitiveness and territoriality for senior corporate executives; in the expected career paths for professional politicians; and so on. Different sectors of society have refined many different ways either for excluding women or for minimizing their participation and restricting their advancement. Today, as Smith suggests, the relations of ruling rely most heavily on abstract media of administration and control and quasi-impersonal ways of converting abstract knowledge and information into patriarchal and often highly personalized political power.

In her work, Smith has also drawn attention to another, hitherto undocumented, aspect of the common everyday experience of women living in a patriarchal society. According to Smith, most women experience, what she calls, a "fault line" which separates their actual *lived experience* from the ideologized forms of consciousness that are imposed on or internalized by women through the relations of ruling. Thus, while women may be induced through the mass media, commercial advertisements and popular culture to think of themselves as canny consumers, fashionistas, sex symbols, earth mothers, equal citizens, pioneers, innovators etc., their everyday experiences constantly contradict or undermine these hegemonic images of power, success and progress. The mundane oppression that many women experience — of the "double-day" and the "glass ceiling," of being a "sex object" and of holding down "dead-end jobs," as well as the humdrum reality of household drudgery — opens up a fault line between the idealized consciousness and women's actual experience. The narratives provided by the mass media and other institutions are frequently belied and contradicted by the raw experiences of daily female existence.

As a feminist standpoint theorist, Smith has also used her work to pioneer new ways of studying the existential dilemmas faced by women in contemporary society. In common with many social theorists of her generation, Smith has been influenced by the "linguistic turn" in social and literary theory and by the corresponding rise of poststructuralism and postmodernism. These combined influences led Smith to pioneer a theoretical perspective which she describes as a "new materialism." This is a perspective that, on the one hand, acknowledges — in a postmodernist vein — that all forms of social reality are constructed through discourse, often through official texts. In this respect, Smith embraces the relativism and pluralism of postmodernist social theory: namely, that all "truths" and all "facts" are best understood as "artifacts" of particular localized, rather than universal, forms of discourse. However, Smith also insists that discourses are only sustained and reproduced through ongoing social practices which "substantiate" and "materialize" these discourses and their discursive objects. The new materialism focuses on the recurrent practices that produce and reproduce the recursive social structures that are substantiated through discourse. These are ideas that have been variously expressed in a number of recent theoretical traditions, including ethnomethodology, structuration theory and poststructuralism. Dorothy Smith assimilated these ideas and gave them a fresh lease on life in her version of standpoint feminism.

Dorothy Smith's entire career has been motivated by a strong commitment to gender justice and progressive social change and to bring an end to the oppression of women and other disempowered minorities. This commitment is widely recognized among feminists and more broadly in the academic world. Smith's legacy is eloquently summarized by the Canadian feminist and health researcher, Marie Campbell (2003:17):

> She recognized that knowing differently was the basis for changing the conditions of women's lives. To begin to undermine oppression, one must be able to identify and challenge the prevailing problems in otherwise unquestioned, taken-for granted, prevailing ways of knowing and acting. That is the sort of inquiry that Smith had wanted to make possible. She imagined that when people begin to see how they participate in their own and others' oppression by using the oppressor's language and tools and taking up actions that are not in their own interests, anti-oppressive work could be advanced.

INTERSECTIONALITY THEORY

As with standpoint theory, intersectionality theory arose because many racialized women, Indigenous women, working-class women, and queer and transgender women rejected what they perceived as a "false universalism" of standard feminist narratives contained in manifestos, declarations, autobiographies, political programs and other types of feminist literature. Some white feminists consciously excluded minority women from their definition of the feminist project (Williams 2019; DiAngelo 2011; Ortega 2006; Accapadi 2007).

The term "intersectionality" was originally coined by Kimberlé Crenshaw, an African American law professor and social theorist, in her 1989 paper "Demarginalizing the Intersection of Race and Sex: A Black

Feminist Critique of Antidiscrimination Doctrine, Feminist Theory and Antiracist Politics." By "intersectionality," Crenshaw refers to the intersecting and interlocking structures of power, wealth and social status that often determine the life opportunities of individuals within a society and may also condition their viewpoints, experiences and personal and social identities. Unlike the standpoint perspective, intersectionality theory is primarily focused on the *structures* of social relations and how these structures and practices may often marginalize and oppress vulnerable groups and individuals, especially in capitalist societies with their extreme stratification of income, wealth and power. Whereas standpoint theory focuses on the perspectives of marginalized or oppressed subjects, not in purely personal terms but more as a critical and reflexive perspective on the experience of injustice and oppression, intersectionality theory focuses far more on the hierarchical and interlocking structures of power and inequality that generate oppression and injustice. At the same time, these two perspectives remain closely aligned. Mann (2013) has suggested that intersectionality theory should be recognized as a social theory, while standpoint theory should be seen as the epistemology, or theory of knowledge, underlying intersectionality theory.

According to intersectionality theorists, there are multiple sources of marginality and oppression generated by intersecting power structures in society or, as Crenshaw (2017) remarked almost three decades after she first introduced this term, "intersectionality is a lens through which you can see where power comes and collides, where it interlocks and intersects. It's not simply that there's a race problem here, a gender problem here, and a class or LBGTQ problem there. Many times, that framework erases what happens to people who are subject to all of these things." Thus, African Canadian women , for example, experience both sexism and racism. And Indigenous women and women of colour who also identify as lesbian or transgender may face at least three intersecting structural sources of prejudice, discrimination and exploitation: racism, sexism and homophobia or transphobia. For intersectionality theorists, it is important that we examine the intersection and interconnection of these structures, rather than treat them as separate dimensions of oppression. As Laurel Weldon (2006: 239) suggests, "theorists of intersectionality insist that we cannot understand the ways that women are disadvantaged as women nor the ways that people of color are oppressed unless we examine the ways these structures interact. Specifically, they claim that certain aspects of social inequality, certain problems and injustices, will not be visible as long as we focus on gender, race and class separately."

Among intersectionality theorists, these structural sources of oppression are known as "vectors of oppression," or "axes of oppression." Other vectors of oppression may include oppression arising from age discrimination (ageism), oppression arising from physical or mental disability (ableism), oppression arising from class prejudice and exploitation (classism), from religion (Islamophobia or anti-Semitism) or from geographic location. Intersectionality theory is primarily oriented towards a study of the hierarchical vectors of power and privilege that determine the life opportunities and expectations of marginalized subjects, especially when these vectors intersect and coalesce into compound structures of domination and oppression. And for Crenshaw, intersectionality theory was conceived as a theoretical, analytical and emancipatory tool in the struggle for social equality and social justice: "A lot of people think that intersectionality is only about identity, but it's also about how race and gender are structured in particular workforces.... If you don't have a lens that's been trained to look at how various forms of discrimination come together, you're unlikely to develop a set of policies that will be as inclusive as they need to be" (quoted in McCauley 2016).

These vectors of oppression and privilege also form the basis of what is known in intersectionality theory as the "matrix of domination," or "matrix of oppression," which outlines the intersecting structures that oppress the lives of women and prevent their full equality and emancipation in society. The matrix of domination was first introduced by African American scholar Patricia Hill Collins (2000), and it charts the various vectors of oppression and privilege: race, sex, gender, sexual orientation, class, ability/disability, religion, and age. It illustrates how these categories combine to trap racialized, sexualized and other marginalized and minoritized subjects into lives burdened by prejudice, discrimination and oppression. In order to confront social injustice, it is necessary to understand the combination of structures in society that generate and reinforce these sources of oppression. According to Collins (2012: xiii), "challenging power structures from the inside, working the cracks within the system, however, requires learning to speak multiple languages of power convincingly." And as Collins (2012: 215) further recognizes, the matrix of oppression serves to reveal just how extensive are these interconnected structures and practices of power and inequality in our society:

"Our task is immense. We must first recognize race, class, and gender as interlocking categories of analysis that together cultivate profound differences in our personal biographies. But then we must transcend these very differences by conceptualizing race, class, and gender to create new categories of connection."

Like any other tradition of social theory, intersectionality has generated its own internal debates and disagreements. One of the central disputes is over whether the structures and dimensions of oppression outlined in the theory may sometimes be seen as separable or autonomous, or whether they must always be seen as interlocking and coalescing structures. This dispute has led one theorist (Weldon 2006) to distinguish between what she calls the "additive" versus the "multiplicative" effects of the vectors of oppression. Rather than polarize this discussion, Weldon suggests that, in all specific cases, the conclusion as to whether different vectors of oppression can function autonomously or whether they are always co-dependent can only be reached on the basis of empirical research, rather than through ideology. Similarly, another theorist (Yuval-Davis 2006: 198) proposes four levels of analysis that may be explored when analyzing specific vectors of oppression: "Social divisions have organizational, intersubjective, experiential and representational forms and this affects the ways we theorize the connections between the different levels." Other debates will doubtless emerge among intersectionality theorists as the living legacy of the work continues to grow. The creativity and social significance of their work is already celebrated among contemporary social theorists. Among their many contributions, they have broadened the conceptual and methodological bases of feminist theory and research; they have extended their structural analysis of oppression and privilege beyond the postmodernist fixation on "identity"; and they have helped to advance the feminist movement beyond its earlier false universalism towards greater diversity and inclusivity.

LGBTQ STUDIES

The emergence of LGBTQ studies took place during the 1970s with the publication of several important works of gay history. Initially inspired by other interdisciplinary departments and similar identity-based academic fields, such as women's studies, African American studies and Indigenous studies, LGBTQ studies also made its way into literature departments, where the emphasis was on literary theory. Queer theory developed later, challenging the "socially constructed" categories of sexual identity.

LGBTQ studies has introduced rich new critical theory around the issue of homosexuality and has ensured that the experiences and perspectives of the LGBTQ community are now recognized in the discourses of the humanities and the social sciences. Emerging as an offshoot of the women's movement, the LGBTQ movement acquired an independence and autonomy that led to the development of its own standpoint perspectives. In recent years, some important developments have taken place within the theoretical perspectives of the LGBTQ community. The advent of LGBTQ studies also coincided with the mounting strength and self-assurance of the LGBTQ community as a powerful political constituency and active social movement. The growth of LGBTQ studies, especially in the area of social and cultural theory, has led to the emergence of distinctive LGBTQ perspectives that articulate the gay experience and express the character of the gay/trans identities and discourses in contemporary society.

The rise of LGBTQ perspectives followed closely in the footsteps of the feminist perspective that emerged from the women's liberation movement of the 1960s. Unlike the feminist perspective, however, the LGBTQ standpoint also emphasizes the evolution of the gay identity and contests and critiques hegemonic heteronormative, heterosexist and homophobic discourses that traditionally stigmatized and demonized the gay lifestyle as unnatural, immoral, deviant, sinful or perverse.

Some LGBTQ writers (Boswell 1994; Crompton 2003) have chosen to emphasize the "natural" character of gay identities. In practice, this has led some gay theorists and activists to assert the biological basis of gay identity: individuals are born gay and do not choose to be gay. This strong assertion of the inherent distinctiveness of the gay identity has recently come under attack from other gay theorists who do not share this viewpoint. For poststructuralist and postmodern theorists, any assertion of inherent (biological) distinctiveness of the gay identity is dismissed as unacceptable "essentialism." The gay identity, for poststructuralists, is always a product of discourse rather than of genes. Every individual is signified through many different intersecting discourses and, thereby, possesses many different intersecting identities, none of which can be said to be fixed, stable, quintessential or exclusive. This clash of viewpoints has, in recent years, opened a division among LGBTQ social theorists, a division that we could characterize as "gay essentialism" versus "gay constructivism." One author (Halley 1994) has defined these two distinct perspectives in the following terms: "Pro-gay essentialism posits that (homo) sexuality is fixed, immutable, and definitional; thus, it should be protected from discrimination…. Pro-gay constructivism posits that (homo) sexual orientations are mutable, once acquired at some point across the lifespan, recognized personally at some moment of choice, or recognized culturally across historical periods, and that social policy should not impede these variations."

In other words, for the essentialist, the gay identity is seen by its defenders and by its detractors as a fixed, probably genetic and permanent characteristic of the individual which remains an unchanging part of their biological inheritance; that is, some people are "born" gay. At the same time, however — like standpoint theory — we can distinguish "strong essentialism" from a weaker or more "strategic" version of gay essentialism. On the other hand, for the constructivist, the gay identity and indeed all gender identities are seen as fluid, malleable and socially constructed identities which can undergo further change and adaptation throughout the lifespan of the individual (Woodson 2012). This mutable and more playful definition of gender identity has been strongly influenced by poststructuralist theory, which sees all identities as discursively constructed and constantly changeable. This version of gay constructivism is commonly known as queer theory.

Thus, traditional LGBTQ essentialists have insisted on the uniqueness and inherent distinctiveness of the gay identity, and indeed the existence of an essential gay identity has usually been seen as an indispensable condition for collective action in the politics of gay liberation. But on the other hand, gay poststructuralist theorists — or queer theorists — not only insist on the instability, indeterminacy and fluidity of the gay identity, but on the instability, indeterminacy and fluidity of *all* identities, whether gay, straight, bisexual, intersex or transgender. The project for gay poststructuralists, therefore, is not only to open up a space for the expression of a distinctive gay identity, but rather for the expression of a gay identity in everyone. In other words, the theoretical project of the new gay theorists is to challenge the binary "heteronormative discourses" that require all individuals to classify and restrict themselves to be either exclusively "masculine" or exclusively "feminine." This is the project of queer theory, and this is how queer theory differs and departs from traditional gay essentialist theory.

QUEER THEORY

The use of the term "queer" has undergone some important changes over the past several decades. Now, "queer" can be used as an adjective, as a noun and even as a verb. Although this term originated as an abusive label to degrade and denigrate "non-straight," gay, lesbian and transgendered individuals, it has acquired a new, more acceptable meaning — referring both to the position and to the perspective of alternative sexual identities and sexual performances. In a word, "queer" introduces us to a more "homocentric" view of our shared social world.

Today, queer theory and queer perspectives do much more than simply describe how different members of the queer community live or perceive and act within society. Queer theory involves a wholesale questioning and reframing of our taken-for-granted social reality and a recalibration of our basic assumptions from the perspectives of those who inhabit the margins and the boundaries of our sociosexual world. Besides deconstructing the texts, discourses, identities and performances of the *heteronormative* world from a homocentric perspective, queer theory also focuses on more general issues of sexual power, inequality, hierarchy and exclusion. In this respect, queer theory reveals its origins as a direct descendant of third wave feminism, intersectionality theory and, most evidently, standpoint theory. In addition, queer theory owes much of its methodology to poststructuralist dconstructionism and much of its political agenda to the influence of critical theory. Beyond these influences, however, it has emerged as a distinct and independent perspective with a unique homocentric view of the world.

In general terms, we can identify several characteristics of queer theory that have contributed to the development of contemporary social theory; among these, several stand out for special mention and attention.

1. Queer theory has developed its own distinctive methods of analysis and representation. These methods are deeply skeptical of the taken-for-granted, i.e., the internalized and normalized, sexual appearances and performances of heteronormative social reality. The methods of queer theory are transgressive and subversive of routinized heteronormative beliefs and practices.
2. Queer theory is committed to the study of society from the outside, from the margins and from the boundaries. Queer theory shares this "underdog" perspective with other standpoint theories; how-

ever, it emphasizes the subversive deconstruction of all fixed and stable conceptions of identity.

3. Queer theory represents the "constructivist" perspective on gay gender identity, committed to recognition of the instability and fluidity of all personal identities and to emphasizing the contingency and performativity of these identities.

4. Queer theory is also closely connected to queer praxis. There is a strong "emancipatory agenda" to queer theory; it is committed to the empowerment of the powerless and to ending the culture of silence among "subaltern" communities. For this reason, we may say that queer theory offers us a "critical pedagogy" (see Luhmann 1998).

The theoretical basis for the critique of hegemonic heterosexualism can be traced back, in part, to the psychoanalytic work of Freud (*Three Essays on the Theory of Sexuality*, 1905) and also to the work of the poststructuralist psychoanalytic theorists (Jacques Lacan, Gilles Deleuze and Felix Guattari). In his writings on the early psychosexual stages of childhood development (oral, anal and phallic), Freud proposed that the earliest stages are characterized by a state of "polymorphous perversity." (His use of the term "perversity" was a descriptive rather than a judgemental or a normative term; "perversity" for Freud actually meant "diversity" not "depravity.") Polymorphous perversity, for Freud, meant that the very young child, up until the age of around five years, seeks sexual gratification from a number of diverse sources, primarily the mother's breast and the child's own body. During this stage of polymorphous perversity, the sexual, or libidinal, drive of the child is unsocialized and unregulated by societal norms and sexual conventions. Thus, the child, as the primal human being, remains potentially open to various and diverse (i.e., polymorphous) forms of sexual gratification through heterosexual, homosexual, autosexual and incestuous stimulation. It is only with the increasing social demand to abandon "deviant" or "perverse" sexual practices (in the usual heteronormative meanings of these terms), that heterosexuality becomes "normalized" and "naturalized" in the child — in preparation for later adult reproduction. In other words, the playful sexual freedom of the child to experiment with diverse forms of sexuality is eventually restricted to a single socially sanctioned form, i.e., genital heterosexuality.

Later psychoanalytic theorists, along with contemporary queer theorists, have reinterpreted the significance of this early "repression" of childhood sexual diversity. Many of these theorists see the repression of the early potential for sexual diversity and experimentation as a traumatic, almost catastrophic, "loss," in which the playful expression of different sexual identities is forever foreclosed. In this sense, the repression of the primal desires of the "Id" and the sublimation of these desires into the "Ego" is seen by queer theorists as a tragic loss of human potential and as a denial of our inherent sexual freedom and fuller humanity. For Judith Butler, this early existential loss carries with it a long-term legacy of melancholia and sadness.

The politics of queer theory is best described as a project of personal and societal sexual emancipation. For queer theorists, the repressive heteronormative sexual ideology imposed on each of us by contemporary Western societies — a mutually exclusive binary identity of masculine: feminine — is both unnatural and unreasonable. According to queer theorists, we live under a particularly repressive sexual regime, one which denies the fluidity of our gender identities and the diversity of our sexual desires. Unlike many other cultures that have, at different times and in different places, tolerated and even celebrated diverse forms of sexual inversion, sexual androgyny and homophilia, our culture has remained a captive to its recent puritanical past.

Under the influence of the French poststructuralist Michel Foucault, queer theorists have referenced numerous historical and cultural examples of institutionalized homophilia and homosexuality, ranging from "berdache," Two-Spirit people and Amazons among the Indigenous Peoples in North and South America, to the tolerance of homosexuality in classical Greece and Rome, and in many other areas of the world, including the Siberian Arctic, Polynesia, India, Southeast and East Asia, Africa and the Middle East (see Parkinson 2013). Today, queer theorists view what they perceive as the rigidly repressive heterosexism of Western societies as abnormal, even "deviant," inasmuch as this homophobic culture denies our inherent potential to perform multiple gender identities and to explore hitherto undiscovered aspects of our fuller humanity.

Judith Butler

Judith Butler is one of the more complex contemporary social theorists. Although she is normally credited as the founder and foremost exponent of queer theory, she has several other strings to her bow. Among other things, Butler pioneered the use of deconstructive techniques in her analyses of sex and gender studies. But one of her most significant accomplishments has been to introduce the topic of the "body" into the discourse of social theory. In these and other ways, Butler is regarded as one of the most original and innovative social theorists writing today.

As a poststructuralist theorist, Butler believes that none of us has knowledge of, or access to, any independent external reality that lies outside the discourses that we use to construct our "realities." The only reality we can ever know is that which is produced, and constantly reproduced, in our discourses and texts and through our recurrent social practices. Life begins and ends for all of us in discourse and with the social practices that sustain and perpetuate this discourse. This is the philosophical starting point for the rest of her work on gender, sexuality, epistemology and ontology.

Some feminists of the second wave and more from the third wave began to distinguish between the concept of "sex" as a biologically determined status based on reproductive organs and the concept of "gender" as a socially constructed status. For Butler, however, both sex and gender are identities, rather than statuses, that are "inscribed" through discourse; neither identity exists independently of the discourse and its corresponding discursive practice which produce and reproduce an identity. The way in which the discourse of sex is "materialized" is through the practices and "performances" that "inscribe" the conventions of the discourse onto the body. In other words, within any culture, the body is a blank biological slate upon which the discourses are inscribed.

In some societies, the sexual discourse of the culture may be inscribed through male and female circumcision or through female genital mutilation; while in other cultures it happens through male scarification, tattoos, body piercing or other forms of ritual or decorative body art. In Western culture, male and female bodies are coded differently and are normally subject to strict and mutually exclusive conventions, especially in regard to the clothing, adornment and public presentation of these discursively "sexed" bodies. This discursive inscription of sexuality onto the body is a much deeper and more fundamental process than the conscious presentation, or performance, of a male or female gendered "self."

Butler sharply distinguishes her concept of "performativity" from Erving Goffman's dramaturgical concept of "performance." Whereas the early Goffman saw the dramaturgical performance of a gendered self as driven by an autonomous social actor, Butler sees the performativity of sex as determined by a hegemonic discourse that inscribes its conventions onto the body through a cultural template developed in many previous iterations. In this respect, Butler suggests that we are all products of the historical and cultural discourses into which we are born. The ways in which we think and act, our "identity," our "self," our relationship to others and our sense of what is possible and what is permissible are all parts of a "discursive regime" that has preceded us and will undoubtedly outlive us. To think otherwise — to assume that we, as individual social actors, are authors of our own life-scripts or stage managers of our own performances — is, according to Butler, nothing more than a "presentist conceit" (1993: 228). We are not the voluntarist authors of our own destiny; we are the products of discourse and of the cultural and historical practices that "materialize" these discourses.

Where does the deconstructive analysis of Butler's version of queer theory ultimately lead us? The politics of queer theory is much more than a simple expression of a gay standpoint. Queer theory has moved beyond the confines of LGBTQ standpoint theory to a theory and politics of total sexual liberation. Butler believes that in any open society, individuals should be free to choose their sexualities, to move between sexualities and to embrace diverse sexualities. She proposes, in a reconceptualization of Freud, that we should all be free to explore the repressed potential sexual identities and energies that we lost in early childhood but which can be recovered through a politics of sexual liberation.

This celebration of sexual freedom was eloquently expressed by another queer theorist, Eve Kosofsky Sedgwick, who wrote: "Queer is a continuing moment, movement, motive — recurrent, eddying, troublant." She continues that it is "the open mesh of possibilities, gaps, overlaps, dissonances and resonances, lapses and excesses of meaning when the constituent elements of anyone's gender, of anyone's sexuality aren't made (or can't be made) to signify monolithically" (quoted in Hanman 2013). In a fully liberated society, an individual's sex can become the site of discursive choice, rather than a biologically determined status. In Butler's liberated world, there is room for a multiplicity of sexual identities — homosexual, trans, bisexual, intersexed — as well as heterosexuals. To open our social and political systems to the possibilities of pansexuality or polysexuality is, for Butler, perhaps the most important way to celebrate diversity and difference as characteristics of a more fully humanized society.

Notwithstanding her heroic status as the originator of queer theory and as a major influence on contemporary gender studies, Butler's work has not escaped criticism. For some socialist feminists, such as Nancy Fraser, Butler's often impenetrable and abstract theoretical language places her work beyond the reach of ordinary people — including other feminists and other feminist scholars. Butler has often been reproached and criticized for her alleged elitism and obscurantism: her work is very difficult and sometimes impossible to understand. Nancy Fraser made her criticisms in a famous exchange between the two theorists. Fraser (1995) contends that Butler's focus on performativity distances her from "everyday ways of talking and thinking about ourselves.... Why should we use such a self-distancing idiom?"

Other political feminists have also criticized Butler's assertion that gender identity is something that is "performed" rather than inherent in the body of the individual. These critics reject what they interpret as the linguistic, or the discursive "reductionism," of Butler's theory of gender identity. Susan Bordo complains that Butler reduces gender wholly to language, thereby overlooking the fact that the body is a major aspect of any gender identity. According to Bordo, in Butler's poststructuralist enthusiasm to avoid essentializing gender identity, she has been blind to the most obvious and inescapable aspect of gender — the body (Hekman 1998). Another vocal feminist critic of Butler's performative conception of gender identity is Martha Nussbaum (1999), who argues that Butler misunderstands philosopher J.L. Austin's concept of a performative utterance. Nussbaum also claims that Butler's reduction of gender identity to the inscriptions of discourse and text robs Butler's female subject identity of any autonomy or capacity for independent action — and resistance. A similar concern has been raised by Aijaz Ahmad of the subaltern studies group, who argues that Butler's poststructuralist/postmodernist conception of a split, fragmented and unstable subject dissolves any conception of a real human subject identity that would be capable of the autonomy and independent action — necessary for the postcolonial subject to resist the strategies of colonial and neocolonial power (Doncu 2017). This brief summary of Judith Butler's key concepts and main theoretical insights provides a general overview of some of her major contributions to the rise of queer theory and has tried to illustrate the contemporary significance of this important branch of standpoint theory.

CRACKS AND FISSURES IN GENDER STUDIES

Looking back at the recent evolution of the feminist and gender movements over the past half century, it is clear that the status of women and of other sexual and gender minorities has improved in many sectors of Western society. At the same time, feminist and gender theories are having internal debates and disagreements, which is common in theory across the social sciences. One contemporary theorist observes:

> The fragmentation of contemporary feminism bears ample witness to the impossibility of constructing modern feminism as a simple unity in the present or of arriving at a shared feminist definition of feminism. Such differing explanations, such a variety of emphases in practical campaigns, such widely varying interpretations of their results have emerged, that it now makes more sense to speak of a plurality of feminisms than of one. (Delmar 1986: 9)

This is nothing new. For years, commentators have reviewed a series of "unhappy marriages" within the feminist tradition as theorists with different and often opposed perspectives have struggled for recognition and respect within the discourse of feminism (see, for example, Hartman 1981; Calhoun 2003; Mann 2013). Sometimes the source of theoretical conflict has been classically political, as in the case of Marxist versus liberal and radical feminists of the second wave. At other times, the conflict has been over the priority that should be given to different forms of oppression: whether "straight" sexism should be prioritized over homophobia or transphobia. However, intersectionality has helped feminists analyze these oppressions differently, so that they are no longer in competition for attention and political action but are understood in terms of axes of oppression that need to be fought holistically.

Current conflicts are over epistemology: whether the poststructuralist and postmodernist agenda of diversity, deconstruction and decentring is compatible with the overwhelming political need to develop a theory and practice of solidarity and unity, especially in the face of the present political crisis in gender relations. The primary division that runs through contemporary feminist and gender theory is the split between the late modernist traditions of intersectionality and standpoint theories on the one hand, and the postmodernist tradition of poststructuralism on the other. And although intersectionality and standpoint theories have each been influenced by some aspects of poststructuralism, both remain opposed to some of the more radical theoretical and political implications of postmodernism and poststructuralism. What then, are some of the main disagreements between late modernist and postmodernist gender theories?

Identity: although most late modernist theories, like standpoint and intersectionality theories, reject the earlier metanarratives of first and second wave feminism, they remain committed to some version of a collective subject identity, such as Black women, Indigenous women, lesbians, working-class women etc. (Epstein 1995; Gitlin 1995). At the same time, these theories see these collective, or generic, identities as intersecting identities within a hierarchical matrix of domination/oppression. Thus, a Black Muslim lesbian woman would be subject to multiple disadvantages of racism, homophobia and Islamophobia, whereas a white American male doctor would enjoy the multiple advantages of race, gender and class.

Poststructuralists, on the other hand, are opposed to the "essentialization" of identity, especially collective identity. For them, the collective, or generic, identity of Black women (or any other category of women) can be infinitely deconstructed into more individual identities: Black immigrant women, Black lesbian women, Black working-class women and so on. Moreover, each of these identities can be further deconstructed: Black lesbian women into Black lesbian young women and Black lesbian old women and so on. In other words, poststructuralism is hostile to the idea of collective, or generic, identity, while standpoint and intersectionality theorists believe that "strategic essentialism" is necessary for the representation and mobilization of women into social movements in order to bring about necessary reforms and social change.

Theoretical practice: This disagreement over the conceptual status of gender identities also reveals a number of other differences between late modernist and postmodernist versions of contemporary feminist theory. Whereas late modernist theories, like standpoint and intersectionality, remain committed to a particular form of collectivism, postmodernism remains radically individualist in its deconstructivist methodology. And although late modernists have abandoned the metanarratives of an earlier age, they continue to assert the objectivity of their knowledge claims, at least within the local contexts, or standpoints, under study. Postmodernists, on the other hand, disavow all claims to "objectivity" and remain, for all intents and purposes, radical relativists. The split between these different versions of contemporary feminist theory, which is also apparent in LGBTQ identity theories, is real and based upon different epistemological, ideological and political agendas. For one writer (Bryson 2004) the way forward beyond the current split between late modernist and postmodernist theories is for feminists to pursue a policy of "theoretical pluralism." Rather than jettison either modernist or postmodernist feminist perspectives of history and society, Bryson suggests that no single perspective has a monopoly over valid or useful knowledge. In place of the "science wars" that have been fought over "truth" and "meaning," Bryson advocates, at least for now, a strategy of theoretical and methodological pluralism.

Today, the state of gender relations in many Western societies appears cloudy and even bleak, and the prospects for further progress remain uncertain. This is a challenging time for the feminist movement. Although significant advances have been made by women and the LGBTQ community in many places, including Canada, some of this progress may yet be overturned and reversed by the return of far-right nationalism, religious fundamentalism and reactionary populism, which are hostile to many aspects of feminist activism and LGBTQ liberation. Unfortunately, these reversals may also be seen in other countries where right-wing populist parties have emerged, for example, France, Germany and the Netherlands, or where far-right governments have been elected, e.g., Hungary, Poland, the Czech Republic and Turkey, with others on the horizon (Flemming, Gilloz, and Hairy 2017). One observer of this rising trend notes:

> Increasingly visible populist right and far right movements try to center white, heterosexual hegemonic masculinities and specific versions of femininities proclaimed to be "traditional" as protecting the future of the nation.... these right-wing discourses project a view of the homely nation into the past. This golden past of social and cultural cohesion around a unified national identity, they argue, was produced and held together by a traditional version of the family ... Such an understanding matters, not only as an intellectual project, but also to bring together social and political struggles against far-right, right-wing populist and conservative

politics targeting gender equality, feminisms, multicultural policies and migrants' rights. (Erel 2017)

The writing is on the wall: the need for political unity and solidarity among women and other sexual and gender minorities has never been greater.

References

Accapadi, M.M. 2007. "When White Women Cry: How White Women's Tears Oppress Women of Color." *College Student Affairs Journal* 26, 2.

Akemi, Romina, and Bree Busk. 2016. *Breaking the Waves: Challenging the Liberal Tendency Within Anarchist Feminism.* <https://theanarchistlibrary.org/library/romina-akemi-and-bree-busk-breaking-the-waves-challenging-the-liberal-tendency-within-anarchist.pdf>.

Baumgardner, Jennifer, and Amy Richards. 2000. *Manifesta: Young Women, Feminism, and the Future.* New York: Farrar, Straus and Giroux.

Berger, Melody (ed.). 2006. *We Don't Need Another Wave: Dispatches from the Next Feminist Generation.* New York: Seal Press.

Borch-Jacobsen, Mikkel. 2001. "Little Brother, Little Sister." In *London Review of Books*, 23, 10 (24 May): 15–17.

Boswell, John. 1994. *Same-Sex Unions in Premodern Europe.* New York: Vintage Books.

Brodribb, S. 1993. *Nothing Mat(t)ers: A Feminist Critique of Postmodernism.* Toronto: James Lorimer.

Bryson, Valerie. 2003. *Feminist Political Theory: Introduction,* 2nd ed. Basingstoke: Palgrave Macmillan.

___. 2004. "Marxism and Feminism: Can the 'Unhappy Marriage' Be Saved?" *Journal of Political Ideologies,* 9, 1.

Butler, Judith. 1993. *Bodies that Matter: On the Discursive Limits of "Sex."* Routledge.

Calhoun, Cheshire. 2003. "Separating Lesbian Theory from Feminist Theory." In Carole McCann and Seung-Kyung Kim (eds.), *Feminist Theory Reader: Local and Global Perspectives.* New York: Routledge.

Campbell, Marie. 2003. "Dorothy Smith and Knowing the World We Live In." *Journal of Sociology & Social Welfare,* 30, 1: 17.

Collins, Patricia Hill. 2000. *Black Feminist Thought: Knowledge, Consciousness, and the Politics of Empowerment.* New York: Routledge.

___. 2012. *On Intellectual Activism.* Philadelphia: Temple University Press.

Crenshaw, Kimberlé. 1989. "Demarginalizing the Intersection of Race and Sex: A Black Feminist Critique of Antidiscrimination Doctrine, Feminist Theory and Antiracist Politics." *University of Chicago Legal Forum,* 1989, Article 8. <https://chicagounbound.uchicago.edu/uclf/vol1989/iss1/8>.

___. 2017. "Kimberlé Crenshaw on Intersectionality, More than Two Decades Later." *Columbia Law School* (June 8). <https://www.law.columbia.edu/pt-br/news/2017/06/kimberle-crenshaw-intersectionality>.

Crompton, Louis. 2003. *Homosexuality and Civilization.* Cambridge, MA: Harvard University Press.

Delmar, Rosalind. 1986. "What Is Feminism?" In Juliet Mitchell and Ann Oakley (eds.), *What Is Feminism?* New York: Pantheon Books

DiAngelo, R. 2011. "White Fragility." *International Journal of Critical Pedagogy* 3, 3.

Dicker, Rory. 2008. *A History of U.S. Feminisms.* Berkeley, CA: Seal Press.

Doncu, Roxana Elena. 2017. "Feminist Theories of Subjectivity: Judith Butler and Julia Kristeva." *Journal of Romanian Literary Studies,* 10: 332–336.

Epstein, Barbara. 1995. "Why Post-Structuralism Is a Dead End for Progressive Thought." *Socialist Review,* 25, 2 (Spring): 83.

Erel, Umut. 2017. "Saving and Reproducing the Nation: Struggles Around Right-Wing Politics of Social Reproduction, Gender and Race in Austerity Europe." *Women's Studies International Forum,* 68 (May/June): 173–182. <https://doi.org/10.1016/j. wsif.2017.11.003>.

Firestone, S. 1971. *The Dialectic of Sex: The Case for Feminist Revolution.* New York: Bantam Books.

Flemming, Matilda, Oriane Gilloz, and Nima Hairy. 2017. "Getting to Know You: Mapping the Anti-Feminist Face of Right-Wing Populism in Europe." *Open Democracy,* 8 May. <https://www.opendemocracy.net/can-europe-make-it/matilda-flemming/ mapping-anti-feminist-face-of-right-wing-populism-in-europe>.

Fraser, Nancy. 1995. "False Antitheses." In Seyla Benhabib, Judith Butler, Drucilla Cornell and Nancy Fraser (eds.), *Feminist Contentions: A Philosophical Exchange.* Routledge.

Freud, Sigmund. 1905. *Three Essays on the Theory of Sexuality.* <http://icpla.edu/ wp-content/uploads/2017/11/Freud-S-Three-Essays-on-the-Theory-of-Sexuality. pdf>.

Gilligan, C. 1982. *In a Different Voice: Psychological Theory and Women's Development.* Cambridge, MA: Harvard University Press.

Gitlin, T. 1995. *The Twilight of Common Dreams Why America Is Wracked by Culture Wars.* New York: Henry Holt.

Halley J.E. 1994. "Sexual Orientation and the Politics of Biology: A Critique of the Argument from Immutability." *Stanford Law Review,* 46, 3: 503–568.

Hanman, Natalie. 2013. "Eve Kosofsky Sedgwick and Judith Butler Showed Me the Transformative Power of the Word 'Queer.'" *The Guardian,* 22 Aug. <https://www.theguardian.com/commentisfree/2013/aug/22/ judith-butler-eve-sedgwick-queer>.

Harding, Sandra. 1991. *Whose Science/ Whose Knowledge?* Milton Keynes: Open University Press.

___. 1993. "Reinventing Ourselves as Other: More New Agents of History and Knowledge." In Linda S. Kauffman (ed.), *American Feminist Thought at Century's End.* Cambridge, MA, Blackwell.

___. 1995. "'Strong Objectivity': A Response to the New Objectivity Question." *Synthese,* 104, 3, Feminism and Science (Sep.): 331–349.

___ (ed.). 2004. *The Feminist Standpoint Theory Reader: Intellectual and Political Controversies.* New York: Routledge.

Hartmann, Heidi. 1981. "The Unhappy Marriage of Marxism and Feminism: Towards a More Progressive Union." In Sargent, Lydia (ed.). *Women and Revolution: A Discussion Of The Unhappy Marriage of Marxism and Feminism.* South End Press

Political Controversies Series. Boston: South End Press.

Hekman, Susan. 1998. "Material Bodies." In Donn Welton (ed.), *Body and Flesh: A Philosophical Reader*. Blackwell Publishing.

Hewitt, Nancy (ed.). 2010. *No Permanent Waves: Recasting Feminism*. New Brunswick, NJ: Rutgers.

Heywood, L., and J. Drake. 2004. "It's All About the Benjamins: Economic Determinants of Third Wave Feminism in the US" in S. Gillis et al. (eds), *Third Wave Feminism*. Basingstoke: Palgrave Macmillan.

hooks, bell. 1984. *Feminist Theory from Margin to Center*. Boston: South End Press.

Jacob, Krista, and Adela C. Licona. 2005. "*Writing the Tools, Tactics, and Tensions of Feminisms and Feminist Time and Place.*" NWSA Journal.

Jacobs, M. 2010. "Getting Out of a Rut: Decolonizing Western Women's History." *Pacific Historical Review*, 79, 4: 585–604.

Labaton, Vivien, and Dawn Lundy Martin (eds.). 2004. *The Fire This Time: Young Activists and the New Feminism*. New York: Anchor Books.

Lacan, J. 1978. *The Four Fundamental Concepts of Psychoanalysis*. New York: W.W. Norton.

Laughlin, K., J. Gallagher, D. Cobble, E. Boris, P. Nadasen, S. Gilmore and L. Zarnow. 2010. "Is It Time to Jump Ship? Historians Rethink the Waves Metaphor." *Feminist Formations*, 22, 1: 76–135.

Luhmann, S. 1998. "Queering/Querying Pedagogy or, Pedagogy Is Pretty Queer Thing." In W. Pinar (ed.), *Queer Theory in Education*. Hillsdale: NJ Lawrence Erlbaum.

Lyotard, J-F. 1984. *The Postmodern Condition: A Report on Knowledge*. Minneapolis: University of Minnesota Press.

Mack-Canty, Colleen. 2005. "Third Wave Feminism and Ecofeminism: Reweaving the Nature/Culture Duality." In Jo Reger, ed. *Different Wavelengths: Studies of the Contemporary Women's Movement*. New York: Routledge.

Mann, Susan A. 2013. "Third Wave Feminism's Unhappy Marriage of Poststructuralism and Intersectionality Theory." *Journal of Feminist Scholarship*, 4 (Spring): 54–73. <https://digitalcommons.uri.edu/jfs/vol4/iss4/5>.

McCauley, Mary Carole. 2016. "Intersectionality Concerns Transcend Straight, White Feminism." *The Baltimore Sun*, 27 September. <https://www.baltimoresun.com/features/women-to-watch/bal-intersectionality-baltimore-feminism-20160926-story.html>.

McLaren, Margaret A. (ed). 2017. *Decolonizing Feminism: Transnational Feminism and Globalization*. Rowman & Littlefield International.

Mohanty, Chandra Talpade. 1993. "Under Western Eyes." In Chandra Talpade Mohanty, Anne Russo and Lourdes Torres (eds.), *Third World Women and the Politics of Feminism*. Bloomington: Indiana University Press.

___. 2003. *Feminism without Borders: Decolonizing Theory, Practicing Solidarity*. Durham, NC: Duke University Press.

Morgan, Robin. 1996. "Light Bulbs, Radishes and the Politics of the 21st Century." In Diane Bell and Klein, Renate (eds.), *Radically Speaking: Feminism Reclaimed*. Chicago: Spinifex Press.

Nader, L. 1969. "Up the Anthropologist: Perspectives Gained from 'Studying Up.'" In D. Hymes (ed.), *Reinventing Anthropology*. New York: Random House.

Nussbaum, Martha. 1999. "The Professor of Parody." In *The New Republic Online*, 22 Feb. <http://faculty.georgetown.edu/irvinem/theory/Nussbaum-Butler-Critique-NR-2-99.pdf>.

O'Brien, M. 1981. *The Politics of Reproduction*. London: Routledge and Kegan Paul.

Ortega, M. 2006. Being Lovingly, Knowingly Ignorant: White feminism and Women of Color. *Hypatia: A Journal of Feminist Philosophy* 21, 3: 56–74.

Paglia, Camille. 2017. *Free Women, Free Men: Sex, Gender, and Feminism*. Pantheon.

___. 2018. *Provocations: Collected Essays*. Pantheon.

Parkinson, R.B. 2013. *A Little Gay History: Desire and Diversity Across the World*. London: British Museum Press and New York: University of Columbia Press.

Parpart, Jane. 1993. "Who Is the 'Other'? A Postmodern Feminist Critique of Women and Development Theory and Practice." *Development and Change*, 24, 3 (July): 439–464.

Power, Nina. 2009. *One Dimensional Woman*. Zero Books.

Reger, Jo (ed.). 2005. *Different Wavelengths: Studies of the Contemporary Women's Movement*. New York: Routledge.

Rich, Adrienne. 1977. *Of Woman Born: Motherhood as Experience and Institution*. London: Virago.

___. 2003 [1980]. "Compulsory Heterosexuality and Lesbian Existence." *Journal of Women's History*, 15, 3 (Autumn): 11–48.

Rowbotham, S. 2000. *Promise of a Dream: Remembering the Sixties*. London: Penguin Books.

Sheinin, Dave, Krissah Thompson, Soraya Nadia McDonald and Scott Clement. 2016. "New Wave Feminism: Betty Friedan to Beyoncé: Today's Generation Embraces Feminism on Its Own Terms." *Washington Post*, January 27. <https://www.washingtonpost.com/national/feminism/betty-friedan-to-beyonce-todays-generation-embraces-feminism-on-its-own-terms/2016/01/27/ab480e74-8e19-11e5-ae1f-af46b7df8483_story.html?utm_term=.a348ec6efd24>.

Smith, Dorothy. 1987. *The Everyday World as Problematic: A Feminist Sociology*. Toronto: University of Toronto Press.

___. 1990. *Texts, Facts and Femininity: Exploring the Relations of Ruling*. Routledge.

Walker, Rebecca (ed.). 1995. *To Be Real: Telling the Truth and Changing the Face of Feminism*. New York: Anchor Books.

Weldon, S. 2006. "The Structure of Intersectionality: A Comparative Politics of Gender." *Politics & Gender*, 2, 2: 235–248.

Williams, Monnica T. 2019 .*How White Feminists Oppress Black Women: When Feminism Functions as White Supremacy*, Jan. 1. <https://chacruna.net/how-white-feminists-oppress-black-women-when-feminism-functions-as-white-supremacy/>.

Willis, Ellen. 1984. "Radical Feminism and Feminist Radicalism." *Social Text*, 9/10—The 60's without Apology (9/10): 91–118.

Woodson, James C. 2012. "I Love You with All My Brain: Laying Aside the Intellectually Dull Sword of Biological Determinism." *Socio-affective Neuroscience & Psychology*, 2: 17334, 15 Mar. <https://www.ncbi.nlm.nih.gov/pmc/articles/PMC3960069/>.

Yuval-Davis, Nira. 2006. "Intersectionality and Feminist Politics." *European Journal of Women's Studies*, 13, 3: 193–209.

CHAPTER 10

THEORIZING OUR COLONIAL HISTORIES

Indigenous Knowledge and Social Thought

COLONIZATION AND KNOWLEDGE

Over the past few years, the voices of Indigenous Peoples have begun to be heard throughout the halls of academia, as well as in the parliament buildings, legislative assemblies, government offices, law courts, health-care agencies and education institutions. Although their growing visibility and audibility in movements such as Idle No More and in memorial marches for the many missing and murdered Indigenous women and girls ("Stolen Sisters") has undoubtedly mirrored the struggles of racial, ethnic, class, gender and sexual grassroots social movements — such as Black Lives Matter, Occupy, #MeToo, Times Up etc. — the identities and challenges of Indigenous Peoples are in many ways unique and independent of those of other minority groups.

There can be no doubt that Indigenous Peoples continue to be severely disadvantaged in terms of their social and economic status, health and general welfare, political and legal status and acceptance within the majority Canadian culture. The tremendous disparities that continue to separate the standards of living and life opportunities of Indigenous Peoples from those of others in Canada are nothing short of a national disgrace and a fundamental human rights issue. Although the problems of racial prejudice and discrimination experienced by First Nations, Metis and Inuit Peoples may, in some respects, be likened to examples of racial intolerance historically directed against other non-white communities in Canada, the case of Indigenous Peoples is unique for a number of reasons. Unlike visible minority groups who entered Canada as immigrants, Indigenous Peoples, as the term implies, are the original inhabitants of this land and have a distinct legal and political position and a unique relationship with the Canadian state.

For thousands of years, Indigenous Peoples have maintained their social and political organizations, knowledge systems and traditional spiritual practices. European settlers tried to undermine and suppress these systems of organization, culture, politics and knowledge, and expropriated and stole Indigenous land. At the same time, the history of colonization is a history of Indigenous resistance and rebellion against the settler colonial state and the culture of occupation. In Canada, this history includes such major events as the 1885 North-West resistance, a five-month insurgency against the Dominion of Canada government, fought mainly by Métis militants and their Indigenous allies in what is now Saskatchewan and Alberta. Another example is the 1990 Oka crisis. This was a seventy-eight-day armed standoff between the Mohawk Nation of Kanesatake, the Quebec provincial police and the Canadian military near the town of Oka, Quebec. The Mohawk Nation was defending their sacred ancestral lands against developers planning to convert this land into a golf course. More recently, Idle no More, which began in 2013 as a mass mobilization against the repressive policies of former Canadian Conservative prime minister Stephen Harper, has developed into a major progressive movement for sovereignty, social justice and Indigenous rights.

In most significant respects, Indigenous Peoples continue to exist at the bottom of the social ladder, at the very base of the vertical mosaic. According to available statistical data, Indigenous Peoples are still denied equality of access to such basic resources as education, employment, housing, health care and self-representation within the judicial system. Moreover, the widespread poverty of many Indigenous communities, both on reserves and in urban areas, has tended to remain invisible to most non-Indigenous Canadians. Unfortunately, the greatest public attention has been paid to the *symptoms* rather than the *causes* of these social problems. Many scholars have noted the propensity of the colonizer to racially stereotype the colonized, and as Raewyn Connell (2007: 97) illustrates, "Colonizers' contempt for the colonized is a common feature of imperialism. North American Indigenous Peoples were slandered as treacherous, Bengalis as effeminate, Chinese as decadent, and so on." Indigenous Peoples have often been stereotyped by other Canadians as a "lazy," "drunken" and "irresponsible" people who prefer the collection of welfare payments to the challenges of securing gainful employment. But the real causes of the serious social problems experienced by Indigenous Peoples across Canada lie deeply embedded in the colonial policies and practices that dispossessed them of their lands and livelihoods; displaced them onto reserves and into residential schools and adoptive and foster families; prohibited their sacred ceremonies, discredited their spiritual beliefs, practices and traditional knowledge; and robbed generations of them of their identities, languages, cultural traditions and collective and individual self-respect.

According to Indigenous Peoples' cyclical and holistic worldviews, land is held in common and in relationship with the nation as a whole. They see land as having been passed down from ancestors and as a legacy for their offspring. Furthermore, the land is to be shared in perpetuity with all living creatures; it is never owned (Dickason 1992: 352–353). In contrast to the Canadian legal system, which is largely based on adversarial relations, Indigenous Peoples' customary laws follow the principles of relations and consensus. Unfortunately, this foundational difference in understanding and interpreting the treaties, and the state's history of breaking its promises and responsibilities to Indigenous Nations, has led to many problems and challenges in the resolution of land claims.

Modern technology and resource development in northern parts of Canada have often led to opposition and protest movements by Indigenous groups who claim that highways, pipelines and hydro projects, industrial activity, mining and logging operations etc. not only encroach upon and diminish traditional hunting, trapping and fishing areas, but also pollute the environment, including water sources, resulting in serious health problems (Dickason 1992: 400–402). The first Canadian Indigenous claims settlement in modern history began in 1971, when Quebec announced its intention to develop a gigantic hydro project in the area of James Bay, an area not under the jurisdiction of any treaties. Economic development was seen as a much higher priority than the welfare of the Indigenous communities who lived in the area, who had not been consulted. After an unprecedented public outcry on behalf of Indigenous land rights, the conflict was temporarily resolved through a compensatory cash settlement, limited Indigenous ownership of land and some hunting, trapping and fishing rights — as well as recognition of an Indigenous veto over certain mineral rights in Quebec. However, the project's four major phases involved a complex system of dams and dikes that have profoundly altered the relationship of water to land in an area the size of France (Dickason 1992: 404–405).

INDIGENOUS KNOWLEDGE

Today, there is greater public recognition and acknowledgement of the colonial crimes committed in Canada by settler governments and religious orders against Indigenous Peoples, including the seizure and dispossession of their land; the abrogation of many treaties; the abduction of the "stolen generation" of their children into residential schools and the child welfare system; the forcible policies of assimilation; the long legacy of government neglect measured in disproportionately high rates of Indigenous poverty, family violence, ill-health, alcoholism and addictions, incarceration, depression, suicide, homicide, missing and murdered Indigenous women and girls, and many other indicators of the broken promises and failures by government agencies. However, there has also been a reaffirmation of Indigenous identity and reclamation of ancestral knowledge and traditional practices. Indeed, it is clear that the current renaissance of Indigenous knowledge and the sponsorship of Indigenous studies programs are essential elements in the ongoing decolonization of Indigenous consciousness and culture and important resources in the resistance to the legacies of colonization. As Angela Cavender Wilson (2004: 70) states:

> When considering the plethora of social problems facing Indigenous communities today (including poverty, chemical dependency, depression, suicide, family violence, and disease), it is profoundly clear that these are the devastating consequences of conquest and colonization. For Indigenous nations, these problems were largely absent prior to European and American invasion and destruction of everything to us. A reaffirmation of Indigenous epistemological and ontological foundations, then, in contemporary times offers a central form of resistance to the colonial forces that have consistently and methodically denigrated and silenced them.

Indigenous knowledge challenges Western social scientists' views of the world and offers an opportunity to understand long suppressed modes of consciousness and practice that — notwithstanding colonization — have endured in North America, as well as in other continents, for thousands of years. Connell (2007: 196) notes: "Social science usually prefers context-free generalization. Special prestige accrues to theory which is so abstracted that its statements seem universally true — the indifference curves of consumption economics, the structural models of Levi-Strauss, the practice models of Bourdieu and Giddens — or which seem applicable to everywhere, such as Foucault's models of power and subjecthood." While Western and Indigenous epistemologies may coexist as alternative modes of discourse in a culture that celebrates and encourages diversity, when one epistemology, such as science, asserts its legitimacy over all others, there is a potential for friction or even for competition and conflict between these alternative theories and practices of knowledge.

Understandably, the primary focus for many recent Indigenous thinkers and writers, including novelists, historians, commentators and activists, has been the decolonization of Indigenous thought and consciousness and the reclamation of Indigenous identity and agency. This emphasis on decolonization has involved a critique of standard Eurocentric perspectives including those that have often framed Western social theory. At the same time, many Indigenous critics of Eurocentrism who have sought to decolonize contemporary social theory have been influenced by current Western (or Northern) social theories — such as postcolonialism, poststructuralism and critical theory — to deconstruct and de-legitimate the Eurocentric worldview. However, as Annette Browne, Victoria Smye and Colleen Varcoe (2005) note, many Indigenous scholars have contributed to postcolonial discourses as a way of reclaiming and repositioning Indigenous voices, knowledge and analyses (see, for example, Battiste 2000). But as Browne, Smye and Varcoe (2005: 23) further suggest, Marie Battiste, a Mi'kmaq scholar, makes an important distinction: for whereas "postcolonial theoretical perspectives ... arise from Western epistemologies and discourses... postcolonial Indigenous knowledge, on the other hand, is grounded in Indigenous epistemologies and is concerned with developing knowledge based on Indigenous ways of knowing, Indigenous worldviews, and Indigenous research processes." While Indigenous knowledge can and should be used to inform postcolonial theories, Indigenous epistemologies represent different intellectual endeavours. This is not to imply that these epistemologies cannot be drawn on together — they are often used and invoked in parallel. As Battiste emphasizes, "although they are related endeavours, postcolonial Indigenous thought also emerges from the inability of Eurocentric theory to deal with the complexities of colonialism and its assumptions" (quoted in Browne, Smye and Varcoe 2005: 23).

Figure 10-1: The Medicine Wheel

Many Indigenous visions of the world emphasize the interconnectedness of all life. Unlike Western scientific social thought, which typically juxtaposes binary oppositions, such as nature/society, individual/collective, body/mind, human/non-human and life/death, Indigenous thought integrates rather than separates these relationships. As Anishinaabe scholar Kathy Absolon (2010: 75) suggests, "wholistic theory includes an intermixing and consideration of time and space: the past, present, future; directions and doorways of life; the ecology of creation such as earth, sun, water and air and all their occupants; and values that retain the balance and harmony of all of the above." In this respect, the medicine wheel represents one of the most important features of Indigenous knowledge: its holism and underlying unity.

THE DECOLONIZATION OF INDIGENOUS KNOWLEDGE

One indicator of the present reawakening of Indigenous knowledge and of the decolonization of Indigenous consciousness and culture, may be seen in the growth of Indigenous studies programs — not only in Canada and the US, but also in Australia, New Zealand and the Torres Strait Islands, the Sami territories of Norway, Sweden, Finland and coastal Russia, as well as in other Indigenous populations around the world. In North America, these programs are known by a number of names: Native

American studies, Aboriginal studies, American Indian studies, Native studies, First Nations studies and Indigenous studies (see Retzlaff 2005). We shall refer to these and similar programs under the generic label of "Indigenous studies" (IS).

According to Clara Sue Kidwell (2009: 4–5), the framework of most IS programs rests upon several distinct assumptions, or premises:

1. The relationship between the people and the land is a "shaping force" in all indigenous cultures. The land, territory or "place" is generally recognized as a foundational aspect of the collective consciousness and social solidarity of indigenous communities. Indeed, it is difficult to overestimate the importance of a "place-based" vision or epistemology in indigenous philosophy and educational practice, as the distinguished Mi'kmaq academic, Marie Battiste, has recognized: "Every conception of humanity and education begins from a human body in territory and a consciousness in which a specific place takes prominence" (Battiste et al. 2005: 8). This emphasis on the concrete, contextual, and ecological significance of place and location contrasts sharply with most Eurocentric social thought which has typically remained abstract, decontextualized and universal in its theoretical focus and scope of application. But, as Alexa Scully (2012: 152) has shown, an ecological sense of place and location can sensitize us to the partial and contextual nature of all social thought, and can encourage greater reflexivity and empathy in our relations with others; "Places are the literal common ground. Exposing the ways that a different experience of a place and the signifiers that make meaning out of place can create rich dialogue and understanding across perspectives. A complex and rich understanding of place can change the view from where one is standing … Sharing perspectives on literal common ground means shared points of reference seen in a whole new way — a whole new set of relations to people and to place; this is the practice that I am employing as a teacher educator in Aboriginal education. *This process begins with an acknowledgment of one's own location.*"

2. The historical contact between European colonial settlers and Indigenous peoples needs to be re-told through indigenous counter-narratives in order to correct the prevailing power and prestige of Eurocentric narratives. Indigenous histories will

necessarily include autobiographical accounts and oral histories passed down through successive generations of elders and story-tellers.

3. A third major assumption of IS programs is that sovereignty, or full control, over their land and natural resources is an inherent right of all Indigenous peoples. In Canada and the US, this sovereignty has traditionally been enshrined in treaties between indigenous nations and the federal government; in too many cases, these rights have often been violated, diminished, or even extinguished.

4. For most IS programs, language is essential for preserving the culture and reaffirming the cultures of indigenous communities. Language embodies a vital vision of the world, and is also the expression of a distinctive indigenous epistemology. The suppression and disappearance of native languages throughout the colonial period — especially in the residential schools and adoption agencies — has played a major role in what most indigenous people now see as a "cultural genocide" committed against their nations.

5. Beyond language, it is now commonly recognized in IS programs that indigenous arts and culture also serve to maintain continuity with past generations and ancestral values.

Athough the work on Indigenous theory and scholarship is thriving, the struggle for decolonization is far from over. There are still plenty of outstanding land claims that remain unresolved and numerous treaties that have been abrogated, violated or diminished in their jurisdictions, and the poverty, racialization, criminalization and social misery of many Indigenous people continues unrelieved. And, as Kidwell (2009: 9) observes, there are many challenges facing IS programs that have yet to be overcome:

> The challenge to American Indian studies as a discipline is to find ways to explicate the nature of contemporary American Indian identity within the constructs of land, historical change, political sovereignty, language, and expressive culture that now constitute one model of a discipline.... The challenge is to find the grounds to assert that Indian communities have maintained their distinctive identities because their

adaptations were based on Indian value systems that are now expressed in ways that can be identified in American society.

At the same time, important steps have already been taken. The projects of decolonizing and indigenizing social knowledge and social theory can also teach us much about the Eurocentric theory that continues to dominate the curricula of most social science departments across North America, even though the rise of "southern theory" and "Indigenous theory" shows that the traditional canon of Western theory has already begun to crumble. It is also important to note that the terms "decolonizing" and "indigenizing" are not synonymous. The "decolonization" of knowledge — for Indigenous communities — refers primarily to the restoration of Indigenous worldviews, knowledge and cultural practices and the deconstruction of Eurocentric social and historical narratives, along with the resurrection of traditional methods of oral history and storytelling. The "indigenization" of knowledge is somewhat different. Although there is no homogenous Indigenous perspective, as worldviews differ across Indigenous Nations, the indigenization of knowledge seeks to recognize the validity of Indigenous worldviews and traditional knowledge by showing how these epistemological perspectives are embedded in specific lands, cultures and communities; identifies opportunities for Indigenous knowledges and practices to be incorporated into Eurocentric institutions such as universities, legislative assemblies, health-care systems and so forth; and advances the project of indigeneity in the interests of sovereignty, social justice and reconciliation. Although these terms are often used interchangeably, many Indigenous scholars and activists note that they are separate but interrelated processes (see Alfred 2009a, 2009b; Alfred and Corntassel 2005; Pete 2015). Indeed, Lisa Korteweg and Connie Russell (2012: 8) remind us that both projects are fundamentally interrelated and need to move forward together, especially in such crucial areas as environmental education and research: "Both decolonizing and Indigenizing energies, as inquiry and sustained action, need to occur simultaneously in environmental education research: decolonizing as critical reflexivity by researchers/educators that makes explicit the present marinade of neocolonialism in mainstream environmentalism and environmental education, and Indigenizing as moving towards an Indigenized future of improved Indigenous–non-Indigenous relations as treaty partners on the same land."

The traditional Eurocentric theoretical focus on the universal, at the expense of the local, has meant that Indigenous perspectives and experiences have been overlooked and excluded from Western social theory. Contemporary social theories, as Indigenous sociologist Duane Champagne reports, "do not easily conceptualize American Indian communities, cultures, and historical experiences and are therefore regarded as outside the main focus of theoretical and empirical interest and focus.... [Indeed] "none of them focus on providing a deep cultural or institutional perspective of American Indians or center American Indian history or individual, group, or cultural experiences" (2007: 354, 359). Champagne further contends that, "since Indigenous experience is not well accounted for by existing theoretical conceptions, Indigenous issues and experiences are under-theorized and often theoretically and conceptually placed in residual categories because they do not work well with existing theoretical conceptions" (365). For these reasons, it is clear that in order for the indigenization of social theory to progress, the decolonization of Eurocentric theory also has to move ahead. The indigenization of social theory necessarily requires the decolonization of colonial, Eurocentric theory.

One of the more influential texts charting a course for the decolonization and indigenization of theoretical and practical knowledge is the book *Decolonizing Methodologies*, by Māori scholar Linda Tuhiwai Smith (2012). For Smith, theory and research are always — directly or indirectly — linked to social practices with real political consequences. Theory is always framed by, frequently unstated, epistemological and ontological premises and, as Dustin Louie and colleagues (2017: 20) suggest, most Western or Eurocentric theory is predicated on administrative and colonial concerns, because theory, like research, "is always a political act and has been used to the benefit of the dominant culture by modelling the core intellectual practices of colonization: defining terms, naming, categorizing and hierarchizing, 'disciplining,' and, ultimately, assigning value."

For Linda Tuhiwai Smith, the activities of theorizing and research are indissolubly linked to the practices of politics and power relations. The frameworks and perspectives of the Western Eurocentric tradition of social theory all originated in the culture of imperialism and colonialism. The conceptual hierarchies and binary oppositions; the segmentation and fragmentation of conceptual categories; and the separation and division of the world into analytical classifications and taxonomies have all been based upon an underlying administrative and colonial imperative (Agrawal 2002). But as Battiste (2002: 11) explains, "Indigenous knowledge ...

defies categorization [because it is] an adaptable, dynamic system based on skills, abilities, and problem-solving techniques that change over time depending on environmental conditions, making the taxonomic approach difficult to justify or verify. Most Indigenous scholars and educators have noted the practical and conceptual limitations of taxonomic categories posing as Indigenous knowledge."

Eurocentric theory has inherited a colonial vision of the social, and natural, world that remains embedded in its intellectual form and content. It is an objectifying worldview based upon the separation of the individual from their natural and social environment and on the alienation of the knowledge-seeker from their place and position in the world. In contrast to this Eurocentric colonial vision, Indigenous thinkers emphasize the holistic, unified, interconnected and spiritual dimensions of knowledge, which, as Kevin Fitzmaurice (2010: 362–363) suggests, stand in sharp contrast to the Western worldview: "Indigenous knowledge suggests more than a world of coherent and separate identities based in fear and competing power. Rather, it offers the possibility of a theoretical, spiritual, and experiential understanding of interconnectivity, interdependence, and community within a view of power that is based in collectivity and spirit rather than being entirely about force."

As part of her strategy for the decolonization and indigenization of theory and research, Linda Tuhiwai Smith has outlined an alternative paradigm that links the pursuit and growth of Indigenous knowledge to political and personal practices designed to further the agency, autonomy and self-determination of Indigenous Peoples. For Smith, there is a necessary connection between the growth of knowledge and the struggle for individual and collective sovereignty among Indigenous Peoples. In other words, theory is always linked to practice, or as the Cree educator, Cora Weber-Pillwax (2001), states, "If my work as an Indigenous scholar does not lead to action, it is useless to me or anyone. I cannot be involved in research and scholarly discourse unless I know ... that such work will lead to some change (out there) in that community, in my community." In advancing her own project for knowledge and action, Smith's paradigm for the acquisition of knowledge and the achievement of personal and political sovereignty is illustrated in a circular conceptual framework. This framework outlines the following four individual and collective dimensions, or "tides," of personal and political change: (1) survival; (2) recovery; (3) development; and (4) self-determination. The

Figure 10-2: Linda Tuhiwai Smith's Paradigm for the Decolonization of Indigenous Knowledge

circle also includes four "directions" for personal and political change: (1) mobilization; (2) healing; (3) decolonization; and (4) transformation. Together, these dimensions are intended to provide an integrated and holistic paradigm for combining (intellectual) enlightenment with the evident need for the individual and collective emancipation, sovereignty and self-determination of Indigenous Peoples. It is also a paradigm that is designed to chart a cyclical course for the personal and political renewal of Indigenous knowledge and Indigenous culture.

Since its original publication in 2012, Smith's work has inspired and informed many other scholars who have sought to address the challenges and opportunities arising from Indigenous knowledge. And, as Louie et al. (2017: 22) suggest, "the principles embedded in *Decolonizing Methodologies* constitute a theoretical framework, even a watershed moment, in Indigenous scholarship, rather than a discipline-specific methodological set." Smith has shown how "'decolonizing and Indigenizing' postsecondary education entails transforming imperialist and assimilative frameworks, validating Indigenous knowledges and epistemologies, and asserting the presence and humanity of Indigenous peoples" (17).

Besdes their distinctive epistemological and ontological premises and its political objectives, Indigenous theory and research use a much broader and more diverse repertoire of methods for information retrieval than those typically used by Eurocentric scholars for the pursuit and growth of knowledge. Thus, for non-Indigenous theorists and researchers, there are important lessons to be learned and valuable insights to be gained from engaging with the principles and practices of Indigenous knowledge and theory. Perhaps the most important, and the most difficult requirement for a Eurocentric theorist who wishes to learn from Indigenous thinkers and educators, is the need to suspend their own epistemic and ontological beliefs and practices and to bracket their own ethnocentric worldviews. Western theorists and researchers need to cultivate a critical reflexive "lens" which can render more transparent their own settler colonial presuppositions and preconceptions and lay bare their latent prejuices and deeply embedded presuppositions. Peggy Macintosh (1989: 10), an American feminist and antiracist activist, described her "invisible knap-sack," which contains all the perks and privileges rouinely conferred upon any member in good standing of white Western middle-class society. For McIntosh, this reflexive recognition of her own unconscious racism came as a shocking epiphany: "White privilege is like an invisible weightless knapsack of special provisions, maps, passports, codebooks, visas, clothes, tools, and blank checks." Becoming reflexively aware of our own skin privileges and socioconomic status is indispensable for any access to an Indigenous perspective and for any understanding of Indigenous tradi-tions of wisdom and knowledge. The purpose for cultivating a reflexive and critical consciousness, especially among those of us who have long enjoyed settler privileges within a colonial culture, is, as Battiste (2002: 9) explains, "to sensitize the western consciousness of Canadians in general and educators in particular to the colonial and neo-colonial practices that continue to marginalize and racialize Aboriginal students and to the unique rights and relationships Aboriginal people have in their homeland."

INDIGENOUS KNOWLEDGE AND WESTERN SCIENCE: BEYOND CONTESTATION TO COLLABORATION

This is a time of unprecedented change and experimentation in the social sciences, a time when the fortress of "scientific knowledge" has finally lowered its drawbridge to allow other traditions of knowledge to enter the hallowed halls of academia and share their insights with the com-munity of scholars, scientists and traditional knowledge-keepers. This is a time when the Western canon of social thought has begun to open up to include social thinkers from around the world: from the Global South and from colonized and marginalized sectors of the Global North. These winds of change have also begun to blow through the various schools of social theory, which have now opened their doors to previously neglected traditions of social thought — including Indigenous theory, but also queer theory, critical race theory, Afrocentric theory, disability theory, along with many others. At the same time, as we have already seen, Indigenous social thought is markedly different from the Eurocentric tradition of social science and social theory in a number of important respects. And these differences are apparent in the distinctive methodologies, types of information and data collection strategies employed in each tradition, as well as in their motives for pursuing their respective intellectual projects. These two traditions of knowledge come from two different worlds: the world of the colonizer and the world of the colonized. The question remains: must they always collide and compete with each other, or can they coexist and collaborate?

As we have seen, one of the most pressing tasks for Indigenous scholars and thinkers at the present time is the decolonization of knowledge and theory. The decolonization project aims to expose how colonialism functions and to restore the respect and recognition once accorded Indigenous knowledge and social thought. The decolonization project has not only critiqued those settler historical accounts that have sanitized the invasion and occupation of Indigenous lands and sanctified the suppression of Indigenous knowledge and cultural practices, but this project has also exposed the oppression and racialization of Indigenous Peoples throughout North America and in all settler colonial states. The decolonization project remains central to the theory and methodology of many Indigenous writers and scholars. For Louie et al. (2017: 17), this project entails "transforming imperialist and assimilative frameworks, validating Indigenous knowledges and epistemologies, and asserting the presence and humanity of Indigenous peoples," while for Champagne (2007: 362), the decolonization project "creates greater consciousness of the effects of colonization on culture, thought ... especially rejection of colonial concepts and understandings of the value and history of indigenous nations."

But in some cases, the rise of Indigenous knowledge, especially its challenges to Eurocentric social thought and its claims for reciprocal recognition and respect, has met with opposition and denial. For example, when confronted with the long-established tradition of inter-generational storytelling as a recognized method of historical information retrieval among Indigenous scholars, some Western academics have scorned this source of historical data as inappropriate within the academy and as "unscientific or atheoretical ... subjective and ... of no professional relevance" (Carr 2004: 8; also Butler 2016: 23).

To a certain extent, as we describe in other chapters of this book, the Western tradition of social science, especially Eurocentric theories and research methods, has come under increasingly critical scrutiny and skepticism among both Western and non-Western thinkers and scholars. Indeed, the rise of poststructuralism, postmodernism, postcolonialism and queer theory, as well as standpoint and intersectionality theories, all bear witness to the current crisis in Eurocentric epistemologies, or as Kidwell (2009: 3) notes, "the slippery nature of truth has become a truism in the academy [and] Post modernism and postcolonialism are the current coin of the realm." And even conventional depictions of the historical logic and consistency of the natural sciences have been questioned and revised by Western philosophers, historians and sociologists such as Thomas Kuhn, Paul Feyerabend, Norwood Russell Hanson, Stephen Toulmin and Bruno Latour, among others. The once iconic status of Eurocentric science has, in many ways, been dislodged from its pedestal and stripped of its monopolistic claims to "truth" and "knowledge."

In the meantime, the renaissance of and the drive to decolonize Indigenous theory and methodology continue to impact both the social and the natural sciences. While some Indigenous educators have made full use of contemporary critical, poststructuralist and postcolonial theories to deconstruct and decolonize Eurocentric discourses, others have eschewed these Westernized perspectives, believing, as African American feminist Audre Lorde (2007 [1984]) once stated, "The master's tools will never dismantle the master's house." Champagne (2007: 358–359) largely rejects the relevance or validity of postmodernist, postcolonial or other Westernized critical perspectives for advancing Indigenous knowledge:

> Postmodern and postcolonial interpretations are imbued with the deep social epistemologies of Western society ... most of the arguments of race, critical theory, class, ethnicity, nation, and postcolonialism make epistemological assumptions usually alien to those made in American Indian communities and traditions and serve the purposes of theories and issues that are often not grounded in American Indian cultures

and institutions, but are sometimes found in the conditions experienced in colonial history.

Similarly, other Indigenous educators, such as Absolon (2010) and Elizabeth Rix et al. (2018), emphasize that, in order to decolonize Indigenous knowledge, it is necessary to avoid Westernized concepts and perspectives and focus instead on Indigenous epistemologies and ontologies. Notwithstanding these strategic differences, the explanatory, interpretative, historical, ecological and spiritual value of Indigenous knowledge is no longer in question. Over the past few years, it has received growing recognition and respect both inside and outside of Indigenous communities.

Some critical educators and scholars do advocate the use of Westernized theoretical perspectives to advance the deconstruction and decolonization of Eurocentric traditions of knowledge. Raymond Morrow (2010: 74), for example, suggests that the decolonization of Western knowledge could be advanced through the "educational theory linked with Habermas [who] provides important foundations for post-Eurocentric understandings of Third World and global education." And although Glen Coulthard (2007) is critical of how the language of "recognition" has been employed in the theories of Charles Taylor, Axel Honneth and Nancy Fraser to analyze the politics of Indigenous self-determination, he turns to the writings of Georg Hegel and Frantz Fanon for a more accurate understanding of the subjective meanings of subordination within the colonial structures of unequal social relations. Others focus primarily on restoring a tradition of Indigenous knowledge uncorrupted by Eurocentric intellectual influences, as Battiste (2013: 20) reminds us, "to avoid the temptation of including Indigenous pedagogies under the banner of Western critical theories." But some researchers have chosen a more collaborative and symbiotic path. Indeed, these researchers attempt to avoid what may be termed a polarization between those who seek to rid Indigenous knowledge of the colonizing influence of any Eurocentric intellectual perspectives, versus those hardcore Eurocentrics who believe that Western science is the only path to truth and knowledge and that assimilation is the only path to justice and equality for Indigenous Peoples.

In his critical response to what he sees as Indigenous "essentialism," Chris Andersen (2009: 96) argues that Indigenous studies should not renounce all Western concepts and theoretical perspectives because Indigenous studies do not "necessarily require an entirely new set of theoretical or methodological precepts that differ from those of main-stream disciplines… Thus, although not fully captured by terms like race, ethnicity or class, such terms nonetheless assist greatly in reflecting upon the relationships between our communities and the various nation-states, and not only because they possess symbolic power in dominant society." Likewise, other scholars encourage collaboration, or even integration, between Indigenous and non-Indigenous forms of knowledge, especially in the conceptualization of empirical observations and the construction of theoretical explanations and in sharing methods of research and data collection. Some writers especially encourage collaboration in the areas of ecological and environmental research. Many of these projects are driven by the growing concern of both settler and Indigenous communities over environmental issues such as threats to biodiversity posed by the contin-ued hunting and harvesting of endangered species, as well as by the local consequences of climate change and global warming. Lesley Green (2012) describes how research projects of Western marine ecologists concerned about depleted fish stocks around coastal South Africa greatly benefitted from the oral reports and firsthand accounts, or "field observations," of native fishers. For these fishers, the "ocean" is understood in much more holistic, cyclical and existential terms than the abstract, analytical and more commodified conceptual framework typical of Western science. Similarly, fish are seen as endowed with their own "intelligence" and practical "logic." These epistemic ways of viewing the natural world, based upon a "relational ontology," have no direct Western counterpart, and as Green makes clear, this "generative dialogue" between Western and Indigenous knowledge reflects the beginnings of a

> paradigm shift in a dialogue on the nature of knowledge in the humanities and sciences. Working with it, public con-sultations on marine conservation might begin to move the conversation beyond a pedagogy that aims to secure compli-ance with science, to projects that explore different ways of knowing the marine environment. With sufficient time for generative dialogue about different ways of knowing the sea, including how to evaluate knowledges, the management of the marine ecosystem as a commons might begin to be a reality in specific locales. (6)

Green argues that the great value of the information and observations of Indigenous knowledge-keepers lies in the recognition that "some ways of knowing lie outside the terrain of formally accredited knowledge … because … they rely on forms of sensory data for which technologies which might measure them have not yet been developed" (7).

The positive prospects of a fruitful dialogue and exchange between Western science and traditional Indigenous knowledge has also been championed by Fulvio Mazzocchi (2006: 465), who suggests:

> Dialogue can become a tool for social cohabitation, as well as for discovering and enhancing knowledge. It should be based on a sense of profound hospitality because it arises from different identities and traditions, which are interested in exchanging their perspectives and experiences. This should not be anathema to Western science — in fact, it is through dialogue that new insights have emerged from the ancient Greek academies to today's laboratory meetings and scientific conferences.

Mazzocchi also reminds us that Article 8 of the (1992) UN Convention on Biological Diversity emphasizes the vital role of Indigenous knowledge and associated cultural practices in the conservation and the protection of endangered species of fauna and flora. Moreover, he notes that Indigenous knowledge is well suited to understand and conceptualize "complex systems" which are often resistant to the reductionist linear models of Western science. In this respect, the methods traditionally employed by Indigenous knowledge-keepers offer some definite advantages over those of Western science: "Not only are they more holistic, but also they seem to be better suited to coping with the uncertainty and unpredictability that are viewed as intrinsic characteristics of natural systems. Western science and traditional knowledge constitute different paths to knowledge, but they are rooted in the same reality. We can only gain from paying attention to our cultural history and richness" (466).

The value of Indigenous knowledge has also been recognized and documented in other official sources, such as the (1987) Brundtland Report (World Commission on Environment and Development and the (1992) Rio de Janeiro UN Conference on Environment and Development (UNCED), also known as the Earth Summit, among others. Indigenous, particularly Inuit, knowledge has also helped to empirically assess many other topics of pressing scientific interest and concern, including historical

changes in caribou and seal populations in the Arctic regions; the recession of polar ice flows and the changing distribution and territorial range
of polar bears; the overpopulation of snow geese and giant Canada geese;
and the use of plants in traditional herbal remedies and their potential
for pharmaceutical use in modern medicine; among many other topics
(Tsuji and Ho 2002). From their survey of the many ways that Indigenous
knowledge has contributed to observation and understanding of the
symbiotic interrelations between different species in the world, Leonard
Tsuji and Elise Ho conclude that a partnership between Indigenous and
Western knowledge would benefit each tradition:

> TEK [Traditional Ecological Knowledge] is a different
> approach to understanding and acquiring knowledge than
> science. If applicable, it may be advantageous to utilize both
> systems.... When there is more than one way of knowing,
> all ways should be used to contribute to a more complete
> understanding of knowledge in general.... TEK and western
> science should be viewed as two separate but complementary
> sources of information and wisdom ... where practitioners of
> both would benefit from a reciprocal flow of knowledge. (346)

INDIGENOUS KNOWLEDGE: COMING IN FROM THE COLD

The stark realities of Indigenous life within what is still a settler colonial
state remain. The grim statistics continue to tell a shameful tale of suffering
and oppression on a scale unparalleled in contemporary Canadian society,
including disproportionately high rates of suicide and homicide; sexual
and physical abuse; trauma, depression and addictions; communicable
diseases and poor health; poverty and malnutrition; homelessness; racial
prejudice, profiling and discrimination; incarceration; and unemployment. Indeed, the suffering of Indigenous communities can be measured
on virtually every index of social inequality and social injustice. And
although the last residential school closed in 1996 and a formal government apology was offered in 2008 and the Truth and Reconciliation
Commission acknowledged some of the historical injustices committed
against Indigenous Peoples in Canada; while Indigenous knowledge and
cultural practices are beginning to receive some recognition and respect;
and Prime Minister Trudeau has promised a new deal or a new legal
framework for Indigenous Peoples in Canada; their trauma and social

misery — experienced over several generations — has not disappeared. Perhaps it will require the full decolonization of all of the major institutions in Canada for Indigenous peoples to finally regain their sense of self-worth and exercise their inherent right of self-determination. In the meantime, their struggles continue and are most poignantly expressed in the words of the Nēhiyaw activist Erica Violet Lee, who describes the predicament of many Indigenous Peoples who continue to inhabit a "wasteland": a place where

> we grow our medicines from the cracks in concrete sidewalks or in between railroad tracks. We have to dig our laws out from underneath gravel logging roads and tend to our worlds in contaminated fields.... For those of us in the wastelands — for those of us who are the wastelands — caring for each other in this way is refusing a definition of worthiness that will never include us. To provide care in the wastelands is about gathering enough love to turn devastation into mourning and then, maybe, turn that mourning into hope. (quoted in King 2017: 8)

But time does not stand still. Today, more than ever, Indigenous Peoples are reasserting their claims to cultural and political autonomy, to their land rights and human rights, and to sovereignty, self-governance and self-determination. Their assertion of these rights is informed by deep cultural, political and spiritual ideals and aspirations. And, as we have already seen, the holistic worldviews of many Indigenous Peoples reflect their strongly localized sense of place and homeland, as well as their living links to ancestral knowledge.

Social theory has a role to play in recovering and celebrating this traditional wisdom and renewing these traditional practices. But social theory also has a responsibility to expand the scope of knowledge for future generations of Indigenous Peoples and to articulate their struggles for greater cultural and political autonomy within a global lifeworld. Eurocentric social theories have often proven inadequate in these respects and have invariably assumed the perspective of the colonizer rather than the colonized. Early evolutionist, assimilationist and modernization theories frequently dismissed Indigenous Peoples' theory and knowledge, first as that of "noble savages" or "racial minorities" and in later versions, assumed its homogeneity and passivity and other fictions of the colonial imaginary. And whereas more recent theories, such as postcolonial, poststructuralist and intersectionality theories have provided some deconstructive tools with which to critique ethnocentric, androcentric and homophobic theoretical perspectives, even these theories remain locked into Eurocentric traditions of social thought. For, as Champagne (2008: 21), suggests,

> Social science theories must be broad enough to understand and conceptualize relations with Indigenous peoples. Social science theories need to understand culture, institutional order, political processes, and the mobilization of Indigenous states within the context of nation-state policies, and international understandings of Indigenous people's land rights.... Consequently, social scientists and policy makers need to develop theories and policies of nation-state groups that systematically include and give understanding to Indigenous people's needs and points of view, and give weight to the negotiation of common cultural and political ground, and establish more consensually democratic relations among Indigenous peoples, nation-states, and international civil society.

References

Absolon, Kathy. 2010. "Indigenous Wholistic Theory: A Knowledge Set for Practice." *First Peoples Child and Family Review*, 5, 2: 74–87. <https://fncaringsociety.com/sites/default/files/online-journal/vol5num2/Absolon_pp74.pdf>.

Agrawal, A. 2002. "Indigenous Knowledge and the Politics of Classification." *International Social Science Journal*, 173: 287–297.

Alfred, Gerald Taiaiake. 2009a. "Redressing Racist Academics, Or, Put Your Clothes Back On, Please!" A Review of Widdowson and Howard's, *Disrobing the Aboriginal Industry*. <https://bermudaradical.wordpress.com/2009/10/26/review-of-"disrobing-the-aboriginal-industry"/>.

____. 2009b. "Colonialism and State Dependency." *Journal of Aboriginal Health*, 5: 2 (November): 42–60.

Alfred, T., and J. Corntassel. 2005. "Politics of Identity IX: Being Indigenous: Resurgences Against Contemporary Colonialism." *Government and Opposition*, 40, 4 (Autumn): 597–614.

Andersen, Chris. 2009. "Critical Indigenous Studies: From Difference to Density [online]." *Cultural Studies Review*, 15, 2 (Sep): 80–100.

Battiste, M. 2002. *Indigenous Knowledge and Pedagogy in First Nations Education: A Literature Review with Recommendations*. Prepared for the National Working Group on Education and the Minister of Indian Affairs Indian and Northern

Affairs Canada (INAC): Ottawa, ON: National Working Group on Education and the Minister of Indian Affairs Indian and Northern Affairs Canada (INAC).
___. 2013. *Decolonizing Education: Nourishing the Learning Spirit.* Saskatoon, SK: Purich.
Battiste, M., M. Bell, I. Findlay, L. Findlay, and J.S. Youngblood Henderson. 2005. "Thinking Place: Animating the Indigenous Humanities in Education." *Australian Journal of Indigenous Education,* 34: 7–19.
Browne, Annette J., Victoria L. Smye, and Colleen Varcoe. 2005. "The Relevance of Postcolonial Theoretical Perspectives to Research in Aboriginal Health." *Canadian Journal of Nursing Research,* 37, 4: 16–37.
Butler, Kathleen. 2016. "Rethinking Sociology, Social Darwinism and Aboriginal Peoples." *International Journal of Critical Indigenous Studies,* 9, 1.
Carr, David. 2004. "Professional and Personal Values and Virtues in Education and Teaching." Philosophy of Education Society of Great Britain Conference Programme and Papers. <http://www.ioe.ac.uk/pesgb/z/Carr.pdf>.
Cavender Wilson, A. 2004. "Reclaiming Our Humanity: Decolonization and the Recovery of Indigenous Knowledge." In D.A. Mihesuah and A. Cavender Wilson (eds.), *Indigenizing the Academy: Transforming Scholarship and Empowering Communities.* Lincoln: University of Nebraska Press.
Champagne, Duane. 2007. "In Search of Theory and Method in American Indian Studies." *American Indian Quarterly,* 31, 3 (Summer): 353–372.
___. 2008. "The Indigenous Peoples' Movement: Theory, Policy, and Practice." 39th Annual Sorokin Lecture, University of Saskatchewan. <https://artsandscience.usask.ca/sociology/documents/39th%20Annual%20Sorokin%20Lecture.pdf>.
Connell, Raewyn. 2007. *Southern Theory: The Global Dynamics of Knowledge in Social Science.* Polity.
Coulthard, Glen. 2007. "Subjects of Empire: Indigenous Peoples and the 'Politics of Recognition' in Canada." *Contemporary Political Theory,* 6, 4 (November): 437–460.
Dickason, O.P. 1992. *Canada's First Nations: A History of Founding Peoples from Ealiest Times.* Toronto: McClelland & Stewart.
Fitzmaurice, Kevin. 2010. "Are White People Obsolete? Indigenous Knowledge and the Colonizing Ally in Canada." In L. Davis (ed.), *Alliances: Re-Envisioning Indigenous-Non-Indigenous Relationships.* Toronto: University of Toronto Press.
Green, Lesley J.F. 2012. "Beyond South Africa's 'Indigenous Knowledge–Science' Wars." *South African Journal of Science,* 108, 7/8, Art. #631. <http://dx.doi.org/10.4102/sajs.v108i7/8.631>.
Kidwell, Clara Sue. 2009. "American Indian Studies: Intellectual Navel Gazing or Academic Discipline?" *American Indian Quarterly,* 33, 1: 1–17.
King, Hayden. 2017. "The Erasure of Indigenous Thought in Foreign Policy." Open Canada.org, July 31. <https://www.opencanada.org/features/erasure-indigenous-thought-foreign-policy/>.
Korteweg, Lisa, and Connie Russell. 2012. "Decolonizing + Indigenizing = Moving Environmental Education Towards Reconciliation." *Canadian Journal of Environmental Education,* 17, 5: 5–14.
Lorde, Audre. 2007 [1984]. "The Master's Tools Will Never Dismantle the Master's

House." *Sister Outsider: Essays and Speeches*. Berkeley, CA: Crossing Press. <https://www.muhlenberg.edu/media/contentassets/pdf/campuslife/SDP%20 Reading%20Lorde.pdf>.

Louie, Dustin William, Yvonne Poitras Prat, Aubrey Jean Hanson, and Jacqueline Ottmann. 2017. "Applying Indigenizing Principles of Decolonizing Methodologies in University Classrooms." *Canadian Journal of Higher Education*, 47, 3: 16–33.

Mazzocchi, Fulvio. 2006. "Western Science and Traditional Knowledge: Despite Their Variations, Different Forms of Knowledge Can Learn from Each Other." *EMBO Reports*, 7, 5 (May). PubMed Central® (PMC) U.S. National Institutes of Health's National Library of Medicine (NIH/NLM). <https://www.ncbi.nlm.nih.gov/pmc/ articles/PMC1479546/>.

McIntosh Peggy. 1989. "White Privilege: Unpacking the Invisible Knapsack." *Peace and Freedom Magazine* (July/August): 10–12. <https://psychology.umbc.edu/ files/2016/10/White-Privilege_McIntosh-1989.pdf>.

Morrow, Raymond A. 2010. "Habermas, Eurocentrism and Education: The Indigenous Knowledge Debate." In Mark Murphy and Ted Fleming (eds.), *Habermas, Critical Theory and Education*. Routledge.

Pete, Shauneen. 2015. "Indigenizing the Academy: One Story." *Aboriginal Policy Studies*, 4, 1: 65–72.

Retzlaff, Steffi. 2005. "What's in a Name? The Politics of Naming and Native Identity Constructions." *Canadian Journal of Native Studies*, 25: 2609–2626.

Rix E.F., S. Wilson, N. Sheehan, and N. Tujague. 2018. "Indigenist and Decolonizing Research Methodology." In P. Liamputtong (ed.), *Handbook of Research Methods in Health Social Sciences*. Singapore: Springer.

Scully, Alexa. 2012. "Decolonization, Reinhabitation and Reconciliation: Aboriginal and Place-Based Education." *Canadian Journal of Environmental Education*, 17: 148–158. <https://cjee.lakeheadu.ca/article/viewFile/1113/660>.

Smith, L.T. 2012. *Decolonizing Methodologies: Research and Indigenous Peoples*, 2nd ed. New York: Zed Books.

Tsuji, Leonard J.S., and Elise Ho. 2002. "Traditional Environmental Knowledge and Western Science: In Search of Common Ground." *Canadian Journal of Native Studies*, 22, 2: 327–360.

Weber-Pillwax C. 2001. "What Is Indigenous Research?" *Canadian Journal of Native Education*, 25, 2: 166–174.

CHAPTER 11

THEORIZING OUR ANXIOUS AGE

Theorists of Late Modernity

WHAT IS LATE MODERNITY?

We are now ready to meet some of those "late," or "high," modernist theorists of the late twentieth century and early twenty-first century who came to prominence in the age of poststructuralism and postmodernism. However, unlike the postmodernist generation, most of whom rejected many of the traditional assumptions of social and sociological theory — such as the pursuit of objectivity and causality in theory and research and the construction of metanarratives — many late modernists have retained their belief in explanatory metanarratives while at the same time remaining sensitive to the concerns and criticisms raised by the postmodernist theorists. Who are these theorists who have tried to adapt their studies to a postmodern world, and how do they differ from the postmodernists?

Any attempt to distinguish between late modernism and postmodernism will be somewhat arbitrary. Different commentators make these distinctions in different ways that will always depend upon their own theoretical predilections. In the ethereal world of social theory, there are few, if any, watertight criteria for classifying, categorizing, defining or otherwise sorting out the similarities and differences between prominent theorists and their respective conceptual frameworks. One obvious commonality between late modernism and postmodernism is that both of these intellectual traditions go beyond modernism and beyond the social theories of the modernist period, which extended well into the mid-twentieth century. In the case of postmodernism and poststructuralism, we have already seen how theorists such as Foucault, Lyotard, Baudrillard, Lacan, Derrida and others embraced the new experiences of the postmodern world. For them, the postmodern world was characterized by a new recognition and celebration of diversity and difference, of pluralism and relativism, and an abandonment of many of the taken-for-granted assumptions of the modernist era. The end of these assumptions was perceived by many postmodernist theorists as a series of "deaths": the deaths of truth, identity, society, reality and history — at least, as these topics had traditionally been understood.

The traditions of postmodernism and late modernism each attempted to confront, describe, analyze and explain the new and unprecedented conditions of the twenty-first century world. Today, perhaps more than anything else, the overwhelming reality in most of our individual and social lives is that of indeterminacy, uncertainty, insecurity and instability. Many of us have experienced the precariousness of employment in the contemporary labour market, and we may already regard ourselves as members of the "precariat" — the precarious contingent workforce employed on short-term contracts, normally without the security of pensions, employer-covered health-care insurance and other employment benefits. Insecurity in our private and public lives has become the distinguishing mark of the twenty-first century. In addition to the insecurities of people's working lives, both postmodernist and late modernist perspectives share a common recognition of many other aspects of this current age of "indeterminacy." Personal identities no longer appear as fixed and permanent as they once did: our gender, sexual, occupational, religious, national, ethnic and even racial identities seem much more fluid and "plastic" than ever before. The way we speak acknowledges this new plasticity: we "identify" as gay or straight, or as bi or trans; as Black or white or Indigenous. Similarly, our society recognizes a far greater diversity and plurality among its members than ever before. Many of these recently recognized groups and individuals have come from former and sometimes current marginalized communities — such as LGBTQ, Indigenous, disabled, Black and Brown communities, among others. Many of these "subaltern" communities are increasingly represented in their own formerly subjugated "discourses," which have now entered into the general universe of discourse within the public and political spheres. In these respects, diversity, plurality, variety and relativity have also become distinguishing marks of the present age of indeterminacy.

Postmodernist and late modernist theorists also both recognize the ways in which the new information and communication technologies have changed our lives by providing us with unprecedented global connectivity and a corresponding compression of space and time around the world. Each of these theoretical traditions also emphasizes the role of "hyperconsumerism" in our neoliberal economies and societies, as well as the more general commodification and globalization of our lives and identities. But if these are some of the ways in which postmodernism and late modernism share a common recognition of this present age of indeterminacy, how do they differ from each other?

Although postmodernism and late modernism both came of age during the transition period between the twentieth century and the twenty-first century, they represent different conceptual frameworks and theoretical perspectives for understanding and adapting to these new realities. Table 11-1 illustrates some of the major differences.

Table 11-1: Late Modernism versus Postmodernism

Late Modernism		Postmodernism
Distinctive Characteristics	**Similarities**	**Distinctive Characteristics**
• grand theories & metanarratives • reason & progress • linear time • human agency • objective reality • faith in big politics: nation, state/province, party, etc. • essentialism • critique of hyperconsumerism and commodification	• indeterminacy • uncertainty • insecurity • precarity • instability • diversity • plurality • hybridity • new information & communication technologies • globalization • reflexivity and self-consciousness: constant re-evaluation of ideas; social and cultural norms and structures seen as unstable and fragmented	• local narratives • moral and epistemological relativism • no independent or objective reality outside of discourse • non-linear and fragmented time • simulacra more powerful than "real"; images and texts with no original referents • no universal "Truth"; only local "truths" • faith in micro-politics, identity politics, local politics etc. • deconstructionism and anti-foundationalism (anti-essentialism) • acceptance of hyperconsumerism

Major Differences Between Postmodernism and Late Modernism

Grand or metanarratives: Whereas both poststructuralism and postmodernism reject the legacy of grand narratives in sociological and social theory, this is not the case for many late modernist social theorists. While poststructuralists and postmodernists have deconstructed many earlier metanarratives, exposing their absences, silences, exclusions and other (androcentric, ethnocentric, Eurocentric, homophobic) biases, many late modernist theorists remain committed to the intellectual project of grand theories and metanarratives. And although late modernists have learned from the critical methods of deconstructivists and poststructuralists, they have continued in their attempts to construct general theories that can encapsulate and analyze some of the central features of our rapidly changing and troubled world of today. Anthony Giddens and Pierre Bourdieu, for example, have become known for their respective theories of structuration; Ulrich Beck for his theory of the risk society; Manuel Castells for his theory of the network society; Axel Honneth for his critical theory of recognition; and Zygmunt Bauman, for his theory of the liquid society. However, most of these theorists have also acknowledged the influence of poststructuralism and postmodernism on their efforts to adapt their theories to local conditions and, in this respect, to construct "local narratives" on particular topics. For example, Bauman focuses on topics such as refugees and asylum-seekers in his book *Wasted Lives*, and Bourdieu focuses on popular cultural distinctions of "taste" and social status and on TV and journalism. And Slavoj Žižek covers numerous topics: film reviews, commentaries on refugees, politics and public issues as well as dense theoretical polemics and ideological critiques. It is in their more local narratives that we can see how late modernists have learned from the decentralized narratives of poststructuralism and postmodernism without abandoning their own pursuit of larger and more inclusive theories of society.

Reason and progress: Another feature that distinguishes the work of many late modernists from their poststructuralist and postmodernists contemporaries is the modernist belief in and commitment to the legacy of the Enlightenment project of "reason" and "progress." Unlike most postmodernists, who have, since the time of Nietzsche and later of Foucault, abandoned any traditional belief in the progressive power of human reason to solve the problems of "humanity," many late modernists, with some exceptions, cling to this belief. Giddens, Bourdieu, Castells and Beck all emphasize the capacity of the social actor for "reflexivity" and for "reflexive modernization." And, of course, the Enlightenment project of rationalism and optimism has remained a central tenet of the critical theorists of the Frankfurt School, most recently for Jürgen Habermas,

Honneth and Nancy Fraser, among others. However, the work of Bauman shows how late modernist theorists may sometimes lose the optimism associated with progressive social thought. Although Bauman is a grand theorist of "liquid modernity," the cultural optimism, or belief in progress, that has traditionally characterized modernism is often absent from his work. In his dark studies of wasted lives, of decomposing societies and of the human capacity for evil, Bauman very rarely alludes to any light at the end of the historical tunnel. Likewise, Žižek disavows any traditional beliefs in the steady march of reason and progress, ideas he rejects as the "sublime objects" of an entrenched liberal capitalist "ideological fantasy." While virtually all late modernists retain some belief in rationalism (the human capacity for reasonable thought and action), in the troubled world that we presently inhabit, this belief is just as likely to be accompanied by cultural pessimism, cultural skepticism or cultural fatalism as by cultural optimism.

Human agency: The belief in the human capacity for reason and for progressive thought and action is often closely associated with a corresponding belief in the human capacity for free will and choice. In the language of social theory, this core belief is often referred to as the "agency" of the social actor. "Agency" implies that the individual has a capacity to choose between alternative courses of action and has the autonomy to at least partially determine their own destiny. This ability to consciously plan, or select, a course of action is known as "intentionality" and is closely related to the idea of "agency." Several schools of social thought have questioned, implicitly or explicitly, or even dismissed this idea of human agency and instead, suggest other causes of social action. When human autonomy is wholly replaced with some other prime causal mechanism for social action, this may be an indicator of a "deterministic," as opposed to a "voluntaristic," theory of social action or human behaviour.

Deterministic social theories have taken many forms over the years. Some versions of Freudian theory have been criticized as examples of psychological determinism, or psychological reductionism. Some versions of sociobiology have been criticized as examples of biological determinism. Some versions of Marxism, historical materialism, have been criticized as examples of historical or economic determinism. Some versions of structural functionalism have been criticized as examples of sociological determinism, or sociologism. And critics fault the more contemporary schools of structuralism, poststructuralism and postmodernism for their linguistic or semiotic determinism, or reductionism. Indeed, in the slippery poststructuralist and postmodernist worlds of smoke and mirrors, of resounding echo chambers, of hidden signifiers, simulacra and deep structures of libidinal desire, nothing is ever as it seems, and the actions of individuals are invariably seen to be driven by forces over which they have little control and even less understanding. Against the influence of these and other deterministic theories, late modernist theorists, such as Giddens, Bourdieu, Castells, Beck, Honneth and even Bauman, have for the most part continued to recognize the autonomy of individuals and their capacity for "agency" and independent, or voluntaristic, social action.

Objectivity: Another sharp distinction that separates the contemporary traditions of postmodernism and poststructuralism from late modernism may be seen in their respective epistemological views on the possibility of "objectivity" when observing and inquiring into the "real world." As we have already seen, poststructuralist and postmodernist theorists largely reject the possibility of "objective," or universalistic, accounts of "reality," "society," "history" or even personal "identity." For these theorists, any attempt to construct "objective" descriptions or explanations of social phenomena is a specious attempt to "essentialize" individuals, objects, structures, processes or events that are always changing and always open to multiple interpretations. For poststructuralists and postmodernists, "objectivity" remains an illusion — a false claim of universalism made within a particular hegemonic discourse. However, even though many late modernist theorists also recognize the indeterminacy of contemporary society, these theorists have not abandoned the pursuit of "objectivity" in their own studies and research. Most late modernist theorists still believe in the possibility of, and the necessity for, providing a general account of our contemporary world from an intentionally objective viewpoint. Thus, Bauman's critical reports on the plight of refugees and asylum-seekers, Castells' examination of our global networks of information and communication and Beck's analysis of the unequal distribution of risks around the world are all presented as "objective" accounts, capable of empirical confirmation or falsification through rational and rigorous methods of testing and research. In this sense, late modernist theorists remain committed to the construction of metanarratives and to the project of objectivity and rationality.

FROM MODERNISM TO LATE MODERNITY: THE SOCIAL THEORIES
OF ANTHONY GIDDENS AND PIERRE BOURDIEU

In many ways, the shift from modern to late modern social theory can best be seen in the work of two contemporary theorists: Anthony Giddens (from the UK) and Pierre Bourdieu (from France), who have each contributed to the transition from the *sociological* theory of the early and mid-twentieth century to the emergent *social*_theory of the late twentieth and early twenty-first centuries. The theme of the loss of individual meaning and autonomy in the face of the growing power of organizations and technology continues to be a connecting thread of much late modernist theory. Giddens's theory of structuration tries to integrate macro and micro levels of social analysis into a single conceptual framework. He does this by borrowing concepts and ideas from a number of different theoretical sources — structural functionalism, symbolic interactionism, ethnomethodology, critical theory and others. The particular force of Giddens's work comes from the fact that he tries to address many of the problems of late modernity, including those raised by postmodernists, within a modernist frame of reference. In other words, Giddens's work tries to emphasize the continuities, rather than the discontinuities, between the present age and those that preceded it. Giddens is also a late modernist in the sense that he believes in the emancipatory project of the Enlightenment. He still believes that individuals, and more particularly communities, can find solutions to the problems of the age by using rational discourse as a basis for collective action. Most late modernist theorists, like Giddens, still subscribe to the notion that, as members of a particular society and culture, most of us share a collective identity and a common sense of history, truth and progress.

Giddens may best be understood as a theorist who attempts to bring together ideas and concepts from a broad range of modernist (twentieth-century) sociological theories. Many of these theories have remained divided along several fault lines: macrosociological theories versus microsociological theories; consensus versus conflict theories; objectivist versus subjectivist theories. Perhaps the most distinctive aspect of Giddens' work is that he tries to reconcile some of these entrenched theoretical divisions, or antinomies, into his own more synthetic or blended theoretical perspective.

STRUCTURATION THEORY OF ANTHONY GIDDENS

Structuration theory is an example of a theory that tries to connect the individual social actor with the larger social structures of society, as well as with the historical and cultural contexts in which all social action takes place. In order to construct a theory that places a reciprocal emphasis on both actor and structure, Giddens has borrowed from several intellectual traditions. His recognition that social structures are always created through "social practices" owes much to a Marxian view of society and history. However, his understanding of the "reflexivity" of practices and the underlying significance of practical consciousness owes much to the insights of ethnomethodology. At the same time, his sense of the growing compression of time and space in modern society has clearly been influenced by postmodernist ideas. There are also other influences at work in Giddens's theory of structuration, including structural functionalism. Thus, we can see that if, as many sociologists believe, Giddens has succeeded at bridging the gap between structure and agency, this has been at a cost. The price that Giddens has had to pay is that of "eclecticism": his theory is one made up of bits and pieces taken from a variety of different and often incompatible, intellectual traditions. These include ideas from the macrosociological theories of structural functionalism, systems theory and neo-Marxist theories and structural conflict theory, and from the microsociological theories of symbolic interactionism, dramaturgy, ethnomethodology, exchange theory, rational-choice theory, among others. In this respect, Giddens follows in a long line of social theorists who attempted to develop general theories of society, including Talcott Parsons' unified theory of social action. Readers must judge for themselves how successful Giddens has been in his attempt to bridge the traditional gaps and divisions that have long existed in sociological theory.

Key Concepts in Giddens' Structuration Theory

Duality of Structure: Perhaps the most important aspect of Giddens' structuration theory is his conception of the relationship between the individual and the larger society. Rather than presenting this relationship as a dichotomy, Giddens suggests that the social structures which make up the larger society and its institutions are best understood as the result of the recurrent, or recursive, routinized and endlessly repeated actions, or social practices, that countless individuals perform on a daily basis.

In other words, structures are best understood as institutionalized, or entrenched, social practices that have become "hardened" over time into habitual patterns of behaviour. These routine patterns often appear to us as "objective" social structures, even though they are derived from the collective social practices of many individuals.

This dynamic conception of social structure — as an abstract artefact of entrenched social practices — is defined by Giddens as the "duality of structure," a conception that in many ways privileges agency over structure. This perspective owes much to the earlier view of Erving Goffman, the dramaturgical theorist, who saw society as the theatrical product of the performances of social actors, and to Harold Garfinkel, the ethnomethodologist for whom the study of "society" was reducible to the "methods of practical reasoning" used by individuals, or "members," to make sense of and produce order in their everyday lives. However, unlike both Goffman and Garfinkel, Giddens tries to balance his focus on social practices with an equal focus on the social structures and social systems that are derived from these practices.

Giddens, therefore, does not view social structures and institutions as lofty, impersonal social edifices that exert an external control over individuals by "socializing" them into accepting the prevailing norms and values of society. This was the view adopted by structural functionalists. But according to Giddens, the structures and processes that appear to govern our conduct in society only seem to be durable and entrenched because all of us continue to reinforce and reproduce these structures in our everyday activities and social practices. In other words, if we all were to change direction and discontinue our routine, recurrent and habitual patterns of behaviour, many of these apparently "objective" structures would collapse before our eyes. Indeed, we have seen dramatic examples of the dissolution of social structures when confronted by the resistance, rebellion or revolution of well-organized oppositional groups. The revolutions in Eastern Europe during the late twentieth and early twenty-first century after the fall of the Soviet Union in 1989 brought about swift and spectacular changes in the governments and political organization of these countries. Similarly, the Arab Spring (between 2010 and 2012), which saw the rise of popular movements against the governments of Tunisia, Egypt, Libya, Syria and the Yemen, sometimes transformed the political regimes of these countries, often with unforeseen tragic consequences. Giddens refers to those occasions when individuals or groups choose to change direction and disrupt the "normal" patterns of social action that continuously reproduce our social structures as "fateful moments." These fateful moments arise from the capacity of individuals or groups to reflect upon their social actions and to change course. Unlike Parsons and the structural functionalists, who emphasized the coercive power of institutionalized norms and values to induce conformity in social actors, Giddens emphasizes the "reflexivity" of individuals and groups and their constant capacity for social change.

It is apparent from his emphasis on the social practices of individuals and groups how much Giddens, as well as Honneth and other social theorists of the new millennium, has been influenced by the new social movements both at home and abroad. The political and social activities of these groups, whether through peaceful democratic protests or through more violent forms of armed struggle, have often changed the political and social landscapes of their respective countries. Although the consequences of these rapid changes are always unpredictable, Giddens fully recognizes (more than the structural functionalists and system theorists who preceded him) the potential of common social practices of ordinary individuals to become powerful agents of social change and equally powerful agents of stability and social stasis.

Rules and resources: For Giddens, social structures are composed from both rules and resources. "Procedural rules" govern how social practices, i.e., routinized social actions and interactions, are performed: how we behave at work, school or college; how we navigate our way through crowded shopping malls; how we greet and address each other and so on. Ethnomethodologists have also analyzed these rules as "methods of practical, or mundane, reasoning." "Moral rules" specify the correct, socially acceptable or socially expected ways of behaving in public and often in private spaces. Moral rules are often codified into norms, mores, customs, traditions and most coercively laws. Moral rules govern how we drive our cars; how we conduct commercial or business transactions; how employers treat employees; how we uphold our contracts and so on. And as Durkheim earlier suggested, these rules exert a coercive, external and objective power over the individual in society. They cannot be ignored, although they can sometimes be violated or transgressed.

"Material, or allocative, resources" refer to the strategic goods and services that are needed to sustain a normal lifestyle, including an income, food and shelter, and other basic necessities of life. "Authoritative resources" refer to social statuses or positions, social class relations, power, prestige and authority relations, social stratification and social mobility and other resources that provide opportunities or constraints in a hierarchically organized society, a community, a business enterprise or any other formal organization.

Figure 11-1: Giddens' Synthetic Approach to Social Theory

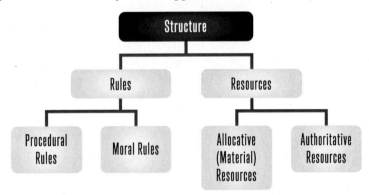

System: Besides the concept of "structure," Giddens also introduces the related concept of "system," and this concept is conceived in more dynamic terms than that of structure. In some ways, Giddens' concept of "system," as a framework of social relations and social integration, resembles that of Parsons. The concept of "system" can refer to many different sets of social relations: from the small nuclear family all the way up to cultural social, political and even global systems. In other words, the concept of "system" can move up and down the ladder of abstraction and across the zones of time and space: from local and intimate social relations, to global and remote social relations. However, Giddens' concept of "system" differs from that of Parsons and from the structural functionalists in three distinct ways:

- Giddens' concept of "system" is always defined concretely in terms of specific time and space, whereas Parsons' conception of "system" was much more abstract, analytical and remote from the real world;
- Giddens has always been more critical of the unequal distribution of allocative and authoritative resources in social systems,

whereas for Parsons, inequality was not a major theoretical concern; and

- Giddens' concept of "system" is more dynamic than that of Parsons and more open to disruption, change and transformation.

Modernity: Giddens is best described as a transitional social theorist whose work serves as a bridge that leads from the earlier mid-modernist, twentieth-century theories of structural functionalists and systems theory, as well as ethnomethodology and symbolic interactionism, to the late modernist, twenty-first-century theorists, such as Bauman, Castells and Beck, among others. And although Giddens' work has clearly been influenced by the postmodernist and poststructuralist writers of the late twentieth century, such as Michel Foucault, Jean Baudrillard, Jean-Francois Lyotard and Jacques Derrida, his work serves as a critical response to the relativism, pluralism and linguistic reductionism of these writers and as an affirmation and defence of the power of the metanarrative and grand theory in contemporary sociology.

Like most other theorists of his generation, Giddens recognizes many novel and distinctive features that contribute to this present era of late modernity, including the globalization of corporate capitalism, the accelerated pace of technological and social change and the profound impact of the new information and communication media on social relations. Late modernity has also seen the rise of identity politics, new social movements and the spread of borderless wars and conflicts, along with global terrorism.

Giddens compares the experience of living in the present age to riding in an out-of-control semi-trailer truck, or what is called in the UK a "juggernaut." He suggests that the rapidity of change in the modern age is both exhilarating and horrifying at the same time. While modernity may offer us endless new opportunities for information, communication, transportation and interaction, it also poses fearsome threats to our very existence — environmental degradation, nuclear apocalypse, terrorism, totalitarianism, war and conflict etc. Above all, modernity remains unpredictable.

Giddens also shows how modernity may greatly undermine the apparent stability and fixity of our "selves" and social institutions. Our identities and institutions may become increasingly changeable. Giddens refers to the idea of "plastic sexuality" as an example of something, sex, that was once assumed to be a fixed biological category but which is now recognized as variable. Similarly, even a basic institution like the nuclear family has become increasingly plastic and may include a step, blended, adoptive, single-parent or same-sex parental family structure. And within this turbulent period of geopolitical and social change, Giddens identifies what he believes to be the major aspects of late modernity.

Distanciation: This concept refers to the compression of space and time that has come to define the age of late modernity. The new information and communication technologies, including cable and internet news services, enable us to witness the unfolding of events in "real time" as they occur in distant locations around the world. Local and global spaces are now interconnected. Sudden digital transfers of wealth can instantly impact the international money markets, causing drops in stock market indexes and the devaluation of national currencies; while the posting of terrorist videos on social media sites can instantly reverberate around the world. We live in a broader and more complex social and cultural environment which presents new possibilities and opportunities, but which also poses new threats and risks.

Power and agency: The interrelated topics of power and agency figure prominently in Giddens' work and in his theory of structuration. Power and authority reside in the rules and resources that positions individuals and groups in hierarchical and stratified social structures and enables some individuals and groups to dominate others. This description and explanation of power and authority is clearly indebted to the ideas of Max Weber. However, because of Giddens' recognition of the "duality of structure," he reminds us that the same social practices that recursively reproduce and reinforce the structures of power and authority may also, under different conditions, undermine, subvert and ultimately overthrow and transform these structures. In other words, Giddens' understanding of power and authority is closely related to his understanding of "agency." He is acutely aware that under the conditions of late modernity, the structures of power and authority are more vulnerable to change and transformation than at any other time in history. Even the most imposing, oppressive and entrenched structures — think of the collapse of the USSR (1989) and of the East European "Peoples' Democracies" throughout the late 1980s and early 1990s; the fall of Apartheid South Africa (1990); and the Arab Spring (2010–11) — can quickly become yesterday's news.

Risk: Late modern societies have become increasingly sensitized to risk factors in their environments. As Giddens suggests, this heightened awareness of risk comes with some ambivalence. On the one hand, unlike premodern societies, which were exposed to a wide variety of unknown natural and social risks, late modern societies are often able to calculate and predict risk factors in their environments. On the other hand, late modern societies face new and more threatening risks, such as environmental degradation, international terrorism, disease pandemics and weapons of mass destruction. Giddens insists that late modernist societies have developed an unprecedented awareness of environmental and existential risks and threats, many of which pose serious challenges to the sustainability and long-term survivability of our habitation on this planet.

Trust: Giddens also suggests that, given our vulnerability to the risks and threats of late modernity, we have become increasingly dependent on our trust relationships with others, especially those which have a strong seal of "legitimacy." This legitimacy may be found in formal organizations, where it is invested in authority figures and respected specialists. However, legitimacy may also be found in informal social relationships, with family members, close friends and established members of the local community. For Giddens, trust has become an important currency in social relations at a time of increasing uncertainty and indeterminacy.

Reflexivity: The last concept from Giddens' theoretical vocabulary in this brief introduction to his basic terms and concepts is that of "reflexivity" (of the self). Unlike the structural functionalists or the systems theorists, for whom the individual was often conceived as a "passive social actor," for Giddens, the individual is very much an active, thoughtful and knowledge-able "agent" who gives as good as they get in their social environment. In other words, the individual is an active agent who is highly responsive to their social situation and capable of exercising free will and of choosing between alternative courses of action. And, as previously mentioned, the individual has a dynamic relationship to their surrounding social struc-tures: they are both shaped by these structures while, at the same time, they actively help to shape these structures through their own actions and social practices. According to Giddens, individuals display three types, or levels, of consciousness in their day-to-day activities and social practices, each of which contributes to the individual's self-development and self-actualization:

- *practical consciousness* refers to the often tacit and taken-for-granted activities in which we all engage during the course of an ordinary day. Whether travelling to work by car, shopping in the local store, taking the dog for a walk or meeting a few friends in a restaurant or local pub, all of these routine activities rely on our "practical consciousness" to ensure that our behaviour is appropriate for the occasion and the setting and that we unthinkingly observe all the unspoken and unwritten rules of social interaction. This concept is closely related to the earlier ethnomethodological concept, "methods of practical, or mundane, reasoning."

- *discursive consciousness* is typically problem-solving in its intent and surfaces whenever we are faced with challenges, threats or even opportunities that require explicit reasoning and cognitive skills. In other words, discursive consciousness becomes most apparent when we are struggling to accomplish a particular task or striving to achieve a particular objective. We enter a state of discursive consciousness when our thinking becomes most "transparent," that is, when we actively and reflexively try to solve a particular problem or puzzle in our own lives. Whether we are struggling to assemble a bookcase, route-finding on a backcountry hike, preparing a speech or addressing problems at work or college, these activities are likely to invoke a level of discursive consciousness.

- *unconscious activity* is a deeper, largely concealed level of consciousness which remains closed to the conscious mind. The unconscious, as Freud and his disciples suggested, refers to the primordial realm of deep sexual drives (the libido), instincts, repressed memories, latent anxieties and neuroses and other unseen and largely unsuspected determinants of our conscious and supposedly rational behaviour. Giddens' recognition of the unconscious is similar to that of Honneth, who realized that some formative experiences remain hidden from us due to what he called the "repression barrier."

Politics: Giddens has become perhaps the most influential sociologist of late modernity in the UK. Besides being a former director of the London School of Economics, Giddens was also a policy advisor to British Prime

Minister Tony Blair and to President Bill Clinton and helped to rebrand the Labour Party as "New Labour." Giddens famously advised Blair and Clinton on the merits of adopting what became known as the "Third Way" in national politics. The Third Way refers to a program and agenda based upon a *centrist* conception of party politics: a politics which intentionally seeks to position itself mid-way between existing political dualities, binaries and polarities. In Britain this approach meant that in order to win general elections (1997, 2001, and again in 2005), the Labour Party (under the leadership of Blair), abandoned much of its traditional socialist program and sought instead to incorporate some aspects of the opposing Conservative Party's agenda. Perhaps, most tellingly, the Labour Party decided to forego its major (Marxist) goal of ending social and economic inequality in favour of a new goal of "social justice." In the US, Clinton announced a similar "reform" in his rebranding of the Democratic Party as a centrist party.

For Giddens, both the traditional politics of the right (conservativism) and of the left (socialism) are now outdated and unable to meet the new political challenges of modernity. In place of the unregulated freedom of the market, advocated by economic conservatives and neoliberals, and in place of a centrally planned economy and traditional welfare state, advocated by socialists, Giddens proposes what he believes to be the best of both worlds. He advocates a politics driven from below rather than from above; decentralization instead of centralization; and the revitalization of democracy through the "reinvention of solidarity." Giddens envisages the rebirth of democracy through the mobilization of social movements, through the growth of popular self-help networks and through the strengthening of local community control at the expense of more remote and unaccountable private corporations and public state agencies. In reviewing Giddens' vision of Third Way politics, several features appear especially significant: Third Way politics proposes a deliberative democracy that is characterized by public dialogue, discussion and debate. In this respect, Third Way democracy differs from populism inasmuch as populism often encourages demagoguery (rather than genuine participation), monologue (rather than dialogue) and passion (rather than reason). Third Way politics addresses many of the "new social issues," including environmental, human rights and global security issues. Third way politics emphasizes the broader issues of social justice over the more traditional issues of socio-economic inequality and the need for economic redistribution. In place of the traditional focus on class inequality, Third Way politics emphasizes social justice in gender, sexual preference, race, and ethnic relations

In retrospect, a couple of observations can be made regarding the legacy of Third Way politics. Notwithstanding his disastrous decision to join the 2003 US invasion of Iraq, Blair's successful attempt to find a compromise peace settlement (the Good Friday Agreement in 1998) between Catholics and Protestants in Northern Ireland certainly fits the pattern of Giddens' synthetic social theory. At the same time, more recent events appear to have thrown into question the centrist strategy of Third Way politics in both the UK and the US. In the wake of the Brexit referendum vote for Britain to leave the European Union, British politics seems to have abandoned any attachment to centrism and has repolarized between the left (Jeremy Corbyn, leader of the Labour Party) and the hard right (UK Independence Party, UKIP). Similarly, in the US, the Bill Clinton–Barack Obama–Hillary Clinton centrist agenda has given way to a repolarization between the hard left (Bernie Sanders) and the hard right (Donald Trump), a division which resulted in the unexpected victory of Donald Trump and the Republican Party in the 2016 presidential and Congressional elections.

Perhaps this demise of centrism in each country exposes a significant problem in both the practice of Third Way politics by Blair and Clinton and in the underlying synthetic social theory championed by Giddens. The results of the Brexit referendum and the US elections have shown that a significant section of the electorate in each country voted against what they perceived to be the "political class" or the "political elite," located far away in Brussels, capital of the European Union, or in Washington. Trump claimed to speak for the forgotten underclasses residing in the rural and rustbelt regions of the US — those most affected by de-industrialization and by the international trade agreements that threatened to outsource and off-shore jobs to countries with cheap labour. In Britain, Nigel Farage (of UKIP) also campaigned to prevent the loss of jobs to other countries within the European Union and to prevent competition for British jobs from European immigrants. In each country, the disaffected, the white working class, felt that their political and economic institutions had betrayed them and that political control was now far removed from them — in Brussels or Washington. These unexpected referendum and election results expressed a raw emotional sense of despair that the cool, analytical, rational politicians and pundits of the established political parties failed to recognize, register or respond to.

The cool, analytical, political distance that separates many centrist politicians from their troubled electorates parallels the analytical distance that separates most social theorists from the subjects of their theories. In this sense, Giddens, like most of his colleagues, tends to over-intellectualize his social theory. He focuses on the reflexivity and duality of social practices and social structures as a cognitive rather than as an emotional process. However, to project an alternative approach to social theory, we can return to Axel Honneth's theory of recognition and respect. Honneth understood the potential for disrespect and non-recognition to drive social movements of protest and defiance. We have reached a point in our history and in our social theory when we can no longer afford to overlook or dismiss the power and passion of raw emotion to turn the wheels of politics and to transform society. It is time for social theory to reconnect with emotion and with lived experience.

Criticisms of Giddens' Social Theory

Like any other social theorist, Giddens has attracted his share of critics. The following are some of the major criticisms that have been made of his version of structuralism:

- Some critics maintain that in his attempt to reduce large scale social structures to the social practices of individuals, Giddens has overlooked any *historical perspective* on the evolution and continuity of social structures. Structures endure throughout historical time and have a reality above and beyond the routinization and recursive reproduction of present social practices.
- Similarly, other critics have suggested that in his attempt to reduce large scale social structures to the social practices of individuals, Giddens has failed to recognize that structures can become separated or alienated from the individuals who first produced and reproduced them. Structures can acquire an independence from individuals and can begin to constrain and control them. In other words, Giddens overlooks the *power of structures to dominate* and subordinate the individual in society.
- Some critics have also exposed what they claim is the Eurocentrism of Giddens' emphasis on the generative potential of social practices to produce and reproduce social structures. There remains

some skepticism as to whether the concept of "social practices" can legitimately be accepted as a cultural universal. Or whether, the concept of "routine," when applied to China or India, for example, may have a rather different (subjective) meaning for individuals in different cultures. According to these critics, Giddens' theory of structuration has yet to demonstrate its cross-cultural and comparative validity.

- Finally, some critics (especially those influenced by the work of Honneth) have objected to what they see as the over-intellectualized or *over-rationalized conception of the individual* in Giddens' version of structuration theory. These critics have complained that Giddens' theory overlooks the emotional aspects of individuals' lives, notwithstanding his recognition of the power of the unconscious to influence both practical and discursive forms/levels of consciousness. As always, readers may form their own conclusion after reviewing Giddens' theory for themselves.

THE STRUCTURATION THEORY OF PIERRE BOURDIEU

The social theory of Pierre Bourdieu has much in common with that of Anthony Giddens but also much to distinguish it. Like Giddens, Bourdieu begins by rejecting the entrenched dichotomies, or antinomies, of much previous sociological theory: those divisions between macro (holistic/collectivistic) versus micro (nominalist/individualistic) theories; between objectivistic versus subjectivist theories; and between determinist versus voluntarist theories. Also like Giddens, Bourdieu introduces his own set of key concepts that are intended to provide a theoretical framework for synthesizing, or integrating, these previous sociological divisions into a unified theory of structuration. While there is considerable overlap in the theoretical and epistemological orientations of Bourdieu and Giddens, the big difference is that Bourdieu's work is primarily focused on the issue of "domination," or more precisely, on the structures of domination in contemporary society and on the practices that reproduce and reinforce these structures. Like Giddens, Bourdieu is interested in how recursive or taken-for-granted social practices contribute to the formation and maintenance of social structures through the process of "structuration." But unlike Giddens, Bourdieu remains fixated on how these practices contribute to relations of domination and structures of power in contemporary capitalist societies.

Given his preoccupation with the study of domination and power, it is easy to spot traces of Marxism in Bourdieu's work. He has, however, remained critical of much Marxian social science because of its (alleged) overemphasis on modes of production and the economy, often at the expense of other sectors of society. In other words, Bourdieu has remained critical of the "economism" and "productivisim" of much traditional and contemporary Marxist theory. Instead, Bourdieu focuses on the cultural aspects of domination, power and inequality — an orientation that undoubtedly owes much to his earlier work as an anthropologist in Algeria. For this reason, Bourdieu is sometimes classified as a critical theorist, although his work should be distinguished from the major tradition of critical theory associated with the Frankfurt School. What then, we may ask, are the unique features of Bourdieu's study of domination and power; how does his version of structuration theory differ from that of Giddens; and how does his critical cultural theory differ from that of the Frankfurt School critical theorists?

In much of his work, Bourdieu has tried to show how many of the mundane and ordinary activities that most of us pursue on a daily basis are profoundly influenced by our position within a stratified set of social relations. Indeed, most of our actions and interactions are conditioned — often without our knowledge — by how we fit into a local power structure and how we behave within a local dominance hierarchy. Without fully realizing it, our behaviour, expectations and sense of what is appropriate are strongly affected by how we view ourselves in comparison to others in any given social situation. Like Giddens, Bourdieu suggests that our social practices are not only conditioned by these structures of power and domination, but our recursive and routinized practices also serve to reproduce and reinforce these structures. Our social identities are at the same time both the products and the producers of our social environments within an unequal class society.

Unlike more traditional Marxian and conflict theories of society, which have normally focused on the macrosocial aspects of inequality (modes of production and distribution, ideology, class consciousness, wealth, power, the state etc.), Bourdieu focuses on the more intimate cultural aspects of domination in contemporary society. He examines how our everyday social practices and social identities are "inscribed" with the markers of our class status. These markers include not only such obvious cultural indicators as the clothes we wear, the food we eat, the entertainment we enjoy and the sports we play and watch, but also the physical markers, such as our physical health and well-being and our appearance. In other words, our social status is "inscribed" on all aspects of our social and physical existence.

For Bourdieu, the social world is a competitive arena composed of local stratified battlegrounds, or "fields," where members of society compete with each other for status and recognition. Much of this competition and struggle has become "second nature" to us and is no longer directly conscious. The many ways in which our behaviour fits our class position in society is reflected in our recursive, routinized and habitual social practices — what Bourdieu calls our "habitus." Each of us enters the different battlegrounds, or fields, of our social world with various resources, or "capital." Each of us, to a greater or lesser extent, has access to different types of capital: economic, social, cultural and symbolic. And our personal access to these material and social resources greatly affects our opportunities for social mobility and self-actualization within the structures of a capitalist class society. In this respect, we could say that Bourdieu undertakes a class analysis of our social world almost from an anthropological perspective, paying close attention to the cultural beliefs and practices that characterize our personal and interpersonal lifestyles and lived experiences. In order to focus more clearly on Bourdieu's version of structuration theory, we turn now to a brief introduction and illustration of some of his basic terms and key concepts.

KEY CONCEPTS IN BOURDIEU'S STRUCTURATION THEORY

Habitus: "Habitus" is one of the central concepts in Bourdieu's structuration theory (sometimes called his "theory of practice"). But rather than a mindless or unthinking mechanical repetition of a habit, Bourdieu's concept refers to a system of "dispositions" internalized from an early age and consolidated and further developed through maturation into adulthood. The habitus of an individual refers to their personal psychological and cultural inheritance acquired from family, friends and close acquaintances throughout their growth and maturation. To take a hypothetical example, the habitus of Donald Trump, acquired from his early days, would include a strong sense of competition and a ruthlessness to succeed at all costs, a mindset and a set of practices originally acquired from his father and later reinforced at the military academy that he attended during his early teenage years. The development of the habitus may also be divided into two stages: the "primary habitus," acquired during early childhood that reflects the values, beliefs and dispositions of the parents and their position within society; and the "secondary habitus," which reflects later experiences in school and in various occupational statuses and roles. In the case of Trump, for example, the secondary habitus would include those dispositions acquired from his military academy schooling and from his later immersion in the world of real estate sales and marketing and from allied business transactions.

Field: For Bourdieu, all social interactions take place within a particular social space, and every social space may be further divided into a variety of social "fields." A social field may include such arenas as art or science, work or leisure, career, recreation and so on. Each social field may be further divided into subfields. Thus, an individual's recreational field may include both individual and team sports; full contact or passive sports, participant or spectator sports etc. For Bourdieu, fields are also the settings, or contexts, in which individual agency and structure interact with each other and where individuals are both produced by, and producers of, these institutions. All actions, or practices, within a field are conducted according to rules and expectations specific to that field. These rules are referred to by Bourdieu as "doxa." But most importantly, fields are also arenas of competition and struggle — for recognition and respect and for material and symbolic rewards (and sometimes costs). Fields are networks of positions and statuses that define relations of dominance and subordination, or power and subservience. There are always some agents who are able to "call the shots" and others who are required to obey. In the case of Trump, for many years one of his primary fields remained his career field: the corporate world in which he presided over a personal office staff, as well as architects, tradespeople, realtors, bankers, municipal and international zoning officials etc. Today, however, his career field has changed into that of the US presidency, with his own administrative staff, congressional and senatorial colleagues and opponents, as well as foreign leaders and diplomats. But the field never ceases to be an arena of competition and struggle, something with which Trump is very familiar.

Figure 11-2: Bourdieu's Structuration

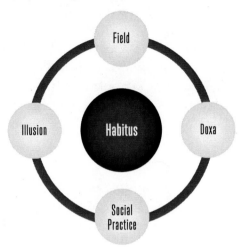

Capital: In order to compete in any social field, an individual requires resources that can be used to gain admission into a field and to achieve upward social mobility within that field. Bourdieu identifies several types of capital: "Economic capital" refers to a person's wealth, assessed in terms of property, revenue, income etc. This type of capital can be readily converted into money, which is the universal currency for economic capital. In the case of Trump, his economic capital includes the sum total of his personal and corporate fortune, measured in property holdings, bank balances, stocks and shares, among other financial instruments. Another form is "social capital," which refers to the range and influence of an individual's network of social relations. The greater the potential scope and influence of one's social contacts and acquaintances, the greater one's social capital. Prestigious social capital can open up opportunities for material and political resources. Bourdieu also includes "cultural capital," which is most commonly expressed in educational qualifications, including academic degrees, professional certificates and diplomas, and other documentary achievements. But cultural capital may also be objectified in the ownership of precious paintings, books, sculptures, monuments or other artistic treasures. In the case of Trump, part of his cultural capital comes from his boast at having been a graduate of the prestigious Wharton School of Finance at the University of Pennsylvania. And finally, Bourdieu refers to "symbolic capital," which is expressed as honour and recognition attained in the larger society. Strictly speaking, symbolic capital is not regarded by Bourdieu as an independent source of capital but is rather based on prestige that has been converted, or transferred, from economic, social or cultural capital. In other words, symbolic capital represents the prestige or status acquired from other forms of capital in specific fields of endeavour. In the case of Trump, the best example of his symbolic capital is his own name brand, which is globally marketed as a mark of business success in the corporate worlds of real estate, hotels, golf courses and other branded merchandise, such as clothing, fragrances, beverages etc.

Figure 11-3: Sources of Personal Capital

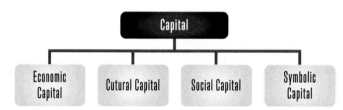

The sociology of Pierre Bourdieu has also tried to accommodate the agency and structures of social action within a unified conceptual framework. Bourdieu's work comes out of a French intellectual heritage and has been heavily influenced by such French traditions as structuralism, existentialism, Marxism and poststructuralism. In much the same way as Giddens, Bourdieu has made the concept of "practice" a link between the social actor and the social and historical structures of society. However, other key concepts used by Bourdieu bear all the distinctive hallmarks of the French intellectual heritage. This is particularly true of his central concept of "habitus," which refers to the collective mental or cognitive structures inherited by social actors as an important part of their social worlds. This notion of collective mental structures has persisted for a long time. We have only to think of the *volonté générale* of Rousseau, the *consensus universalis* of Comte, the *conscience collective* of Durkheim, the *mentalités* of Lévi-Bruhl and Lévi-Strauss and the *discursive regimes* of Foucault to see that this has been an enduring theme in French social thought. Even the distinction between "habitus" and "field" — between the ideational world of mental structures and the material world of social structures — owes something to Durkheim's distinction between the structures of social solidarity and the structures of the conscience collective. In reading Bourdieu, one sometimes gets a sense of déjà vu: *plus ça*

change, plus c'est la même chose (the more things change, the more they stay the same). At the same time, the international prestige accorded to his work shows that Bourdieu has been successful in adapting his theoretical framework to the needs of practical research. In this respect, Bourdieu, who died in 2002, significantly advanced the integration of theory and research in his own sociological work.

ZYGMUNT BAUMAN AND THE TRAGIC SENSE OF LIFE

Another of the great contemporary late modernist social thinkers was the sociologist Zygmunt Bauman (born in Poland in 1925 and died in England in 2017), although there is no clear agreement among social theorists as to how Bauman should be labelled. Indeed, he has been variously called a postmodernist, a critical modernist, a critical theorist and a critical humanist, among other designations. But he may also be classified, along with other theorists in this discussion, as a late modernist: someone who was strongly influenced by postmodernism and poststructuralism but without accepting all of the assumptions and conclusions of these perspectives. Instead, he forged his own distinctive theoretical and conceptual framework with which to understand the often bewildering and alarming events that are transforming our contemporary world.

In many ways, Bauman was one of the most compelling and colourful recent characters in contemporary sociology. Besides being a prolific writer with a rich personal biography, Bauman constantly used his work to highlight the suffering of some of the most vulnerable members of our global society. In this respect, Bauman always identified with the "underdogs" in the world and through his own work, sought to tell their story, to bear witness to their suffering and to alleviate their plight. This is a social theorist with a clear moral conscience and a strong sense of moral purpose.

Bauman's own life history sensitized him to the horrors of political and racial persecution, as well as to other forms of social and economic injustice experienced by vulnerable groups and individuals around the world. As a Polish Jew, he and his immediate family were forced to escape from Poland into the USSR during the Second World War, where he served in the Red Army. After the war, Bauman returned to Poland and taught at the University of Warsaw until 1968, when growing political repression and anti-Semitism forced him with his family into exile: first to Israel and then to the UK. In subsequent years, Bauman became one of the most celebrated and revered sociologists of his generation, and his prolific publication record remains a testament to his lasting intellectual achievements.

Perhaps the single most important distinction that Bauman made in his work is that between the "sociology of postmodernism" versus "postmodernist sociology." While Bauman's work can accurately be described as the sociology of postmodernism, he certainly cannot be accurately described as a postmodernist sociologist. This distinction means that although Bauman was fascinated and often alert to many aspects of contemporary, or postmodern, society — such as its uncertainty, its unpredictability and what we have called its "indeterminacy" — he did not share many of the assumptions or conclusions of postmodernist social theorists. In other words, unlike many postmodern theorists who have implicitly or explicitly accepted the postmodern "deaths" of "reality," "society," "history," "objectivity" or core "identity" in contemporary social relations, Bauman continued to study postmodern society within a cautious modernist conceptual framework and theoretical perspective. He remained committed to describing and explaining the changes and transformations of contemporary society within a modified grand theory or metanarrative. In his investigations of the horrors of the Holocaust, or the marginalization of refugees and asylum-seekers, or the poverty and powerlessness of the urban underclasses, Bauman never lost his belief in the value of empirical research that could still provide an accurate and "objective" picture of dismal reality.

Although Bauman may not have shared many of the theoretical and epistemological beliefs of the postmodernists, he remained skeptical of more traditional modernist beliefs. His landmark sociological study of the Holocaust robbed him of any faith in the Enlightenment "emancipatory project" and cast considerable doubt on any facile rationalist hopes for the triumphal march of "reason" and "progress" in the future development of humanity. If Bauman can be regarded as a residual modernist in any meaningful sense, then it is only as a disillusioned and fatalistic late modernist. At various points in his writings, he makes clear his abandonment of the traditional Enlightenment project:

> Two features, nonetheless, make our situation — our form
> of modernity — novel and different. The first is the gradual

collapse and swift decline of early modern illusion: of the belief that there is an end to the road along which we proceed, an attainable telos of historical change, a state of perfection to be reached tomorrow, next year or next millennium, some sort of good society, just society and conflict-free society in all or some of its many postulated aspects. (2000: 29)

Bauman pursued a number of major themes in his research and scholarly studies. When viewed alongside many other sociologists of this period (from the mid- to late twentieth century into the early twenty-first century), Bauman's orientation appears quite critical — even radical. Indeed, much of his work may be read as an extended critique of the policies and practices of neoliberalism and of its local and global impact on social relations. Bauman's investigations convinced him that neoliberalism had directly contributed to the growing inequality of wealth and income in society and to the inevitable polarization and stratification that resulted from this inequality. He remained critical of the policies of privatization, deregulation, marketization and commodification of public resources and basic goods and services under late capitalism and of the corresponding erosion of personal security, safety, autonomy and liberty that so often accompanied these policies. The following major themes emerged from his critiques of neoliberalism:

Liquid society: Bauman's idea of a "liquid society" is characterized by high levels of job insecurity (the rise of the "precariat"), community decline, family breakdown and a general instability and unpredictability, or what we have called the "indeterminacy" of social relations.

Globalization: This refers to the loss and transfer of power and sovereignty of the nation state to more global institutional actors, such as transnational and multinational corporations, as well as to international government agencies, such as the World Bank and the International Monetary Fund, also trade deals like the North American Free Trade Agreement, or NAFTA.

End of welfare and the social state: Neoliberalism has led to the collapse of "society" as a protective welfare or social state and the privatization, deregulation and outsourcing, off-shoring and sub-contracting of many former public utilities and social services to private, for-profit companies and agencies.

Violence of abstraction: The preoccupation of modernism (both as a discourse and as a set of discursive practices) with abstraction, homogeneity, control, order, stability, certainty and inflexibility is reflected in neoliberalism. For Bauman, modernism was typically represented in hegemonic systems of bureaucratic classification which often only served to include insiders and to exclude outsiders. The dysfunctional extreme to which this process of bureaucratic classification could sometimes lead was exemplified, for Bauman, in the horrors of the Holocaust. In some ways, Bauman's critique of bureaucratic and abstract solutions to political and moral problems is similar to that of Derek Sayer (1987), who offered his own critique of the "violence of abstraction."

Postmodern ethics: The decline of modernism also raises the problem of postmodern ethics in the contemporary world. Whereas modernism erected abstract, systematic and logical frameworks, such as constitutions, charters, bills of rights etc., to define and resolve problems of ethics and morality, many of these abstract systems have lost their authority and credibility to resolve ethical problems in the postmodern period. We have entered a new age of cultural relativism and pluralism which rejects universalizing, totalizing and essentializing discourses, even ethical discourses. The decline of modernity and the rise of postmodernity has presented what Bauman saw as the new challenges and new opportunities of postmodern ethics.

Ambivalence: Perhaps the quintessential aspect of Bauman's social theory and sociological studies is his emphasis on "ambivalence," a theme that haunts his work in a number of ways. Bauman remained ambivalent throughout his studies as to whether the present age could or should be characterized as either late modern or as postmodern. Although he readily acknowledges most attributes of contemporary postmodern society — such as its constant flux and change; its technological compression of space and time; its uncertainty and unpredictability; its hyperreality; and its pluralization of structures, discourses and identities — Bauman was still unable to embrace the relativism of postmodern theory or to fully abandon the metanarratives, and holistic perspectives of modernist theory and history. In this respect, Bauman remained a *child of two worlds* — caught in the interstices between them. Besides his own theoretical dilemma, the theme of ambivalence runs throughout Bauman's writings on the unpredictability of contemporary society and on the ethical problems posed by these uncertainties, instabilities and insecurities. He attempts to reach an accommodation with the present age in all its chaos and complexity by recognizing that although this age presents new challenges to our former modernist assumptions and conclusions about life and knowledge, this new century also offers us new opportunities for reflexive self-consciousness and for new forms of recognition, understanding and social justice. Bauman refers to this perspective, perhaps a little ironically, as "postmodern wisdom":

> What the postmodern mind is aware of is that there are problems in human and social life with no good solutions, twisted trajectories that cannot be straightened up, ambivalences that are more than linguistic blunders yelling to be corrected, doubts which cannot be legislated out of existence, moral agonies which no reason-dictated recipes can soothe, let alone cure. The postmodern mind does not expect any more to find the all-embracing, total and ultimate formula of life without ambiguity, risk, danger and error, and is deeply suspicious of any voice that promises otherwise. The postmodern mind is aware that each local, specialized and focused treatment, effective or not when measured by its ostensive target, spoils as much as, if not more than, it repairs. The postmodern mind is reconciled to the idea that the messiness of the human predicament is here to stay. This is, in the broadest outlines, what can be called "postmodern wisdom. (1993: 245)

The Liquid World of Zygmunt Bauman

As a public intellectual, Bauman is probably most famous for his theory of "liquid modernity." Bauman remained ambivalent regarding the terminology of postmodernism and postmodernity even though he recognized that the contemporary age and contemporary society were very different from the modern age of the early and mid-twentieth century. Unwilling to use the terms "postmodernity" or "late modernity," Bauman decided to use "liquid modernity" to capture the distinctive and quintessential qualities and dimensions of the time in which we currently live. In one of his most quoted observations, Bauman distinguished this present period of human history from that which immediately preceded it: "In a liquid modern life there are no permanent bonds, and any that we take up for a time must be tied loosely so that they can be untied again, as quickly and as effortlessly as possible, when circumstances change — as they surely will in our liquid modern society, over and over again" (2003).

Bauman incorporated many of the characteristics and dimensions of postmodernity into his own conception of liquid modernity. Thus, liquid modernity, or liquid society, is defined in terms of its diversity and plurality; mobility and short-term perspective; compression of space and time through telecommunications via social media and the internet; multiple and hybrid identities; global reach and economic dependence on service, commercial and financial industries (rather than on manufacturing or primary resource extraction industries); the precariousness of work; and the shallowness and superficiality of personal and social relations, as well as an abiding sense of insecurity and anxiety about the present and the future. In other words, for Bauman, liquid modernity is the antithesis of what he calls "heavy, or solid, modernity."

Heavy modernity was everything that liquid modernity is not. Thus, heavy modernity was based on manufacturing (or primary resource extraction) industries with typically immobile capital assets and a stable workforce. The goods produced in a solid society were designed to be durable, unlike the disposable products of a liquid society. Solid society emphasized unity and homogeneity and fixed identities, in contrast to the emphasis on diversity, heterogeneity and the multiple mutable identities of liquid societies. Moreover, solid society and heavy modernity ensured greater job security and relatively stable work and social relations and also encouraged confidence in future progress. On the other hand, members of liquid society experience job insecurity and high employee turnover, or "churn rates," shallow and superficial personal and social relations and general anxiety and concern about the future. For Bauman, these two types of modernity stand in stark contrast to each other.

In some ways, it could be said, perhaps unkindly, that Bauman wanted to have his cake and eat it, too. While he incorporated all the symptoms of postmodernity into his own theoretical and empirical studies, he was unwilling to adopt a postmodernist interpretation which might imply a philosophy of "anything goes." Bauman resisted the postmodernist perspective and steered clear of the relativism, localism and indeterminacy typically associated with postmodernism. At the same time his own perspective, which remained suspended between the relativism of postmodernism and the determinism of modernism, eventually became the target of criticism from other social theorists (see, for example, Tester 2002; 2004).

Some of the sterner critics of Bauman's theory of liquid modernity have denied that Bauman's perspective constitutes a "theory" at all. Instead, they claim that Bauman's use of the term "liquid" is nothing more than a descriptive metaphor devoid of any generalizable causal analysis, explanatory power or empirically testable validity (Jacobsen and Marshman 2008). A number of critical essays on Bauman's work have been published in two edited collections (Elliott 2007; Jacobsen 2008). There have also been some objections to Bauman's analysis of the Holocaust set out in his book *Modernity and the Holocaust* (see, for example, Freeman 1995; Mann 2005; Vetlesen 2005; Cannon 2016; Sznaider 2016); while his views on consumerism have not gone unchallenged either (see, for instance, Warde 1994a; 1994b). Critics of Bauman's analysis of the Holocaust have suggested that he underemphasized and underestimated the regressive ideological content of Nazism, especially its extreme racism, anti-Semitism and brutal dehumanization, in his view of the Holocaust as a product of the modern bureaucratization of society.

Other critics have suggested that Bauman's metaphorical conception of liquidity and his preoccupation with the instabilities and uncertainties of contemporary life are rooted in a deeply Eurocentric and metrocentric (city-based) view of social reality (see Rattsani 2014, 2016). This privileged view, say the critics, has little relevance for those developing societies of the Global South, whose populations face far more fateful and urgent challenges to their ways of life than those relatively privileged denizens of the "liquid societies" of the Global North. Another indictment of Bauman's work from a political perspective is that, in the absence of any viable theory of society, Bauman's ideas provide little support for any politically progressive social change or for any significant policy reforms. In other words, to echo Karl Marx, while Bauman may have offered some philosophical interpretations of the social world, he has done little to change it.

However, other criticisms of Bauman's work have been more measured and less dismissive. These more tempered criticisms concede that Bauman has managed to capture the novelty, flux and indeterminacy of liquid modernity, although he has overlooked those residual aspects of heavy or solid modernity that continue to co-exist alongside liquid institutions, perspectives and practices. While many aspects of contemporary society may conform to Bauman's description of liquid modernity, there are others that still correspond to more traditional and customary beliefs and practices (see, for example, Smart and Shipman 2004; Dawson 2012). Some examples of these remaining forms of solid modernity were seen in the 2016 US presidential election. Many commentators have noted that part of the success of Trump's electoral campaign came from his promise of a halt to the fast-eroding "solid modernity" of the US economy, a promise which involved the return of previously outsourced and off-shored full-time jobs to the manufacturing and heavy industrial centres, and a reversion of the evolving precarious "gig" economy back to a stable and well paid workforce that could once again see progress and growth in its standard of living. This is the promise that won Donald Trump the support of the uneasy working-class constituencies of "middle America," and a similar promise won the British Prime Minister Boris Johnson the election in 2019: a promise to fully restore a "solid economy." Indeed, much of Trump's campaign was based on an explicit repudiation of globalism and on his expressed intention to regain US economic and political sovereignty by withdrawing from international trade deals and from other international multilateral accords, such as the Paris climate agreement. Similar examples may be found across Europe where other far-right nationalist politicians are exploiting public fears of global terrorism and popular resentments over international trade deals that seem only to benefit the corporate elites, as well as widespread disaffection — such as Brexit in 2016 — with multinational political unions that appear to reduce national sovereignty and to encourage economic immigrants and political refugees. However we interpret these signs, it appears that some politicians — with the support of selective media outlets — have tried to capitalize on these concerns with appeals to deeply conservative values that seek to restore an earlier age of heavy modernity.

Finally, some critics have taken issue with Bauman's rather critical views on what he calls the "liquid identities" that reflect the conditions of contemporary social life. Bauman appears to lament the passing of the more traditional or core identities that were characteristic of earlier solid modernity, and he appears critical of the proliferation of multiple, mutable, hybrid and constantly changing liquid identities that are characteristic of contemporary society. Indeed, Bauman implies that contemporary liquid identities are essentially narcissistic in nature and represent a new age of "manic individualism":

> Liquid modernity casts all of us as outsiders, outcasts, strangers, others; it encourages reflexive experimentation in our self-constitution — a manic individualism; it accelerates the liquefaction of identity into privatised, episodic fabrications performed under "constant erasure," drifting along schizoid, fragmentary twisted trajectories. This world is as much about contested meanings as about material complexity; and the liquid mode of experience courts vulnerability, insecurity, ambivalence, confusion, and loss of orientation. Liquid life is a series of new beginnings that demand swift and painless endings, resulting in a constant state of uncertainty and uprootedness. (2005)

Critics have challenged Bauman on at least two fronts: first, that he overlooks the persistence of stable, core identities in contemporary society (see, for example, Paterson 2006); and second, that he fails to appreciate the emancipatory implications of an age in which diverse and multiple (sexual, ethnic, racial, generational, national) identities can be acknowledged and celebrated. Indeed, these critics charge Bauman with being too conservative and basically regressive in his judgements of the age of liquid identities (see, for example, Gane 2004).

A Humanistic Epitaph

There can be little doubt that Bauman focused on those who have been silenced and oppressed in the world today: "The task for sociology is to come to the help of the individual. We have to be in service of freedom. It is something we have lost sight of" (quoted in Rameesh 2010). He focused his research on the life experiences of immigrants, refugees, asylum-seekers, the urban underclasses and other people whose lives have been uprooted and often terrorized by the impersonal and dehumanizing forces of state repression, protectionism, xenophobia, marginalization and global indifference. And, of course, he introduced the concept of "liquidity" into sociological discourse and published books on liquid modernity, liquid society, liquid life, liquid times, liquid identity, liquid love, liquid fear and most recently, liquid evil. Each of these books illustrates the strong sense of engagement and empathy that Bauman clearly felt towards the subjects of his scholarly studies — the poor, the oppressed, the marginalized and the excluded; in other words, to use the words of Frantz Fanon (1963), the "wretched of the earth."

Opinions remain divided as to the value of Bauman's writings when assessed as examples of social theory or rigorous sociological research. However, when read as a works of art, as powerful and lyrical descriptions of contemporary social reality experienced by the most vulnerable members of our global society, the value of Bauman's contributions would seem to be self-evident. Rarely has a sociologist or social theorist written with such passion and compassion and with such empathy for the grim realities faced by the socially marginalized and excluded. For this alone, his work is well worth reading.

SLAVOJ ŽIŽEK, THE JOCULAR ICONOCLAST

One of the most popular social theorists writing today is the Slovenian philosopher Slavoj Žižek, a social thinker whose observations on popular culture and contemporary politics have conferred upon him a celebrity status in both the mass media and academia. Born in the former Yugoslavia, Žižek grew up under the communist regime of Josip Broz Tito. Although this was a more liberal regime than those which ruled in the USSR and in other Eastern Bloc states, Žižek suffered some official retaliation for his independent ideas and was dismissed from his university post for his political non-conformity. During the late 1980s and early 1990s, however, Žižek began to achieve international recognition as a social theorist and public intellectual. Since his first English-language publication, *The Sublime Object of Ideology* (1989), Žižek has acquired a reputation as an original and provocative social thinker whose work offers frequent critical commentaries on many current cultural and political events.

In many ways, Žižek is, at least for the novice reader, a difficult and often frustrating writer to comprehend. His language is often arcane and full of neologisms, or coinages, and his arguments are replete with references to a wide range of sources, including literature, music and popular culture as well as philosophy and politics. His style has been dismissed by some critics for its "obscurantism" and unnecessary erudition and by others for its frivolous and sometimes vulgar irony and humour. Žižek is a provocative thinker and writer whose work has attracted both adulation and condemnation in the court of public opinion.

Although there are many different ways to characterize Žižek's contributions to social theory, it is probably simplest to describe him as a
latter-day critical theorist. However, unlike the original critical theorists
of the Frankfurt School, Žižek has been influenced by, and has settled his
accounts with, the age of postmodernism and poststructuralism. Like
the postmodernists, Žižek remains attentive to the power of language
and discourse and to the significance of the local: he is often focused on
the details of everyday life and on the worlds of popular culture. But in
a clear departure from postmodernism, Žižek rejects what he sees as the
relativism, pluralism, subjectivism and irrationalism of postmodernism.
Instead, he seeks in his work to restore more traditional notions of truth,
materialism, universality and the self as essential categories of philosophical and social analysis. At the same time, Žižek's theoretical work carries
the imprint of his own inimitable style: his work is among other things
*idiosyncrat*ic (highly individualistic), *eclectic* (borrows ideas from many
unrelated sources), *esoteric* (only understood by a small, privileged, intellectual elite) and *iconoclastic* (critically targets well respected canonical
authorities).

Some of Žižek's harsher critics (see, for example, Kirsch 2008) remain
convinced that his work is wholly eclectic and disconnected from the
mainstream traditions of philosophy and social theory. Other, more
sympathetic readers have discerned a method to his philosophical "madness" and have concluded that Žižek is a "systematic" thinker (Dean 2006,
2007; Johnston 2009). However one views the overall configuration of
his work, there are several main themes that emerge from his writings
which, together with some of his key concepts, begin to define the shape
of his intellectual project.

Žižek is best understood as a critical theorist and his main theoretical
project remains the "critique of ideology." In developing his perspective,
Žižek acknowledges a number of intellectual influences that have shaped
his approach to the critical study of ideology: German idealism (notably
Kant, Hegel and Schelling), Marxism and the psychoanalytic theories of
Jacques Lacan, a major representative of the school of French poststructuralism. But aside from his indebtedness to these earlier thinkers, especially
Lacan, Žižek's work may also be seen as a challenge to postmodernism.
Although Žižek has passed through the age of postmodernism, his work
may be read as a vigorous counter-attack on postmodernist theory and
a repudiation of some of its most fashionable tenets. Žižek impatiently

rejects the postmodernist view that the "Real" is only ever constructed through language and discourse, or that "Truth" is always relative to and only ever derived from a particular discourse and its corresponding practices. Instead of resigning himself to difference and diversity, Žižek seeks to restore the categories of universality, materiality and reality to the language of philosophy and social theory.

Inescapable ideology: Žižek claims that all members of society remain trapped in an "ideological fantasy": ideology is like the air we breathe; we cannot escape from it. It frames our perceptions and observations of the world in which we live; it is inscribed in our actions and daily practices. Ideology may be thought of as the "spectacles we wear behind our eyes." According to Žižek, we live in a dream world of ideology, which filters our perceptions and experiences of the "Real." Or, as one perceptive commentator observed, for Žižek, "ideology provides an idealized vision of a `society' that cannot really exist" (Elliott 1995: 242, quoted in García and Sánchez 2008: 11).

In many respects, Žižek is heavily indebted to Jacques Lacan, in his choice of key concepts, his underlying theory and his methods of social analysis. For Žižek, as for Lacan, all of us struggle with a deep sense of loss, or what Lacan called "desire," a feeling that derives from our inability to return to the primal state of the Real. With the acquisition of language, we are forever banished from the nurturing state of pre-linguistic maternal care and comfort. According to Žižek, much of the latent energy for politics and public activity is generated from what he calls "surplus" or "excess" enjoyment or "*jouissance,*" that is, from a deep need to recover the unrecoverable pleasures of the primal state.

For Žižek, political extremism — in its various forms of racism, ultra-nationalism, xenophobia, ethnocentrism etc. — may be understood as a "displacement" of deep libidinal energy, or surplus enjoyment, and its "projection" onto externalized human objects. These external objects become representatives of the Other: foreign, alien, strange and "legitimate" targets and objects of fear and hatred. The attack on the Other — as an expression of "transgressive pleasure," or surplus enjoyment — is able to covert pain of absence or loss into pleasure (at the discomfort of others) and thereby becomes a means of reducing or resolving the inner psychic tensions of "desire" within the individual.

There is certainly room for considerable debate or doubt when evaluating Žižek's psychoanalytical theory of ideology. However, the following useful lessons may be learned from his analysis:

- Ideology is not simply a belief system within our minds, but also a code of conduct inscribed and embedded in our actions, practices and institutions. Ideology is all around us: the invisible net in which we are all entangled.
- Our strong negative feelings towards those we choose to dislike and exclude, and our psychological need to construct the "other," often spring from deep-seated inner psychic tensions. Our psychic pain can be converted into transgressive pleasure when we are able to displace our pain onto "others."
- Our perceptions and interpretations of others are always filtered through and framed by our ideological preconceptions and biases. In this sense, all social interaction is an expression of our imaginary fantasies and symbolic desires.

Ideology-critique: Žižek's most enduring contribution to contemporary social theory has been to the long-neglected field of ideology-critique. Žižek's own understanding of ideology-critique — unlike that of popular usage — focuses on how ideology is expressed and embedded in the actual *practices* of individuals, as much as in their overt beliefs and opinions. Žižek also employs a method for detecting the presence of strong or extremist ideological values, a method that focuses on the presence of incompatible, or contradictory, beliefs within an apparently unified worldview. Žižek suggests that it is common for individuals who may express extremist, especially racist or ethnocentric, worldviews to hold contradictory beliefs about the despised or hated objects of their beliefs, without recognizing or acknowledging these contradictions. In this respect, Žižek emphasizes that all ideologies, especially those that seek to target or scapegoat certain groups or individuals, are highly adaptable, flexible and revisable and often embrace contradictory elements in order to preserve a political or social prejudice within an apparently unified worldview.

In general terms, Žižek intends his critique of ideology to supersede the traditional Marxist theory on a number of different levels. For Žižek, ideology is no longer conceived as "false consciousness," a condition which can be rectified through class struggle and the progressive development of an authentic "class consciousness." Whereas orthodox

Marxism concluded that authentic class consciousness inevitably led to a "true" recognition of one's position in society (i.e., within the system of "productive relations"), Žižek denies that there is any such vantage point that offers a "true" or "objective" view of social reality. Instead, Žižek maintains that ideology has become a pervasive and inescapable aspect of our social existence and social consciousness. In other words, ideology has not really disappeared from the political landscape; it has become fully embedded, or "inscribed," into this landscape. Ideologies, understood as political discourses, now function to secure the "voluntary consent" of the population to policies and programs that are frequently controversial, sometimes unpopular and often strongly contested. The effectiveness of ideology, however, lies not in its ability to "brainwash" the population, but to convince them that their consent is obtained through their free "subjectivity," in other words, their freedom to choose between alternatives. Žižek claims that the success of contemporary ideology derives from the "illusion of choice" and from the supposed distance that it allows individuals to have towards its stated ideals and goals. This distance is referred to by Žižek as "ideological dis-identification." (In some ways, this idea is reminiscent of Herbert Marcuse's expression, "repressive tolerance").

In his analysis of ideology, Žižek suggests that ideologies often contain references to certain "sacred or sublime objects," such as "God" (in a theocracy), the "Party" or the "People" (in a totalitarian dictatorship) or even "freedom and democracy" (in a liberal democracy). A current example from the US is the second amendment right, which many Americans proclaim in order to resist government attempts at gun control, even after the many high school rampages and other mass shootings that have occurred since the Columbine massacre in 1999. In Canada, the policy of multiculturalism, although eroded over the years by ever more restrictive immigration requirements as well as rising rates of anti-immigrant hate crimes (Habib 2019), still serves as a convenient liberal myth for distinguishing Canadian race and ethnic intergroup relations from the American myth of the "melting pot." Hence, the myth of the "multicultural mosaic" provides another example of a sublime object of ideology. These legitimating signs, also called the "big Other" by Žižek, operate as "master signifiers," as representations which serve to evoke mass loyalty to the goals and ideals of the ideological discourse. Indeed, it is in the name of these sublime objects that individuals will transgress ordinary moral codes and, on occasion, even lay down their lives.

According to Žižek, most people accept the legitimacy of these master signifiers without really knowing what these signs actually represent. The Moscow "show trials" engineered by Stalin in the 1930s convicted many of his internal critics as "Rightists and Trotskyists," including Nikolai Bukharin, a Marxist theorist and former head of the Communist International, along with many other communist leaders purged (executed) between 1936 and 1938. And of course, Leon Trotsky was assassinated by Stalin's agent in Mexico in 1940. Most of Stalin's victims were designated as enemies of the "People," although, for most of the population, the "People" did not refer to any actual constituency.

When George W. Bush decided to invade Afghanistan in 2001 and Iraq in 2003 to defend the "values of freedom and democracy," this expression also lacked a clear and concrete reference. Similarly, when Donald Trump declared throughout his presidential election campaign that he was going to "make America great again," "America" was a sublime object, a signifier without a specific reference. Whose America was he referring to? It was certainly not the America of Hispanic immigrants, Indigenous Peoples, Muslims or many African Americans, women or those in the LGBTQ community. Most of the time, therefore, master signifiers are employed to obtain the loyalty and obedience of a population and do not refer to any real or tangible objects. In this sense, they are also "zero signifiers": they are empty signifiers without a signified, or empty representations without a referent. In practical terms, Žižek reminds us that there is no more effective political gesture than to declare some controversial or contestable topic above political contestation or scrutiny. Today, in the West, terms such as "human rights," "national interest," "national security," "humanitarian missions" and "freedom and democracy" have all acquired the status of incontestable ideological signifiers. Žižek further suggests that, for most of us, the various manifestations of the "big Other" occupy our thought-worlds as "spectral presences" — things we may not be fully conscious of but which offer us comfort and security at a deeper unconscious level.

Žižek also suggests that most individuals in contemporary society are what he calls "split subjects" (another concept borrowed from Jacques Lacan): their selves are divided between their conscious awareness and their unconscious beliefs and commitments. In addition to what they consciously think and say about politics, all individuals carry deeply held unconscious feelings about their political systems and their leaders.

Žižek concludes that many of the strongest attachments that we have to our political belief systems, or ideologies, are unconscious and, therefore, unreflexive. These unconscious attachments allow us to reproduce and perpetuate what Žižek calls an "ideological fantasy." An ideological fantasy refers to a deeply held, unconscious framework that allows individuals and communities to constantly reconcile their core beliefs with any discrepant or contradictory information or evidence. Ideologies are self-contained and logically elastic systems of ideas that are able to rearrange themselves in order to reconcile any new information with deeply held core beliefs. In this sense, ideologies are empirically irrefutable.

Some of the most powerful examples of the "elastic and adjustable nature of ideology" come from the racist ideologies which emerged over the past several centuries: in Nazi ideology, the Jewish people were represented as "the Jew," portrayed as rich and exploitative and as "parasitic" on the backs of the German people. The Nazis often referred to the "international Jewish conspiracy" to vilify Jews as an international capitalist class which had no loyalty to nation or local community. After the Nazis began to demonize the communists, who were, of course, anti-capitalist, the Jews were then accused of being both capitalists and communists. This contradiction was resolved by signifying the Jew as both "cosmopolitan" and "parasitic" — labels which reframed the doctrine of hatred and provided a new internal coherence to Nazi ideology. (In his anti-Semitic attacks on the Jewish community in the USSR, Stalin also reverted to using the ancient slander of "rootless cosmopolitans" against the Jews). Similarly, the earliest racist stereotypes of African Americans emphasized "the Negro" as "child-like," "simple," "happy-go-lucky," "lazy," "superstitious" and "ignorant." After the slave revolts and armed insurrections, American racists had to recalibrate their representations to accommodate new often contradictory images of "the Negro" as "dangerous," "primitive," "cunning" and "aggressive." Ideologies are flexible, adaptable and opportunistic.

Parallax view: Ideologies are not only abstract belief systems, but they are also "material forces" in society. Ideologies inform social practices and are, therefore, "materially" reproduced in the daily actions of individuals in society. Above all, ideologies provide us with the perspectives we use to observe, interpret and experience "reality," or what Žižek calls the "Real." Any real object can be viewed from a number of perspectives or vantage points. Most of the time, these perspectives are incommensurable, or mutually exclusive. Thus, in any given situation, we may understand human conduct to be the result either of free will or of biological determination but not both at the same time. However, unlike the postmodernists and the poststructuralists, Žižek does not claim that the Real is wholly constructed through discourse, or that each perspective produces its own "reality." Instead, Žižek invokes what he calls the "parallax view." This interpretation (taken from homologies in physics and astronomy) suggests that any view of the Real is always structured by the angle and by the line of sight of the observer. In other words, there are many possible views, or perspectives, from which to observe the Real. But while the Real is not a product or an artefact of the perspective, any view of the Real is always structured and limited by the perspective through which it is apprehended.

One of the most striking examples of the parallax view is that of the complementarity thesis of Niels Bohr in quantum physics. Bohr concluded that an electron may be observed both as an elementary particle and as a wave, depending upon the mode of observation. Although the electron could at different times be observed as either a wave or a particle, it could never be seen as both at the same time. Each mode of observation was mutually exclusive of the other. The Real, in this case, existed as a wave and as a particle but also as much more: that which had yet to be discovered. The point of the parallax view is that neither perspective can be reduced to the other; nor can they be translated into an external meta-perspective. Similarly, Žižek insists that when Marx used the economy to "decode" politics and politics to "decode" the economy, there is no meta-language outside either language from which to understand the whole of the Real. The Real is always more than what can ever be fully known. The parallax gap is the space between two perspectives that cannot be reduced to either one of them. This gap is a productive site; it is not a question of bridging, or transcending the gap, but of conceiving it as "becoming."

Whereas postmodernists reject any conception of the Real as a transcendental category, or metanarrative, for Žižek, the Real exists as an actual point of reference, even though it can never be apprehended in its entirety. In this sense, the Real may be understood as the "non-All," for it can never be fully symbolically represented or theorized. There is always something left over; something which exists elsewhere. For this reason, Žižek distinguishes between the "abject Real" (which cannot be symbolized) and the "symbolic Real" (which can). As we saw in our earlier

discussion of Lacan in the chapter on postmodernism and poststructuralism , the Real is that which is outside, or beyond, language, that which
resists signification or symbolization.

ŽIŽEK'S POLITICS

Žižek has achieved a celebrity status that is unusual for an academic, even
one who is recognized as a global public intellectual. With the exception
of a handful of intellectual celebrities, such as the late Bertrand Russell
and Jean-Paul Sartre, as well as Michel Foucault, Noam Chomsky and
Edward Said, very few scholars have managed to capture the public
imagination this way. But in spite of, or maybe because of, all his fame
and media exposure, Žižek has remained something of an enigmatic and
controversial figure. Much of his present reputation rests on his dazzling
deconstructions of popular culture — psychoanalytic reviews of iconic
movies and ironic commentaries of contemporary events, such as the
Balkan wars, the Middle East conflicts, the 9/11 terror attacks, the global
war on terror, the Iraq and Syrian wars, refugees and asylum-seekers,
Brexit and Donald Trump. However, his contributions to social theory
and philosophy and his flirtation with revolutionary politics are often met
with controversy and skepticism, and sometimes derision.

Žižek has had a somewhat ambiguous relationship to postmodernism and poststructuralism. On the one hand, his thinking has clearly
been influenced by the "linguistic turn" in contemporary social theory,
and much of his terminology has been borrowed from the poststructuralist psychoanalytic lexicon of Jacques Lacan. Žižek also shares the
postmodernist skepticism towards traditional positivist conceptions of
"truth," "meaning" and "reality." In these respects, Žižek may be classified
as a "post-positivist" social thinker. On the other hand, much of Žižek's
work involves a polemic, or counter-attack, against postmodernism and
against the new left or liberal establishment, especially what he regards
as the relativism, subjectivism and pluralism of postmodernist theory
and political practice. But it is when we turn to examine some of Žižek's
political writings that things become more controversial.

The golden thread that runs throughout much of Žižek's work is his
critique of ideology. Unlike classical Marxists, for whom ideology was a
state of "false consciousness" imposed on the minds of the masses by the
ruling class, Žižek sees ideology as an inescapable part of our cultural

landscape. For him, ideological discourse — as a system of signification — serves to consolidate the unity and compliance of the populations in nations, societies, communities and other collectivities. It is through the perpetuation and reproduction of myths and other "sublime objects" of ideological discourse that national communities construct their collective identities and legitimate their authority figures. Ideology, in other words, is the glue that holds a society together. From his close observation of the Yugoslav Wars (1991–99), Žižek quickly recognized that ideologies, especially nationalist ideologies, can sometimes become malignant and destructive forces in human affairs. Xenophobic, racist and extreme nationalist ideologies were integral to the hostilities that unfolded in the former Yugoslavia between the Serbs, Bosnians, Croats and Kosovars. Žižek also suggests that comparable "ideological fantasies" are constructed in the West around "sublime objects" and founding myths, such as "human rights," "multiculturalism," "humanitarianism," "democracy," "national security" and "tolerance." These ideological "objects" tranquilize public opinion and limit popular scrutiny and criticism of and opposition to many controversial issues, such as poverty and inequality, racism, the financial crisis, corporate corruption scandals, environmental catastrophes, the wars in Afghanistan, Iraq, Syria and Yemen and so on.

Žižek's critique of ideology leads him to his primary political project: the traversing of ideological fantasy. "Traversion," for Žižek, entails a recognition by human subjects that the "sublime objects" of their ideological fantasies are self-constructed and self-perpetuated projections of deeply embedded psychological needs. (This idea resembles Herbert Marcuse's concept of "repressive de-sublimation.") Traversing the fantasy enables the political subject to realize the deepest form of self-recognition, but it is also a necessary precondition for undertaking any radical, or revolutionary, social change. To traverse the fantasy is to cross the barrier from unconscious compliance and subordination to active and fully conscious self-determination.

In order to traverse the fantasy of ideology, Žižek insists that an active, practical intervention into the political world is necessary. Indeed, for Žižek, traversing the fantasy requires an "Act" which challenges the normalized frameworks of political speech and action. It is only though an exceptional Act that political action is capable of "touching the Real" — and of redefining the parameters of political discourse and political practice. But what exactly does Žižek have in mind when he calls for the performance of a transformative Act?

The violence of the Act: The declared aim of Žižek's politics is to find a way to break through what he regards as the present impasse of contemporary politics in the West. On the one hand, he wants to break through the corporate, profit-driven, neoliberal ideology of the political right and, on the other hand, to break through what he sees as the fatalistic and passive postmodernist ideology of the political left. In short, Žižek wants to rehabilitate a revolutionary tradition of hard political action, a tradition which is capable of penetrating ideological fantasy and exposing its fraudulent and illusionary nature. For this reason Žižek and his intellectual colleague Alain Badiou are often referred to as "neo-communists." It is at this point that Žižek is in danger of losing some, perhaps many, of his readers. Žižek believes that "authentic" politics has largely disappeared in the West. Conservatives, liberals, socialists and even communists and radicals have — through their alliances, coalitions, compromises and "loyal" opposition — colluded in depoliticizing their societies and leaving their populations apathetic, cynical and powerless. Contemporary societies in the West, he concludes, can best be described as "post-political" societies.

Instead of politics, Žižek suggests, we now have a largely conflict-free collusion or "collaboration of enlightened technocrats (economists, public opinion specialists) and liberal multiculturalists" (1999: 198), who negotiate a series of compromises and attempt to engineer a pseudo "national consensus." The depoliticized politics of consensus runs throughout Western societies: Tony Blair's New Labour; the former Conservative-Liberal Democrat coalition (UK); Bill Clinton's New Democrats; Barack Obama's congressional bi-partisanship; and so on. Moreover, the fragmented single-issue and identity politics of special interest groups — business, labour, consumers, environmentalists, Indigenous Peoples, women, African-descended peoples, the LGBTQ community, antiwar activists etc. — ensures that no unified or broad-based opposition will arise to seriously contest or change the rules of the present political game. At the same time, in his denunciation of "single issue" politics, Žižek overlooks the considerable overlaps and co-constitutive nature of many of these social justice struggles, something that intersectionality theorists are at pains to emphasize. But for Žižek, multiculturalism, broadly defined, is part of the problem rather than a part of the solution. Even though Žižek certainly distained the politics of Trump, he has suggested that Trump's election could be useful for destabilizing, disrupting or traversing the consensual politics of the political elite.

It is when he begins to articulate his own political vision that Žižek starts to run into trouble. At different points in his political writings, he invokes very diverse sources of inspiration, including philosophers Hegel, Kant, Schelling and Heidegger; psychoanalyst Lacan; political economist Marx; and fierce Christian evangelist St. Paul. As some critics have observed, there are aspects of Žižek's call for a "return to politics" that are deeply troubling. In his more recent works, such as his book *In Defence of Lost Causes* (2008) and in his essay "Repeating Lenin," Žižek not only calls for a return to Marxism but, more specifically, for a return to Leninism and a de facto call for a "neo-communism." Neo-communism, at least in practical political terms, is generally understood to mean the return of a Leninist revolutionary political party led by a group of "cadres" or committed political leaders whose role is to ensure that the revolutionary party takes on a "vanguard" role in mobilizing and organizing the "masses" for effective political action and revolutionary transformation. However, socialists, social democrats, anarchists and other grassroots activists see "vanguardism" as top-down political "elitism" and try to practise "participative democracy" as an alternative to the "democratic centralism" of traditional communist parties (Isaac 2013).

This return to the politics of the hard left reflects the growing influence on Žižek of the French Maoist philosopher Alain Badiou. However, Žižek's attempt to rehabilitate dialectical materialism raises some troubling questions regarding the *role of violence* in his political philosophy. For Žižek, Lenin signifies the importance of the revolutionary Act, an Act which frees the political subject from the constraints of the old political game and opens up a space for genuine, authentic, political transformation. But for Žižek, "repeating Lenin" does not mean turning back the historical clock. Whereas Lenin saw himself as the leader of a working-class revolution, for Žižek, the "working class" is no longer an agent of revolutionary change. Lenin (as well as Trotsky, Mao and St. Paul) is invoked as a signifier for the Act: for a radical and violent break with the existing political establishment. But the call for revolution without a material basis, without a working class, reduces the Act of revolution to the politics of violence for its own sake. Indeed, as several critics (Gray 2012; Boyton 1998; Kirsch 2008; Hardy 2010; Johnson 2009, 2011a, 2011b, 2015) have observed,

Žižek's celebration of the violent Act, of "egalitarian terror" and of "ruthless discipline," carries with it some troubling historical echoes. In these respects, the self-proclaimed new muscular neo-communism of Žižek and Badiou — in its authoritarianism and elitism — carries more than a hint of the past ideology of fascism or of "direct-action" anarchism, which promoted the "propaganda of the deed," i.e., "terrorism." Although Žižek provides us with much that is enlightening and entertaining in his political commentary and cultural criticism, his prescriptions for political action sometimes seem dangerously muddled and misguided.

The 9/11 terror attacks: In his short book *Welcome to the Desert of the Real*, Žižek provides us with a striking example of his iconoclastic personal style and his method of ideology critique. The title is taken from the movie *The Matrix*, in which most of the characters inhabit a virtual reality generated and coordinated by a gigantic mega-computer. Behind this virtual reality, however, lies an original "actual reality" to which most of the characters remain oblivious. This actual reality consists of a devastated wasteland — the horrific remains of a global thermonuclear war. When the hero of the movie, Neo (played by Keanu Reeves), awakens to this grim reality, he is greeted ironically by the resistance leader, Morpheus (played by Laurence Fishburne), who exclaims: "Welcome to the desert of the Real."

Žižek's main point is that the 9/11 terrorists deliberately launched a symbolic as well as an actual attack on the virtual world of global capitalism — the world of abstract financial transactions accomplished through the digital purchase and sale of shares, stocks, bonds, debentures, securities, derivatives and other financial commodities traded through cyberspace. Behind this virtual (First) world of extravagance, privilege, indulgence, entitlement and corruption lies a "real" (Third) world of exploitation, oppression, poverty, disease, violence, famine and war. But the corporate and political elites who inhabit the virtual "bubble" of the First world remain largely oblivious and indifferent to the realities of this Third underworld. It was only when this underworld attacked America that the privileged elites of the First world were forced to directly confront and respond to the Third world. Predictably, this confrontation has been framed through the cultural "cobweb" of the First world ideological perspective. 9/11 is now represented as a confrontation between Them and Us and between "fundamentalism" and the "free world" and as the "clash of civilizations" (according to Samuel P. Huntington 1996 and Bernard

Lewis 1990, 2002). Žižek tries to show how these representations are inscribed in an ideological fantasy which is oblivious to its own internal contradictions, inconsistencies and hypocrisies. Using his own method of ideology-critique, he deconstructs the ideology of the global war on terror, especially in the way that this ideology most fully reveals itself in what it actually conceals.

One of the themes that has haunted Žižek's coverage of the events of 9/11 is the idea that the "Evil" we perceive in the Other is an echo of the sublimated "evil" we recognize in ourselves. In other words, our horror over the cruelty and callous indifference to human life exhibited in the 9/11 attacks is an inverted image of the much greater suffering that our Western colonial legacy has inflicted on the rest of the world. Evil never solely resides in the Other; it lives within us as well. Nowhere is this idea expressed more forcefully than by Jean Baudrillard (2002: 14):

> When the world has been so thoroughly monopolized, when power has been so formidably consolidated by the techno-cratic machine and the dogma of globalization, what means of turning the tables remains besides terrorism? In dealing all the cards to itself, the system forced the Other to change the rules of the game. And the new rules are ferocious, because the game is ferocious.

But once we have recognized this "transparency of evil" in ourselves as well as in the Other, it is no longer possible to ideologize these events. The binary oppositions between the so-called "free world" and the fundamentalists, the rational and the fanatic, are, for Žižek, simply projections from the dark side of our historical identity onto the face of the Other. Similarly, any defence of the retaliatory attacks, such as the invasions of Afghanistan (2001) and Iraq (2003); drone strikes against Pakistan; or missile attacks in Syria, Somalia, Yemen and elsewhere, clothed in the ideological rhetoric of "democracy," "freedom," and "humanitarianism," misses an important point.

Rather than asking the particularistic questions: "Why did these attacks happen here?" or "Why do they hate us?" Žižek suggests that the events of 9/11 could have opened up a space in which a broader universalistic question could be asked: "Why should such attacks happen anywhere?" Rather than isolating America from the rest of the world, 9/11 provided an unprecedented opportunity for America to empathize with those who suffer similar attacks on a regular basis — whether in Palestine, the Congo, Chechnya, Afghanistan, Iraq, Pakistan, Northern Nigeria or elsewhere. 9/11 provided an opportunity for America to confront the universality of global pain and suffering. It could have become the Event that produced a new generational "truth," a new cosmopolitan consciousness, a new sense of global citizenship. Instead, as Žižek remarks, 9/11 simply served to re-fortify America and to launch a new age of global virtual warfare.

> We should therefore invert the standard reading according to which the WTC explosions were the intrusion of the Real which shattered our illusory Sphere: quite the reverse — it was before the WTC collapse that we lived in our reality, perceiving the Third World horrors as something which was not actually part of our social reality, as something which existed (for us) as a spectral apparition on the (TV) screen — and what happened on September 11th was that this fantastic screen apparition entered our reality. It is not that reality entered our image: the image entered and shattered our reality (i.e., the symbolic coordinates which determine what we experience as reality). (Žižek 2002: 16–17)

The ideology of human rights: Žižek also addresses the significance that the concept of "human rights" has acquired in the current ideological discourse of the West. And although most of us may uncritically accept the defence of human rights as a moral, indeed noble, principle of foreign policy, for Žižek, nothing is ever as simple as it seems. According to Žižek, the reconfiguration of our post-Cold War ideology around the centrality of "human rights" has led to some unfortunate consequences. First, the ideology of "human rights" has introduced a polarization between "freedom" (in the West) and "fundamentalism" (in the Muslim world). Islam, in many ways, has now replaced communism as the evil Other imaginary in our ideological fantasy. Second, the demonization of Islam as the evil Other eradicates from our collective memory the history of tolerance and pluralism in premodern Muslim societies. Under the "millet system," administered in the Ottoman Empire, for example, religious minorities (including Jews and Christians) were protected from persecution and given local autonomy, as long as they paid their taxes (see, for example, Masters 2001).

The ideological amnesia that allows us to forget the history of tolerance in premodern Islam also allows us to forget the history of intolerance in the West (see, for example, Maalouf 1984). Žižek reminds us that many of the current ethnic, religious and nationalist conflicts around the world — including those in some Muslim countries — originated in the colonial modernizing pressures from the West. The *gaze_*that perceives the evil in the Other is the same gaze that sees the inverted evil in ourselves. A further consequence of the ideology of human rights has been to provide a rationale for so-called "humanitarian" military interventions into "failed" or "rogue" states, such as the 2001 NATO military mission in Afghanistan and its earlier mission during the breakup of the former Yugoslavia, as well as the 2003 invasion of Iraq led by the US and the so-called "coalition of the willing." This ideology has a special significance in Canada, for it was a Canadian public intellectual, Michael Ignatieff, who played a major role in developing the doctrine of "responsibility to protect" (R2P), which has codified the ideology of humanitarian interventions into an international policy.

The ideological fantasy which leads us to bifurcate the world into their fundamentalism versus our freedom also blinds us to some deep inconsistencies and hypocrisies in our own claims to freedom. Žižek cites several examples of spurious or "pseudo" freedoms, or "unfreedoms," in which the freedom to choose between alternatives is more apparent than real. Thus, the decision by a Muslim woman in the West to wear a hijab, niqab or burqa is more likely to be reviled by most Westerners as "fundamentalism" than respected as "freedom of choice." Similarly, the dismantling of the welfare state, the privatization of health care and the deregulation of many service industries initiated in the later decades of the twentieth century by politicians such as Margaret Thatcher in the UK, Ronald Reagan in the US, Nicolas Sarkozy in France and in 2017 by Donald Trump in the US has usually been sold to the resistant public under the banner of "increased competition" and greater "freedom of choice." This is certainly the argument used by the US Republican Party when attempting to repeal the Affordable Care Act (aka Obamacare). These are all examples of the ways in which a rhetorical cliché, such as "freedom of choice," can mask the Real and thereby lock us into an ideological consensus which ensures the continuation of "business as usual." For Žižek, this is the politics of the "post-political," a politics which banishes the substantive issues of inequality, injustice, oppression and exploitation from the realm of public discourse in favour of the "formal" issues of management, administration, leadership and governance. This is how ideology has drained politics of its flesh and blood and replaced it with abstractions. This is how the demons of radical protest and opposition have been exorcised from the contemporary discourse of politics.

Besides our own convoluted claims to "freedom of choice," the ideological division of the world into Them and Us may rebound in countless other inconsistent and hypocritical ways. The polarization of our culture of pleasure (hedonism) to their culture of sacrifice (fundamentalism) is also based upon a false dichotomy. As Žižek suggests, it requires certain "sacrifices" to pursue a culture of pleasure, just as a strong commitment to a culture of sacrifice offers certain rewards or pleasures. Ideological distinctions are often slippery, and the boundaries between supposedly clear moral categories can easily become blurred. While war is officially condemned and peace applauded, in the liberal ideology of the West, war has become the default way to impose peace on "unpeaceful" populations, especially on , "rogue" or "failed" states. Similarly, while democracy is lauded and dictatorship is lambasted, the "wrong" democracy may well be overturned (as in Haiti in 2004) or punished (as in Palestine in 2006 and Bolivia and Venezuela in 2019). The bottom line is: democracy is OK as long as it is our approved democracy.

What Žižek calls the "anti-politics," or the "post-politics," of the post-millennial era can best be seen in the military interventions justified by the ideology of "human rights." As Žižek observes, when military interventions, which are after all always violent events, are ideologically repackaged and marketed as "humanitarian missions," the intention of this depoliticized discourse is to mask the inherent conflicts and antagonisms of the Real. In this way, the real intentions and actions of the superpower and other states are mystified — if not to their enemies — at least to a majority of their own citizens. The clinical and impersonal discourse of human rights, therefore, conceals more than it reveals. And in some important ways, this discourse has helped to ignite the fuse that now sends soldiers on "humanitarian'" combat missions to "trouble spots" around the globe.

At the same time, Žižek has expressed his reluctance to abandon the notion of universal human rights. Even though he concedes that the ideology of human rights has served to mask the self-interested intentions of nation-states and has polarized the discourse of international relations, he still believes that the idea carries an as yet unrealized potential for mass mobilization and political action. Unlike traditional Marxists and later deconstructionists, who were content to dismiss ideology as an illusion fostered by a ruling class onto the masses, Žižek believes in the power of the people to traverse, reverse and invert ideology. In this sense, the ideology of universal human rights still possesses what Žižek refers to as "symbolic efficiency," an ability to animate and activate those who exist outside the realms of justice and due process. For Žižek, therefore, the ideology of human rights — traditionally used by the powerful to dominate the powerless — can turn into its opposite and become a counter-ideology of the dispossessed. "Much more interesting is the … process, in which something that was originally an ideological edifice imposed by colonizers is all of a sudden taken over by their subjects as a means to articulate their 'authentic' grievances" (Žižek 2005: 130).

It is clear from much of his work that Žižek is first and foremost a conflict theorist who believes that contemporary society is based upon fundamental conflicts that are inherent in the present system of late capitalism. Moreover, Žižek recognizes that in any conflict there are ideological divisions which usually signal a deeper material division of opposing class or social interests. For Žižek, each party to any particular conflict has its own ideological viewpoint, and neither viewpoint can be reduced to that of the other. Thus, Žižek employs the "parallax view" of recognizing the specific concerns of each conflicted party, even though these concerns may mask more fundamental divisions. While opponents of Donald Trump may reject his sexism and racism, and while supporters may embrace his economic nationalism and populism, both sides may fail to detect the more fundamental contradiction: the exploitation of labour by monopoly capitalism. The fact remains that in any ideological conflict, no particular view can ever fully access a total "truth." Universal truth and absolute reality always remain inaccessible and lie beyond the apprehension of anyone.

At the same time, Žižek is skeptical of the common liberal democratic view that compromise solutions can always been found whenever conflicting parties agree to reach some "middle ground." In Žižek's opinion, many conflicts cannot and should not be negotiated away; these conflicts often express irreconcilable divisions or antagonisms in society. Even though each party may have its own viewpoint, Žižek concludes that it is sometimes necessary to choose sides and to push for radical, even revolutionary or violent, social change. For Žižek, the purpose of politics and of ideology-critique is to show that there is always an *alternative* to the present situation. While this alternative may not bring resolution to all political and social problems, it will likely release society from its old problems before introducing a set of new problems. Žižek does not believe in happy endings or in permanent solutions to ever-changing problems. While some critics may see him as a cynic, a nihilist, a narcissist, a "deadly jester" or even as a fascist, he sees himself as a world-weary realist.

ALAIN BADIOU: THE ARMCHAIR REVOLUTIONARY

Another contemporary social thinker whose work has often been classified as post-Marxist is the French philosopher Alain Badiou. In many ways, it is probably more accurate to define Badiou, along with his colleague Slavoj Žižek, with whom he is often paired, as a "neo-communist." This is because Badiou's ideas constitute more of a philosophy of revolutionary action rather than a theory of history or society in the grand tradition of classical Marxism. In this respect, Badiou follows in the footsteps of Nietzsche, Sartre and even of Lenin and especially Mao. Part of the problem of classifying Badiou's work derives from the arcane and sometimes obscure language in which his ideas are formulated and communicated. Like many recent European, especially French, philosophers, Badiou employs a language in which terms and concepts are often used in novel and unfamiliar ways. Like Žižek, Badiou's language is also partly borrowed from the French psychoanalytic traditions of Jacques Lacan and Gilles Deleuze, partly derived from mathematical set-theory and partly a product of his own neologisms. His resultant text, especially in English translation, can be demanding for readers.

The void: Much of Badiou's work is organized around recurrent and interrelated themes. The most important of these themes, influenced by Lacan, are those of the "void," the "event," and the "subject." Together, these ideas form the intellectual axes around which much of Badiou's work is organized. For Badiou, the void represents what may be described as the "circle of contingency" that surrounds our known world. The void refers to the unknowable realm of infinite possibility that can never be known in advance and which exists beyond our current horizons of experience and understanding. The void consists of the unknown, the unthought, the unpredictable and the unrealized.

The event: An "event" is something that erupts from the void: a one-time, never-to-be-repeated singularity that can change the course of human history. An event is a point at which the real and the possible converge; it is, to use Badiou's terminology, the "meridian hour." An event provides its agents with the opportunity to translate the possible into the real, to make their own history, to create their own "truth." According to Badiou, examples of events — as landmarks, turning points or tipping points in history — include Beethoven's Third Symphony, Newton's laws of gravitation, and transformative political acts, such as the French, Russian, Chinese and Iranian revolutions; the Paris Commune; the Chinese Cultural Revolution; the Zapatista insurrection in Chiapas, Mexico; the Paris student-worker revolt in 1968; and the Arab Spring. In the case of such political events, Badiou suggests that these singular occurrences provide collective subjects (the revolutionaries and their supporters) with an opportunity to create new historical "truths."

Truth: For Badiou, "truth" refers to the action, or practice, of forging coherence and meaning out of the chaos of the void. But the process of establishing "truth" requires what Badiou calls a "fidelity" to the event: a "truth procedure" that organizes and consolidates the consequences of the event. Badiou's conception of truth, therefore, goes far beyond that of empiricism or positivism. Truth is not composed of facts; instead, it involves, in the case of politics, the birth of a new political "subject." Truth, for Badiou, is more of an existential, or ontological, concept than an epistemological concept. Truth, in this sense, is never "discovered"; it is always "performed." Moreover, the concept of truth, for Badiou, is universal and eternal. In this respect, as in many others, Badiou is deeply hostile to any relativistic or pluralistic conception of "truth," especially as championed by postmodernists and poststructuralists.

How do Badiou's ideas translate into politics or social theory? As we have already suggested, his ideas may best be understood as a philosophy of action, or as a politics of praxis. His main concern is how to burst what he regards as the bubble of complacency, hypocrisy and self-deception that envelops the present state of politics in the West. Badiou wants to break through the ideological consensus that lies at the heart of Western politics and holds together the political regimes of Western societies. Today, we live in an age in which nation states can violate the rights of ethnic and religious minorities with impunity in the name of "national security," "immigration control," "counter-terrorism," "law and order" and so on; or when invasions or wars of aggression can be re-branded as "humanitarian missions," or as "muscular diplomacy." Under these conditions, the rhetoric of "bourgeois humanism," with its endless appeals to human rights, free enterprise, democracy and tolerance, only serves to deepen our self-deception and further entrench our complacency about our own society and its relation to the rest of the world. For Badiou, the time has come to break through this ideological baggage with a decisive event that will shock the system and its ideology and forever change the rules of the game.

In these respects, Badiou remains a child of the 1960s. The source of much of his political inspiration can be traced back to the spontaneous student and worker uprisings in France during the early months of 1968, which nearly tumbled the government of Charles de Gaulle. In common with many other revolutionary theorists, Badiou's project is focused on how to reactivate a revolutionary program that can bring about a global social transformation. His work is built upon an explicit critique of militarism, imperial sovereignty, neoliberalism, consumerism and a host of other evils that are, he believes, generated within the present capitalist world system. The aim of his philosophy is to make an "interpretive intervention," or a radical gestalt switch, which will usher in an event that will change the rules of the present political game. All successful revolutions have managed to change the rules of the game and have — through the "fidelity" of their militant supporters — gone on to produce the fresh revolutionary "truths" needed to construct new social orders. Changing the rules, however, is nearly always accompanied by, or even engineered through, violence and terror.

Most historical revolutions were brought into existence through violence and (revolutionary) terror, including those in America (1776), France (1789), Russia (1917), China (1949) and Iran (1979). More recent attempts to impose revolutionary programs on unwilling or recalcitrant populations have invariably ended in bloodshed, famine and widespread, sometimes genocidal, slaughter. This was certainly the case with the forced collectivization of the USSR (1930–1940), the Great Leap Forward in China

(1958 to 1962), the Chinese Cultural Revolution (1966–1976), the Khmer Rouge revolution in Cambodia (1975–1979), the Shining Path guerrilla insurgency in Peru (1980s) and the FARC insurgency in Colombia. Badiou appears to accept that violence and cruelty are inevitable in all revolutionary events. Indeed, some critics have even accused him of romanticizing or glorifying such violence (see, for example, Jenkins 2008; Toscano 2006).

Like Franz Fanon, a generation earlier, Badiou has written passages that seem to commend revolutionary violence as necessary to purge the old society and liberate its potential for rebirth. In a world of repressive political regimes that often brutally oppress their captive populations, it is almost inconceivable that a revolutionary event could ever be initiated or consolidated without violence and cruelty. Revolutionary action, in Badiou's eyes, is always motivated by a "passion for the real," a desire to intervene in the causality of human affairs. Such a passion transcends the shallow limits of conventional morality and extends beyond good and evil. Whether we applaud him for his realism or reproach him for his callousness, there is no doubt that Badiou has tried to confront the ontological implications of his philosophy of action. And one of the implications of "traversing the Real" and of forming a new political subject is the inevitability of violence. Rather than evading this implication, Badiou embraces it.

CONTROVERSIAL CONCLUSIONS

The overall impact of Žižek and Badiou, at least on an English-speaking audience, is not easy to assess. For one thing, both of these theorists are still very much alive (in 2020), and each is still busily engaged in producing his own legacy. Their intellectual careers are a work in progress. At the same time, their work has proven to be divisive and has often polarized their defenders against their critics. Žižek, in particular has become a contentious figure on the theoretical stage, especially in light of some of his political observations. However, notwithstanding the incomplete and often controversial status of their work, several general observations can be made and tentative conclusions drawn.

There is no doubt that Žižek is a social theorist and philosopher who has acquired a celebrity status with a broader public audience. Indeed, he has even been labelled the "Elvis of social theory." Much of his reputation with the general public has been built on his often ironic and critical interpretations of popular culture: his philosophical readings of films, commercial advertisements, popular fiction, social movements and of course, politics. In addition, his frequently shabby appearance and obsessive mannerisms, his comical and jocular demeanour and his penchant for irony and parody have only further served to endear him to an enthusiastic network of admirers.

Žižek's primary strength lies in his skillful capacity for ideology-critique. He has shown how ideology should be understood as a set of often unacknowledged and unrecognized routinized practices that "interpellate" the individual subject into the norms and conventions of the dominant culture. However, as a self-proclaimed Marxist (and Leninist), Žižek's ideology-critique remains primarily focused on the liberal-democratic "consensus" of late capitalist societies and on the inability or unwillingness of the left opposition to engage in any real contestation or practical critique of the political culture of capitalism. Thus, in the UK, the formal opposition to the Conservative prime minister Margaret Thatcher was Tony Blair, the leader of the opposition Labour Party and succeeding prime minister, who continued the neo-liberal economic policies first introduced by Thatcher and who proved to be even more belligerent than Thatcher in his foreign policy support for the US invasion of Iraq in 2003. Similarly, in the US, Bill Clinton continued many of the neoliberal policies of Ronald Reagan at home and abroad. These are some of the "bipartisan" policies that illustrate the unholy consensus that lies at the heart of liberal-democratic politics in most late capitalist societies today. And this consensus is the focus of Žižek's critique. Without any real political challenge to this culture, Žižek asserts that there can be no transformation into a more egalitarian and humane society.

Thus, for Žižek and Badiou, we have reached an impasse in the possibility for any radical or revolutionary social change in the liberal-democratic cultures of late capitalist Western societies. Most of these states, including Canada, are bound together through a fundamental political consensus of all parties, a consensus that precludes the possibility of radical social change. This "ideological fantasy" has integrated all political constituencies around a set of "sublime objects" of ideology, including such "master signifiers" as the national interest, national security, human rights, the constitution and other symbols of national identity. The function of these sublime objects of ideology has been to place any real possibility for radical social change beyond the present parameters of political discourse and contestation. It is in this sense that Žižek and Badiou claim that late capitalist states have now become "post-political" societies — societies that have effectively excluded the possibility of real political change from their agendas.

However, as Žižek makes clear, these post-political societies also permit and often encourage a degree of internal criticism and debate over such identity issues as racism, sexism, homophobia, human rights etc. in order to provide a release valve for any real threat that these controversies might otherwise pose to the established social order. In other words, political contestation around specific issues is permitted in order to avoid any fundamental contestation of the culture and structure of late capitalism itself. Internal criticism and debate is largely confined within the political parameters of possible reforms and incremental changes. But the over-arching culture of capitalism — the "ideological fantasy" in which we all are trapped — is never seriously questioned. For Žižek, this false toler-ance for internal criticism that only serves to reinforce the status quo is termed "ideological dis-identification" (what Marcuse called "repressive tolerance").This is why Žižek remains critical of struggles for piecemeal reforms, expressed in identity politics, protests movements against rac-ism, sexism, homophobia etc., and why he dismisses the significance of campaigns for human rights (Žižek 2005). According to Žižek, in late capitalist societies, the ideology of human rights has been used primarily to justify neocolonial military interventions into countries of the Global South and to demonize as "terrorists" or "insurgents" those who often seek to overthrow neoliberal regimes supported and often installed by the West.

Žižek rejects the political struggles of our post-political societies because most of these struggles are limited to a "politics of the possible." In other words, most political protests and struggles remain within the political parameters of our present ideological fantasy. They fail to ques-tion or contest the limits of political possibility by confining themselves to the identity politics of particular groups and social movements. They also fail to mobilize a universal collective identity which is a necessary condition for "traversing the fantasy" and for transforming the present capitalist system. For Žižek, "authentic politics … is the art of the impos-sible — it changes the very parameters of what is considered 'possible' in the existing constellation" (1999: 199).

There can be little doubt that both Žižek and Badiou have provided penetrating insights into the morally compromised nature of the current political establishments of late capitalist societies and the failure of the political opposition to effectively challenge or contest this political consensus and the ideological fantasy on which it is based. Žižek has also provided a vigorous theoretical critique of postmodernism and poststructuralism and of the identity politics of the post-political age. He has also been applauded for his intellectual links to Descartes, Hegel, Marx and Lacan; as had Badiou, for his links to Sartre. There is, however, a darker side to these theorists, especially their prescription for radical and revolutionary political and social change in liberal-democratic, late capitalist societies. Indeed, some of Žižek's comments, observations and examples have inspired outrage and consternation in many of his readers.

For Žižek and Badiou, any authentic revolutionary change requires an "Act" which is capable of "traversing the fantasy" of popular culture and "touching the Real": that is, of going beyond the horizon of the politically "possible" and producing an unprecedented political "event." According to Žižek and Badiou, an event is a unique and unrepeatable action — a singularity — in time and space that forever changes a society. Žižek (2014) explains:

> What's an event? It's a difficult question not because we lack definitions but because there are too many definitions … I focus on event in the sense of something extraordinary takes place … Within a certain field of phenomena where things go on the normal flow of things, from time to time something happens which, as it were, retroactively changes the rules of what is possible in the sense that something happens. It is generated by that situation.

An event can refer to a devastating natural disaster or to the latest celebrity scandal, a political victory of the people or a brutal political regime change, an intense experience of a work of art or an intimate personal decision. An event is the effect that seems to exceed its causes. In order to produce a political event, an Act must be performed on behalf of a unified collective identity, or what Žižek calls "the universal freedom of humanity," which is empowered to reach beyond the horizon of the "possible" in its attempt to achieve the "impossible." In this sense, an Act breaks out of the ideological fantasy of the past and present and forever changes the rules of the game.

However, Žižek's examples of singular transformative political events are of some of the most violent and bloody events of the past century. Indeed, it almost appears from his observations and conclusions that Žižek believes that any genuine event, one that "traverses the fantasy" and "touches the Real," can only be accomplished through "divine" violence (named after Walter Benjamin) and terror. But, in order to qualify as an event, in Žižek's eyes, a political revolution has to totally transform and replace the culture and structures of capitalism. Thus, even when a political Act is accomplished through violence and terror, if it fails to replace the culture and structures of capitalism, it is insufficient to produce a radical political transformation. This somewhat mystical conception of the Act leads Žižek to make disturbing observations and draw alarming conclusions. When reflecting on the birth of the Nazi Third Reich and the rise of Adolph Hitler, Žižek suggests that

> crazy, tasteless even, as it may sound, the problem with Hitler was that he was "not violent enough," his violence was not "essential" enough…. The true problem of Nazism is not that it "went too far" in its subjectivist-nihilist hubris of exercising total power, but that it did not go far enough, that its violence was an impotent acting-out which, ultimately, remained in the service of the very order it despised. (2012: 902)

And again, the rise of the Khmer Rouge in Cambodia (when it was known as the Democratic Republic of Kampuchea), which resulted in the deaths of 1.7 to 2.5 million people out of a 1975 population of roughly 8 million, is dismissed as insufficiently radical: "The Khmer Rouge were, in a way, not radical enough: while they took the abstract negation of the past to the limit, they did not invent any new form of collectivity, they just replaced the old order with a primitive regime of egalitarian control and ruthless exploitation…. Even so, revolutionary violence should be celebrated as 'redemptive,' even 'divine'" (2010: 389–390). For some critics, like John Gray (2012), this apparent celebration of political violence is a troubling echo of other forms of political extremism and fanaticism, both from the far right and the far left. Fascist writers such as Maurice Barrès and Georges Sorel and even Nazi theorists such as Carl Schmidt have promoted, or at least condoned, political violence; while anarchists, including theorists such as Errico Malatesta, also have a turbulent history of advocating political violence, assassination and of the "propaganda of the deed" — a sanitized expression for political terrorism. It is hardly surprising, therefore, that critics have been deeply disturbed that Žižek's views on political violence share a dark and dangerous pedigree with some of the most malevolent political philosophies of modern times.

Throughout Žižek's discussions of revolutionary events, he is clear about the role of violence and terror in forging a new transformative social order: "What matters is not the brutal violence and terror in China, but the enthusiasm generated by this spectacle in its Western observers.... (And, why not, one could claim the same for the fascination of Nazi Germany for some Western observers in the first four years of Hitler's rule when unemployment fell rapidly, etc.!)" (2008:108). It is sometimes difficult to know when to take Žižek seriously and when to recognize that he is being provocative or ironical (Fried 2007: 2). But the accumulation of so many quotations explaining or justifying violence and terror make it difficult to discount these numerous statements as merely ironic rhetoric. And, when concerned critics have expressed their discomfort over these apparent celebrations of violence, Žižek's response has been terse and dismissive: "If this radical choice is decried by some bleeding-heart liberals as Linksfaschismus (i.e., left-wing fascism), then so be it!" (Laclau, Butler and Žižek 2000: 326).

However, it has not only been "bleeding heart liberals" who have found Žižek's prescription for political action unacceptable. Hardline Marxists have often dismissed Žižek's own claims to be a Marxist and Leninist. For many of these critics, Žižek's and Badiou's embrace of thinkers such as Hegel, Nietzsche, Schelling, Heidegger and Lacan clearly signals their retreat from historical materialism and descent into idealism. This idealism is evident in the absence of any consistent reference to the working class in Žižek's writing and the lack of any realistic program for social and political change (Van Auken and Haig 2010; Hardy 2010; Schwarz 2016). Moreover, Žižek's apparent celebration and glorification of violence and terror has led many critics, Marxist and non-Marxist, to decry him as a Jacobin, a Blanquist (after Louis Blanqui) or even a "decisionist" and an elitist in the tradition of fascist theorists such as Martin Heidegger and Carl Schmitt.

More recently, Žižek has been criticized for what sometimes appears to be his callous indifference towards, and stereotyping of, refugees, asylum-seekers and other migrants seeking shelter and protection on European shores. Žižek has warned against the idealization of migrants, and has resisted attempts by "humanitarians" to downplay and minimize the extent of cultural differences between the migrant strangers and their host societies. Some of his rhetoric rings harsh, unwelcoming and indifferent to the horrific conditions from which most refuges and asylum-seekers are escaping:

> We tend to forget that there is nothing redeeming in suffering: being a victim at the bottom of the social ladder does not make you some kind of privileged voice of morality and justice.… even if many immigrants are more or less victims who have fled from devastated countries, this does not prevent them behaving despicably.…The fact that someone is at the bottom, does not make them automatically a voice of morality and justice. (Žižek 2016a)

At times, it almost seems as though Žižek has allied himself with the voices of the far right — like Marine Le Pen, Nigel Farage and even Donald Trump — all of whom are ready to sound the alarm that countless foreign migrants are ready to overrun our borders and occupy "our" lands: "It is a simple fact that most of the refugees come from a culture that is incompatible with Western European notions of human rights … The problem here is that the obviously tolerant solution (mutual respect of each other's sensitivities) no less obviously doesn't work" (quoted in Merelli 2016).

The valuable lessons that both Žižek and Badiou have to teach us — about our political culture, our own complacency and hypocrisy and our failure to become active agents of change and social justice — are sometimes lost in the provocative rhetoric, the irony and parody and the complexity of many of their ideas. But given the fact that Žižek is best known as an iconoclast and as an idiosyncratic commentator on current affairs and philosophical issues, perhaps his vision of life and learning is best expressed in a recent quote: "The recognition that we are all, each in our own way, weird lunatics, provides the only hope for a tolerable co-existence of different ways of life" (2016b).

References

Baudrillard, Jean. 2002. *The Spirit of Terrorism: And Requiem for the Twin Towers*. Verso.

Bauman, Zygmunt. 1993. *Postmodern Ethics*. Oxford: Blackwell.

___. 2000. *Liquid Modernity*. Cambridge: Polity.

___. 2003. *Liquid Love: On the Frailty of Human Bonds*. Cambridge, UK: Polity.

_____. 2004. *Wasted Lives: Modernity and Its Outcasts.* Cambridge, UK: Polity.

_____. 2005. *Liquid Life.* Cambridge, UK: Polity.

_____. 2006. *Liquid Fear.* Cambridge, UK: Polity.

_____. 2006. *Liquid Times: Living in an Age of Uncertainty.* Cambridge, UK: Polity.

Boyton, Robert S. 1998. "An Excitable Slovenian Philosopher Examines the Obscene Practices of Everyday Life — Including His Own." *Lingua Franca* 7, 8 (October). <http://linguafranca.mirror.theinfo.org/9810/Žižek.html>.

Cannon, Bob. 2016. "Towards a Theory of Counter-Modernity: Rethinking Zygmunt Bauman's Holocaust Writings." *Critical Sociology*, 42, 1: 49–69. <http://journals.sagepub.com/doi/pdf/10.1177/0896920513516023>.

Dawson, Matt. 2012. "Reviewing the Critique of Individualization: The Disembedded and Embedded Theses." *Acta Sociologica*, 55, 4.

Dean, Jodi. 2006. *Žižek's Politics.* Routledge.

_____. 2007. "Why Žižek for Political Theory?" *International Journal of Žižek Studies*, 1, 1: 18–32.

Elliott, Anthony (ed.). 2007. *The Contemporary Bauman,* 1st edition. Routledge.

Fanon, Frantz. 1963. *The Wretched of the Earth,* trans. Constance Farrington. New York: Grove Weidenfeld.

Freeman, Michael. 1995. "Genocide, Civilization and Modernity." *British Journal of Sociology*, 46, 2 (June): 207–223.

Fried, Gregory. 2007. "Where's the Point? Slavoj Žižek and the Broken Sword." *International Journal of Žižek Studies*, 1, 4.

Gane, Nicholas. 2004. "Zygmunt Bauman: Liquid Sociality." *The Future of Social Theory.* London: Continuum.

García, George I., and Carlos Gmo. Aguilar Sánchez. 2008. "Psychoanalysis and Politics: The Theory of Ideology in Slavoj Žižek." *International Journal of Žižek Studies*, 2, 3.

Gray, John. 2012. "The Violent Visions of Slavoj Žižek." *New York Review of Books*, 59, 12 (July 12).

Habib, Jacky. 2019. "Far-Right Extremist Groups and Hate Crime Rates Are Growing in Canada." *The Passionate Eye*, CBC Saturday, July 13. <https://www.cbc.ca/passionateeye/features/right-wing-extremist-groups-and-hate-crimes-are-growing-in-canada>.

Hardy, Simon. 2010. "Slavoj Žižek, An Idealist Trojan Horse." *League for the Fifth International,* 28 October. <http://www.fifthinternational.org/content/slavoj-Žižek-idealist-trojan-horse>.

Huntingdon, Samuel P. 1996. *The Clash of Civilizations and the Remaking of World Order.* New York: Simon & Schuster.

Isaac, Jeffrey C. 2013. "The Mirage of Neo-Communism." *Dissent* (Summer). <https://www.dissentmagazine.org/article/the-mirage-of-neo-communism>.

Jacobsen, Michael Hviid. 2008. *The Sociology of Zygmunt Bauman: Challenges and Critique,* 1st ed.; ed. by Poul Poder. Routledge.

Jacobsen, Michael Hviid, and Sophia Marshman. 2008. "Bauman's Metaphors: The Poetic Imagination in Sociology." *Current Sociology*, 56, 5.

Jenkins, Joseph. 2008. "Violence in Badiou's Recent Work." *Cardozo Law Review*, 5, 1: 2121–2131.

Johnson, Alan. 2009. "The Reckless Mind of Slavoj Žižek." *Dissent*, 56, 4 (Fall): 122–127.

___. 2011a. "The Power of Nonsense." *Jacobin*, July 14. <https://www.jacobinmag.com/2011/07/the-power-of-nonsense>.

___. 2011b. "Slavoj Žižek's Theory of Revolution: A Critique." *Global Discourse*, 2, 1: 135–151. doi: 10.1080/23269995.2011.10707889.

___. 2015. "Slavoj Žižek's Linksfaschismus." In Gregory Smulewicz-Zucker and Michael J. Thompson (eds.), *Radical Intellectuals and the Subversion of Progressive Politics: The Betrayal of Politics*. New York: Palgrave Macmillan.

Kirsch, Adam. 2008. "The Deadly Jester: Review of *In Defense of Lost Causes*." *New Republic* (2 December). <http://www.newrepublic.com/article/books/the-deadly-jester>.

Laclau, Ernesto, Judith Butler, and Slavoj Žižek. 2000. *Contingency, Hegemony, Universality: Contemporary Dialogues on the Left*. Verso Books.

Lewis, Bernard. 1990. "The Roots of Muslim Rage." *The Atlantic Monthly*, September.

___. 2002. *What Went Wrong? The Clash Between Islam and Modernity in the Middle East*. Weidenfeld & Nicolson.

Maalouf, Amin. 1984. *The Crusades through Arab Eyes*. New York: Schocken Books.

Mann M. 2005. *The Dark Side of Democracy*. New York: Columbia University Press.

Masters, Bruce. 2001. *Christians and Jews in the Ottoman Arab World: The Roots of Sectarianism*. Cambridge: Cambridge University Press.

Merelli, Annalisa. 2016. "Marxist Philosopher Slavoj Žižek Explains Why We Shouldn't Pity or Romanticize Refugees." *Quartz*, 9 September. <https://qz.com/767751/marxist-philosopher-slavoj-Žižek-on-europes-refugee-crisis-the-left-is-wrong-to-pity-and-romanticize-migrants/>.

Paterson, M. 2006. *Consumption in Everyday Life*. Routledge.

Rameesh, Randeep. 2010. "The Sociologist Influencing Labour's New Generation." *The Guardian*, 3 Nov. <https://www.theguardian.com/society/2010/nov/03/zygmunt-bauman-ed-miliband-labour>.

Rattsani, Ali. 2014. "Zygmunt Bauman: An Adorno for 'Liquid Modern' Times?" *The Sociological Review*, 62: 908–917.

___. 2016. "Race, Imperialism and Gender in Zygmunt Bauman's Sociology: Partial Absences, Serious Consequences." In Michael Hviid Jacobsen (ed.), *Beyond Bauman: Critical Engagements and Creative Excursions*. Routledge.

Sayer, Derek. 1987. *The Violence of Abstraction: The Analytic Foundations of Historical Materialism*. Oxford: Basil Blackwell.

Schwarz, Peter. 2016. "Slavoj Žižek: From Pseudo-Left to New Right." World Socialist Web Site, 8 February. <http://intsse.com/wswspdf/en/articles/2016/02/08/zize-f08.pdf>.

Smart, C., and B. Shipman. 2004. "Visions in Monochrome: Families, Marriage and the Individualization Thesis." *British Journal of Sociology*, 55, 4: 491–509.

Sznaider, Natan. 2016. "Multiple Modernities and the Nazi Genocide: A Critique of Zygmunt Bauman's Modernity and the Holocaust." *The Society Pages*, 15 August, Center for Holocaust & Genocide Studies. <https://thesocietypages.org/holocaust-genocide/multiple-modernities-and-the-nazi-genocide-a-critique-of-zygmunt-baumans-modernity-and-the-holocaust/>.

Tester, K. 2002. "Paths in Zygmunt Bauman's Social Thought." *Thesis Eleven*, 70: 55–71.

___. 2004. *The Social Thought of Zygmunt Bauman*. Basingstoke: Palgrave Macmillan.

Toscano, Alberto. 2006. "Can Violence Be Thought? Notes on Badiou and the Possibility of (Marxist) Politics." *Identities: Journal for Politics, Gender and Culture*, 5, 1 (Winter).

Van Auken, Bill, and Adam Haig. 2010. "Žižek in Manhattan: An Intellectual Charlatan Masquerading as 'Left.'" World Socialist Web Site, 12 November. <https://www.wsws.org/en/articles/2010/11/zize-n12.html>.

Vetlesen, A. 2005. "The Ordinariness of Modern Evildoers: A Critique of Zygmunt Bauman's Modernity and the Holocaust." In *Evil and Human Agency: Understanding Collective Evildoing*. Cambridge Cultural Social Studies. Cambridge: Cambridge University Press.

Warde Alan. 1994a. "Consumption, Identity-Formation and Uncertainty." *Sociology*, 28, 4: 877–898.

___. 1994b. "Consumers, Identity and Belonging: Reflections on Some Theses of Zygmunt Bauman." In N. Abercrombie, R. Keat, and N. Whiteley (eds.), *The Authority of the Consumer*. London: Routledge.

Žižek, Slavoj. 1989, *The Sublime Object of Ideology*. Verso Books.

___. 1999. *The Ticklish Subject: The Absent Centre of Political Ontology*. Verso.

___. 2002. *Welcome to the Desert of the Real*. Verso.

___. 2005. "Against Human Rights." *New Left Review*, 34 (July–August): 115–131.

___. 2007. "Why Heidegger Made the Right Step in 1933." *International Journal of Žižek Studies*, 1, 4.

___. 2008. *In Defence of Lost Causes*. Verso.

___. 2010. *Living in the End Times*. Verso.

___. 2012. *Less Than Nothing: Hegel and the Shadow of Dialectical Materialism*. Verso.

___. 2014. *Event: A Philosophical Journey through a Concept*. Melville House.

___. 2016a. "The Cologne Attacks Were an Obscene Version of Carnival." *New Statesman*, 13 (January). <https://www.newstatesman.com/world/europe/2016/01/slavoj-Žižek-cologne-attacks>.

___. 2016b. "What Our Fear of Refugees Says about Europe." *New Statesman*, 29 February. <https://www.newstatesman.com/politics/uk/2016/02/slavoj-Žižek-what-our-fear-refugees-says-about-europe>.

CHAPTER 12

THEORIZING OUR SHRINKING WORLD

Globalization and Its Discontents

THE GLOBAL AGE

In this final chapter, we turn to what is perhaps the most significant aspect of contemporary social relations: the process of globalization — the ever-increasing interconnectedness of our thoughts and actions with others around the world. While the definition and the concept of "globalization" is flexible, contemporary social theorists have focused on many different aspects of the rapidly changing global relations of our time. As we have already seen in earlier chapters, some social theorists, like Zygmunt Bauman, have focused on the growing interdependency of nation states, either as political allies (or adversaries) or as trading partners (or economic rivals). Bauman has also focused on how the growing power of transnational corporations and international government organizations, such as the World Bank, the International Monetary Fund and the World Trade Organization, has begun to erode the sovereignty and independence of individual nation states. Other theorists, such as Manuel Castells, have focused on the impact that new forms of "connectivity" — through information and communications technologies — have had on our economics, politics and daily lives. Ulrich Beck, on the other hand, has emphasized how globalization has introduced new risks and threats — environmental, economic, financial, political, military and cyber — into our societies and communities. We shall examine the main ideas of these globalization theorists in greater detail below.

Today, the impact of globalization on our lives is evident in many ways, some of which are positive and uplifting while others are negative and sometimes devastating. On the upside, globalization has greatly increased our personal orbits of communication and transportation. We can now video-chat with our friends and relatives in remote parts of the world, an impossibility only a few decades ago. And those of us fortunate enough to live relatively privileged lives in the Global North can travel as immigrants, tourists, visitors, employees and medical patients to most countries around the world; we can consume produce and products that originate in faraway places; and we can vicariously witness, in our own living rooms, news events around the globe as they occur in real time, via cable TV or the internet. In this sense, the whole world is now on our doorstep.

Globalization also has a much darker aspect. One dramatic example of this can be seen in the unprecedented power of transnational corporations to move their financial assets to tax-free havens, to outsource and off-shore their manufacturing plants to cheap labour markets and to increase the exploitation of workers in the Global South (Klein 1999). Another example is our growing vulnerability to cyber-crimes from overseas computer hackers. According to monitoring agencies like the Center for Strategic and International Studies in Washington, DC, while some attacks may originate with unaffiliated individual hackers, many over the past decade appear to originate from other nation states such as Russia, China, North Korea and Iran with the covert support, or even sponsorship, of their respective governments. The potential devastation of these attacks may be seen in the "ransomware" cyber-attacks of May 2017, which showed how overseas hackers can disrupt computerized operational systems ranging from airline schedules to health-care records and from electricity grids to postal services (see Wong and Solon 2017).

The dark side of globalization is not only apparent in deliberate criminal attempts to sabotage basic services but may also be seen in the unintended effects of global interdependency. The increased travel by international migrants, tourists, visitors and others between countries around the world has also facilitated the transmission and spread of deadly diseases, such as West Nile virus, swine flu, Zika and Ebola, among others. And, of course, the destabilization of many countries by the US with its invasion of Afghanistan and Iraq and its ongoing aerial bombardment and drone strikes in Somalia, Sudan, Syria, Libya, Pakistan, Yemen and elsewhere, has contributed to the displacement of populations and to a growing number of refugees and asylum-seekers. The costs of these neoimperialist military interventions by the US and other major powers are invariably borne by poorer neighbouring states, such as Lebanon, Turkey or Bangladesh, which are obliged to provide refuge to these desperate victims of war and violence. And in many Western countries, the plight of these victims of war, rape and ethnic cleansing has often been met with racism and the resurgence of far-right political movements and events like the Brexit referendum vote in the UK and the anti-immigrant campaign rhetoric of Trump. The growth of anti-immigrant sentiment has, of course, also been exacerbated by the deadly attacks, such as those in Paris, Brussels, Nice, Syria, Orlando, Manchester and London, and the many more attacks in the Middle East and North Africa inspired by borderless global terrorist networks, such as ISIS, Al-Qaeda, the Taliban, al-Shabaab, Boko Haram and Abu Sayyaf, among others. There are now many moving pieces on the global chessboard, and it has become increasingly difficult to predict their impact on international relations.

But looming above the wars, disease pandemics, migrant flows, terrorist and cyber-attacks is a much greater threat to our societies and indeed to our long-term survival as a species on the planet, and that is the threat of climate change and global warming. Although this threat may be defined as more of a biological or environmental problem than a purely social problem, most twenty-first century social theorists have recognized the challenges that climate change poses for social relations and for long-term ecological planning and resource management on our planet.

The Dimensions of Global Modernity

The new age of what we shall call "global modernity" has become a hot topic for contemporary social theorists. Some, like Ulrich Beck, have emphasized the new threats and hazards that haunt this global "risk society." Others, like Manuel Castells, have emphasized the impact of the new information and communications technologies on the "network society." John Urry has emphasized the role of new forms of mobility, while Zygmunt Bauman has focused on the new "liquidity" of global society in the twenty-first century. And, as we have already seen, Anthony Giddens and Pierre Bourdieu have emphasized the new "reflexivity" exhibited by members of this global society in their social actions and practices. In order to summarize some of these various insights, we can outline the main dimensions of global modernity in the following terms:

Connectivity: The age of the internet, smart phones, tablets, social media and cable TV provides us with historically unprecedented opportunities for information retrieval and for high-speed local and global communications. Today, there are millions of users of Facebook, YouTube, Twitter,

Figure 12-1: The Main Dimensions of Global Modernity

Snapchat, Instagram, WhatsApp and other social media sites that allow individuals to "network" with each other around the world. As many social theorists have observed, this new age of high-speed connectivity has resulted in a "space-time compression" (Harvey 1989), or a "space-time instantiation" (Giddens 1990), whereby events can be viewed simultaneously anywhere in the world as they occur in real time. This new age of connectivity has massive implications for many aspects of social life, including financial transactions, war journalism, terrorist attacks, sporting events and interpersonal communications between friends and relatives separated by geographical distance.

Mobility: The present global age is witness to unprecedented mobility, not only of people but also of information, goods and services, capital, financial commodities, images, ideas and many other items. People travel more than ever before, for business and pleasure, education, diplomacy, medical treatment, to join wars and to escape from wars, and for many other reasons. Besides the movement of people, the present age is also distinguished by the export of capital from high-priced to low-priced labour markets, the travel of labour for jobs and economic opportunities, the transfer of financial assets for tax avoidance or for massive cash hoarding and investment, the movement of global terrorist networks and cells across national borders, the flight of refugees and asylum-seekers and the travel of scientists, scholars, diplomats and many others. Sometimes it seems as though everyone is on the move. But it is normally those with the economic means and opportunity who comprise the ranks of voluntary migrants, while those who move to escape war and persecution, famine or economic hardship comprise the ranks of involuntary migrants.

Liquidity: another aspect of the global age, which is closely linked to and even derived from the connectivity and mobility of the times, is the "liquidity," or "de-materialization," of goods and services. For example, much of the information that is publicized and distributed around the world is digital and virtual, rather than actual and material. The internet news sources are rapidly replacing printed newspapers and magazines, and in colleges and universities e-texts are displacing printed texts. Many financial transactions are now accomplished online, rather than though "hard currency" exchanges. And outsourced "call centres," reachable only via telephone or websites, have overtaken face-to-face office staff. And for some online consumers, "bitcoins" have replaced real money transactions (see Ball 2011). This tendency to convert from print to digital forms of communication is seen as environmentally friendly, conserving energy and resources, such as trees. For this reason, the process of "de-materialization" is often described as the "greening" of commercial transactions and industrial processes and products (see UNIDO 2009; Harris and Roach 2017).

This trend towards greater liquidity and de-materialization is not only apparent in the economy and the spread of telecommunications but also in the more intimate world of personal identity. Whereas a sexual identity was once seen as fixed, today it can be more fluid; even the most intimate aspects of an individual have assumed a more liquid and de-materialized form in the age of global modernity.

Reflexivity: Many social theorists have cited the greater "reflexivity" of social actors as a distinguishing feature of this period of late modernity and global modernity. When used by theorists such as Giddens, Bourdieu, Bauman, Beck and Castells and by feminist scholars like Margaret Archer (2007); Sandra Harding (1983), Rosanna Hertz (1997) and R.R. Wasserfall (1997), among others, "reflexivity" refers to the propensity of social actors to understand the motives and underlying causes that drive their social actions. "Reflexivity" also implies the ability to learn from and adjust one's action or conduct as a result of this understanding. More than ever before, our actions and practices have become increasingly "transparent"; we can recognize their causes and effects and use this practical knowledge to readjust or redirect our actions towards a revised goal. In earlier modernist sociological theories of Parsons, Merton, Mead and Goffman and Garfinkel etc., this reflexive dimension of social action was referred to as "voluntaristic" in order to distinguish it from "deterministic" — action that is controlled by internal or external forces over which the actor has little or no control. Thus, the concept of "reflexivity" has been used by theorists to emphasize the autonomy or "agency" of the social actor. Reflexivity is normally invoked by theorists who are critical of social theories that advance an "oversocialized" conception of the social actor (Wrong 1961) or portray the social actor as a "judgemental dope," or "cultural dope," incapable of free will or voluntaristic action (Garfinkel 1967: 68). The long list of deterministic theories includes organicism, structural functionalism, structuralism and poststructuralism, as well as various forms of biological, genetic, psychological, economic, environmental and even linguistic determinism. The emphasis on reflexivity represents a repudiation of this deterministic legacy.

Above and beyond these abstract debates among social theorists, "reflexivity" has acquired a more compelling meaning in the present age of global modernity. The pervasiveness of telecommunications media, including smart phone cameras, closed circuit cameras and other surveillance media, means the actions of individuals have attained an unprecedented visibility in both the private and public spheres. This transparency has resulted in a new type of reflexivity which has had a significant impact on individual and collective action. The viral images in the US social and mass media of the police killings of African Americans (such as Trayvon Martin, Michael Brown, Eric Garner, Tamir Rice, Walter Scott, Freddie Gray and Sandra Bland, among many others) not only exposed racialized police brutality but also led directly to the rise of the Black Lives Matter movement. Similarly, the viral images of US torture (what the US government euphemistically calls "enhanced interrogation" techniques) used at Abu Ghraib and Guantanamo detention centres directly contributed to the rise of global jihadism, including ISIS and other terror networks. The transparency of our actions may result in unpredictable and sometimes undesirable forms of reflexivity and retaliation, both at home and abroad.

Vulnerability: Finally, as many social theorists have observed, especially Ulrich Beck, although global modernity has brought us unprecedented benefits in terms of scientific and technological advances in medicine, information retrieval, telecommunications, transportation and travel, food production etc., the present age has also introduced unparalleled threats and risks to our long-term survival. The list of risks to our security and survival is a long one, which includes, above all, unprecedented levels of corporate irresponsibility and unaccountability that contribute to many global problems. These largely unacknowledged and unprosecuted corporate crimes have played a major role in many contemporary global problems: climate change and extreme weather events; interstate and trans-state wars and conflicts; large-scale involuntary migration; terrorist attacks; thermonuclear weapons; industrial accidents, such as major oil spills (e.g., Exxon Valdez in 1986 and Deepwater Horizon in 2010), the 1984 toxic leaks from the chemical plant at Bhopal and the radiation leaks from the nuclear power plants at the Three Mile Island Nuclear Generating Station in Pennsylvania in 1979 and at Chernobyl in 1986; global inequalities of income and wealth; global economic recessions or depressions; cyber-warfare, data theft and fraud; global disease pandemics; among many other concerns. In these respects, we now live in an age of numerous vulnerabilities. And the knowledge and fear of these vulnerabilities are magnified by the images of catastrophic events circulated via the mass media, the internet and social media. Whether these images are of brutal beheadings or suicide bombings by jihadists groups; or of the victims of US political surrogates' aerial or artillery bombardments of residential neighbourhoods in war-torn Syria, Iraq, Afghanistan, Yemen or Palestine; or of the tragic drowning deaths of refugees and asylum-seekers; or of victims of diseases such as Ebola; or of the victims of extreme weather events like the Haiti earthquake (2010), Hurricane Katrina (2005), the Indian Ocean Tsunami (2004), the European Heat Wave (2003) and Hurricanes Harvey, Irma and Maria in the US (2017) or Dorian in the Bahamas (2019); these images spread rapidly around the world and heighten our sense of insecurity and uncertainty in the age of global modernity.

THE MANY VOICES OF GLOBALIZATION THEORY

Globalization is a hotly contested topic in the social sciences, especially in the theoretical and political debates over globalization. These debates have focused on several related issues, including definitions and conceptualizations of "globalization," as well as the practical consequences of globalization processes and policies for businesses, communities, nation states, and ordinary citizens. Indeed, "globalization" can be defined and conceptualized in a number of ways, depending upon who is proposing the definitions. For some, "globalization" has become a synonym for neoliberalism and the related policies and practices of marketization, privatization, deregulation, outsourcing and off-shoring. For others, "globalization" refers primarily to the contemporary global networks of communication and information, as well as to the increased "mobilities" of capital, labour, transmigration, travel and tourism.

Figure 12-2: Globalization Theories

When it comes to defining, describing, analyzing and explaining the process of what has become known as "globalization," we are confronted with a bewildering number of popular views and academic theories. To add to this confusion, the current crop of globalization narratives contains theories which often pull us in very different directions: some theories celebrate globalization, while others are more inclined to critique it; some theories are optimistic, while others are pessimistic or even fatalistic; some theories are strongly ideological and judgemental, while others are more empirical and pragmatic. And to further complicate matters, globalization theories come from a variety of disciplines: from economics, international relations, political science, sociology and anthropology, as well as more specialized areas, such as education studies, media studies, global studies, environmental studies and cultural studies.

Different theorists emphasize different criteria — spatial, temporal, economic, technological, political, cultural and even psychological — to capture the essence of globalization. According to numerous commentators (Held et al. 1999; Hay and Marsh 2000; Archibugi 2004; Robinson 2008; Martell 2010), the current diversity of globalization theories has evolved through at least three distinct "waves," or generational perspectives, each of which reflects a steady growth in the proliferating theory and research of globalization studies. These waves include the first wave of "hyperglobalization" theories and their corresponding first wave of radical critics, the second wave of "skeptical" theories and the third wave of "transformationalist" theories.

Table 12-1: Definitions of Globalization

Source	Definition of Globalization
Immanuel Wallerstein, *The Modern World System: Capitalist Agriculture and the Origins of the European World-Economy in the Sixteenth Century* (cited in Holton 1998: 11).	"Globalization represents the triumph of a capitalist world economy tied together by a global division of labour."
David Harvey, *The Condition of Postmodernity* (cited in Holton 1998: 8).	"The compression of time and space."
Martin Albrow, *Globalization, Knowledge and Society* (1990: 8).	"All those processes by which the peoples of the world are incorporated into a single world society."
Anthony Giddens, *The Consequences of Modernity* (1990: 64).	"Globalization can thus be defined as the intensification of worldwide social relations which link distant localities in such a way that local happenings are shaped by events occurring many miles away and vice versa."

Arjun Appadurai, "Disjuncture and Difference in the Global Cultural Economy" (1990: 308).	"The critical point is that both sides of the coin of global cultural process today are products of the infinitely varied mutual contest of sameness and difference on a stage characterized by radical disjunctures between different sorts of global flows and the uncertain landscapes created in and through these disjunctures."
Peter Dicken, *Global Shift: The Internationalization of Economic Activity* (1992: 1, 87).	"Globalization is 'qualitatively different' from internationalization…. It represents 'a more advanced and complex form of internationalization which implies a degree of functional integration between internationally dispersed economic activities.'… The degree of interdependence and integration between national economies."
Kenichi Ohmae, *The Borderless World: Power and Strategy in the Global Marketplace* (cited in RAWOO Netherlands Development Assistance Research Council 2000: 14).	"Globalization means the onset of the borderless world."
Roland Robertson, *Globalization: Social Theory and Global Culture* (1992: 8).	"Refers both to the compression of the world and the intensification of consciousness of the world as a whole."
OECD, *Intra-Firm Trade* (cited in Brinkman and Brinkman 2002: 730–731).	"Understood as the phenomenon by which markets and production in different countries are becoming increasingly interdependent due to the dynamics of trade in goods and services and the flows of capital and technology."

Source: Al-Rodhan and Stoudmann 2006.

First Wave: Hyperglobalism

The first wave of contemporary globalization theories made its appearance in the mid-twentieth century and became known as the wave of "hyperglobalism": theories that have promoted and celebrated the, primarily economic and technological, trends of globalization . Hyperglobalism can be traced back to the early post-industrial theories of Alain Touraine (1971), Daniel Bell (1974) and Francis Fukuyama (1989, 1992), among others. Some of the main points emphasized in the post-industrialism thesis include the following: the expansion of the service sector and the contraction of the manufacturing sector in modern economies; the growing importance of knowledge as a source of human capital; the decline of blue-collar, unionized work, including manual labour; and the rising importance of both white-collar commercial and human service workers, as well as professional workers (e.g., scientists, marketing professionals and IT professionals). Bell famously declared that this global transition to post-industrialism was destined to result in the "end of ideology," as the two superpowers of the mid-twentieth century, the US and the USSR, were rapidly converging in their economic and technological characteristics and becoming more alike. Economics and technology would soon displace ideology as the primary focus of national interest and international relations. Similar sentiments were later expressed by Francis Fukuyama, who in 1989 proclaimed the "end of history" in this new age of post-industrialism and globalization: "At the end of history it is not necessary that all societies become successful liberal societies, merely that they end their ideological pretensions of representing different and higher forms of human society.... that is, the end point of mankind's ideological evolution and the universalisation of western liberal democracy as the final form of human government" (1989: 280). Unlike Bell, Fukuyama never claimed that ideology had ended, only that the best possible ideology had finally evolved. However, the "end of history" and the "end of ideology" arguments have the same effect: they both proclaim the triumph of the Western way of life. Needless to say, in light of the rise of religious fundamentalism, far-right nationalism and anti-establishment populism in the twenty-first century, this type of global optimism now seems hopelessly naïve. Indeed, just after its publication, Fukuyama's neoconservative vision of the triumph of liberal democracy and the advent of a post-ideological world was critiqued by commentators from both ends of the political spectrum for its narrow US-centric perspective on the world and for its geopolitical implausibility (Huntingdon 1989; Said 2001; Kurtz 2002; Moores 2006; Nye 2007; Mahdavi and Knight 2012).

More recently, the major representatives of hyperglobalism most often cited are the *New York Times* journalist Thomas Friedman and the organizational theorist Kenichi Ohmae. Each in his own way has promoted and boosted the main aspects of globalization in the contemporary world. Although Friedman's books (1999, 2005) purport to describe and explain the process of globalization, they may also be read as a celebration and endorsement of this new age of global integration and connectivity:

> [Globalization] is the inexorable integration of markets, nation states, and technologies to a degree never witnessed before — in a way that is enabling individuals, corporations and nation-states to reach around the world farther, faster,

deeper, and cheaper than ever before and in a way that is enabling the world to reach into individuals, corporations, and nation states farther, faster, deeper, and cheaper than ever before. (1999: 9)

For Friedman, the age of globalization is irreversibly driven, not only by the demands of global economic competition, but also by the new technologies of communication, information and transportation that have revolutionized connectivity, interactivity and mobility on our planet. In this respect, Friedman is something of a technological determinist. At the same time, he is honest enough to remind us that the export of open markets, free trade and liberal democratic values (the American way of life) often requires the harder reinforcement of the US military to implement these neoliberal "reforms" in client states and overseas territories: "The hidden hand of the market will never work without a hidden fist. McDonald's cannot flourish without [the corporate defence contractor] McDonnell Douglass.... And the hidden fist that keeps the world safe for Silicon Valley's technologies to flourish is called the U.S. Army, Air Force, Navy and Marine Corps" (1999: 373).

Kenichi Ohmae is also an enthusiastic apologist for globalization. Indeed, Michael Haralambos and Martin Holborn (2013, quoted in Thompson 2017) describe Ohmae as "one of the most uncompromising and wholeheartedly enthusiastic advocates of globalisation from a right-wing neoliberal perspective who sees economic change as the driving force of globalization." But whereas Friedman seems like a technological determinist, Ohmae appears more like an economic determinist. Ohmae's work emphasizes what he sees as the benefits of international free trade, transnational corporations, economic deregulation, consumer sovereignty and open borders. Like Friedman, Ohmae believes that economic globalization brings with it geopolitical benefits, such as a decline in the sovereignty of the nation state and the gradual eclipse of nationalism, a decline in militarism and armed conflict and the increasing spread of liberal democracy and human rights around the world.

Neoliberalism: The Ideology of Privilege

Both Friedman and Ohmae have embraced the core of hyperglobalism: the ideology of neoliberalism. This doctrine privileges and empowers the interests of capital over those of labour; the interests of the private sector over those of the public sector; the interests of the producer and distributor over those of the consumer; and the interests of the corporation over those of the citizen. The key aspects of the doctrine of neoliberalism include the following:

De-regulation: In the interests of free trade and open markets, neoliberalism opposes all trade tariffs, even if they are designed to protect the jobs of domestic workers. Neoliberalism is also opposed to most other types of regulation enforced on private enterprise, such as environmental protections, labour rights (i.e., protections against the exploitation of sweated labour); animal rights (i.e., protections against cruel practices of rearing or slaughtering livestock and poultry); as well as opposition to any financial restrictions or any interference in private business (including rent controls for landlords).

Precarious employment: Neoliberal policies and practices threaten domestic job security and bring lowered wage levels through the "outsourcing" of many public sector jobs to private sector companies. This is the case when transferring the jobs of public sector transport workers (who drive the buses, trains, garbage trucks etc.) to private companies; the jobs of public sector airport baggage-handlers and security guards to private firms and so on. Also, domestic job security has been threatened by the "off-shoring," or foreign displacement, of jobs to cheaper and more docile labour markets in the Global South, for example, through the relocation of manufacturing and assembly plants, including automotive plants, from North America to Mexico, and apparel factories (Nike, Reebok, Adidas) to China, Indonesia, Pakistan, Vietnam and the Philippines.

Privatization: Neoliberal policies strongly encourage the privatization of public services and utilities. Under former British prime minister Margaret Thatcher and former American president Ronald Reagan, the US and the UK saw the privatization of public transportation services (buses and trains), public broadcasting channels and public utilities (telephone, electricity and natural gas), as well as garbage collection, airport security and even, in the US, prisons. Canada also has not escaped the impact of neoliberal policies of privatization: "a number of major Canadian Crown corporations were privatized between 1985 and 1996, including Air Canada, CN Railway, Petro-Canada, Fishery Products International, Potash Corporation of Saskatchewan, Eldorado Nuclear Limited and

Saskatchewan Mining Development Corporation (now Cameco), Alberta Government Telephones (now Telus), Suncor and Nova Scotia Power" (Fraser Institute Nd). And in some countries with public health-care insurance plans, including Canada, there is always the looming threat of privatization if a neoliberal government is elected into office. The long-term effect of neoliberalism has been to hollow-out and drastically reduce the services and coverage provided by the welfare state, or what neoliberals call "the nanny state."

Taxes: Neoliberal policies are designed to lower corporate tax rates, supposedly to free up funds for increased capital investment in order to create more jobs and stimulate economic growth. This was the rationale used by Donald Trump to market his tax "reform" legislation in 2017 (known as the Tax Cuts and Jobs Act). However, there is considerable evidence that many corporations use these tax cuts primarily to buy back their own shares and to offer one-time inflated bonuses to senior executives (Phillips 2018). Also, many companies, as well as many financial oligarchs, political dictators and other members of the global elite, take advantage of so-called "loopholes" to avoid paying full taxes by diverting their corporate earnings to off-shore tax havens or shell companies in locations like the British Virgin Islands, the Cayman Islands, Bermuda, the Isle of Man, Jersey, Guernsey, Mauritius, Seychelles, Singapore, Hong Kong and Shanghai. Canada, also, has helped to provide safe sanctuaries for the rich and super-rich to hide their wealth from the tax authorities, as was documented by Alian Deneault in his revelatory book *Legalizing Theft*. In 2016, journalists first revealed the extent of corporate tax evasion by leaking the Panama Papers, followed by a second batch of leaks, the Paradise Papers (Garside 2017). At the same time, lower taxes for the corporate elite lead to major cutbacks in social services, health-care provision and many other public investment projects, including environmental protection and conservation, alternative energy sources, higher education, infrastructure, public transit etc.

First Wave Critics

The enthusiasm of the hyperglobalists and their passionate endorsement of neoliberalism is not shared by everyone. Indeed, early hyperglobalism generated a negative response from the first wave of critics, who questioned and often rejected many of the claims and predictions of the optimists. At the same time, this first wave of critics was itself divided, between conservative cultural conflict theorists on the one hand and more radical Marxist critics on the other. While virtually all of these first wave critics contest the optimistic predictions of the hyperglobalists, most share their conclusion that globalization is now a reality and that the power and influence of multinational and transnational organizations has spread around the world at an unprecedented rate. In this respect at least, both hyperglobalists and their critics agree that globalization is changing the economic and political rules of the game; however, they differ wildly in their evaluations of this recent historical trend and on its probable long-term consequences.

Global culture conflict: One of the most famous cultural critics of hyperglobalism is the American political scientist Samuel Huntington, whose book *The Clash of Civilizations* (1996) paints an alarming picture of the growing cultural and military conflict between the secular West, with its liberal democratic values, and other major civilizations that do not share Western values but are now able to project their power and influence onto their immediate neighbours and increasingly around the world. For Huntington, China offers the gravest potential threat to the West, both as a rising economic power and as a potential military adversary. However, he also recognizes a threat from what he calls the "Islamic resurgence," related to the theocratic regimes and terror networks within the Islamic world, led by Saudi Arabia and Iran. In this regard, he is joined by another cultural conflict theorist, Bernard Lewis (1990, 2004). The emergence of fundamentalist groups such as the Taliban, Al Qaeda and ISIS from the ruins of Afghanistan, Iraq, Libya and Syria, as well as the rise of other jihadist groups such as Al Shabab (East Africa), Boko Haram (Northern Nigeria) and the Philippines' Abu Sayyaf etc., may appear to have put more flesh on the bones of Huntington's gloomy thesis, at least in the minds of the general public (see also Robbins 1997). In addition, Huntington recognizes what he calls several major "swing states," such as Russia, India and Japan, as well as such "torn countries" as Turkey and Mexico, whose loyalty may switch to either side of the major clash between Occidental and Oriental civilizations. Although Huntington's clash of civilizations has been variously criticized as "racist" and "Islamophobic" by Edward Said (2001, 2004: 293) and as "imperialist" by Noam Chomsky (2007), among others, his work remains an example of the more conservative criticisms of hyperglobalism offered by the first wave critics.

Global class conflict: Hyperglobalism, especially neoliberalism, has been strongly attacked by Marxist and other radical left critics (David Harvey; Frederic Jameson; Göran Therborn; Alex Callinicos; Ellen Meiskins Wood; H-J Chang, among others). In many ways, these left-wing criticisms of neoliberalism may be seen as updated versions of earlier Marxist criticisms of colonialism and imperialism. This tradition hearkens back to Marx himself, but was later refined by some of his intellectual protégés — Vladimir Lenin, Nicolai Bukharin and Rosa Luxemburg — and further updated by dependency theorists of the mid-twentieth century, such as Andre Gunder Frank, and by world systems theorists, such as Immanuel Wallerstein. Today, there is no shortage of critiques from the left. Some of the major Marxist criticisms of neoliberalism include the following concerns.

Global inequality: Like their orthodox Marxist predecessors, current Marxist critics of neoliberalism condemn the tremendous socioeconomic inequality between the super rich and the impoverished masses around the world. The global gap in wealth and income, exacerbated by the policies and practices of neoliberalism, continues inexorably to widen. We know that, according to Oxfam, 82 percent of the global wealth generated in 2017 went to the most wealthy 1 percent (Elliott 2018); and according to a Credit Suisse report, the wealthiest 1 percent of the world's population now owns more than half of the world's wealth, and 70.1 percent of the world population holds only 3 percent of global wealth (Frank 2017). For Marxists, inequality has always been a target of theoretical criticism and a motivation for practical political action. And in capitalist societies, whether national or transnational, the accumulation of corporate profit has always been explained as a process of local and global exploitation of the working class.

Labour exploitation: Marxists also argue that, in the competition between companies in local and global markets, capitalist enterprises always display an inherent tendency to exert a downward pressure on the level of wages, the so-called "wage repression." Low wages increase the volume of surplus value that can be extracted from the process of production. In the global market of transnational capitalism, the cheapening of workers' wages is often achieved through the relocation of manufacturing and assembly plants and the corresponding outsourcing and off-shoring of jobs to the low-wage economies of the Global South. "As wages rise so capital is moving offshore to lower-wage locations in Bangladesh, Cambodia and other parts of South East Asia" (Harvey 2010).

Decline of national sovereignty: The compulsion of transnational corporations (TNCs) to invest their capital, locate their enterprises and recruit their labour forces in markets that will produce the highest return on investments has begun to erode the sovereignty of the nation state, especially the less powerful states in the world. Driven by the pressures of global competition and the need to maximize the accumulation of profit, transnational enterprises now often operate outside the regulative and legislative limits of the nation state. Neoliberal policies have eroded the jurisdiction of the nation state and have weakened its legislative and enforcement procedures. One commentator observes: "There is a 'wide consensus' that some kind of 'erosion' of sovereignty has taken place. The standard neoliberal interpretation of globalization sees a decline in state territoriality. According to this view, state sovereignty has been 'compromised' by the competing interests of nonstate actors" (Ip 2010). The erosion of the autonomy of the state has sometimes enabled TNCs to circumvent national labour codes, environmental regulations and consumer protection legislation and to avoid national taxation by transferring their corporate earnings to off-shore tax havens and shell companies. In order to counter the growing financial, economic and political impunity of TNCs, national governments now have to resort to new methods of regulation and control, while international government organizations have also attempted to impose regulative regimes to enforce taxation, environmental protection, fair labour practices and other matters of global concern. But for most Marxists, international government agencies, like the World Bank, International Monetary Fund and World Trade Organization, fall under the influence and control of hegemonic states like the US and the UK, as well as transnational business interests. These financial institutions are not seen as "honest brokers" in the contemporary world of global trade. But at the same time, public pressure, sometimes seen in the rise of populist movements on both the far right and the far left has led some politicians to campaign in favour of trade tariffs for domestic job protection and for the repatriation of manufacturing plants, and to campaign against neoliberal trade deals, such as NAFTA, which threaten to further hollow-out the manufacturing base in the homeland. In this respect, socialists like Bernie Sanders and nationalists like Donald Trump may sometimes sing from the same hymn book.

Anti-democratic: For most Marxists and socialists, the various problems of neoliberalism, including the export of jobs and manufacturing plants, the super-exploitation of Global South labour, the erosion of state sovereignty and the legal and political unaccountability of TNCs all pose serious challenges to the "democratic project" of a welfare state and a planned and regulated economy. TNCs continue to evade national taxation and their unregulated movement of financial assets has serious implications for national budgets and economic planning. The corporate elite also "purchases" favoured politicians and pays for its preferred political agendas. In the US, for example, the 2017 tax "reforms" resulted in spectacular tax cuts for the financial elite and is a clear example of the close interlocks between the financial and the political elites. The corporate neoliberal agenda can also punish recalcitrant nation states by imposing severe austerity programs through international government agencies, like the IMF, or thorough other neoliberal national governments. This is what happened to debtor countries Greece, Spain, Portugal and Ireland within the monetary Eurozone of the European Union. As the American philosopher Noam Chomsky observed, "In Europe the way democracy is undermined is very direct. Decisions are placed in the hands of an unelected troika: the European Commission, which is unelected; the IMF, of course unelected; and the European Central Bank. They make the decisions. So people are very angry, they're losing control of their lives" (Lydon 2017). For Marxists and for other critics, neoliberalism has shown its power and its willingness to frustrate and to sabotage the democratization of societies within the global system. And as Chomsky concluded: "In sum, neoliberalism is the immediate and foremost enemy of genuine participatory democracy, not just in the United States but across the planet, and will be for the foreseeable future" (McChesney 1999: 11).

Second Wave Skeptics

Since the rise of the first wave hyperglobalists, along with their first wave (conservative and radical/Marxist) critics, a second wave of skeptics emerged during the first decade of the twenty-first century with various concerns about claims made by pro-globalization theorists. However, the tone of this second wave of dissent has been more moderate, more empirical and less ideological than their first wave critical counterparts (Hirst and Thompson 1996). For this reason, we may label them as "skeptics" rather than "critics" in order to differentiate them from their more ideological first wave cousins. This point is made explicitly by Colin Hay and David Marsh (2000: 2–3), who state that their main objective is to "cast a critical and in large part skeptical gaze over some of the often wildly exaggerated … claims made in the name of globalization" (see also Martell 2007: 181). These second wave skeptics share the following common concerns:

Globalization is not unprecedented: A growing number of skeptics question the hyperglobalist claim that contemporary globalization is unique and unprecedented in world history. Several scholars have shown that there was more international trade in the pre-WW1 era ("La Belle Époque," 1871–1914). For many countries during this period, international trade contributed more as a percentage of national income than it does today (O'Rourke and Williamson 1999; Osterhammel and Petersson 2005; Martell 2007). According to these skeptics, therefore, there is no novelty in globalization, although the speed and intensity of contemporary globalization is without historical parallel.

Globalization or regionalization: For many second wave skeptics, the hyperglobalist narrative of a homogenous process of globalization throughout the world, whereby diverse cultures are drawn into a uniform trend of Westernization, is a myth which fails to pass the smell-test of empirical scrutiny (Hirst and Thompson 1996; Krugman 1996). Several skeptical theorists recognize a process of "regionalization," claiming that much of the world's trade is actually confined to several large regional trading blocs: the Americas, Europe and the Pacific Rim countries of South and East Asia (China, India, Japan, Hong Kong, South Korea etc.), but that many other countries — especially those in Africa, the Middle East and elsewhere — have long remained excluded from the primary circuits of international trade and commerce. This focus on regionalization, rather than globalization, has led some skeptics to recognize the very different models of capitalism that are presently driving the process of globalization. David Held and Anthony McGrew (2001) note this diversity: "Dismissing the idea of a unified global economy, the sceptical position concludes that the world is breaking up into several major economic and political blocs, within which very different forms of capitalism continue to flourish." The dynamism of China's "red capitalism" is very different from the liberal free enterprise capitalism of most Western states, and the "oligarchical capitalism" of Vladimir Putin's Russia is also very different from the theocratic petro-capitalism of Saudi Arabia and Iran. For these reasons, many skeptics dismiss as a gross oversimplification the idea that contemporary globalization is driven by a homogenous Western model of free enterprise and free trade capitalism.

Obdurate nationalism: Similarly, many skeptics challenge the popular belief that globalization, besides rapidly advancing the economic, financial and cultural integration of the world, is also de-nationalizing most contemporary states and greatly diminishing traditional nationalist sentiments. Some skeptics counter-claim that, for many countries, there has been a recent return to "hard" nationalism and a strong reassertion of national interests (Smith 1990; Kennedy and Danks 2001). This return to hard nationalism is apparent in several examples: in the US, the 2018 trade tariffs against China, the European Union and other countries, as well as heightened concerns over border security and undocumented migrants; in the UK, the 2016 Brexit referendum vote to quit the EU; the rise of far-right populist movements across Europe, the UK and the US; and a return by many countries to protectionist trade policies. In addition, the revival of nationalism among the major powers is apparent in the tough reassertion of their strategic geopolitical interests and a willingness to wage proxy wars in other countries: the US in Afghanistan, Iraq and Libya; Russia in Georgia, Ukraine and Syria; Saudi Arabia and Iran in Yemen; and Turkey in Syria. As Held and McGrew (2001) observe: "Rather than a new world order, the post-Cold War global system has witnessed a return to old style geo-politics and neo-imperialism, through which the most powerful states and social forces have consolidated their global dominance." Even China's president, Xi Jinping, has reasserted a territorial claim for the full reintegration of Taiwan and Hong Kong into the Peoples Republic of China, threatening "to fight bloody battles against our enemies" [in order to] "take our due place in the world" (Haas 2018). None of these examples support the globalist narrative of a "new world order," integrated through global trade and commerce and supported by an increasingly cosmopolitan global culture. If anything, history appears to be moving in the opposite direction.

Globalization versus social democracy: Finally, many second wave skeptics share with radical first wave critics a concern that the process of capitalist, or corporate, globalization and its underlying neoliberal agenda will hasten the death of social democracy and abolish the welfare state. Although second wave skeptics, unlike many first wave Marxist critics, identify more as social democrats and social reformers rather than as hard socialists, they remain strongly committed to the projects of income redistribution, greater socio-economic equality and social justice, environmental protection and conservation, and greater democratic accountability. In all these respects, the corporate model of hypergloblization threatens to frustrate and negate the prospects of building social democracy around the world.

Third Wave Transformationalists

The final and third broad category of globalization theory that evolved in the wake of hyperglobalism and its critics and skeptics is what Held and colleagues (1999) call "transformationalism." Arguably, a more appropriate name for this third wave could be "reflexive globalism," because most of the theorists who endorse this perspective distance themselves from the earlier hyperglobalism of the neoliberals and internalize many of the questions, concerns and objections raised by critics and skeptics of globalization theory. For these reasons, third wave globalization theorists are more nuanced, more cautious and far less ideological than the earlier hyperglobalists. In the words of Held and McGrew (2001), "The third-wave perspectives have been ones that do not go as far as the skeptics in that they do not deny that real significant changes have happened. They acknowledge the reality of globalizing changes and so defend a globalist position but one that is modified to be more complex than that of the hyperglobalists." There are several ways in which this third wave can be distinguished from both the first and second waves of globalization theory:

Distinctive but not unique: Most transformationalists recognize that globalization is not unique to the twentieth and twenty-first centuries, for, as many skeptics have shown, globalization also occurred during other historical periods, often helping to define them (Abu-Lughod 1991; Frank and Gills 1993). For example, the period of early modern globalization, or what is now called "proto-globalization" (Hopkins 2003; Bayly 2004), spanned the years between 1600 and 1800, following the period of archaic globalization. Increasing trade links and cultural exchange characterized this period immediately preceding the advent of so-called "modern glo-balization" in the nineteenth century. Third wave theorists also recognize that that the current process of globalization has a number of distinctive features: the unprecedented compression of space and time made possible through new flows of information (Giddens 1990) and new networks of communication and mobilities of travel and transportation (Castells 1996). Contemporary globalization has also advanced the processes of market integration — through trade, commerce and finance — and cultural homogenization to levels never before seen in the history of the world.

Voluntarism rather than determinism: Third wave theorists have also abandoned the deterministic models of globalization favoured by hyper-globalists and often by their Marxist critics. Whereas first wave theorists saw globalization as an inevitable linear trend leading to a complete integration of financial and commercial markets, unified networks of information and communication, the eclipse of the nation state by mul-tilateral institutions and eventual cultural homogenization and world governance, transformationalists are unconvinced. Instead they recognize that globalization remains a hotly contested process, opposed by some countries and by a growing number of anti-globalization movements around the world. For Global South theorists, there is nothing inevitable about globalization; it is not a *telic,* or "teleological," process (Holton 2005).

Instead, globalization has often proven to be an uncertain and unpre-dictable process, with stops and starts, advances and retreats. It is apparent that globalization has greatly expanded transnational transactions in commerce, trade and finance and has also accelerated the distribution of material production around the world. According to Held and McGrew (2001), "Multinational corporations now account, according to some estimates, for at least 20 per cent of world production and 70 per cent of world trade." But there are two sides to this process. While globalization has enriched those who own and control transnational enterprises and multinational corporations, it has simultaneously impoverished those who are marginalized and excluded from the benefits of international trade, commerce and manufacturing, in some regions of North America and Europe and in the forgotten hinterlands of the Global South. While glo-balization has the power to integrate, it also has the power to alienate and divide. Today, the global gap in wealth and income has never been greater, and the level of inequality between rich and poor is without precedent. But the blowback is growing stronger and is expressed in various forms of opposition, ranging from religious fundamentalism and jihadism, to political populism, anti-globalization movements, resurgent nationalism and even terrorism. For many of its victims and survivors, globalization remains an ambiguous project. And transformationalists are keenly aware of these contradictions.

Multidimensional: Unlike the hyperglobalists, who see globalization as a process leading to one global culture, largely determined by economic causes and economic outcomes, transformationalists recognize that globalization is a multidimensional process, with multiple causes and consequences. Thus, while some third wave theorists continue to prioritize economic globalization, others focus on cultural globalization (Robertson 1992; Appadurai 1996) or on political globalization (Steger 2003; Delanty and Rumford 2008); while still others focus on technological globalization (Castells 1996; Scholte 2005). There are many different dimensions to globalization, and third wave theorists have pioneered new areas of theory and research within their multivariate perspective. One of the more important lessons learned from adopting a multidimensional paradigm is the recognition that globalization is a *heterogeneous* process rather than the homogenous process previously portrayed in the oversimplified hyperglobalist accounts and oversimplified Marxist critiques. This recognition has enabled transformationalist theorists to show, for example, that even the Americanization of food cultures in other countries — through the Coca-colonization of beverages and the McDonaldization of fast food — may be filtered and mediated through the lenses of local cultural influences. And other Westernized products of globalization, such as the Disney theme park in Hong Kong, have also been adapted to local conditions (Matusitz 2009).

The process of local adaptation to the larger forces of globalization has resulted in a new focus on what postcolonial theorists call the process of "hybridization" or "creolization" (Garcia Canclini 1990; Kraidy 2005; Nederveen 1994; Acheraiou 2011), or more commonly known in the recent globalization literature as "glocalization" (Robertson 1992; Appadurai 1996). This concept is best defined by the theorist who introduced the term: "By glocalization, Robertson means that ideas about home, locality and community have been extensively spread around the

Glocalization of American Food Culture

In the Netherlands, McDonald's serves a McKroket (a fried beef croquette on a bun); in Germany, it offers shrimp with cocktail sauce.... There's a burger on pita bread for the Greek market (the Greek Mac, of course), and a McKebab for Israel. Naturally, you can get guacamole on your burger in Mexico; you can also order McMolletes — refried beans and salsa on an English muffin...

For its Japanese stores, McDonald's has found that novelty is the way to go, and the company has introduced lots of special menu items. You can pair your Teriyaki McBurger, made from pork, with a bag of Seaweed Shaker fries (add the seaweed powder yourself). You can get a Croquette Burger or a Bacon Potato Pie. Probably the most distinctively Japanese dish is the Ebi Filet-O, a fried shrimp patty on a bun ("ebi" means shrimp in Japanese)....

Dunkin' Donuts has made a big splash in South Korea, popularizing bagels and doughnuts as breakfast treats. Besides the standard American glazed and filled versions, it offers red bean and glutinous rice doughnuts as well as sweet potato muffins and a sesame tofu ring. There are savory fried croquettes filled with lentil curry or kimchi, spicy pickled cabbage.

Source: Stern 2010.

world in recent years, so that the local has been globalized, and the stress upon the significance of the local or the communal can be viewed as one ingredient of the overall globalization process" (quoted in Robinson 2008: 135). This recognition that local cultures retain the capacity and agency to modify and customize for their own particular needs the broader process of globalization contradicts the claims of hyperglobalists — such as Friedman (2005), Barber (1995) and Ritzer (2004, 2013) — that we now all inhabit a "flat" world, a McDonaldized world and a fully Americanized or Westernized world, in other words, a global culture. The recognition of the multidimensionality of globalization has simultaneously led to a growing recognition of the vitality and sustainability of local cultures and local contexts (Featherstone 1996; Hall 1997).

The politics of transformationalism: The global politics of the third wave transformationalists is best understood as an attempt to steer a middle course between the brash optimism of the neoliberal hyperglobalists versus the pessimism and fatalism of their first and second wave critics and skeptics. Perhaps a good description of the politics of the third wave is that of qualified or cautious "possibilism." The major hope of most transformationalists is pinned to the rise of a new cosmopolitan politics developed from local, national and regional "communities of practice" that already exist around the world. Unlike the hyperglobalists, the third wave theorists do not foresee the imminent demise of the nation state or the end of its sovereignty. Instead, they believe that the infrastructure of a cosmopolitan civil society is already underway (Archibugi and Held 1995). However, these academic disagreements between the "optimism" of the third way globalists and the "pessimism" of their first and second wave predecessors can more realistically be understood as a family dispute between earlier more pragmatic proponents of the hegemony of global capitalism versus their more openly imperialistic contemporary neoliberal colleagues. In this sense, all these theorists are ideologues of global capitalism, and the search for a middle way was always a search for the most efficient way to ensure the global accumulation of private capital and the most effective way of exploiting a powerless global working class.

The main elements of this new constitutional democracy can already be seen in a number of evolving transnational institutions. Chief among these are the international government agencies — such as the World Trade Organization, the International Monetary Fund and the World Bank — as well as others, such as the United Nations Food and Agriculture Organization, International Labour Organization, Organization for Economic Cooperation and Development, UN Conference on Trade and Development, UN Environment Programme, World Health Organization, World Organization for Animal Health, World Intellectual Property Organization and, of course, the United Nations. Each of these multilateral institutions helps to set the international rules for conducting trade, commerce and finance, as well as many other global activities. Alongside these agencies, a system of cosmopolitan law has begun to evolve which legislates, arbitrates and regulates a host of international issues, including labour codes, environmental protection and conservation, human rights, arms sales and shipments, drug smuggling, human trafficking, disease pandemics, war crimes and crimes against humanity. These concerns have been addressed in a number of judicial settings, including the International Criminal Court, the European Court of Human Rights, the International Court of Justice, special courts and tribunals and other legal settings. Transformationalists believe that this judicial infrastructure is laying the groundwork for a system of cosmopolitan law that will advance the cause of worldwide universal justice.

In addition to these formal organizations, there are many officially recognized international non-governmental organizations (INGOS), including associations, social movements, advocacy workers and citizens groups which organize and operate across national boundaries and borders around the world. Examples of INGOS include the Red Cross, Greenpeace, the World Wildlife Fund, Oxfam and Amnesty International, among many others. While most INGOS are found in scientific, technical, business, industry, medical and professional domains, many are also active in areas such as sports and recreation, development, education, women's rights etc. "This explosion of 'citizen diplomacy' creates the basis of communities of interest or association which span national borders, with the purpose of advancing mutual goals or bringing governments and the formal institutions of global governance to account for their activities" (Held and McGrew 2001).

Transformationalism in Retrospect

The political project of cosmopolitan democracy has attracted a variety of critics and skeptics (Archibugi 2004). Self-proclaimed "realists," such as Danilo Zolo (1997) and David Chandler (2003), are convinced that in the final analysis all states are motivated by their perceived national interests and will use military force when necessary to secure these interests. The term "realism" among theorists of international relations refers to the view that the international order is basically anarchic, that states will invariably act in their own rational interests and that — if necessary — power or force will be used to secure these interests. For them, any hope of replacing national interest with an idealized cosmopolitan democracy is utopian and unworthy of serious consideration. Some realists also reject the goal of a world government, which they mistakenly believe to be the logical conclusion of any project for cosmopolitan democracy; there is no evidence that any of the advocates of cosmopolitan democracy have ever advocated such a centralized political model. Most third wave theorists have only pursued the goal of the transnational rule of law and democratic accountability. A further extension of this realist critique may be called the "hegemonist" argument. These realists insist that the major powers, especially the US, already control many of the transnational institutions (IGOS) that transformationalists see as the backbone of a cosmopolitan democracy. Any attempt to limit the hegemony of a major power would likely be met with military force: e.g., the US in Panama, Afghanistan and Iraq; the Russians in Ukraine, Crimea, Georgia and Syria; India in Kashmir; China in Tibet etc.

Critics and skeptics from other standpoints have also questioned the project of cosmopolitan democracy. Marxists insist that true "internationalism" can only be achieved through the struggle for socialism and a classless society: the unity of working people throughout the world (Gilbert 1999; Brennan 2001). Other communitarians and multiculturalists are convinced that cosmopolitanism is inherently *elitist* and that transnational institutions will always remain dominated and manipulated by cosmopolitan elites (Kymlicka 1995). According to these skeptics, the best guarantee for advancing a democratic politics around the globe is the nation state, where governments and political agendas can be held more directly accountable to public opinion and the electorate. Finally, some critics argue that cosmopolitan constitutionalism is not the same thing as cosmopolitan democracy (Morgan 2003). In other words, the establishment of global rules of law and transnational constitutional procedures is very different from democracy. Whereas "democracy" implies mass and equal participation in the political process, constitutionalism and proceduralism can easily promote a specialized stratum of experts and technocrats, i.e., governance by an elite.

The third wave transformationalist globalization theorists occupy a precarious position. On the one hand, they reject the brash optimism of the hyperglobalists and the pessimism and fatalism of the first wave critics. But on the other hand, they have acknowledged and learned from the concerns expressed by both first wave critics and second wave skeptics. Third wave theorists have tried to advance their own theoretical perspective of "reflexive globalization" at a time when there appears to be a resurgence of nationalism around the world. This has been apparent in the recent appearance of far-right nationalist movements in Europe and North America and in the adoption of economic protectionism, political isolationism and aggressive foreign policies by a growing number of nation states. In the face of this resurgent nationalism, the project of cosmopolitan democracy, however noble in sentiment and intent, seems further away than ever.

Table 12-2: Waves of Globalization Theory

Social Theory	Key Concepts	Major Representatives
First Wave Hyperglobalists		
Post-industrial theorists	End of ideology; end of history	Daniel Bell; Francis Fukuyama
Hyperglobalists	neoliberalism; laissez-faire; free trade; open borders; homogenization; economic determinism	Thomas Friedman; Kenichi Ohmae; Theodore Levitt; Tony Blair; Bill Clinton
First Wave Critics		
Cultural conflict theorists	Clash of civilizations; fundamentalism; nationalism & nativism	Samuel Huntington; Bernard Lewis; Benjamin Barber; Mary Daly
Marxist theorists and radical anti-imperialist theorists	World systems theory; anti-neoliberalism; anti-capitalism & anti-imperialism; critiques of corporate & late capitalism; pro-socialism and radical democracy	Immanuel Wallerstein; Rosa Luxemburg, Jane Addams, David Harvey; Frederic Jameson; Göran Therborn; Alex Callinicos; Ellen Meiksins-Wood; Ha-Joon Chang; Noam Chomsky
Post-colonial theorists	orientalism; hybridism	Edward Saïd; Gayatri Spivak; Homi J. Bhabha; Chris Weedon; Sarojini Sahoo
Second Wave Skeptics		
Social democratic theorists	Welfare state; economic & environmental regulations	Paul Hirst & Grahame Thompson; Mike Featherstone; Leslie Sklair; Alison Mary Jaggar; Nancy Fraser
Revised globalization theorists	Resource curse & extractive industries; economic geography; agglomeration & economies of scale; information asymmetry	Jeffrey Sachs; Paul Krugman; Joseph Stiglitz; Valentine Moghadam
Multicultural theorists	Cultural homogenization and hybridism	Jeremy Seabrook; George Ritzer; Maxine Baca Zinn
Third Wave Transformationalists		
Network society theorists	Connectivity; mobility; flows	Manuel Castells; John Urry; Arjun Appadurai; Pragya Agarwal

Risk society theorists	Indeterminism; threats; hazards; risks	Ulrich Beck, Mary Douglas
Information society (or knowledge society) theorists	Space/time compression; space/time instantiation; global village	Marshall McLuhan; Anthony Giddens; Jan Aart Scholte; Wendy Harcourt; Nancy Hafkin, Nancy Taggart
Late modernity theorists	Liquid modernity/society	Zygmunt Bauman
Global postmodernist theorists	Hegemonic discourse, de-materialization & deterritorialization; subaltern; strategic essentialism	Michael Hardt & Antonio Negri; Martin Albrow; Chandra Talpade Mohanty; Gayatri Chakravorty Spivak
Globalism and localism theorists	Glocalization; global cities	Robert Robertson; Arjun Appadurai; Michael Burawoy; Saskia Sassen
Cosmopolitan democratic theorists	Cosmopolitan & global democratization & humanization	David Held & Anthony McGrew; Daniele Archibugi; Jürgen Habermas; Ulrich Beck; Richard Falk; Mary Kaldor; Martha Craven Nussbaum; Mary Robinson

MANUEL CASTELLS AND THE NETWORK SOCIETY

One of the most influential contemporary theorists to analyze the more distinctive features of global modernity is the Spanish social theorist Manuel Castells. In his studies of globalization, Castells focuses on how the new technologies of information and communication (sometimes called the Third Industrial Revolution) have revolutionized social relations in the twenty-first century. In particular, he has shown how high-speed digital communication has transformed and compressed our experience of space and time and has also led to the redesign and restructuring of organizations, especially business enterprises competing in a global market.

For Castells, there are several prominent features that together illustrate the distinctive nature of social life in the age of global modernity. The instantaneous and simultaneous transmission and reception of real-time information — whether of news reports, flows of currency or financial assets, or of simultaneous "flash mobilizations" of political protests and demonstrations in different cities or different parts of the world — has transformed our lives forever. As Castells suggests, this reduction of space to "flows of time" through the new digital economy and the new liquid society has led to further changes. The old bureaucratic design of organizations with hierarchal authority structures and vertical chains of command has been superseded in some sectors, such as information and communication companies in the digital economy, producer cooperatives for sporting equipment, housing etc., by organizations with flatter and more fluid structures that are far better adapted to respond to rapid changes in the global marketplace. However, as several critics (Freeman 1972; Pfeffer 2013; Finley 2014; Baker 2015; Spicer 2018) have shown, the benefits of a more horizonal and supposedly democratic organizational structure are frequently more illusory than real. Feminist sociologist Jo Freeman (1972) argues, in "The Tyranny of Structurelessness," that structurelessness easily "becomes a smokescreen for the strong or the lucky to establish unquestioned hegemony over others." Other commentators have observed that the absence of formalized rules and procedures or of an established chain of command can lead to the growth of a vicious new informal power structure, with fresh opportunities for personal, sexual and workplace abuse. With the disappearance of official executive officers, new powerful workplace "barons" can pursue their own interests with few limitations. At the same time, the days when material manufacturing still constituted the primary economic base of capitalist societies in the Global North have also disappeared. The primary production of many late capitalist societies today is centred on dematerialized commodities — information, finance and services. For these reasons, Castells concludes that the classical themes of social theory, which focused on material production and bureaucracy, have become less relevant to the present conditions of global modernity: "I grew increasingly dissatisfied with the interpretations and theories, certainly including my own, that the social sciences were using to make sense of this new world" (Castells 2002: 125).

Networks

Castells refers to the distinguishing mode of organization for the early twenty-first century as the "network." The network is a "chain" (of organization, communication and information) comprised of a number of links or "nodes." Unlike the typical organization of the pre-global period, contemporary networks are flat, flexible, fluid and often ephemeral; they may appear and disappear depending upon prevailing economic, political and social conditions. Networks are also open structures, capable of rapid and infinite expansion, and they are highly decentralized, often unified on the basis of "trust" and common communication codes. According to Castells, networks, which are formed within a "space of flows" (i.e., within an environment in which space and time are digitally compressed), include three main elements: "connectivity" (via information and communication technologies); "nodes" (which constitute the links in the network chain of relations); and "people" (typically members of a cosmopolitan managerial elite who commute from country to country).

Figure 12-3: Castells' Concept of Network

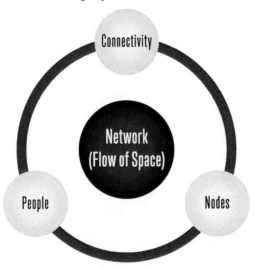

Although most of the examples that Castells provides of typical networks are of legitimate enterprises in our society, such as global businesses, financial enterprises, news media, education institutions and international agencies, networks are also used by more unsavoury global actors, such as criminal syndicates and terrorist groups. Thus, a global jihadist group, such as ISIS or Al Qaeda, may be described as a "network," complete with its own connectivity, nodes and people. For ISIS, its connectivity is used to promote its ideology on the internet, to attract potential recruits and to showcase its atrocities: beheadings, bombings and military attacks. The ISIS network also has a number of nodes which function as operational links in its chain of activities. These would doubtless include funding sources (from sympathetic nations such as Saudi Arabia), arms suppliers (for battlefield weapons), recruitment contacts (for attracting foreign fighters) and distribution contacts (for propaganda and other publications).

And of course, ISIS also needs people: those who travel from different countries to combat zones in Syria, Iraq and etc., as well as those who are radicalized within particular countries in sleeper, or lone-wolf, operative cells. In this respect, networks have become the primary mode of organization for many agencies, enterprises and groups with a global reach.

Criticisms of Castells

Within the quarrelsome world of social theory, almost every theoretical perspective is likely to attract some criticisms from other social theorists who identify weaknesses or shortcomings that in their opinion need to be addressed. The network theory of Manuel Castells is no exception. Some of the main criticisms that have been made of this theory include the following:

Overgeneralized conception of "network": According to some critics, Castells has employed the concept of "network" too promiscuously in his work. It sometimes appears that, for Castells, all forms of social interaction and social organization can be reduced to network analysis. Some critics conclude that Castells uses this term too broadly and, consequently, has impoverished its meaning and significance (Webster 2002: 115). If all forms of interaction can be described as "networks," then we are left with no way to compare and contrast more fixed and durable bureaucratic structures with those that are more fluid and fleeting. We also are left with no way to distinguish relatively strong ties of interaction from those that are much weaker.

Technological determinism: Castells' theory has been critiqued for its alleged "technological determinism." Some critics reject Castells' assumption that the power of technology has primarily been responsible for propelling our world in a new age, the global network society. Especially for Marxist theorists, this *technological bias* is problematic for a number of reasons. First, it overlooks the historical context of class relations and neglects to consider the role that technology plays in the development of capitalist society. Technology, as a means of production, is always under the ownership and control of the capitalist class. As Nicholas Garnham (2004: 174) suggests, "the informational mode of development is developed for and put at the service of a set of property relations and the goal of accumulation, not vice versa." Second, Castells is sometimes accused of exaggerating the uniqueness of the network society and overlooking the extent to which the roots of post-industrial technology extend back to an earlier age of industrialism. While the network society may be distinctive in many ways, it remains a product of earlier stages in the development of the capitalist means of production. In this respect, Castells' theoretical perspective may be seen as "ahistorical." Third, Castells' definition of "informational labour" has been criticized for its *vagueness*. Unlike most sociological definitions of labour, which refer to relatively homogenous occupational groups, Castells includes a strange assortment of occupations in his definition of "informational labour." As Geoffrey Glass (2005) observes, Castells includes such diverse occupations as "journalists, stockbrokers, and surgeons. The relations between these occupations and the information they deal with is anything but consistent, and the group as a whole anything but homogeneous. (Is it level of education? communication? influence?)."

Eurocentrism: Another criticism of Castells' theory of the network society is that "networks" have typically been associated with the rise of high-tech information and communications companies, such as Microsoft, Apple and Google. Such companies, with their relatively decentralized, flat and fluid organizational structures, exemplify the new networks of information, communication and organization that have revolutionized the worlds of business, commerce and social relations. However, although the network form of organization has now spread into many other spheres of human activity, this is primarily the case for Western countries, characterized by high-tech industries, advanced capitalist societies and consumer-driven markets for goods and services. Many critics conclude that the network society is less likely to be found within the much poorer conditions of the Global South. The charge against Castells is that his global generalization of the network society reflects his basic Eurocentrism and his failure to recognize the huge organizational and "digital divide" that separates the Global North from the Global South.

Notwithstanding these criticisms, Castells has greatly contributed to our understanding of the transformative power of digital technology in late modernity and helps us to recognize more clearly the distinctiveness of the globalizing world we inhabit.

ULRICH BECK AND THE RISK SOCIETY

Another contemporary thinker who has analyzed the present era of global modernity is the German social theorist Ulrich Beck (1944–2015). However, whereas Castells has focused on the "network society," Beck has focused on the "risk society." More than any other contemporary theorist, Beck's work highlights the risks associated with the present age. But unlike earlier theorists, for whom natural hazards and catastrophes, such as earthquakes, tsunamis, floods, storms, tornados, hurricanes, landslides etc., were once considered arbitrary and unforeseeable "natural" disasters, contemporary theorists now view many of today's catastrophic events as predictable and calculable risks and as clear dangers that result from human activity. For Beck, the techno-scientific advances of our present age are accompanied by proliferating risks — of climate change, of environmental degradation, of resource depletion, of the growing potential for a thermonuclear holocaust or chemical catastrophe and of many other human-made risks to our long-term survival on this planet.

Figure 12-4: Beck's Hazards versus Risks

Beck's Risk Society

Like all the theorists discussed in this book, Beck has introduced his own vocabulary of basic terms and key concepts, all of which play an important part in his theory of the risk society. Some of the more significant concepts are identified below:

Reflexivity: Besides his concerns with the growing risks encountered by individual and collective social actors in the present age of global modernity, Beck also focuses on the problems of what he calls "reflexive modernization." By this he means the particular form of individual and collective consciousness that has evolved in contemporary societies around the world. According to Beck, the conditions of social life in the twenty-first century, including the dramatic advances in science and technology and especially the invention of personalized mobile communications and social media, have combined to produce a high level of "reflexivity" in social actors, by which he means a capacity to learn from past experiences and to use this knowledge for more informed and educated future actions. In other words, more than ever before, the actions and practices of social actors are subject to considerable self-scrutiny and self-criticism. This concept of reflexivity is similar to that introduced by Anthony Giddens. The main difference is that for Beck, the reflexivity of social actors is deeply influenced by their constant awareness of the prevailing risks that threaten their sense of security and safety and even their long-term survival. Today, the scope and scale of societal and individual self-examination is unprecedented in human history. At first sight, it might seem that this reflexivity could only be a good thing. But, as Beck is at pains to point out, this focus on collective or individual self-examination also has a more sinister side.

According to Beck, the great paradox of reflexivity in the present age is that even though there is now more knowledge and information available on the risks and perils of human-made industrial, environmental, technological, epidemiological, financial and other possible catastrophic "accidents," there are also more ways of evading, ignoring or even denying these risks. The present capacity for reflexive individual and societal self-examination of our human-made risks has also evolved a corresponding capacity for avoidance, minimization and denial of these risks. Beck refers to these individual and societal mechanisms of cognitive dissonance as "individual self-confrontation" and "societal self-confrontation." And in each case, self-confrontation may result in "organized irresponsibility," that is, techniques for reducing cognitive dissonance by denying the reality or the magnitude of current risks and threats to our long-term security and safety. An obvious example of this type of irresponsibility may be seen in counter-claims by climate change deniers and capitalists who prioritize traditional job creation in the fossil fuel industries over and above climate concerns.

Individualization: As an extension of his concept of "reflexive modernization," Beck focuses on the process of "individualization" that characterizes personal lifestyles and social relations in the present era of global modernity. Beck refers to the unprecedented range of personal choices available to many social actors in terms of their lifestyles, identities, occupations, practices and beliefs, among many others. Many of the restrictions that were once placed on who we could marry, which occupations were legally open to us, where we were permitted to live and what religion we were obliged to practise have been lifted.

However, as Beck suggests, these new private freedoms often come with new public responsibilities and obligations. For example, although we may choose to adopt a child into our family, that decision involves a number of legal obligations and responsibilities that may limit our personal freedoms. Similarly, a decision to undertake gender reassignment, or gender affirmation, surgery entails legal requirements related to personal ID documentation. In many ways, Beck's concept of "individualization" raises some of the issues that were first raised over a century ago by Emile Durkheim with his concept of *homo duplex*:

> Far from being simple, our inner life has something like a double centre of gravity. On the one hand is our individuality.... On the other is everything in us that expresses something other than ourselves. Not only are these two groups of states of consciousness different in their origins and their properties, but there is a true antagonism between them. (1973: 152)

Although the dissolution of traditional lifestyle values and normative codes now allows us greater personal freedom, we can also encounter greater tensions between our split private and public lives and identities.

The Risks in a Risk Society

Throughout much of his work, Beck provides a powerful overview of our growing awareness of the potential threats to our future existence on the planet. In a compelling summary of his own theory of the risk society, delivered as a public lecture at the London School of Economics, Beck explained what he means by the concept of "risk" and how our awareness of global risks can change our politics, our social relations and even our conception of sociology. This lecture provides a fitting conclusion for many of the topics covered in this book, and it also suggests some of the ways in which we can — as a global population — plan for greater safety and security in an age of uncertainty and indeterminacy.

Beck begins by distinguishing between intended and unintended dangers in contemporary global societies. Intended dangers arise from deliberate actions that are designed to endanger others, most commonly acts of terrorism or warfare. On the other hand, unintentional dangers arise either from natural catastrophes or from human-made accidents, such as those highlighted in Figure 12-5. However, as Beck is quick to point out, the distinction between some natural catastrophes and human-made accidents is murky, even spurious, because some natural disasters have been connected to human activities. For example, there is evidence to suggest that "fracking" (hydraulic fracturing) has contributed to earthquakes and that deforestation has contributed to avalanches and mud/rock slides. Although it is clear that such fracking and logging consequences as well as mining catastrophes are always the result of corporate decisions to exploit natural resources and are never "accidents," it is becoming more difficult to disentangle natural disasters from social accidents.

Beck also distinguishes the new global "risks" from the old traditional "dangers" that have long confronted and challenged humanity. The "risks" that we face today, according to Beck, differ from earlier dangers in at least three ways:

- *Spatial*: The new risks traverse national borders and are often global in their causes and consequences. The burning of fossil fuels can occur in any part of the world, but the impact of these practices is felt by all of us though global warming and climate change.
- *Temporal*: The new risks may have a long incubation period. Radioactive materials may have a long half-life before they finally decay and are rendered harmless. Or a lone-wolf terrorist operative or a terrorist "sleeper-cell" may remain dormant within a community for some time before becoming active. Many other new global risks may remain invisible for long periods of time before they detonate.
- *Social*: It may often be difficult to separate the cause from the effect of some new global risks. Attempts to prevent the risks of authoritarian rule through "regime change" may then produce a backlash (as in Afghanistan, Iraq, Libya and Syria), which may lead to new risks of local and global terrorism. Sometimes, efforts to prevent the poaching of endangered species (such as elephants, rhinos or lions) result in a greatly increased regional or global demand that may intensify poaching activities for an underground market.

Figure 12-5: Beck's Different Types of Dangers

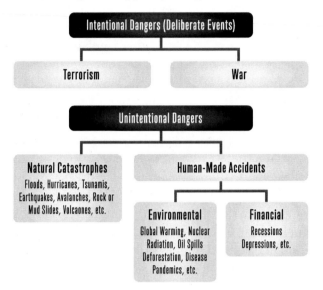

The Irony of Global Dangers

Perhaps the most important part of Beck's lecture is his conception of danger as "ironic," by which he signifies several different aspects of contemporary global dangers:

Hazards are unknown and incalculable: Unlike "risks" or "dangers," which are known and often predictable, "hazards" in Beck's vocabulary are unknown. Hazards are "ironic" in the sense that we do not, and cannot, know these "unknowns." This irony was most famously expressed by Donald Rumsfeld, former US Secretary of Defense, when he stated: "As we know, there are known knowns; there are things we know we know. We also know there are known unknowns; that is to say we know there are some things we do not know. But there are also unknown unknowns — the ones we don't know we don't know" (Graham 2014). For this reason, hazards form a dark background to our lives — invisible and unknowable and yet omnipresent.

Risks are ambiguous: While risks pose obvious threats to our health, well being and survival, they also provide opportunities for creative responses, through rational planning, international cooperation and the formation of new alliances, even between former adversaries. Global climate confer-ences are now sometimes attended by rival nation states, such as China and the US, except that President Trump withdrew in 2017 from the 2015 Paris Agreement on climate change. Although risks may generate threats, they may also provide new opportunities for what Beck calls a "cosmopolitan moment." This capacity and potential for risk to become a two-edged sword (threat versus opportunity) is also referred to by Beck as the "ruse of history" and at other times as the "ruse of risk." Risks may also prove to be "ironic" in the sense that the very means used to combat particular (environmental, financial or security) risks — whether these means are techno-scientific, monetary or military — may sometimes contribute to the risks they are designed to prevent.

Risks are disruptive: Some observers have said that digital information and new communication technologies are "disruptive" in the sense that they have contributed to the decline of printed products, for example, as well as to the elimination of other technologies — such as the land-line telephone, VHS cassette tapes, DVDs, etc. — through the use of new technologies such as smart phones, video streaming, podcasts and so on. Because they are feared and unknown, some global dangers have similarly disrupted established institutions and social practices and have generated new forms of organization. The absolute sovereignty of the nation state has been disrupted by concerns over climate change and global warming. Nation states within the European Union, for example, have ceded some of their national sovereignty in the greater interest of confronting environmental challenges. Similarly, other states have ceded some of their sovereignty over national security by sharing cross-border information in an effort to thwart global terrorism and other global crimes, such as human trafficking. An example is the G5 Sahel security alliance — comprising Burkina Faso, Chad, Mali, Mauritania and Niger, which face a number of security challenges, including the growing threat of terrorism and organized crime, climate change and demographic growth. Besides multilateral security alliances between NATO and EU countries, there is also the Moscow-dominated Collective Security Treaty Organization (CSTO) and the Eurasian Economic Union (EEU), which consists of partially failed states — Moldova, Ukraine, Georgia and Azerbaijan. Canada is a member of the Five Eyes, often abbreviated as FVEY, which is a multilateral anglophone intelligence and security alliance comprising Australia, Canada, New Zealand, the United Kingdom and the United States.

Global Cosmopolitanism

The final section of Beck's lecture focuses on the possible future political organization of human societies in an age of global risks. Beck suggests that two competing alternative states are in the process of emerging. One is the "neoliberal state," which closely resembles the vision of America espoused by Donald Trump and the Republican Party. This state emphasizes individualism, minimal government, reduced social services and personal responsibility for health care, social insurance etc. It also emphasizes such neoliberal policies and practices as privatization, deregulation and full marketization and commodification of everything.

On the other hand, the "cosmopolitan state" is perhaps best exemplified by the ideal member state of the European Union. Strongly influenced by the European Convention on Human Rights, the ideal member state upholds the rights of same-sex marriage, as well as open access to abortion, contraception and divorce. The cosmopolitan state, according to Beck, enshrines constitutional protections for such basic freedoms as freedom of speech and assembly and freedom of religion, as well as protections from arbitrary arrest and search or seizure of personal property. The cosmopolitan state is also characterized by a strong commitment to social justice and a willingness to form multilateral and transnational partnerships, alliances and coalitions for environmental protection and shared cross-border security against terrorism, human trafficking, drug trafficking and other aspects of global crime. As with all ideal types, aspects of each may be found co-existing within a single state. For example, Canada shares some characteristics of the neoliberal state in its participation of free trade agreements like NAFTA (now replaced with the United States–Mexico–Canada Agreement, or USMCA), but in other respects — such as its health-care, pension and social service programs — it resembles some member countries of the European Union.

Beck's distinction between the neoliberal state and the cosmopolitan state has been criticized by several theorists, who have pointed to its Eurocentrism and spurious nature (Archibugi 2000; Gowan 2001; Martell 2009; Mythen 2007; Ormrod 2013). Indeed, Janet Bujra (2000: 63) dismisses both of these ideal types as models of the modern state and charges Beck's theory of modernization with reproducing "an evolutionist and

THEORIZING OUR SHRINKING WORLD 545

westernized model of social development." Other critics argue that, in a world dominated by transnational capital and US geopolitical hegemony, any distinction between a neoliberal state and a cosmopolitan state is illusory. Peter Gowan (2001: 89) concludes: "In this empire, we find substantial unity between the states and market forces of the core countries rather than the antagonism suggested by theorists of globalization and liberal cosmopolitanism." Also, while Beck suggests that "humanitarian military interventions" are part of the democratic mandate of the cosmopolitan state, other critics see these interventions in geopolitical terms as US neoimperialism — ultimately designed to stabilize regional trade and commerce and to secure access to natural resources, as well as to consumer and cheap labour markets. Many of these criticisms, as Luke Martell (2009: 21) notes, are part of a broader critique of Beck's advocacy of cosmopolitanism as an enlightened strategy of globalization and internationalism: "Beck's approach effectively disguises conflicts, inequalities and injustices in world society and harmonises contradictions with a benign and optimistic view of international relations."

Beck has become one of the leading proponents of what he calls "global cosmopolitanism" or "methodological cosmopolitanism." These terms emphasize the positive and progressive aspects of contemporary global connectedness — through information and communication networks, through transportation and travel and through the greatly enhanced mobility of contemporary population flows. In this respect, Beck has much in common with those theorists, already discussed, who have advanced their project for cosmopolitan democracy. According to Beck, global cosmopolitanism entails a new age of potential global unity and cooperation extending across the borders of many different nation states. For Beck, this new age brings promises and potentialities for overcoming traditional national divisions, hostilities and antagonisms. But most of all, Beck's global cosmopolitanism has become a strong critique, or counter-ideology, to the policies, principles and practices of neoliberalism, or more specifically, neoconservatism. If Beck is a leading proponent of global cosmopolitanism, he is at the same time a leading opponent of neoconservativism (and neoliberalism). Whereas "neoliberalism" is an economic ideology that promotes open and cross-border trade policies, full marketization, privatization and deregulation etc., "neoconservatism" is a political ideology that promotes the export of "democracy," "human rights" and "civil liberties" throughout the world, sometimes through military intervention and "regime change," especially to those states governed by "unfriendly" rulers (examples are the US military interventions in Panama in 1989, Afghanistan in 2001, Iraq in 2003 and Libya in 2011).

In general terms, Beck distinguishes between two contrasting ideological programs, or agendas, for the exercise of power through political action. On the one hand, he refers to "methodological nationalism" as an ideology dedicated to national sovereignty, to secure national borders and to the projection of a strong national identity. This is the ideology of Donald Trump's "Make America Great Again" campaign: an ideology that is deeply suspicious of immigrants, of transnational trade deals and of international regulative agencies. It is also the ideology of far-right politicians such as Marine Le Pen in France and of the Brexit supporters in the UK. On the other hand, Beck believes "methodological cosmopolitanism" represents the best aspects of global modernity: the potential for international unity, solidarity and cooperation, the erosion of national borders and the growth of global understanding. For Beck, the EU is, in a sense, a paradigm case of methodological cosmopolitanism inasmuch as the EU is a union of federated democratic states with open borders (Schengen Agreement), a common currency (euro), progressive transnational laws on human rights, environmental protection, civil liberties etc. and a freely elected central European government in Brussels. For Beck, the EU, although far from perfect, illustrates a path towards global cosmopolitanism.

According to Beck, the way forward is clear enough. In order to meet and creatively respond to the current risks of global modernity, old fixations on national sovereignty need to make way for much greater transnational collaboration and cooperation in the face of unprecedented global risks and existential threats to our very survival on this planet. And, as an addendum, he underlines the need for a reflexive and "cosmopolitan sociology" that is capable of identifying, analyzing and studying the social impact of these new global risks upon our own lives and our own selves.

Criticisms of Beck

Beck's theoretical perspective of the risk society and his vision of global cosmopolitanism has not escaped the critical scrutiny of some social theorists, who have expressed concern over weaknesses and limitations of his perspective, notwithstanding his novel and valuable focus on the significance of risk in the contemporary age of global modernity. Among these various criticisms, the following have received particular attention:

Exaggeration: Some critics (Dingwall 1999) suggest that Beck has exaggerated the distinctiveness of contemporary risks while underestimating many of the hazards that were present in traditional societies, including the bubonic plague and other communicable disease pandemics such as influenza and syphilis, among others, all of which claimed millions of victims in the premodern world. Along with this criticism is the related concern that Beck exaggerates the extent to which the reflexive awareness of threats and risks penetrates deeply down into the private lives and personal relations of contemporary social actors. Many critics conclude that Beck has failed to provide any evidence to support this claim. Similarly, other critics suggest that Beck projects an over-rationalized conception of the social actor — a conception that is wholly focused on rational reflexivity and decision-making to the exclusion of any consideration of emotional or affective aspects of the individual.

Decontextualized concepts: Other theorists (Sørensen and Christiansen 2012) suggest that Beck's concept of "risk" does not take into account the particular historical, cultural, socioeconomic or geopolitical context in which these risks are identified and assessed. In other words, Beck is critiqued for introducing a universal or overgeneralized concept of risk that overlooks the specificity of local contexts and conditions. These critics insist that the meaning of "risk" is always dependent upon a specific context and that the impact of a risk may also differ from one context to the next. For example, if a fully democratic society were to exist, the impact of a major catastrophe would be equally distributed among all social actors. However, in a sharply stratified society, divided by caste, class, gender, sexual orientation, ethnicity, race etc., the impact of a devastating event is likely to be disproportionately borne by the most vulnerable social actors.

Power and domination: Closely related to the above critique is the concern that Beck overlooks the structures of power, domination and oppression in contemporary societies around the world, but also underestimates the power of political social movements to secure greater national sovereignty from global capitalist corporations (Weiss 1998). The presence of severe social inequality in many counties ensures that the impact of major threats and risks will be felt most intensely by the most vulnerable members of society — the poor and destitute — while the rich and affluent can normally afford the means to insulate and protect themselves from the worst effects of catastrophic dangers and perils.

Naïve optimism: Some critics (Omrod 2013; Elliott 2002, 299) find Beck's optimistic view, that traditional divisions of social class and social status are being eroded in the new risk society, implausible. Beck appears to believe that the challenge of global risks, such as climate change, will serve to erode entrenched class divisions and to unify populations in the face of a shared and common threat to humanity. However, as already noted, in stratified societies, the impact of a major event is likely to be unequally distributed. Beck also seems to suggest that the new "information and knowledge society and economy" will also eradicate traditional socioeconomic divisions. But many critics show how the benefits of knowledge and information are also unequally distributed in most societies. In other words, the announcement of the post-capitalist age is both premature and unrealistic.

Anti-Americanism: Some critics suggest that Beck's celebratory vision of global cosmopolitanism is animated and distorted by a strong expression of anti-Americanism. At times, Beck's sociological analysis of global cosmopolitanism becomes an increasing politicized ideological counterattack against neoliberalism and neoconservativism. Anthony Elliott (2014: 343) draws attention to this ideological animus:

> Beck packs a considerable punch against the neo-liberal creed. With a formidably stinging intelligence, he equates neo-liberalism with a US global dictatorship. As he writes (2006: 160), "Americans are now exporting American pessimism by infecting everyone else with their terror phobia." But Beck's sociology is more than merely the latest form of anti-imperialism. For, as he argues at length, the new cosmopolitanism must deal with a whole host of emergent global risks — xenophobic nationalisms, religious fundamentalisms, multinational monopolies.

In the eyes of some critics, Beck's critique of imperialism is mistaken for anti-Americanism, and these critics suggest that this perspective does a disservice to an otherwise innovative and novel theory of global cosmopolitanism.

Postmodernism: Other critics (Latour 2003) charge Beck with inconsistency, for although he has sharply criticized postmodernism as a relativistic and non-empirical theoretical perspective, he has failed to acknowledge its influence on his own conception and understanding of the contemporary globalized world. It was, after all, postmodernists who first identified many features of global modernity, including the compression of space/time, the power of global connectivity through new information and communications technologies and the emergence of borderless networks of business, finance, terrorism, transmigration etc.

Idealism: Theorists (Wilkinson 2001), especially those from the political left, critique the idealism of Beck's global cosmopolitanism. These critics are quick to assert that Beck's celebration of global cosmopolitanism fails to acknowledge that its benefits, such as global travel, business, commerce, finance, information and communication, are disproportionately enjoyed by a new privileged global elite composed of corporate leaders, top politicians and diplomats and celebrities, as well as affluent travellers. Most of the world's population, especially those locked in poverty or oppression, will never get to experience these benefits. And those from the Global South who do get to experience the new realities of borderless travel are often the most desperate and oppressed populations on the move — civilian refugees from war, combat and terror; economic migrants fleeing famine, starvation and poverty; and other minority populations escaping persecution and oppression. For the most part, the benefits of global cosmopolitanism accrue to the wealthy and the powerful, while its costs are borne by the most vulnerable among us.

Geopolitics, inequality and conflict: Other more intractable problems with Beck's perspective have been recognized and recorded by other critics. Like many advocates of cosmopolitanism, Beck often appears to minimize the imperatives of national interest and geopolitical advantage, which continue to drive the policies and practices of many nation states. This under-recognition of the "realpolitik" pursued by most states, especially major powers such as the US, UK, Russia, China and India, signals an unmistakable naïveté and utopianism in Beck's theory of cosmopolitan globalization. At the same time, other aspects of Beck's theoretical project appear to some critics to reinforce global inequalities rather than provide a path for their abolition and transformation. For example, Beck advocates a global division of labour between low-skilled jobs in the developing world and high-skilled jobs in the developed world. Rather than encourage low-skilled workers to migrate to the West in search of employment, Beck suggests that low-skilled work should be exported to them in their home countries. In other words, the export of low-skill work would serve the double purpose of encouraging capital investment in the Global South, and would discourage labour migration to the Global North: two birds with one stone! But as Martell (2009: 257–258) suggests, the long-term consequences of this policy would only serve to entrench and reproduce existing global inequalities and reduce cosmopolitanism. Finally, some critics express concern that Beck's vague and naïve conceptualization of cosmopolitanism also permits a poorly defined role for "military human-ism," or humanitarian military interventions. The problem is that Beck provides an almost indiscriminate justification for these interventions — lumping together the need to prevent ethnic cleansing and genocide with the need to preempt the development of weapons of mass destruc-tion. According to Beck, preventive war may sometimes be necessary — whether in Bosnia, Rwanda or Iraq. Thus, Beck conflates very different provocations and in effect is willing to sign an almost blank cheque to authorize the use of lethal force for dissimilar situations. This logic led Beck to endorse George W. Bush's global war on terror, a judgement that some critics have found deeply troubling. Martel concludes his critical review of Beck's cosmopolitanism with this final verdict: "Beck's approach effectively disguises conflicts, inequalities and injustices in world society and harmonizes contradictions with a well meant but benign and opti-mistic view of international relations" (2009: 271).

References

Abu-Lughod, Janet L. 1991. *Before European Hegemony: The World System A.D. 1250–1350*. Oxford: Oxford University Press.

Acheraiou, Amar. 2011. *Questioning Hybridity, Postcolonialism and Globalization*. London: Palgrave Macmillan.

Albrow, Martin. 1990. "Introduction." In M. Albrow and E. King (eds.), *Globalization, Knowledge and Society*. London: Sage.

Al-Rodhan, Nayef R.F., and Gérard Stoudmann. 2006. "Definitions of Globalization: A Comprehensive Overview and a Proposed Definition." <http://citeseerx.ist.psu.edu/viewdoc/download?doi=10.1.1.472.4772&rep=rep1&type=pdf>.

Appadurai, A. 1996. *Modernity at Large: Cultural Dimensions of Globalization.* Minneapolis, MN: University of Minnesota Press.

___.1990. "Disjuncture and Difference in the Global Cultural Economy." In M. Featherstone (ed.), *Global Culture: Nationalism, Globalization and Modernity.* London: Sage.

Archer, M.S. 2007. *Making Our Way Through the World: Human Reflexivity and Social Mobility.* Cambridge: Cambridge University Press.

Archibugi, Daniele. 2000. "Cosmopolitical Democracy." *New Left Review,* 4 (July-August): 137–150.

___. 2004. "Cosmopolitan Democracy and Its Critics: A Review." *European Journal of International Relations,* 1, 3: 437–447.

Archibugi, Daniele, and David Held (eds.). 1995. *Cosmopolitan Democracy: An Agenda for a New World Order.* Cambridge: Polity Press.

Ball, James. 2011. "Bitcoins: What Are They, and How Do They Work?" *The Guardian,* 22 June. <https://www.theguardian.com/technology/2011/jun/22/bitcoins-how-do-they-work>.

Barber, Benjamin R. 1995. *Jihad vs. McWorld: How Globalism and Tribalism Are Reshaping the World.* Crown.

Bayly, C.A. 2004. *The Birth of the Modern World: Global Connections and Comparisons, 1780–1914.* Malden, MA: Blackwell.

Beck, Ulrich. 2006. "Living in the World Risk Society." A Hobhouse Memorial Public Lecture given on Wednesday 15 February 2006 at the London School of Economics.) *Economy and Society,* 35, 3 (August): 329–345.

Bell, Daniel. 1974. *The Coming of Post-Industrial Society.* New York: Harper Colophon Books.

Brennan, Timothy. 2001. "Cosmopolitanism and Internationalism." *New Left Review,* second series (7): 75–84.

Brinkman, R., and J. Brinkman. 2002. "Corporate Power and the Globalization Process." *International Journal of Social Economics,* 29, 9.

Bujra, Janet. 2000. "Risk and Trust: Unsafe Sex, Gender and AIDS in Tanzania." In Pat Caplan (ed.), *Risk Revisited.* London: Pluto Press.

Castells, M. 1996. *The Rise of the Networked Society.* Oxford: Blackwell.

___. 2002. "An Introduction to the Information Age." In G. Bridge and S. Watson (eds.), *The Blackwell City Reader.* Oxford: Blackwell. Originally published in *City,* 7: 6–16 (1996).

Chandler, David. 2003. "New Rights for Old? Cosmopolitan Citizenship and the Critique of State Sovereignty." *Political Studies,* 51, 2: 332–349.

Chomsky, Noam. 2007. "On the Samuel P. Huntington 'clash of civilizations,' Islam, and the West's relationship to the most extreme Islamic state—Saudi Arabia, a 'key ally,' according to Tony Blair." YouTube. <https://www.youtube.com/watch?v=qT64TNho59I>.

Delanty, Gerard, and Chris Rumford. 2008. "Political Globalization." In George Ritzer (ed.), *The Blackwell Companion to Globalization.* John Wiley & Sons.

Deneault, Alain. 2018. *Legalizing Theft: A Short Guide to Tax Havens.* Halifax: Fernwood Publishing.

Deng, N. 2005. "On the National Literature's Tactics in the Globalization's Language

Environment." *Journal of Human Institute of Humanities, Science and Technology*, 1: 39–41.

Dicken, Peter. 1992. *Global Shift: The Internationalization of Economic Activity.* London: Guilford Press.

Dingwall, Robert. 1999. "Risk Society: The Cult Theory of the Millennium?" *Social Policy and Administration* 33, 4.

Durkheim, Emile. 1973. "The Dualism of Human Nature and Its Social Conditions." In *Emile Durkheim on Morality and Society*, ed. Robert Bellah. Chicago: University of Chicago Press.

Elliott, Anthony. 2002. "Beck's Sociology of Risk: A Critical Assessment." *Sociology*, 36, 2: 299.

___. 2014. *Contemporary Social Theory: An Introduction.* Routledge.

Elliott, Larry. 2018. "Inequality Gap Widens as 42 People Hold Same Wealth as 3.7bn Poorest." *The Guardian*, 22 Jan. <https://www.theguardian.com/inequality/2018/jan/22/inequality-gap-widens-as-42-people-hold-same-wealth-as-37bn-poorest>.

Featherstone, Mike. 1996. "Localism, Globalism, and Cultural Identity." In Rob Wilson and Wimal Dissanayake (eds.), *Global/Local: Cultural Production & the Transnational Imaginary.* Durham: Duke University Press.

Finley, Klint. 2014. "Why Workers Can Suffer in Bossless Companies Like GitHub." *Wired*: Business, March 20. <https://www.wired.com/2014/03/tyranny-flatness/>.

Frank, Andre Gunder, and Barry K. Gills (eds.). 1993. *The World System: Five Hundred Years or Five Thousand?* London: Routledge.

Frank, Robert. 2017. "Richest 1% Now Owns Half the World's Wealth." CNBC, 14 Nov. <https://www.cnbc.com/2017/11/14/richest-1-percent-now-own-half-the-worlds-wealth.html>.

Fraser Institute. Nd. "Time to Privatize: Governments Should Begin Selling Off Assets" <https://www.fraserinstitute.org/article/time-privatize-governments-should-begin-selling-assets>.

Freeman, Jo. 2013. "The Tyranny of Structurelessness." *Women's Studies Quarterly*, 41, 3&4: 231–246.

Friedman, Thomas L. 1999. *The Lexus and the Olive Tree: Understanding Globalization.* New York: Farrar, Straus & Giroux.

___. 2005. *The World Is Flat: A Brief History of the Twenty-First Century.* New York: Farrar, Straus & Giroux.

Fukuyama, Francis. 1989. "The End of History." *The National Interest* (Summer). <https://www.wesjones.com/eoh.htm>.

___. 1992. *The End of History and the Last Man.* Free Press.

García Canclini, Néstor, 1990. *Hybrid Cultures.* Minneapolis: University of Minnesota Press.

Garfinkel, Harold. 1967. *Studies in Ethnomethodology.* Englewood Cliffs, NJ: Prentice-Hall.

Garnham, Nicholas. 2004. "Information Society Theory as Ideology." In F. Webster (ed.), *The Information Society Reader.* New York: Routledge.

Garside, Juliette. 2017. "Paradise Papers Leak Reveals Secrets of the World Elite's Hidden Wealth." *The Guardian*, 5 November.

Giddens, A. 1990. *The Consequences of Modernity.* Cambridge: Polity Press.

Gilbert, Alan. 1999. *Must Global Politics Constrain Democracy?* Princeton: Princeton University Press.

Glass, Geoffrey. 2005. "Manuel Castells's Network Society." Blog, November, 30. <http://www.geof.net/research/2005/castells-network-society>.

Gowan, Peter. 2001. "Neoliberal Cosmopolitanism." *New Left Review,* 11 (September–October): 79–93.

Graham, David. 2014. "Rumsfeld's Knowns and Unknowns: The Intellectual History of a Quip." *The Atlantic,* March 27.

Haas, Benjamin. 2018. "Xi Jinping Warns He Is Ready to 'Fight Bloody Battles' Against China's Enemies." *The Guardian,* 20 Mar. <https://www.theguardian.com/world/2018/mar/20/xi-jinping-warns-fight-bloody-battles-chinas-enemies>.

Hall, Stuart. 1997. "The Local and the Global: Globalization and Ethnicity." In Anthony D. King (ed.), *Culture, Globalization and the World-System: Contemporary Conditions for the Representation of Identity.* University of Minnesota Press.

Haralambos, Michael, and Martin Holborn. 2013. *Sociology Themes and Perspectives,* 8th edition. Collins Education.

Harding, Sandra. 1983. "Common Causes: Toward a Reflexive Feminist Theory." *Women & Politics,* 3, 4: 27–42.

Harris, Jonathan M., and Brien Roach. 2017. *Environmental and Natural Resource Economics: A Contemporary Approach,* 4th edition. Routledge.

Harvey, David. 1989. *The Condition of Post-Modernity.* London: Blackwell.

___. 2010. "The Enigma of Capital and the Crisis This Time." Paper prepared for the American Sociological Association Meetings in Atlanta, 16 August. <http://davidharvey.org/2010/08/the-enigma-of-capital-and-the-crisis-this-time/>.

Hay, Colin, and David Marsh (eds). 2000. *Demystifying Globalization.* Palgrave Macmillan.

Held, David, and Anthony McGrew. 2001. "Globalization." In *The Oxford Companion to Politics of the World,* 2nd edition. <http://www.polity.co.uk/global/globalization-oxford.asp>.

Held, David, A. McGrew, D. Goldblatt, and J. Perraton. 1999. *Global Transformations: Politics, Economics and Culture.* Stanford: Stanford University Press.

Hertz, R. (ed.). 1997. *Reflexivity and Voice.* Thousand Oaks, CA: Sage.

Hirst, Paul, and Grahame Thompson. 1996. *Globalization in Question: The International Economy and the Possibilities of Governance.* Polity Press.

Holton, Robert. 2005. *Making Globalization.* Basingstoke: Palgrave.

Hopkins, A.G. (ed.). 2003. *Globalization in World History.* New York: W.W. Norton & Company.

Huntington, Samuel P. 1989. "No Exit: The Errors of Endism." *The National Interest,* 17 (Fall): 3–11.

___. 1996. *The Clash of Civilizations and the Remaking of World Order.* Simon & Schuster.

Ip, Eric. 2010. "Globalization and the Future of the Law of the Sovereign State." *International Journal of Constitutional Law,* 8, 3 (July): 636–655. <https://doi.org/10.1093/icon/moq033>.

Kennedy, Paul, and Catherine J. Danks (eds.). 2001. *Globalization and National Identities: Crisis or Opportunity?* London: Palgrave.

Klein, Naomi. 1999. *No Logo: Taking Aim at the Brand Bullies*. Knopf Canada, Picador.

Kraidy, Marwan. 2005. *Hybridity: Or the Cultural Logic of Globalization*. Philadelphia: Temple.

Krugman, Paul. 1996. *Pop Internationalism*. Boston: MIT Press.

Kurtz, Stanley. 2002. "The Future of History." *Policy Review*, 113 (1 June).

Kymlicka, Will. 1995. *Multicultural Citizenship*. Oxford University Press.

Latour, B. 2003. "Is Re-Modernisation Occurring — and If So, How to Prove It? A Commentary on Ulrich Beck." *Theory, Culture and Society*, 20, 2: 35–48.

Lewis, Bernard. 1990. "The Roots of Muslim Rage." *The Atlantic*, 1 September.

___. 2004. *The Crisis of Islam: Holy War and Unholy Terror*. New York: Random House.

Lydon, Christopher. 2017. "Noam Chomsky: Neoliberalism Is Destroying Our Democracy: How Elites on Both Sides of the Political Spectrum Have Undermined Our Social, Political, and Environmental Commons." *The Nation*, June 2. <https://www.thenation.com/article/noam-chomsky-neoliberalism-destroying-democracy/>.

Mahdavi, Mojtaba, and Andy White. 2012. *Towards the Dignity of Difference? Neither "End of History" nor "Clash of Civilizations,"* Routledge.

Martell, Luke. 2007. "The Third Wave in Globalization Theory." *International Studies Review*, 9: 173–196.

___. 2009. "Global Inequality, Human Rights and Power: A Critique of Ulrich Beck's Cosmopolitanism." *Critical Sociology*, 35, 2: 253–272.

___. 2010. *The Sociology of Globalization*. Polity.

Marx, Karl. 2010 [1848]. *The Manifesto of the Communist Party*, Section 1, paragraph 18, lines 12–14. Harriman House Ltd.

Matusitz, J. 2009. "Disney's Successful Adaptation in Hong Kong: A Glocalization Perspective." *Asia-Pacific Journal of Management*, 28: 667–681.

McChesney, Robert W. 1999. *Rich Media, Poor Democracy: Communication Politics in Dubious Times*. New Press.

Moores, Colin (ed.). 2006. *The New Imperialists: Ideologies and Empire*. Oxford University Press.

Morgan, Glyn. 2003. "Democracy, Transnational Institutions, and the Circumstances of Politics." In Bruce Morrison (ed.), *Transnational Democracy: A Critical Consideration of Sites and Sources*. Aldershot: Ashgate.

Mythen, G. 2007. "Reappraising the Risk Society Thesis: Telescopic Sight or Myopic Vision?" *Current Sociology*, 55, 6: 793–813.

Nederveen Pieterse, J. 1994. "Globalisation as Hybridization." *International Sociology*, 9, 2: 161–184.

Nye, Joseph. 2007. *Understanding International Conflict: An Introduction to Theory and History*. New York: Pearson.

OECD. 1993. *Intra-Firm Trade*. Paris: OECD.

Olofsson, A., and S. Öhman. 2007. "Views of Risk in Sweden: Global Fatalism and Local Control –— An Empirical Investigation of Ulrich Beck's Theory of New Risks. *Journal of Risk Research*, 10, 2: 177–196.

O'Rourke, Kevin H., and Jeffrey G. Williamson. 1999. *Globalization and History: The Evolution of a Nineteenth-Century Atlantic Economy*. Cambridge, MA: MIT Press.

Ormrod, J.S. 2013. "Beyond World Risk Society? A Critique of Ulrich Beck's World Risk Society Thesis as a Framework for Understanding Risk Associated with

Human Activity in Outer Space." *Environment and Planning D: Society and Space,* 31, 4: 727–744.

Osterhammel, Jürgen, and Niels P. Petersson. 2005. *Globalization: A Short History,* translated from the German by Dona Geyer. Princeton, NJ: Princeton University Press.

Pfeffer, Jeffrey. 2013. "You're Still the Same: Why Theories of Power Hold over Time and Across Contexts!" *Academy of Management Perspectives,* 27, 4: 269–280.

Phillips, Matt. 2018. "Trump's Tax Cuts in Hand, Companies Spend More on Themselves than on Wages." *New York Times,* February 26. <https://www.nytimes.com/2018/02/26/business/tax-cuts-share-buybacks-corporate.html>.

RAWOO Netherlands Development Assistance Research Council. 2000. "Coping with Globalization: The Need for Research Concerning the Local Response to Globalization in Developing Countries." Publication No. 20.

Ritzer, George. 2004. *The Globalization of Nothing.* Thousand Oaks, CA: Pine.

___. 2013. *The McDonaldization of Society: 20th Anniversary Edition.* Thousand Oaks, CA: Sage.

Robertson, Roland. 1992. *Globalization: Social Theory and Global Culture.* London: Newbury Park, and New Delhi: Sage Publications.

___. 1995. "Glocalization: Time-Space and Homogeneity-Heterogeneity." In M. Featherstone, S. Lash, and R. Robertson (eds.), *Global Modernities.* London: Sage.

Robins, Kevin. 1997. "What in the World's Going On?" In P. du Gay (ed.), *Production of Culture/Productions of Culture.* London: Sage Publications.

Robinson, William I. 2008. "Theories of Globalization." In George Ritzer (ed.), *The Blackwell Companion to Globalization.* Blackwell Publishing.

Said, Edward. 2001. "The Clash of Ignorance: Labels Like "Islam" and "the West" Serve Only to Confuse Us About a Disorderly Reality." *The Nation,* 22 October.

___. 2004. *From Oslo to Iraq and the Road Map.* New York: Pantheon.

Scholte, Jan Aart. 2005. *Globalization: A Critical Introduction.* Basingstoke Palgrave.

Smith, Anthony D. 1990. "Towards a Global Culture?" *Theory, Culture, and Society,* 7: 171–191.

Sørensen, Mads P., and Allan Christiansen. 2012. *Ulrich Beck: An Introduction to the Theory of Second Modernity and the Risk Society.* Routledge.

Spicer, André. 2018. " No Bosses, No Managers: The Truth Behind the 'Flat Hierarchy' Façade." *Guardian,* July 30. <https://www.theguardian.com/commentisfree/2018/jul/30/no-bosses-managers-flat-hierachy-workplace-tech-hollywood>.

Steger, Manfred B. 2003. *Globalization: A Very Short Introduction.* Oxford University Press.

Stern, Steven. 2010. "Fast-Food Chains Adapt to Local Tastes." CNN, April 8. <http://www.cnn.com/2010/LIVING/homestyle/04/08/fast.food/index.html>.

Thompson, Karl. 2017. "Kenichi Ohmae, The Borderless World — Neoliberal Radical Globalism." *ReviseSociology,* June 1. <https://revisesociology.com/2017/06/01/kenichi-ohmae-the-borderless-world-neoliberal-radical-globalism/>.

Touraine, A. 1971. *The Post-Industrial Society: Tomorrow's Social History: Classes, Conflicts and Culture in the Programmed Society.* New York: Random House.

UNIDO (United Nations Industrial Development Organization). 2009. *A Greener Footprint for Industry: Opportunities and Challenges of Sustainable Industrial*

Development. Vienna. <http://www.unep.or.jp/ietc/spc/news-nov09/UNIDO_GreenIndustryConceptEbook.pdf>.

Wallerstein, Immanuel. 1974. *The Modern World System: Capitalist Agriculture and the Origins of the European World-Economy in the Sixteenth Century.* New York: Academic Press.

Wasserfall, R.R. 1997. "Reflexivity, Feminism and Difference." In R. Hertz (ed.), *Reflexivity and Voice.* Thousand Oaks, CA: Sage.

Webster, F. 2002. *Theories of the Information Society.* Routledge.

Wilkinson, I. 2001. "Social Theories of Risk Perception: At Once Indispensable and Insufficient." *Current Sociology,* 49, 1: 1–22

Wong, Julia Carrie, and Olivia Solon. 2017. "Massive Ransomware Cyber-Attack Hits Nearly 100 Countries Around the World." *The Guardian,* 12 May. <https://www.theguardian.com/technology/2017/may/12/global-cyber-attack-ransomware-nsa-uk-nhs>.

Wrong, Denis. 1961. "The Oversocialized Conception of Man in Modern Sociology." *American Sociological Review,* 26, 2: 183–193.

Zolo, Danilo. 1997. *Cosmopolis: Prospects for World Government.* Cambridge: Polity Press.

THE EXPANDING UNIVERSE OF SOCIAL THEORY

Today, perhaps more than at any time since the end of the Second World War, many in both the Global North and the Global South are living with anxiety and uncertainty. In the Global South, people's lives have been disrupted and homes displaced by wars and armed conflicts, famines, floods, disease pandemics, environmental devastation, climate change and the unrelenting pressures of the global capitalist policies of neoliberalism and neocolonialism. In the Global North, many of the established diplomatic conventions and practices of the twentieth century no longer appear relevant. Indeed, events in the twenty-first century have shaken the foundations of our world. The century began with the 9/11 terrorist attacks on the World Trade Center, an event which triggered an endless series of wars in Afghanistan, Iraq, Libya, Syria, Somalia, Sudan and now Yemen. The results of these catastrophic wars have also awakened global terrorist networks and led to flows of refugees and asylum-seekers escaping violence, conflict, persecution and destitution. And in many Western societies, instead of compassion and empathy for people facing these calamities, there has been a rise of far-right, ultra-nationalist, anti-immigrant political parties.

The present age of global modernity has affected the lives of a new generation that entered the workforce in the late twentieth century and early decades of the twenty-first century. For many of this new generation, the possibility of obtaining long-term employment in any particular occupation has greatly diminished. The days of permanent and secure jobs are over, and most employment opportunities in the current labour market are short term, underpaid, unpensioned, uninsured and insecure. Among the working class of most postindustrial countries, the proletariat has been replaced by a new, unstable "precariat" (see Standing 2011). Moreover, these new stressful, insecure and unstable conditions of work have necessitated the development of new attitudes and aptitudes, new habits, mindsets and social practices and new labour organizing for the many individuals seeking and competing for employment in the new precarious labour market. Today's "gig economy," an unregulated market system in which temporary positions are common and organizations contract with independent workers for short-term engagements, involves the labour of freelancers, independent contractors, project-based workers and temporary or part-time hires.

These psychological and social characteristics of the new worker have sometimes been labelled as the "new individualism" — a "cultural logic" that places a high value on personal flexibility, adaptability, distinctive identity and instant availability (Elliott and Lemert 2006). This new individualism extends far beyond the world of work into popular culture and the private lives and personal selves of individuals. The age of global modernity has become the age of the *ephemeral*: of transient and dispos-able social structures, social relationships and personal identities. These are some of the social and cultural attributes of what has been called in this book the "age of indeterminacy."

What contributions can social theory or sociology make in the present state of global conflict, change and radical uncertainty? Is there a viable future for social theory and sociology? The major achievements of social theorists have been, and continue to be, their informed and insightful contributions to public education and public debates over social and political policy. The ability to adopt various theoretical perspectives in order to interpret the views of diametrically opposed sides to any debate or conflict is also a defence against dogmatism and a recipe for empathic understanding. A major mission of social theory continues to be the extension of "social literacy" in the public sphere and the cultivation of an enlightened citizenry. This is not an isolated sentiment, as Steven Seidman (1991: 144) suggests: "Our broader social significance would lie in encouraging unencumbered open public moral and social debate and in deepening the notion of public discourse. We would be a catalyst for the public to think seriously about moral and social concerns." In this regard, social theorists and social researchers have contributed both as critics of ideology and social policy and as advocates of social reform and enlightened social change.

FROM THE CRUMBLING WESTERN CANON TO THE HIDDEN GLOBAL HERITAGE

There have been many justifications and rationales provided for creating social theory. One of the more enduring definitions, which described social theory as a "sociological imagination" and has inspired many Western social theorists and social scientists over the years, remains that of American sociologist C. Wright Mills (1959: 185), who saw the social theorist in liberating terms:

> That is to say ... his [sic] public role has two goals: What he ought to do for the individual is to turn personal troubles and concerns into social issues and problems open to reason — his aim is to help the individual become a self-educating man, who only then would be reasonable and free. What he ought to do for the society is to combat all those forces which are destroying genuine publics ... his aim is to help build and to strengthen self-cultivating publics.

During the early to mid-twentieth-century debates around race relations and civil rights, sociologists such as W.E.B. Du Bois, E. Franklin Frazier, Oliver Cromwell Cox and other African American sociologists, as well as European sociologists like Gunnar Myrdal, provided important insights that contributed to the constitutional and legislative changes that eventually ended legalized racial discrimination throughout the US (Bhambra 2014). In Canada, sociologists such as John Porter (1965, 1979) provided an academic perspective that facilitated the passage of the federal government policy on multiculturalism. Today, the role of the "public intellectual" has been assumed by numerous social theorists, including many covered in this book. Anthony Giddens became a theoretical advisor to Western leaders Tony Blair and Bill Clinton, and Pierre Bourdieu, Zygmunt Bauman, Judith Butler and others have provided a voice and academic advocacy for those who have been socially marginalized and excluded. Other social theorists have provided opportunities for women, members of the LGBTQ community and Indigenous, racialized and colonized groups around the world to have their voices heard and their standpoints and viewpoints recognized and respected.

Although many of these theorists have tried and sometimes succeeded in contributing to progressive public policy and to increasing the general level of social literacy, they still only represent Western social theory.

But, as we have seen throughout this book, the tide is turning and the theoretical universe is expanding. The historical chronicle of Western social thought is no longer the definitive guide to global social theory. The Western canon of social theory is crumbling and losing its imperial authority and influence. Since the closing decades of the twentieth century and into the opening decades of the twenty-first century, a new generation of global theorists has arisen to challenge and critique many of the Eurocentric biases of the Western tradition. While many theorists of this new generation are from the Global South — such as Chandra Talpade Mohanty, Gloria E. Anzaldúa and Gayatri Spivak — those regions whose intellectual traditions have been long overlooked or even suppressed by colonial and neocolonial ideas and practices, Global North–based theorists like bell hooks, Patricia Hill Collins, Kimberlé Crenshaw, Audre Lorde and Adrienne Rich have offered critical insights that have much to add to our understanding of the modern world. For this reason, rather than lamenting the "crumbling Western canon," we should celebrate the rise of critical thought that is enriching, deepening and expanding the world of social theory.

This is not to say that the recognition and acceptance of the new wave of global theories entails the wholesale rejection of the European and North American traditions. But for these traditions to retain any value or significance, they must be re-evaluated and re-contextualized. This means that the ideas of Parsons, Habermas and others must be understood within their original contexts, as descriptions and explanations of parts of the societies of their birth. In other words, these theories must be stripped of their false universalizations: they need to be decentred, deconstructed and seen as local narratives of actual societies rather than as abstract metanarratives for all humankind. This re-reading of the crumbling canon of social theory requires us to deconstruct these ideas and assess their relevance and accuracy for the changing conditions of the modern world. In the final analysis, social theory will always have a role to play in analyzing and in recommending transformative changes in our political, economic and social landscape which may minimize the existential risks of war, inequality, climate change and social collapse and help to transform our global society into one that is more compassionate, inclusive, equitable, sustainable and connected. If there is a chain that links the best of social theory from one generation to the next, then it is the pursuit of social justice. This, it would appear, is the golden thread that runs throughout the most inspired work within our discipline. And, as one distinguished social theorist observes:

> Social theories derive from the serious attempts of women and men [sic] to make sense out of the unthinkable social things that harm, constrain, repress or damage life; social theories are of value when they most directly engage, and seek to transform, the political and ideological turmoil out of which they were born, and in the process offer alternative visions of how our personal and social lives could be lived otherwise. (Elliott 2014: 376)

References

Bhambra G.K. 2014. "A Sociological Dilemma: Race, Segregation and US Sociology." *Current Sociology. La Sociologie contemporaine*, 62, 4: 472–492. doi:10.1177/0011392114524506.

Elliott, Anthony. 2014. *Contemporary Social Theory: An Introduction*. Routledge.

Elliott, Anthony, and Charles Lemert. 2006. *The New Individualism: The Emotional Costs of Globalization*. Routledge.

Mills, C. Wright. 1959. *The Sociological Imagination*. Oxford University Press.

Porter, John. 1965. *The Vertical Mosaic: An Analysis of Social Class and Power in Canada*. Toronto: University of Toronto Press.

____. 1979. *The Measure of Canadian Society: Education, Equality and Opportunity*. Toronto: Gage.

Seidman, Steven. 1991. "The End of Sociological Theory: The Postmodern Hope." *Sociological Theory*, 9, 2 (Autumn): 131–146.

Standing, Guy. 2011. *The Precariat: The New Dangerous Class*. Bloomsbury.

INDEX